GERMANY

R. Mattès/MICHELIN

Editorial Director   Cynthia Clayton Ochterbeck

THE GREEN GUIDE GERMANY

Editor   Alison Coupe
Contributing Writer   Andrea Schulte-Peevers
Production Manager   Natasha G. George
Cartography   Peter Wrenn
Photo Editor   Lydia Strong, Yoshimi Kanazawa
Layout & Design   John Higginbottom, Natasha G. George
Cover Design   Laurent Muller, Ute Weber

Contact Us: The Green Guide
                                   Michelin Maps and Guides
                                   One Parkway South
                                   Greenville, SC 29615
                                   USA
                                   www.michelintravel.com
                                   michelin.guides@us.michelin.com

                                   Michelin Maps and Guides
                                   Hannay House
                                   39 Clarendon Road
                                   Watford, Herts WD17 1JA
                                   UK
                                   ☎ (01923) 205 240
                                   www.ViaMichelin.com
                                   travelpubsales@uk.michelin.com

Special Sales: For information regarding bulk sales,
                                   customized editions and premium sales,
                                   please contact our Customer Service
                                   Departments:
                                   USA   1-800-432-6277
                                   UK   (01923) 205 240
                                   Canada 1-800-361-8236

Note to the Reader

One Team...
A Commitment to Quality

There's just one reason our team is dedicated to producing quality travel publications—you, our reader.

Throughout our guides we offer **practical information**, **touring tips** and **suggestions** for finding the best places for a break.

Michelin driving tours help you hit the highlights and quickly absorb the best of the region. Our descriptive **walking tours** make you your own guide, armed with directions, maps and expert information.

We scout out the attractions, classify them with **star ratings**, and describe in detail what you will find when you visit them.

Michelin maps featured throughout the guide offer vibrant, detailed and easy-to-follow outlines of everything from close-up museum plans to international maps.

Places to stay and eat are always a big part of travel, so we research **hotels and restaurants** that we think convey the essence of the destination and arrange them by geographic area and price. We walk you through the best shopping districts and point you towards the host of entertainment and recreation possibilities available.

We **test**, **retest**, **check and recheck** to make sure that our guidebooks are truly just that: a personalized guide to help you make the most of your visit. And if you still want a speaking guide, we list local tour guides who will lead you on all the boat, bus, guided, historical, culinary, and other tours you shouldn't miss.

In short, we remove the guesswork involved with travel. After all, we want you to enjoy exploring with Michelin as much as we do.

The Michelin Green Guide Team

PLANNING YOUR TRIP

INTRODUCTION TO GERMANY

T. Krieger/MICHELIN

CONTENTS

DISCOVERING GERMANY

HOW TO USE THIS GUIDE

PLANNING YOUR TRIP

The blue-tabbed PLANNING YOUR TRIP section at the front of the guide gives you **ideas for your trip** and **practical information** to help you organize it. You'll find tours, practical information, a host of outdoor activities, a calendar of events, information on shopping, sightseeing, kids' activities and more.

INTRODUCTION

The orange-tabbed INTRODUCTION section explores Germany's **Nature** and geology. The **History** section spans *Homo heidelbergensis* through WW II to today. The **Art and Culture** section covers architecture, art, literature and music, while the **Country Today** delves into modern Germany.

DISCOVERING

The green-tabbed DISCOVERING section features Germany's Principal Sights, arranged alphabetically and by region,

featuring the most interesting local **Sights**, **Walking Tours**, nearby **Excursions**, and detailed **Driving Tours**.

🛈 Contact information, ⌖ admission charges, 🕐 hours of operation, and a host of other **visitor information** is given wherever possible. Admission prices shown are normally for a single adult.

STAR RATINGS★★★

Michelin has given star ratings for more than 100 years. If you're pressed for time, we recommend you visit the ★★★, or ★★ sights first:

★★★	Highly recommended
★★	Recommended
★	Interesting

Address Books - Where to Stay, Eat and more...

WHERE TO STAY

We've made a selection of hotels and arranged them within the cities by price category to fit all budgets (*see the Legend on the cover flap for an explanation of the price categories*). For the most part, we've selected accommodations based on their unique regional quality, their regional feel, as it were. So, unless the individual hotel embodies local ambience, it's rare that we include chain properties, which typically have their own imprint.
See the back of the guide for an index of where hotels featured throughout the guide can be found.

WHERE TO EAT

We thought you'd like to know the popular eating spots in Germany. So, we selected restaurants that capture the regional experience—those that have a unique regional flavor (*see the Legend on the cover flap for an explanation of the price categories*). We're not rating the quality of the food per se; as we did with the hotels, we selected restaurants for many towns and villages, categorized by price to appeal to all wallets.
See the back of the guide for an index of where restaurants featured throughout the guide can be found.

MAPS

- Regional **Driving Tours** map and **Places to Stay** map.
- Germany map with the **Principal Sights** highlighted.
- Maps for major **cities** and **villages**.
- **Local tour** maps.

All maps in this guide are oriented north, unless otherwise indicated by a directional arrow. The term "Local Map" refers to a map within the chapter or Tourism Region. A complete list of the maps found in the guide appears at the back of this book, as well as a comprehensive index and list of where restaurants and accommodations are to be found.
See the map Legend at the back of the guide for an explanation of map symbols.

ORIENT PANELS

Vital statistics are given for each principal sight in the DISCOVERING section:

- **Information:** Tourist Office/Sight contact details.
- ▶ **Orient Yourself:** Geographic location of the sight with reference to surrounding boroughs, towns, and roads.
- **P Parking:** Where to park.
- **Don't Miss:** Unmissable things to do.
- **Organizing Your Time:** Tips on organizing your stay; what to see first, how long to spend, crowd avoidance, market days and more.
- **Kids Especially for Kids:** Sights of particular interest to children.
- **Also See:** Nearby PRINCIPAL SIGHTS featured elsewhere in the guide.

SYMBOLS

Spa	**Spa Facilities**	🚶	**Tours**
Kids	**Interesting for Children**	P	**On-site Parking**
	Also See	▶	**Directions**
	Tourist Information	✕	**On-site eating Facilities**
🕐	**Hours of Operation**	⚐	**Swimming Pool**
🕐	**Periods of Closure**	△	**Camping Facilities**
⛌	**Closed to the Public**	⚏	**Beaches**
⊚	**Entry Fees**	☕	**Breakfast Included**
⊘	**Credit Cards not Accepted**	🐌	**A Bit of Advice**
♿	**Wheelchair Accessible**	🐌	**Warning**

Contact - Addresses, phone numbers, opening hours and prices published in this guide are accurate at the time of press. We welcome corrections and suggestions that may assist us in preparing the next edition. Please send your comments to:

UK
Michelin Maps and Guides
Hannay House
39 Clarendon Road
Watford, Herts WD17 1JA
travelpubsales@uk.michelin.com
www.michelin.co.uk

USA
Michelin Maps and Guides
Editorial Department
P.O. Box 19001
Greenville, SC 29602-9001
michelin.guides@us.michelin.com
www.michelintravel.com

*Beach with wicker chairs,
Fischland peninsula*
T. Krieger/MICHELIN

MICHELIN DRIVING TOURS

Local Driving Tours

In the *Discovering Germany* section you will find local driving tours with maps for the following sights:

- DEUTSCHE-ALPENSTRASSE
- BAYREUTH
- BODENSEE
- EIFEL
- ERZGEBIRGE
- HARZ
- MOSELTAL
- OBERSCHWÄBISCHE BAROCK-STRASSE
- RHEINTAL
- SÄCHSISCHE SCHWEIZ

- SAUERLAND
- SCHWÄBISCHE ALB
- SCHWARZWALD
- THÜRINGER WALD
- **Also see:** BADEN-BADEN, BERGSTRASSE, LAHNTAL, MECKLEN BURGISCHE SEENPLATTE, MÜNCHEN, NÜRNBERG, PASSAU, RÜDESHEIM AM RHEIN, ROMANTISCHE STRASSE, UNTERES SAARTAL, OBERES SAALETAL, WÜRZBURG, XANTEN.

Regional Tours

See the Driving Tours map

HAMBURG AND SCHLESWIG-HOLSTEIN 1

550km/342mi-tour leaving from Hamburg.

This tour through the Länder of Hamburg and Schleswig-Holstein meanders through the far north of Germany, a region with a glorious Hanseatic past. The country's second largest city, **Hamburg** is a bustling port set on the banks of the Elbe estuary; its central districts are ideal for a stroll and the richly endowed museums will be much appreciated by art lovers. A mere 70km/43mi from Hamburg is **Lübeck**. This delightful town in northern Germany has been on UNESCO's World Heritage list since 1987. Remarkably preserved, it boasts an exceptional collection of houses and monuments from many different periods. Not far from Lübeck, **Travemünde**, on the shores of the Baltic Sea, is renowned for its sandy beaches, extensive seafront promenade and its casino. The tour continues northwards with the next port of call being **Kiel**, the gateway to Scandinavia. Capital of Schleswig-Holstein, Kiel combines a long marime tradition with a modern atmosphere. The route then takes a northwesterly direction along the Baltic coast to **Schleswig**, an ideal place to relax and explore. Heading westwards, from one sea to the other takes you to the island of **Sylt** and the other North Frisian islands. Their fragile sandy shores are pitted against the North Sea in a constant battle against marine erosion. Lastly, the peaceful seaside town of **Husum**, birthplace of the writer Theodor Storm, offers all the attractions of a modern tourist resort.

BALTIC SEA, MECKLENBURG-VORPOMMERN 2

650km/380mi-tour leaving from Neubrandenburg.

This itinerary will give you a glimpse of a region of Germany that is wild and captivating and little known among foreign visitors. The town of **Neubrandenburg** has a surprise in store with its imposing medieval ramparts, miraculously spared by the Second

World War. The journey continues westwards through the **Mecklenburg lake district**, a well-preserved region and one of the least populated in Germany. With countless lakes and a wide range of activities, it is of particular appeal to nature-lovers. **Schwerin** is without a doubt one of the most pleasant towns in northern Germany. Its refined architecture and the majestic charm of its castle set atop an island facing the old town add to the appeal of this city, the state capital of Mecklenburg-Vorpommern. Our itinerary then takes us north to the coast where **Wismar**, with its trove of red-brick buildings, provides an excellent introduction to the Baltic coast. The town's historic center was classed a UNESCO World Heritage site in 2002, along with that of **Stralsund**. Along with **Rostock** and **Bad Doberan,** Stralsund is well worth a visit on your way to the island of **Rügen**. Here, an astonishing variety of landscapes awaits: bands of sandy dunes, land reclaimed from the sea, salt meadows, cultivated fields, endless mudflats (Watt, or Wadden) and prehistoric tumuli. Rügen, like the neighboring island of **Usedom**, is a very popular vacation destination with delightful seaside, health and spa resorts and unique late 19C spa architecture. Last stop on the itinerary is **Greifswald**, whose very old architecture reveals a Scandinavian influence.

BREMEN, HAMBURG AND LOWER SAXONY ③

550km/342mi-tour leaving from Bremen.
The bustling town of **Bremen** is a true delight. A large port and city of artistic interest where the Weser Renaissance style flourished, it has a number of parks and a charming riverside promenade. After a stop in **Hamburg**, 125km/78mi to the northeast (◔ *see description in itinerary* ①), the tour next takes you to **Lüneburg**, which owes its longstanding prosperity to salt and marks the gateway to the vast expanse of the **Lüneburg Heath**. In the face of the increasing advances of

agriculture, attempts are being made to preserve this wild environment which is characterized by picturesque copses of birch, pine and juniper. From mid-August to mid-September, the purple carpet of heather in bloom will have you burning up the pixels in your digicam. South of the heath awaits the dignified city of **Celle**. There are many reasons to stop here; treasures from the old city, a magnificently restored ducal palace and a folklore and history museum to name but a few. For car fanatics, a quick detour to **Autostadt** – a vast automobile complex set up by Volkswagen not far from Braunschweig – is a must. Here you will find generously landscaped areas of park and water, dotted with architecturally striking buildings. A stop in **Braunschweig** is followed by a leisurely look around the beautiful city of **Wolfenbüttel** with its exceptional collection of Renaissance houses. Further west, after **Hildesheim**, **Hannover** awaits with its famous Herrenhausen gardens.

BERLIN AND BRANDENBURG ④

600km/373mi-tour leaving from Neubrandenburg.
After a look around **Neubrandenburg** (◔ *see description in itinerary* ②), head south to explore Schloss **Rheinsberg** where Frederick the Great, by his own account, spent the happiest years of his life as a young man. **Berlin**, Germany's vibrant capital, is a mere

Salzspeicher in Lübeck

J. Bouraly/MICHELIN

Schloß Sanssouci, Potsdam

Partner für Berlin/FTB-Werbefotografie

– literature and music flourished. **Leipzig** is a city of artistic interest that can be proud of its exceptional musical heritage; Bach, Wagner and Mendelssohn all lived here at one time and the city remains very much in the foreground of the German music scene. Around 60km/37mi south, **Naumburg** stands among hills cloaked in vineyards and forests. The town is renowned in particular for its cathedral that is an exceptionally harmonius blend of Romanesque and Gothic style elements. **Weimar**, **Jena**, **Erfurt** and **Eisenach** are all names with strong connotations in German culture through their association with such key figures as Luther, Goethe and Schiller. Offering a pleasant distraction from the "cultural pilgrimage", the Thuringian Forest and, farther north, the Harz mountains take you right to the very heart of nature. The latter is an area steeped in legend and lore and offers a limitness menu of year-round outdoor pursuits. Next, steer towards **Magdeburg** for a look at its fantastic Gothic cathedral before heading to **Wittenberg**, where Martin Luther posted his 95 Theses again church corruption. For this reason, the twon is considered the cradle of the Reformation. The route continues via **Dessau**, famous for its Bauhaus legacy and a gateway to the Garden Realm, a 18C wonderland of landscape gardens with **Wörlitzer Park** as its finest jewel.

90km/56mi further south. The buzzing city offers a wealth of culture and an after-dark scene not only night-owls will love. it is an amazing metropolis that will captivate you with its world's class museums and art galleries, a lively café scene, monumental landmarks, huge parks and gardens and the easy-going attitude of the locals. Another town marked by the personality of Frederick the Great, who held a brilliant and cosmopolitan court here, **Potsdam** is a genuine "Rococo treasure" of universal appeal. Carry on westwards and, after the small town of **Brandenburg** in the heart of the Havelland lake region, stop off at **Tangermünde**, which is still enclosed within its late 14C ramparts. **Stendal**, just a few kilometres away, was until the mid-16C the most important town in the Brandenburg March before the ravages of the Thirty Years' War sent it on a downward spiral. Several monuments typical of the Gothic brick architecture still attest to this former period of prosperity. Further north you can admire the beautiful cathedral of **Havelberg**, a pretty town set on the banks of the River Havel. The itinerary ends with a foray into the picturesque **Mecklenburg lake district.**

HARZ, THURINGIA, SACHSEN-ANHALT AND LEIPZIG ⑤

750km/466mi-tour leaving from Leipzig.
This route is tailor-made for culture vultures, taking you into a region where – particularly in the 18C

SACHSEN (DRESDEN) AND ERZGEBIRGE ⑥

650km/380mi-tour leaving from Dresden.
Saxony is a region that has played a key role in Germany's history. A city of art and culture, **Dresden** has undergone extensive restorations of its its Baroque treasures (most famously the complete rebuilding of the Frauenkirche), making it once again "the Florence of the Elbe". Southeast of here, the **Sächsische Schweiz** charms with its whimsically eroded sandstone formations and winding gorges gouged from the rock—this region is truly one of Germany's most spectacular natural

wonders. The towns of **Bautzen** and **Görlitz** provide an opportunity to sample the culture of the Sorbs. An ethnic German minority, their homeland today straddles the Länder of Saxony and Brandenburg. Not only do Sorbs still speak their own language, but they have also kept alive many traditions. These include the decoration of eggs at Easter and the wearing of the Sorbian national costume and tall embroidered headdresses. Heading northwards takes you to **Branitz**, a stone's throw from Cottbus where Prince Hermann von Pückler-Muskau built a palace and – indulging his passion for garden design – a fabulous park. Heading back to Dresden, make a stop at **Schloss Moritzburg** and **Meissen**, renowned for its porcelain. If you have the time, extend your tour with a trip through the **Erzgebirge**, a wooded region with a long tradition in both mining and toy making. Make **Annaberg-Buchholz** with its impressive Flamboyant Gothic church, a key stop before heading back to Dresden.

PFALZ, RHEINTAL AND MOSELTAL [7]

950km/570mi-tour leaving from Cologne.
Not far from the borders with Belgium, Luxembourg and France, this extensive loop takes in key sights in western Germany. The Rhine valley is full of surprises; steeply terraced vineyards and rocky outcrops dominated by lofty castles, the route from **Koblenz** to **Rüdesheim** or **Bingen** affords some magnificent views. Take a stroll around the historic center of **Mainz** with its maze of little alleyways and old houses. After **Darmstadt**, take the **Bergstrasse** southwards to historic **Heidelberg**, a symbol of German Romanticism, whose hillside castle leaves a lasting impression. The route continues west to **Speyer**, whose enormous Romanesque cathedral is the burial place of several Holy Roman Emperors. Heading north takes you along the German Wine Route through the **Pfalz**, a region blessed with a mild microclimate conducive to

the cultivation of exotic fruits. Next up is **Worms**, which competes with **Trier** for the title of oldest town in Germany; both were founded by the Romans. From Trier to Koblenz, the winding course of the **Moselle** takes you past picturesque villages, castles and vineyards. Cruises, hiking and cycling are among the activities that beckon along here. **Aachen**, on the border with Belgium and Holland, is next on the agenda. The town is indelibly associated with Charlemagne, who made it capital of his Frankish Empire. Nearly three dozen princes were crowned king or emperor in its cathedral between 936 and 1531. From Aachen it won't be long before the famous twin spires of the cathedral of **Cologne** come into view. This delightful town on the Rhine is also known for its Romanesque churches, colorful historic houses, top-notch art museums and raucous beer taverns serving the local brew called Kölsch.

NÜRNBERG AND FRANKEN [8]

650km/380mi-tour leaving from Nürnberg.
This itinerary provides a chance to explore the age-old sights of northern Bavaria. It begins with **Nürnberg**, an old bronze casters' and gold-beaters' town and one of the most beautiful medieval cities in Germany. Farther south, **Eichstätt** is distinguished by a harmonious mix of Rococo and contemporary architecture. Passing through river valleys and fertile hills, the **Romantische Strasse** recalls at every stage some aspect of the past that could only belong to the history of Germany. As the route unfolds, it evokes life in the great medieval cities (**Nördlingen, Dinkelsbühl, Rothenburg ob der Tauber**). In Würzburg, the mid-17C grandeur of the three prince-bishops of the Schönborn family is reflected in the splendid Residenz Palace. Next up is **Bamberg** with its pretty-as-a-penny historic quarter (a UNESCO World Heritage Site since 1993) and imposing hilltop cathedral. Our Bavarian route dips into the

Kloster Bebenhausen, Tübingen

R. Chéret/MICHELIN

neighboring Land of Thuringia, passing through **Coburg** and the nearby **Wallfahrtskirche Vierzehnheiligen**. This pilgrimage church is a Baroque masterpiece by Balthasar Neumann with a truly captivating wealth of decoration. **Bayreuth**, last stop on the tour, is a high point for fans of Wagner's music and the Rococo style.

BADEN-WÜRTTEMBERG AND BODENSEE ⑨

850km/510mi-tour leaving from Freiburg.

Southeast Germany has an astonishing number of remarkable tourist attractions. The easy-going atmosphere of the old university town of **Freiburg** is infectious and its paved alleyways beg to be explored. The town is the gateway to the **Schwarzwald**, a region steeped in legend and endowed with surprising variety of scenery. Add to that its picturesque villages, a passion for cuckoo clocks and the possibilities of hiking in summer and skiing in winter, and it is easy to see why this mountainous region is one of Germany's most popular tourist destinations. Passing through towns such as the elegant spa resort of **Baden-Baden**, which attracts a wealthy clientele all year round, and **Karlsruhe**, the route takes you up to **Bruchsal** (ⓒ*see KARLSRUHE*) whose sumptuous 18C palace houses a museum entirely devoted to mechanical musical instruments.

A short distance southeast of here looms **Kloster Maulbronn**; built in 1147, it was one of the earliest Cistercian abbeys in Germany. The school established here since the Reformation (1557) has seen the flowering of such diverse scientific, literary and philosophical talents as those of Kepler, Hölderlin and Hermann Hesse. The road south leads to **Tübingen** and **Ulm**. Tübingen's maze of narrow sloping streets lined with old half-timbered houses, combined with its animated student life, create a relaxed and happy atmosphere away from the throng of tourists. In Ulm, you can take a stroll between the canals and the Danube and admire the town's extraordinary cathedral. The Upper Swabian Plateau is dotted with Baroque churches whose dazzling decoration and architecture combining light effects and symmetry are in perfect harmony with the landscape. **Zwiefalten** and **Weingarten** are two superb illustrations of the Baroque style that flourished so extensively in southern Germany. The tour ends with the magnificent **Bodensee**, a vast lake that also borders Switzerland and Austria. It is regarded by Germans as their very own "Riviera".

MUNICH AND THE BAVARIAN ALPS ①⓪

650km/380mi-tour leaving from Munich.

A tour through this far southern region, with its magnificent alpine scenery and wealth of culture, will undoubtedly be a high point in your exploration of Germany. The country's second most popular tourist destination after Berlin, **Munich** – Bavaria's vibrant capital – is a prosperous and lively city. Art lovers will delight in its fabulous museums and Baroque churches. A little over 100km/62mi to the east, on the Austrian border, **Burghausen** is crowned with the biggest medieval fortress in Germany. Its defense system, reinforced at the beginning of the 16C in the face of a threatening invasion by the Turks, stretches for around 1km/0.6mi. The much-traveled **Deutsche Alpenstrasse** kicks off in **Berchtesgaden**, where you can explore underground salt mines, hike in the shadow of the mighty Watzmann mountain or take a cruise on the magical Königssee. The Alpenstrasse is an intensely scenic route passing dreamy villages, bucolic meadows as well as famous ski resorts such as **Garmisch-Partenkirchen**, which is lorded over by the Zugspitze, Germany's tallest mountain. When the Alpenstrasse reaches Füssen, be sure to make a side trip to **Neuschwanstein**, the famous fantasy castle of "fairytale king" Ludwig II. Füssen is also the southern terminus

Neue Pinakothek, one of many museums on offer inMunich

of the equally fabled Romantische Strasse, which you follow as far as **Augsburg**.

WHEN AND WHERE TO GO

When to Go

Whatever the season, the weather in Germany is subject to enormous variation. The period when you are most likely to find good weather extends from May to October (🌞it can get very hot during high summer in Baden-Württemberg and Bavaria). Spring and fall, when tourist sights are fewer, can be the perfect time to discover the country. It is sensible to pack some waterproof clothing whenever you plan to go. Before you leave, don't forget to find out about any festivals, fairs or other events which may considerably increase the number of visitors in certain towns and make finding a room difficult (🌙see Calendar of Events). Skiers will find snow-covered slopes from the end of November until late February.

Where to Go

Clearly signposted, these "thematic" itineraries provide a handy means of crisscrossing the country and getting to know it better. They include:

- **Badische Weinstraße (Baden Wine Route)**, from Baden-Baden to Lörrach *(170km/105.6mi)*. Breathtaking scenery, superb cuisine, plenty of sunshine and some of the finest wines in the country await in Germany's southeastern corner.
- **Burgenstrasse (Castle Road)**, from Mannheim to Bayreuth and then on to Prague *(975km/605mi in total)*. Plunge back into medieval times as you skirt the 70 legend-shrouded castles of this meandering route.
- **Bocksbeutelstrasse (Middle Franconian Wine Route)**, *50km/31mi* south east of Würzburg. Sample delicious Franconian wines bottled in their signature flagons called "Bockbeutel" right at time-honored wine estates.
- **Deutsche Alleenstrasse (German Avenues)**, from Sellin on Rügen Island to Goslar. Let nature embrace as you travel beneath a shady canopy of mature beeches, chestnuts and oaks arching over the highway.
- **Deutsche Ferienstrasse Ostsee-Alpen (German Holiday Route)**, links the Baltic Sea (Puttgarden) with the Alps (Berchtesgaden). From dune-fringed beaches to snowy mountains, the entire quilt

of Germany's varied landscapes unfolds on this epic north-south journey.

- **Deutsche Weinstrasse (German Wine Road**, from Bockenheim/ Palatinate to Wissembourg/Alsace *(91km/56.5mi)*. Spring arrives early along this sweet, unhurried route dotted with charming villages steeped in history and hemmed in by rambling vineyards.
- **Deutsche Fachwerkstrasse (Route of Half-timbered Buildings)**, nine routes through Lower Saxony, Hessen and Baden-Württemberg. There is an undeniable fairytale quality to these centuries-old higgledy-piggledy half-timbered houses, each of which is decorated with individual fancy and artistry.
- **Alte Salzstraße (Old Salt Road)**, from Lüneburg to Lübeck *(100km/62mi)*. Horsecarts needed 3 weeks to transport salt—the "White Gold"—along this historic trading route. You can do it in just a day or two!
- **Straße der Romanik (Romanesque Road)**, loop leaving from Magdeburg. European history was made a 1 000 years ago in towns along this route of dignified cathedrals, fierce fortresses and rambling abbeys.
- **Romantische Straße (Romantic Road)**, from Würzburg to Füssen *(315km/195.7)*. On this dreamy

route you can check off many of Germany's most famous destinations, including Rothenburg and Neuschwanstein.

- **Silberstraße (Silver Route)**, from Zwickau to Dresden *(115km/71.4mi)*. This enchanting "ribbon of riches" winds through rural, mountaineous countryside steeped in ancient traditions.
- **Klassikerstraße Thüringen (Thuringian Classical Route)**, Goethe to Gropius *(300km/186.4mi)*. Germany's legacy as a land of poets, thinkers and innovators is confirmed along this intensely cultural route.
- **Oberschwäbische Barockstraße (Upper Swabian Baroque Route)**, from Ulm to Lake Constance (Bodensee) *(455m/282.7mi)*. This route links the "greatest hits" (churches, abbeys, libraries) of the wonderfully exuberant southern German Baroque and Rococo styles.
- **Straße der Weser-Renaissance (Weser Renaissance Route)**, Münden to Bremen *(400km/248.5mi from Hann)*. In the 16C, merchants and the nobility expressed their prosperity in large manors festooned with frilly turrets, gables, oriels and balconies. This route preserves some of the style's finest examples.

🖰 www.germany-tourism.de

KNOW BEFORE YOU GO

Useful Websites

GENERAL INFORMATION

One of Germany's most popular tourist destinations is the *Romantische Straße*, the Romantic Road. Half-timbered houses, medieval fortresses and city walls, Alpine vistas and flower-filled balconies stretch along the route. **www.romantischestrasse.de** offers

detailed travel information and maps for each of the cities along the route. Germany's most romantic castles are located along the *Burgenstraße*, Castle Road, that stretches across the country. For maps and details about the route, visit **www.burgenstrasse.de**. The German *Weinstraße*, or Wine Road, website is **www.deutscheweine. de**. The site offers information about each of Germany's wines and wine regions and a listing of the nation's wine festivals.

Germany is home to 14 national parks, 15 biosphere reserves and 100 nature parks. **www.naturpark.de** offers detailed information and maps for each of Germany's parks.

Spas and wellness centers have long been considered by Germans an important part of healthy living. A visit to The German Spa Association's website, **www. deutscher-heilbaedervband.de**, provides links to spas nationwide, including lists of those with English-speaking therapists.

Parents traveling with young children may want to visit **www.zoo-infos.de** prior to traveling in Germany. This comprehensive website includes information about and links to all of the zoos and animal parks in the country.

Oktoberfest is one of the world's most famous festivals. Visitors to Munich interested in up-to-date festival information can visit **www.oktoberfest.de**.

CULTURAL ORGANIZATIONS

The Goethe-Institut websites for each of the cities below can be accessed via www.goethe.de

- **Goethe-Institut Johannesburg**, 119 Jan Smuts Ave, Parkwood 2193, Johannesburg, ☎(011) 442 3232, fax (011) 442 3738.
- **Goethe-Institut London**, 50 Princes Gate, Exhibition Road, London SW7 2PH, ☎(020) 7596 4000, fax 020-7594 0240.
- **Goethe-Institut New York**, 1014 Fifth Avenue, New York, NY 10028, ☎(212) 439-8700, fax (212) 439-8705.
- **Goethe-Institut Ottawa**, Saint Paul University 223 Main St, Suite 128 Ottawa, ON, K1S 1C5 ☎613 2329000, fax (613) 232 9000
- **Goethe-Institut Sydney**, 90 Ocean Street, Woollahra, NSW 2025, ☎(02) 8356 8333, fax (02) 8356 8314.

Tourist Offices

TOURIST ORGANIZATIONS

Information on travel arrangements and accommodation and a variety of brochures are available from the **German National Tourist Office**. For online information refer to www.germany-tourism.de, the German National Tourist Office website. Every sight throughout the *Discovering Germany* section of this guide has sight-specific tourist office details.

Chicago
German National Tourist Office Chicago PO Box 59594, Chicago, IL 60659-9594 ☎(773) 539-6303, fax (773) 539-6378, heike.pfeiffer@gntoch.com, www.cometogermany.com

Johannesburg
German National Tourist Office, c/o Lufthansa German Airlines, PO Box 412246, Craighall, 2024 Johannesburg ☎(011) 325 1927, fax (011) 325 0867

London
German National Tourist Office, PO Box 2695, London W1A 3TN ☎(020) 7317 0908, ☎09001 600 100 (24hr brochure line, calls cost 60p/min), fax (020) 7317 0917 gntolon@d-z-t.com, www.germany-tourism.co.uk

New York
German National Tourist Office, 122 East 42nd Street, New York, NY 10168-0072 ☎(212) 661-7200, toll-free (800) 651-7010, fax (212) 661-7174, gntonyc@d-z-t.com, www.cometogermany.com

Sydney
German National Tourist Office, GPO Box 1461, Sydney NSW 2001 ☎(02) 8296 0488, fax (02) 8296 0487, gnto@germany.org.au

Toronto
German National Tourist Office,
480 University Avenue, Suite 1500,
Toronto, ON, M5G 1V2
☎ (416) 968-1685, fax (416) 968-0562,
info@gnto.ca,
www.cometogermany.com

TOURIST INFORMATION ON SITE

Tourist offices
Tourist offices are marked on the town plans in this guide by the 🛈 symbol. Every sight throughout the *Discovering Germany* section of the guide has tourist office information.

International Visitors

GERMAN EMBASSIES AND CONSULATES ABROAD

In Australia
- Embassy of the Federal Republic of Germany, 119 Empire Circuit, Yarralumla ACT 2600
  ☎ (02) 6270 1911, fax (02) 6270 1951, info1@germanembassy.org.au
  www.germanembassy.org.au

- Consulate General of the Republic of Germany, Sydney, 13 Trelawney Street, Woollahra NSW 2025,
  ☎ (02) 9328 7733,
  fax (02) 9327 9649,
  info@sydney.diplo.de,
  www.sydney.diplo.de

In Canada

- Embassy of the Federal Republic of Germany, 1 Waverley Street, Ottawa, ON, K2P 0T8
  ☎ (613) 232-1101,
  fax (613) 594-9330,
  germanembassyottawa@on.aibn.com, www.ottawa.diplo.de
  Postal address: PO Box 379, Postal Station "A", Ottawa, ON, K1N 8V4

- Consulate General of the Federal Republic of Germany, 77 Bloor Street West, Suite 1703, Toronto, ON, M5S 2T1

☎ (416) 925 28 13, fax (416) 925 28 18, mail@germanconsulatetoronto.ca, www.toronto.diplo.de
Postal address: Consulate General of the Federal Republic of Germany Postal Station "P" Box 523 Toronto, ON, M5S 2T1

In South Africa

- Embassy of the Federal Republic of Germany, 180 Blackwood Street, Arcadia, Pretoria 0083,
  ☎ (012) 427 89 00,
  fax (012) 343 94 01,
  germanembassypretoria@gonet.co.za, www.pretoria.diplo.de
  Postal address: PO Box 2023, Pretoria 0001

- Consulate-General of the Federal Republic of Germany, 19th Floor, Safmarine House, 22 Riebeek Street, Cape Town 8001
  ☎ (021) 405 30 00,
  fax (021) 421 04 00, info@german consulatecapetown.co.za
  Postal address: PO Box 4273, Cape Town 8000

In the United Kingdom

- Embassy of the Federal Republic of Germany, 23 Belgrave Square, London SW1X 8PZ,
  ☎ (020) 7824 1300,
  fax (020) 7824 1435,
  www.london.diplo.de

- Consulate General of the Federal Republic of Germany, 16 Eglinton Crescent, Edinburgh EH12 5DG, Scotland,
  ☎ (0131) 337 2323,
  fax (0131) 346 1578

In the United States

- Embassy of the Federal Republic of Germany, 4645 Reservoir Road NW, Washington, DC 20007-1998
  ☎ (202) 298-4000,
  www.germany.info

- Consulate General of the Federal Republic of Germany, 871, United Nations Plaza (1st Avenue @ 49th Street), New York, NY 10017 ☎(212) 610-9700, fax (212) 940 04 02, www.new-york.diplo.de

FOREIGN EMBASSIES AND CONSULATES IN GERMANY

- **American Embassy,** American Embassy, Pariser Platz 2, 10117 Berlin, ☎030-830 50, fax 030 238 62 90

- **American Consulate-General,** Willi-Becker-Allee 10, 40227 Düsseldorf, ☎0211-7 88 89 27, fax 0211-7 88 89 36

- **Australian Embassy,** Wallstraße 76–79, 10179 Berlin, ☎030-88 00 88-0, fax 030-88 00 88-210, www.australian-embassy.de

- **Australian Consulate-General,** Neue Mainzerstr. 52-58, 60322 Frankfurt am Main, ☎069-90 55 80 80, fax 069-90 55 81 19

- **British Embassy Berlin,** Wilhelmstraße 70-71, 10117 Berlin, ☎030-20 45 7-0, fax 030-20 45 7-579, www.britischebotschaft.de

- **British Consulate-General,** Wilhelmstraße 70, Düsseldorf 40476, ☎0211-94 48-0, fax 0211-48 81 90

- **Canadian Embassy,** Leipziger Platz 17, 10117 Berlin, ☎030-20 31 20, fax 030-20 31 25 90, www.kanada-info.de

- **Consular Services Section,** Canadian Embassy, Leipziger Platz 17, 10117 Berlin, ☎030-2031-2470, fax 030-2031-2457

- **South African Embassy,** Tiergartenstraße 18, 10785 Berlin, ☎030-22 07 30, fax 030-22 07 31 90, www.suedafrika.org

- **South African Consulate-General,** Sendlinger-Tor-Platz 5, 80336 München, ☎089-2 31 16 30, fax 089-23 11 63 63

Entry Requirements

Passports and Visas

Citizens of European Union countries need a national identity card or a passport to visit Germany; there is no limit to the length of their stay. Under the visa-waiver program, citizens of certain nations (including Australia, Canada, New Zealand and the US) require only a passport, but no visa, in order to be admitted to Germany and are permitted to stay for up to three months as tourists. Citizens of all other countries, including South Africa, need to apply for a Schengen Visa at the German consulate in their home country. Regulations change from time to time. Check www.auswaertiges-amt.de for the latest details.

Driving licence

A valid national or international driving licence is required to drive in Germany and third-party insurance cover is compulsory; it is advisable to obtain an International Insurance Certificate (Green Card) from your insurer. If you are bringing your own car into the country, you will need the vehicle registration papers.

Customs Regulations

UK citizens should spply to the Customs Office (UK) for a Customs guide for travellers, available from HMRC, http://customs.hmrc.gov.uk.

For **US citizens**, the US Customs Service offers a publication called *Know Before You Go*, which is available as a downloadable pdf from www.cbp.

gov/xp/cgov/travel/vacation/kbyg or visit www.customs.gov.

Health

Be sure to obtain adequate travel health insurance before going on your trip. If you are a citizen of the European Union, you are entitles to free or reduced-cost emergency medical treatment while visiting Germany as long as you carry your European Health Insurance Card (EHIC). It is available free of charge through your national health authority. Applications can usually be made online. Contact your local office or see http://ec.europa.eu/employment_social/healthcard for full details.

Citizens from countries outside the EU should check with their health insurance provider is they are covered for medical emergencies while travelling in Germany. If not, definitely obtain travel insurance, preferably one that covers emergency repatriation to your home country. Most German doctors and hospitals require visitors to pay at the time of service. Make sure you understand what kind of documentation your insurance requires for reimbursement.

For referrals to an English-speaking doctor, contact your embassy or consulate in Germany.

If you take regular medications, bring a sufficient supply as well as letter from your physicians stating that they are required to treat your medical condition.

Accessibility

Many of the sights described in this guide are accessible to people with special needs. Sights marked with the symbol j offer access for wheelchairs. However, it is always best to call ahead.

An excellent source is the annually updated guide *Handicapped-Reisen Deutschland* (16.80€, plus postage) published by FMG-Verlag GmbH, Postfach 2154, 40644 Meerbusch, b 02159-815622, fax 02159-815624, www.fmg-verlag.de. It lists specific details about hundreds of wheelchair-friendly hotels, apartments and youth hostels and is available at bookstores or directly from the publisher online, by phone or in writing.

Disabled motorists should take note that a disabled car badge/sticker does not entitle them to unrestricted parking, as it does in the UK (local disabled residents are granted special parking permits only in exceptional circumstances). Apart from this, Germany is on the whole a well-equipped country for disabled visitors.

GETTING THERE AND GETTING AROUND

By Plane

Numerous airlines operate regular services to Germany's airport, the busiest of which are Frankfurt and Munich. Others are in Berlin, Bremen, Dresden, Düsseldorf, Hamburg, Hannover, Köln/Bonn, Leipzig, Nürnberg, Saarbrücken and Stuttgart. The German national carrier **Lufthansa** can be contacted on the following numbers:

- ♦ **Australia**, ☎1300 655 727
- ♦ **Canada**, ☎1-800 563 59
- ♦ **South Africa**, ☎0861 842538
- ♦ **UK**, ☎0871 945 9747
- ♦ **USA**, ☎800 399-5838

Information about flights to and within Germany can also be obtained, and reservations made, on their website at www.lufthansa.com.

Numerous budget airlines, notably **Ryanair** and **easyJet** also fly to several destinations in Germany from throughout Europe. They are both ticketless airlines. Ryanair serves Berlin, Bremen, Weeze (near Düsseldorf), Hamburg, Leipzig, Friedrichshafen and Karlsruhe/Baden from London Stansted airport. For information and reservations, visit www.ryanair.com or contact one of their European call centers. Dial ☎0871 246 0000 (£0.10/min) from within the UK, at ☎0900 116 0500 (0.62€/min) in Germany and at ☎+353 1 249 7700 from the rest of the world.

Web-based airline **easyJet** flies to Berlin, Cologne/Bonn, Dortmund, Hamburg and Munich from various airports in the UK. For information and reservations, visit www.easyjet.com, or call ☎0905 821 0905 (£0.62/min) in the UK.

INLAND FLIGHTS

There are numerous internal flights in Germany, most of them operated by **Lufthansa** (☎0180 583 84 26, www.lufthansa.com). Other carriers with domestic services include **Air Berlin** (☎01805-73 78 00, www.airberlin.com) and **Germanwings** (☎0900-191 91 00, www.germanwings.com).

By Ship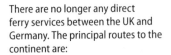

There are no longer any direct ferry services between the UK and Germany. The principal routes to the continent are:

- ◆ Dover to Calais, France (sailing: 1hr 15min);
- ◆ Folkestone to Calais, France (sailing: 2hr);
- ◆ Harwich to Hook van Holland, Netherlands (sailing: 6hr 15min)
- ◆ Hull to Zeebrugge, Belgium (12hr30min)

By Train

International high-speed rail links from London St Pancras to Aachen and Cologne (Eurostar to Brussels, then Thalys) make the train an attractive alternative to plane, coach or car in terms of time, price and convenience. Visitors leaving London can reach Aachen in just 4 hours and Cologne in less than 5 hours.

TICKETS AND FARES

Deutsche Bahn (DB), Germany's leading railway, is also the quickest and most reliable option for getting around the country. Most cities are served by DB's high-speed InterCity-Express (ICE) trains or InterCity/Euro-City (IC/EC) services; regional centers are connected by a fleet of RegionalExpress (RE), RegionalBahn (RB) and S-Bahn trains.

Special tickets: **German Rail Pass** (www.raileurope.com) – valid for 4 days of travel anywhere in Germany (available only to non-European residents); **Bahncards** (www.bahn.de) – 25% or 50% discount for frequent travelers within Germany; **InterRail One Country Pass** (www.interrail.net)– the classic rail pass for unlimited rail travel within Germany for 3, 4, 6 or 8 days of travel within 1 month (available only to European residents).

In addition, various saver tickets, seasonal promotions and discounted fares for children, seniors, students and groups are also available.

S-Bahn Station Sign

©Tobias Machhaus/istockphoto.com

For further information and reservations, contact:
Deutsche Bahn UK Booking Centre, ☎08718 808 066 (🕐open Mon-Fri 9am-5pm), sales@bahn.co.uk, www.bahn.co.uk. Information can also be obtained from Deutsche Bahn's main website, www.bahn.de.
Rail Europe, 178 Piccadilly, London W1, ☎08448 484 064 (brochure hotline: ☎08448 484 055), www.raileurope.co.uk.
DER Travel Service, 18 Conduit Street, London W1R 9TD, ☎0871 231 3433, fax 020 7629 7442, tours@dertour.co.uk, www.dertravel.co.uk.

By Coach

Eurolines serves many cities in Germany from the UK. The coaches are all well-equipped for maximum comfort and have air conditioning, WC, TV/video, reclining seats, etc. Journey times can be quite long (from London Victoria it takes around 18hr to Berlin, 19hr to Munich and 13hr to Cologne), but tickets are inexpensive, especially when booked in advance (a 30-day advance return to Berlin costs around 82€). For information and reservations, call ☎08717 818 181 in the UK, or visit the Eurolines website at www.eurolines.co.uk.
The **Eurolines Pass**, valid for 15 or 30 days allows you to travel for a set price between a choice of 40 cities across Europe, with numerous internal connections available within Germany (low/high season prices for adults 199€/329€ for a 15-day pass and 299€/439€ for a 30-day pass). There are discounts for children, youths (under 26) and senior citizens. Children under 4 travel free.
For further details, call ☎01582 404 511 in the UK or visit www.eurolines-pass.com.

By Bus

The bus can be invaluable traveling within Germany, especially in areas where there is no train service.

Bus stations are generally found near railway stations. For prices and timetables, contact **Deutsche Touring GmbH**, Am Römerhof 17, 60486 Frankfurt am Main, ☎(069) 790 35 01; www.touring.de.

By Car

When driving to the Continent, the fastest and easiest way is via the Eurotunnel. These shuttle trains whisk cars, motorbikes, bicycles and coaches from Folkestone through the Channel Tunnel to Coquelles (near Calais, France) in about 35 minutes. For fares and details check with your travel agent, call ☎08705-353 535 in the UK or visit www.eurotunnel.com.
There are no longer an direct ferry services from the UK to Germany. The closest port to the German border is Hook van Holland in the Netherlands, which is served from Harwich. There are also ferries from Dover and Folkstone to Calais, France and from Hull to Zeebrugge, Belgium. See the section By Ship earlier for details. From these ports there is a wide choice of routes using autobahns and national roads into Germany.
Michelin offers drivers and motorcyclists a free online route planning service at www.ViaMichelin.com. For a proposed journey, you can determine possible stopovers between departure point and destination and define your required route using various criteria (such as time, distance, use of motorways, road tolls, etc.). You are given information on mileage, journey time, hotels and restaurants along the way (selected from the *Michelin Guide Germany*), and map extracts that can be printed out.

Distances
- Calais to Frankfurt via Cologne 600km/374mi.
- Hook van Holland to Munich via Bonn, Mainz, Stuttgart and Augsburg 845km/525mi.
- Zeebrugge to Munich via Karls-ruhe, Stuttgart and Augsburg 853km/530mi.

◆ Calais to Cologne via Aachen
   417km/259mi.

DRIVING REGULATIONS

Traffic in Germany drives on the right.
Drivers in cities with trams should
be especially careful before crossing
tramlines. The maximum speed in
built-up areas is 50kph/31mph. On the
open road the maximum increases to
100kph/62mph. There is no official limit
on motorways (Autobahnen), but drivers are recommended not to exceed
130kph/81mph. There is a compulsory
speed limit of 80kph/50mph on roads
and motorways for vehicles with
trailers. In Germany careless or reckless
driving is considered a serious offence
and fines can be stiff. The maximum
limit for alcohol in the blood is 0.5ml/g.
German motorways (signposted 'A'
for Autobahn) are toll-free and well
equipped with service areas, usually
open round the clock and providing:
petrol, spare parts and accessories,
washrooms, toilets, public telephones,
refreshments, accommodation and
first-aid equipment.
City centers are often reserved for
pedestrians but there are usually
plenty of signposted parking garages
(Parkhaus).
Seatbelt usage is compulsory in the
back as well as the front of the car.
Children under age 12, or less than
1.5m/4ft 11in tall, are required by law
to be fastened in a suitable child car
seat; there are fines for non-compli-
ance. It is a legal requirement to carry
the regulation red emergency triangle,
for warning other motorists of a breakdown or enforced roadside halt, and
a first-aid box (including disposable
gloves and rescue blanket).
In Germany emergency services are
always given priority and drivers
should pull over to the side of the road.

BREAKDOWN SERVICE

For 24-hour service on motorways and
main roads, call ☎ 0180/2 22 22 22
(or ☎ 22 22 22 from mobile phones).
Service is provided on main roads and
autobahns by the ADAC (www.adac.

Important Warning Signs:	
Anfang	beginning
Ausfahrt	exit
Baustelle	roadworks, building site
Einbahnstraße	one-way street
Einfahrt	entrance
Ende	end
Gefahr	danger
LKW	HGV; truck
PKW	private car
Rechts einbiegen	turn right
Links einbiegen	turn left
Rollsplitt	gravel chippings
Stau	hold-up, traffic jam
Unfall	accident
Umleitung	diversion
Verengte Fahrbahn	road narrows
Vorfahrt	priority
Vorsicht	Look out!

de). Roadside breakdown services can
be called from one of the emergency
phones – small arrows on the roadside
posts indicate the direction of the
nearest emergency phone.
On-the-spot repairs are free, as only the
cost of replacement parts or towing is
charged. Motorists ringing this service
should ask specifically for the "Straßen-
wachthilfe" (road patrol assistance).
The *Michelin Guide Deutschland* lists
the numbers to use to contact the
ADAC service in all big towns.

GASOLINE

The following grades of petrol (gas)
are available in Germany:
🚗 *Super Plus Bleifrei*:
   Super unleaded (98 octane)
🚗 *Normal Bleifrei*:
   Standard unleaded (95 octane)
🚗 Diesel

Leaded petrol is no longer available.
A lead substitute can be added to the
fuel tank of those vehicles that require

it; the additive can be purchased at petrol stations.

CAR HIRE

The minimum age for car hire is 25, although some companies may rent to drivers ages 21 to 24 at a surcharge. You also need to have had your driving licence for more than one year. The major car hire firms have offices at airports and main stations and in large towns, but it is generally cheaper to arrange car hire before travelling to Germany. Some useful numbers (in Germany) include:

- **Avis**: ☎01805 217 702, www.avis.com
- **Europcar**: ☎01805 80 00, www.europcar.com
- **Hertz**: ☎01805 33 35 35, www.hertz.com
- **Sixt**: ☎01805 25 25 25, www.e-sixt.com

WHERE TO STAY AND EAT

Where to Stay

Hotel and Restaurant recommendations are located in the Address Books throughout the *Discovering Germany* section of this guide. For coin ranges and for a description of the symbols used in the Address Books, see the Legend on the cover flap.

ADDRESSES IN THE GUIDE

We have selected accommodations for their value, location or character, trying to cater to all budgets. However, popular tourist regions, resorts and big cities are more expensive than others. Likewise, there is often a significant price difference between high and low season.

During festivals and other cultural events last-minute accommodations are very hard to find.

Tourist information offices have lists of local lodging, including apartment rentals, rural guesthouses and castle hotels and are able to reserve rooms on your behalf.

For advance reservations, consult such online booking services as www.venere.com, www.hotel.de, www.expedia.de and www.opodo.de. For last-minute bargains, consult Hotel Reservation Service (☎0870 243 0003 in the UK, ☎0221 2077 600 in Germany, www.hrs.com).

BED AND BREAKFAST

The sign *Zimmer frei* outside private houses indicates that guestrooms are available. Final prices quoted usually include tax, service charges and breakfast.

CAMPING

With around 2 500 campsites, Germany has plenty of scope for camping. Most are closed between November and March, but a few remain open all year. Fees are usually composed of a charge per person (2.50€ to 7€), for your tent (4€ to 8€) and for your car (2€ to 5€). More information is available from **Bundesverband der Campingwirtschaft in Deutschland (BVCD)**, www.bvcd. de and from **ADAC**, ☎01805 10 11 12, www.adac.de. The latter publishes an annually updated guide called *ADAC Camping and Caravaning Führer* (in German).

DJH YOUTH HOSTELS & BACKPACKER HOSTELS

Germany has almost 600 youth hostels, which are managed by the Deutsches Jugendherbergswerk (DJH, see www.djh.de for a complete list) and affiliated with the Hosteling International (HI). They are open to everyone, young and old, although

In Bavaria priority is given to families and travelers under 27 if space is tight. Staying at a hostel requires membership in an HI association. Nonmembers can obtain cards directly at the hostels. Advance booking is recommended during the holiday season and at city center youth hostels. Bookings can be made by phone, fax, email and, in some cases, online.

There is now also a growing number of independent **backpacker hostels** that don't require membership. They are especially prevalent in big cities, Berlin in particular, and generally cater more to individual travelers than groups or families. Standards vary widely. Consult Backpacker Network (www.backpackernetwork.de). Reservations are available through www.hostelworld.com.

Lunch by the River Wümme

Bremer Touristik-Zentrale

whole host of details on Germany's hotels and restaurants.

APARTMENT LIVING

Renting a furnished apartment for a short period of time is common practice in Germany.
Local tourist offices normally have information on availability.

FARMS

This type of accommodation is particularly well developed in Bavaria and in the wine-growing regions and very popular with families.
For details, check www.landtourismus.de or www.bauernhofurlaub.de.

CASTLE HOTELS

For information about hotels and restaurants in castles and other historic buildings, contact your country's German National Tourist office or try **Histohotels**, Eduard-Rosenthal-Str. 30, 99423 Weimar, ☎01805 891 791, www.histohotels.de.

THE MICHELIN GUIDE DEUTSCHLAND

For a more exhaustive list of hotels and restaurants consult *The Michelin Guide Deutschland* which provides a

Where to Eat

Restaurants are described in the **Address Books** within the *Discovering Germany* section. Meal prices are indicated according to the following key:

⊜⊜⊜⊜	Over 40€
⊜⊜⊜	25€ to 40€
⊜⊜	14€ to 25€
⊜	Less than 14€

GERMAN CUISINE

German food is more varied and balanced than is generally supposed. Breakfast **(Frühstück)** is usually a generous spread including cold meats, cheese and a wonderful assortment of fresh bread and rolls. Lunch **(Mittagessen)** is traditionally a hot meals consisting of soup and a main course revolving around fish or meat. Many modern Germans, though, eat their main meal at dinnertime, preferring a light meal at midday. Snack stands are called **Imbisse** and are ubiquitous throughout the country. Sausages, especially the grilled **Bratwurst** are a staple here, often paired with potato salad or sauerkraut. Choices are greater and more international in the big cities, where the Turkish doner kebab is a popular tummy filler. Many Germans still indulge in an afternoon coffee break in a café. Most offer

Regional specialities

Bavaria and Franconia
- **Leberknödel:** Dumplings of liver, bread and onion, sometimes in broth.
- **Leberkäs:** Minced beef and pork (no liver), cooked in the form of a loaf.
- **Knödel:** Dumplings of potato or soaked bread.
- **Steckerlfisch:** Skewered grilled mackerel, often served at festivals such as Oktoberfest.
- **Rostbratwürste:** Small sausages grilled over beechwood charcoal.

Baden-Württemberg
- **Schneckensuppe:** Soup with snails.
- **Spätzle:** Egg-based handmade pasta in long strips.
- **Maultaschen:** Pasta stuffed with a mixture of veal and spinach.
- **Geschnetzeltes:** Thinly sliced veal in a cream sauce.

Rhineland-Palatinate
- **Sauerbraten:** Beef marinated in wine vinegar, served with potato dumplings.
- **Reibekuchen:** Potato pancakes served with apple or blueberry sauce.
- **Saumagen:** Stuffed pork belly with pickled cabbage.
- **Schweinepfeffer:** Highly seasoned pork ragout, thickened with blood.
- **Federweißer:** Partially fermented new wine accompanied by an onion tart.

Hessen and Westphalia
- **Sulperknochen:** Pork ears and tail served with cabbage and pease pudding.
- **Töttchen:** Ragout of brains and calf's head, cooked with herbs.
- **Pfefferpothast:** Stew cooked with pepper, lemon and capers.

Thuringia
- **Linsensuppe mit Thüringer Rotwurst:** Lentil soup with Thuringian sausages.

Saxony
- **Leipziger Allerlei:** Vegetable medley e.g. of peas, carrots, asparagus.
- **Dresdener Stollen**: Dense butter cake with dried fruits.

Lower Saxony and Schleswig-Holstein
- **Aalsuppe:** Sweet-and-sour eel soup with prunes, pears, vegetables and bacon.
- **Labskaus:** Favorite sailor's dish, beef, pork and salted herrings with potatoes and beetroot, served with gherkins and fried egg.
- **Grünkohl mit Pinkel:** Minced kale cooked with smoked sausage and onion.

a large selection of cakes, such as **Schwarzwälder Kirschtorte** (Black Forest cherry cake) or **Käsekuchen** (cheesecake).

They also serve the somewhat lighter fruit tarts and the famous **strudel**, a mixture of fruit wrapped in crisp pastry. The evening meal **(Abendessen)** is either a cold supper of meats, cheese and bread or a simple cooked dinner, sometimes paired with a salad.

Although each region has its own specialities, certain dishes are served all over the country: **Schnitzel** (breaded and panfried pork cutlet), **Eisbein** (boiled knuckle of pork), **Schweinebraten** (roast pork) **Sauerbraten** (vinegar-marinated braised beef) and **Gulasch** (either in the form of soup or as a stew).

Beer and Wine

Germans are justifiably proud of their national beverage, produced by nearly 1 200 breweries throughout the country. Although no longer required by law, most German brewers still adhere to a purity law *(Reinheitsgebot)* decreed in 1516, whereby nothing but barley, hops and plain water may be used in the making of beer (with the addition, today, of yeast).

German vineyards cover 102 000ha/252 000 acres, extending from Lake Constance to the Saaletal, and from Trier to Dresden. Growers produce a variety of wines from a wide range of grapes. The most famous German grape is the noble Rieslings, which accounts for 21% of vineyard area, followed by Müller-Thurgau with 14%. Wines from the Middle Rhine, Moselle, Saar and Ruwer rivers are aromatic and refreshing, those from the Rheingau delicate and from the Nahe full-bodied and elegant. Also try the potent, dry wines of Franconia and the varied wines of Baden and Württemberg. Among the **red wines**, choice examples come from Rheinhessen and Württemberg. The Palatinate and the Ahr are known for their well-balanced reds, especially the Spätburgunder.

Ph. Gajic/MICHELIN

WHAT TO SEE AND DO

Outdoor Fun

PARKS

National Parks

Germany's 14 national parks are wonderful playgrounds for nature-lovers and active types. Further information is available from **Europarc Deutschland**, Friedrichstraße 60, 10117 Berlin, ☏(030) 28 87 88 20, www.europarc-deutschland.de.

- **Bavaria:** Bavarian Forest (Bayerischer Wald), Berchtesgaden.
- **Schleswig-Holstein:** Schleswig-Holstein mudflats (Wattenmeer).
- **Lower Saxony:** Lower Saxon mudflats (Niedersächsisches Wattenmeer), Harz.
- **North Rhine-Westphalia:** Eifel.
- **Hamburg:** Hamburg mudflats (Wattenmeer).
- **Saxony-Anhalt:** Harz.
- **Mecklenburg-Western Pomerania:** Jasmund, Müritz, Vorpommersche Boddenlandschaft.
- **Saxony:** Swiss Saxony (Sächsische Schweiz).
- **Brandenburg:** Lower Oder valley (Unteres Odertal).
- **Thuringia:** Hainich.

Theme Parks

For a list of the best known and most popular amusement parks in Germany, see www.germany-tourism.de/ENG/culture_and_events/theme_parks.htm.

SPORTS

For nature-lovers and outdoor sports fans alike, Germany's varied landscapes provide an ideal setting for all sorts of activities. Some very useful information in this respect can be found at www.germany-tourism.de (under Nature, Activity & Recreation).

Hunting

For information on hunting in Germany, contact **Jagdschutz-Verband**, Johannes-Henry-Straße 26, 53113 Bonn, ☏(0228) 94 90 620, www.jagd-online.de.

Cycling

Cycling can be a very practical, healthy, economical and delightful way to explore the German countryside. There are plenty of long-distance routes as well as dedicated bike paths in many cities. Information is available from the **Allgemeiner Deutscher Fahrad Club** (ADFC, ☏0421 34 62 90, www.adfc.de. Another good source is www.germany-

Park/Place	☎/Website	Nearest motorway exit
Bavaria-Filmstadt/ Geiselgasteig (Bayern)	(089) 64 99 20 00 www.bavaria-filmstadt.de	A 99: Oberhaching (4)
Churpfalzpark Loifling/ Cham (Bayern)	(099 71) 303 40 www.churpfalzpark.de	A 3: Straubing (106)
Erlebnispark Schloß Thurn/ Heroldsbach (Bayern)	(091 90) 92 98 98 www.schloss-thurn.de	A 73: Baiersdorf Nord (10)
Erlebnispark Tripsdrill/ Cleebronn-Tripsdrill (Baden-Württemberg)	(071 35) 99 99 www.tripsdrill.de	A 81: Mundesheim (13)
Erlebnispark Ziegenhagen/ Witzenhausen (Hessen)	(055 45) 246 www.erlebnispark-ziegenhagen.de	A 75: Hann.-Münden (75)
Europa-Park/Rust (Baden-Württemberg)	(01805) 77 66 88 www.europapark.de	A 5: Ettenheim (57
Fränkisches Wunderland/ Plech (Bayern)	(092 44) 98 90 www.wunderland.de	A 9: Plech (46)
Freizeit-Land/Geiselwind (Bayern)	(095 56) 92 11 92 www.freizeitlandgeiselwind.de	A 3: Geiselwind (76)
Filmpark Babelsberg/ Potsdam (Brandenburg)	(0331) 721 27 50 www.filmpark-babelsberg.de	A 115: Potsdam-Babelsberg (5)
Fort Fun Abenteuerland/ Bestwig-Wasserfall (Nordrhein- Westfalen)	(029 05) 811 23 www.fortfun.de	A 46: Bestwig (71)
Hansa-Park/Sierksdorf (Schleswig-Holstein)	(045 63) 47 40 www.hansapark.de	A 1: Eutin (15)
Heide-Park/Soltau (Niedersachsen)	(01805) 91 91 01 www.heidepark.de	A 7: Soltau-Ost (44)
Holiday Park/Haßloch (Rheinland-Pfalz)	(018 05) 00 32 46 www.holidaypark.de	A 65: Neustadt-Süd (13)
Phantasialand/Brühl (Nord-rhein-Westfalen)	(02232) 36-200 www.phantasialand.de	A 553: Brühl-Süd (2)
Potts Park/Minden-West (Nordrhein-Westfalen)	(0571) 510 88 www.pottspark-minden.de	A 2: Porta Westfalica (33)
Ravensburger Spieleland/ Meckenbeuren	(075 42) 40 00 www.ravensburger.de/spielelandL	A 96: Wangen-West (5)
Hollywood- und Safari-park/Schloß Holte-Stukenbrock (Nordrhein- Westfalen)	(052 07) 95 24 25 www.safaripark.de	A 2, then A 33: Stukenbrock-Senne (23)
Legoland (Günzburg)	(082 21) 70 07 00 www.legoland.de	A 7, then A 8: exit Günzburg
Serengetipark/Hodenhagen (Niedersachsen)	(05164) 97 99 90 www.serengeti-park.com	A 7: Westenholz (7)
Taunus-Wunderland/ Schlangenbad (Hessen)	(061 24) 40 81 www.taunuswunderland.de	A 66: Wiesbaden-Frauenstein (2)
Vogelpark Walsrode/ **Walsrode** (Niedersachsen)	(051 61) 60 440 www.vogelpark-walsrode.de	A 27: Walsrode-Süd (28)
Movie Park Germany/ Bottrop-Kirchhellen (Nordr-hein- Westfalen)	(020 45) 89 90 www.movieparkgermany.de	A 31: Kirchhellen-Feldhausen (40)

touism/cycling, a free route finder with maps and planning tips put together by the German National Tourist Office.

Horseback riding

Lists of equestrian centers can be obtained from regional and local tourist offices, or contact the **Deutsche Reiterliche Vereinigung**, Freiherr von Langen-Straße 13, 48231 Warendorf, ☎(02581) 636 20, www. pferd-aktuell.de.

Golf

High-quality golf courses are abundant in both metropolitan areas and the German countryside. For information, contact the **Deutscher Golf Verband**, Viktoriastraße 16, 65189 Wiesbaden, ☎(0611) 99 02 00, www. golf.de. Greens fees range from 35€ to 75€ for a one-day pass during the week, rising to about 45€ to 90€ on weekends.

Fishing

A German fishing license is required. For information contact the **Deutscher Anglerverband**, Weißenseer Weg 110, 10369 Berlin, ☎(030) 97 10 43 79, www.anglerverband.com or the **Verband Deutscher Sportfischer**, Siemensstraße 11-13, 63071 Offenbach, ☎(069) 857 06 95, www.vdsf.de.

Walking

The Federation of German Mountain and Walking Clubs can provide details on hikes organized by regional associations and also publishes guides and maps.
Contact details: **Deutscher Wanderverband**, Wilhelmshöher Allee 157-159, 34121 Kassel, ☎(0561) 93 87 30, www.dt-wanderverband.de.
Another source of information on mountain trails, shelters and overnight huts is the **Deutscher Alpenverein** (DAV, German Alpine Club), Von-Kahr-Straße 2-4, 80997 München, ☎ (089) 14 00 30, www.alpenverein.de.
For up-to-the-minute details on refuge opening times, weather reports, trail conditions, etc, contact the DAV's **Alpine information center** (Alpine Auskunft) at ☎(089) 29 49 40, Mon-Fri

Sailing on the Aussenalster, Hamburg

Hamburg Tourismus GmbH

9am-noon, Mon-Wed 1pm-4pm and Thu 1pm-6pm. For the Alpine weather forecast, call ☎0900 129 50 70.

Canoeing and Kayaking

Those interested in canoeing and kayaking or rafting should get in touch with **Bundesvereinigung Kanutouristik,** Hannah-Arendt-Straße 3-7, 35037 Marburg, ☎(06421) 168 91 60, www.kanutouristik.de.

Winter Sports

Although the Alps and the Black Forest remain the most popular skiing areas in Germany, snow sport is also possible in the central upland regions of the Harz mountains, the Thuringian Forest and the Sauerland.

Sailing & Windsurfing

Sail sports are hugely popular all along the North Sea and Baltic Sea coast as well as on such lakes as the Lake Constance, Lake Müritz and Lake Starnberg, near Munich. Information can be obtained from the German Sailing Federation, **Deutscher Seglerverband**, Gründgensstraße 18, 22309 Hamburg. ☎(40) 632 00 90. www.dsv.org.

Spas

Spa treatments have been around Roman times and Germans still consider them an important component of a healthy lifestyle. The frantic pace of modern life is driving an increasing number of visitors to follow suit at one of Germany's many spa resorts. Not only are spas used for the treatment or prevention of certain illnesses, they are also an ideal place to recharge your batteries.

Spa resorts have access to mineral water with medicinal properties and offer proper facilities for applying the necessary treatments. They are usually found in beautiful natural settings and are an interesting alternative for those wishing to have a quiet vacation, enjoy nature and enhance their well-being.

Information on all of the country's spa resorts can be obtained from the German Spa Association, the **Deutscher Heilbäderverband**, Schumannstraße 111, 53113 Bonn, ☎(0228) 20 12 00, www.deutscher-heilbaederverband. de. Another useful website is www. baederkalender.de.

Activities for Children 🄺🄸🄳🄨

In this guide, sights of particular interest to children are indicated with a KIDS symbol 🄺🄸🄳🄨. Some attractions may offer discount fees for children.

Zoos and Animal Parks – Kids love animals, of course, and Germany has plenty of places to meet cuddly koalas, pet a sheep or marvel at tiger teeth. An excellent online resource with detailed information about nearly 800 zoos throughout the country is www.zoo-infos.de.

Deutsche Spielzeugstrasse (German Toy Road)— This enchanting tourist route travels for 300km/186mi from Waltershausen in Thuringia to Schwabach in Franconia, passing through 30 towns where toys, dolls, teddy bears and other playthings are being produced, often in traditional fashion.

For the full scoop, contact Deutsche Spielzeugstraße, Bahnhofsplatz 1, 96515 Sonneberg, ☎(036 75) 88 02 65, www.spielzeugstrasse.de.

Kinderland Bayern – The Kinderland intitative in Bavaria is a network of more than 300 lodging properties, restaurants and leisure facilities such as theme parks, fun pools, museums, cable cars, and zoos. Members are classified with three, four or five "bears" according to their family-friendliness. For more information, see Kinderland Bayern, Leopoldstraße 146, 80804 Munich, ☎(0 89) 212 39 70, www.kinderland.by.

Calendar of Events

Listed below are the main events and festivals taking place year-round in Germany. More details can be obtained from tourist offices and at www.germany-tourism.com.

See also under 'Festivals' in certain blocks in the Address Book section.

JANUARY 1

New Year's Day International Ski Jump, part of the Vierschanzentournee (Four Hills Tournament) — **Garmisch-Partenkirchen**

SUNDAY BEFORE SHROVE TUESDAY

"München narrisch" Carnival — **Munich**

SHROVE MONDAY

Rosenmontagszug: procession and street carnival — **Cologne, Düsseldorf, Mainz, Munich**

SHROVE MONDAY AND TUESDAY

Narrensprung Carnival: elaborate traditional costumes and expressive wooden masks; Dance of the Fools — **Rottweil**

MAUNDY THURSDAY TO EASTER MONDAY

Traditional Sorbian Easter Egg Market — **Bautzen**

EASTER

Sorbian Easter Egg market — **Oberlausitz**

APRIL 30/MAY 1

Walpurgisnacht: Witches' Sabbath Festival — **Various towns in the Harz region**
Marburg townspeople and students sing in the month of May — **Marburg**

MAY TO MID-SEPTEMBER EVERY SUNDAY AT NOON

Rattenfängerspiel: pageant retracing the legend of the Pied Piper — **Hameln**

FRIDAY AFTER ASCENSION

Blutritt: equestrian cavalcade in honor of the Holy Blood relic — **Weingarten**

EARLY MAY TO EARLY JUNE

Festival of Classical Music — **Schwet-zingen**

SECOND HALF OF MAY

International horse racing at Iffezheim — **Baden**-Baden

WHITSUN

Kuchen und Brunnenfest: dance of the salt-workers in traditional 16C costume — **Schwäbisch Hall**
Meistertrunk: performance of the legend of the "Long Drink" during the Thirty Years' War by locals in period costume — **Rothenburg ob der Tauber**

WHIT MONDAY

Pfingstritt: equestrian parade — **Kötzting**

WHIT TUESDAY

Historische Geißbockversteigerung: auctioning of a goat in period costumes with folk dancing and a local fair) — **Deidesheim**

CORPUS CHRISTI

Solemn procession through the decorated town — **Munich**
Mühlheimer Gottestracht: procession of boats along the Rhine — **Cologne**
Procession through flower-decked street — **Hüfingen**

LAST SATURDAY OF MAY

Wildpferdefang: capture and auction of young stallions — **Merfelder Bruch**

14 DAYS AFTER WHITSUN, FROM FRIDAY TO MONDAY

Salatkirmes: Salad Fair commemorating the introduction of the potato to the Hessen region; traditional local costumes — **Schwalmstadt**

1ST WEEKEND IN JUNE AND SEPTEMBER, 2ND WEEKEND IN JULY

Castle illuminations (firework displays) — **Heidelberg**

JUNE-AUGUST

Summer Music Festival: concerts of classical music in the Cistercian abbey — **Chorin**
Festival of Drama and Opera in the abbey ruins; theatre, opera — **Bad Hersfeld**

JUNE TO SEPTEMBER (EVERY 5 YEARS, NEXT: 2012)

Documenta: world's largest international exhibition of contemporary art — **Kassel**

LAST WEEK OF JUNE

Kiel Week: international sailing regatta; local festival — **Kiel**

LAST WEEKEND OF JUNE

Bergparade in historical costumes — **Freiberg**

FOUR SUNDAYS FROM END OF JUNE (EVERY 4 YEARS, NEXT: 2009)

Fürstenhochzeit (Landshut Royal Wedding): historical pageant in period costume — **Landshut**

DURING SUMMER MONTHS

Mecklenburg-Vorpommern Summer Music Festival, held in historic mansions, castles and churches — **Throughout Mecklenburg-Vorpommern**

JULY TO AUGUST

Schleswig-Holstein Music Festival — **Throughout Schleswig-Holstein**

1ST WEEKEND IN JULY

Spreewald Festival: Sorbian folklore and traditions — **Lübbenau**

EARLY JULY

Archers' Festival: procession of archers — **Hannover**

MID-JULY (EVERY 4 YEARS, NEXT: 2009)

Fischerstechen (Fishermen's Festival) — **Ulm**

3RD WEEKEND IN JULY (SATURDAY TO MONDAY)

Kinderzeche: commemorating the saving of the town by a deputation of children (historical costumes) — **Dinkelsbühl**

PENULTIMATE MONDAY IN JULY

Schwörmontag: river procession on the Danube — **Ulm**

3RD SUNDAY AND MONDAY IN JULY

Tänzelfest: historical procession by school children — **Kaufbeuren**

LAST SATURDAY IN JULY AND 1ST SUNDAY IN AUGUST

Summer music festival — **Hitzacker**

END OF JULY TO END OF AUGUST

Bayreuther Festspiele: Wagner Opera Festival — **Bayreuth**

JULY-AUGUST

Festival on the cathedral steps — **Erfurt**
Der Rhein in Flammen (The Rhine in Flames): Fireworks and illuminated casteles and boats along Rhine valley between Koblenz and Bingen— **Koblenz-Oberwesel, St Goar**

2ND SATURDAY IN AUGUST

Seenachtsfest: evening lakeside festival — **Constance**

2ND WEEK IN AUGUST

Further Drachenstich (Slaying of the Dragon): pageant of the legend of St George, in period costumes — **Furth im Wald**

SATURDAY AFTER AUGUST 24

Schäferlauf: shepherds' race (barefoot over a field of stubble) — **Markgrö-ningen**

LAST WEEK IN AUGUST

International horse racing at Iffezheim — **Baden-Baden**

SEPTEMBER

Festival with firework display — **Rothenburg ob der Tauber**

END OF SEPTEMBER TO EARLY OCTOBER

Cannstatter Volksfest: popular local fair — **Bad Cannstatt**

Oktoberfest

DECEMBER 24 AND NEW YEAR'S EVE

Weihnachtsschießen und Neujahrs-schießen: Christmas and New Year shooting matches — **Berchtesgaden**

Shopping

Germany is a shopper's paradise with malls, department stores, boutiques and specialty shops often conveniently clustering in pedestrianized city centers. Most towns also have weekly farmers' markets selling whatever fruit and vegetables are in season. Flea markets, meanwhile, are great for picking up some offbeat souvenirs. Generally, though, souvenirs are best purchased directly in the region where they hail from. So in the Black Forest you might acquire a cuckoo clock, in Bavaria a beer stein or a pair of lederhosen, in the Rheingau a bottle of excellent Riesling wine, in Meissen handpainted porcelain, in Nuremberg spicy gingerbread, in Lübeck delicious marzipan and in Berlin an authenticated piece of the Wall.

Other popular items to bring back home include natural cosmetics by Dr Hauschka, Birkenstock sandals, stuffed toys made by Steiff, collectible Käthe Kruse dolls and Solingen-made cutlery. Dedicated shoppers might want to visit in December, when you can stock up on enchanting ornaments and beautiful decorations at dozens of Christmas markets lighting up nearly every town square.

TWO WEEKS PRECEDING FIRST SUNDAY IN OCTOBER

Oktoberfest: Beer Festival. The largest popular festival in the world attracts around 6 million people to the Bavarian capital every year. — **Munich**

1ST AND 2ND WEEKEND IN OCTOBER

Weinlesefest: Wine Fair and election of the Queen of Wine — **Neustadt an der Weinstraße**

LAST 10 DAYS IN OCTOBER

Bremer Freimarkt: largest popular fair in northern Germany — **Bremen**

SUNDAY BEFORE NOVEMBER 6

Leonhardifahrt: similar celebration to that at Bad Tölz (below) — **Benediktbeuern**

NOVEMBER 6

Leonhardifahrt: prior to a Mass in honor of St Leonard, gaily decorated horse-drawn carts process through town to the church — **Bad Tölz**

ADVENT

Christkindlesmarkt: Christmas markets (Christmas tree decorations and gifts); seasonal performances by children — throughout Germany but especially in **Nuremberg, Munich, Dresden**

Christmas Fair in Kassel

Sightseeing

The *Discovering Germany* section gives the opening times and admission charges for monuments, museums, churches, etc. On account of the ever-increasing cost of living and frequent variations in the opening times of these monuments, this information should only be used as a rough guide. It is intended for tourists who are travelling on their own and are not entitled to any reduction. With prior agreement, groups can obtain special conditions as regards both times and charges. Enquire at the ticket office before purchasing your tickets; age-related reductions, in particular, are available. It is always a good idea to make enquiries by phone before setting off, since certain monuments may be temporarily closed for restoration. Visiting conditions for churches are only specified if the interior is of particular interest, if there are set opening times or if there is an admission charge. Churches can generally not be visited during services. If a church is open only during services, visitors should behave respectfully.

MUSEUMS

Museums are usually closed on Mondays. Art museums often have a late-night opening one evening per week. Ticket offices usually close between 30min to 1hr before closing time.

Books

HISTORY AND BIOGRAPHY

- **A Concise History of Germany** – Mary Fulbrook
- **The Reformation** – Owen Chadwick
- **The Thirty Years' War** – Veronica Wedgwood
- **The Rise and Fall of the Third Reich** – William Shirer
- **The Last Days of Hitler** – Hugh Trevor-Roper

- **The Wall: The People's Story** – Christopher Hilton
- **Stasiland** – Anna Funder

THE ARTS

- **Bauhaus** – Frank Whitford
- **The Expressionists** – Wolf Dieter Dube
- **The Weimar Years:** *A Culture Cut Short* – John Willett

LITERATURE

- **Nibelungenlied** – Anonymous
- **The Lost Honor of Katharina Blum** – Heinrich Böll
- **Caucasian Chalk Circle; The Threepenny Opera; Mother Courage** – Bertolt Brecht
- **The Tin Drum; The Flounder; From the Diary of a Snail; My Century**– Günter Grass
- **The Glass Bead Game; Narcissus and Goldmund; Steppenwolf** – Hermann Hesse
- **Runaway Horse** – Martin Walser
- **The Reader** – Bernhard Schlink
- **Buddenbrooks; The Magic Mountain** – Thomas Mann
- **The Wall Jumper** – Peter Schneider
- **All Quiet on the Western Front** – Erich Maria Remarque
- **A Model Childhood** – Christa Wolf
- **Berlin Alexanderplatz** – Alfred Döblin

TRAVEL AND MODERN GERMAN SOCIETY

- **A Time of Gifts** – P Leigh Fermor (Penguin)
- **A Traveller's Wine Guide to Germany** – K Brady Stewart et al (Interlink Publishing Group)
- **A Tramp Abroad** – M Twain
- **Deutschland: A Winter's Tale** – H Heine
- **Germany and the Germans** – J Ardagh (Penguin)

- **Goodbye to Berlin** – C Isherwood (Hunter Publishing)
- **The Simon & Schuster Guide to the Wines of Germany** – I Jamieson (Simon & Schuster)
- **The Germans** – GA Craig (Plume Books)
- **The Origins of Modern Germany** – G Barraclough (WW Norton & Company)
- **Vanishing Borders** – M Farr (Penguin)

Films

- **The Lives of Others (2006)** – Academy Award-winning film about the all-pervasiveness of the East German secret police, the Stasi.
- **Sophie Scholl – The Final Days (2005)** – A dramatization of the final days of Sophie Scholl, co-founder of the Nazi resistance group, The White Rose.
- **Downfall (2004)** – A gripping account of Hitler's final days cooped up in a Berlin bunker.
- **Goodbye Lenin (2003)** – A son must protect his sick mother from learning that her beloved GDR has vanished while she lay in a coma.
- **Run Lola Run (1998)** – Fast-paced movie about woman who has 20 minutes to find and bring 100 000 Deutschmarks to her boyfriend so he does not rob a supermarket.

- **The Nasty Girl (1990)** – True story about a young woman who meets denial and hatred when investigating the Nazi past of her home town as a school project.
- **Wings of Desire (1987)** – An angel in postwar Berlin falls in love with a trapeze artist and decides to become human and thus mortal.
- **Das Boot (1981)** – Blood, sweat, fear, claustrophia and cameraderie experienced by a German World War II submarine crew under attack.
- **The Enigma of Kaspar Hauser (1974)** – True story set in 1820s Nürnberg about a young man who emerges after being held captive in a dungeon since birth.
- **Ludwig (1973)** – The tragic life and mysterious death of King Ludwig II of Bavaria.
- **Triumph of the Will (1935)** – Leni Riefenstahl's infamous propaganda film of the 1934 Nazi Party rally in Nürnberg.
- **The Blue Angel (1930)** – A nerdy professor's life goes on a downward spiral after he marries a sexy lounge singer (Marlene Dietrich).
- **Metropolis (1927)** – Fritz Lang's silent epic about the uprising of a proletarian class working underground.

USEFUL WORDS & PHRASES

ja, nein	yes, no	**Sprechen Sie Englisch?**	Do you speak English?
danke	thank you	**Ich spreche kein Deutsch.**	I don't speak German.
bitte	please		
Hallo (informal)	Hello	**Was kostet das?**	How much is it?
Tschüss (informal)	Bye	**Das ist zu teuer**	That's too expensive
Guten Tag (formal)	Good day	**Wo ist...?**	Where is...?
Auf Wiedersehen (formal)	Goodbye	**Ich heisse...**	My name is...
eins, zwei, drei	one, two, three	**Wieviel Uhr ist es?**	What time is it?
vier, fünf, sechs	four, five, six	**Ist der Tisch frei?**	Is that table taken?
sieben, acht	seven, eight	**Die Rechnung, bitte.**	The bill, please
neun, zehn	nine, ten	**Wieviel Uhr ist es?**	What time is it?
links, rechts	left, right		
Wie geht es Ihnen?	How are you?		

37

Haben Sie ein Zimmer frei?	
Are there any rooms available?	
Wo ist die Toilette?	Where is the loo?
Hilfe!	Help!
Entschuldigung	Sorry
Montag	Monday
Dienstag	Tuesday
Mittwoch	Wednesday
Donnerstag	Thursday
Freitag	Friday
Samstag	Saturday
Sonntag	Sunday
Ein Bier, bitte	A beer, please

Frühstück	Breakfast
Mittagessen	Lunch
Abendessen	Dinner
Imbiss	Snack
Polizei	Police
Krankenhaus	Hospital
Rufen Sie einen Arzt!	Call a doctor!
Es ist ein Notfall!	Emergency!
gut	good
schlecht	bad
Ich habe mich verirrt.	I'm lost
Wie weit ist es...?	How far is it?

BASIC INFORMATION

Business Hours

BANKS

Banks are open from 8.30am to 4pm Monday to Friday (sometimes to 6pm on Thursday) and closed on weekends. Branches in rural and suburban areas usually close for lunch between noon and 1pm. Bureaux de change *(Wechselstuben)* tend to keep longer hours.

SHOPPING

German shopkeepers are able to keep any hours they want, but most stick with the traditional pattern of opening around 9am or 10am and closing between 6.30pm and 8pm Monday to Friday and around 2pm or 4pm on Saturday.

In big cities, some supermarkets and shopping malls are experimenting with staying open until 10pm on Friday and Saturday.

Only bakeries and flower shops open for a few hours on regular Sundays. All stores are allowed to open on up to 10 predetermined Sundays per year, including throughout December.

Gas stations and stores at big city train stations are your main options for stocking up on basics after hours.

Communications

The international dialing code for Germany is **49**, so from the UK, for example, you would dial 00 49 + local dialing code **omitting** the initial 0 + subscriber's number.

International dialing codes from Germany:

- ☏ 00 44 for the UK
- ☏ 00 353 for Ireland
- ☏ 00 1 for the USA and Canada
- ☏ 00 61 for Australia
- ☏ 00 27 for South Africa.

National directory enquiries
☏11 833

International directory enquiries
☏ 11 834

Public telephones: phonecards *(Telefonkarten)* for the largely card-operated public telephones are sold at post offices and newspaper kiosks. Some phones also take bank cards.

☏Note that phone calls from hotel rooms are generally expensive.

Cell (mobile) phones operate on the GSM900/1800 network. If you have an unlocked phone, you can easily obtain a local German number by buying a SIM card at a telecom store such as those operated by T-Moible, Vodafone or E-plus. SIMs cost about 15€ and come with prepaid airtime that can be recharged by buying scratch-off cards at newsagents or supermarkets. If your phone is not unlocked, you can buy a prepaid phone for around 30€ at a major electronics stores such as Saturn or Media Markt.

🙂Please note that it is illegal to use your phone while driving.

Electricity

Voltage is 220V and appliances use two-pin plugs. Appliances operating on 110V, such as those from North America, require a transformer. Most electric shavers and laptops run on both 110V and 220V.

Emergencies

Police:	☎110
Fire brigade	☎112
Medical emergencies	☎112
Traffic accidents	☎110

Mail/Post

Yellow is the trademark color of the Deutsche Post, as the German postal service is called. Most post offices are open Mondays to Fridays from 8am to 6pm and on Saturdays from 8am to noon. Smaller and rural branches may observe a lunch break, while those in city centers may keep slightly longer hours. Postal rates are 0.55€ for standard letters (up to 20g) sent within Germany, 0.70€ to countries within Europe and 1.70€ for letters destined for overseas.

Media

NEWSPAPERS

Regional daily newspapers are widely read in Germany. The conservative *Frankfurter Allgemeine* and Munich's centrist *Süddeutsche Zeitung* enjoy a broad readership throughout Germany. Berlin's most popular daily is the *Tagesspiegel*, but the *Berliner*

Zeitung and the *taz* are also popular with readers in the capital. Among the national newspapers, the sensationalist daily *Bild* has a print run of over 5 million copies, but *Die Welt* offers better quality news. *Focus* and *Der Spiegel* are excellent weekly news magazines, while *Stern* and *Bunte* belong more in the tabloid category.

The main foreign newspapers are, of course, available at airports, stations and the larger newspaper kiosks.

TELEVISION

Germany has two national state television channels, **ARD** and **ZDF**. There are also regional channels such as Cologne's Westdeutscher Rundfunk (WDR) and Munich's Bayerischer Rundfunk (BR), and the Franco-German cultural television channel **Arte**. In addition, many private channels features a mix of soap operas, sitcoms, game shows and movies. Although most of them target the general public (RTL 2, PRO 7, SAT 1), there are some theme channels, such as the music channel VIVA – the German equivalent of MTV – and the sports channel DSF.

Money

The euro has been the unit of currency in Germany since the beginning of 2002. Foreign currency can be exchanged at the airports, in banks, at hotels and at currency exchange offices such as those operated by Reisebank and usually located in major train stations. To check on the latest currency exchange rates, consult www.xe.com or www.oanda. com.

CREDIT CARDS

Cash is still the dominant method of payment in Germany, especially in rural areas, although credit cards are slowly gaining in popularity. You can usually whip out your plastic at gas stations, travel agents, international hotels and better restaurants and boutiques, but it is always best to check first.

In the event of loss or theft of your card, call the following numbers immediately: **Visa** ☎ (0800) 814 91 00, **Eurocard-Mastercard** ☎ (069) 79 33 19 10, **American Express** ☎ (069) 97 97 10 00.

ATMS

Generally, the easiest and most convenient way to obtain cash is by using your bank card at a local ATM in Germany. Most are linked to such international networks as Cirrus, Maestro and Star. Credit cards may also be used but are generally more expensive.

Public Holidays

Jan 1, **Jan 6** (in Baden-Württemberg, Bayern and Sachsen-Anhalt only), **Good Friday**, **Easter Sunday**, **Easter Monday**, **May 1**, **Ascension**, **Whit Sunday and Monday (Pentecost)**, **Corpus Christi** (in Baden-Württemberg, Bayern, Hessen, Nordrhein-Westfalen, Rheinland-Pfalz, Saarland, Sachsen, Thüringen and those communities with a predominantly Roman Catholic population only), **Aug 15** (in Roman Catholic communities in Saarland and Bayern only), **Oct 3** (Day of German Unity), **31Oct 31** (Reformation Day, celebrated only in Brandenburg, Mecklenburg-Vorpommern, Sachsen, Sachsen-Anhalt and Thüringen only), **Nov 1** (in Baden-Württemberg, Bayern, Nordrhein-Westfalen, Rheinland-Pflaz and Saarland only), **Buß- und Bettag** (Day of Repentance and Prayer, usually third Wed in Nov, observed in Sachsen only), **Dec 24** (afternoon), **25**, **26** and **31** (afternoon).

Reduced Rates

By Train
See *Getting Around: tickets and fares* for information on special ticket offers available through Deutsche Bahn.

By Air
Fares are generally cheaper, the earlier you book them. For flying between European cities, discount carriers such as easyJet, German Wings and Ryanair usually offer the best fares. If you are under 26 or a student, you may qualify for cheaper fares with major carriers. Check with such travel agents as STA Travel or Flight Centre. Children under the age of 2 usually travel free.

Smoking

Germany was the last major European country to do so, but in January 2008 strict anti-smoking laws kicked in even in this final bastion of nicotine.
 There are slight variations between the individual Länder (states) but generally, smoking is no longer allowed in public buildings, hospitals, trains and train stations. It is also not permitted in restaurants, cafe's, bars and nightclubs. In some regions, smoking is permitted in such places if there is a separate room designated for smokers or if the establishment serves primarily beverages and no food. Beer gardens, street cafés and festivals are usually exempt.

Time

German clocks are set to Central European Time, which is Greenwich Mean time + 1 hour. When it is 12pm in Berlin, it is 6pm in New York, 11am in London and 12pm in Paris.

Tipping

A service charge of 15% is already included in the bill at German restaurants and cafes, so no additional tip is required. However, it is common to round your bill up to the nearest €. If the service has been especially good, an additional 5% tip may be given, 10% if the service was exceptional. Don't leave the tip on the table; pay the waiter in person. Taxi drivers typically receive a 5% tip. Porters and others assisting with your luggage expect 1€ per bag.

CONVERSION TABLES

Weights and Measures

	🇺🇸	🇬🇧	
1 kilogram (kg)	**2.2 pounds (lb)**	**2.2 pounds**	*To convert*
6.35 kilograms	14 pounds	1 stone (st)	*kilograms*
0.45 kilograms	16 ounces (oz)	16 ounces	*to pounds,*
1 metric ton (tn)	**1.1 tons**	**1.1 tons**	*multiply by 2.2*
1 litre (l)	**2.11 pints (pt)**	**1.76 pints**	*To convert litres*
3.79 litres	1 gallon (gal)	0.83 gallon	*to gallons, multiply*
4.55 litres	1.20 gallon	1 gallon	*by 0.26 (US)*
			or 0.22 (UK)
1 hectare (ha)	**2.47 acres**	**2.47 acres**	*To convert*
1 sq. kilometre	**0.38 sq. miles**	**0.38 sq. miles**	*hectares to*
(km²)	**(sq.mi.)**		*acres, multiply*
			by 2.4
1 centimetre (cm)	**0.39 inches (in)**	**0.39 inches**	*To convert metres*
1 metre (m)	**3.28 feet (ft) or 39.37 inches**		*to feet, multiply*
	or 1.09 yards (yd)		*by 3.28; for*
			kilometres to miles,
1 kilometre (km)	**0.62 miles (mi)**	**0.62 miles**	*multiply by 0.6*

Clothing

Women	🇪🇺	🇺🇸	🇬🇧		Men	🇪🇺	🇺🇸	🇬🇧
	35	4	2½			40	7½	7
	36	5	3½			41	8½	8
	37	6	4½			42	9½	9
Shoes	38	7	5½		Shoes	43	10½	10
	39	8	6½			44	11½	11
	40	9	7½			45	12½	12
	41	10	8½			46	13½	13
	36	6	8			46	36	36
	38	8	10			48	38	38
Dresses	40	10	12		Suits	50	40	40
& suits	42	12	14			52	42	42
	44	14	16			54	44	44
	46	16	18			56	46	48
	36	06	30			37	14½	14½
	38	08	32			38	15	15
Blouses &	40	10	34		Shirts	39	15½	15½
sweaters	42	12	36			40	15¾	15¾
	44	14	38			41	16	16
	46	16	40			42	16½	16½

Sizes often vary depending on the designer. These equivalents are given for guidance only.

Speed

KPH	10	30	50	70	80	90	100	110	120	130
MPH	6	19	31	43	50	56	62	68	75	81

Temperature

Celsius (°C)	0°	5°	10°	15°	20°	25°	30°	40°	60°	80°	100°
Fahrenheit (°F)	32°	41°	50°	59°	68°	77°	86°	104°	140°	176°	212°

To convert Celsius into Fahrenheit, multiply °C by 9, divide by 5, and add 32.
To convert Fahrenheit into Celsius, subtract 32 from °F, multiply by 5, and divide by 9.
NB: Conversion factors on this page are approximate.

Chiemsee
T. Krieger/MICHELIN

INTRODUCTION TO GERMANY

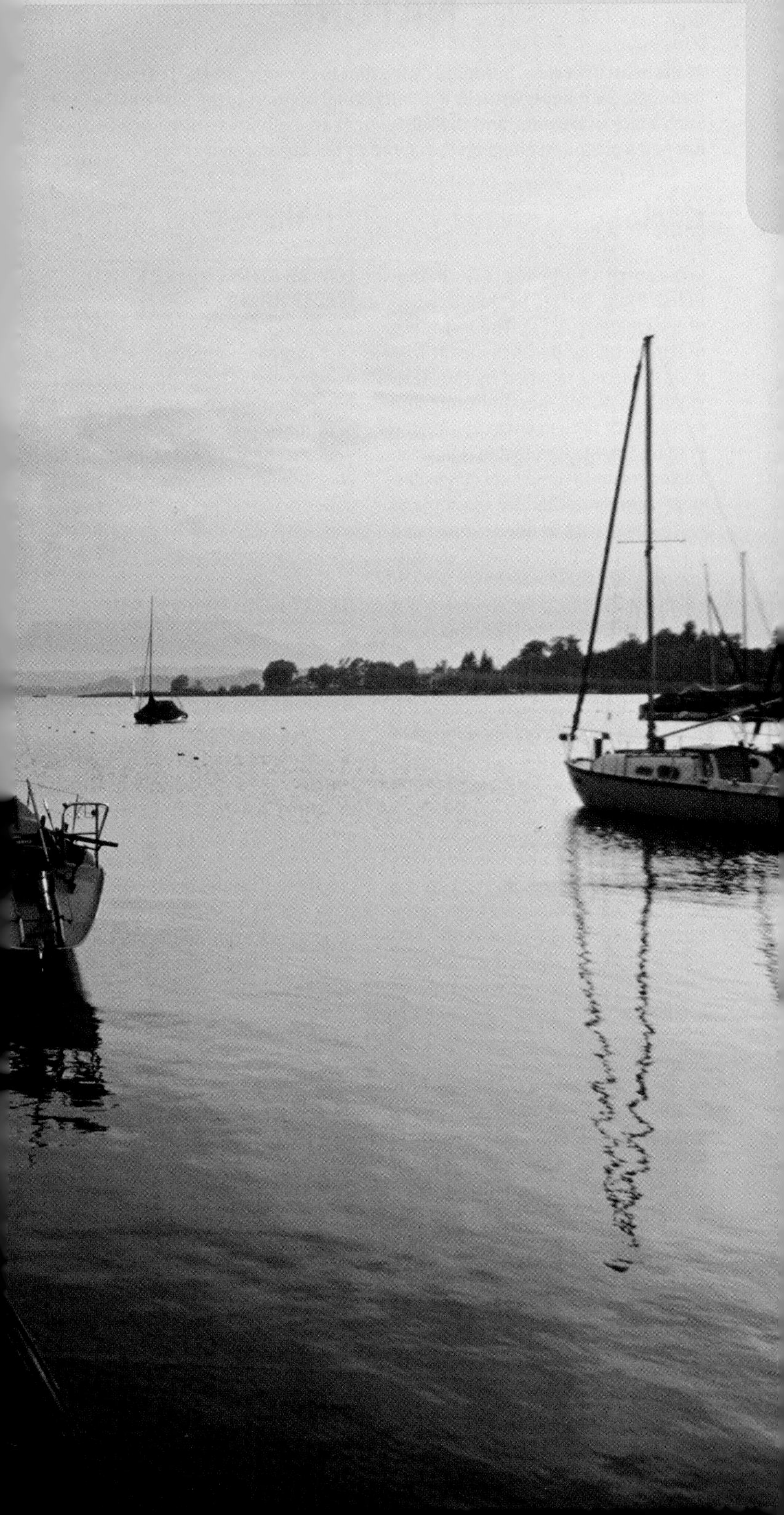

NATURE

At the heart of Europe, bordered by the Alps to the south and by the Baltic Sea to the north, Germany is virtually without natural frontiers to the east and the west. Such a lack of barriers, and the subsequent accessibility to outside influences has had a profound effect on the country's history and civilization.

Geology

In the **north** is the immense **Germano-Polish Plain**, formed by the glaciation of the Quaternary Era. The resistance of its crystalline bedrock meant that it was scarcely touched by the Hercynian and Alpine mountain-building movements. In the **center**, during the Primary Era, the formidable Hercynian folding created a complex of minor massifs—now smoothed by erosion and for the most part wooded—separated by geographic depressions. The most important of these Hercynian massifs are the Black Forest, the Rhenish schist massif, and—encircling Bohemia in the Czech Republic—the Bavarian Forest, the Erzgebirge (Ore Mountains) and the Sudeten Mountains. On the edges of this Hercynian zone accumulated the coal-bearing deposits of the Ruhr and Silesia which led to the industrial expansion of the 19C.

The sedimentary basin of Swabia-Franconia, its vast area drained by the Main and the Neckar Rivers, offers a less dramatic landscape. Abutting the Black Forest to the west and the Swabian Jura to the south, the limestone plateau is patterned with lines of hills sculpted according to the resistance of the varied strata.

In the **south**, the Alpine portion of Germany is delimited by the **Pre-Alps** (*Voralpen*) where the debris torn up and crushed during the final exertions of Quaternary glaciation formed the Bavarian plateau—a huge area stretching in a gentle slope as far as the Danube.

Northern Germany

LOWER RHINE VALLEY AND WESTPHALIA

Lush, green and flat, protected from flooding, the plain of the Lower Rhine brings to mind the landscape of the neighboring Netherlands. There is similar scenery around Münster, on the Westphalian plain, where farmlands patterned by hedges and trees offer the additional attraction of many moated castles *(Wasserburgen)*.

GREAT NORTHERN PLAIN

Despite its apparent monotony, this enormous area (which extends eastwards into Poland) does offer a certain variety of landscapes.

In the south, below the Weser and Harz foothills, the Börde country lies between the Weser and the Elbe—a region covered by an alluvial topsoil whose fertility is legendary. Farms and market gardens flourish in this densely populated zone, which is favored also with mineral deposits rich in iron and potassium. Farther north, on either side of the Elbe, is the Geest—a region of glacial deposits (sand, gravel, clay) with little to recommend it geographically, since it was covered by the Scandinavian glaciers right up to Paleolithic times. This has resulted in poor drainage and soils that are too sandy; between Berlin and the Baltic, the Mecklenburg plateau is scattered with shallow lakes interspersed with morainic deposits that bear witness to the prolonged glacial presence. The Spree and the Havel, meandering through the flatlands, supply the lakeland regions of the Spreewald and Potsdam. West of the Lower Weser, and in the Worpswede neighborhood north of Bremen, peat bogs (*Moore*) alternate

The red-sandstone cliffs of the island of Helgoland, North Sea

Bremer Touristik-Zentrale

with very wet pastureland. Most of the peat moors are now under cultivation, after having been drained using Dutch methods. The nature reserve south of Lüneburg, however, has preserved for all time a typical stretch of the original moorland.

THE BALTIC COAST

The German section of the Baltic Coast, which stretches from Flensburg all the way to the Stettin Haff, is a murrain landscape, which, in addition to very flat parts also has a few elevations that rise above the 100m/320ft mark. Because of the relatively limited tidal differences of the shallow (on average 55m/180ft deep) Baltic Sea, the coastline has only been subject to little change. That's why numerous cities with long traditions have evolved here. Between the bays of Lübeck and Kiel lies the Holsteinische Schweiz (Holstein Switzerland), the hilly and lake-dotted remainders of a ground and end moraine from the Ice Age. The arms of the sea, which are the fjords and bays left over from the glaciers of the last Ice Age, cut deep into the land and form excellent natural harbors. Their banks are lined with beaches, forests and little fishing villages. Further to the east, the Baltic Coast is marked by shallow, water-filled inlets from the post-Ice Age period. Four islands lie offshore, the largest is the water-washed Rügen.

NORTH SEA COAST

Because of the winds and waves, the North Sea Coast between the Netherlands and Denmark is constantly undergoing change. The tides raise and lower the water level by 2m/6.4ft to 3m/9.6ft twice daily. Several island groups lie off shore in the «Watt», a 5x30km/3x18mi strip of land that is washed by the sea when the tide is in, but is above sea level at ebb times. The Watt ecosystem is home to nearly 2 000 species, from sea lions to creatures 1/10 of a millimeter in size. A strip of marshland created over centuries lies along the coast. Once upon a time, the tides used to bring in animal and plant particles together with fine sand, which formed a fertile base for agriculture in the marshlands. Behind this is the less fertile, hilly "Geest". Broad moors have formed in the depressions, some of which have been turned over to farming. Germany's two largest seaports, Hamburg and Bremen, lie at the inner ends of the funnel-shaped Elbe and Weser estuaries.

Central Germany

THE RHENISH SCHIST MASSIF

This ancient geological mass, cut through by the Rhine—the only continuous natural channel of communi-

H. Spiering/MICHELIN

Lindau in Bavaria

cation between the north and south of the country—the Lahn and the Moselle, comprises among others the highlands known as the Eifel, the Westerwald, the Taunus and the Hunsrück.

They share the same inhospitable climate and the same evidence of volcanic activity as the crater lakes, known as the *Maare*, of the Eifel plateau.

The Eifel will be familiar to motoring enthusiasts as the home of the Nürburgring Grand Prix race circuit. The Upper Sauerland, a thickly wooded, mountainous region (alt 841m/2 760ft), with its many dams, acts as a water reserve for the Ruhr industrial area.

MOUNTAINS OF UPPER HESSEN AND THE WESER

Between the Rhenish Schist Massif and the Thuringian Forest (*Thüringer Wald*) lies an amalgam of heights, some of them volcanic (Vogelsberg, Rhön), and depressions which have been used as a highway, linking north and south, by German invaders throughout the ages. Between Westphalia and the north, the Weser Mountains—extended westwards by the Teutoburger Wald—form a barrier that is breached at the Porta Westfalica, near Minden. Farther to the east, the Erzgebirge (Ore Mountains) form a natural frontier with the Czech Republic.

HARZ MOUNTAINS

This relatively high range (alt 1 142m/ 3 747ft at the Brocken) has a typical mountain climate, characterized by heavy snowfalls in winter.

Southern Germany

PLAIN OF THE UPPER RHINE

Between Basle and the Bingen Gap, a soil of exceptionally fertile loess—accompanied by a climate combining light rainfall, an early spring and a very hot summer—has produced a rich agricultural yield (hops, corn and tobacco) and a terrain highly suitable for the cultivation of vines. The whole of this low-lying, productive tract has become a crossroads for the rest of Europe, which is why certain towns—Frankfurt, for instance—have profited internationally from their development.

SCHWARZWALD (BLACK FOREST)

This crystalline massif (alt 1 493m/4 899ft at the Feldberg), which overlooks the Rhine Gap, is relatively well populated. The region's healthy climate and many thermal springs, with their attendant, highly reputed spa resorts, draw large numbers of tourists here every year.

SWABIAN-FRANCONIAN BASIN

Franconia, formed by vast, gently undulating plateaux, is bordered to the south-east by the small limestone massif of the Franconian Jura which produces Germany's building stone, and to the north and north-east by the wooded crystalline ranges flanking Bohemia and Thuringia. Swabia, once ruled by the kings of Württemberg, offers a variety of landscapes—barred to the south by the blue line of the Swabian Jura, which rises to 874m/2 867ft. Small valleys, enlivened by orchards and vineyards, alternate here with the gentle slopes of wooded hillsides.

THE ALPS AND THE BAVARIAN PLATEAU

The Bavarian Alps and the Allgäu Alps offer contrasts between the sombrer-green of their forests and the shades of gray of their rocks and escarpments, an impressive sight when seen against the backdrop of a blue sky. The Zugspitze, the highest point in Germany, reaches an altitude of 2 962m/9 720ft. Torrents such as Isar, Lech, Iller and Inn, have over time carved out corridors with broad, flat floors suitable for the cultivation of the land and the development of towns (Ulm, Augsburg and Munich).

HISTORY

Long divided into a number of autonomous states, Germany was slow to achieve unity. This nation of great diversity, which was for a long time marked by feudalism and whose regions still hold considerable powers, is today one of the main spearheads of European unity.

Time Line

GERMANS AND ROMANS

The earliest evidence of human life on German territory today is the lower jaw bone dating back over 500 000 years of the so-called *Homo heidelbergensis*, which was discovered near Heidelberg in 1907. The Middle Paleolithic Age (200 000–40 000 BC) is considered the age of the Neanderthal Man (*see DÜSSELDORF: Excursions*). The first "modern people", the Homo sapiens, who survived on fishing, hunting and gathering, lived during the Late Paleolithic, an epoch of the Stone Age within the last Ice Age. During the Neolithic Era, people began to settle in village-like communities, where they lived for a while, grew plants and began raising animals.

The last prehistoric period, the Iron Age, began around 1000 BC, following the Bronze Age, thus named because that material was widely used to make implements, weapons and jewelry. The Iron Age is divided up into the La Tène Culture and the Hallstatt Culture.

Economic and political power started becoming more concentrated, evidence from graves suggests a stratified social system.

In the first millennium before Christ, Germanic tribes began resettling towards Central Europe. The occurrence and extent of this movement was under the auspices of numerous population groups of various origins and cultural levels living in the area between the northern German flatlands and the central mountain ranges. The first written reference to "Germania" is in the works of the Roman author Poseidonius (1C BC). Julilus Caesar, too, used this term in his *De Bello Gallico* to describe the non-Gallic regions north of the Alps.

The wars conducted by the Kimbers and the Teutons against the Romans around 100 BC were the first military conflicts between German tribes and the Roman civilization. The expansion of the western German tribes was stopped by Caesar's conquest of Gaul (58–55 BC). The aims of foreign policy until Emperor Augustus also covered the inclusion of Germania into the Roman Empire all the way to the Elbe, an objective that was never met.

During the 1C AD, the **Limes** was built: A 550km/341.7mi fortified line that sealed the Roman sphere of influence from the Rhine to the Danube. Skirmishes did break out every now and then, but there were also alliances, trade and cultural exchanges. New towns arose where Roman camps stood and at river crossings (e.g. Cologne, Koblenz, Regensburg).

In the 2C–3C AD, large tribes like the Franks, the Saxons and the Alemanni joined forces. The military kingdoms of the age of mass migration gave way to early medieval states.

AD 9 Three Roman legions under General Varus are annihilated by Germanic troops under prince **Arminius**, resulting in Roman relinquishment of bastions on the Rhine.

314 One year after announcing the Edict of Tolerance, Emperor Constantine establishes the first German bishopric, in Trier.

375 Beginning of the *Völkerwanderung*, the "movement of the peoples": The Huns drive the Goths (eastern Germans) to the west. The former *Imperium Romanum* breaks into partial empires.

800 End of the West Roman Empire brought about by German general Odoaker, who is in turn

---

La Tène Culture

The name for this cultural epoch supported by Celtic tribes (5C–1C BC) originated at an excavation site on Switzerland's Neuenburg Lake. Over 2 500 objects were found, including grave furnishings and treasures. The La Tène Culture was located primarily in southwestern Germany, along the northern edge of the Alps and in the Main-Moselle area. Fortifications expanded into settlements, the first north of the Alps. The advance of Germanic tribes and the expansion of the Roman Empire brought the La Tène Culture to an end.

---

murdered by the Ostrogoth Theodorich.

THE FRANKISH EMPIRE

The tribal union of the Franks expanded slowly south. Their king, Clovis I, eliminated the remains of the West Roman Empire and adopted Christianity. In the 7C, the Merovingians lost their hegemony to the Carolingians, formerly the highest royal officials under the Merovingians.

Since the 8C, the general term *thiutisk* developed from a derivation of the word for tribe to describe the peoples speaking Germanic languages. There was still no supra-regional language spoken to the east of the Rhine, the area of the Franks, until the 11C. In the 10C, the term *Regnum Teutonicorum* appeared for the first time in relation to the Eastern Frankish tribes. During the 11C and 12C it slowly established itself as a term.

751 Pope Zacharias agrees to the deposition of the last of the Merovingian kings, Childeric III, in favor of the palatine Pippin. Three years later the Pope places Rome under the protection of the Frankish kings.

768 Charlemagne becomes ruler. He conquers, among others, the Lombards, divides up Bavaria and defeats the Saxons after a long war.

800 Coronation of Charlemagne in Rome. The emperor legally assumes sovereignty over the former empire.

843 The Treaty of Verdun divides the Carolingian Empire among Charlemagne's grandchildren. The East Frankish Kingdom is given to Ludwig the German. The final division, determined by the treaties of Mersen (870) and Verdun/Ribemont (879–80), would evolve into Germany and France

911 The East Franks elect the Frankish duke Konrad to become their king, separating themselves from the West Franks.

Charlemagne crowned as Emperor on Christmas Day AD 800, in Chroniques de France ou de Saint Denis (14C)

THE HOLY ROMAN EMPIRE

The Holy Roman Empire consisted of an elective monarchy in which the king was crowned emperor by the Pope. From the 11C onwards, the emperor could rely on being king of not only Germany and Italy, but also of Burgundy. An especially "German" Imperial concept gave way to a Roman-universal idea of an emperor, a fact underscored in 1157 by the additional title *sacrum Imperium*. During the time of the Staufer dynasty, in the mid-13C, the claim to rule in Italy came to an end. In the 15C, the term "Holy Roman Empire of the German Nation" was finally established, implying the politically active community of the German Imperial estates, who acted as a counterweight to the emperor.

Ruling this empire, which during the High Middle Ages stretched from Sicily to the Baltic, was difficult without central administration and technical, financial and military wherewithal. By granting land and privileges (e.g. customs rights), administrative responsibility, security and imperial expansion were domains of the aristocracy.

Beginning in the second half of the 11C, the **Investiture Controversy** pitted the Pope against the Emperor on the issue of the right to invest bishops. This weakened the empire and shook up Christianity. The dispute ended with the Concordat of Worms (1122), declaring that ecclesiastical dignitaries had to be separated from worldly goods. The position of the bishops became similar to that of the princes, since they became vassals of the empire.

Charlemagne's Empire

After being crowned Emperor in St Peter's Basilica in Rome in 800, Charlemagne followed the lead of the Roman emperors. His empire stretched from Spain to the Elbe, from Rome to the English Channel. Charlemagne's reign introduced the "Carolingian Renaissance" as well as a new administrative structure. The emperor instituted a county constitution, disposing of independent duchies and tribal states. Each administrative district was governed by an officer chosen from the Frankish aristocracy, thus ensuring the coherence of the empire. Vulnerable borders were secured by border marches under authorized margraves. And emissaries with royal powers watched over the Imperial administration. The king constantly traveled his empire, visiting the "Pfalzen", which grew into major economic and cultural centers, and overnighting in Imperial abbeys.

These vassals gradually accumulated more power owing to the heredity laws of the fiefs and regalia. In the long term this weakened the empire, paving the way to the rise of numerous territorial states. The regional princely territorial states replaced the personal union state.

962   In Rome, Otto the Great, having been crowned king in 936, is crowned emperor by the Pope. The Ottonian dynasty rules until the death of Henry II in 1024, and is followed by that of the Salians (Franks).

1073   Pope Gregory VII elected. The reformer disputes the role of secular power in the church. The crux of the conflict was the penitent journey to Canossa (1077) by King Heinrich IV to receive absolution from the Pope, who had excommunicated him.

1152–90   Rule of the Staufer emperor Frederick I Barbarossa, who strengthens Imperial power (*Restauratio Imperii*) and captures the duchies of Bavaria and Saxony from the Guelph duke Henry the Lion (*see BRAUNSCHWEIG*). He also strives to limit papal power.

1212–50   Frederick II stays in southern Italy and Sicily for much of his reign, holding little interest in the area north of the Alps. Two Imperial edicts (1220–31) confirm the power over the territories of the secular and religious princes.

1254–73   The years between the death of Konrad IV and the election of Rudolf of Habsburg are known as the **Interregnum**. It is a time of lawlessness under "foreign" kings and anti-kings, finally eliminating the empire's power in the High Middle Ages.

THE LATE MIDDLE AGES

After the Interregnum, the power of the Habsburgs grew. Building up and consolidating family power by the 15C though the Luxembourg, Nassau and Wittelsbach families occasionally won the throne. The emperors tried to have a son elected king during their lifetime in order to maintain the ranking of their own dynasties. But during the Renaissance, the Imperial crown surrendered its holiness.

In the Late Middle Ages, the "Hoftage", or Imperial meetings, became the **Reichstag**, a meeting of 350 secular and religious Imperial estates, foreshadowing a sharp dualism between the emperor and his estates. At the Reichstag in Worms (1495), fundamental reforms created the preconditions for transforming the Reich into a unified legal and pacified territory. The proclamation of the *Ewiger Landfrieden* (eternal peace in the land) prohibited personal feuds, favoring a new legal basis. A Permanent Imperial Chamber Court ensured compliance. After a long debate, financial reform was pushed through raising the *Common Penny*, a combination of wealth tax, income tax and poll tax. Later *Reichstage* divided up the empire into administrative units—the Reichskreise, or Imperial districts. In 1663, the Permanent Reichstag was set up in Regensburg.

Inspired by the Humanists, the concept of a "German nation" began to arise politically as well as culturally, legitimized by the rediscovery of literary monuments such as "Germania" by Tacitus. Until around 1500, Europeans spoke of the *Deutsche Lande* (German lands); after 1500 the term "Deutschland" in the singular became common.

1273   After a warning from the Pope, electors choose as king Count Rudolf of Habsburg (dynastic power in the Breisgau, Alsace and Aargau).

1346–78   Charles IV of Luxembourg emerges as the most important ruler of the Late Middle Ages.

1386   Founding of the University of Heidelberg, Germany's first.

1414–18   Council of Constance; the largest church meeting of the Middle Ages to date.

1438   After the death of the last Luxembourg emperor, the electors choose the Habsburg duke Albrecht V to become King Albrecht II.

c. 1450 Invention of movable type printing by Johann Gutenberg from Mainz; flourishing and spread of Humanism.

1452 During a military campaign by Frederick III, the last imperial coronation takes place in Rome.

1493 Maximilian I becomes king. As of 1508 he is the "elected Roman Emperor". His successors adopt the Imperial title immediately after the royal coronation in Aachen, avoiding the difficult and dangerous journey to Rome.

1519–56 Emperor Charles V, Maximilian's grandchild, gathers more power during his term than any ruler since the Carolingians.

THE REFORMATION AND THE THIRTY YEARS' WAR

Engraved frontspiece to Luther's bible (1648)

In 1503, **Martin Luther** (1483–1546) entered the Augustinian monastery of Erfurt. A dedicated cleric, he was tormented by the problem of salvation. Appointed Professor of Theology in Wittenberg (1512–17), he found in the Holy Scriptures his answer: "We cannot earn forgiveness for our sins through our deeds, only God's mercy justifies us in our faith in it." Man's salvation, Luther argued, lies entirely within the grace of God. This concept led him to attack the Church's dealing in indulgences. On October 31, 1517, he nailed to the doors of Wittenberg Church his "95 Theses" condemning such practices and reminding the faithful of the importance of Christ's sacrifice and the Grace of God. Luther disagreed with Catholicism's pre-

scribed acts of atonement (confession, monetary contributions) as the only way to achieve salvation. He condemned the priest's role as "mediator" between man and God, advocating instead the "direct line" approach: man and God alone.

Luther was denounced in the court of Rome, refused to recant, and in 1520 burned the Papal Bull threatening him with excommunication. Subsequently he attacked the institutions of the Church. He objected to the primacy of the clergy in spiritual matters, arguing the universal priesthood of Christians conferred by baptism.

Refusing again to recant before the Diet of Worms (1521), where he had been summoned by Charles V, Luther was

The Golden Bull

Beginning in the 10C, the number of electors for the king began to decline. At the same time the election process became more regulated and formalized. In 1356, the Golden Bull promulgated an Imperial law regulating royal election, defining an institutional framework and limiting the power of the empire. From now on, the king would be elected by three religious electors (the archbishops of Mainz, Cologne and Trier) and four secular ones (the king of Bohemia, the margrave of Brandenburg, the duke of Saxony and the Palatine of the Rhine) and then crowned emperor. The election was set in Frankfurt/Main, and the coronation in Aachen; papal confirmation was no longer necessary. This law, announced by the Luxembourg emperor **Charles IV,** is considered the empire's first constitution and a basis for a federal system of state.

The Hanseatic League

The Hanseatic League existed between the 12C and the 17C. Its basic structure was established by about 1300. Thirty larger and numerous smaller cities joined to safeguard their shipping and trade interests. This union went through its Golden Age in the 14C: Over 100 cities, under Lübeck's leadership, formed the most significant economic force in northern Germany. After the Thirty Years' War, the Hanseatic tradition only continued in Hamburg, Lübeck and Bremen.

placed under a ban of the Empire and his works were condemned.

The patronage of Frederick the Wise, Duke of Saxony, enabled the reformer to seek refuge in Wartburg Castle where he translated the Bible from Latin into "everyday" German, making God's Word available to the German-speaking layperson. Indeed, his translation of the Bible is considered the first literary work in modern German. Luther's Bible and 95 Theses were a direct cause of the ensuing split of the Protestants from Roman Catholicism.

The Council of Trent (1545-63) resulted in the renewal of Catholicism and the Counter Reformation, which was resolutely supported by the Emperor. The internal struggles of the Protestants and the feud between Rudolf II and his brother Matthias ended the Peace of Augsburg. The Protestant Union led by the Electorate of the Palatinate now faced the Catholic League with the Duchy of Bavaria at its head. The Bohemian Rebellion of 1618 led to the outbreak of the Thirty Years' War, which began as a religious conflict and soon engulfed all of Europe.

The war, which was almost exclusively fought on German territory, devastated the land, caused general havoc, left cities in rubble and ruined economic life in the countryside. By the end of the war, only individual territorial states showed some gain in authority; the empire's significance dwindled.

1530 Invited by Charles V to Augsburg, theologians of the opposing faiths fail to agree. Luther's assistant, Melanchthon, draws up the "Confession of Augsburg," the charter of Protestantism.

1555 The Peace of Augsburg establishes a compromise, and Lutheran Protestantism is recognized as equal to Catholicism. The empire loses its sovereignty over religious matters to the territories.

1618 The Bohemian estates refuse to recognize Archduke Ferdinand, the successor of Emperor Matthias, as the Bohemian king. Instead, they elect the Protestant Elector Frederick V from the Palatinate to be their ruler. After the Defenestration of Prague in May (when the Bohemian king's representatives were thrown out of a window by nobles protesting reduced privileges), the situation intensifiea and leads to the Thirty Years' War.

1618–23 The first phase of the war (Bohemian-Palatinate War) is decided by the defeat of Frederick V at the battle of Weißer Berg in 1620 against an army commanded by Tilly.

1625–29 Phase two (the Danish-Dutch War) ends with Denmark's Protestant soldiers defeated by Imperial troops under Wallenstein.

1630–35 Sweden enters the war on the Protestant side (Swedish War). King Gustav Adolph II dies in battle near Lützen.

1635–48 France, under the leadership of Richelieu, participates in the alliance with Bernhard von Weimar (French-Swedish War).

1648 Peace of Westphalia: peace treaty in Münster and Osnabrück after five years of negotiations (see MÜNSTER).

1688–97 Palatinate War of Succession. Louis XIV lays claim to the left bank of the Rhine; French troops under Louvois devastate the Palatinate.

Prussian Reforms: The Revolution from Above

The reforms already prepared by the General Land Law of 1794 were initially set in motion by Baron von Stein, and, after his dismissal, by Baron von Hardenberg. The two men went about installing new structures for government and society virtually by decree and with almost revolutionary energy. Abolition of serfdom by the Edict of 1807 was of particular importance, as was the lifting of guild compulsion and the introduction of a free crafts market. Educational reforms followed, resulting in the founding of the university in Berlin by Wilhelm von Humboldt (1810) and a military reform. Other reforms included the emancipation of Jews and the modernization of the administration.

THE RISE OF PRUSSIA

In 1415, Burgrave Frederick of Hohenzollern was granted the Electorate of Brandenburg. The Duchy of Prussia, 203 years later, also came under the authority of his dynasty. Frederick William (1640–88), the Great Elector, turned the small country into the strongest, best-governed northern German state thanks to successful power policies, deprivation of the estates' power, a centralized administration and the creation of a standing army. He also expanded the country, adding eastern Pomerania, which he received in the Peace of Westphalia: two peace treaties which ended the Thirty Years' War. After the revocation of the Edict of Nantes in France, thousands of Huguenots fled to Brandenburg and built up the economic basis of Berlin.

His grandson, King Frederick William I continued his efforts by laying the foundations to a Prussian military and official state. Fulfillment of one's duty, industriousness, economy and strict discipline were aspects inspired by the "Soldier King".

His son, **Frederick the Great** (1740–86), took the throne in a country with an exemplary administration, and within a few years it became the second imperial power. The Silesian War and the Seven Years' War won him Silesia, and the division of Poland extended his power eastwards. This connoisseur of music and literature, the friend and correspondent of Voltaire, was considered an "enlightened ruler" and had a high reputation among European scholars. The rule of "Old Fritz" left Prussia with a well organized administration and a close relationship between the king and the nobles, all cornerstones of Prussian power.

1701 Elector Frederick III is crowned Frederick I King of Prussia in Königsberg.
1740–48 War of Austrian Succession/Silesian Wars: The legality of the Pragmatic Sanction (1713) pronounced by Charles VI is disputed. The war is triggered by Frederick II's troops marching into Silesia.
1756–63 Prussia joins forces with England against the Emperor during the Seven Years' War. By the end of the war, Prussia is the fifth European power; the system of power will guide Europe until World War I.

THE WAY TO A GERMAN NATIONAL STATE

Since 1792, war had raged between France and the other powers of Europe. The Peace of Lunéville, signed in 1801, resulted in the loss of German territories on the left bank of the Rhine. The Decision of the Deputation of German Estates (1803) destroyed the political and legal foundations of the old Empire. Bavaria, Prussia, Baden and Württemberg benefitted, gaining territory, while the latter two received Elector ranking. Sixteen of the southern and western German states left the Imperial Union and founded the Confederation of the Rhine in 1806 in Paris under the protection of France.

At the **Congress of Vienna** (1814–15) leaders discussed the geographical reor-

The Deutscher Bund

The Deutscher Bund, or German Confederation, a loose federation with little authority, was founded in 1815. The confederation included 39 politically autonomous states; four free cities; the kings of Holland, Denmark and the Low Countries; and portions of Prussia and Austria. The Bundestag (Parliament) included 11 governmentally-appointed representatives who met in Frankfurt and were led by Austria. Prince Metternich, who came from the Rhineland, played a decisive role in this union after he became Austrian chancellor. In collaboration with Prussia, he mercilessly crushed the libertarian and national movements. The restoration policies of the Bundestag gave rise to a period of extreme calm (Biedermeier period).

ganization, including restoration of the political status quo of 1792, legitimization of the *Ancien Régime*, and solidarity among the princes in combating revolutionary ideas and movements.

Since the 18C, literature, philosophy, art and music had melded, giving rise to a single German culture that preceded patriotism. The ideals of the French Revolution, the end of the Holy Roman Empire, the experience of French occupation and other reforms led to the growth of a 19C movement toward a free, unified German national state. One important stage on the way to unity was an economic one: the foundation of the German Zollverein (Customs Union) at the behest of Prussia.

On March 31, 1848, a pre-Parliament met in Frankfurt and held a National Convention, which opened on May 18 in the Paulskirche in Frankfurt. The aim was to pass a liberal constitution and consideration of the future German state. On the table were the Greater German Solution, with the Habsburg empire under Austrian leadership; and the Smaller German Solution, i.e. without Austria, but with a Hohenzollern emperor at the top. The latter was finally voted in. However, Prussian King Frederick William IV refused the Imperial crown brought to him by a delegate from the Paulskirche Parliament.

Otto von Bismarck, appointed Minister-President of Prussia in 1862, needed only eight years to bring about unification under Prussian rule. With the loyalty of an elite bourgeoisie created by the advances of industry and science, and aided by the neutrality of Napoléon III, he pursued a policy of war aggressively. After joining forces with Austria in defeating Denmark in 1864, Prussia declared war on her German ally and defeated the Imperial troops at the battle of Sadowa, thus ending Austrian-Prussian dualism for good. A year later, Bismarck created the North German Alliance, including all German states north of the River Main; Hannover, Hessen and Schleswig-Holstein already belonged to Prussia. The Franco-Prussian War of 1870–71 completed the task of unification.

1806 Napoleon marches into Berlin. Emperor Francis II of Austria surrenders the Imperial Crown ending the Holy Roman Empire going back to Charlemagne.

1813 Prussia commands the Coalition in the Wars of Liberation against Napoleon, who is defeated in the Battle of Nations at Leipzig.

1814–15 Congress of Vienna establishes the German Confederation; Holy Alliance between Russia, Prussia and Austria.

1819 The Decisions of Karlsbad include press censorship, prohibitions of

©2008 Hip/Scala, Florence

Otto von Bismarck

FORMATION OF GERMAN UNITY (1866-1871)

Kingdom of Prussia in 1865	
Prussian annexations in 1866	
Limits of German Empire in 1871	—
K= Kingdom	GD = Grand Duchy
D = Duchy	● = Free City

fraternities, monitoring of universities.

1833-34 Founding of the German Customs Union (*Zollverein*), an economic unification of most German states—except Austria—led by Prussia.

1835 First German railway line opens between Nuremberg and Fürth.

1848 Unrest in France in February spreads to Mannheim and then, in March, to all German states. But the "March Revolution" quickly turns into a bourgeois reform movement.

THE GERMAN EMPIRE (1871–1918)

The immediate cause of the Franco-Prussian War of 1870/71 was the claim by the House of Hohenzollern (Leopold von Hohenzollern-Sigmaringen) to the Spanish throne. Bismarck succeeded in kindling national pride on both sides of the border. France then declared war on Prussia. The southern states united with the states of the North German Union led by Prussia. The German princes all stood against France as they had signed secret alliances with Prussia. After the victory of Sedan (September 2), the southern states opened negotiations with Prussia on the issue of German unification.

The first years following the founding of the German Reich in 1871 were marked by an exceptional economic boom, the **Gründerzeit**, financed in part by the receipt of five billion francs in French war reparations. The advantages of the larger boundary-free economic area and efforts to standardize coins, measures and weights combined to create rapid growth in the financial, industrial, construction and traffic sectors.

1871 On January 18, William I is crowned German Emperor in the Mirror Room of Versailles. Imperial Germany, enlarged by the acquisition of Alsace-Lorraine, remains in theory a federation, but is in fact under Prussian domination. Germany is transformed from an agricultural to an industrial economy.

1888 William II succeeds his father Frederick III's brief reign.

1890 After numerous altercations, the Emperor forces Bismarck's resignation. The Emperor's unabashed expansionary policies and dangerous foreign policy provokes the enmity of England, Russia and France.

WORLD WAR I AND THE WEIMAR REPUBLIC

The assassination of the Austrian Archduke Franz Ferdinand and his wife at Sarajevo on June 28, 1914 unleashed an intense international reaction. Austria-Hungary's declaration of war against Serbia mobilized the great powers of Europe. Germany launched into wars on two fronts: German troops moved into France, halting only once they reached the River Marne; in the east, German troops invaded large sections of Russian territory.

1914 Germany declares war on France and Russia on August 3.

1917 The armistice agreed with Russia is shattered by revolution. The USA enters the war after Germany declares indiscriminate submarine warfare.

1918 On October 28–29, the sailors of the German naval fleet at Wilhelmshaven raise up in mutiny. Revolution erupts in Germany, with workers' and soldiers' councils springing up throughout the land. The revolution is suppressed by the provisional government under Friedrich Ebert with the support of military supreme command. On November 9, William II abdicates and Philipp Scheidemann proclaims the German Republic in Berlin. Two days later, Matthias Erzberger signs the armistice at Compiègne.

After the November revolution, which dwindled in early 1919 due to the unrest caused by the Spartacists, the model of a liberal democratic state with a strong president was established. On August 11, 1919, Germany adopted a Republican Constitution in Weimar, where the National Convention was meeting. This "republic without republicans" shouldered the burden of the Treaty of Versailles, which took effect in 1920: Acceptance of responsibility for the war, diminution of national territory (including important agricultural and industrial areas), loss of colonies, demilitarization and high reparations.

The only truly republican parties accepting the constitution, the SPD (Social Democrats), the Center Party, and the DDP (German Democratic Party) had a parliamentary majority after 1920. The Weimar Republic had 16 government changes, an average of one every eight-and-a-half months. Galloping inflation erupted, brought about by economic crisis, difficulties in relaunching the industrial sector and by high government debt: the bourgeoisie was ruined, and all financial assets except real estate were worthless.

Germany experienced an economic upswing and relative tranquility from 1924 to 1929 in spite of major economic burdens and high unemployment. The Dawes Plan can be credited with those successes; it managed German reparations, ended the French occupation of the Ruhr and committed to capital investment. Germany was even accepted into the League of Nations (1926) during the incumbency of Chancellor and Foreign Minister Gustav Stresemann. A year earlier in Locarno, Germany and France signed a pact pledging not to use violent means to revise borders—a corresponding agreement could not be signed for the eastern borders.

However, the world economic crisis hit the Weimar Republic in 1929. High foreign debt, sharp export declines, inflation, and dramatic unemployment all led to the rise of radical political parties, especially the German National Socialist Worker's Party, after 1930. They presented a theory that solving social problems would require a people's community, or "Volksgemeinschaft," based on race. Nazi storm-troops and Communist groups increasingly fought in the street. Social elites and the business community saw in **Adolf Hitler** a bulwark against Communism: on January 30, 1933, Hitler was named Chancellor of the Reich by President Von Hindenburg; it was the end of the Weimar Republic.

1919 The National Convention meets in Weimar, Friedrich Ebert (SPD) is named its first President (February 11); Versailles Peace Treaty is signed (June 28).

1923 Occupation of the Ruhr region on January 11 by France, because of Germany's failure to make reparation payments. The NSDAP (the National Socialist German Workers' Party) attempts a coup in Munich on November 8-9 led by Adolf Hitler, who had joined the party in 1919. The coup is foiled, Hitler is jailed but released in 1924.

1925 After the death of Friedrich Ebert, former Field Marshall General Paul von Hindenburg is elected President of the Republic.

1930 An electoral defeat in the Reichstag (Parliament) ushers in several presidial cabinets (Brüning, Von Papen, Von Schleicher), i.e. governments without parliamentary majorities.

1932 At the Reichstag elections in July, the NSDAP assumes leadership with almost 38% of the votes. Together with the Communists, the Nazis have an absolute majority, which lets the radical parties block all other parliamentary minorities.

THE NAZI DICTATORSHIP AND WORLD WAR II

No sooner had the NSDAP taken power under Hitler than it began to organize a totalitarian dictatorship and eliminate all democratic rules. In a climate of propaganda, intimidation and terror on the part of the SA, SS and Gestapo, all parties, associations and social organizations were liquidated or dissolved, with the exception of the churches. The NSDAP was declared the sole legal party. Opponents were thrown into concentration camps and murdered. Their power and societal control allowed the party to penetrate every level of state government. Competing authorities and rivalries quietly coexisted, but art and literature were subjected to censorship, forcing numerous artists into exile.

The Nuremberg Laws promulgated at the Reich party rally (September 1935) codified Jewish persecution on racist grounds; prohibitions, loss of civil rights and mass arrests were the instruments of the anti-Semitic ideology. As early as April 1, 1933, the NSDAP had ordered a "boycott of the Jews," initiating the gradual exclusion of Germany's 500 000 Jews from public life. In the night of November 9–10, 1938, the Nazis organized a pogrom *(Reichskristallnacht)* during which synagogues, Jewish homes and shops were damaged or destroyed.

The improved worldwide economic situation helped reduce unemployment as did a program of public works (autobahns, drainage schemes), a policy of rearmament and the recruitment of youth into para-governmental organizations. The National Socialist Reich stood at the zenith of its power: materially speaking and otherwise, many Germans had profited up until that point.

The assault on Poland on September 1, 1939, launched **World War II**. German preparations for an annihilation war had been underway since 1936 in the hopes of eliminating other peoples and creating a European area dominated by *Aryan* Eurasians. But the war reached German civilians as soon as the British and the Americans began dropping explosive and incendiary bombs on war-related and residential targets. By the end of the war, Germany lay in ruins, the bulk of the inhabitants suffered from under-nourishment and millions had been driven out of the eastern regions. With the liberation of the concentration camps, the world discovered with what cruelty and meticulousness the Nazis had carried out their policy of genocide against the Jews.

GERMANY FROM POST-WAR 1945 TO THE PRESENT

1945 Germany and Berlin are divided into four zones of occupation. According to the agreement, American and British forces pull out of Saxony, Thuringia and Mecklenburg and redeploy in the western sector of Berlin. At the Potsdam Conference (see POTSDAM) the victorious powers decide to demilitarize and democratize Germany and administer it jointly.

Dresden in ruins, 1945

1946 Amalgamation of the British and American zones.

1948 End of the Four-Power administration of Germany after the Soviet delegate leaves the Allied Control Council (March 20). Soviet blockade of the western sectors of Berlin, the city is supplied by the airlift.

1949 Creation (May 23) of the Federal Republic in the three western zones. The Soviet zone becomes (October 7) the German Democratic Republic.

Under Konrad Adenauer, Chancellor until 1963, and Ludwig Erhard, Minister of Economic Affairs, the Federal Republic enjoys a spectacular economic rebirth and re-establishes normal international relations.

1952 Soviet leadership offers to create a single, neutral, democratic Germany, a reunification initiative which fails.

1961 Construction of the "Berlin Wall" begins (August 12–13).

1972 Signature of a treaty between the two Germanies (East and West), a milestone in Chancellor Willy Brandt's policy of openness toward the East (*Ostpolitik*).

Reunification: the Fall of the Berlin Wall

1989 Citizens of East Germany occupy West German embassies in Prague, Budapest and Warsaw with the aim of traveling to West Germany. The opening of the border between Austria and Hungary launches an East German mass migration. On November 4 the largest demonstration ever brings together over one million people in East Berlin. On the night of November 9–10, the internal German border is opened, the Wall is breached. On December 7, the Round Table meets for the first time as an institution of public control, with representatives from the

Willy Brandt

Germany in the EU

The European Union is the result of a decades-long process of economic and political integration. It began in the 1950s with the goal of putting an end to centuries of bloody wars pitting neighboring nations against each other and culminating in World War II. Germany was one of the six founding countries, along with Italy, France, Belgium, Holland and Luxemburg. The EU currently has 27 members, 15 of which share a common currency, the euro. Germany, which held the EU Council Presidency in the first half of 2007, is a strong supporter of the 2007 Treaty of Lisbon that promotes collaboration among EU members on global challenges such as climate change, security and sustainable development.

political parties and the citizens' movements.

1990 Treaty of reunification drawn up; on October 3 the German Democratic Republic (DDR) joins the Federal Republic of Germany (BRD) according to Article 23 of the Basic law. On December 2, the first joint German parliamentary elections take place.

2005 Angela Merkel is elected German Chancellor.

2005 Bavaria-born Cardinal Joseph Ratzinger is elected Pope Benedikt XVI, becoming the first German pope since 1523.

2007 Merkel hosts the world's richest industrialized nations at the G8 summit in the Baltic Sea resort of Heiligendamm.

Keen to achieve rapid reunification, on November 28, 1989 West German Chancellor **Helmut Kohl** put forward a ten-point plan providing for the initial constitution of a confederation. On October 3, 1990 (now one of Germany's national holidays) parliament sitting in the Reichstag in Berlin ratified the treaty of reunification. Helmut Kohl won the elections in December 1990, and, in 1991, the Bundestag chose Berlin as capital of the reunified country. With the withdrawal of the last Allied troops in 1994, Germany became a sovereign state. It set its sights on the construction of a unified Europe. After the Federal President's move to Berlin, Parliament followed suit in 1999. On April 19 the new Plenary Room of the Reichstag building, crowned by a dome designed by British architect Lord Norman Foster, was inaugurated.

Reunification caused considerable economic and social problems: a drop in competitiveness, high unemployment in the new Länder and high taxes in the West to finance the modernization of the East fueled growing discontent. These problems eventually led to the loss of Helmut Kohl's CDU-CSU party in the 1998 elections and the ascendancy of Social Democrat **Gerhard Schröder** in coalition with the Green Party.

Under Schröder, Germany succeeded in reclaiming a post-World War leadership role within Europe and on the international stage. Germany is considered a leading political and economic force within the European Union, and its military has played an active peace-keeping role in war-torn Kosovo (1999) and also sent troops to Afghanistan.

But while the country has re-emerged as a positive force internationally, economic stresses continued to take their toll in the early 2000s. High unemployment and taxes coupled with decreased competitiveness due to economic globalization helped to oust Schröder's SPD from office. In its place, the CDU-CSU coalition regained a parliamentary majority in the 2005 federal election, with the role of Chancellor going to **Angela Merkel**.

Merkel's election reflected several historical milestones for Germany. She was the country's first female chancellor; the first former citizen of East Germany to head a reunified German government; and was the youngest person to be chancellor since World War II.

ART AND CULTURE

Religious architecture

Plan of a church

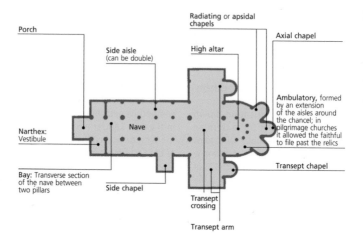

Porch

Side aisle (can be double)

Radiating or apsidal chapels

Axial chapel

High altar

Narthex: Vestibule

Nave

Ambulatory, formed by an extension of the aisles around the chancel; in pilgrimage churches it allowed the faithful to file past the relics

Bay: Transverse section of the nave between two pillars

Side chapel

Transept chapel

Transept crossing

Transept arm

Cross section of a church

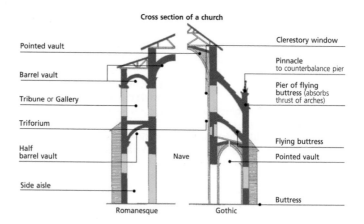

Pointed vault

Barrel vault

Tribune or Gallery

Triforium

Half barrel vault

Side aisle

Clerestory window

Pinnacle to counterbalance pier

Pier of flying buttress (absorbs thrust of arches)

Flying buttress

Pointed vault

Nave

Buttress

Romanesque

Gothic

Hall Church

Unlike a basilica, a hall church has aisles the same height as the central nave and covered with one roof: their windows let light inside the edifice.

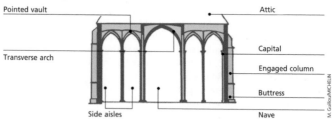

Pointed vault

Transverse arch

Attic

Capital

Engaged column

Buttress

Side aisles

Nave

M. Guillou/MICHELIN

SPEYER – East End of the Cathedral (11C)

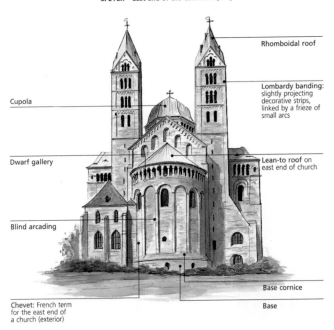

Rhomboidal roof

Lombardy banding: slightly projecting decorative strips, linked by a frieze of small arcs

Cupola

Lean-to roof on east end of church

Dwarf gallery

Blind arcading

Base cornice

Base

Chevet: French term for the east end of a church (exterior)

FREIBURG – Cathedral Altar (14C-16C)

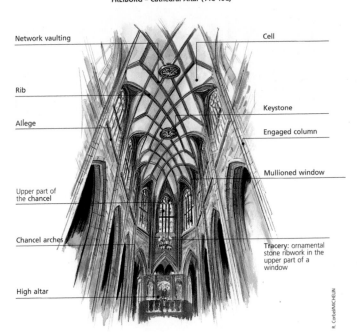

Network vaulting

Cell

Rib

Keystone

Allege

Engaged column

Mullioned window

Upper part of the chancel

Chancel arches

Tracery: ornamental stone ribwork in the upper part of a window

High altar

R. Corbel/MICHELIN

61

COLOGNE CATHEDRAL (1248 to 1880), South façade

The construction of the cathedral began in 1248 and took more than 600 years to complete. It was the first Gothic church in the Rhineland and the original design was based on those in Paris, Amiens and Reims. The twin-towered western façade marks the peak of achievement in the style known as Flamboyant Gothic. Stepped windows, embellished gables, slender buttresses, burst upwards, ever upwards, slimly in line with the tapering spires that reach a height of 157m/515ft.

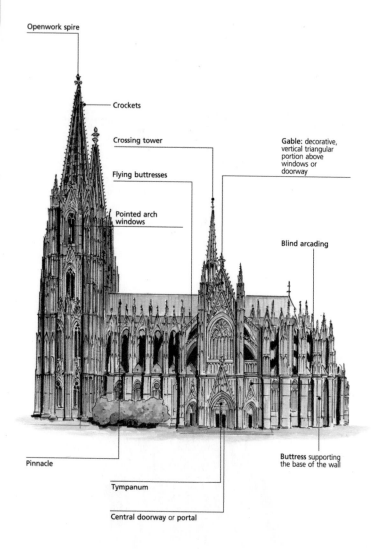

Openwork spire

Crockets

Crossing tower

Flying buttresses

Pointed arch windows

Gable: decorative, vertical triangular portion above windows or doorway

Blind arcading

Pinnacle

Buttress supporting the base of the wall

Tympanum

Central doorway or portal

R. Corbel/MICHELIN

Schloß BRUCHSAL – Garden façade (18C)

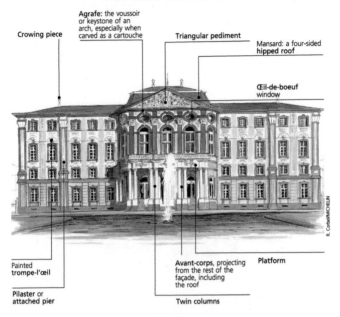

Crowing piece

Agrafe: the voussoir or keystone of an arch, especially when carved as a cartouche

Triangular pediment

Mansard: a four-sided hipped roof

Œil-de-boeuf window

Painted trompe-l'œil

Pilaster or attached pier

Avant-corps, projecting from the rest of the façade, including the roof

Twin columns

Platform

R. Corbel/MICHELIN

POTSDAM – Sanssouci Palace and Park
(Georg Wenzelaus von Knobelsdorff and Friedrich II, 1745-47)

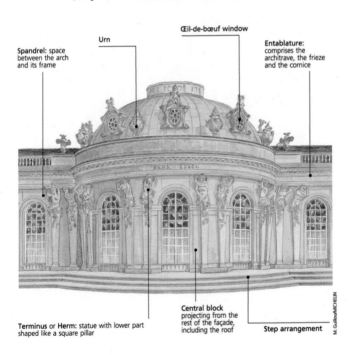

Spandrel: space between the arch and its frame

Urn

Œil-de-bœuf window

Entablature: comprises the architrave, the frieze and the cornice

Terminus or Herm: statue with lower part shaped like a square pillar

Central block projecting from the rest of the façade, including the roof

Step arrangement

M. Gaillou/MICHELIN

OTTOBEUREN Abbey Church (18C)

Ottobeuren is characteristic of other Bavarian churches with its dazzling ornamentation and plays of light and symmetry.

Painted vaulting

Spandrel: triangular space between the curve of an arch and the frame in which it is set

Stuccowork

Cornice with projecting ornamental motifs

Retable or altarpiece

Tabernacle

Pulpit (or ambo): elevated stand from which sermons were preached

Sounding board

R. Corbel/MICHELIN

"Uncle Tom's Cabin" estate
(Bruno Taut, Hugo Häring, Otto Rudolf Salvisberg, 1926-32)

Designed to house 15 000 people, this estate built under the supervision of Martin Wagner, does not convey an impression of monotony. There is a U-Bahn Station in its centre as well as a shopping centre and a cinema.

Terraced roof

All the buildings are of a moderate size

The simplicity of the façades painted with bright colours, hence the nickname of "parrot estate", is due to a rational building plan and the use of standard, relatively cheap, materials.

The natural surroundings are in keeping with the concept of **garden cities** at the beginning of the century.

Individual houses have re-entrant angles and tall windows characteristic of the style of Salvisberg who designed the buildings along Riemeisterstraße.

Philharmonie (Hans Scharoun, 1960-63) and Chamber Music Hall
(Edgar Wisniewski, from a drawing by Scharoun, 1984-88)

In 1957, during a congress, H Scharoun expressed his wish to build "an adequately shaped hall for music making, where listening to music would be a common experience". The audience sits round the orchestra, which occupies the very heart of the arena.

Aluminium sheeting: perforated, it was only added in 1978-81. Before that time, the concrete roof was painted in an ochre colour.

Philharmonie

The internal structure and the outside appearance are closely related. The place occupied by the orchestra determines the type of structure (three imbricated pentagons in the case of the Philharmonie, a hexagon in the case of the Chamber Music Hall): the tent-shaped roof provides good acoustics and adds a dynamic element to the visual aspect.

Chamber music hall

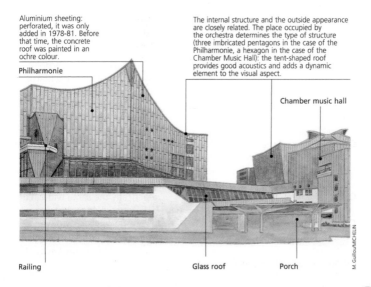

Railing

Glass roof

Porch

M. Guillou/MICHELIN

65

Glossary of Architecture

Absidiole or **apsidiole chapel**: Small apsidal chapel opening on the ambulatory of a Romanesque or Gothic church.

Aisles: Lateral divisions running parallel with the nave.

Ambulatory: Formed by an extension of the aisles around the chancel; in pilgrimage churches it allowed the faithful to file past the relics.

Apse: Rounded or polygonal end of a church; the outer section is known as the chevet.

Archivolt: Ornamental moulding around the outside of an arch.

Atlantes (or **Telamones**): Male figures used as supporting columns.

Atrium (or **four-sided portico**): Court enclosed by colonnades in front of the entrance to a early Christian or Romanesque church.

Basilica: Rectangular religious building, built on the Roman basilica plan with three or five aisles.

Bossage: Architectural motif or facing made of bosses, uniformly projecting blocks on the outer wall. They are surrounded by deep carving or separating lines. Bossage was in vogue during the Renaissance.

Buttress: External mass of masonry projecting from a wall to counterbalance the thrust of the vaults and arches.

Capital: Crowning feature of a column, consisting of a smooth part, connecting it to the shaft, and a decorated part. There are three orders in classical architecture: Doric, Ionic (with double volute), and Corinthian (decorated with acanthus leaves). The latter is often found in 16C-17C buildings.

Chancel: Part of the church behind the altar set aside for the choir, furnished with variously decorated wooden stalls.

Chevet: French term for the east end of a church (exterior).

Choir screen or **rood screen**: Partition separating the chancel from the nave.

Ciborium: Canopy over an altar.

Console (or **corbel** or **bracket**): Element of stone or wood projecting from a wall to support beams or cornices.

Corbelling: Projecting course of masonry.

Corbie gable: Triangular section crowning a wall, with steps on the coping.

Cornice: In Classical architecture, projecting ornamental moulding along the top of a building. Also designates any projecting decoration around a ceiling.

Cross (church plan): Churches are usually built either in the plan of a Greek cross, with arms of equal length, or a Latin cross, with shorter transept arms.

Crossing: Central area of a cruciform church, where the transept crosses the nave and choir. A tower is often set above this space.

Crypt: Underground chamber beneath a church, where holy relics were placed. Often a chapel or church in its own right.

Diagonal arch: Diagonal arch supporting a vault.

Drum: Circular or polygonal structure supporting a dome.

Embrasure: Recess for a window or door, splayed on the inside.

Entablature: In Classical architecture, the section above the columns consisting of architrave, frieze and cornice.

Gable: Decorative, triangular section above a portal.

Gallery: In early Christian churches, an upper story opening on the nave. Later used in exterior decoration.

Grotesque: Fanciful ornamental decoration inspired by decorative motifs from Antiquity. The term comes from the old Italian word *grotte*, the name given to the Roman ruins of the *Domus Aurea*, uncovered in the Renaissance period.

Hall-church: Church in which the nave and aisles are of equal height and practically the same width, communicating right to the top.

High relief: Sculpture with very pronounced relief, although not standing out from the background (half-way between low relief and in-the-round figures).

Jamb or **pier**: Pillar flanking an opening (doorway, window, etc.) and supporting the lintel above.

Keystone: Wedge-shaped stone at the crown of an arch.

Lantern: Turret with windows on top of a dome.

Lesene: Slightly projecting pilaster used for decoration.

Lintel: Horizontal beam connecting pilasters or columns and constituting the lower part of the entablature (in Classical buildings such as temples).

Lombard strips: Romanesque decoration consisting of vertical bands in slight relief or lesenes joined at the top by an arched frieze.

Low relief: Bas-relief, carved figures slightly projecting from their background.

Misericord or **miserere**: Bracket on the underside of a hinged choir stall used for support by canons or monks.

Modillion: Small console supporting a cornice, beginning of an arch, etc.

Moulding: ornamental shaped band which projects from the wall.

Mullion window: Window with two arches divided by a central post.

Narthex: Portico preceding the nave of a church.

Nave: Central main body of a church, flanked by aisles.

Oriel window: Window projecting from a wall on corbels.

Ovolo moulding: Egg-shaped ornamentation.

Pediment: Usually triangular ornament above buildings, doors, windows, recesses.

Pendentive: Triangular section of vaulting rising from the angle of two walls enabling the transition from a square space to an octagonal or circular dome.

Polyptych: Painted or carved work consisting of more than three folding leaves or panels.

Predella: Base of a polyptych or altarpiece.

Pulpit (or **ambo**): Elevated stand in various locations from which sermons were preached in a church.

Retable or **altarpiece**: Vertical structure, either painted or carved, above or set back from the altar. Monumental altarpieces are often found in Baroque churches.

Rib: Projecting band on the surface of a dome or vault that disperses the weight onto the structures below.

Rococo: Type of decoration in the late Baroque period typified by abstract combinations of shells and volutes.

Rose window: Circular window usually inserted into the front elevation of a church, decorated with delicate fan-shaped stone tracery (small columns, volutes, patterns).

Spandrel: Triangular space between the curve of an arch and the frame in which it is set.

Squinch: Arches placed diagonally across the internal corner angles of a square tower, converting the square into an octagonal form, thus enabling it to support a drum.

Stalls: Wooden seats reserved for the clergy, grouped together in the chancel.

String course: Ornamental, horizontal band on an exterior wall marking the division between storys.

Stucco: Form of plaster widely used from the Renaissance period for decoration in relief on walls and ceilings.

Transept: Transverse arms set at right angles to the nave and giving the church a cruciform shape.

Tribune: Upper platform in a church, overlooking the interior.

Triforium: In a Gothic church, a wall-passage above the aisles, opening on the nave, often via a blind arcade.

Triptych: Work comprising three painted or carved panels, whose outer sections can be folded over the central section.

Tympanum: In buildings, doors and windows, the triangular section between the horizontal entablature and the sloping sides of the pediment.

Vault: Arched structure forming a roof or ceiling.

Westwerk or **westwork:** The west end of a church containing a second chancel. A massive structure, often flanked by two stair turrets, typical of Carolingian and Ottonian architecture, sometimes reserved for the emperor.

Architecture

Germany's geographical location and history have left it open to the influence of artistic currents from the rest of Europe—mainly French in the Gothic period and Italian in the Renaissance period. Each style has been interpreted and adapted according to regional tastes. This inventiveness has allowed Germany to develop an originality that is reflected in the sumptuous decoration of the Baroque abbeys in Bavaria and in the Expressionism of the interwar years.

ROMANESQUE ARCHITECTURE

Carolingian Architecture (9C and early 10C)

Under the impetus of the emperor and the great prelates, a large number of religious buildings were built in Germany on a basilical or central plan (Palatine chapel at Aachen), both inherited from Antiquity. Carolingian architecture is marked by the building of churches with two chancels: at the west end, a particular form emerged, the **Westwerk**, a tall square structure attached to the nave and often flanked by two towers, like at Corvey, for instance. The Westwerk constitutes almost a church in itself, where the emperor may have worshipped and where a special liturgy developed. It had a long-lasting effect on German Romanesque architecture.

Ottonian Architecture (10C and early 11C)

The restoration of Imperial power by Otto I in 962 was accompanied by a revival of religious architecture in Saxony and in the regions of the Meuse and Lower Rhine. The huge churches of this period, characterized by deeply projecting transepts and wide aisles, feature wooden roofs that were usually painted. The alternation of piers and columns broke up the uniformity of the central portion, and east and west choirs were linked by the nave, with a skillful use of proportion giving a harmonious effect. The churches of St Michaelis at Hildesheim and St Cyriacus at Gernrode date back to this period.

Rhineland Romanesque Style

At Cologne and in the surrounding countryside, several churches feature a distinctive ground plan with a triple apse designed in the form of a cloverleaf, a style dating back to the 11C. A fine example can be seen at the church of St Maria im Kapitol in Cologne. These trefoil extensions are adorned on the outside with blind arcades and a "dwarf gallery" *(Zwerggalerie)*—a motif of Lombard origin.

In the Middle Rhine region, the style achieves its full splendor in the majestic "Imperial" cathedrals of Speyer (the first church to be entirely vaulted), Mainz and Worms. Typical of these cathedrals are floor plans with a double chancel and no ambulatory, but sometimes a double transept. The exterior features numerous towers, blind arcades and Lombard bands. A characteristic of these Rhineland towers is a pointed roof in the form of a bishop's mitre, the base decorated with a lozenge pattern.

The churches of Limburg and Andernach and the cathedral at Naumburg, which were built early in the 13C, mark the transition between two periods. They are built in a style which combines Romanesque aesthetics and Gothic structures, with pointed rib vaulting and triforia.

GOTHIC ARCHITECTURE

The gradual emergence of the Gothic style (13C)

The French style of Gothic architecture, which attempted to free itself of Romanesque austerity, did not flourish in Germany until the mid-13C. Architecture then reached new heights of refinement, producing such masterpieces as the cathedral in Cologne with its vast interior, two tall slender towers framing the façade in the French style and its soaring pointed vaulting. Also inspired by the French Gothic style are the cathedrals of Regensburg, Freiburg im Breisgau, Magdeburg and Halberstadt. A further manifestation of the predominance of French architecture can be seen in the establishment of Cistercian monasteries between 1150 and 1250. Their churches, usually without towers or belfries and often later modified in the Baroque manner, were habitually designed with squared-off chancels flanked by rectangular chapels. The abbey of Maulbronn is one of very few Cistercian complexes preserved in almost its entirety still extant in Europe.

The originality of German architecture

The German imprint first emerged in the use of brick. In the north of the country the most imposing edifices were brick, complete with buttresses and flying buttresses. Typical of this brick Gothic style (known in German as Backsteingotik) are the Nikolaikirche at Stralsund, the Marienkirche in Lübeck, the town halls of those two cities, Schwerin Cathedral and the abbey church at Bad Doberan. Also unique to Gothic German architecture is the adoption of a new layout inspired by Cistercian architecture and manifested in the **hall-churches** (Hallenkirche). In these buildings, the aisles are now the same height as the nave, which therefore has no clerestory windows, and are separated from it only by tall columns. In the Elisabethkirche in Marburg, the three aisles are separated by thin supports, giving an impression of space and homogeneity.

Late Gothic Architecture
(Spätgotik)

The lengthy Late Gothic period (14C, 15C and 16C) witnessed the widespread construction of hall-churches, including Freiburg cathedral, the Frauenkirche in Munich and the Georgskirche, Dinkelsbühl. The vaulting features purely decorative ribs forming networks in the shape of stars or flowers in stark contrast to the austerity of the walls. St Annenkirche at Annaberg-Buchholz epitomizes this artistic virtuosity, free of all constraints.

Secular Architecture in the Late Middle Ages – Commercial prosperity among merchants and skilled craftsmen

Mainz Cathedral

in the 14C and 15C led to the construction in town centers of impressive town halls and beautiful gabled and half-timbered private houses, frequently adorned with painting and sculpture. Examples of such architecture are still to be seen in the old town centers of Regensburg, Rothenburg ob der Tauber, Goslar and Tübingen.

THE RENAISSANCE

The Renaissance (1520–1620) is no more than a minor episode in the history of German architecture. Long held at bay by the persistence of the Gothic style, it was finally eclipsed by the troubles of the Reformation. Renaissance-style buildings are therefore rare in German towns. Augsburg is the lone exception. Its beautiful mansions lining Maximilianstraße and its town hall were designed by **Elias Holl** (1573–1646), Germany's most important Renaissance builder.

Southern Germany shows a marked Italian influence: elegant Florentine arcading was used by Jakob Fugger the Rich as decoration for his funerary chapel at Augsburg (1518); the Jesuits, building the Michaelskirche in Munich (1589), were clearly inspired by their own Sanctuary of Jesus (Gesù) in Rome; and in Cologne, the town hall with its two-tier portico reflects Venetian influence.

Northern Germany, on the other hand, was influenced by Flemish and Dutch design. In the rich merchants' quarters, many-storied gables, such as those of the Gewandhaus in Brunswick, boast rich ornamentation in the form of obelisks, scrollwork, statues, pilasters, etc. The castles at Güstrow and Heidelberg and the old town of Görlitz are important examples of Renaissance architecture, while the buildings of Wolfenbüttel, Celle, Bückeburg and Hameln are steeped in the particular charm of the so-called "Weser Renaissance" (&see HAMELN).

THE SPLENDOURS OF BAROQUE ARCHITECTURE

After the disruption of the Thirty Years' War (1618–48), the ensuing revival of artistic activity provided an opportunity for the principalities to introduce Baroque architecture by welcoming French and Italian architects. Characterized by an irregularity of contour and a multiplicity of form, the Baroque style seeks, above all, the effect of movement and contrast. Taken to its extreme, it was soon saturated by Rococo decoration, which originated in the French *Rocaille* style; this style was originally secular and courtly but subsequently used in religious buildings.

From the mid-17C, Baroque influence was felt in southern Germany, encouraged by the Counter-Reformation's exaltation of dogmatic belief in Transubstantiation, the cult of the Virgin Mary and the saints, and in general all manifestations of popular piety. The aim was to achieve an emotional response from the spectator. This exuberance did not spread to Protestant Northern Germany.

The Masters of German and Danubian Baroque

There were exceptionally talented individuals in Bavaria who displayed equal skill across a variety of techniques, and who tended to prefer subtle ground plans, such as a round or elliptical focal shape. **Johann Michael Fischer** (Dießen, Zwiefalten and Ottobeuren), the **Asam brothers** (Weltenburg and the Asamkirche in Munich) and **Dominikus Zimmermann** (1685–1766, Steinhausen and Wies) were the virtuosi

Zwiefalten Church

of this Bavarian School; their vibrant creations are covered by a profusion of Rococo decoration.

The Baroque movement in Franconia, patronized by the prince-bishops of the Schönborn family, who owned residences in Mainz, Würzburg, Speyer and Bamberg, was closely linked with the spread of similar ideas in Bohemia. The Dientzenhofer brothers decorated the palaces in Prague as well as the one in Bamberg. Perhaps the greatest of all Baroque architects was **Balthasar Neumann** (1687–1753), who worked for the same prelates, and whose breadth of cultural knowledge and creativity, enriched by his contact with French, Viennese and Italian masters, far surpassed that of his contemporaries. One of his finest creations was the Vierzehnheiligen Church near Bamberg, where he managed to combine the basilical plan with the ideal of the central plan. In Saxony, the Zwinger Palace in Dresden—joint masterpiece of the architect **Matthäus Daniel Pöppelmann** (1662–1736) and the sculptor Permoser—is a consummate example of German Baroque with Italian roots. The refinement of the Rococo decor in Schloss Sanssouci at Potsdam is even more astonishing given the reputed Prussian tendency towards austerity, but is explained by the periods of study undertaken in France and Italy by **Georg Wenzeslaus von Knobelsdorff** (1699–1753), official architect and friend of Frederick the Great.

Churches

A sinuous movement, generally convex in line, animates the façades, while the superposition of two pediments, different in design, adds vitality to the whole. They are additionally adorned with twin domed towers. Inside, huge galleries stand above the lateral chapels, at the height of pilaster capitals with jutting abaci. Chapels and galleries stop at the level of the transept, giving it a much greater depth. Clerestory windows at gallery level allow plenty of light to enter.

Bohemian and Franconian Baroque is typified by **complex vaulting**, round or oval bays being covered by complicated structures in which the transverse arches bow out in horse-shoe shape, only to meet in their keystones.

Illusion is the keyword as regards the often **Rococo** decoration, using the effects of the white stucco, colored marble and gilding. The numerous paintings and sculptures enhance this celebration of the sacred.

The monumental altarpiece or reredos

Reminiscent of a triumphal arch, in carved wood or stucco, the reredos became the focal point of the church, framing a large painting and/or statuary (Ottobeuren Abbey Church). Columns twisted into spiral form accentuate the sense of movement which characterizes Baroque art, and back lighting from a hidden source, with its striking contrasts of brightness and shadow, is equally typical of the style.

Palaces

The one-story construction of these country residences was often lent additional importance by being built on a raised foundation. The focal point was a half-circular central bloc with the curved façade facing the garden.

Monumental stairways with several flights and considerable theatrical effect are often the centerpieces of the larger German castles and palaces built in the 18C. The staircase, embellished with arcaded galleries and a painted ceiling, leads to the first floor state room which rises majestically to a height of two storys. Such elaborate arrangements characterize many of the great abbeys of this period, often complemented by that other ceremonial room, the library.

FROM NEOCLASSICISM TO NEO-GOTHIC

The ideal of an original austerity

From 1750 on, Winckelmann's work on the art of Antiquity, and the excavations taking place at Pompeii, threw a new light on Greco-Roman architecture. At the same time, the example of Versailles inspired in Germany a new style of court life, particularly in the Rhineland and the Berlin of Frederick II. Many French architects were employed by the Electors of the Palatinate, of Mainz, of Trier and of Cologne; mainly, they produced plans for country mansions with names such as Monrepos ("my rest") or Solitude. Other German architects, such as **Carl Gotthard Langhans** (1732–1808), were instrumental in the transition from the Baroque to the Neoclassical style (Brandenburg Gate and the Charlottenburg theater in Berlin).

Features such as unadorned pediments, balustrades at the base of the roofs, columned porticoes at the main entrance, all indicate a desire for unobtrusive elegance. A new fashion arose, in which architects favored the Doric style coupled with a preference for the colossal—pilasters and columns of a single "order" no longer stood one-story high but always two.

The interior decoration, carried out with a lighter touch, confined itself to cornucopias of flowers mingled with Rococo motifs that were now a little more discreet (garlands, urns, vases and friezes of pearls).

Architecture was now responding to a demand for rationality that had emerged in reaction to the Late Baroque and Rococo styles.

Karl-Friedrich Schinkel (1781–1841)

Appointed state architect by Frederick William III in 1815, he designed many buildings, including the Neue Wache, Altes Museum and Schauspielhaus in Berlin. In a refined approach using elements inspired by Antiquity, this great exponent of Romantic Classicism constantly sought to blend his constructions in with their surroundings. The grandiose style of his buildings with their long Neoclassical colonnades, the dramatic contrasts of light and the use of Gothic elements are typical of the Romantic trend.

The 19C and the Neo-Gothic

19C architecture was characterized by a great diversity of styles. By 1830, the Neoclassical movement had become sterile; it was superseded, except in Munich, by a renewed interest in the Gothic, emblematic for the Romantics of "the old Germany".

At the same time, the **Biedermeier** style—lightweight, cushioned furniture with flowing lines, glass-fronted cabinets for the display of knick-knacks—corresponding perhaps with the later Edwardian style in England, was popular in middle-class homes between 1815 and 1848.

1850 marks the beginning of the **Founders' Period** *(Gründerzeitstil)* with E. Ludwig and A. Koch pursuing an up-to-date style. But the wealthy industrialists fell for pretentious medieval or Renaissance reproductions, also to be found in public buildings such as the Reichstag in Berlin.

20C MOVEMENTS

In the late 19C, artists began exploring new avenues in a desire to move away from past styles and into the modern age. **Art nouveau** or **Jugendstil**, a European movement, became the vogue in Germany. The architects' idea was to create a complete work of art accessible to all, combining structure, decoration and furniture. This ideal, based on cooperation with industry, its methods of production and the use of its newest building materials (glass, iron, cement), resulted in the fundamental concept of an industrial aesthetic, brought to the fore by such pioneers as Peter Behrens, **Ludwig Mies van der Rohe** and **Walter Gropius**.

This style flourished mainly in Munich, Berlin and Darmstadt (with the Mathildenhöhe artists' colony). The artists' commitment, expressed within the Secessions (Munich 1892, Berlin 1899), was coupled with a political demand for independence.

The Bauhaus

In 1919, Walter Gropius founded the **Bauhaus** (Weimar: 1919–25, Dessau: 1926–32), a school of architecture and applied arts which radicalized the movement for modernisation, displaying an even greater interest in industrial production. The quest for unity between art and technique was a fundamental element. Architecture remained, in principle at least, the preferred form of expression since it combined structure and decoration and enabled application of the principles of functionality and rationality (🧭 see DESSAU and WEIMAR). The movement instigated modern reflections on architecture and habitat and lent its vocabulary to modern design.

The school, which was critical of society, was closed in 1933 by the Nazis, who adopted a pompous and monumental style of architecture intended to reflect their power. It was, in most cases, to be destroyed.

At the end of the war, the reconstruction effort inspired a wide variety of architectural creations. Architects such as Dominikus Böhm and Rudolf Schwartz were among the craftsmen who were brought to light by this renewal of interest in sacred work, many of their designs being markedly austere.

New concepts, too, characterized the construction of municipal and cultural enterprises such as Hans Scharoun's Philharmonie in Berlin and the Staatsgalerie in Stuttgart by British architect James Stirling—buildings of an architectural audacity only made possible by the development of entirely new materials and construction techniques. Architectural creation is still very much alive in Germany today, particularly in Berlin with centers such as Friedrichstrasse or Potsdamer Platz—showcases of the avant-garde—and creations such as the Jüdisches Museum, completed by Daniel Liebeskind in 1998.

Art

GERMANY'S GREAT PAINTERS AND SCULPTORS

15C

In the fields of painting and architecture, Germany remained for a long time attached to the Late Gothic tradition, which denied the realism so sought after in Italy. The country was divided into a large number of local schools under Dutch influence. Now came the time to seek an outlet for emotional expression and give vent to the religious concerns that marked the end of the Middle Ages.

Stefan Lochner (c. 1410–51)

This leading master of the Cologne School perpetuated the tradition of international Gothic, giving it a lyrical and refined touch with his sweet expressions and an exquisitely delicate palette. The use of gold backgrounds afforded him a certain amount of leeway as regards the requirements of perspective. (*Adoration of the Magi*, Cologne cathedral; *Virgin and Rose Bush*, Wallraf-Richartz-Museum, Cologne).

Veit Stoß (c. 1445–1533)

Sculptor, painter and engraver with a distinctive, powerful style; one of the greatest woodcarvers of his age. His figures were generally of a pathetic nature (*Annunciation*, Lorenzkirche, Nuremberg; *Reredos of the Nativity*, Bamberg Cathedral).

Tilman Riemenschneider (c. 1460-1531)

Sculptor of alabaster and wood, he was master of an important studio where he created many altarpieces. His intricate works are executed with great finesse and richness of expression (*Tomb of Henry II the Saint*, Bamberg Cathedral; *Adam and Eve*, Mainfränkisches Museum, Würzburg; *Altarpiece to the Virgin*, Herrgottskirche, Creglingen).

The Master of St Severinus (late 15C)

The intimacy and iridescent colors of his works reflect Netherlandish influence (*Christ before Pilate*, Wallraf-Richartz-Museum, Cologne).

The Master of the Life of the Virgin (late 15C)

Painter of original works, influenced by the Flemish artist Van der Weyden (*Scenes from the Life of the Virgin*, Alte Pinakothek, Munich; *Vision of St Bernard*, Wallraf-Richartz-Museum, Cologne).

Engraving

First emerging in Germany around 1400, engraving was espoused by the greatest German masters. One pioneer was the unidentified engraver **Master E.S.**, known by the monogram with which he signed his engravings, whose work dates from between 1450 and 1467. Copperplate engraving techniques were later perfected and best demonstrated by virtuosi such as **Martin Schongauer** (c. 1450–91), whose designs were later followed by Albrecht Dürer.

16C

The German Renaissance did not emerge until the 16C with Dürer. The observation and idealizing of nature resulted in works of increasing refinement. The Danube School showed a new interest in landscape, encouraging its development as a genre, while Holbein breathed new life into the art of portrait painting with his striking realism.

Matthias Grünewald (c. 1480–1528)

An inspired painter of the Late Gothic period, producing works of great emotional intensity capable of expressing the pain of humanity (*Crucifixion*, Staatliche Kunsthalle, Karlsruhe; *Virgin and Child*, Stuppach parish church).

Self-Portrait (1498) by Albrecht Dürer

©1994, Photo Scala, Florence/Prado, Madrid

Albrecht Dürer (1471–1528)

The greatest artist of the German Renaissance, he was fascinated by the art of Antiquity and the Italian Renaissance, with which he was able to lend Nordic gravity. Based in Nuremberg, Dürer produced woodcuts achieving some magnificent light effects and a broad range of grays (*The Apocalypse*). His religious scenes and portraits are of an extraordinary intensity (*The Four Apostles*, *Self-Portrait with Cloak*, Alte Pinakothek, Munich; *Charlemagne*, Germanisches Nationalmuseum, Nuremberg).

Lucas Cranach the Elder (1472–1553)

Official painter to the prince-electors of Saxony and master of an important studio, he was the portraitist of the most eminent men of the Reformation, most notably of his friend Luther. His works reflect a strong sense of the wonders of nature, allying him with the painters of the Danube School. As court painter in Wittenberg, he produced Lutheran-inspired religious paintings. The more Expressionist works of his youth gave way to paintings full of grace and nobility, typical of the refinement towards which 16C German art was heading. (*The Electors of Saxony*, Kunsthalle, Hamburg, *The Holy Family*, Städel museum, Frankfurt; *Portrait of Martin Luther*, Germanisches Nationalmuseum, Nuremberg).

Albrecht Altdorfer (c. 1480–1538)

Leading member of the Danube School and one of the founders of landscape painting, his use of chiaroscuro creates dramatic and moving works, with the focus on landscapes shrouded in mystery (*Battle of Alexander*, Alte Pinakothek, Munich).

Hans Baldung Grien (c. 1485–1545)

His complex compositions feature dramatic lighting effects, unusual colors and tortured movement (Altarpiece: *The Coronation of the Virgin*, Freiburg Cathedral).

Hans Holbein the Younger (1497–1543)

Painter of German merchants and subjects from court circles and the high

Venus and Cupid Carrying the Honeycomb (c. 1531) by Lucas Cranach, the Elder

©1990, Photo Scala, Florence/Galleria Borghese, Rome/Ministero Beni e Att. Culturali

aristocracy, he breathed new life into the art of portrait painting. His subjects are depicted with incredible precision in skillfully composed settings that illustrate their office. His compositions, both solemn and realistic, mark a definitive departure from the Gothic tradition (*Portrait of the Merchant Georg Gisze*, Museum Dahlem, Berlin).

17C and 18C

Italian influence remained evident during these two centuries. Court circles played host to many French and Italian artists who introduced an increasingly exuberant Baroque style.

Adam Elsheimer (1578–1610)

Elsheimer's often small scale mythological and biblical paintings reflect a combination of Italian influence and a concept of landscapes peculiar to Flemish and German painting. At the same time as Caravaggio, he experimented with the power of light in the evocation of nature, notably in his dramatic nocturnal landscapes (*The Flight into Egypt*, 1609, Alte Pinakothek, Munich).

Andreas Schlüter (c. 1660–1714)

This master of Baroque sculpture in northern Germany and talented architect produced some very powerful works (*Statue of the Great Élector*, Schloss Charlottenburg, Berlin; *Masks of Dying Warriors*, Zeughaus, Berlin).

The Merians (17C)

A family of engravers specializing in plates illustrating German towns.

Balthasar Permoser (1651–1732)

Sculptor to the Court of Dresden, Permoser studied in Rome, Vienna and Venice. His masterful works reflect the exuberant style of the Italian Baroque, particularly at the Zwinger (*Wallpavillon* and *Nymphenbad*, Zwinger, Dresden).

Antoine Pesne (1683–1757)

This French-born painter in the service of the Prussian court became the portraitist of Frederick II, who admired his coloristic talent. He produced a great number of portraits and some mythological ceiling paintings and murals

Atlantes in the Zwinger Palace, Dresden

R. Mattes/MICHELIN

Barbara Campanini Dancing by Antoine Pesne

(*Portrait of Frederick II and his sister Wilhelmina,* apartments of Schloss Charlottenburg, Berlin).

Joseph Anton Feuchtmayer (1696–1770) and Johann Michael II Feichtmayr (1709–72)

These members of a family of German painters and sculptors helped to perpetuate the Rococo style with their fanciful compositions (decoration of the abbey churches of Ottobeuren and St Gall).

Matthäus Günther (1705–88)

A pupil of CD Asam, master of Rococo painting in southern Germany, Günther is famous for his decoration of many churches in Swabia and Bavaria (Amorbach, Rott am Inn).

19C

The 19C was first of all dominated by the **Biedermeier style** (1815–48) which glorified middle-class values and way of life, as perfectly illustrated by the genre painting of GF Kersting. Then came the time for rebellion. Romanticism called the Classical values into question, launching a dialogue between reason and feeling. Realism and Impressionism, which both originated in France, allowed German artists to express certain budding socialist ideas. All of these

various forms of artistic expression came in response to the moral crisis of modern Europe.

Caspar David Friedrich (1774–1840)

German Romantic painter whose landscapes were represented as manifestations of the divine and places of wonderment ideal for meditation (*The Monk by the Sea, The Cross on the Mountain, Alte Nationalgalerie,* Berlin; *Rambler Above a Sea of Clouds,* Kunsthalle, Hamburg).

Friedrich Overbeck (1789–1869)

Member of the Lucas Brotherhood, he was the most important member of the group of **Nazarenes** who occupied the abandoned monastery of San Isidoro in Rome in 1810. Advocating a form of painting that glorified moral values in a reaction against Neoclassicism, they revived medieval art and sought the purity of the early Italian and Flemish masters of the 15C. (*Italia and Germania,* Neue Pinakothek, Munich).

Adolf von Menzel (1815–1905)

Representative of German Realism, initially illustrating anecdotal themes and later producing powerful portrayals of the industrial world, tempered by the influence of Impressionism (*Rolling Mill,* Nationalgalerie in Berlin).

Wilhelm Leibl (1844–1900)

Master of German Realism, he was influenced by Courbet and mostly painted scenes of village life (*Three Women in Church*, Kunsthalle, Hamburg; portrait of *Mina Gedon*, Neue Pinakothek, Munich).

Adolf von Hildebrand (1847–1921)

German sculptor based in Munich, whose measured taste in monumental sculpture, inspired by the most austere Greek style, was in contrast to the excesses of most 19C artists. (*Wittelsbach Fountain*, Munich).

Max Liebermann (1847–1935)

Greatly influenced by French Realism and Naturalism, he painted the universe of peasants and workers in all its harsh reality. Later, under the influence of Impressionism, he allowed light to suffuse his already rich palette. He led the Berlin "Sezession" movement in 1899, advocating freedom and realism as opposed to the patriotic insipidness of the court painters (*Jewish Street in Amsterdam*, Wallraf-Richartz-Museum, Cologne).

20C

The Expressionism which marked the beginning of the century gave way to a new form of revolt and glorification of subjective feeling. The shock of World War I and the ensuing social crisis plunged art into a period of darkness and disillusionment. Political and social dissent were embodied in a succession of new avant-garde movements. More than ever before, art was driven by a desire to change society and expose its failings.

Expressionism

German Expressionism introduced an emotionally charged, often violent or tragic vision of the world to modern painting. The movement owed much to Van Gogh and the Norwegian painter Edvard Munch (1863–1944), whose work had a marked influence in Germany. In Dresden and then in Berlin, the **Brücke (Bridge) Group** united from 1905 to 1913 such painters as Erich Heckel, Ernst Ludwig Kirchner and Karl Schmidt-Rottluff, whose work, with its use of pure color, recalls that of the Fauves in France. See the works of **Emil Nolde** (1867–1956) at Seebüll, and of Expressionism in general at the Brücke-Museum, Berlin.

Der Blaue Reiter (The Blue Rider Movement)

Association of artists founded in Munich in 1911 by **Wassily Kandinsky** and **Franz Marc**, later to be joined by **August Macke** and **Paul Klee**. Although the work of the artists involved differed widely, they were united by a general aim to free art from the constraints of reality, using bold colors and untraditional forms, thus opening the way to abstraction (*Deer in the Forest* by **Franz Marc**, Orangerie Staatliche Kunsthalle, Karlsruhe; *The Dress Shop* by **August Macke**, Folkwang-Museum, Essen). The movement broke up during the war.

The Bauhaus

This movement, which united all art forms, attracted a host of avant-garde painters and sculptors including Klee and Kandinsky, Oskar Schlemmer, Laszlo Moholy-Nagy, **Lyonel Feininger** and **Joseph Albers**.

Neue Sachlichkeit (New Objectivity)

An artistic movement affecting all the arts which grew up in the early 1920s, aiming to produce a realistic illustration of social facts and phenomena. It corresponds to the harshness of the post-war period. Pioneers of this movement were **Otto Dix** and **George Grosz** (*War* by **Otto Dix**, 1932, Albertinum in Dresden). The Dada movement, present in Cologne and Berlin, and in Hannover with **Kurt Schwitters**, used art for political ends. On the sidelines of these movements, **Max Beckmann** (1884–1950), who was also deeply affected by the war and its consequences, shared his very bleak view of humanity.

Second half of the 20C

The Nazi regime brought an abrupt end to these artistic experiments labelled as "degenerate art", replacing them with a Neoclassical style glorifying race, war and family. This "Nazi art" died out at the end of the Reich in 1945.

Social Realism, an official art form which served the regime's ideology, was predominant in East German painting until the 1960s–70s. The painters of Leipzig in particular won international acclaim, among them Bernhard Heisig, Wolfgang Mattheuer, Willi Sitte and Werner Tübke. In East Germany in the years leading up to reunification, non-conformist artists were also given the opportunity to express themselves.

The 1960s saw a turning point in German artistic creativity. **Gruppe Zebra** took up the credo of New Objectivity against German Abstract art, while the members of **Gruppe Zero** (Heinz Mack, Otto Piene, Güntheb Uecker) concentrated on using kinetic art to transform thoughts into material objects. In the 1970s, **Joseph Beuys**, together with the artists of the school of **Constructivist Sculpture** in Düsseldorf, strove to create a direct relationship between the artist and the viewing public in his Happenings and Performances, and to redefine the role of art and the artist in contemporary society (**Neue Nationalgalerie** in Berlin; **Hessisches Landesmuseum** in Darmstadt; **Staatsgalerie** in Stuttgart).

From the 1980s, a new generation of German artists managed to break through onto the international scene with "new Fauves" (Neue Wilde) **Georg Baselitz** and **Markus Lüpertz** developing a new form of Expressionism, **Sigmar Polke**, closer to pop art, and **Anselm Kiefer**, with his focus firmly on German history.

Literature

German literature, from the reign of Charlemagne up to the present day, has demonstrated an enduring vitality, constantly breaking with tradition and inventing new forms of expression. In the wake of Goethe's monumental influence in the 18C, the best authors have been guaranteed international renown.

FROM THE MIDDLE AGES TO THE 17C

German literature in the Middle Ages was written in a great variety of dialects. Largely drawing on the oral tradition, it was characterized by lyrical poetry and genres that can be described—not in any pejorative way—as popular: plays, ballads, songs and epics. One of the earliest works, dating back to Charlemagne's reign, is the **Lay of Hildebrand** (Das Hildebrandslied, 820), of which only a 68-line fragment has survived. The national folk saga of the **Nibelungen**, an anonymous work from the late 12C, draws on the sources of Germanic mythology and celebrates the heroic spirit that faces up to trials and tribulations without ever giving up. One of the big names in courtly epics was **Wolfram von Eschenbach**; his poem Parzival (c. 1200), which **recounts the** quest for the Holy Grail, revolves around religious and chivalrous themes. The 14C was an age of mystic literature, with writers such as **Meister Eckhart**. In a departure from the dryness of scholastic teaching, he sometimes forsakes Latin to discuss religious topics in powerful and eloquent German.

Satire took center stage in the 16C (The Ship of Fools by **Sebastian Brant** appeared in 1494) along with folk songs and the poetry of the Meistersänger (master singers). **Hans Sachs** (1494–1576), a poet-cum-cobbler from Nuremberg, was a prominent figure in the latter genre, which provides the theme of Wagner's opera Tannhäuser. **Luther**'s contribution during this period also marked a turning point; his hymns and translation of the Bible (1534) paved the way for the writing of literary works in a common, modern German language. The late 16C witnessed the publication of the Faust Book (1587) by **Johann Spies**, a work of remarkable depth, which draws the captivating portrait of a man driven by an unquenchable thirst for knowledge which distances him from God.

The ravages of the Thirty Years' War (1618–48) profoundly marked the collective psyche; 17C literature bears echoes of this traumatic time. Among the recurrent themes of these often edifying works is the vanity of human things and man's need to find God in order to ensure his salvation. *Adventurous Simplicissimus* (1669) by **Grimmelshausen** (1622–76) is a picaresque novel whose hero, having experienced the suffering of war, finally chooses a life of retreat and meditation.

"AUFKLÄRUNG" (AGE OF ENLIGHTENMENT)

The 18C marked the beginning of the golden age of German literature, as its influence began to extend well beyond the German-speaking countries.

The spotlight was now on philosophical and moral themes, the flourishes of language belying a pursuit of the natural. The influence of **Leibniz** (1646–1716), whose *Theodicy* in French and Latin uses rational arguments to justify evil and show that we live in "the best of all possible worlds", still remains strong. **Rationalism**, apparent in the works of **Christian Wolff** (1679–1754), coexisted with the tenacious survival of Pietism, which highlights the emotional experience in any religious phenomenon.

This explains how **Lessing** (1729–81), in his writings on religion (*The Education of the Human Race*, 1780), strives to combine a rationalist deism with a belief in revelation. In the purely literary field, Lessing also set the principles of new German theater by creating middle-class drama (*Emilia Galotti*).

His contemporary, **Immanuel Kant** (1724–1804), endeavored to define the limits of what can be known; only that which is determined by pure forms of understanding can be the subject of rational knowledge. Whatever eludes such determination (the soul, God, etc.) can, of course, be "thought" and give rise to "belief", but cannot be "known". In the practical field, Kantianism defines the balance between liberty and the "moral law" that governs every rational being: man finds liberty by submitting to the "categorical imperative" and renouncing the influence of his "sensitivity".

"STURM UND DRANG" AND CLASSICISM

In reaction to the strict rationalism of the Aufklärung, the **Sturm und Drang** (Storm and Stress) movement, encompassing authors such as **Herder** (1744–1803) and **Hamann** (1730–88), exalts freedom, emotion and nature. Poetry, "the mother tongue of the human race", takes pride of place and the past is revisited, with particular emphasis placed on folk songs. The works of the young **Johann Wolfgang von Goethe** (1749–1832), such as *The Sorrows of Young Werther*, bear witness to the influence of Sturm und Drang. However, Goethe—poet and universal genius—soon tempered this fashionable enthusiasm with a move towards the **classical humanist** tradition. As the leading light of German literature prior to the emergence of the Romantic trend, in which he never became involved, he penned a great number of works. Classical dramas (*Iphigenie auf Tauris*, *Egmont*, and *Torquato Tasso*), novels (*Elective Affinities*, *Wilhelm Meister's Apprenticeship*) and *Faust* (Parts I and II, 1808 and 1832) contain the quintessence of Goethe's philosophy. After settling in Weimar in 1775, Goethe was joined by Herder, **Wieland** and **Schiller** (1759–1805). The historical dramas of the latter, a poet and dramatist of genius, are undisguised hymns to liberty (*Don Carlos, Wallenstein, Wilhelm Tell*).

Two major literary figures emerged during the transitional period between Weimarian Classicism and actual Romanticism: **Friedrich Hölderlin** (1770–1843), a tragic, lyric author (*Hyperion, The Death of Empedocles*) with a passion for Ancient Greek civilization, produced some powerful odes before sinking into madness at the age of 36. The novelist Johann Paul Friedrich Richter (1763–1825), better known as **Jean Paul**, had a creative imagination, although a somewhat labored style.

19C: BETWEEN ROMANTICISM AND REALISM

The **Romantic movement** charts the individual soul's quest for the infinite in all its forms. Besides literature, it incorporates the fine arts, philosophy, politics and religion. First Jena, then Heidelberg and Berlin were centers from which the movement blossomed. After initially being theorized by the **Schlegel brothers**, the Romantic doctrine was put into powerful poetic form by **Novalis** (1772–1801); a poet and mystic, Novalis exalts the art and religion of the Middle Ages and his "Blue Flower" symbol comes to represent the Absolute, or object of Romantic longing (*Heinrich von Ofterdingen*). While in the process of theoretical elaboration, budding Romanticism was exposed to the influence of post-Kantian idealist philosophers, in particular **Fichte** (1762–1814), **Schelling** (1775–1854) and **Hegel** (1770–1831). It also reflects a heightened interest in popular literature, often seeking inspiration in the sources of myths and legends, as can be seen in the tales of the **Brothers Grimm** (1812) or the more disturbing tales of **Hoffmann** (1776–1822). On the sidelines of the Romantic movement, the playwright **Heinrich von Kleist**, who, tragically, committed suicide in 1811, wrote some remarkable plays, notably *The Prince of Homburg* (1810): A play about a man of action led away by his dreams.

The exuberant idealism of Romanticism was succeeded by a search for greater realism. An outstanding figure and "defrocked Romantic" poet of the *Loreley*, **Heinrich Heine** (1797–1856), treats the naivety of his age with bitter irony and enthuses about St Simonian ideals. **Hebbel** (1813–63), a fine psychologist, wrote plays often inspired by biblical or mythical subjects, focusing on conflict between the individual and the existing moral order (*Judith, Herodes und Mariamne, Agnes Bernauer*). Toward the mid-19C, a number of writers sought to bring literature closer to life and everyday experience; novelists such as **Stifter** (1805–68) and **Keller** (1819–90) were among the main exponents of this "Realist" trend. Some of them, such as **Fontane** (1819–98) and **Raabe** (1831–1910), focus on the social and political conditions of human existence. Social drama is brilliantly illustrated by **Hauptmann** (1862–1946), a prolific author whose Naturalist writing is at times allegorical and symbolic, drawing inspiration from legend and mythology *(The Atrides Cycle)*.

In the field of philosophy, **Schopenhauer** (1788–1860), pessimistic theorist of the will to live, describes the will as reality's true inner nature, and this will as suffering (*The World as Will and Idea,* 1819); he had a crucial influence on the thinking of authors such as Nietzsche, Freud and Wittgenstein. Political thought, moreover, took a new direction with **Karl Marx** (*The Communist Manifesto* was published in 1848); rejecting Hegelian idealism, Marx, who was both a philosopher and an economist, developed the theory of "historical materialism", a powerful conceptual tool enabling the analysis of human societies according to their historical development. Together with **Engels**, Marx cofounded "scientific socialism", in opposition to so-called "utopian" socialism, and launched the modern international workers' movement.

THE MODERN PERIOD

Friedrich Nietzsche (1844–1900) belongs as much to the history of philosophy as to the history of literature. His tremendous influence over the history of literature and western thought is still in evidence today. His fundamentally life-affirming philosophy called, with

© World Pictures/Photoshot

Jakob and Wilhelm Grimm

great lyricism, for mankind to surpass itself (*Thus Spake Zarathustra*, 1886).

Focusing on the often irreconcilable duality of the mind and the senses, the irrational and the rational, the works of **Thomas Mann** (*Buddenbrooks, The Magic Mountain*) and **Hermann Hesse** (*Der Steppenwolf*) bear the stamp of Nietzscheism; the sanatorium in Davos in *The Magic Mountain* symbolizes the "disease" that runs rife in decadent European societies. In this struggle between life and morbid instincts, the shadow of Thanatos hangs over our western civilizations. The Czech-born German-language writer **Franz Kafka** (1883–1924) differs from these authors in both style and thought; his nightmarish novels *(The Trial, The Castle, America)* contain a vision of a dehumanized world dominated by anxiety and the absurd. The works of Vienna-born **Stefan Zweig**, one of Kafka's contemporaries, were of a less tortured nature. This highly cultivated man; citizen of the world, traveler and translator proved in his best short stories *(Amok, Conflicts, The Royal Game)* to be a remarkable story teller with humanist sympathies.

The early 20C also witnessed a revival in poetry. **Stefan George** (1868–1933) published poems which, in their formal perfection, ally him with the French Symbolists, while the Austrians **Rainer Maria Rilke** (1875–1926) and **Hugo von Hoffmannsthal** (1874–1929) reach the peak of lyrical impressionism.

The 1930s and 40s were marked by an intensified search for the meaning of life; spurred on by Husserlian phenomenology, **Heidegger** and, to a lesser degree, **Jaspers**, put the question of being back at the heart of philosophy. Based on our essential finiteness, Heideggerian existentialism distinguishes between an existence marked by a sense of being and an "inauthentic" existence, led astray into the impersonal self.

The world of theater was dominated by **Bertolt Brecht** (*The Threepenny Opera, Mother Courage, Galileo*). A committed socialist, he rejected the "theater of illusion", advocating "Verfremdungseffekt" (the alienation effect): the spectator must observe the action on stage with a critical eye and be able to decipher the

Ernst Jünger

methods by which the strong exploit the weak.

National Socialism forced numerous poets and writers into exile (Walter Benjamin, Alfred Döblin, Lion Feuchtwanger, Else Lasker-Schüler, Thomas and Heinrich Mann, Carl Zuckmayer, Stefan Zweig). **Gottfried Benn** (1886–1956) withdrew into silence, while **Ernst Jünger** (1895–1998) courageously published his novel *On the Marble Cliffs* in 1939: "...Such are the dungeons above which rise the proud castles of the tyrants... They are terrible noisome pits in which a God-forsaken crew revels to all eternity in the degradation of human dignity and human freedom."

POST-1945 LITERATURE

Twelve years under National Socialist rule had broken the flow of literary creation in Germany, necessitating repair work in this domain too. The association of authors known as **Gruppe 47** (after the year of its founding), which centered upon **Hans Werner Richter** and **Alfred Andersch**, was instrumental in putting Germany back onto the map as far as world literature was concerned. This loosely associated group of writers served as a forum for reading, discussion and criticism, until its last conference in 1967, exerting a lasting and formative influence on the contemporary German literary scene. Authors associated with

Gruppe 47 included **Paul Celan**, **Heinrich Böll** (Nobel Prize winner in 1972), **Günter Grass** (Nobel Prize winner in 1999), **Siegfried Lenz**, **Peter Weiss** and **Hans Magnus Enzensberger**. By the end of the 1950s, works of international standing were being published: Günter Grass' masterpiece *The Tin Drum* is an extraordinary novel in the tradition of Celine; **Uwe Johnson**'s *Speculations about Jacob*, **Heinrich Böll**'s *Billiards at Half Past Nine* and **Martin Walser**'s novel *Marriages in Philippsburg*. Increasing politicisation was what finally put an end to Gruppe 47's activities. Authors not associated with Gruppe 47 were hard at work also; **Arno Schmidt** developed a very original and high-quality body of work, while **Wolfgang Koeppen** produced some wickedly satirical novels on contemporary society. The literature of the 1960s was characterized by a wave of criticism, but, by the following decade, German literary concerns were withdrawing to a newly discovered "inner contemplation". A particularly prolific amount of good writing was produced by women during the 1970s and 1980s (**Gabriele Wohmann**, **Karin Struck**, **Verena Stefan**).

In the world of theater, dominated initially by the dramatic theory of Bertolt Brecht, a new band of writers began to emerge, with works by **Tankred Dorst** (*Toller*, 1968), **Peter Weiss** (*Hölderlin*, 1971) and **Heinar Kipphardt**. **Rolf Hochhuth** was particularly successful with his "documentary dramas" in which he examines contemporary moral issues (*The Representative*, 1963), and **Botho Strauß**, the most widely performed modern German dramatist, has won international acclaim with plays such as *The Hypochondriac* (1972), *The Park* (1983) and *Final Chorus* (1991).

The political division of Germany was also reflected in German literature. In the old East German Republic, the leadership viewed literature's *raison d'être* as the contribution it might make to the socialist programme for educating the masses. The Bitterfelder Weg, a combined propaganda exercise and literary experiment launched at the Bitterfeld chemical factory in 1959 as part of the East German Republic's cultural programme under Walter Ulbricht, was intended to unite art and everyday life and break down class barriers. Factory visits were organized for writers, so they could observe workers and then portray them glowingly in their novels, poems or plays, while the workers themselves were encouraged to write about their lives.

The results of the project were mixed, and although it gave authors a clearer idea of the primitive conditions that most East German workers were obliged to tolerate, those who wrote too honestly about what they saw found their works censored.

Poetry was the literary form least easily subject to Communist censorship, and poets such as **Peter Huchel**, **Johannes Bobrowski** and **Erich Arendt** produced some remarkable work. From the early 1960s the prose work of **Günter de Bruyn**, **Stefan Heym** (d. 2001) and **Erwin Strittmatter** was widely appreciated. **Anna Seghers**, who returned from exile in America after the war, was considered the greatest East German writer of the older generation, while rising star **Christa Wolf** won acclaim in both Germanies. Important contributions to the theater were made by playwrights **Ulrich Plenzdorf**, **Peter Hacks** and above all **Heiner Müller** (*The Hamlet Machine*, 1978).

Any overview of German-language literature since World War II must, of course, acknowledge the enormous contribution made by **Max Frisch** and **Friedrich Dürrenmatt**, of Switzerland, and **Ilse Aichinger**, **Ingeborg Bachmann** and **Thomas Bernhard** of Austria.

Music

Germany and the German-speaking world have made a considerable contribution to western music. After reaching an initial high point in the 18C with the Baroque period, German music was propelled back into the limelight by the genius of composers such as Beethoven and Wagner. Modern experimentation since the emergence of the twelve-tone system testifies to the continuing vitality of German music.

FROM MINNESÄNGER TO MEISTERSÄNGER

In the 12C and 13C, feudal courts constituted the main forum for musical expression. The **Minnesänger** (essentially troubadours—"minne" meaning "love" in Middle High German), who were often noble knights, such as **Wolfram von Eschenbach** and **Walther von der Vogelweide**, drew inspiration for their songs from French lyric poetry. They would perform their love songs before the nobility, accompanying themselves on the lute.

The Meistersänger, or mastersingers, of the 14C–16C preferred a more sedentary lifestyle and organized themselves into guilds. They introduced polyphony to German music and clearly set the musical forms of their art. Anyone wanting to become a Meistersänger had to prove himself in a public contest. Among the prominent figures of the time was **Heinrich von Meißen** (1250–1318) who marked the transition from Minnesang (courtly love song/lyric) to the poetry of the Meistersänger. **Hans Sachs** (1494–1576), a cobbler by trade and an ardent supporter of Luther, was also a prolific poet; many of his compositions were turned into Protestant chorales. Sachs later became the subject of Wagner's opera *The Mastersingers of Nuremberg*.

FROM THE RENAISSANCE TO THE 17C

In the wake of the Reformation, German music began to develop an individual identity with the emergence of the chorale, the fruit of the collaboration between **Luther** and **Johann Walther** (1496–1570). *"Ein' feste Burg ist unser Gott"* (A Mighty Fortress is Our God) composed by the two men in 1529 was reworked by Bach. Originally a hymn with a simple melody, the chorale—sung in the vernacular—soon opened up to the secular repertoire, embracing popular genres of music. It subsequently gave rise to the German cantata and oratorio.

Religious music maestro, **Heinrich Schütz** (1585–1672) managed to produce a skillful combination of German and Italian elements. He composed the first German opera, *Dafne*, a work which was sadly lost. *The Seven Words of Christ* (1645) shows the influence of Monteverdi who, along with Gabrieli, was one of Schütz's masters.

The second half of the 17C witnessed a proliferation of organ schools, one of the most famous of which was in Nuremberg. An inspiration for Bach, who is said to have walked hundreds of kilometers (1km = 0.6mi) to hear him play in Lübeck, **Dietrich Buxtehude** (1637–1707) organized the first concerts of sacred music. **Johann Pachelbel**

Munich Philharmonic Orchestra in concert

Munich Tourist Office

(1653–1706) was the great master of the organ school in southern Germany; the only surviving piece of his work is the *Canon in D Major*.

BACH AND BAROQUE MUSIC

His consummate skill as a composer, his genius for invention and his mastery of counterpoint enabled **Bach** (1685–1750) to excel in every kind of music he wrote. Based in Weimar until 1717, he spent several years at the court of Köthen, during which he composed *The Brandenburg Concertos*. In 1723, he was appointed "Cantor" at St Thomas' School, Leipzig. Bach's duties included the composition of a cantata for every Sunday service, as well as the supervision of services at four other churches. He also taught Latin and voice and still found time to write his own instrumental and vocal works. His masterpieces include *The Well-Tempered Clavier* (1722 and 1744) and the *St Matthew Passion* (1727).

A brilliant court composer, influenced by his travels in Italy, **Georg Friedrich Händel** (1665–1759) excelled in both opera and oratorio (*The Messiah*, 1742). Born in Halle, he was organist at the town's cathedral before pursuing his career at the Hamburg opera. Based in England from 1714, he spent most of the last forty years of his life in London, and even obtained British nationality.

Händel's friend, **Georg Philipp Telemann**, (1681–1767) was influenced by French and Italian composers, and was himself a particularly prolific composer. He turned from counterpoint to harmony and composed chamber music and church music as well as operas. Telemann was godfather to Bach's second son, **Carl Philipp Emmanuel** (1714–88), who popularized the sonata in its classic form.

FROM THE MANNHEIM SCHOOL TO BEETHOVEN

In the mid 18C, the musicians of the **Mannheim School**, under the patronage of Elector Palatine Karl Theodor, helped establish the modern symphonic form, giving a more prominent role to wind instruments. Influenced by the innovations from Mannheim, **Christoph Willibald Gluck** (1714–87) undertook a "reformation of opera", producing refined works where the lyrics took pride of place; he provoked the enthusiasm of the innovators—and the horror of fans of traditional, Italian-inspired opera—by staging, in Paris, his *Iphigenia in Aulis* and *Orpheus*. This period was also marked by the appearance in Germany of the **Singspiel**, a popular opera in which dialogue is interspersed with songs in the form of Lieder. Mozart's *Magic Flute* (1791) and Beethoven's *Fidelio* (1814) are excellent examples of this genre later identified with operetta.

The contribution of Viennese Classicism during the second half of the 18C proved to be crucial. **Joseph Haydn** (1732–1809) laid down the classical form of the symphony, the string quartet and the piano sonata. **Wolfgang Amadeus Mozart** (1756–91) perfected these forms and created some truly immortal operas (*The Marriage of Figaro*, *Don Juan*).

Born in Bonn, **Ludwig van Beethoven** (1770–1827) went to Vienna to study under Haydn and Antonio Salieri. With his innovative harmonizations, he developed a highly individual style and transformed existing forms of music, heralding the Romantic movement. The depth of his inspiration, ranging from pure introspection to a wider belief in the force and universality of his art, emanates from his work with extraordinary power, perhaps most particularly in his symphonies. It was in 1824, when he had already been suffering from total and incurable deafness for five years, that Beethoven's magnificent *Ninth Symphony*—inspired by one of Schiller's odes—was performed for the first time.

ROMANTIC MUSIC AND WAGNER

Franz Schubert (1797–1826) brought Romantic music to its first high point. He focused much creative energy on the Lied (song), blending folk and classical music in a unique style.

Carl Maria von Weber (1786–1826), created Germany's first Romantic opera, *Freischütz* (1821), paving the way for the characters of Wagnerian drama. It was a resounding success when first performed in Berlin, due in part to the use of folk songs. As for the lofty world of **Felix Mendelssohn-Bartholdy** (1809–79), it was far removed from the forces of evil that inhabit the *Freischütz*. Although espousing classical music forms, Mendelssohn, who was a conductor, pianist and founder of the Leipzig Conservatory, also reveals a Romantic influence.

Robert Schumann (1810–56), passionate and lyrical in turn, but brought up in the Germanic tradition, strives to reconcile a classical heritage with personal expression. A talented music critic (he founded the *Neue Zeitschrift für Musik* newspaper in 1834), he initially wrote for piano alone *(Carnival, Scenes from Childhood)*. Then, spurred on by his admiration for Schubert and the advice of his friend Mendelssohn, he began to compose Lieder *(Dichterliebe)*, subsequently turning his attention to symphonies and chamber music. A close friend of Schumann whose wife Clara he loved with a passion, **Johannes Brahms** (1833–97) exemplified a more introverted style of German Romanticism. After long being accused of formalism, he was rediscovered in the 20C, notably thanks to the influence of Schönberg *(Brahms the Progressive)*.

Crowning glory of the German Romantic movement, the work of **Wagner** (1813–83) revolutionized opera. Wagner claimed that music should be subservient to drama, serving as "atmosphere" and a "backdrop of sound" without which the opera's message could not be fully conveyed. Orchestration thus becomes of paramount importance. Libretto and plot unfold continuously, preserving dramatic reality. Wagner introduces the use of "leitmotifs"—musical phrases used recurrently to denote specific characters, moods or situations—making them essential to the continuity of the action. *Lohengrin* was first performed in 1850 in Weimar, under the supervision of **Franz Liszt**. Designed by Wagner himself as a stage for the performance of the entire work (Gesamtkunstwerk), the Bayreuth Theater was inaugurated in 1876 with *The Ring of the Nibelung (Rheingold, Walküre, Siegfried* and *Götterdämmerung)*. The

fruit of 22 years' work, the magnificent first public performance of *The Ring* lasted 18 hours. Although its artistic success was undeniable, the Bayreuth episode ended in financial ruin for the composer. *Parzival*, Wagner's last opera, revolves around the theme of redemption through sacrifice, and was first performed in Bayreuth in 1882.

At the end of the 19C, **Gustav Mahler** (1860–1911), Czech-Austrian composer and creator of the symphonic Lied, and **Hugo Wolf** (1850–1903) developed a new musical language which forms a bridge between Romanticism and dodecaphony.

Richard Strauss (1864–1949) excelled in orchestra music *(Thus Spake Zarathustra)*, uniting a certain harmonic audacity with a dazzling and multifaceted style.

CONTEMPORARY MUSIC

Contemporary musical experimentation is derived principally from the Austrian school of atonal, or serial (especially 12-note systems) music, represented by **Arnold Schönberg** and his two main disciples **Alban Berg** and **Anton von Webern**. Introducing a new method of composing music, the twelve-tone system was first revealed to the public by Schönberg in 1928 in the *Variations for Orchestra*. Berg applied his master's innovation to lyrical drama *(Lulu)*, while Webern, turning his back on Romanticism, focused on the concision of form. The brilliant **Paul Hindemith** (1893–1963), initially influenced by Romanticism, remained untouched by Schönberg's innovations; in a break with German tradition, he forged a path of his own between atonality and dodecaphony.

Carl Orff (1895–1982), creator of the Orff Schulwerk, propounded innovative ideas about music education. His highly original theatrical compositions combine drama, speech and song in a fascinating rhythmic framework: his powerful collection of secular songs with infectious rhythms, *Carmina Burana* (1937), soon gained international renown. The compositions—mainly opera and ballet music—of **Werner Egk** (1901–83), a student of Carl Orff, reveal the influence of Igor Stravinski and Richard Strauss. As for **Kurt Weill** (1900–50), influenced at the beginning of his career by the atonal composers, he returned under the impact of jazz to tonal music, and composed *The Threepenny Opera* (1928) in collaboration with Brecht.

Although **Wolfgang Fortner** (1907–87) was influenced initially by Hindemith, he nonetheless later turned to modal 12-tone serial music. His mature works introduce electronic elements into his musical compositions.

Bernd Alois Zimmermann (1918–70) perceived past, present and future as one, and the multiple layers of reality are reflected in his composition technique. Quotations and collage were particularly important to him. His major work is the opera *The Soldiers*.

From 1950, a younger generation of musicians developed the potential of electronic music under the aegis of **Karlheinz Stockhausen** (b. 1928). **Hans Werner Henze** (b 1926) created expressive operas, in which modernity and tradition, and atonality and tonality are combined. **Wolfgang Rihm** (b. 1952), a student of Fortner, like Henze, also mixes traditional stylistic elements with new techniques in his extremely complex musical language.

Cinema

After producing a number of masterpieces during the Expressionist period of the 1920s, German cinema fell into a decline from which it did not emerge until the 1960s. Although now struggling to make its mark in the face of the American productions, it has managed to produce some remarkable international award-winning works.

THE GOLDEN AGE OF EXPRESSIONISM

The creation in 1917 of UFA (Universum Film Aktiengesellschaft), a production company of considerable means which, from 1921, was directed by producer **Erich Pommer**, led to some lavish productions. The Expressionism that was apparent in literature, theater and painting also seeped into film production in the troubled post-war political and social scene. Deliberately turning its back on Realism, it often revelled in angst-ridden atmospheres, cultivating an exaggeration of forms and contrasts; it was typified by the use of chiaroscuro lighting effects and the geometric stylization of the décor. Very few works could actually be classed as purely Expressionist, but among them is **Robert Wiene**'s masterpiece *The Cabinet of Dr Caligari* (1919), which was well received in the United States and France. Nevertheless, Expressionism was a great source of inspiration for German cinema in the 1920s; this period was dominated by the films of **FW Murnau** (*Nosferatu the Vampire*, 1922; *The Last Laugh*, 1924; *Faust*, 1926) and **Fritz Lang** (*Dr Mabuse*, 1922; *Metropolis*, 1925). Lang's German work reached its high point in 1931 with *M*, the director's first talking picture. Initially entitled *Murderers Among Us* (the title was changed under pressure from the Nazis), *M* paints the picture of a diseased society which, unable to cure its own ills, seeks scapegoat sinners on whom to place the blame. *The Last Will of Dr Mabuse* in 1932 attracted Nazi censure. Soon after being invited by Goebbels to supervise the Reich's film production, Lang went into exile, first moving to Paris and then to California, where he pursued his film-directing career.

The 1920s in Germany also witnessed a shift towards Realism and away from the dominant Expressionist trend. Examples of this new trend include the films of **GW Pabst** (*The Joyless Street*, 1925; *Diary of a Lost Girl*, 1926; *Lulu*, 1929) and **Josef von Sternberg**'s *The Blue Angel* (1930) starring **Marlene Dietrich** and **Emil Jannings**.

AN ABRUPT HALT

The promising surge of German cinema after World War I was sadly stopped in its tracks with the arrival of the Third Reich. Many actors and directors went into exile. The Nazis turned cinema into a tool to serve the regime's ideology. Filmmaker **Leni Riefenstahl** (1902–2003) stands out in the generally disappointing and inartistic genre of propaganda

The Berlinale

As one of the pioneers of cellu-loid history, it's only natural that Germany should be home to one of the world's most prestigious film festivals: The Berlinale (☞ see BERLIN), which brings hundreds of international stars to the German capital every February.

Founded in 1951 with the encour-agement of the Western allies, the festival hundreds of flicks from around the world with some of them competing for the coveted Golden and Silver Bear trophies (www.berlinale.de). Munich and Hamburg also host major festivals and there quite literally dozens of smaller others, many specialized in particular genres such as docu-mentaries, animated films, short films, children's cinema and gay & lesbian movies.

Berlin International Film Festival 2008

Poster for the 2008 Berlinale Film Festival

films, with her productions of amazing cinematic beauty, such as *The Gods of the Stadium*, a glorification of the 1936 Berlin Olympics.

The period immediately after World War II was a cultural desert. While "Socialist Realism" prevailed in East Germany, film production in the Fed-eral Republic of the 1950s was of poor quality. Only a few films, such as *The Last Bridge* (1954) and *The Devil's General* (1955) by **Helmut Kaütner**, managed to escape the pervasive mediocrity. The 1962 **Oberhausen Manifesto**, signed by 26 young filmmakers, signalled the birth of a new cinematographic lan-guage; the long-awaited revival was here at last.

THE REVIVAL OF THE 1960s AND BEYOND

In the 1960s and 1970s makers of "New German cinema" rose up in the wake of the French *nouvelle vague*, seeking to distance themselves from old-style cinema with its run-of-the-mill com-mercial superficiality. Films made by **Werner Herzog, Volker Schlöndorff**

(*Young Törless*, 1966) and **Alexander Kluge** (*Artists at the Top of the Big Top: Disorientated*, 1968) quickly met with success. It was not long—the mid 1970s—before this younger generation had reestablished German cinema on an international scale. **Volker Schlöndorff** made *The Lost Honor of Katharina Blum* (in collaboration with **Margarethe von Trotta**, 1975), and *The Tin Drum* (1979). **Werner Herzog** went on to explore a fantastic, often quite exotic world in *Aguirre, Wrath of God* (1972), *Nosferatu the Vampyre* (1979), and *Fitzcarraldo* (1982). Prominent figures in the **Munich School** include **Rainer Werner Fass-binder** (1945–82), who also worked in television, and who was responsible for a considerable number of excellent films (*Fear Eats the Soul (Angst Essen Seele Auf)*, 1973; *The Marriage of Maria Braun*, 1978; *Berlin Alexanderplatz*, a 14-part televi-sion series, 1980), and **Wim Wenders** (*The American Friend*, 1977; *Paris, Texas*, 1984; *Wings of Desire*, 1987; *Buena Vista Social Club*, 1999). Important and innova-tive women film directors include **Mar-garethe von Trotta** (*Rosa Luxemburg*, 1986; *Das Versprechen*, 1995). Wolfgang Peterson's fantasy world in *The Never-*

ending Story (1984) was a resounding commercial success.

Edgar Reitz won international acclaim with his film epic *Heimat* (1984) and its sequel *Heimat 2* (1993).

However, West German cinema has been characterized by a strongly individual narrative feel which perhaps makes it less approachable to outsiders. One refreshing filmmaker worthy of note is **Doris Dörrie** who, with *Men... (Männer)* (1985) and *Bin ich schön?* (1998), reduced the Zeitgeist to a humorous point. Other successful films include **Tom Tykwer**'s 1999 *Lola rennt* (*Run Lola Run*) and **Wolfgang Becker**'s *Goodbye Lenin*, which won the Best European Film award at the 2003 Berlin Film Festival. The most successful German film of late has been *The Lives of Others*, written and directed by **Florian Henckel von Donnersmarck**, which won the Academy Award for Best Foreign Language Film in 2007.

CINEMA IN THE FORMER EAST GERMAN REPUBLIC

East German cinema, like all other art forms, was compelled by the state to fulfil a didactic function. Thus a number of films used literary classics as a theme, since directors felt unable to confront issues relevant to contemporary East Germany. **Konrad Wolf** made his mark on three decades of East German filmmaking, with films such as *Sterne* (1958), which won him recognition worldwide. In *Solo Sunny* (1979), he put forward the case for individualism, thus paving the way for a breakthrough in the East German film industry. **Egon Güntheb** made the highly successful *Der Dritte* (1971), while the greatest hit was **Heiner Carow's** *Die Legende von Paul und Paula* (1973).

1984 was a particularly fruitful year, with **Hermann Zschoche**'s *Hälfte des Lebens*, **Iris Gusner**'s *Kaskade Rückwärts*, and **Helmut Dzuiba**'s *Erscheinen Pflicht*. One of the leading East German filmmakers of the 1970s and 1980s was **Rainer Simon** (*Das Luftschiff*, 1982; *Die Frau und der Fremde*, 1985).

Finally, **Lothar Warneke** studied the problems of everyday life, and endeavored to dismantle rigid ideological points of view (*Bear Ye One Another's Burdens* (*Einer trage des anderen Last*), 1988).

THE COUNTRY TODAY

Germany is a highly decentralized federal state whose human, political and administrative facets reflect very individual traits that are rooted in its history. This brief, factual portrait highlights some of the aspects peculiar to the German nation and to life in Germany today.

Economy

After World War II, the economy of West Germany made a spectacular recovery, generally referred to as an **"economic miracle"** *(Wirtschaftwunder)*. Indeed, the considerable reconstruction effort coupled with judicious fiscal and monetary policy propelled the West German economy to third place worldwide, behind the United States and Japan. Good relations between employers and trade unions and a powerful banking system helped maintain this growth. The **"social market economy"** (state intervention to correct the perverse market effects) long provided the context of this development, which was also stimulated by a favorable economic climate.

Despite the strong development of service-sector activities, industry remains the cornerstone of Germany's economic strength.

The industrial sector, which represents around one third of Gross Domestic Product GDP), consists of large international groups with varied activities (Thyssen-Krupp, Bayer, Hoechst, Siemens, Bosch, BMW, Volkswagen, etc.)

and countless small but dynamic companies.

The **reunification** of the two Germanies in 1990 was an enormous challenge; the high cost of the economic integration of the former German Democratic Republic severely impacted the competitiveness of the Federal Republic. The modernization of the new Länder and social support for employees in the East put a great strain on the federal budget. However, the massive investments made by the Federal Government, increased taxation, and structural aid from Europe finally allowed the East to make the transition from a planned economy to a market economy. Today, Germany is the world's largest exporter (mostly car, machinery and metals) and has the third-largest economy globally. After a long period of stagnation with an average growth rate of 0.7% between 2001–05 and chronically high unemployment, stronger growth led to a major drop in unemployment to about 7.7% in late 2007 (vs 11.7% in 2005) and a concurrent economic growth of 2.6%. In 2008 a fall in growth rate to below 2% was anticipated as the strong euro, high oil prices, tighter credit markets and slowing growth abroad take their toll.

Government and Administration

THE BIPARTITE SYSTEM

Since 1949, two parties—the CDU and the SPD—have dominated political life in the Federal Republic. A rare alliance between these two groups arose in 1966 with the formation of the "great coalition" (Große Koalition). One of the most significant recent developments in German politics is the rise of the ecology party, Die Grünen (*The Greens*).

The conservative Christian Democratic Union **(CDU)** and their Bavarian counterpart, the CSU, joined with liberal allies from the FDP in 1949 to elect **Adenauer** as chancellor. The party returned to power under the aegis of **Helmut Kohl**, who was elected Chancellor four times (1983, 1987, 1991 and 1994).

The Länder Regions

The Federal Republic comprises 16 Länder, 11 of which formed the old West Germany and five of which were added in 1990, re-constituted from the 15 districts of the former East German Democratic Republic. Each Land organizes its constitution within the terms of the Basic Law. The Länder have a legislative assembly **(Landtag)** elected by universal suffrage and an executive body consisting of a council of ministers with a President **(Ministerpräsident)**. Areas involving the sovereignty of the state, such as foreign affairs, defense or monetary policy, fall under the responsibility of the Federal Government alone, but the Länder possess broad powers; they have exclusive jurisdiction over education and culture, and are actively involved in the areas of justice and the economy.

The Social Democrat Party **(SPD)** came to power for the first time in 1969 led by **Willy Brandt**. The SPD allied with the liberals again in 1974 under **Helmut Schmidt**. They also claimed victory in the 1998 elections under the leadership of **Gerhard Schröder**.

RECENT DEVELOPMENTS

Schröder governed in a coalition with the Green Party was re-elected in 2002. The Free Democratic Party **(FDP)**, capable of making alliances with either of the two main parties, has for a long time acted as referee on the political chessboard. Chairman of the party (and Leader of the Opposition), **Guido Westerwelle**, is the archetypal dynamic politician. Successor of the SED, East Germany's former communist party, the Party of Democratic Socialism **(PDS)** has a considerable following in the new Länder.

In 2005, the PDS entered an electoral alliance with the western Germany-based Labor and Social Justice—The Electoral Alternative (WASG) and won 8.7 percent of the vote in Germany's

September 2005 federal elections (more than double the PDS' 4% share in the 2002 election).

On June 16, 2007, the two groupings merged to form a unified party called The Left (Die Linke).

In 1983, **Die Grünen** entered the Bundestag. As part of the 1998 coalition with the SPD their leader, **Joschka Fischer**, took up office as Foreign Secretary in Schröder's government.

Continued frustration with high unemployment, high taxes and slow economic growth (due in part to Germany's reunification in 1990, and in part to the economic globalization that has affected Western industrial nations worldwide) led to an impatience with the liberal SPD-Green coalition in federal elections in 2005. The more conservative CDU/CSU regained majority status in the Bundestag, resulting in the naming of **Angela Merkel** as German Chancellor.

Merkel serves as Germany's first female chancellor; its first East German chancellor since reunification; and its youngest chancellor since World War II.

A Federal State

Subdivided throughout history into largely autonomous regions, owing allegiance to no single capital (prior to 1945 Berlin was only capital of the Reich for just over 70 years), Germany has naturally gravitated towards a federal governmental structure. Today it is a highly decentralized state whose Länder, or regions enjoy considerable powers.

The **Basic Law** established in 1949 guarantees individual liberties and defines the institutions of a republic founded on democratic principles. The Federal Parliament is composed of two chambers: the **Bundestag**, a national assembly of 656 members elected by universal suffrage, is invested with legislative power, chooses the chancellor, and controls the government; the **Bundesrat**, a federal council comprising members drawn from the local governments administering the Länder, is concerned with certain aspects of legislative power, particularly when they affect the Län-

The Reichstag in Berlin

der. The Bundesrat also exercises certain control over the government, with the government being required to submit all bills to it.

The **Chancellor** holds executive power and is elected by the Bundestag, to whom she is accountable. He is invested with wide-ranging powers and defines the broad lines of government policy. The government introduces laws (adopted by the Bundestag) and is responsible for their implementation. The role of the Federal President (**Bundespräsident**) is essentially representative: it is he/she who concludes treaties with foreign states, and appoints or removes judges, federal functionaries and federal ministers suggested by the Chancellor. Lastly, the supreme judicial authority of the Federal Republic is the **Constitutional Court**, based in Karlsruhe. It ensures compliance with the Basic Law, guards constitutional principles, and acts as arbitrator in disputes between the Federal Government and the Länder.

Population

With over 82 million inhabitants, Germany is the most highly populated country in the European Union and the second most populous in Europe after Russia. It has been in demographic decline for about 25 years and is experiencing an accelerated ageing of the population (the average age—over 43.4—is the highest in Europe).

Nearly 90% of Germans live in towns with more than 2 000 inhabitants, and the western part of the country has by far the highest population densities. Although immigration has, since the 1960s, provided a significant additional source of labor, the tightening of legislation has considerably reduced the influx of people from abroad. About 7.2 million foreigners live in Germany, including about 2 million Turks, 700 000 people from the former Yugoslavia, 600 000 Italians, 360 000 Greeks and 280 000 Poles.

Traditions and Customs

Germany is a completely modern nation but one with strong traditions and links with its past.

It can be completely "en vogue" (Berlin, Hamburg) or somewhat conservative (Munich). In southern Germany especially, folkloric garments such as Lederhosen and Dirndl dresses, are worn regularly by people of all ages and from all walks of life.

You can almost never go wrong with using the formal 'Sie' instead of the informal 'Du' when addressing someone. 'Kaffee und Kuchen' (coffee and cake) on Sunday afternoons is as time-honored as popping down to a beer garden with friends or screaming your lungs out at soccer games. Children and the elderly are well respected, as are dogs and the rights of bicyclists on their dedicated paths. The automobile is a bit of a sacred cow where even so much as a fingerprint may well elicit scorn.

Food and Drink

Although there is some regional variation, German food is generally rather rich and hearty. Typical dishes pair potatoes with a piece of meat (most likely pork—often sausages) and a cooked vegetable (e.g. sauerkraut or red cabbage).

Of late, though, a new generation of energetic chefs has been busy modernizing traditional menus by using fresh, locally sourced and seasonal ingredients and making dishes lighter and healthier. Thanks to Germany's large immigrant population, especially in the cities, you are never far from pizza, doner kebab, or Chinese food!

Schloss Moritzburg to the north of Dresden
R. Mattes/MICHELIN

AACHEN

POPULATION 260 000

Aachen is a bustling college town with a special place in German history. Its natural hot springs were already popular with Celtic tribes, but it was the Romans who built the first thermal baths. Charlemagne (747–814) made Aachen capital of his Frankish Empire in 794 and, after being crowned emperor in 800, unleashed his military campaigns on Saxony and Bavaria from here. He's buried in the spectacular cathedral that also saw the coronation of 31 German kings between 936 and 1531.

- **Information:** Elisenbrunnen, Friedrich-Wilhelm-Platz, 52062 Aachen. ☎(0241) 180 29 60 and 180 29 61. www.aachen-tourist.de.
- **Orient Yourself:** Situated among the northern foothills of the Ardennes (Hohes Venn), near the Belgian and Dutch borders, Aachen is Germany's most westerly town, easily accessible by road from Cologne, Düsseldorf and Liège, Belgium.
- **Parking:** Public parking is available in lots near the main train station, near the market, near the cathedral, and near Kaiserplatz. Electronic signs throughout town indicate lot availability and free spaces.
- **Don't Miss:** The Cathedral and its treasury.
- **Organizing Your Time:** Allow at least a half day for the Cathedral District.
- **Also See:** MONSCHAU, KÖLN, EIFEL.

Cathedral District

Dom★★★ (Cathedral)

⏱Open daily 7am–7pm (Nov–Mar 6pm). Guided tours daily. ⊕4€. ☎(0241) 47 70 90. www.aachendom.de.

The first German monument to be included on UNESCO's list of World Heritage Site, Aachen's soaring cathedral towers above the historic district. The oldest part, Charlemagne's palace chapel *(Pfalzkapelle)* was completed around 800 and is a superb example of Carolingian architecture.

The Gothic chancel was added in 1414 to accommodate the growing number of pilgrims. The cathedral is still an important pilgrimage site today, attractions the faithful by the thousands every seven years (next in 2014).

Exterior

Starting at the Katschhof (north side), walk around the cathedral.

Exterior chapels of note include those of St. Nicholas (pre-1487) and of Charles-Hubert (1455–74).

The Carolingian entrance hall features bronze doors embellished with lions' heads (c. 800).

Interior

Aachen's cathedral is remarkable for the harmonious design of the domed Carolingian palace chapel, an octagonal structure surrounded by a 16-sided gallery awash in mosaics.

It is also a treasure trove of quality art works, most notably the 11C **ambo★★★**, a copper pulpit decorated with precious stones and donated by Henry II. Other highlights are the magnificent 12C wheel-shaped **chandelier★★**, courtesy of Emperor Frederick I Barbarossa; the 13C **Shrine of Mary★**; the 14C Virgin of Aachen statue; and the high altar adorned with a **Pala d'Oro★★★**, a gilded panel relief depicting the Passion of Christ (c. 1020).

Behind the altar rests the **Shrine of Charlemagne★★★** (Karlsschrein: 1200–15), a hand-worked gold and silver reliquary containing the emperor's bones. His **marble throne** in the upper gallery was also used as the coronation throne of 30 German kings *(must be seen on guided tour; meet in the treasury).*

Domschatzkammer (Cathedral Treasury)★★★

Access via Klostergasse. ⏱Open year-round, Mon 10am–1pm; Jan–Mar, Tue–Sat

Address Book

For coin ranges, see the Legend on the cover flap.

WHERE TO STAY

Haus Press – *Trierer Straße 842–844.* (0241) 92 80 20. www.haus-press.de. *15 rooms. Restaurant.* This unpretentious family hotel has functional rooms furnished in rustic country-style, including some family rooms with three beds. The restaurant serves regional cuisine, while the beer garden and pub are good unwinding spots.

Forsthaus Schöntal – *Korneli münsterweg 1 (3mi/5km southeast of town center, toward Kornelimünster).* (0241) 55 94 30. www.forsthaus-sch-oental.de. *11 rooms. Restaurant.* Rooms are clean, and comfortably furnished in pine at this clean and well-run guesthouse. It's in a charming brick building close to town and the forest and sports a relaxing beer garden out back.

WHERE TO EAT

Zum Schiffgen – *Hühnermarkt 23.* (0241) 335 29. www.zum-schiffgen.de. Enjoy traditional regional specialities at this long-running favorite. In summer, the terrace on the pedestrian zone offers delightful views of the Town Hall.

Gallo Nero – *Kaiserplatz 6.* (0241) 401 4930. *Closed Mon.* This charming bi-level restaurant in a historical townhouse with stucco ornamentation exudes an elegant ambience. Locals give it high marks for the feistily flavored Italian cuisine prepared with local ingredients whenever possible.

NIGHTLIFE

Café Molkerei – *Pontstraße. 141 (northeast of Markt).* (0241) 489 82. An Aachen institution right on lively Pontstraße, this cafe, lounge and cocktail bar is beautifully lit at night and buzzes with students, artists and families enjoying drinks or light meals.

Magellan – *Pontstraße 78 (northeast of Markt).* (0241) 401 64 40. This cafe-bar/restaurant is particularly pleasant in the summer because of its shady terrace. Weekdays between 11am and 3pm Turkish dishes and set menus are served. At the bar, choose from 40 cocktails.

Van den Daele Alt Aachener Kaf-fee- und Weinstuben – *Büchel 18/Körbergasse.* (0241) 357 24. www.van-den-daele.de. Sample delicious cakes and the town's speciality, Printen (spicy ginger) in this traditional coffeehouse in a historical building from 1655. Leather-covered walls and antique furniture in a warren of rooms create quintessential old-world ambience.

10am–5pm; Apr–Dec, Tue, Wed, Fri–Sun 10am–6pm (Thu 9pm). Closed Jan 1, Carnival, Good Friday, Dec 24, 25 & 31. 4€. Guided tours daily. (0241) 47 70 90.
The treasury is one of the most important north of the Alps, with over 100 outstanding artworks arranged in five thematic sections.
Highlights include several major silver and gold reliquaries including the bust of Charlemagne (1349) and the Lothar Cross (c. 1100).
Also note the the Aachen Altarpiece (c. 1520); and a unique ivory situla (c. 1000) for holy water.

Rathaus (Town Hall)

Markt. Open 10am–1pm, 2pm–5pm. Closed major holidays and during special events. 2€. (0241) 432 73 10. www.aachen.de.
The Gothic 14C Town Hall has sprouted from the foundations of Charlemagne's palace of which only the Granus Tower remains. The palatial building overlooks the market square with its **fountain** and **emperor's statue**. The most important room is the **Reichssaal** decorated in the 19C by Alfred Rethel with romanticized scenes from Charlemagne's life.
The same room also contains replicas of the imperial insignia, including the crown, the orb and several swords (originals in Vienna).

Excursion

Kornelimünster

10km/6.2mi southeast.

This is an enchanting village with slate-roofed, blue and grey stone houses typical of the Eifel region. Its key sight is the **Abbey Church**★ with origins in the Carolingian period, although the current Baroque version dates only from 1728. The octagonal Kornelius chapel contains the reliquary of 3C Pope Cornelius for whom the town is named.

Monschau

33km/20.5mi SE. Coming from Aachen via B 258, enjoy a superb view★★ *of the town.*

Pretty Monschau, with its tall, narrow, slate-roofed houses clustered in a winding river gorge, is lorded over by a ruined medieval castle but is otherwise predominantly Baroque in style.

A highlight is the **Rotes Haus**★ *(Red House;* ⏱*open Good Fri–Nov, Tue–Sun 10am, 11am, 2pm, 3pm and 4pm;* ✎*2.50€;* ☎*(024 72) 50 71)* of 1765, a one-time residence of a local clothmaker and merchant. Rooms provide a peak into the bourgeois lifestyle of the 18C and 19C. Of special note is the free-standing, three-story **Rococo staircase**★. **Haus Troistorff** *(Laufenstraße 18)* is another magnificent residence from 1783.

The North Eifel Lakes

85km/52.8mi Leave Monschau on B258.

The road rises rapidly, and after a mile there is a **look-out point**★ giving a good view of the village. Leaving the town of Schmidt, the ruined **Burg Nideggen** (NIdeggen Castle) lies straight ahead. Until the 15C the rose-colored sandstone castle was the residence of the counts and dukes of Jülich. The restored 12C church has a Romanesque chancel with frescoes.

Rurtalsperre★ (Rur Dam)

In a wild stretch of countryside, this reservoir forms with the Urft reservoir to the south the largest stretch of water in the Eifel. Motor boat services operate on both.

DEUTSCHE ALPENSTRASSE★★★

GERMAN ALPINE ROAD

The splendors of mountain scenery combined with renowned sites like the Wieskirche and the castles of Ludwig II of Bavaria make the Alpenstraße an unforgettable journey. When passing through the region's villages, where life goes on much as it has for centuries, stop to sample local culinary or cultural traditions, or head off for a walk in the woods or across alpine meadows.

- **Information:** Deutsche Alpenstraße, Radolfzeller Straße 15, 81243 Munich. ☎(089) 829 21 80. www.deutsche-alpenstrasse.de.
- ▶ **Orient Yourself:** Running from Lindau on Lake Constance (Bodensee) to Berchtegaden near the Austrian border, this 450km/279.6mi scenic route traverses spectacular high mountain country accented by pristine alpine lakes. It meanders along the foothills of the Allgäu and the Bavarian Alps, paralleling the southern German border and linking world-famous ski resorts, bucolic villages, onion-domed churches, royal castles and the lofty peaks of the Zugspitze (2 964m/9 724.4ft) and the Watzmann (2 712m/8 897.6ft).
- **Don't Miss:** Beautiful panoramas appear around every corner, but the best lie atop the Wendelstein and along the final part of tour ④ below.
- **Organizing Your Time:** Allow at least 3 days to explore this alpine region.
- **Kids Especially for Kids:** Hohenschwangau and Neuschwanstein castles; cable car rides up the Wendelstein.
- **Also See:** ROMANTISCHE STRASSE, KONSTANZ, CHIEMSEE.

Driving Tours

① The Allgäu★

▶ *From Lindau to Füssen*
112km/69.6mi – half a day

The Allgäu is home to the Swabians, an Allemanic tribe that settled in the area around the 2C AD. It's a fairytale landscape where lazy cows graze on steep mountain pastures and farmers still produce wonderful artesanal cheese in their own dairies.

Lindau★★ *see LINDAU*

Paradies

Engineers gave this name to a viewpoint between Oberreute and Oberstaufen, along a sweeping curve, from which the distant Swiss Appenzell Alps can be seen.

Oberstaufen

This charming ski resort sits at the foot of the Hochgrat massif (1 832m/6 010ft). From the mountain station at 1 708m/5 600ft, you'll have a 360-degree view★★ across the Allgäu, Lake Constance and into Switzerland.

▶ *The road now climbs the alpine valley of the Iller, which runs to the foot of Grünten, the "guardian" of the Allgäu.*

Bad Hindelang★

Together with its neighbor, Bad Oberdorf, this romantic flower-decked village is a popular **Spa** spa and vacation resort perfectly suited for mountain walks in summer and skiing in winter.

Above Bad Hindelang, the climbing **Jochstraße★** delivers idyllic views over the jagged summits of the Allgäu Alps. From the **Kanzel★** viewpoint, near the summit, take in the splendid panorama embracing the Ostrach Valley and surrounding mountains.

▶ *Descending on the far side, the road crosses the Wertach valley, skirts the Grüntensee and passes near the sprawling Pfronten ski resort before arriving at Füssen.*

Hindelang seen from the Jochstraße.

Füssen★ (*see FÜSSEN*)

2 The Ammergau★

▶ *From Füssen to*
Garmisch-Parten kirchen.
67km/41.6mi – 1 day.

The road bypasses the Ammergau Alps to the north, then crosses countryside seamed and broken by the moraines deposited by the ancient Lech glacier. This rolling land is punctuated by villages with onion-domed churches.

Hohenschwangau and Neuschwanstein★★★ Kids
See NEUSCHWANSTEIN

Steingaden★

Long before reaching the village of Steingaden, the distinctive onion-domed silhouette of its 12C Premonstratensian abbey church rises from the misty horizon. Numerous alterations have all but obscured its Romanesque origins. The Gothic entrance bears a painted genealogy of the Welf family who founded the abbey in 1147. But first and foremost it

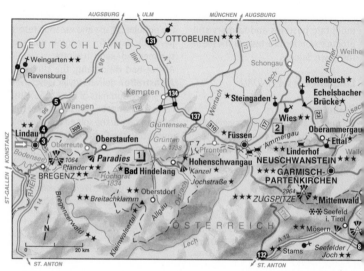

is luxuriant Baroque flourishes that now give the interior its dynamic and uplifting character. Ten gleaming pillars guide the eye toward the pastel-colored ceiling fresco depicting the ascension of Mary and enhanced with breathtaking stuccowork. Only the cloister, where the architect Dominikus Zimmermann is buried, retains its comparatively austere 13C Romanesque columns.

Wieskirche★★ See WIESKIRCHE

Rottenbuch

First built as an Augustinian monastery, the **Mariä-Geburts-Kirche**★ (Church of the Nativity of the Virgin) was remodelled in Baroque and Rococo styles in the 18C. The School of Wessobrunn, of which Joseph and Franz Schmuzer were masters, crafted the magnificent stucco. Matthäus Günther's ceiling fresco depicts the death of St. Augustine in perfect visual harmony with the extravagantly sculpted décor. The pulpit, organ loft and altars by Franz Xaver Schmädl are heavily adorned with statues and giltwork in pure Rococo tradition.

Echelsbacher Brücke (Echelsbacher Bridge)

Opened in 1929, this was Germany's first bridge made of reinforced concrete. Almost 90m/295.3ft long, it spans the deep Ammer gorge. Walk to the middle of the bridge for an impressive view.

Oberammergau★

This small town of farmers and craftspeople, encircled by the wooded foothills of the Ammergau, is internationally famous for its Passion Play, staged every ten years (next in 2010) by hundreds of local amateur actors. The tradition derives from a vow made by the inhabitants in 1634 after being spared by a plague epidemic. Performances are held at the **Passionstheater** (guided tours (45min) Mar–Oct & Dec daily 9.30am–5pm, 4€, (8822) 923 10), where tours give you insight into the play's history, meaning and production.

Oberammergau is also renowned for its trompe l'oeii facades painted in a style called *Lüftlmalerei* (roughly 'air painting'). These are colorful frescoes depicting both secular and religious themes, from fairytales to Biblical scenes.

Linderhof★★
See Schloss LINDERHOF

Ettal★

A blossoming of the Benedictine tradition and the local veneration of a Virgin statue explain the vast dimensions of **Ettal Abbey**★, founded by Emperor Ludwig the Bavarian in 1330. The original Gothic church succumbed to a fire in 1774 after which it was rebuilt by Baroque star architect Enrico Zuccalli and Joseph Schmuzer of the School of

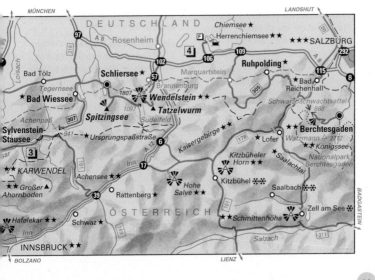

Address Book

For coin ranges, see the Legend on the cover flap.

WHERE TO STAY

Gästehaus Weißes Rössl – *Dorfstraße 19, 83242 Reit im Winkl.* ☎(08640) 982 30. www.weissesroessl-riw.de. *20 rooms.* This low-key inn in the Chiemgau Alps offers self-catering apartments perfect for families along with comfortable rooms, all with balconies. Cooll off in the outdoor pool or wrap up your day in the sauna or gym.

Gasthaus Zum Stern – *Dorfstraße 33, 82487 Oberammergau.* ☎(08822) 867. www.gasthaus-stern-ogau.de.vu. *12 rooms. Restaurant (⊜⊜). Closed Wed.* Right in the village, this delightful inn in a 16C building has modest but well-tended rooms. A restaurant enjoys a fine reputation and serves light meals and three-course dinners. The snug *Biergarten* in back is especially inviting on balmy summer nights.

Gasthaus Zum Fischerwirt – *Linderhofer Straße 15, 82488 Ettal.* ☎(08822) 63 52. www.zum-fischerwirt.de. *Closed Nov–mid-Dec and 2 weeks at Easter. 10 rooms. Restaurant (⊜⊜).* A traditional, pleasant hotel with charmingly decorated sparkling rooms and a restaurant serving reasonably-priced regional favorites.

Villa Bellaria – *Ludwigstraße 22, 83636 Bad Tölz.* ☎(08041) 800 80. www.villa-bellaria.de. *18 rooms.* This peaceful villa in the spa district welcomes guests with contemporary, classically furnished rooms and a breakfast room overlooking the garden.

Alpenlandhotel Hirsch – *Kurze Gasse 18, 87541 Bad Oberdorf.* Spa ☎(08324) 308. www.alpengasthof-hirsch.de. *Closed 3 weeks in Nov. 25 rooms. Restaurant (⊜).* Tradition meets modern comforts at this family-run hotel with spotless rooms, some with kitchenette or sitting area. There's a playroom for kids, a spa for grown-ups and a restaurant for everyone to enjoy.

Alpengasthof Winklmoo-salm – *Dürrnbachhornweg 6, 83242 Reit im Winkl.* ☎(08640) 974 40. www.winklmoosalm.com. *Closed Nov–Dec. 18 rooms. Restaurant (⊜⊜).* You'll sleep well in the fresh mountain air of this well-maintained inn in a famous ski area. Enjoy panoramic views and organic dishes in the cheerfully decorated restaurant.

Hotel Lederer am See – *Bodenschneidstraße 9, 83707 Bad Wiessee.* ☎(08022) 82 90. hotel@lederer.com. *Closed Nov–mid-Dec. 89 rooms. Restaurant (⊜⊜⊜).* Four traditional-style houses make up this appealing hotel complex with a popular country-style restaurant overlooking the lake.

WHERE TO EAT

Ratskeller – *Rathausstraße 1a, 83727 Schliersee.* ☎(08026) 47 86. www.ratskeller-schliersee.de. *Closed Mon.* Reasonably priced traditional rustic restaurant in a pleasant food.

Obere Mühle – *Ostrachstraße 40, 87541 Bad Hindelang. Closed Tue.* ☎(08324) 28 57. www.obere-muehle.de. *Reservations required.* This country-style restaurant in a 1433 mill oozes plenty of old-world charm. You'll dine well on regional cuisine and dishes prepared over a wood fire. Don't miss the cheese made in the on-site dairy.

Freihaus Brenner – *Freihaus 4, 83707 Bad Wiessee.* ☎(08022) 820 04. www.freihaus-brenner.de. *Closed year-round Tue, Nov–Apr also Wed. Reservations recommended.* Rustic yet upscale, this restaurant spoils you with updated regional cuisine and sweeping views over the mountains and Lake Tegernsee beneath the wooden beamed ceiling of the dining room.

Wessobrunn *(see above).* The dazzlingly detailed dome **fresco** showing St. Benedict and his followers is a masterpiece by Johann Jakob Zeiller.

The monastery is still active today with several dozen monks keeping busy running a hotel, a brewery, a distillery and other ventures.

▶ *The road rejoins the Loisach Valley. To the south, the cragged Wetterstein range reveals the peaks of the Zugspitze, Alpspitze and Dreitorspitze. Continue to Garmisch-Partenkirchen.*

Garmisch-Partenkirchen★★★
See GARMISCH-PARTENKIRCHEN

3 The Upper Isar Valley and the Lake District★

▶ *From Garmisch-Partenkirchen to Schliersee. 93km/57.8mi – 1 day.*

Mittenwald★ *See GARMISCH-PARTENKIRCHEN: Excursions*
At Wallgau, the route heads north along the B11 into the Tölzer Land, a wonderful outdoor playground with gorgeous scenery that inspired such painters as Franz Marc and Wassily Kandinsky.

Walchensee★
See MÜNCHEN: Driving Tours

Kochel Am See★
Kochel worked its considerable charms on German painter Franz Marc (1880–1916), a co-founder of the Blue Rider artist group, who settled here in 1914. The newly organized and enlarged **Franz Marc Museum** *(Herzogstandweg 43; open Tue–Sun 10am–6pm (Nov–Mar 5pm); 7.50€, 08851 71 14; www. franz-marc-museum.de)* presents his work along with such contemporaries as Ernst Kirchner and post-WWII expressionists including Willi Baumeister.

Benediktbeuern★
See MÜNCHEN: Driving Tours

Bad Tölz★
See MÜNCHEN: Driving Tours

Tegernsee★
Splendidly embedded in forested Alpine foothills, Lake Tegernsee has long been popular with the rich, famous and powerful. It is surrounded by four villages, each with its own flavor. Spa **Bad Wiessee** on the western shore is a fashionable spa resort with a sparkling new

casino. **Rottach-Egern** in the south is the ritziest enclave and has the best restaurants and chic houses. On the western shore, the village of **Tegernsee** is the most historical with origins as a Benedictine monastery founded in 746. It has a famous beer hall, the Bräustüberl. Finally, **Gmund** in the north is the most low-key village and popular with families.

Schliersee
Beside the lake of the same name, this small community—together with Fischhausen, Neuhaus and Spitzingsee (*see itinerary below*)—offers interesting day trips. The **St. Sixtus Parish Church**★ (Pfarrkirche) was rebuilt in the Baroque between 1712 and 1714. The interior frescoes and delicate stucco were executed by Johann Baptist Zimmermann (1680–1758), brother of the architect of the Wieskirche (*see WIESKIRCHE*).

4 The Sudelfeld and the Chiemgau Mountains★

▶ *From Schliersee to Berchtesgaden. 172km/106.8mi – one day*

Spitzingsee
Less than 0.6km/1mi from the summit, the steep access road offers views of the Fischhausen-Neuhaus plain and Lake Schliersee. Soon after, the road stops at the Spitzingsee.

▶ *Shortly (3km/1.8mi) before Bayrischzell, the road passes the cable-car terminal to the Wendelstein summit.*

Tatzelwurm Wasserfall (waterfall)
From the Naturdenkmal Tatzelwurm parking lot, a short trail leads to this cascade.

Wendelstein★★
Cable car: daily 9am–5pm (Nov–Apr 4pm); round-trip 24.50€. Cogwheel train: daily 9.15am–4pm (Nov–Mar 4pm); round-trip 17.50€. (08034) 30 80. www.wendelsteinbahn.de.
Kids To ascend the Wendelstein, take either the **cable car** from Bayrischzell-

©Mattana/Wikimedia Commons

Frescoes on the dome of the Ettal Abbey

Osterhofen *(7min)*, or the **cogwheel train** *(Zahnradbahn)* from Brannenburg *(25min)*. From the mountain station at 1 738m/5 702ft, a trail leads another 100 vertical meters to the peak. Crowned by a solar observatory and an 18C chapel, it offers an unforgettable **panorama**★★ and access to four geological trails (Geo-Wanderwege). We recommend the Gipfelweg, which circles the summit in about 2hr 30min.

▶ *From Wendelstein follow the A8 Munich–Salzburg autobahn to the shore of Lake* **Chiemsee**★. *Turn south onto the B305 which winds through the Chiemgau, a delightful region of lakes, moors, valleys and lakes with top skiing, hiking and mountain biking in the villages of Reit im Winkl, Inzell and Ruhpolding.*

Ruhpolding★

This popular cross-country skiing resort also has a famous art work: a 12C Romanesque statue of the Virgin Mary in the twin onion-domed parish church of **St. George.**

▶ *The Schwarzbachwacht pass reveals the contrast between the austere wooded Schwarzbach valley and the open pastures on the Ramsau slopes.*
The drive offers **panoramas**★★ *of the Watzmann peak and the Hochkalter with its Blaueis glacier. The German Alpine Road ends at Berchtesgaden.*

Berchtesgaden★★
ⓒ*See BERCHTESGADEN*

Der Blaue Reiter

The symphony of nature in the Tölzer Land—a pastiche of glassy lakes, muscular mountains and soft meadows—greatly inspired key members of the artists' group Der Blaue Reiter (The Blue Rider), founded in 1911 by Wassily Kandinsky and Franz Marc. Along with fellow artists Gabriele Münter, Paul Klee, August Macke, Alex Jawlensky and others, they spent summers here and Kandinsky and Marc eventually ended up buying houses in Murnau on the Staffelsee and Kochel am See, respectively. Blue Rider artists may have developed different artistic styles but all shared a desire to translate emotion and spirituality onto canvas. The clear, reflective light of the Alpine foothills, the intensity of the colors (especially the blue of the sky and the lakes) and the harmony of the landscape were all conducive to their vision. The group disbanded at the outbreak of World War I in 1914. Both Marc and Macke died on the battlefield.

ANNABERG-BUCHHOLZ★

POPULATION 23 000

After the discovery of silver and tin ore in 1491 and 1496, Annaberg and Buchholz experienced an economic boom; at its peak, 600 mines enriched the capital of the Erzgebirge (Ore Mountains). In the 16C, as the silver petered out, lace production became Annaberg's most important industry. Today the town's principal attraction is its Gothic cathedral.

Information: Markt 1, 09456 Annaberg-Buchholz. ☎(03733) 194 33. www.annaberg-buchholz.de.

▶ **Orient Yourself:** Annaberg-Bucholz lies in the Erzgebirge region of Saxony, about 60 mi/100km southwest of Dresden, near the border with the Czech Republic.

Don't Miss: St. Annen-Kirche

Organizing Your Time: Annaberg-Buchholz can be seen in about half a day.

Also See: CHEMNITZ, FREIBERG, ERZGEBIRGE.

Sights

St. Annen-Kirche★★

Open year-round, Mon–Sat 10am–5pm, Sun noon–5pm. ☎(037 33) 231 90. www. annenkirche.de.

Built between 1499 and 1525, St. Anna's is one the most important Late Gothic hall churches in Germany. Twelve slender pillars support the vaulted ceiling, each yoke covered by a "blossom baldaquin." The gallery parapets feature scenes from the Old and New Testaments. Especially noteworthy are the **Schöne Tür★★** (beautiful door), a multicolored portal designed in 1512 by Hans Witten, one of this region's most accomplished wood carvers of the Late Gothic period. He also created the church Madonna sculpture and the delicate baptismal font. References to Annaberg's mining past are evident in the **pulpit★★** (1516), which is decorated with the relief figure of a miner.

Also note the painted panels behind the **Miners' Altar★** (Bergmannsaltar, c. 1520), depicting various stages of mine work in that period.

The tower, which is still inhabited by the keeper, can be climbed from May to September.

Erzgebirgsmuseum mit Besucherbergwerk

Open year-round, daily 10am–5pm. Closed Dec 24. 5.50€ (museum and mine). *Guided tours daily. ☎(037 33) 234 97.*

This museum retraces local history with an emphasis on mining and has some endearing examples of local folk art. Annexed to the museum is the **Im Gößner** mine, which opened at the height of Annaberg's prosperity c. 1498. *The entrance shaft is in the museum courtyard.*

Technisches Museum Frohnauer Hammer

Guided tours (50min) daily year-round 9am–noon, 1pm–4pm. Closed Jan 1, Dec 25. 3€. ☎(037 33) 220 00. www.annaberg-buchholz.de/hammer.

This 15C mill complex south of the old town started out as a flower mill, then housed a coin mint and in the 17C was converted into an iron forge.

On tours you get to see close-ups of the historic hydraulic bellows and the power-hammers, some of them massive in size. Upstairs is a wide array of objects produced at the forge, while the gallery opposite presents artistic wood carvings.

Visits wrap up in the former miller's mansion where you can observe a lace maker at work.

Excursion

Erzgebirge★ *see ERZGEBIRGE*

AUGSBURG★★

POPULATION 268 000

Bavaria's third-largest city (after Munich and Nuremberg) and a key stop on the Romantic Road, Augsburg has long been associated with luminaries, including 16C artist Hans Holbein the Younger, Mozart's father Leopold (b. 1719–1787) and the dramatist Bertolt Brecht (1898–1956). Today, the Renaissance city continues to enchant visitors with its artistic beauty and lively cultural scene.

- **Information:** Maximilianstraße 57, 86150 Augsburg. ☎(0821) 50 20 70. www.augsburg-tourismus.de.
- **Orient Yourself:** Augsburg is one hour west of Munich by the A8 and 30 min by train. The river Lech, a tributary of the Danube, crosses the town and feeds into a canal in the lower town.
- **Parking:** Public lots and garages are located throughout the city, including near the main train station and the Rathaus. Electronic signs indicate lot availability and the number of free spaces.
- **Don't Miss:** Maximilianstraße and the Cathedral.
- **Organizing Your Time:** Budget about one day to see Augsburg.
- **Also See:** ROMANTISCHE STRASSE, MÜNCHEN.

A Bit of History

Roman origins – Founded in 15 BC by Drusus and Tiberius, stepsons of Emperor Augustus, Augsburg is, along with Trier and Cologne, one of Germany's oldest cities.

It became a trading center en route to Italy and, at the fall of the Roman Empire, an Episcopal See. By the late 13C it was a Free Imperial City and the seat of the Diet.

The Fuggers – Augsburg reached its historical peak at the end of the 15C, Augsburg when it became the financial center of Europe because of two wealthy merchant families, the Fuggers and the Welsers.

History has preserved the name of Jakob Fugger the Rich (1459–1529), renowned as the Empire's banker and the financier of the Habsburgs. He was powerful enough to rebuke Charles V, reminding him: "It is well known that, without my help, Your Majesty would no longer wear

The Town Hall and the Perlachturm

AUGSBURG		Grottenau	Y	16	Maximilianstr.	Z	
		Haunstetter Str.	Z	18	Mittlerer Graben	Y	27
Annastr.	Y	Hoher Weg	Y		Perlachberg	Y	32
Bahnhofstr.	YZ	Karlstr.	Y		Predigerberg	Y	33
Bgm.-Fischer-Str.	Y 5	Karolinenstr.	Y	22	Rathauspl.	Y	34
Dominikanergasse	Z 8	Lechhauser Str.	Y	23	Unterer Graben	Y	39
Frauentorstr.	Y 12	Leonhardsberg	Y	24	Vorderer Lech	Z	43
Fuggerstr.	Y 13	Margaretenstr.	Z	25	Wintergasse	Y	44

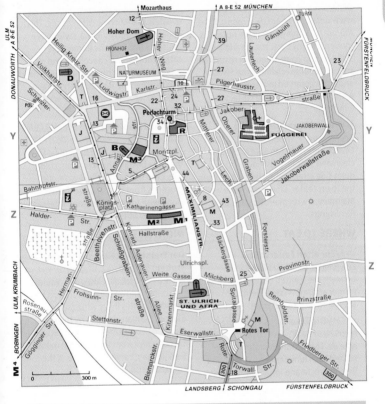

Heilig-Kreuz-Kirchen	Y D	Schaezlerpalais	Z M¹	Staatsgalerie	
Maximilianmuseum	Y M³	St. Anna-Kirche	Y B	In der Kunsthalle	Z M⁴
Rathaus	Y R	Staatsgalerie alter Kunst	Z M²		

the crown of the Holy Roman Empire"
The unpaid debt of the Habsburgs to
their Augsburg bankers has been esti-
mated at four million ducats.

The Augsburg Confession – In 1530
Charles V, disturbed by the growing
strength of the Reformation, called an
Imperial Diet at Augsburg with the hope
of dissipating the religious troubles.
The Protestants, inspired by Luther,
thereupon proclaimed a "Confession"
of the basic tenets of their beliefs. The
statement was rejected, and it was not
until the **Peace of Augsburg** in 1555
that German Protestants won freedom
of worship.

Sights

Rathausplatz
(Town Hall Square)

Augsburg's hulking **Town Hall** ranks
among the most important secular
Renaissance buildings north of the
Alps. Built by Elias Holl between 1615
and 1620, its two onion-domed tow-

Address Book

⚙ For coin ranges, see the Legend on the cover flap.

WHERE TO STAY

⊝⊝**Unterbaarer Hof** – *Ulmer Straße 218.* ☎*(0821) 43 13 00. www.unterbaarer-hof.de. 6 rooms. Restaurant (⊝).* This good-value hotel has modern if fairly basic rooms and a huge self-catering apartment. The restaurant specializes in specialties from Swabia and Bavaria served in a cozy ambience with plenty of wood and curtained windows.

⊝⊝**Hotel Garni Georgsrast** – *Georgenstraße 31.* ☎*(0821) 50 26 10. Closed Christmas–Jan 6. 24 rooms.* A clean and simple guesthouse on a quiet side street about 1km/0.6mi from the town center. Small rooms are well maintained with plain, light-colored furnishings.

WHERE TO EAT

⊝⊝**Zur alten Feuerwache** – *Zeugplatz 4.* ☎*(0821) 51 16 85.* Dine beneath the vaulted ceilings of the 16C former armory. A large Biergarten offers a relaxing respite out front.

⊝⊝⊝**Die Ecke** – *Elias-Holl-Platz 2.* ☎*(0821) 51 06 00. www.restaurant-die-ecke.de.* This historic restaurant once hosted such luminaries as Mozart and Bertolt Brecht and ingeniously melds

rustic and modern styles in an elegant setting. Great for special occasions.

TAKING A BREAK

Caféhaus Eber – *Philippine-Welser-Straße 6 (opposite the Town Hall).* ☎*(0821) 3 68 47. www.cafe-eber.de.* This endearingly stuffy Vienna-style coffee house is famous for its homemake cakes, cookies and chocolates and also serves a few hot dishes at lunchtime. In fine weather, the Rathausplatz terrace makes for an excellent people-watching perch.

Stadtmarkt – *Annastraße 16 (accessible also from Fuggerstraße 12).* ☎*(0821) 324 39 22.* Pick up a snack or light meal from the city's bustling market stalls: cold cuts from the meat hall *(Fleischhalle)*; groceries from the *Viktualienhalle*, along with fresh produce and international specialties.

NIGHTLIFE

Der Weinbäck (Laxgangs Weinstuben) *Spitalgasse 8.* ☎*(0821) 379 11. www.weinbaeck.de. Closed Sun.* Vaulted 16C cellars and an idyllic courtyard set the scene at this lively wine tavern. Sample German vintages by the glass alongside complimentary homemade bread or pick from the seasonal menu. Suckling pig, carved tableside, is the signature dish.

---

ers frame a pediment adorned with the traditional pine cone. Inside, the Golden Hall *(Goldener Saal (⊙ open year-round, daily 10am–6pm; ⊜2€),* with its restored coffered ceiling, can be visited. The **Perlachturm** was originally a Romanesque watchtower amd can be climbed in summer. A yellow flag is flown when views are clear enough to spot the distant Alps.

St Anna-Kirche

Fuggerstraße 8. ☎*(0821) 34 37 10.* When Luther came to Augsburg in 1518 to defend his reformed thesis, he stayed at what was then a Carmelite monastery. The rooms, accessed via a flight

of wooden stairs *(Lutherstiege)* now house a small exhibit about the man and his times. The **Fugger Chapel**★ *(Fuggerkapelle),* where Jakob Fugger and his brothers are buried, is a prime example of Renaissance architecture. Note the three works by Lucas Cranach the Elder in the east chancel.

Fuggerei★

Enter via Jakoberstraße.
⊙*Open Apr–Sept, daily 8am–8pm; Oct–Mar, daily 9am–6pm. ⊜2€.* �&*(0821) 31 98 81 14. www.fugger.de.*
Known as the 'town within the town', the Fuggerei is the world's oldest social housing compound and was founded in

1516 by Jakob Fugger the Rich. To this day it provides simple but permanent housing for impoverished local Catholics in exchange for a symbolic annual rent of 0.88€ and a daily prayer for the souls of the founders.

Dom St. Maria

Hoher Weg. ☎(0821) 316 63 53.
Augsburg's cathedral has origins in the 10C but didn't get its Gothic shape until the 14C. Noteworthy features include the **Jungfrauenportal**★★ (Virgin's Door), as well as 11C Romanesque bronze door **Türflügel**★ (panels). Four of the nave altars are adorned with **paintings**★ by Holbein the Elder. Outside the cathedral look for remains of the Roman city.

Maximilianstraße★

Elegant Maximilianstraße is flanked by the mansions of wealthy Renaissance-era Augsburgers (including Fugger's at no. 36) and punctuated by two monumental 16C fountains depicting Mercury and Hercules. The latter is outside the recently renovated **Schäzlerpalais** at no 46, whose highlight is a grand **Festsaal**★★ (ballroom) canopied by a lush ceiling fresco and stuccowork. The building also houses a gallery of German Baroque paintings and another featuring works by Hans Holbein the Elder and Albrecht Dürer and southern German masters.

Glaspalast Augsburg

Am Glaspalast 1.
Open year-round, Tue 10am–8pm, Wed –Sun 10am–5pm. ☎(0821) 324 41 55. www.glaspalast-augsburg.de.
A former textile plant has taken on a new life as an art and cultural center. The two main galleries are the H2 Zentrum für Gegenwartskunst and the Staatsgalerie Moderne Kunst both present changing exhibitions of contemporary art. The latter is an offshoot of the famous Munich Pinakothek museums.

Basilika St. Ulrich und Afra★

Ulrichsplatz 19. ☎(0821) 34 55 60.
At the end of Maximilianstraße looms this former Benedictine abbey built in 1474 in late-Gothic style with Renaissance and Baroque additions. it boasts the shrines of the town's patron saints as well as three lavishly gilded Baroque altars and a bronze *Crucifixion* (1607). St. Simpert's chapel features a lovely gallery topped by terracotta **Statues of the Saints**★.
The Catholic basilica hugs the much smaller Protestant **Ulrichkirche** in reflection of the religious compromise achieved at the Peace of Augsburg.

BADEN-BADEN★★

POPULATION: 54 000

From Brahms to Queen Victoria to Bill Clinton, the spa resort of Baden-Baden has long been a favorite playground of the wealthy, famous and powerful. There's plenty to lure them, including an idyllic location on the little Oos River, hot mineral springs that worked miracles on the aching joints of ancient Roman generals, and superb cultural institutions. A highlight is the Casino, a lavish Belle Epoque extravaganza that inspired Dostoyevski's novel *The Gambler* and Prokofiev's eponymous opera.

- **Information:** Kaiserallee 3, 76530 Baden-Baden. ☎(07221) 27 52 00. www.baden-baden.de.
- **Orient Yourself:** Wedged into the Oos Valley on the edge of the Black Forest and surrounded by the Baden vineyards, Baden-Baden is 60km/37.3mi from Strasbourg via the A 5 Autobahn.
- **Don't Miss:** Lichtentaler Allee, Casino, Museum Frieder Burda.
- **Organizing Your Time:** Allow at least one day to visit the sights and Casino and relax in one of the spas or gardens.
- **Also See:** RASTATT, KARLSRUHE.

A Bit of History

Spa – Sample the restorative powers of Baden-Baden's mineral springs in two spa complexes: the **Friedrichs-bad**, a neo-Renaissance style bathing palace with a Roman-Irish Bath; and the modern **Caracalla-Therme** with pools, saunas, whirlpools, grottoes and other relaxation stations. Both are open daily but admission depends on the length of your stay and treatment menu.

Sights

Lichtentaler Allee★★

This riverside promenade has been the place to see and be seen for over a century. Napoleon III, Queen Victoria, Bismarck and Dostoevsky all whiled away the hours here and in the equally enchanting **Gönneranlage**★ nearby.

Kurhaus & Casino★

Casino tours (25min) Apr–Oct, daily 9.30am–noon; Nov–Mar, 10am–noon. Closed major holidays. 4€. (07221) 302 40. www.casino-baden-baden.de. If you plan to gamble, dress nicely (men in tie and jacket) and bring a passport.

The majestic 19C Kurhaus hosts balls, festivals, concerts and society events but is really most famous for its elegant casino. A symphony of red velvet and gilded chandeliers, the Belle Epoque venue was designed by Benazét to resemble a French palace.

Museum Frieder Burda★

Lichtentaler Allee 8b.

Open year-round, Tue–Sun 10am–6pm. Closed Dec 24 & 31. 9€. (07221) 39 89 80. www.sammlung-frieder-burda.de

Right in the Kurpark, a stunning building by New York-based architect Richard Meier houses this equally stellar art collection. The focus in on 20C works with outstanding works by Max Beckmann, August Macke, Picasso, Jackson Pollock, Mark Rothko, Georg Baselitz and Gerhard Richter.

Stadtmuseum★ (Town Museum)

Lichtentaler Allee 10.

Open year-round, Tue–Sun 10am–6pm (Wed 8pm). Closed major holidays. 4€. (07221) 93 22 72. Two thousand years of town history are engagingly chronicled in this new glass pavilion. Keep an eye out for rare coins gambling paraphernalia, sculpture from across the epochs and an enchanting assortment of historical toys.

Neues Schloss (New Castle)

The former hilltop residence of the local margraves is not open to the public but is still a great place to enjoy a signature panorama of the town and surrounding

Baden-Baden

Address Book

For coin ranges, see the Legend on the cover flap.

GETTING AROUND

Baden-Baden is linked to Karlsruhe by city train line S 4 and regional RE trains. Check ticket prices and schedule with **Stadtwerke Baden-Baden** (*(072 21) 7 71; www.stadtwerke-baden-baden.de*) or with **Deutsche Bahn** (*www.bahn.de*).

Airport – Karlsruhe/Baden-Baden Airport (10 km west of town) has flights serving Berlin, London, Hamburg and other destinations. *(07229) 66 20 00 or www.baden-airpark.de.*

SIGHTSEEING

Tourist bus – City-Bahn trolley tours are offered from March to October *(55min, 5€).*

WHERE TO STAY

Haus Rebland – *Umwegerstraße 133, 76534 Baden-Baden-Varnhalt. (07223) 951 18 80. www.haus-rebland. de. Closed mid-Nov –mid-Dec.* 24 rooms. *Restaurant ( ).* Set amid the vineyards of Varnhalt, this family-run establishment features balconies in all its guestrooms. The rustic restaurant has a country feel and pretty views over the Rhine valley.

Hotel Bayerischer Hof – *Lange Straße 92. (07221) 935 50. www.hotel-bayrischerhof.de.* 38 rooms. Restaurant( ). It would be difficult to find a more convenient hotel – the town's sights are all virtually on your doorstep and the Festival Theater *(Festspielhaus)* is across the street.

WHERE TO EAT

Yburg – *Burgruine 1. (07223) 95 75 43. www.burggaststaette-yburg. de.* This popular tourist haunt in a medieval hilltop castle offers sweeping views of the Rhine and the wine country and serves inspired regional dishes made with locally sourced, seasonal ingredients.

Medici – *Augustaplatz 8. (07221) 258 54. www.medici.de.* This trendy spot combines a restaurant, bar, internet café, sushi bar and library under one roof.

It serves international food cleverly infused regional touches to a moneyed and famous clientele that has included Nelson Mandela and Bono from the world-famous Irish band, U2.

TAKING A BREAK

Café König – *Lichtentaler Straße 12. (07221) 2 35 73. www.chocolatier. de.* This legendary coffeehouse has counted Tolstoy and Liszt among its guests and is the best place in town to sample the famous liqueur-laced Black Forest cake. In summer, sit outside on the lime-tree shaded terrace.

NIGHTLIFE

In der Trinkhalle *Kaiserallee 3 (west aisle of the Trinkhalle, entrance from back). (07221) 30 29 05. www. in-der-trinkhalle.de.* This chic café-bar with leather armchairs is the place to see and be seen while sipping latte or champagne. The tranquil terrace offers relaxing views of the spa park.

---

hills. Money troubles forced the Margravial family to auction off all interiors in 1995. The palace itself was sold in 2003 to a Kuwaiti investor group that apparently has plans to turn it into a luxury hotel.

Stiftskirche (Collegiate Church)

Climb the stairs up to Marktplatz (market square) to visit the burial place of the Baden margraves from the 14C to the 18C. Several of their epitaphs are remarkable works of art that invite closer inspection. Of particular note is the 5.6m/18ft-high sandstone **Crucifix**★, a 1467 masterpiece by Nicolaus Gerhaert von Leyden and a fine example of late medieval sculpture.

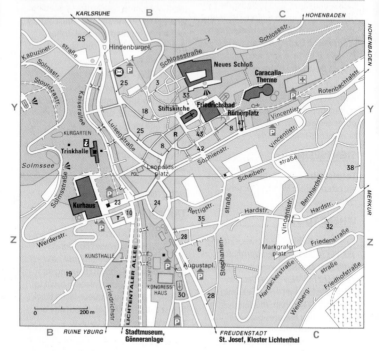

Driving Tours

Baden Vineyards★

▶ *34km/21mi, 2hr. Leave town on Kaiser-Wilhelm-Straße then Fremersbergstraße.*
Follow the signposts marked 'Badische Weinstraße'.

The **Badische Weinstraße★★★** winds sinuously from village to village through the vineyards on the lower slopes of the Black Forest.

▶ *At Altschweier, leave the Wine Road to get to Altwindeck.*

Burg Altwindeck★

This ancient fort, built on a circular plan, has been transformed into a restaurant with panoramic views. From its precincts there is a wide **view★** of the plain.

▶ *Rejoin the Wine Road and head toward Kappelrodeck.*

Oberkirch★

This beautiful town is surrounded by orchards, vineyards and forests and retains charming half-timbered houses dating from the 17C.

Schwarzwald-Hochstraße (Black Forest Crest Road)

☝ *See SCHWARZWALD.*

BAMBERG★★

POPULATION: 71 000

Established in the Middle Ages, transformed in the 17C and 18C and spared wartime bomb-raids, Bamberg is one of Germany's most delightful towns with 2 300 well-preserved buildings in styles ranging from the Romanesque to the Baroque. UNESCO honored Bamberg by giving it World Heritage status in 1993. Among its many gastronomic delights are traditionally prepared carp (Karpfen), and smoked beer (Rauchbier) which, oddly, tastes a bit like bacon.

- **Information:** Geyerswörthstraße 3, 96047 Bamberg. ☎ (0951) 87 11 61. www.bamberg.info.
- **Orient Yourself:** Bamberg was built on seven hills and lies smack dab in the heart of Franconia. The River Regnitz and the Rhine-Main-Danube Canal bisect the town, with the historic center in the upper part of town.
- **Parking:** Garages are in the Old Town, at Geyerswörtherstr. 5; on the south side at Schützenstr. 2; and on the north side at Am Georgendamm and Hornthalstr.
- **Don't Miss:** The Old Town, especially the Kaiserdom and the Rathaus.
- **Organizing Your Time:** Plan on spending a full day to properly sample Bamberg's treasures (and beers).
- **Also See:** WALLFAHRTSKIRCHE VIERZEHNHEILIGEN, BAYREUTH, NUREMBERG, ROMANTISCHE STRASSE, VOLKACH.

The Old Town

Kaiserdom★★
(Imperial Cathedral)

Open year-round, daily 8am–5pm.
Dominating Bamberg's skyline with its four towers, the Cathedral of St. Peter and St. George was completed in 1237 in a transitional style bridging the Romanesque and the Gothic. The older of its two apses, the eastern Georgenchor, stands upon a raised terrace, while the western Peterschor is entirely Gothic. The finest of the cathedral entrances is the **Fürstenportal** (Princes' Gate) facing the Domplatz.

It comprises 10 receding arches supported by fluted, ribbed columns decorated with apostels and prophets with Christ propped up in the tympanon. The **Adamspforte** (Adam's Door) features diamond and dog-tooth carving.

M. Hertlein/MICHELIN

Bamberg

The interior brims with artistic masterpieces including the celebrated 13C statue of an equestrian knight only known as **(1) Bamberg Rider**★★★ *(Bamberger Reiter)*, and the statuary group, **(2) The Visitation**. At the center of the nave is the **(3) tomb**★★★ of Emperor Henry II and his wife Kunigunde. It took native son Tilman Riemenschneider 14 years to complete the tomb. The **(4) Christmas Altar**★ depicting the Nativity is a stellar 1523 work by Veit Stoß. The **(5)** funerary statue, **(6)** statue representing the Christian church, and another **(7)** symbolizing the Jewish Faith (in the form of a blindfolded woman) are also worthy of closer inspection.

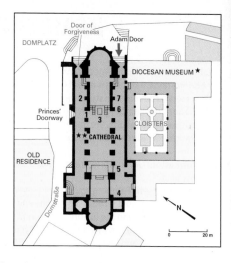

Alte Hofhaltung (Old Residence)

🕐*Courtyard is open until dusk.*

Near the dome stands the 16C episcopal palace whose ornate doorway—called the **Schöne Pforte** (Beautiful Gate) leads to a delightful inner **courtyard**★★ *(Innenhof)* framed by half-timbered Gothic buildings. Inside, the moderately interesting Historical Museum chronicles Bamberg's cultural history.

Neue Residenz (New Palace)

Domplatz 8.

✏*Visit by guided tour (45min) only: Apr–Sept, daily 9am–6pm; Oct–Mar, daily 10am–4pm.* 🕐*Closed Jan 1, Shrove Tue,* *Dec 24, 25 & 31.* 💶*4€.* ♿☎*(0951) 51 93 90.* *www.schloesser.bayern.de*

This palace, the largest building in Bamberg, includes two early 17C Renaissance wings *(on Obere Karolinenstraße)*; and two late 17C Baroque wings *(on the Domplatz)*, by local architect Leonard Dientzenhofer.

On the first floor you can peruse paintings by Lucas Cranach the Elder and other Old German masters, while on the second floor the Imperial apartments wow with intricate parquet floors, Baroque furniture and authentic Gobelins tapestries.

The **Emperors' Hall** *(Kaisersaal)* is outstanding for its portraits and allegorical frescoes.

▶ *Follow Karolinenstraße to the lay quarter of the old town, built on the banks of the River Regnitz.*

The Bamberg Christmas Crèche Tour

During Christmas time (December to January 6) Bamberg is deluged by thousands of visitors eager to follow the city's unique Christmas Crèche Trail *(Bamberger Krippenweg)*. Dozens of churches, museums and squares are decorated with splendid, handcrafted Nativity scenes. The route kicks off in the Cathedral with Veit Stoß's famous 1523 Navitity altar as well as a modern crèche that tells the famous story in eight enchanting scenes. Other tour highlights include multiple crèches in the peaceful *Maternkapelle*, which is surpassed only by the exhibit in the *Obere Pfarre* featuring more than 200 individual movable figures averaging 45cm/1.5ft in height. But each of the 33 stations is an artwork in itself, from the enormous manger in Schönleinsplatz with life-size figures in traditional local costume to the tiny crib in the church of St. Gandolf, seen through a special viewer.

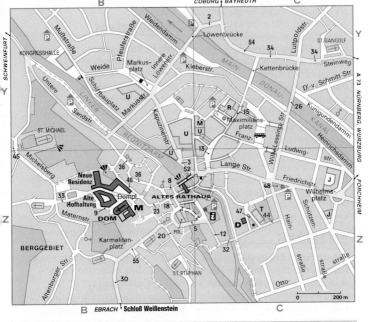

Take time to explore some of the adjoining streets, particularly around Judenstraße (note the statues of the Virgin Mary on the house corners).

Altes Rathaus★ (Old Town Hall)

Standing alone on an islet in the river, Bamberg's unusual medieval townhall is Gothic at its core but got a Baroque makeover in the 18C. Its charms include vividly painted trompe l'oeil façades, a bridge tower and a small half-timbered annex, known as the Rottmeisterhaus,

Excursions

Schloss Pommersfelden★

21km/12mi south.

The Noble Dynasty of Saxe-Coburg

In a history of intrigue and diplomacy spanning centuries, the noble dynasty of Saxe-Coburg was related either directly or through marriage to nearly every royal family of Europe: Belgian, Portuguese, Russian, Swiss and Bulgarian. The marriage between Edward, the Duke of Kent, and the Coburg Princess Victoire produced Queen Victoria; she, in turn, married a cousin: Prince Albert of Saxe-Coburg.

Address Book

🪙*For coin ranges, see the Legend on the cover flap.*

WHERE TO STAY

🍽🍽**Romantik Hotel Weinhaus Messerschmitt** – *Lange Straße 41.* ☎*(0951) 29 78 00. www.hotel-mess-erschmitt.de. 67 rooms. Restaurant (*🍽🍽🍽*).* This yellow and white-fronted hotel is the ancestral home of aviation pioneer Willy Messerschmitt. A recent expansion has added an annex with 49 modern and stylish rooms to the 18 in the historic building. The restaurant has a charming terrace overlooking a fountain-studded courtyard.

🍽🍽**Barock-Hotel am Dom** – *Vorderer Bach 4.* ☎*(0951) 540 31. www.barockho-tel.de. Closed Feb. 19 rooms.* Next to the cathedral, this sweet hotel occupies a building from 1520 later sheathed by an elegant 18C Baroque facade. Design details abound and breakfast is served beneath a Gothic vault.

WHERE TO EAT

🍽**Historischer Brauereiausschank Schlenkerla** – *Dominikanerstraße 6.* ☎*(0951) 560 60. www.schlenkerla.de. Closed Tue in Jan–Apr.* This beautiful half-timbered building is a little piece of Bamberg's history: Franconian speciali-ties are served here, including smoked beer *(Rauchbier)*, brewed on-site and drawn directly from the barrel, in the traditional manner.

🍽🍽🍽 **Würzburger Weinstube** – *Zinkenwörth 6 (west of Schönleins-platz).* ☎*(0951) 2 26 67. www.restaurant-wuerzburger-weinstuben.de. Closed Tue evening & Wed.* This wine tavern and restaurant is central but tucked off the beaten path inside a Late Gothic half-timbered building. Franconian wines and food specialties are served here. In the summer, enjoy refreshments on the terrace canopied by ancient chestnut and lime trees.

TAKING A BREAK

Café im Rosengarten – *Domplatz (in the Neue Residenz).* ☎*(0951) 98 04 00. www.hotel-graupner.de. Closed Nov–Easter.* Sweet treats from the Graupner pastry shop at Lange Straße 9 and light meals are served in the formal pavilion or on the rose garden terrace.

NIGHTLIFE

Bars cluster along Austraße (west of Grüner Markt) and Obere Sandstraße.

Klosterbräu – *Obere Mühlbrücke 1–3.* ☎*(0951) 5 77 22. www.klosterbraeu. de.* Choose from a large selection of speciality beers in the oldest brewery in town (since 1533), with delightfully rus-tic rooms. In summer the hearty local cuisine is best enjoyed on a terrace.

Palais Schrottenberg – *Kasernstr. 1 (between Dominikanerstr. and the Regnitz).* ☎*(0951) 95 58 80. www.palais-schrottenberg.de.* Built in the 18C by Johann Dientzenhofer, this café-bar offers a choice of style and ambience: Baroque-style lounge, modern winter garden, bar or idyllic courtyard. The menu unites dishes and flavors from around the world.

🚶*Visit by guided tour (1hr) only: Apr–Oct, daily 10am–5pm.* 🎫*6€.* ☎*(09548) 981 80. www.pommersfelden.de.* Also known as **Weißenstein**, this building designed by Dientzenhofer and Hildeb-randt in the 18C quickly became one of Germany's finest Baroque palaces with a stunning **double staircase**★. On the ground floor, an artificial grotto opens onto the garden, while the marble hall on the first floor features frescoes by Rottmayr. You'll also get to peak at the Elector's apartments, a gallery with paintings by Rubens, Titian and Cranach, and the dizzying hall of mirrors.

Coburg★

46km/29mi north.

Dominated by a mighty fortress (🔎*see below*), Coburg was once the capital of the dukes of Saxe-Coburg. Coburg is rich with beautiful facades, especially around the Marktplatz. The **Gymnasium Caimirianum**★ *(opposite the Moritzkirche)* dates from 1605.

Veste Coburg (Fortress)★★

🕐*Open Apr–Oct, daily 9.30am–5pm, Nov–Mar, Tue–Sun 1pm–4pm.* 🕐*Closed Dec 24, 25 & 31.* ⊚*5€.* ☎*(095 61) 87 90. www.kunstsammlungen-coburg.de.*
One of the best-preserved medieval fortresses in Germany, the Veste is guarded by a triple ring of fortified walls. The original 11C castle was replaced in the 16C. Martin Luther famously sought refuge in Veste Coburg during the Diet of Augsburg Confession; the rooms where he stayed now present exhibits on the famous reformer. The precious **art collections**★ *(Kunstsammlungen)*, include paintings by Dürer and Cranach.

In the central wing *(Carl-Eduard-Bau)* a decorative arts display includes the largest Venetian glassware collection in Europe.

Schloss Ehrenburg

👁‍🗨*Visit by guided tour (50min – hourly) only, Apr–Sept Tue–Sun 9am–5pm; Oct–Mar 10am–3pm.* 🕐*Closed Jan 1, Shrove Tue, Nov 1, Dec 24, 25 & 31.* ⊚*4€.* ☎*(095 61) 80 88 32. www.sgvcoburg.de.*
This castle was the residence of the dukes of Coburg from 1547 to 1918. Today the Renaissance palace features a Baroque interior with an early 19C English Neo-Gothic façade. Castle rooms house sumptuous Empire and Biedermeier furniture.
An art gallery contains works by German and Dutch masters.

BAUTZEN★

POPULATION: 42 000

Crowning a rocky outcrop skirted by the Spree River, Bautzen has managed to retain its old-fashioned charm despite wars and the deprivations of the East German regime. It has been the cultural and political capital of the Sorbs, **Germany's only ethnic minority**, for over 100 years. Sorbs descended from a Slavic people and speak a language related to Czech and Polish. Signs are bilingual, women wear tall embroidered headdresses during traditional festivities such as the symbolic *Hexenbrennen* **(witches' burning)** on April 30.

🛈 **Information:** Hauptmarkt 1, 02625 Bautzen. ☎(035 91) 420 16.
www.bautzen.de.

▸ **Orient Yourself:** Bautzen is on the A4 Autobahn linking Dresden and Görlitz.

🕐 **Organizing Your Time:** Allow at least four hours to see the cathedral, Ortenburg Castle and to wander along the ramparts.

👁 **Also See:** GÖRLITZ, DRESDEN, SÄCHSISCHE SCHWEIZ.

Sights

Hauptmarkt
The old market square is surrounded by nicely restored Baroque houses and a three-story 18C Town Hall built by Johann Christoph Naumann. Reichenstraße leads east from the market square to the **Reichenturm** *(Tower of the Rich;* 🕐 *open Apr–Oct, daily 10am–5pm;* ⊚*1.40€;* ☎*(03591) 46 04 31; www.bautzen.de)*, a 56m/179ft severely leaning tower that offers an excellent view of the city.

Dom St. Peter★
This hall church (1213–1497) is used both by Roman Catholics and Protestants (Catholic Masses in the chancel; Protestant services in the main nave). Construction began early in the 13C, with the southern section enlarged in the 15C.
In 1664, the 85m/279ft tower was crowned with a Baroque cupola. Inside the cathedral, note the large **Crucifix** (1714) by Balthazar Permoser; the **Baroque high altar** (1722–24) by G Fossati in the chancel; an **altar painting** by

Address Book

For coin ranges, see the Legend on the cover flap.

WHERE TO STAY

Villa Antonia – Lessingstraße 1. ☎(03591) 50 10 20. www.hotel-villa-antonia.de. 16 rooms. Restaurant (⊜⊜). This charming little hotel in a late 19C villa has bright and timelessly furnished rooms. The restaurant specializes in Austrian cuisine.

Dom Eck – Breitengasse 2. ☎(03591) 50 13 30. www.wjelbik.de. 12 rooms. Shadowed by the cathedral, this artist-decorated and family-owned hotel delivers Sorbian hospitality in modern and comfortable rooms.

Goldener Adler – Hauptmarkt 4. ☎(03591) 486 60. www.goldeneradler.de. 30 rooms. Restaurant (⊜⊜). Right in the heart of the historic center is this upscale hotel in lovingly restored 16C building. Rooms lack no mod-cons, while the restaurant sports a romantic cross-vaulted ceiling.

WHERE TO EAT

Mönchshof – Burglehn 1. ☎(03591) 49 01 41. www.moenchshof.de. Time-travel back to the Middle Ages at this congenial inn where you'll be eating without utensils amid historical vaults or on the terrace with sweeping views.

Schlossschänke – Burgplatz 5. ☎(03591) 30 49 90. www.schloss-schaenke.net. Exposed brick walls, wooden beams and vaulted ceiling create a wonderfully cozy ambience in this 600-year-old tavern. The German and regional cuisine is light, modern, seasonal and fresh.

Wjelbik – Kornstraße 7. ☎(03591) 420 60. www.wjelbik.de. Come to this historic restaurant to sample Sorb culinary specialities such as elderberry soup or braised beef with horseradish. Dishes are mostly made with locally sourced ingredients.

GA Pellegrini; and the Princes' Loggia (1674) in the Protestant section.

▸ *Follow the road that runs past the cathedral as far as the monastery.*

Remnants of the **monastery** date back to 1683, while the southern façade with its imposing portal is from 1755.

▸ *Now follow Schloßstraße.*

This charming street with restored Baroque houses leads to Ortenburg Castle.

Schloss Ortenburg

Where Ortenburg stands today was once a fortified complex completed c. AD 600 and expanded in 958 by Heinrich I. Two early 15C fires destroyed the original, but in the late 15C, when the region fell under Hungarian rule, Hungarian king Matthias Corvinus had it rebuilt in Late Gothic style. A relief portrait of the king graces the tower of the north wing. The

Thirty Years' War left profound scars, removed by renovations after 1648. In 1698, three Renaissance gables were added.

Sorbisches Museum/ Serbski Muzej

🕐Open Apr–Oct, Mon–Fri 10am–5pm, Sat–Sun 10am–6pm; Nov–Mar, Mon–Fri 10am–4pm, Sat–Sun 10am–5pm. 🕐Closed Dec 24 & 31. ⊜2.50€. ♿ ☎(03 591) 424 03. www.museum.sorben.com. In the former Salt House, an annex added to Ortenburg palace in 1782, the **Sorbian Museum** illustrates the history, culture and way of life of the Sorbs from the 6C to the present.

Town ramparts★

The 17 surviving medieval fortification towers give the town its distinctive silhouette.
A walk along the ramparts is like traveling back centuries in time. En route, you'll pass the enchanting ruins of the **Nikolaikirche** and its historic cemetery

with ornate headstones that are veritable works of art.

Alte Wasserkunst★

🕐Open daily 10am–5pm (Nov–Mar 4pm). ☜2€. ☎(03591) 415 88.
This formidable defensive and water tower has been standing since 1558. Testament to its sturdiness is the astonishing fact of its having supplied the town's water until 1965. Recently restored, it houses a fascinating technological exhibits and delivers sprawling views from the top.

Excursion

Zittau

45km/28mi southeast.
Zittau is Germany's southeastern-most city and boasts a crumbling but largely original historic center.
From the tower of the **Johanniskirche**, views extend into three countries: Germany, Poland and the Czech Republic. Zittau's most famous and rare attraction is the 1472 **Zittau Lent Cloth** (*Grosses Zittauer Fastentuch*), displayed in a former church that's now part of the **Museum Kirche zum Heiligen Kreuz** (🕐 open Apr–Oct, daily 10am–6pm; Nov–Mar, Tue–Sun 10am–5pm; ☜4€; ☎ (03583) 500 89 20; www.zittau.de/museen).
It is 8.2m/27ft high and 6.8m/21ft wide and depicts stories from the Bible in 90 vividly painted scenes.
A smaller (4.3m/14ft x 3.5m/11ft)—but no less precious—cloth from 1573 hangs in the **Kulturhistorisches Museum Franziskanerkloster** (🕐open year-round daily 10am–5pm; ☜2€; ☎(03583) 55 47 90; www.zittau.de/museen).
Zittau's most imposing building is the palace-style **Town Hall** (*Rathaus*), which was designed by Prussian building master Karl Friedrich Schinkel in the 19C and blends Renaissance and Neoclassical elements.

BAYREUTH★

POPULATION: 74 400

Bayreuth is the Holy Grail to Wagner fans, and the Bayreuth Festival attracts many of them every August. Wagner was not the only one to leave his mark on the town: The Margravine Wilhelmina, one of the most cultivated women of the 18C, transformed Bayreuth into the cultural center it remains.

🎫 **Information:** Luitpoldplatz 9, 95444 Bayreuth. ☎(0921) 885 88. www.bayreuth.de.
▶ **Orient Yourself:** Bayreuth is located in northern Bavaria, between the wooded heights of the Fichtelgebirge and the, desolate landscape of Swiss Franconia. The A9 autobahn linking Munich and Berlin runs near the town.
🅿 **Parking:** Parking garages are located throughout the city of Bayreuth.
🚫 **Don't Miss:** The Bayreuth Festival if you're an opera fan, but make your plans well in advance (🕐see A Bit of Advice).
🕐 **Organizing Your Time:** Bayreuth's highlights can be seen in half a day unless you plan to enjoy the city's musical performances.
Kids **Especially for Kids:** Cave explorations in Excursions 1 and 3.
👁 **Also See:** WALLFAHRTSKIRCHE VIERZEHNHEILIGEN, NUREMBERG.

A Bit of History

Princess Wilhelmina – Wilhelmina, sister of Prussian King Frederick the Great, had the great misfortune to be paired with a rather dull husband: Margrave Friedrich of Brandenburg-Bayreuth. A gifted artist, writer, composer and patroness, she turned her energy toward transforming Bayreuth into an artistic and cultural hub and surrounding herself with clever personages of the age. Some

Sumptuous Markgräfliches Opernhaus in Bayreuth

©Dickbauch/Wikimedia Commons

subsequently, his son Siegfried, then his grandsons Wieland (d. 1966) and Wolfgang, who ended his leadership on August 28, 2008, aged 88. At the time of writing, Wolfgang's successor had not been named.

Sights

Markgräfliches Opernhaus (Margravial Opera House)★

🕐 *Open Apr–Sept, daily 9am–6pm; Oct–Mar, daily 10am–4pm.* 🕐*Closed Jan 1, Shrove Tue, Dec 24, 25 & 31.* 🎫*5€.* ♿,☎*(0921) 759 69 22.*

Margravine Wilhelmina commissioned this gorgeous baroque theatre in 1748 as a venue for the opera and ballet. The austere façade gives no clue to the exuberance of the **interior decoration**★ by Giuseppe Galli Bibiena of Bologna. The reds, greens and browns harmonise perfectly with the gilded stuccowork on the columns; the interior is constructed entirely of wood. Visitors are treated to a 45-minute light and sound show about the theater and its patroness.

of Bayreuth's finest buildings date back to her lifetime (1709–58).

Wagner and the festival – Wagner moved to Bayreuth in 1872 along with his wife Cosima, the daughter of the Hungarian composer **Franz Liszt**. Wagner's music was stimulated by admiration for his father-in-law, who is said to be indirectly responsible for many of Wagner's masterworks. The writer and composer of *Parzival* and *Tannhäuser*, Richard Wagner searched far and wide for the ideal music venue. With the support of Ludwig II of Bavaria, he designed his own Festival Theatre *(Festspielhaus)*, revolutionary in its day for its generous audience space as well as its outstanding acoustics.

The first festival took place in 1876. After his death in 1883, the tradition continued under his daughter, Cosima and,

Neues Schloss (New Palace)

🕐 *Open Apr–Sept, daily 9am–6pm; Oct–Mar, Tue–Sun 10am–4pm.* 🕐*Closed Jan 1, Shrove Tue, Dec 24, 25 & 31.* 🎫*5€.* ♿,☎*(0921) 75 96 90.*

After a fire destroyed their old residence, Wilhelmina directed the construction of this palace and even designed some its most memorable features, including the **Broken Mirrors Cabinet**★ *(Spiegelscherbenkabinett)*. Elsewhere the lavish **decorations**★ reflect the masterful Rococo flourishes of stucco artist Jean Baptiste Pedrozzi. Wilhelmina's private

---

Bayreuth Festival

From 25 July until 28 August, Bayreuth reverberates to the sound of Wagner. Hotels within 10km/6.2mi of the town tend to be fully booked, and hotel rooms are reserved far in advance. Bookings can only be made by post and the lucky few who get a room endure poor seating and stifling heat while listening to the marathon operas. But each year the exceptional program mesmerizes opera enthusiasts.

Write to Bayreuther Festspiele, Kartenbüro, Postfach 100262, 95402 Bayreuth. Information and program (in German) is posted on www.festspiele.de. Prices vary year to year but are comparable to the usual cost of opera tickets. At 6am of performance day queuing begins for sales of any unused tickets.

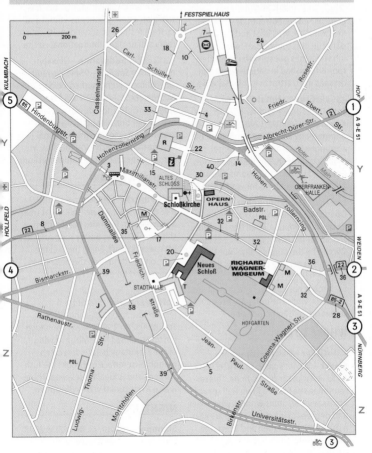

quarters were on the first floor of the north wing. On the ground floor are a small exhibit about this remarkable woman and a collection of Bayreuth porcelain. Elsewhere you can admire 18C Dutch and German paintings, including the *Four Seasons* cycle by Jan Brueghel the Elder.

Richard-Wagner-Museum★

ⓘ *Open Apr–Oct, 9am–5pm (Tue & Thu 8pm); Nov–Mar, daily 10am–5pm.* ⓘ *Closed Dec 24.* ⬡*4€.* ☏ *(0921) 75 72 80. www.wagnermuseum.de.*

Wagner's private mansion, built with funds supplied by Ludwig II and called **Haus Wahnfried**, is a major stop on any Wagnerian pilgrimage. The only remaining original feature of the house is the façade.

Displays including furniture, manuscripts, pianos and Wagner's death mask, evoke the maestro's life and work as well as the history of the Bayreuth Festival. The composer and his wife Cosima lie buried in the garden. Franz Liszt, Wagner's great friend and father-in-law, who died during the 1886 festivals, is buried in the town

Address Book

For coin ranges, see the Legend on the cover flap.

WHERE TO STAY

Goldener Löwe – *Kulmbacher Straße 30.* ☎*(0921) 74 60 60. www. goldener-loewe-bayreuth.de. 13 rooms. Restaurant.* Well kept and run with panache, this traditional Franconian inn welcomes guests with countrified rooms furnished in natural wood and dressed in an attractive color scheme.

Grunau Hotel – *Kemnather Str. 27 (east of Wieland-Wagner-Str. and Königsallee).* ☎*(0921) 798 00. www. grunau-hotel.de.* On the upper floor of a shopping mall and fitness center, this multifloor hotel has modern, spacious, quiet and comfortable rooms. Guests get discounted access for workouts.

Goldener Anker – *Opernstraße 6.* ☎*(0921) 650 51. www. anker-bayreuth.de. Closed Dec 24–mid-Jan. 35 rooms. Restaurant (   ).* Owned by the same family since the 15C, this venerable hotel oozes historical flair from every nook and cranny. Each room has its own style, but all are spacious, while the intimate restaurant serves upscale French cuisine.

WHERE TO EAT

Oskar – Das Wirtshaus am Markt – *Maximilianstr. 33.* ☎*(0921) 516 05 53. www.oskar-bayreuth.de.* This restaurant in the former Town Hall sprawls across several rooms with varying styles and degrees of intimacy. There are also a pretty winter garden and a terrace. Bavarian specialties (great dumplings!) make up the bulk of the earthy menu.

Lohmühle – *Badstraße 6.* ☎*(0921) 530 60. www.hotel-lohmuehle.de. Closed dinner Sun.* The gleaming white walls form a nice contrast to the dark wooden beams at this congenial restaurant where Franconian dishes dominate the menu. You can't go wrong with the fish raised by the chef himself in a basin right on the premises.

Landhaus Gräfenthal – *Obergräfenthal 7– 95448 Bayreuth-Wolfsbach (southeast along Nürnberger Str.).* ☎*(0921) 98 40. www.schlosshotel-thiergarten.de. Closed Sun & Mon.* A petite margravial Baroque palace has taken on a new identity as a hotel and upscale restaurant serving multi-course menus of inspired international cuisine.

Zur Sudpfanne – *Oberkonnersreuther Straße 6 – 95448 Bayreuth-Oberkonnersreuth (southeast along Nürnberger Str.)* ☎*(0921) 528 83. www. sudpfanne.de.* This popular restaurant in a former brewery building is well known for its creative international cuisine infused with local touches. In summer, the leafy beer garden beckons.

TAKING A BREAK

Café Funsch – *Sophienstr. 9.* ☎*(0921) 6 46 87. www.funsch.de.* The sweet treats and marzipan figurines handcrafted at this long-standing pastry shop are like little works of art. Enjoy them in the cafe, on the terrace on the pedestrian zone or and take some home as a souvenir.

Café Orangerie – *Eremitage 6 (east of town along Wieland-Wagner-Str.).* ☎*(0921) 79 99 70. www.eremitage-gastro.de. Closed Nov–Mar.* In a wing of the Eremitage palace, this cafe's magnificent terrace overlooks the lush gardens and is ideal for relaxing. There is also a restaurant with a *Biergarten*.

NIGHTLIFE

Sinnopoli – *Badstr. 13.* ☎*(0921) 6 20 17. www.sinnopoli.de.* Popular with a youthful crowd, this outpost changes stripes depending on the time of day serving big breakfasts to light lunches to more than 40 cocktails, both alcoholic and non-alcoholic. Prices are discounted during happy hours.

Schinner Braustuben – *Richard-Wagner-Straße 38.* ☎*(0921) 676 73. www.schinner-braustuben.de.* Immerse yourself in Franconian hospitality and locally made suds at this traditional brew-pub near the former Wagner villa. In summer, the pilsner, brown ale and lager taste best in the beer garden.

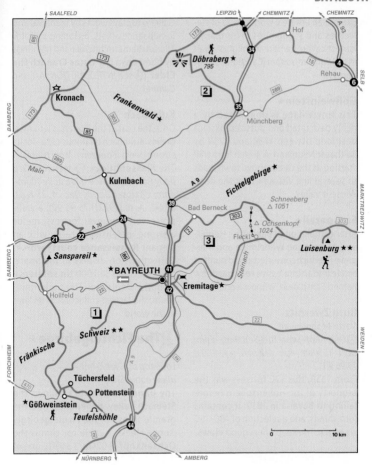

cemetery (Stadtfriedhof—*entrance on Erlanger Straße*)

Schloss Eremitage (Hermitage Palace)★

4km/2.5mi east by ② on the town plan.
🕒*Open Apr–Sept 9am–6pm; Oct 1–15 10am–4pm.*⬤*2.50€.*♿⬤*(0921) 759 69 37.*
This summer palace was a gift from her husband to the Margravine Wilhelmina, who couldn't wait to remodel it and turn it into a playground retreat. She also built the **new palace** *(Neues Schloss)*, and created the magnificent English-garden-style **Schloßpark**★.
It is filled with pavilions, follies and fountains, most famously the Upper Grotto with its writhing figures and the **Lower Grotto**, a vast basin with sculptured fountains whose jets blend with water gushing from the surrounding arcade.

Excursions

1 Swiss Franconia★★ (Fränkische Schweiz) and Sanspareil

Round-trip tour of 105km/65mi – allow one day

Pottenstein

The castle, a former residence of the elector-bishops of Bamberg, overlooks the town. Natural wonders, like gorges and caves, dot the local countryside.

Teufelshöhle (Devil's Cave) Kids

🔹*Visit by guided tour (45min) only: Apr–Oct, daily 9am–5pm; Nov–Feb, Tue & Sat–Sun 10am–3pm (Dec 26–Jan 6 daily).*
🕒*Closed Dec 24 & 25.*⬤*3.80€.*⬤*(092 43) 708 41; www.teufelshoehle.de.*

Explore an ethereal wonderland of stalactites and stalagmites in Germany's
largest caverns where highlights await
in the *Barbarossadom* (Cathedral of Barbarossa).

Gößweinstein★

This tiny village is dominated by a
richly deocrated and outsized basilica
designed btween 1730 and 1739 by
Balthasar Neumann. A 45min loop trail
starting at the castle above town leads
to several fine vistasa★ over the deep
Wiesent valley.

Sanspareil★

After completion of Bayreuth's Hermitage, Margravine Wilhelmina and Margrave Friedrich converted an old hunting
estate into an impressive **rock garden**★
named Sanspareil ("without equal").

Burg Zwernitz

North of Sanspareil.
⊙*Open Apr–Sept, Tue–Sun 9am–6pm;
Oct 1–15 10am–4pm. ⊚2.50€. ♿☎(0921)
75 96 90.*
From 1338, this 12C fortress was the
property of the Hohenzollern before
falling to Bavaria in 1810. It contains
furnishings, and a selection of 16C–18C
weapons. The keep offers good **views**.

② The Franconian Mountains★ (Frankenwald)

Round-trip of 125km/78mi – allow 5hr

Döbraberg★

*45min round-trip walk. Climb to the look-
out tower (795m/2 608ft).*
The majestic **panorama**★ extends as far
as the Thuringian Mountains in the north
and the Fichtelgebirge in the south.

Kronach

Festung Rosenberg (16C–18C), one
of the largest medieval fortresses in
Germany, towers over the small town
of Kronach and the wooded heights of
the Frankenwald. Inside, the Franconian

Gallery displays works by medieval and
Renaissance artists, including sculptor
Tilman Riemenschneider and paintings
by hometown boy **Lucas Cranach the
Elder** (ⓒ *see INTRODUCTION: Art and
Culture*).

Kulmbach

Once the seat of the Hohenzollern margraves, Kulmbach is famous today for its
strong beers *(Kapuziner, Mönchshof)*.
The **Plassenburg**★(⊙*open Apr–Oct,
daily 9am–6pm; Nov–Mar, daily 10am–
4pm;* ⊙*closed Jan 1, Dec 24, 25 & 31;*
⊚*4€;* ♿☎*(09221) 75 96 90)*, a well-
preserved medieval fortress, melds
a strong, defensive exterior with an
elegant **Renaissance courtyard**★★.
Collections on display in the apartments include 300 000 **tin soldiers**★
from the Deutsches Zinnfigurenmu-
seum, the largest collection of its kind
in the world.

③ The Fichtelgebirge★

*Loop trip of 92km/57mi –
allow about 5hr*
The **panoramic route**★ follows the
Steinach Valley, penetrating into the
granite massif of the Fichtelgebirge.
Above Fleckl, a cable car climbs the
Ochsenkopf (1 024m/3 360ft), one of
the region's highest peaks.

Luisenburg★★   Kids

This labyrinth of enormous granite
boulders makes for a pleasant hike
along a pine-shaded, hilly path *(blue
arrows indicate the way up, red the way
down)*. Several look-out points along the
way afford views of the Fichtelgebirge.
Goethe, then minister to the court of
Weimar and a geology enthusiast, was
the first to explore this unique natural
formation with a scientific approach in
1785. Since 1914, professional outdoor
theater has been presented on a natural
stage framed by rocks and forest.

▸ *Return to Bayreuth on road nº 303,
which passes through the small
spa of Bad Berneck.*

BERCHTESGADEN★★

POPULATION: 7 800

Journey's end of the German Alpine Road (Deutsche Alpenstraße), Berchtesgaden has a sublimely beautiful setting embraced by half a dozen mountain ranges and anchored by the painterly Königssee lake. Much of the landscape is protected as the Berchtesgaden National Park and an year-round outdoor playground. The only stain on the region's legacy came during the Nazi years when Adolf Hitler chose the Obersalzberg as the site of his southern headquarters.

- **Information:** Königsseer Straße 2, 83471 Berchtesgaden, ☎(08652) 96 70. www.berchtesgaden.de and www.berchtesgadener-land.de.
- ▶ **Orient Yourself:** Berchtesgaden is the main town of the Berchtesgadener Land region, which also includes the town of Schönau adjacent to Lake Königssee 5km/3mi south of town, Obersalzberg 4km/2.5mi east, Marktschellenberg 9km/6mi north, Ramsau 9km/6mi west, and Bischofswiesen 5km/3mi north.
- **Don't Miss:** Königssee, Eagle's Nest, Roßfeld-Höhenringstraße.
- **Organizing Your Time:** Allow a full day, preferably two, to enjoy this region's outstanding natural beauty.
- **Especially for Kids:** Salt Mines.
- **Also See:** DEUTSCHE ALPENSTRASSE, CHIEMSEE, BURGHAUSEN.

Sights

Schlossplatz★

This triangular square is the heart of Berchtesgaden. On the western side is the Getreidekasten, the former granary furnished with an arcade in the 16C. Lombard influence is evident in the façade of the **Church of St. Peter and St. John** *(Stiftskirche St. Peter and Johannes),* decorated with multicolored stones.

Schloss (Palace)

🕑 *Visit by guided tour (50min) only: mid-May–mid-Oct, Sun–Fri 10am–noon, 2pm–4pm; rest of the year Mon–Fri 11am & 2pm. ☜7€. ☎(08652) 94 79 80. www. haus-bayern.com.*

Once a monks' priory, this sumptuous palace is still owned—and sometimes used—by the Wittelsbachs, Bavaria's royal family. The palace museum displays weapons, religious art, French tapestries and Nymphenburg porcelain. A **guided tour** allows a close-up look at the palace. Visit the highest terrace for unforgettable views of the Watzmann.

©Sándor Kelemen/istockphoto.com

Chapel of St. Bartholomä

Obersalzberg

Adolf Hitler first visited and fell in love with the Obersalzberg area in 1923 and began spending summers in the Wachenfeld House in 1928. After seizing power in 1933, he has the property enlarged and turned into the elegant Berghof chalet. Many of the party brass built their own estates, including Martin Bormann and Hermann Göring, thus gradually turning the Obersalzberg into the southern Nazi party headquarters alongside Berlin.

Most of the compound was destroyed by British and American bombs in April 1945. The Bavarian government demolished the remaining ruins in 1952; a year later the American military made the area a recreation zone.

Salzbergwerk (Salt Mines)★★ Kids

Visit by guided tour (1hr) only: May–Oct, daily 9am–5pm; Nov–Apr, daily 11.30am–3.30pm. Closed Jan 1, Good Friday, Pentecost, Nov 1, Dec 24,25 & 31. 14€. (08652) 60 02 20. www.salzzeit reise.de.

The Berchtesgaden salt mines, which started operating in 1517, brought prosperity to a once very poor region. The salty rock is washed by water and the resulting brine (*Sole*) is piped to Bad Reichenhall to be refined. On the **tour**, visitors get to dress in miner's overalls, take a small train, whoosh down wooden slides and raft across an illuminated underground lake.

Dokumentationszentrum Obersalzberg★★

Salzbergstraße 41.

Open Apr–Oct, daily 9am–5pm; Nov–Mar, Tue–Sun 10am–3pm; Closed Jan 1, Nov 1, Dec 24, 25 & 31. 3€. (08652) 94 79 60. www.obersalzberg.de.

After the American military handed the Obersalzberg back to the Bavarian government in 1996, the decision was made to document the area's sinister past in a multilingual, multimedia exhibition center. Open since 1999, it stands on the foundations of the former Nazi guest-house "Hoher Göll". A visit here is an essential, if disturbing, epxerience.

Kehlsteinhaus★★ (Eagle's Nest)

Buses operate May–Oct, daily 7.20am–4pm. 15€. (08652) 2969. www.kehl steinhaus.de

One of the region's most impressive **panoramas**★★ unfolds from the Eagle's Nest lodge atop Mt Kehlstein at 1834m/6020ft. A restaurant today, it was originally a gift from the Nazi party to Hitler on his 50th birthday and is the only remaining Third Reich-era building.

It took 3000 workers 13 months to build the steep **road**★★★ leading all the way up the mountain. Today, special shuttle buses make the vertigo-inducing ascent from the parking lot at Hintereck. At the end of the road, a lift ascends the final 100m/328ft. **Views**★★★ extend across the German and Austrian Alps, while the Königssee shimmers below like an emerald jewel.

Königssee★★

Boats leave year-round approx every 30min. Allow 1hr 45mins, plus at least 1hr for possible short trips ashore. 12€ to St. Bartholomä, 15€ to Salet. (08652) 96 36 18; www.seenschifffahrt.de.

This long, narrow lake is one of the most romantic sites in Bavaria and the heart of the Berchtesgaden National Park. With the Watzmann, Germany's second highest mountain (2 713m/8 900ft) looming above, the lake narrows at St. Bartholomä, where you can visit the onion-domed pilgrimage **Chapel of St. Bartholomä**. From here, an easy to moderate one-hour trail leads to the mysterious **Eiskapelle**★★, an ice grotto formed by avalanches and constantly changing shape and size (do not enter—dangerous!).

More trails leave from the final boat stop at Salet, including the easy 15min trek to the **Obersee** and the 400m/1 312ft Röthbach falls.

For birdseye-views of the lake and the surrounding peaks, take the Jennerbahn

Address Book

For coin ranges, see cover flap.

WHERE TO STAY

Neuhäusl – *Wildmoos 45, along Roßfeld-Höhenringstr 7km/4.3mi east.* (08652) 94 00. www.neuhaeusl.de. *Closed Nov–mid-Dec. 32 rooms. Restaurant (*). Enjoy magnificent alpine countryside by day and the comfort of well-furnished rooms and apartments at this well-cared-for mountain inn with pretty spa and beauty area.

Alpenhotel Denninglehen – *Am Priesterstein 7.* (08652) 978 90. www.denninglehen.de. *Closed Dec 1–18, Jan 15–30. 24 rooms. Restaurant (*). About 7km/4.3mi outside town, this country-style hotel is surrounded by mountains and close to winter sports. The good-sized rooms are endearingly appointed with rustic painted furniture; some have canopied beds.

Hotel Fischer – *Königsseer Straße 51.* (08652) 95 50. www.hotel-fischer.de. *Closed Mar & late Oct–mid-Dec. 54 rooms. Restaurant (*). A few minutes' walk from the town center, this hotel is a convenient option for those eager to engage in leisure activities. Rooms are well presented and most lead onto a balcony or terrace. Ski instruction is available by reservation. Wrap up a day on the slopes or the trails with a few laps in the indoor pool or a soothing session in the sauna or steam room.

---

cable car up the 1 800m/5 900ft Mt Jenner (*19.50€ round-trip*).
Maps and information can be picked up at the **Nationalpark-Haus** *(Franziskanerplatz 7;* (08652) 643 43; *www.nationalpark-berchtesgaden.de)* in central Berchtesgaden.

Excursions

Roßfeld-Höhenringstraße★★
Round-trip of 29km/18mi east of Berchtesgaden (anti-clockwise) 1hr 30min. Toll 4.30€ car & driver, 1.70€ per additional person. (08652) 574 10; *www.rossfeldpanoramastrasse.de.*
The **Roßfeld Road** *(open year-round)* ascends the crest of the Austrian valley of the Salzach and overlooks the Tennengebirge. The Dachstein, recognizable by its glittering glaciers, fills the background. On the other side of the ridge is a view of the countryside around Berchtesgaden and Salzburg and of the Hoher Göll, Kehlstein and Untersberg peaks. From the Hennenkopf parking lot, it is only a few minutes' climb to the beacon and the Hennenkopf Cross at 1 551m/5 089ft. The road plunges down from the crest after the Roßfeldhütte (Inn) and winds through the charming valleys of the Oberau region.

Hintersee★
12km/7.4mi west via B 305.
The road climbs the narrow Ramsau Valley to reach this lake framed by the domes of the Reiteralpe and the teeth of Hochkalter. The eastern shore, the "enchanted forest" *(Zauberwald)* bordering it, and the shady lakeshore make this a popular destination for hikers, especially families.

Almbachklamm (Almbach Gorge)★★
5km/3mi north via the B 305.
Considered one of the prettiest gorges in the Bavarian Alps, this one is carved into the cliffs behind a traditional inn and 17C marble mill that still grinds big chunks of rocks into smooth balls.
A trail follows the gushing creek past several frothy waterfalls and crystal-clear pools, crossing more than two dozen iron footbridges along the way. From the top of the gorge, you can either return the same way or continue via a steepish trail to the village of Ettenberg with its lovely confection-like pilgrimage chapel. Budget about 90min for the gorge only or 2hr 30min for the trek to Ettenberg.

BERGSTRASSE

The Bergstraße, or Mountain Road, follows an ancient Roman trading route *(strata montana)* winding through gentle forest- and vineyard-covered hills and sunny escarpments sloping toward the Rhine River. "This is where Germany starts to turn into Italy," is how Emperor Joseph II described this lovely landscape. Dotted with castles and half-timbered villages, orchards and wineries, it holds much appeal for hikers, cyclists and others craving outdoor pursuits.

- **Information:** Grosser Markt 9, 64646 Heppenheim. ☎(06252) 13 11 70. www.diebergstrasse.de.
- ▶ **Orient Yourself:** The Bergstraße runs north from Heidelberg to Darmstadt following a course parallel to the A67 autobahn, which intersects it at Frankfurt.
- **Don't Miss:** The scenic town of Heidelberg.
- **Organizing Your Time:** If you want to explore Heidelberg, plan to spend a full day on the Bergstraße.
- **Also See:** HEIDELBERG, DARMSTADT, WORMS, FRANKFURT AM MAIN, MAINZ.

Driving Tour

From Heidelberg to Darmstadt

58km/36mi – about 3hr.

Heidelberg★★ – *see HEIDELBERG*

Weinheim

Sun-splashed Weinheim is the first town on the Bergstraße to see springtime. The 13C agricultural community is today the seat of local government. It has a charming **old town** centered upon a romantic market square with a 16C *Altes Rathaus* (old Town Hall). Nearby, the Büdinger Hof *(Judengasse 15–17)* is another attractive building. The **Schloss** (castle) abuts an English-style park that segues into the 19C **Exotenwald★** (Exotic Forest), with a wonderful variety of trees. The castle ruins of **Burg Windeck** and **Wachenburg** stand watch over the town.

Heppenheim an der Bergstraße

The charming **Marktplatz★** is framed by the medieval Liebig pharmacy, the 16C Town Hall and the vast Neo-Gothic "Bergstraße Cathedral".

Lorsch

A key stop on the Bergstraße, tiny Lorsch is home to **Kloster Lorsch**, an 8C Carolingian abbey that once ranked among the most important in Europe. In 1991 it was listed as a UNESCO World Heritage site, largely because of the well-preserved 8C **Königshalle★★** (Royal Hall, also known as *Torhalle*).

Presumed to be a gate house, it sports arches, an elaborate façade and is one of the few surviving pre-Romanesque architectural relics in Germany.

The building opposite houses a trio of **museums** *(Museumszentrum Lorsch; NibelungenStraße 35;* ○ *open year-round, Tue–Sun 10am-5pm;* ○ *closed Jan 1, Shrove Tue, Dec 24;* ⊕ *3€;* ♿☎*(06251) 10 38 20; www.kloster-lorsch.de).*

One details the history of the abbey, another presents Hessian folklore and traditions and the third focuses on tobacco.

Bensheim

This "town of flowers and wine" is proud of its **old town**.

Quaint half-timbered houses line the Marktplatz, the Haupstraße and Wambolterhofstraße. In a sheltered valley is the **Fürstenlager★★**, once the summer residence of the landgraves of Hessen, now surrounded by a park.

To the north, the imposing **Auerbacher Schloss** (○ *open year-round, daily 10am–5pm;* ☎ *(06251) 729 23; www.schloss-auerbach.de)* commands a view of the whole region.

Darmstadt – *see DARMSTADT*

BERLIN★★★

POPULATION: 3 404 040

No other European capital has been in the crosshairs of history as much as Berlin. In the 20C alone, it was torn asunder by war, became ground zero of Hitler's fascist regime, was split into two during the Cold War and finally reunited in 1989. Out of such adversity has grown a city that is adaptable in the extreme. Today's Berlin buzzes with a giddying energy and an unbridled zest for experimentation. Nightlife and partying here are nonstop and new trends in fashion, music, design and architecture emerge practically on a daily basis fuelled by an influx of creatives from around the planet. But Berlin is also a place of incredible beauty in its forests, rivers and historical sites. Culture blossoms everywhere and dining is an international smorgasbord.

- **Information:** *See Address book.*
- ▶ **Orient Yourself:** Berlin has two city centers: the Mitte district around Alexanderplatz in the east, where most historic sights are located, and Charlottenburg around Zoo Station in the west. The two are linked by the vast Tiergarten Park. The new Potsdamer Platz quarter is south of Mitte. Outlying districts of interest include Dahlem in the southwest, Spandau in the northwest and Köpenick in the southeast.
- **Parking:** Parking garages abound throughout Berlin. Visit http://wap.parkinfo.com for a complete listing of locations and charges.
- **Don't Miss:** Museum Island (especially Pergamon Museum), Charlottenburg Palace, Gemäldegalerie (Picture Gallery), "Historic Center" Walking Tour.
- **Organizing Your Time:** You could spend a week in Berlin and not see everything. Prioritize your visit. Allow 2 days for Mitte, including the government quarter and historic center, and 1 day for Charlottenburg, including the palace.
- **Especially for Kids:** Berlin Zoo & Aquarium, German Museum of Technology, Story of Berlin, TV Tower, Museum of Natural History.
- **Also See:** POTSDAM.

A Bit of History

Early History – The German capital originated from two 13C villages: Cölln and Berlin. Built on a sandy Spree island along a major trade route, each was inhabited by fishermen and itinerant merchants. The Hohenzollern Electors of Brandenburg became rulers of Berlin in 1417, built a palace and miraculously managed to remain in power until 1918.

The Great Elector (1640–88) – **Frederick-William of Brandenburg** fortified the town, constructed quays along the Spree and established laws making Berlin a civilized, well-governed town. His most important contribution, though, was granting residence to thousands of French Huguenot refuges in 1685, many of them trained craftsmen, theo-logians, doctors and scholars. Within a few years, nearly one in five Berliners was of Huguenot descent.

Berlin becomes a kingdom

The Great Elector's son, Elector Friedrich III, was an ambitious type who elevated himself to king of Prussia in 1701, making Berlin a royal residence. His son, **Frederick-William I** (1713–40)—otherwise known as the **Soldier King**—laid the foundations of Prussian military power by introducing the draft and building up an army of 80,000 men. He also laid out a new town, Friedrichstadt, beyond the city's original bastions along Leipziger Straße, Friedrichstraße and Wilhelmstraße.

Frederick II the Great (1740–86), son of the Soldier King, sent this army to various battlefields but also embraced the ideals of the Age of Enlightenment, surrounding himself with the finest thinkers of the day, including Voltaire. His reign also saw the construction of the Forum Fridericianum (today Bebelplatz) and other buildings along Unter den Linden, many designed by Georg Wenzeslaus von Knobelsdorff (1699–1753). Major monuments completed were the Brandenburg Gate (1789) and the *Neue Wache* (1818).

19C Berlin – Napoléon's defeat of Prussia in 1806 and the three-year occupation by the French of Berlin was a humiliating moment for the fledgling kingdom. However, it also imbued Prussians with a greater sense of patriotism, led to a number of civic reforms and ultimately paved the way for the Industrial Revolution and the formation of the German Empire in 1871 with Berlin as its capital. As the city boomed economically, politically and culturally, its population rose to one million around 1870 and twice that by 1900.

Greater Berlin – In 1920 the city united six urban suburbs, seven towns, 59 villages and 27 demesnes under a single administration encompassing four million inhabitants. Despite the upheavals following World War I, the 1920s saw immense intellectual and artistic growth. A highlight was the 1928 premiere of Bertolt Brecht and Kurt Weill's *Threepenny Opera*.

The blossoming of this talent was violently interrupted by Hitler's regime, when, along with the persecution of the Jews, a wealth of German artistic and literary heritage was banned or destroyed in the campaign against "degenerate art."

The Taking of Berlin – From April 21 to May 3, 1945 the German capital was a battlefield. The Red Army marched against the remnants of the German army, destroying everything above ground, including 120 of Berlin's 248 bridges. On 30 April 1945, the Reichstag was captured and Hitler committed suicide.

Berlin Divided – After the German surrender on 8 May, the four victorious allies – Great Britain, the United States, France and the Soviet Union – took over administration of greater Berlin. But political developments in the Soviet Sector hindered the municipal administration. The Berlin Blockade, provoked by Soviet opposition to currency reform in the western sectors, was undermined by an airlift of supplies from the west (June 26, 1948 to May 12, 1949).

Although this effort prevented Berlin's absorption into the Soviet state, it did not prevent the division of Germany. In 1949, Berlin's Soviet sector became the capital of the German Democratic Republic (GDR), while West Berlin remained under the control of the western Allies. At the

Großer Müggelsee

H. Champollion/MICHELIN

M. Hertlein/MICHELIN

Sir Norman Foster's lofty Reichstag dome

height of the Cold War, in 1961, the city's division was completed with the construction of a concrete and barbed-wire wall by the East Germans. The goal? To prevent an exodus of its own people seeking freedom and opportunity in West Berlin and the Federal Republic of Germany (West Germany).

The "Fall" of the Wall – In November 1989, the GDR government, bowing to increased public pressure, agreed to re-establish free passage between the two Germanies. A night of wild celebration, especially around the Brandenburg Gate, followed the official "opening" of the Berlin Wall on November 9.

In June 1991, the Bundestag (German parliament) selected Berlin as the capital of a reunited Germany. Since then, Berlin has experienced an extraordinary building boom and the two city halves have grown back together, though the differences in architecture, housing and shops are still clear.

An Outdoor City – Berlin, the biggest city in Germany, covers an area eight times the size of Paris. Devastated by the war, the capital lost much of its historical heritage and is now essentially a modern city shaped by leading architects of the 20C and 21C, including Le Corbusier and Hans Scharoun and, more recently, Daniel Libeskind, Renzo Piano, Helmut Jahn and others. Berlin is also a very green city, with the vast Tiergarten Park

at its heart, numerous neighborhood parks and a green belt stretching along its periphery. Waterways, including the Spree River, which cuts through the central city, the Havel River along its eastern edge and various lakes, including the Wannsee and Grunewaldsee, further provide open spaces and recreational opportunities.

A Lively Cultural Scene – Berlin justly enjoys a reputation for the quality and diversity of its cultural scene. Fashion, art, design and music are all exploding, fueled by scores of artists and creative spirits from around the world. In February, a galaxy of stars descends for the Berlinale (*see INTRODUCTION: Art and Culture, Cinema*), one of Europe's most prestigious film festivals.

There are venues everywhere, but much of the nightlife action centers on the **Scheunenviertel**, the old Jewish Quarter, in the Mitte district, just north of Alexanderplatz. The **Prenzlauer Berg** quarter just north of here also teems with bars, restaurants and clubs. Major hubs are Kollwitzplatz and Helmholtz-platz squares. The **Kreuzberg** district, south of Mitte, has a more alternative, multicultural flair, especially along Bergmannstraße, Schlesische Straße and Oranienstraße. **Potsdamer Platz** and Gendarmenmarkt areas have the most high-brow venues, including the Konzerthaus and Philharmonie for classical music. Theaters also flank

Brandenburg Gate, symbol of Berlin

Ph. Gajic/MICHELIN

Kurfürstendamm in Charlottenburg and Friedrichstraße in Mitte.

The cosmopolitan sophistication that's in evidence throughout Berlin also extends to its cuisine. In fact, restaurants serving traditional local dishes such as pig's knuckles (*Eisbein*) with sauerkraut and pease-pudding have become a dying breed while gourmet restaurants catering to a sophisticated, international clientele are on the rise.

Walking Tour

Historic Center★★

The itinerary starts at the Reichstag and follows the celebrated Unter den Linden ("Under the Lime Trees") boulevard from Pariser Platz to Schlossplatz.
Most of the great monuments of the former Prussian capital flank this grand avenue, which originated as a bridle path leading from the city palace to the Tiergarten hunting reserve.

Reichstag★★

This massive Neo-Renaissance government building was inaugurated in 1894, damaged by fire in 1933, and heavily bombed in 1945. It was restored during the 1970s, but without the landmark dome that had been dynamited in 1954. After reunification the Reichstag was returned to its former glory thanks to British architect, **Lord Norman Foster**, who embarked upon a top-to-bottom renovation in 1995. In 1999, the sparkling new glass dome, became a shining beacon of the reunited city. Poignantly, it sits right above the Plenary Hall where the German parliament (*Bundestag*) again convenes since 1999. Brave the inevitable line for the free elevator ride to the **viewing platform**★★ and take in the fantastic views of the historic center and vast Tiergarten Park. And don't miss a stroll up the dome's ramp spiralling around its mirror-clad central funnel.

▶ *From the Reichstag head south on Eberstraße toward the Brandenburg Gate.*

Brandenburger Tor (Brandenburg Gate)★★

This triumphal arch was for almost three decades the symbol of the city's division, trapped just behind the Berlin Wall. Inspired by the Propylaea of the Parthenon, the gate was built by Carl Gotthard Langhans in 1788–91 and is surmounted by Gottfried Schadow's famous Quadriga, a sculpture of the Goddess of Victory (1793). It was removed to Paris after one of Napoléon's campaigns and returned to Berlin in 1814. Today, the gate is the emblem of the reunited city.

▶ *Head southeast on Eberstraße to Behrenstraße*

Address Book

For coin ranges, see the Legend on the cover flap.

PRACTICAL INFORMATION

TELEPHONE AREA CODE: 030

TOURIST INFORMATION

Berlin Tourismus Marketing *(BTM; info hotline, room & ticket reservations ☎(030) 25 00 25; www.visitberlin. com; Mon–Fri 8am–7pm, Sat–Sun 9am–6pm.* **Infostores:** Brandenburg Gate, *Pariser Platz, South Wing, daily 10am–6pm;* Hauptbahnhof, *ground floor near Europa Platz entrance, daily 8am–10pm;* Alexa Shopping Center, *Grunerstraße 20, near Alexanderplatz, Mon–Sat 10am–10pm, Sun 11am–4pm;* Reichstag, *ScheidemannStraße, daily 10am-6pm;* Neues Kranzlereck, *Kurfürstendamm 21, Mon–Sat 10am–8pm, Sun 10am–6pm.* All Infostores may offer extended hours between April and October.

ENTERTAINMENT

Listings: The bi-weekly city magazines *Zitty* and *Tip* and the monthly *Berlin-Programm* (available at bookshops and kiosks) are the best sources for event listings. All are in German. The monthly English-language *Ex-Berliner* magazine also has some listings and reviews.
Tickets can be booked via www.visitberlin.com or call the BTM hotline ☎(030) 25 00 25. The multilingual staff can also help with room reservations, a free service with a best-price guarantee.

POST OFFICES WITH LATE HOURS

The branch at Joachimstaler Straße 7 near Bahnhof Zoo is open Mon–Sat 9am–8pm and has a 24/7 self-service section; near Alexanderplatz, the branch at Rathausstraße 5 is open Mon–Fri 8am–7pm, Sat 8am–4pm. For additional branches, call ☎(01802) 33 33 or check www.deutschepost.de.

DAILY PAPERS

Berliner Morgenpost, Tagesspiegel, Berliner Zeitung, Die Tageszeitung

INTERNET

www.berlin.de
www.berlinonline.de
www.berlin-info.de
www.visitberlin.com
www.berlin-life.com
www.people-in-berlin.de

TRANSPORTATION

AIRPORT

For general information about any of Berlin's two airports, call ☎0180 500 0186. From **Tegel (TXL)**, northwest of Berlin, bus nos. 109 and X9 travel through the western city center to Zoo Station (Bahnhof Zoologischer Garten), while Jet Express Bus TXL serves Alexanderplatz in the eastern city center. **Schönefeld (SFX)** is southeast of town and linked by Airport Express train to the city center.

PUBLIC TRANSPORTATION

Berlin's public transportation system consists of buses, trams, S-Bahn (light rail) and U-Bahn (subway). For trip planning and general information, contact the 24hr hotline at ☎19449 or www.bvg.de. In-person information is available at the kiosk on Hardenbergplatz *(outside Bahnhof Zoo; open 6.30am–8.30pm)* and at many U-Bahn and S-Bahn stations. Berlin and its environs (e.g. Potsdam) are divided into fare zones A, B and C. For rides within the city, a Zone AB ticket suffices. Tickets are available from vending machine in all U-Bahn and S-Bahn stations, in trams and from bus drivers. They must be stamped prior to your journey.
Single tickets cost 2.10€ for Zone AB, day passes (valid to 3am the following morning) are 6.10€. A 7-day pass costs 26.20€. Tariffs increase every year or so.
The **Berlin Welcome Card** (www.visitberlin.de/welcomecard) costs 16.50€ for 48hrs and 21.50€ for 72hrs and is good for unlimited public transportation within Zone AB and discounts to 130 sights, attractions and tours. The Berlin & Potsdam version is valid for travel in Zone ABC for one adult and up to three children under 14. Cards are sold at BTM Infostores, BVG outlets and through ticket vending machines.

Construction in Berlin can lead to delays and detours in local transport.

Useful Tip: Bus no. 100 shuttles between Bahnhof Zoo and Alexanderplatz, passing by many of Berlin's major sights. Bus no. 200 follows a more southerly route via Potsdamer Platz and the Kulturforum museums.

SIGHTSEEING

BUS TOURS

Severin & Kühn (☎880 41 90; www.severin-kuehn.de); Berolina Sightsseeing (☎88 56 80 30); BBS (☎35 19 52 70; www.bbsberlin.de); Tempelhofer Reisen (☎752 40 57; www.tempelhofer.de) all provide hop-on-hop-off bus tours with taped commentary taking in all major city attractions. Buses run at 15- or 30-minute intervals between 10am and 5pm and leave from Kurfürstendamm or outside the Park Inn Hotel on Alexanderplatz.

WALKING & BIKING TOURS

The following companies all provide excellent English-language walking and biking tours: New Berlin Tours (☎51 05 00 30; www.newberlintours.com), Original Berlin Walking Tours (☎301 91 94; www.berlinwalks.de), Brewer's Berlin Tours (☎22 48 74 35; www.brewers-berlin.de), Insider Tour ☎692 31 49; www.insidertour.com). Look for their flyers in hotel lobbies and the tourist offices.

BOAT TOURS

Stern- und Kreisschiffahrt (☎536 36 00; www.sternundkreis.de) offers 1hr cruises along the Spree River through the historic city center from various landing docks, including in the Nikolaiviertel and FriedrichStraße. Longer tours go out to Charlottenburg Palace, along the Landwehrkanal or Berlin's green suburbs.

SPECIALTY TOURS

Trabi Safari (☎2759 2273; www.trabi-safari.de) Imagine: you behind the steering wheel of a tinny GDR-era Trabi car exploring Berlin's Wild East following your guide in another vehicle. The ultimate "Ostalgia" tour (i.e. nostalgia for the East).

WHERE TO STAY

⊜⊜**Am Wilden Eber** – Warnemünder Straße 19, 14199 Berlin-Wilmersdorf. ☎(030) 89 77 79 90. www.hotel-am-wilden-eber.de. 15 rooms ☜. This simple hotel in a leafy suburb has well-kept and quiet rooms, and a small pool and sauna in the basement.

⊜⊜ **Hotel Am Anhalter Bahnhof** – Stresemannstraße 36, 10963 Berlin-Kreuzberg. ☎(030) 258 00 70. www.hotel-anhalter-bahnhof.de. 35 rooms. The best thing about this no-frills but good-value property is its central location near Potsdamer Platz and a bus stop on its doorstep. Basic rooms are clean and cheap, but only some have private facilities; others must share bathrooms down the hall.

⊜⊜**Hotel Econtel** – Sömmeringstraße 24, 10589 Berlin-Charlottenburg. ☎(030) 34 68 10. www.econtel.de. 205 rooms. Restaurant ⊜, closed Sun. This pet-friendly modern hotel near Schloss Charlottenburg is a winner with groups and offers rooms in three categories: Economy, Business and Comfort, as well as Family Rooms (with bunk beds) sleeping up to four.

⊜⊜**Hotel Arte Luise** – Luisenstraße 19, 10117 Berlin-Mltte. ☎(030) 28 44 80. www.luise-berlin.com. 47 rooms. At one of Berlin's most eclectic hotels you'll sleep in rooms that each reflect the vision of a different artist. Themes range from cabaret to Hollywood, bird's nest to safari—all of them classy, artsy and unique. The cheapest rooms must share facilities.

⊜⊜**Hotel Berlin-Plaza** – Knesebeck straße 63, 10719 Berlin-Charlottenburg. ☎(030) 88 41 30. www.plazahotel.de. 131 rooms. Restaurant ⊜. This dog-friendly hotel puts you close to Ku'damm shopping and has modern, clean and plain rooms.

⊜⊜⊜ **Hotel Hackescher Markt** – Große Präsidentenstraße 8, 10178 Berlin-Mitte. ☎(030) 28 00 30. www.loock-hotels.com. 31 rooms. Charmingly decorated in English country style, this intimate boutique hotel occupies a modern building concealed by a historic façade. It is right in the heart of the happening Scheunenviertel nightlife district, so get a room facing the small inner courtyard for extra quiet.

⊖⊖⊜⊜ **Grand Hotel Esplanade** – *Lützowufer 15, 10785 Berlin-Tiergarten. ☎(030) 254 788 255. www.esplanade. de. 386 rooms. Restaurant ⊖⊖⊜.* This updated urban designer hotel features elegant rooms dressed in natural hues and accented with wood and chrome. The generous pool and sauna are welcome relaxation zones while four restaurants feed tummy and soul.

⊖⊖⊜⊜ **Hotel Adlon Kempinski** – *Unter den Linden 77, 10117 Berlin-Mitte. ☎(030) 226 10. www.hotel-adlon. de. 382 rooms. Restaurant ⊖⊖⊜.* A faithful replica of the 1907 original, this quintessential grand hotel delivers luxury, elegance and unparalleled service. Overlooking the Brandenburg Gate, it is a favorite with stars, politicians and blue bloods.

WHERE TO EAT

⊖⊜ **Marjellchen** – *Mommsenstraße 9, Charlottenburg. ☎(030) 883 26 76. Closed Sun.* This homey Berlin restaurant serves substantial dishes from eastern Prussia and Silesia that taste just like in the old days.

⊖⊜ **Mutter Hoppe** – *Rathausstraße 21, Mitte. ☎(030) 241 56 25. www. prostmahlzeit.de/mutterhoppe.* A rustic restaurant near the Nikolaiviertel, Mutter Hoppe celebrates Old Berlin nostalgia in its warren of rooms filled with faded photographs and yesteryear's memorabilia. On Fri and Sat nights, live bands play music from the 1920s and '30s.

⊖⊜ **Zum Nußbaum** – *Am Nußbaum 3, Mitte. ☎(030) 2472 6969.* Berlin's oldest tavern has been serving cold beer and hearty Berlin food since 1571. Painstakingly rebuilt after World War II, its wood-paneled wallls and low ceilings feel as authentic as ever.

⊖⊜⊜ **Borchardt** – *Französische Straße 47, Mitte. ☎(030) 81 88 62 62.* With impressive gilded columns, stuccoed ceilings and refined furniture, this chic restaurant attracts celebrities, politicians and the merely monied. The wiener schnitzel is reportedly the best in town.

Turkish market in Kreuzberg

H. Champollion/MICHELIN

⊖⊜⊜ **Diekmann** – *Meinekestraße 7, Charlottenburg. ☎(030) 883 33 21. www.j-diekmann.de. Closed Sun lunchtime. Reservation necessary.* With its wooden flooring, simple chairs and old-style décor this restaurant resembles a colonial boutique. Budget-priced business lunch menus are available.

⊖⊖⊜ **Neuer Bamberger Reiter** – *Regensburger Straße 7, Charlotten burg. ☎(030) 23 13 74 94. www.neuer-bamberger-reiter.de. Closed Sun.* Soft music, candlelight, and an elegant bistro flair combine to give this dining room a romantic vibe. The kitchen rotates an intriguing repertory of light, market-fresh dishes inspired by the cuisines of France and Italy.

⊖⊖⊜ **Mao Thai** – *Wörther Straße, Prenzlauer Berg. ☎(030) 441 92 61. www.maothai.de.* At this Thai stalwart, authenticity and quality matter more than high turnover. A haze of tantalizing aromas envelops you as you step inside the elegant dining room, subtly accented with imported art and antiques.

⊖⊖⊜ **Vino e Libri** – *TorStraße 99, Mitte. ☎(030) 44 05 84 71. www. vinoelibri.de.* This family-run Italian ristorante dazzles with class not glitz and serves excellent thin-crust pizzas and innovative mains. The service is friendly service and the ambience unpretentious.

⊖⊖⊜ **Zander** – *Kollwitzstraße 50, Prenzlauer Berg. ☎(030) 44 05 76 78. www.zander-restaurant.de. Closed Mon. Reservations recommended.* This bi-level bistro serves freshly prepared regional and international dishes with a creative, modern touch. The menu changes weekly.

⊜⊜🍽🍽🍽**Facil** – *Potsdamer Straße 3, at Mandala Hotel, Tiergarten.* ☎(030) 590 051 234. www.facil-berlin.de. *Closed Sat–Sun.* The purist design of this glass pavilion is the perfect foil for Michael Kempf's creative Mediterranean culinary compositions.

⊜⊜🍽🍽**Fischers Fritz** – *Charlottenstraße 49, at Regent Hotel, Mitte.* ☎(030) 20 33 63 63. www.fischersfritzberlin. com. Kitchen wizard Christian Lohse specializes in fish dishes, prepared both classically and innovatively.

CAFÉS

Café Einstein – *Kurfürstenstraße 58, Schöneberg.* ☎(030) 261 50 96. www. cafeeinstein.de. This Vienna-style coffeehouse in the former villa of silent-movie star Henny Porten is popular with artists, intellectual types and politicians. Enjoy breakfast, a light lunch, afternoon coffee and cake or Austrian dishes at dinnertime.

Ephraim's – *Spreeufer 1, Mitte.* ☎(030) 24 72 59 47. www.ephraims.de. Nostalgia rules at this café-restaurant in the Nikolaiviertel serving Berlin specialities, homemade cakes and a warm atmosphere. In fine weather, sit outside with views of the Spree River.

Telecafé – *Panoramastraße 1a, Mitte.* ☎(030) 242 33 33. www.berlinerfernsehturm.de. Pinpoint Berlin landmarks from this TV Tower café at a lofty 207m/680ft height. It completes a full revolution in 30 minutes.

NIGHTLIFE

Useful Tips – Berlin's nightlife is decentralized and constantly evolving. Current hot spots cluster in the Scheunenviertel and around Gendarmenmarkt in Mitte; Kollwitzplatz, Kastanienallee and Helmholtzplatz in Prenzlauer Berg; Bergmannstraße, Schlesische Straße and Paul-Lincke-Ufer in Kreuzberg; Winterfeldtplatz in Schöneberg; and Savignyplatz in Charlottenburg.

Clärchen's Ballhaus – *Auguststraße 24–25, Mitte.* ☎(030) 282 92 95. www. ballhaus.de. *Closed Mon.* This 19C dance hall draws young and old with tango, swing, ballroom, disco and more. Live bands perform on Fri and Sat night and dance lessons are offered, too. In the daytime, there's German food and thin-crust pizza.

925 Loungebar – *Taubenstraße 19, Mitte.* ☎(030) 20 18 71 77. At this ritzy cocktail bar on Gendarmenmarkt everything is bathed in scarlet red, except for the bar, which is plated with 925 sterling silver.

Die Tagung – *Wühlischstraße 29, Friedrichshain, east of Warschauer Straße.* ☎(030) 29 77 37 88. This funky been-here-forever bar is a tongue-in-cheek celebration of 'Ostalgia' with a hodgepodge of retro busts, signs, posters and other memorabilia.

Universum Lounge – *Kurfürstendamm 153, Charlottenburg.* ☎(030) 89 06 49 95. www.universumlounge. de. A cool crowd of cashed-up locals, theater-goers and hipsters convenes for cocktails and conversation in this sleek, space-age themed lounge. It's right in the Schaubühne theater, designed by Expressionist architect Erich Mendelsohn in the 1920s.

Zillemarkt – *Bleibtreustraße 48a, Charlottenburg.* ☎(030) 881 70 40. www.zillemarkt.de. This Old Berlin hangout with its cobbled courtyard, bric-a-brac décor and earthy cooking is much beloved by tourists and locals alike.

Prater Berlin – *Kastanienallee 7–9, Prenzlauer Berg.* ☎(030) 448 56 88. www.pratergarten.de. Dating back to 1873, this is Berlin's oldest, largest and most beautiful beer garden. Quaff a

H. Champollion/MICHELIN

Café terrace on the banks of the Spree

cold one sitting at long blond-wood tables beneath mature chestnut trees.

Philharmonie – *Herbert-von-Karajan-Straße, Tiergarten. ☎(030) 25 48 81 32. www.berliner-philharmoniker.de.* Enjoy supreme acoustics, a top notch orchestra led by Sir Simon Rattle and renowned soloists in one of Germany's finest concert halls, built by Hans Scharoun in the 1960s.

Staatsoper Berlin – *Unter den Linden 7, Mitte. ☎(030) 20 35 45 55. www.staatsoper-berlin.org.* The most prestigious

among Berlin's three opera houses, the National Opera is helmed by Daniel Barenboim and features world-class performers in a spectacular setting.

Wintergarten Varieté – *Potsdamer Straße 96, Schöneberg. ☎(030) 25 00 88 88. www.wintergarten-berlin.de.* This glittery variety theater captures the glamor of 1920s Berlin beautifully with nightly shows featuring magicians, clowns, jugglers, acrobats and other world-class artistes.

Holocaust-Mahnmal (Holocaust Memorial)★★

Built to honor the memory of the millions of Jews killed by the Nazis, this powerful memorial was designed by Jewish German-American architect Peter Eisenman. Stretching over two hectares (five acres) just south of the Brandenburg Gate, it consists of over 2 700 concrete pillars of differing heights. The underground information center *(Ort der Information)* provides historical context on the Holocaust and includes one room where the names of all known victims are read out aloud continuously. The memorial was inaugurated on May 10, 2005, 60 years after German capitulation.

▶ *Return to the Brandenburg Gate and turn right onto Unter den Linden.*

Unter den Linden★★

Berlin's most elegant boulevard was conceived by Great Elector Frederick William in 1647. It is lined by embassies, banks and expensive stores as well as by a parade of beautifully restored monuments and buildings dating back to the 17C.

▶ *Follow Charlottenstraße south to the Gendarmenmarkt.*

Gendarmenmarkt★★

Berlin's most beautiful square was named after the "Gens d'Armes", a Prussian regiment made up entirely of Huguenots who had settled here after having being forced out of their native France in 1685. The square is bookended by the **Deutscher Dom**★ (German Cathedral) and the **Französischer Dom**★ (French Cathedral), both of which now harbor exhibits. The tower of the latter can be climbed.

Konzerthaus★★ (Concert Hall)

Linking the two Gendarmenmarkt churches is the Konzerthaus, built by Karl Friedrich Schinkel in 1821. Originally a theater called the Schauspielhaus, it is now a classical concert hall. Schinkel found inspiration in Greek antiquity: note the grand staircase leading to a portico supported by six pillars. Destroyed during World War II, the structure was rebuilt between 1980 and 1984. Although not an exact reproduction, the elaborately decorated concert halls are truly magnificent.

▶ *Take Markgrafenstraße north, turn right on Behrensstraße and follow it to Bebelplatz.*

Bebelplatz★

This wide open square was once the heart of the Forum Fridericianum, a neoclassical arts and cultural complex conceived by Frederick the Great and designed by Knobelsdorff. Since the king's military exploits diminished his cash flow, only some structures were completed. The most magnificent is **Staatsoper Berlin** (opera house) on the west side. The ensemble also encompasses the baroque Old Library on the western side, the Hotel de Rome in a 19C bank building on the south side and St. Hedwig Cathedral in the southeastern corner. In 1994, Micha Ullman created the below-ground **Versunkene Biblio-**

The Huguenots, France's Contribution to Berlin

In 1685, in response to Louis XIV's Revocation of the **Edict of Nantes**, the Great Elector Frederick William of Brandenburg issued the **Edict of Potsdam** granting asylum to French Calvinists.

These Protestants, or Huguenots, came in droves. In fact, 100 000 passed through Frankfurt-am-Main alone in 20 years' time. 15 000 Huguenots came to Brandenburg, including 6 000 to Berlin, representing one quarter of the population. Most settled in the Friedrichstadt area around Gendarmenmarkt, developing trades, a textile industry and fruit and vegetable husbandry. They also introduced several popular new dances: the cotillon, the gavotte and the minuet. Until the 19C, Berlin's French community had its own ecclesiastical and legal organization.

thek (sunken library), a glass-fronted, empty-shelved room in the square's center. It commemorates the first official book-burning held by the Nazis on Bebelplatz on 10 May 1933.

St. Hedwigs-Kathedrale
Knobelsdorff drafted the plans for this copper-domed Catholic church (1773), closely modeled on the Pantheon in Rome. Since Frederick the Great had been victorious in capturing Silesia, the church was dedicated to St. Hedwig, the patron saint of Silesia. It was badly damaged during World War II and rebuilt with a modern interior.

Staatsoper Unter den Linden★
Built by Knobelsdorff between 1740 and 1743, the national opera house burned down in 1843; Langhans' reconstruction follows the original plans. Destroyed again during World War II, it was rebuilt by Richard Paulick between 1951 and 1955 and is home to one of Germany's most prestigious ensembles.

Alte Königliche Bibliothek★
(Old Library)
Designed by Georg Friedrich Boumann in Viennese Baroque style for the royal book collection, this library was inaugurated in 1780 and now houses part of the university law school.

Humboldt-Universität
Opposite the Opera House.
The palace of Frederick the Great's brother, Prince Heinrich, built in 1753, became a university in 1810 and now enrolls around 37 000 students. Left of

the main entrance on Unter den Linden a statue of founder Wilhelm von Humboldt faces that of his brother, the explorer and geographer Alexander von Humboldt. The philosophers Fichte and Hegel and the scientists Einstein and Planck all taught here; Heine and Marx were students.

▶ *Continue east on Unter den Linden.*

Neue Wache (New Guardhouse)
Designed by Schinkel in 1818, this former guardhouse is now Germany's central memorial "for the victims of war and violence." The austere interior houses the Käthe Kollwitz sculpture called *Mother with Dead Son.*

Deutsches Historisches Museum★★
(German Historical Museum)
🕐*Open year-round, daily 10am-6pm.*
🕐*Closed May 1, Dec 24 & 31.* ✆*5€.*
♿✆*(030) 20 30 40. www.dhm.de.*
Housed in the Baroque former armory (*Zeughaus*), this comprehensive exhibition uses multimedia exhibits and original artifacts to trace over 2 000 years of German history. The upper floor covers the period from the first century AD to the end of the German Empire in 1918, while the ground floor details events of the Weimar Republic, the Nazi and Cold War years and modern reunification.

Friedrichswerdersche Kirche★
(Friedrichswerdersche Church)
🕐*Open year-round, daily 10am–6pm.*
♿✆*(030) 20 90 55 77. www.smb.spk-berlin.de.*

Schinkel, the architect who left his mark on Berlin more than any other, also designed this Neo-Gothic brick church just south of Unter den Linden. Completed in 1830, it now houses the **Schinkelmuseum**★ showcasing sculptures by its namesake and his contemporaries.

▸ *Cross the Spree canal via the Schloßbrücke adorned with Schinkel sculptures to get to Museum Island (see below). In front of your looms the Berlin Cathedral.*

Berliner Dom★ (Berlin Cathedral)

🕐 *Open Apr–Sept, Mon–Sat 9am–8pm, Sun noon–8pm (Oct–Mar, daily until 7pm). ⊗8€. ♿☎(030) 20 26 91 36. www.berlinerdom.de.*

This Italian Renaissance cathedral was consecrated in 1905 and features a magnificent **interior**★★. The sarcophagi of Frederick I and his second wife Sophie Charlotte, carved by Andreas Schlüter, are of special artistic merit. More members of the Prussian royal family are buried in the **crypt**. For closeups of the massive dome and a sweeping panorama of Museum Island and the central city, climb up the 270 stairs to the viewing gallery.

▸ *Continue east along Karl-Liebknecht-Straße to Alexanderplatz.*

Alexanderplatz★

Named for Tsar Alexander, who visited Berlin in 1805, this square—known as "Alex"—is the commercial and traffic hub of the eastern city center. It was completely destroyed in World War II and rebuilt in an austere socialist style that is still in evidence today, despite improvements.

On your way to the Alex, you will pass by the 14C **Marienkirche** (St. Mary's Church) with its macabre Dance of Death fresco that recalls the ravages of the Black Plague. The red-brick pile just south of here is the **Rotes Rathaus** (Red Town Hall), where the Berlin mayor makes his home. Above it all looms the 365m/1 200ft-high **Fernsehturm**★ (TV Tower) with a viewing platform and revolving restaurant about halfway up.

Nikolaiviertel★ (St. Nicholas Quarter)

With its narrow cobbled streets and old taverns, this quarter teems with restored period houses like the **Knoblauch House**★ (Knoblauchhaus— Poststraße 23; 🕐 open year-round, Tue & Thu–Sun 10am–6pm, Wed noon–8pm; 🕐 closed Dec 24 & 31; ☎(030) 27 57 67 33; www.stadtmuseum.de) and the **Ephraim Palace**★ (Ephraim-Palais – Poststraße 16; 🕐 open: see Knoblauchhaus; ⊗5€, Wed free; ☎(030) 24 00 21 21; www.stadtmuseum.de). The Nikolaiviertel is dominated by the bell-towers of the Late Gothic 1230 **Nikolaikirche**★, Berlin's oldest church.

Tiergarten District★

Berlin's oldest public park stretches almost 3km/1.8mi from Ernst-Reuter-Platz to the Brandenburg Gate. Originally a royal hunting reserve, it was a military exercise area and in the 19C was transformed into a delightful English-style park by landscape architect Peter Joseph Lenné (1789–1866).

Siegessäule (Victory Column)

🕐 *Open Apr–Oct, Mon–Fri 9.30am–6.30pm, Sat–Sun 9.30am–7pm; Nov–Mar, Mon–Fri 10am–5.30pm, Sat–Sun 10am–5pm. ⊗2.20€. www.monument-tales.de.*

All of 67m/220ft high, this landmark monument, surmounted by a gilded sculpture of the Goddess of Victory (nicknamed Gold Else), commemorates the Prussian campaigns of 1864, 1866 and 1870 against Denmark, Austria and France. From the top (285 steps), **views**★ extend across Tiergarten Park to the Spree, the Hansa residential quarter and the Brandenburg Gate.

Schloss Bellevue

Built in the Neoclassical style by Philipp Boumann in 1785, this was the summer palace of Frederick the Great's younger brother, Prince Augustus-Ferdinand. Today it is the official residence of the German president and is backed by a lush park that is not accessible to the public.

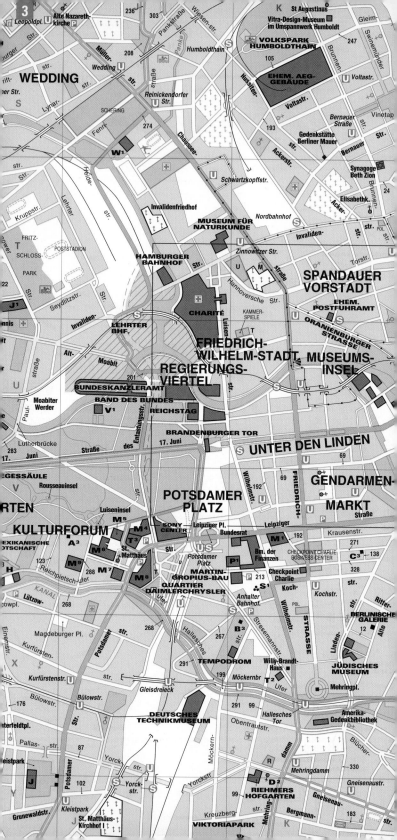

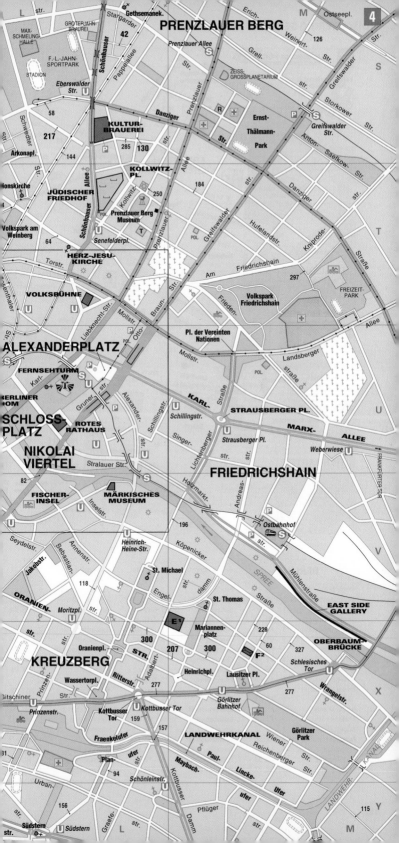

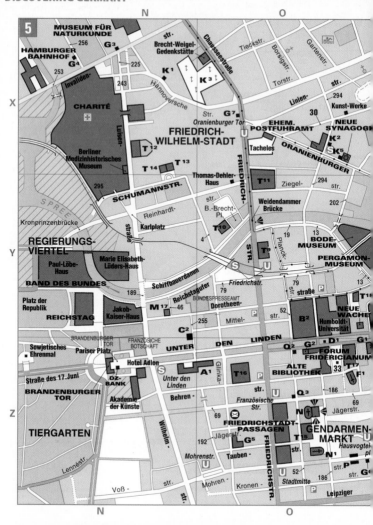

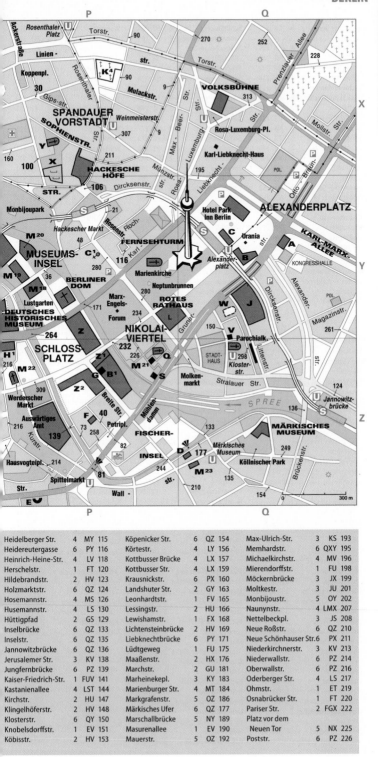

Berlin Zoo & Aquarium ★★ [Kids]

Hardenbergplatz 8.
Open Apr–mid-Sept, daily 9am–7.30pm; mid-Sept–Oct, 9am–7pm; Nov–Mar, 9am–5pm. 12€. (030) 25 40 10. www.zoo-berlin.de.

Some 14 000 creatures make their home in Berlin's venerable zoo, including Knut, possibly the world's most famous polar bear. Next door is the **Aquarium** *(entry via the zoo or from Budapester Straße; open year-round, daily 9am–6pm; 12€; (030) 25 40 10; www.aquarium-berlin.de)* which has some 650 different species, including some fearsome crocodiles on the first floor. *Combination tickets with the zoo are 18€.*

Around Kurfürstendamm ★

Kurfürstendamm★★

This busy 3.5km/2mi-long boulevard started life as a riding path to the royal hunting lodge in the Grunewald forest. In the 1880s, Bismarck transformed it into the prestigious thoroughfare known as the "Ku'Damm." With its many department stores and boutiques, it is still Berlin's major shopping street and also lined by cafés, restaurants, theaters and galleries.

Kaiser-Wilhelm-Gedächtniskirche★ (Kaiser Wilhelm Memorial Church)

Open year-round, daily 9am–7pm. (030) 218 50 23. www.gedaechtnis kirche-berlin.de.

This Neo-Romanesque church was consecrated in 1895 in honor of Emperor Wilhelm I. After World War II its ruined tower was left standing as a reminder of the horrors of war. A much photographed Berlin landmark, it stands next to a modernistic octagonal new house of worship (1961) famous for its deep blue glass walls made in Chartres. The original church entrance beneath the tower is now a **Memorial Hall**.

Breitscheidplatz

The square next to the Gedächtniskirche turns into a lively Christmas market in

Knautschke the Survivor

The end of the war was a difficult time for the animals at the zoo; the locals used them for food, just as they used trees from the Tiergarten for heat. One writer, Stefan Reisner (*Stadtfront, Berlin West Berlin*, 1982), recalls his father melting a camel's hump in a frying pan. However, the hippopotamus Knautschke was more fortunate. He stayed underwater during the conflict, re-emerging a true hero once the bombardments were over.

December but is a popular gathering spot year-round. It is anchored by an unusual fountain officially known as **Weltbrunnen** (World Fountain) but irreverently called "Wasserklops" ("water meatball") by the ever-creative Berliners. Beyond the fountain looms the **Europa-Center** shopping complex, which was Berlin's first high-rise building when it opened in 1965.

Tauentzienstraße

South of the Gedächtniskirche, this fashionable shopping street is home to Europe's second-largest department store, the **"KaDeWe."** The abbreviation stands for Kaufhaus des Westens: Department Store of the West.

Museum für Fotografie/Helmut Newton Sammlung★ (Museum of Photography/Helmut Newton Collection)

Jebensstraße 2.
Open year-round, Tue–Sun 10am–6pm (Thu 10pm). 6€, free Thu 6pm–10pm. (030) 266 21 88. www.smb.spk-berlin.de.

A former Prussian officers' casino built in 1909 has been reinvented as an Art Library and Museum of Photography. Exhibits of the latter are often drawn from the collection that the late fashion photographer Helmut Newton donated to the city of Berlin shortly before his death in 2004. Downstairs are Newton's recreated Monte Carlo office, a wall of his magazine covers and assorted memorabilia.

Story of Berlin [Kids]

Kurfürstendamm 207.
🕐*Open year-round, daily 10am–8pm.*
📷*9.80€.* ♿📷*(030) 88 72 01 00. www. story-of-berlin.de.*

This interactive, multimedia journey through the history of Berlin—from the city's 13C founding to the fall of the Berlin Wall—culminates with a tour of an original atomic bunker located beneath the building.

Museumsinsel★★★ (Museum Island)

The brainchild of Frederick William III, this vast museum complex occupies the northern end of the Spree island where Berlin's settlement first began in the 13C. The four (soon-to-be five) museums represent 6 000 years of art and cultural history of Europe and beyond have been included on UNESCO's list of World Heritage Sites since 1999. Under a master plan conceived by British architect David Chipperfield, the compound is undergoing a complete overhaul. It includes not only the restoration of the existing four museums but also the reconstruction of the Neues Museum (New Museum, destroyed during World War II), the addition of an Archeological Promenade linking all museums and the construction of a modern new entrance called the James Simon Gallery from which all museums can be accessed. The projected completion date is 2015 but the New Museum is expected to

reopen with the Egyptian Collection and the Museum of Pre- and Early History in 2009.

Pergamonmuseum★★★ (Pergamon Museum)

Entry on Kupfergraben. 🕐*Open year-round, daily 10am–6pm (Thu 10pm).* 📷*10€, free Thu 6pm–10pm.* ♿📷*(030) 20 90 55 77. www.smb.spk-berlin.de.*

The most important museum was also the last to be completed, in 1930. It harbors three world-class collections. The **Collection of Classical Antiquities** ★★★ *(Antikensammlung)* features the **Pergamon Altar**★★★, a masterpiece of Hellenistic art (2C BC); the market gate of Miletus★★ (2C AD); and Greek and Roman sculptures. The **Museum of the Ancient Near East**★★ *(Vorderasiatisches Museum)* includes the **Processional Way and Ishtar Gate**★★ from ancient Babylon, 580 BC; the Plinth of Asachadon, 7C BC; and the façade of the Temple of Irmin at Uruk. Highlights of the **Museum of Islamic Art**★★ *(Museum für Islamische Kunst)* include the Façade of Mshatta Palace (8C) from Jordan; the painted Aleppo room (early 17C); and miniatures (15C–17C).

Alte Nationalgalerie★★ (Old National Gallery)

Entry on Bodestraße. 🕐*Open year-round, Tue–Sun 10am–6pm, Thu 10pm.* 📷*8€, free Thu 6pm-10pm.* ♿📷*(030) 20 90 55 77. www.smb.spk-berlin.de.*

This museum exhibits European paintings and sculptures from the 19C.

The Museums of Berlin

The Altes Museum, the first museum in Berlin, was built in 1830 by Karl Friedrich Schinkel. It was followed under Frederick William IV by the Neues Museum and Nationalgalerie on the Museumsinsel. Wilhelm von Bode, director of the Berlin museums from 1906 onward, painstakingly organized the city's collections, bringing them to the attention of connoisseurs worldwide.

Reconstruction of the destroyed museums began after World War II – no small task considering collections had to be gathered from storage or reacquired from victorious pillagers. Post-war Germany further divided the museum collections between East and West. The Stiftung Preußischer Kulturbesitz (Foundation for Prussian Cultural Property) preserved the collections in the west while eastern artifacts gathered at the traditional spot: the "Museumsinsel".

In 1992, soon after Germany's reunification, Berlin's museums rejoined under the umbrella of the Stiftung Preußischer Kulturbesitz – Staatliche Museen zu Berlin.

H. Champollion/MICHELIN

Altes Museum on Museumsinsel, Berlin's first public museum

Romantic artists take center stage on the top floor, with outstanding works by **Caspar David Friedrich** and Karl Friedrich Schinkel. Galleries on the middle floor are dedicated to French Impressionists, Realists including Max Liebermann and Wilhelm Leibl, and German and Flemish historical scenes. On the ground floor are works by Berlin artists (**Adolph Menzel**, Krüger, Schadow) along with Realist landscapes (Constable, Courbet).

Bode-Museum★★

Entry via Monbijoubrücke. ◯*Open year-round, daily 10am–6pm (Thu 10pm).* ⊛*8€, free Thu 6pm–10pm.* ♿⊛ *(030) 20 90 55 77. www.smb.spk-berlin.de.*
Housed in a splendid 1904 Neo-Baroque edifice at the northern tip of Museumsinsel, this museum emerged from a thorough renovation in 2006 and once again delights visitors with its stunning **Sculpture Collection.**
Particular strengths lie in medieval Italian sculpture (e.g. *Man of Sorrows* by Giovanni Pisano), Late Gothic German works by such masters as Tilman Riemenschneider and Hans Leinberger, and Rococo sculpture by Ignaz Günther and Jean Antoine Houdon.
The museum also features a sprinkling of objects from the **Museum of Byzantine Art** such as the "Great Berlin Pyx" (around AD 400), a small vessel carved of ivory. There are also the rare and precious coins of the **Numismatic Collection** and selections from the Gemäldegalerie (Picture Gallery).

Altes Museum★★ (Old Museum)

Enter from Lustgarten. ◯*Open year-round, daily 10am–6pm (Thu 10pm).* ⊛*8€, free*

Thu 6pm–10pm. ♿⊛ *(030) 20 90 55 77. www.smb.spk-berlin.de.*
Designed by Schinkel and open since 1830, Berlin's first public museum is a Neoclassical architectural masterpiece fronted by 18 Ionic columns.
The ground floor presents the smaller works of the **Antikensammlung** (Collection of Antiquities—the monumental ones are in the Pergamonmuseum), mostly from Greece. Upstairs is the temporary home of the **Egyptian Museum** until the completion of the Neues Museum (New Museum). The core of the exhibit is formed by objects from the time of **Pharaoh Akhenaton** (ruled 1353–1336 BC) excavated by German explorers in Tell-el-Armana between 1911 and 1914. Take special note of the ebony head of **Queen Teje★★** and the world-famous **Bust of Queen Nefertiti★★★**.
Made of painted plaster over limestone, it served as a model for other effigies of the queen.

5-7-9

The three-naved foyer of the Gemäldegalerie, a wonderfully designed space, boasts a single work of art: a sculpture by the American conceptual sculptor Walter De Maria entitled *The 5-7-9 Series*. It consists of 27 polygonal, highly polished steel staffs ordered in three rows in a granite water basin. The geometric staffs are assembled according to various mathematical combinations. This artwork is a good conclusion to a visit to the Gemäldegalerie: It brings the viewer back to earth, tests his or her imagination and simply permits a rest.

Amenhotep IV's Revolution

Upon his accession to the throne, **Amenhotep IV** imposed the idea of a single god. Other gods were abandoned in favour of **Aton**, the disk of the sun whose rays terminate in human hands holding the hieroglyph for life *(Ankh)*. **Amenhotep** changed his name to **Akhenaton, "One Useful to Aton"**, set up court in Tell el-Amarna and banned worship, priests and temples of all other gods, offending a rich and powerful clergy. The reign of his son-in-law **Tutankhamen**, who abandoned Tell el-Amarna after two or three years, marked the end of the revolution.

Potsdamer Platz & Kulturforum Area

A clutch of museums and cultural venues, the **Kulturforum** was designed, in the late 1950s, to become the West Berlin counterpart to the Museumsinsel in the eastern part of the city.

Just east of here, the **Potsdamer Platz**★★ quarter stands as the biggest of Berlin's post-reunification developments. Before World War II, the area was a busy traffic hub and entertainment zone. Completely destroyed, it was bifurcated by the Berlin Wall during the Cold War. After reunification some of the world's top architects collaborated in its reincarnation. Today, Potsdamer Platz is again a lively quarter teeming with hotels, theaters, restaurants, a casino, museums and shops.

Gemäldegalerie★★★ (Picture Gallery)

Open year-round, Tue–Sun 10am–6pm (Thu 10pm). 8€, free Thu 6pm–10pm. (030) 266 29 51. www.smp.spk-berlin.de.

This collection was born of the passion of the Great Elector (1620–88) and Frederick the Great (1712–86). But it was **Wilhelm von Bode**, director of the Gemäldegalerie who, beginning in 1890, tirelessly acquired European paintings from the 13C to the 18C. Despite war losses (400 paintings were destroyed), the collection is still considered one of the finest in the world.

The modern building's 53 rooms are arranged in a horseshoe around a foyer and provide space for over 1 100 paintings. Works are presented in chronological order and arranged by school:

Rooms I–III, Galleries 1–4: German School, 13C–16C (Late Gothic/Renaissance) Notably illustrated by Martin Schongauer *(The Birth of Christ)*, Lucas Cranach the Elder *(Venus und Amor, Adam and Eve)*, Hans Holbein the Younger *(The Merchant Georg Gisze)* and Albrecht Dürer *(Portrait of Hieronymus Holzschuher)*.

Rooms IV-VI, Galleries 5–7: Dutch School, 15C–16C (Late Gothic/Renaissance) Features works by Gérard David, Hans Memling, Hugo Van der Goes, Jan Gossaert, Jan Van Eyck, Quentin Metsys and Pieter Bruegel the Elder (including his famous painting *Dutch Proverbs*).

H. Champollion/MICHELIN

Showcase of Berlin's avant-garde architecture: the Sony Center on Potsdamer Platz

Rooms VII–XI, Galleries 8–19: Flemish and Dutch Schools, 17C (Baroque). Extensive section including Peter Paul Rubens *(Child with a Bird, Virgin and Child)*, his pupil Anthony van Dyck *(Portrait of a Wealthy Genoan Couple)*, Matthias Stomer *(Esau Sells his Birth Right)*, Rembrandt *(Self-portrait, Moses Shatters the Decalogue, Susanna and the Two Old Men, The Man with the Golden Helmet)*, Jacob van Ruisdael *(Oaks by the Lake with Water Lilies)*, Jan Bruegel the Elder *(Flower Bouquet)*, Frans Hals *(Singing Child with Flute)*, Jan Vermeer van Delft *(The Glass of Wine)*.

Galleries 20–22: English, French and German Schools, 18C (Rococo/Neoclassicism) Artists include Thomas Gainsborough *(The Marsham Children)*, Antoine Watteau *(The Dance)*, Jean-Baptiste-Siméon Chardin *(The Painter)*, Antoine Pesne *(Frederick the Great as Crown Prince)*.

Rooms XII–XIV, Galleries 23–26, 28: Italian School, 17C–18C (Baroque/Mannerism); **French School, 17C; Spanish School, 16C–17C** (Mannerism/Baroque). Exhibits here include Francesco Guardi *(Canal Grande in Venice)*, Canaletto *(Canal Grande with View of the Rialto Bridge)*, Velázquez *(Portrait of a Lady)*, Caravaggio *(Amor as Victor)*, Claude Lorrain *(Ideal Roman Landscape)*, Nicolas Poussin *(Self-portrait)* and Georges de La Tour *(Peasant Couple Eating Peas)*.

Rooms XV–XVII, Galleries 29–32: Italian School, late 15C–16C (Late Renaissance/Mannerism). This part of the museum contains works by Correggio *(Leda with the Swan)*, Parmigianino *(Christ's Baptism)*, Titian *(Venus with the Organizt, Portrait of a Bearded Young Man)*, Tintoretto *(Virgin and Child)*, and several paintings by Raphael (including the *Madonna Terranuova*).

Gallery 34: miniatures, 16C–18C, including *Katharine of Bora* (Martin Luther's wife) by Lucas Cranach the Elder.

Room XVIII, Galleries 35–41: Italian School, 13C–late 15C (Gothic/Early Renaissance) Includes Botticelli *(Saint Sebastian, Virgin Enthroned)*, Giovanni Bellini, Andrea Mantegna *(Representation of Christ in the Temple)*, Fra Angelico *(The Day of Judgement)* and Lorenzo Monaco *(The Last Supper)*.

Kunstgewerbemuseum★★ (Museum of Decorative Arts)
Matthäikirchplatz.

◐*Open year-round, Tue–Fri 10am–6pm, Sat–Sun 11am–6pm.* ◦*8€, free Thu 2pm–6pm.* &◦*(030) 266 29 02. www.smb.spk-berlin.de.*

The vast treasures of the Museum of Decorative Arts are displayed in two locations. The Kulturforum branch presents a broad overview of European applied arts and design from the Middle Ages to the present. The second part of the collection is at Schloss Köpenick.

At the Kulturforum branch, Gallery I *(ground floor)* is devoted to the Middle Ages. Inside the entrance is the Enger-Herford (Westphalia) **Treasure of Dionysius★**, with a remarkable reliquary purse decorated with precious stones (late 8C). In the center of the gallery, the **Guelph Treasure★★★** includes a reliquary resembling a Byzantine church (Cologne c. 1175). Gallery II *(ground floor)*: Italian furniture and majolica from the 14C to the 16C, Venetian glassware from the 16C to the 17C. Gallery III *(ground floor)*: **Lüneburg's municipal silver★★★** (Late Gothic and Renaissance) and jewelry from Nuremberg. Gallery IV *(first floor)*: the splendid **Pommern Cabinet★** and its contents. Gallery V *(first floor)*: 17C–18C porcelain from China and Germany. Gallery VI *(first floor)*: Biedermeier and Jugendstil objets d'art, a paneled glass cabinet from Schloss Wiesentheid in Franconia (1724). Gallery VII *(first floor)*: porcelain, glazed earthenware and Art Nouveau and Art Deco period glass. Galleries IX and X *(basement)*: modern international design by such practitioners as Charles Eames and Philippe Starck.

Kupferstichkabinett★ (Museum of Prints and Drawings)
Matthäikirchplatz. Exhibition: ◐*Open year-round, Tue–Fri 10am–6pm, Sat–Sun 11am–6pm.* Study room: ◐*Open Tue–Fri 9am-4pm.* ◦*8€, free Thu 2pm–6pm.*

&⌨ *(030) 266 29 51. www.kupferstich kabinett.de.*

In 1652 the Great Elector laid the foundation for this internationally renowned **collection** of 500 000 prints and 110 000 watercolors, oil sketches, drawings and pastels from the 14C to the 20C. Many famous Italian, Old German and Old Dutch masters are represented, including including Rembrandt, Botticelli and Dürer, along with 20C Pop Art, Conceptual Art and Minimal Art.

Neue Nationalgalerie★★ (New National Gallery)

Potsdamer Straße 50.

Ⓒ*Open year-round, Tue, Wed & Fri 10am–6pm, Thu 10pm, Sat–Sun 11am–6pm.* ⌨*8€, free Thu 6pm–10pm.* &⌨*(030) 266 29 51. www.neue-nationalgalerie.de.*

This steel and glass "temple of the arts", designed in 1968 by Ludwig Mies van der Rohe, houses paintings and sculptures from the early 20C to the 1960s. Particularly impressive is the collection of **German Expressionists** which includes a smattering of works by members of the artist group *Die Brücke* (&*see INTRODUCTION: Art and Culture, Art)*, including Kirchner, Schmidt-Rottluff and Heckel. The **Bauhaus** is represented by such artists as Klee and Kandinsky, **Surrealism** by Max Ernst and Dalí, and **Cubism** by Picasso and Gris. The collection ends with **American paintings** from the 1960s featuring works by Frank Stella, Ellsworth Kelly and others.

Philharmonie★★★

Herbert-von-Karajanstraße 1.

Guided tour (1hr) at 1pm. Meeting point: stage door. Ⓒ*Closed Jan 1, Dec 24–26 & 31.* ⌨*3€.* &⌨*(030) 25 48 89 99. www.berliner-philharmoniker.de.*

The roof of this asymmetrical building designed by **Hans Scharoun** (1963) resembles a giant wave. It is the home base of the Berlin Philharmonic Orchestra, directed by **Sir Simon Rattle**, and surrounded by terraced seats accommodating up to 2 200 people. The **Chamber Music Hall** (1988) next door seats up to 1 150 under a tent-shaped roof.

Musikinstrumenten-Museum★ (Musical Instruments Museum)

Enter from Ben-Gurion-Straße 1.

Ⓒ*Open year-round, Tue, Wed, Fri 9am–5pm, Thu 10pm, Sat–Sun 10am–5pm.* ⌨*4€, free Thu 6pm–10pm.* &⌨*(030) 25 48 11 78. www.mim-berlin.de.*

Keyboards, strings and percussion instruments from the 16C to today are on display, including a mammoth 1929 Wurlitzer theater organ and flutes played by Frederick the Great.

Gedenkstätte Deutscher Widerstand (German Resistance Memorial Center)

Stauffenbergstraße 13–14.

Ⓒ*Open year-round, Tue, Wed, Fri 9am–6pm, Thu 9am–8pm, Sat–Sun 10am–6pm.* Ⓒ*Closed Jan 1, Dec 24–26 & 31.* ⌨*(030) 26 99 50 00. www.gdw-berlin.de.*

This documentary exhibit details German resistance to the Nazis and occupies the very rooms where Claus Schenk, Count of Stauffenberg and his co-conspirators planned their ill-fated assassination of Hitler on 20 July 1944.

Museen Dahlem★★★

The leafy residential suburb of Dahlem is home to the Freie Universität (Free University), which was founded in 1948 and has about 34,000 students. The main visitor attraction, though, is a remarkable **museum complex** (Ⓒ*open year-round, Tue–Fri 10am–6pm, Sat–Sun 11am–6pm;* ⌨*8€, free Thu 2pm–6pm;* &⌨ *(030) 830 14 38; www.smb.spk-berlin.de).* Aside from collections detailed below, it also harbors the child-oriented 🄺🄸🄳🅂**Junior Museum**.

Ethnologisches Museum★★★ (Museum of Ethnology)

Enter on Lansstraße 8.

This museum is home to 400 000 outstanding ethnographic objects divided into several permanent collections.

Archeology of the Americas★★★

A journey through 1 400 of pre-Hispanic cultures through Central and South America reveals such treasures as **carved stelae** from Guatemala, painted

stone vessels of the Maya, Aztec **stone figures** of gods and **gold objects** from Central America, Colombia and Peru.

North American Indians★

This exhibits showcases the cultural and artistic diversity that developed among Indian cultures throughout North America and also seeks to debunk myths created by western fiction and modern media, movies in particular. Items include moccasins, medicine pouches, tomahawks and peace pipes.

South Seas★★

Among the items gathered during sea voyages since the 18C, some by Captain James Cook, note the painted **masks** and **wooden sculptures** from New Guinea, the spectacular boats from **Oceania**, and the **feathered cloak** of the king of Hawaii.

Africa★★

The most interesting objects in this collection include **terracotta heads from Ife** (Nigeria), **bronzes** from the ancient kingdom of Benin, and Berber jewelry, along with wooden sculptures from Cameroon.

East Asia★

Everyday culture in China at the end of the imperial period and folk art from Japan are the focus of this collection. Expect **amulets**, cult objects, devotional items, ivory, **lacquer** and ceramic art from the third millennium BC to the present.

Music Ethnology

Open again since late 2007, this section documents global music culture and encompasses more than 150 000 **sound recordings**. One of the earliest is from 1900, when the psychologist Carl Stumpf used an Edison phonograph to record a group of Thai musicians performing in Berlin.

Museum für Asiatische Kunst★★ (Museum of Asian Art)

Enter from LansStraße 8.

The East Asian collections cover art and artifacts from China, Japan and Korea and were recently combined with the Museum of Indian Art into the Museum of Asian Art. Galleries display objects from the 4th millennium BC to today, including stone sculpture, ceramics, cult objects, Japanese woodcuts and lacquer arts, most notably a **17C imperial throne**★★ made of palisander wood with mother-of-pearl laid into lacquer and gold. Another highlight is the **Japanese tea room**★, which is occasionally used for tea ceremonies and a **video installation**★ by Korean artist Naim June Paik.

Museum Europäischer Kulturen★ (Museum of European Cultures)

Focused on everyday European culture from the 18C to the present, this museum is undergoing major renovations and is expected to remain closed until at least mid-2010.

Schloss Charlottenburg★★★

Schloss Charlottenburg is a summer residence commissioned by King Friedrich I for his wife Sophie-Charlotte. Designed by Arnold Nering and later expanded by Johann Friedrich Eosander, it is Berlin's most exquisite Baroque palace. An equestrian statue of the Great Elector by Andreas Schlüter greets visitors arriving in the front courtyard. Budget a full day to see all of Schloss Charlottenburg's features.

Altes Schloss★★ (Old Palace)

Ground floor of central block.

Visit by guided tour (50min) only, year-round, Tue–Sun 10am–6pm (Nov–Mar 5pm). ⊙ *Closed Dec 24.* ⊙10€. ⌖☎(030) 32 09 11. www.spsg.de.

After viewing models of the 18C palace and gardens, visitors approach three small rooms in the **Mecklenburg Apartment.** The official function rooms span 140m/460ft overlooking the gardens. They house family portraits of the Houses of Hohenzollern and Hanover, finely lacquered furniture and Sophie Charlotte's harpsichord. The famous **Porcelain Room**★★ features a magnificent collection of Asian porcelain, while the **Palace Chapel**★ (*Schlosskapelle*) is

© Partner für Berlin/FTB-Werbefotografie

Schloss Charlottenburg

occasionally used as a concert venue. Above the royal pew an enormous crown carried by two allegorical figures bears the Prussian eagle. The fine free-standing **staircase** by Eosander (1702) was the first of its kind in Germany. Passing through the upper rooms overlooking the courtyard and gardens, the tour proceeds to the **apartments of Frederick William IV**, the last king to live at the palace. The painting *Parade along Unter den Linden in 1837* by Franz Krüger features some of this avenue's most important buildings, still recognizable today. Adjoining rooms exhibit part of the East Prussian noble Schlobitten Collection, including paintings, tapestries, porcelain and metalwork. The **Crown Prince's silverware**★★ is particularly interesting. It was a gift to Crown Prince William at his betrothal to Cecilie of Mecklenburg-Schwerin in 1904.

Neuer Flügel★★ (New Wing)

East of the central block.

⏰*Open year-round, Tue–Sun 10am-6pm (Nov–Mar 5pm).* ⬤6€. ♿☎*(030) 32 09 11. www.spsg.de.*

Also known as the Knobeldorff Wing after its architect, the New Wing was commissioned by Frederick the Great and completed in 1746. Stairs lead up to the **White Room** *(Weißer Saal)* used by Frederick II as a dining and throne room. The ceiling painting is a modern work by Hann Trier which replaced the original by Antoine Pesne destroyed in 1943. The 42m/138ft-long **Golden Gallery**★★ is a Rococo music room and dance hall restored to its original pastel green, pink and gold hues. Frederick II's apartments, which follow, feature white and gold Rococo décor and important 18C French paintings by Watteau: **Gersaint's Signboard**★★★ (1720) in

The Crown Prince's Silverware

This masterpiece of 20C German craftsmanship was a gift from 414 Prussian cities at the marriage of Crown Prince William to Duchess Cecilia of Mecklenburg-Schwerin in 1904. Completed in 1914, the dinner service never belonged to the couple. Following the Hohenzollerns' abdication, it became property of the Berlin Senate and is now on long-standing loan to Schloß Charlottenburg. The service originally contained 2 600 pieces for fifty at a 16m/53ft-long table. Terrines, plates and salad bowls are displayed on a magnificent sideboard. A group of six, including architects, sculptors and the director of the Museum of Decorative Arts, supervised the creation of the dinner service, which is in classical and *Jugendstil* style. The statuettes include elephants surmounted by an obelisk, equestrian statues and candelabra, all part of a long tradition of royal dinner services.

the concert hall and **Embarkation for Cythera**★★★.

Winter apartments★

Frederick the Great's successor, Frederick William II, lived in these apartments in the late 18C and early 19C. These south-facing rooms display the disciplined elegance of early Prussian Neoclassicism. **Queen Louise's Bedchamber**★ is decorated in harmonious mauve tones and draped in white net. The final room contains a fine collection of **portraits**★ by court painter Antoine Pesne.

On the ground floor a model shows the **Berlin City Palace** (*Berliner Stadtschloss*), blown up in 1950 on the orders of the East German government. In the adjoining room are Baroque tapestries and portions of Frederick the Great's **antique collection**. The **Chinese Gallery and Chinese Room**, part of Frederick William II's summer apartments, overlook the gardens.

Museum für Vor- und Frühgeschichte★ (Museum of Pre- and Early History)

Ⓒ*Open year-round, Tue–Fri 9am–5pm, Sat–Sun 10am–5pm.* ⓢ*3€, free Thu 1pm–5pm.* ♿℡*(030) 32 67 48 40. www. smb.spk-berlin.de.*

In the former palace theater designed by Carl Gotthard Langhans in 1791, this museum is dedicated to the cultural history of Europe from the Stone Age to the Middle Ages. Prized exhibits include the **Trojan antiquities**★★ unearthed by archeologist Heinrich Schliemann in 1870, Ice Age art, a Neanderthal hominid from Le Moustier and the amazing **Goldsaal** (Gold Room) where the trophy exhibit is the cone-shaped 1m/3ft-tall **Berliner Goldhut**★★ (golden hat).

Schlossgarten★★

This English-style park is an oasis of tranquillity and great for strolling, picnicking, sunning by the pond or lounging beneath shady trees. To the west, at the end of a yew and cypress walk, a small **mausoleum** (Ⓒ*open Apr–Oct, Tue–Sun 10am–6pm, Nov–Mar, noon–5pm;* ⓢ*2€*) contains the marble sarcophagi of Frederick William III and his wife Queen Louise carved by Christian Daniel Rauch, as

well as those of Emperor Wilhelm I and Queen Augusta. More royal family members are buried in the crypt, which is not accessible to the public.

The **New Pavilion**★ **(Schinkel Pavilion)** *(east of the New Wing)* was built in 1824 as a summer residence for Frederick William III and was under restoration at press time.

North of the lake, toward the Spree, is the **Belvedere**★ (Ⓒ*open Apr–Oct, Tue–Sun 10am-6pm, Nov–Mar noon–5pm;* ⓢ*2€*), a gleaming white miniature palace overlooking a shaggy meadow. It houses an exhibit of precious historic porcelain made by the *Königliche Porzellan Manufaktur* (KPM), the Prussian royal manufactory established in 1763.

Around Schloss Charlottenburg

Museum Berggruen★★

SchlossStraße 1a.
Ⓒ*Open year-round, Tue–Sun 10am–6pm.* ⓢ*6€, free Thu 2pm–6pm.* ♿*(partly)* ℡*(030) 32 69 58 15. www.smb.spk-berlin.de.*

Art dealer Heinrich Berggruen was an avid collector of **Pablo Picasso** and his contemporaries and donated a sizeable portion of his private collection to this intimate museum in a former royal guard barracks built by Friedrich August Stüler in 1859. On display are about 100 Picassos from all his creative periods, including the famous *Horses on a Hill* (1909). These are cleverly juxtaposed with works by Cézanne, Van Gogh, Matisse, Giacometti and others, as well as African tribal art. The second floor features over 60 works by **Paul Klee:** *Stadtartiger Aufbau* (Urban Structure), *Betrachtung beim Frühstück* (1925, watercolor), and *Klassische Küste* (1931). A museum expansion began in 2008.

Museum Scharf-Gerstenberg★★

Schlossstraße 70.
Ⓒ*Open Tue–Sun 10am–6pm.* ⓢ*6€.* ℡*030 34 35 73 15. www.smb.museum.*

Opposite the Museum Berggruen, in another building by Stüler, this new museum opened in mid-2008 and showcases works by **Surrealist artists** and the people who inspired them.

It features more than 250 paintings, sculptures and works on paper by such famous artists as Dalí, Magritte, Max Ernst and Dubuffet. French Symbolism is represented by the paintings of Odilon Redon and Gustave Moreau, as is its German counterpart in the form of graphic cycles of Max Klinger. Displays are augmented by a film program, including the classic surrealist films by Luis Buñuel and Salvador Dalí.

Bröhan Museum★
Schloßstraße 1a.
Open year-round, Tue–Sun 10am–6pm. Closed Dec 24 & 31. 5€. (030) 32 69 06 00. www.broehan-museum.de.
Fine art, furniture and decorative objects from the **Art Nouveau, Art Deco and Functionalism** periods (1889–1939) get the star treatment at this museum. Downstairs are period rooms by Hector Guimard and Peter Behrens, while the upper floor is dedicated to paintings by artists from the **Berlin Secession** movement, including Willy Jaeckel and Hans Baluschek.
A special exhibit on the third floor shines the spotlight on Belgian multi-talent **Henry van de Velde**.

Gipsformerei der Staatlichen Museen
Sophie-Charlotten-Straße 17–18.
Open year-round, Mon–Fri 9am–4pm (Wed 6pm). Closed public holidays. (030) 326 76 90.
The world's largest plaster-cast workshop fashions near-identical replicas of some 7 000 famous sculptures.

Additional Sights

Museum für Kommunikation Berlin★ (Museum of Communication)
Leipziger Straße 16.
Open year-round, Tue–Fri 9am–5pm, Sat–Sun 10am–6pm. 3€. (030) 20 29 40. www.museumsstiftung.de.
Considered the world's oldest postal museum, this exhibit counts an ultra-rare **Blue Mauritius** stamp, entertaining robots and decades' worth of communication devices among its treasures.

Deutsches Technikmuseum Berlin★★ (German Museum of Technology) Kids
Trebbiner Straße 9.
Open year-round, Tue–Fri 9am–5.30pm, Sat–Sun 10am–6pm. Closed May 1, Dec 24, 25 & 31. 4.50€ (child 2.50€). (030) 90 25 40. www.dtmb.de.
This temple of technology takes you on an eye-opening journey past the milestones of transportation, energy, communication and production. It features outstanding exhibits on air and space **travel**★★, an early computer designed by pioneer Konrad Zuse, a historical brewery and an entire hall of **historic locomotives**★★. Interactive displays, live demonstrations and experiments further enliven visits.

Hamburger Bahnhof – Museum für Gegenwart Berlin★★ (Hamburg Station – Museum of Contemporary Art)
Invalidenstraße 50–51.
Open year-round, Tue–Fri 10am–6pm, Sat 11am–8pm, Sun 11am–6pm. 8€, free Thu 2pm–6pm. Guided tours (1hr) Sun 2pm, Thu 2.30pm. 3€. (030)39 78 34 11. www.hamburgerbahnhof.de.
Berlin's key contemporary art museum occupies a former railway station built in the 1840s, closed in 1884 and converted into a transportation museum in 1906. Today the main building and a recent addition present artworks from 1960 to the present. The collection includes such top producers as Anselm Kiefer, Richard Long *(Berlin Circle)*, Bruce Naumann and Cindy Sherman along with Cy Twombly, Robert Rauschenberg and Andy Warhol. An entire wing is devoted to Joseph Beuys.

Käthe-Kollwitz-Museum★
Fasanenstraße 24.
Open year-round, Wed–Mon 11am–6pm. Closed Dec 24 & 31. 5€. (030) 882 52 10. www.kaethe-kollwitz.de.
In a lovely villa, this small museum presents a broad survey of one of the most important German women artists, the Berlin-born Käthe Kollwitz (1867–1945). Highlights include engravings *The Weavers' Revolt* (1893–98) and *The Peasants' War* (1903–08), woodcuts titled *War*

(1920–1924) and *The Proletariat* (1925), and self-portraits and lithographs labelled *Death*. 1920s-era posters such as *Nie wieder Krieg (No More War)* underline Kollwitz's pacifist ideals; sculptures on the upper floor include *Muttergruppe (Mother Group*, 1924–37).

Martin-Gropius-Bau★★ (Martin Gropius Building)

Stresemannstraße 110.

🕐*Open year-round, Thu–Tue 10am–8pm.* ✎*Varies with exhibition.* ♿☎*(030) 25 48 60. www.gropiusbau.de.*

A stately Italian Renaissance-style building by Martin Gropius (great uncle of Walter Gropius) and Heino Schmieden originally served a museum of decorative arts and now houses traveling exhibitions of international rank.

Topographie des Terrors (Topography of Terror)

🕐*Open May–Sept 10am–8pm, Oct–Apr 10am–dusk.* 🕐*Closed Jan 1, Dec 24 & 31.* ♿ ☎*(030) 25 48 67 03. www.topographie.de.*

Next to the Gropiusbau is a short stretch of the **Berlin Wall**★ and beyond it an empty field where once stood the key institutions of oppression and persecution in Nazi Germany: the Gestapo headquarters, the SS central command, the SS Security Service and, after 1939, the Reich Security Headquarters. The compound was completed destroyed in World War II but since 1997 an outdoor **memorial exhibit** has commemorated the site's fearsome legacy. In 2007, construction began on a permanent documentation center, which is expected to open in 2010.

Viktoriapark★

Kreuzberg hill, the highest natural elevation in central Berlin (66m/216ft), is entirely covered by the Viktoriapark. The top is crowned by Karl Friedrich Schinkel's monument to the "Wars of Liberation" and delivers nice city views. There are also a children's playground and a leafy beer garden.

Luftbrückendenkmal (Airlift Memorial)

Platz der Luftbrücke.

Outside Tempelhof, the main airport used during the Berlin Airlift (1948/9), this memorial honors this amazing effort and the people that died making it happen. The three arcs symbolize the three air corridors used by the western Allies to supply the city with the basic necessities.

Jüdisches Museum Berlin★★ (Jewish Museum)

Lindenstraße 9–14.

🕐*Open year-round, Mon 10am–10pm, Tue–Sun 10am–8pm.* 🕐*Closed Rosh Hashanah, Yom Kippur, Dec 24.* ✎*5€.* ♿☎*(030) 259 93 30. www.juedisches-museum-berlin.de.*

American architect Daniel Libeskind designed this spectacular lightning-bolt-shaped museum, which opened in 2001. A veritable labyrinth, with hall-

---

The Wall

Masterminded by the East German government in 1961, the Berlin Wall divided the city's western districts from the east and the surrounding Brandenburg region for 28 years. Since 1989, the bricks, watchtowers, barbed wire and machine guns have been replaced by new construction or parks, but a few sections of the Wall still commemorate this unique period in history.

The longest stretch, and the most rewarding for visitors, is the **East Side Gallery**, which runs for 1.3km/0.8mi along MühlenStraße, parallel to the Spree River, just south of Ostbahnhof train station. After reunification, artists from around the world were asked to turn turn it into an outdoor art gallery. The picture of a Trabi car bursting through the Wall is one of the most iconic images. There are also shorter Wall remnants on Niederkirchner Straße near the Topography of Terror exhibit, on Potsdamer Platz and at the **Berlin Wall Memorial Site** (*Gedenkstätte Berliner Mauer*) on Bernauer Straße, a documentary center that combines an exhibit, an outdoor installation and a memorial chapel.

H. Champollion/MICHELIN

The Jewish Museum designed by Daniel Liebeskind

ways leading into empty spaces called "voids", the building is an architectural metaphor for the torturous experiences of German Jews. The exhibition traces 2 000 years of their history, with special emphasis given to the cultural and artistic contributions made by prominent Jewish Berliners—such as the philosopher Moses Mendelssohn—between the 18C and the 20C. A special section examines the post-reunification renaissance of the local Jewish community.

Berlinische Galerie
Alte JakobStraße 124–128.
⏱Open year-round, Wed–Mon 10am–6pm. ⏱Closed Dec 24 & 31. ⊚6€. ⭑⏱Guided tours Sat and Sun 3pm. ⭑⏱(030) 78 90 26 00. www.berlinische galerie.de.
A former glass warehouse has found new purpose as a repository of art created in Berlin between 1870 and today. All major movements are represented in this crisp, bi-level space: Berlin Secessions to Dada to Expressionism and contemporary creativity.

Museum Haus am Checkpoint Charlie★ (Berlin Wall Museum) 🅺🅸🅳🆂
Friedrichstraße 43–45.
⏱Open year-round, daily 9am–10pm. ⊚12.50€. ⏱(030) 253 72 50. www.mauer museum.de.

The Berlin Wall Museum houses Wall-related artifacts and illustrates the often hair-raising escapes attempted by East Germans trying cross over into the West aboard a tractor, hidden in the boot of a car, in a suitcase, even via a chairlift. Many expeditions, of course, ended unsuccessfully, usually resulting in the incarceration of the brave souls. A separate section spotlights modern human and civil rights movements.

Märkisches Museum★ (Berlin Regional History Museum)
Am Köllnischen Park 5.
⏱Open year-round, Tue–Sun 10am-6pm, Wed noon–8pm). ⏱Closed Dec 24 & 31. ⊚4€, free Wed. ⏱(030) 24 00 21 62. www.stadtmuseum.de.
This rambling red-brick building (1908) tells the history of Berlin and the surrounding region (called the March of Brandenburg) from the Middle Ages onwards. A copy of a 1474 Roland figure—a symbol of civic liberties and privileges—guards the museum entrance.

Museum für Naturkunde★ (Museum of Natural History) 🅺🅸🅳🆂
InvalidenStraße 43.
⏱Open year-round, Tue–Fri 9.30am–5pm, Sat–Sun 10am–6pm. ⊚6€. ⏱(030) 20 93 85 91. www.naturkundemuseum-berlin.de.
Founded in 1889, Berlin's natural history museum counts some 30 million specimen in its collection, making it one of the largest in the world. A thoughtfully put-together selection is on display in an exhibit called "Evolution in Action", or EVA. Highlights Include the skeletal remains of a building-sized brachiosaurus and a fossilized archeopteryx.

Kunstgewerbemuseum★ (Museum of Decorative Arts)
In Schloss Köpenick (Schloßinsel).
⏱Open year-round, Tue–Sun 10am-6pm. ⊚4€. ⭑⏱(030) 65 66 17 49. www.smb. spk-berlin.de.
The Museum of Decorative Arts occupies a restored 17C Baroque palace on a little peninsula in the southeastern Berlin suburb of Köpenick. The 16C–19C furniture is especially interesting, as are

Address Book

SHOPPING

Useful Tips Berlin's main shopping streets are Kurfürstendamm and Tauentzienstraße in Charlottenburg and Friedrichstraße in Mitte. The biggest malls are the Potsdamer Platz Arkaden in Tiergarten and the new Alexa mall near Alexanderplatz. Independent boutiques cluster in the Scheunenviertel in Mitte, along Bergmannstraße in Kreuzberg; on Bleibtreustraße and Fasanenstraße in Charlottenburg; and on Kastanienallee in Prenzlauer Berg.

DEPARTMENT STORES

Berlin's most famous department store is **KaDeWe** on Tauentzienstraße in Charlottenburg with a wonderful food hall on the 6th floor. **Galeries Lafayette** brings Parisian style and fashion to Friedrichstraße in Mitte. On Alexanderplatz, the Galeria Kaufhof has been redesigned by architect JosefPaul Kleihues and is now an elegant place to max out those credit cards.

Art galleries – Galleries abound around Savignyplatz and along FasanenStraße in Charlottenburg, on ZimmerStraße near Checkpoint Charlie along AugustStraße, both in Mitte.

Flea markets – Flohmarkt am Tiergarten, Straße des 17. Juni, Charlottenburg, *Sat–Sun 11am–5pm*; Flohmarkt am Mauerpark, Bernauer-straße 63–64, Prenzlauer Berg, *Sun 8am-6pm*; Flohmarkt am Arkonaplatz, Prenzlauer Berg, *Sun 10am–5pm*.

Farmers' markets – Winterfeldplatz, Schöneberg, *Wed 8am–2pm, Sat 8am–4pm*; Turkish market Maybachufer, Kreuzberg, *Tue and Fri 11am–6.30pm*; Kollwitzplatz, Prenzlauer Berg, *Thu noon–7pm, Sat 9am–4pm*.

---

the **paneled room**★ from Haldenstein castle (Switzerland, 16C), the **Treasury**★, with jewelry and 16C Baroque gold- and silverware, the silver **sideboard**★★ from the Knights' Room in the old Berlin city palace and the **coats of arms hall**★.

Botanischer Garten & Museum★★ (Botanical Gardens & Museum)

Königin-Luise-Straße 6–8.
🕐*Open year-round, daily 9am-dusk, latest 9pm.* 🕐*Closed Dec 24.* 🚫*5€, incl museum.* ♿🕾*(030) 83 85 01 00. www. bgbm.org.*
At 43ha/106 acres, Berlin's botanical garden is one of the world's largest and most diverse with more than 22 000 plant species. Vegetation is arranged geographically from mountains to plains. Rare species of trees and shrubs are in the **Arboretum**, while 15 **greenhouses** shelter a wealth of tropical and subtropical plants.
The **Botanical Museum**★ *(Botanisches Museum;* 🕐*open year-round, daily 10am-6pm;* 🚫*2€, museum only)* chronicles the evolution of flora and documents common plant uses.

Brücke-Museum★

Bussardsteig 9.
🕐*Open year-round, Wed–Mon 11am–5pm.* 🕐*Closed Dec 24 & 31.* 🚫*4€.* ♿🕾*(030) 831 20 29. www.brueckemuseum.de.*
This museum contains works by members of the **Die Brücke** (The Bridge), an artist group of German Expressionists. It was founded in Dresden in 1905 by architecture students Erich Heckel, Ernst Ludwig Kirchner, Fritz Bleyl and Karl Schmidt-Rottluff. Rejecting traditional painting styles taught at the art academies, they sought to explore new forms of expression, especially by employing bold color and working with distorted compositions. In 1911, the group moved to Berlin where it disbanded two years later. The small museum, which was founded by Schmidt-Rottluff himself and opened in 1967, presents works by all major Brücke members, including Max Pechstein, Otto Mueller and Emil Nolde in addition to those by its founders.

Olympic Games of 1936

When Germany beat Barcelona in 1931 to become the host of the 1936 Olympic Games, no one could have predicted that the country would by then have fallen under the rule of Adolf Hitler and his totalitarian National Socialist Party. The United States almost boycotted the Games, largely because of the regime's anti-Semitic policies, but was assuaged when Hitler declared that athletes of all races and confessions would be allowed to participate. Ironically, it was African American runner Jesse Owens who became the star of the show as the winner of four gold medals in the sprint and long jump events. On August 1, 1936 Hitler opened the Games at Berlin's new Olympic Stadium in front of 100,000 people. It marked the second time that the Olympic Flame was used but the first time that it was carried from Olympia, Greece in a torch relay by thousands of runners.

Grunewald★★

A hunting reserve of the prince-electors in the 16C, this mixed forest covers 3 100ha/745 acres and is bounded by a chain of small lakes.

Near one of them, the Grunewaldsee, is **Jagdschloss Grunewald★** (*open May–Oct, Tue–Sun 10am–6pm; Nov–Apr, Sat–Sun 10am–5pm; 2€; (030) 813 35 97; www.spsg.de*), an elegant hunting lodge built in 1542. Originally a Renaissance pavilion, it was converted into the Baroque style for King Frederick I some 160 years later. The building overlooks a courtyard bordered by ancient beech trees. The storehouse features an exhibit on the royal hunt, but the palace itself is undergoing major restoration expected to last through 2009.

To the west, the Grunewald forest is bordered by **Lake Havel★★**, whose eastern shore is paralleled by the picturesque Havelchaussee road. It leads south to the beaches of the **Wannsee★★**, a hugely popular recreational area in summer.

Pfaueninsel★★ (Peacock Island)

Ferries leave from the landing at the end of Nikolskoer Weg, May–Oct daily 8am–9pm, Mar–Apr and Sept–Oct 9am–6pm, Nov–Feb 10am–4pm. 2€.

There's a dreamy quality about this park-like island in the Havel River, which was turned into a romantic retreat by King Frederick William II in the 18C. It is still a popular escape from the city bustle with gardens landscaped by Peter Joseph Lenné inviting extensive strolling. Paths lead to a snowy-white fairytale **castle★** (1794–97) (*visit by guided tour (30min) only, Apr–Oct, Tue–Sun 10am–5pm; 3€; (030) 80 58 68 30; www.spsg.de*) that displays souvenirs of Queen Louise in salons paneled with exotic woods.

Funkturm (Radio Tower)

Open year-round, Tue–Sun 10am–11pm. Closed Jan 1 & Dec 24. 3.60€. (030) 30 38 29 96.

Known to Berliners as "Langer Lulatsch" (lanky laddie), this 150m/492ft tower looms above the trade show grounds and looks like a smaller brother of Paris' Eiffel Tower. Designed in the 1920s by Heinrich Straumer, it features a viewing platform at 126m/413ft and a restaurant about halfway up.

Olympia-Stadion★ (Olympic Stadium)

Open Jun–mid-Sept, daily 9am–8pm; Apr–May & mid-Sept–Oct 9am–7pm, Nov–Mar 9am–4pm; restricted hours on event days. 4€. (030) 25 00 23 22. Guided tours (60–75min) available. 8€. www.olympiastadion-berlin.de.

Designed for the 1936 Summer Olympics by Nazi-era architect **Werner March**, this massive coliseum-style stadium got a complete overhaul for the 2006 FIFA World Cup for which it hosted the final. Learn more about the 1936 Games and enjoy wonderful views from the newly remodeled **Glockenturm** (*Bell Tower; open Apr–Oct, daily 9am–6pm; Nov 10am–4pm; 3.50€; www.glockenturm.de*) behind the stadium.

It overlooks the huge **Maifeld**, which was used for Nazi mass rallies and later by the British as a military training ground.

Bauhaus-Archiv/Museum für Gestaltung★ (Bauhaus Archives/Museum for Design)

Klingelhöferstraße 14.

🕙*Open year-round, Wed–Mon 10am–5pm.* 🕙*Closed Dec 24.* ⮑*6€ (Wed–Fri),* ⮑*7€ (Sun–Mon).* ♿⮑*(030) 254 00 20. www.bauhaus.de.*

In a building designed by Bauhaus founder **Walter Gropius**, this museum and archive highlights the concepts and philosophy of this early 20C aesthetic movement that greatly influenced modern design and architecture. Exhibits include sculptures, blueprints, models and paintings by Schlemmer, Moholy-Nagy, Feininger, Kandinsky, Klee and other Bauhaus School members.

Gedenkstätte Hohenschönhausen★ (Hohenschönhausen Memorial)

Genslerstraße 66.

👁‍🗨*Visit by guided tour (90min) only: year-round, Mon–Fri 11am & 3pm, Sat–Sun hourly 10am–4pm; Mar–Oct, Mon–Fri 3pm.* ⮑*4€.* ⮑*(030) 9860 8230. www.stiftung-hsh.de.*

Scenes from the Academy Award-winning film *The Lives of Others* (2006) were filmed at this original Stasi prison, where the East German secret police held and tortured scores of its own citizens—many of them innocent—until the regime's demise in 1989.

Tours of the site (*also in English*) are sometimes led by former prisoners and provide a fascinating glimpse behind bars and the inhumane machinations of a totalitarian government.

Gedenkstätte Plötzensee (Plötzensee Memorial Site)

🕙*Open year-round, daily 9am-5pm (Nov–Feb 4pm).* 🕙*Closed Jan 1, Dec 24–26 & 31.* ♿⮑*(030) 26 99 50 00. www.gedenkstaette-ploetzensee.de.*

This memorial to victims of the Nazi regime occupies the former execution chamber in Plötzensee prison. Between 1933 and 1945 over 3 000 prisoners were killed here, usually by guillotine or hanging.

Spandauer Zitadelle★ (Spandau Citadel)

🕙*Open year-round, daily 10am-5pm.* ⮑*4.50€.* ♿⮑*(030) 354 94 40. www.zitadelle-spandau.de.*

In the historic northwestern suburb of Spandau, this citadel was built in the 16C on the site of a medieval castle at the confluence of the Havel and the Spree. It is one of the best preserved Renaissance fortresses in Europe, protected by turreted walls and arrow-shaped bastions. Cross the moat via the a drawbridge, walk through the gateway and reach the armory that now houses a **local history museum** (*Stadtgeschichtliches Museum Spandau*). The fortress' 32m/105ft-high **Juliusturm** (Julius Tower), the only remnant of the original 13C castle, has become the emblem of Spandau and can be climbed for panoramic views.

© Partner für Berlin/FTB-Werbefotografie

Olympic Stadium

Excursions

Potsdam★★★   *19km/11.8mi W.*
See POTSDAM.

Gedenkstätte und Museum Sachsenhausen (Sachsenhausen Memorial Site and Museum)

31km/19.2mi north of Berlin.
Open mid-Mar–mid-Oct, daily 8.30am–6pm (rest of year 4.30pm). Closed Jan 1, Dec 24, 25 & 31. (033 01) 20 00.
The Nazi-era concentration camp of **Sachsenhausen** near the town of Oranienburg north of Berlin opened in 1936. More than half of the 220 000 prisoners that passed through its gates perished. Exhibits occupy such sites as the camp commander's house, the kitchen, the hospital wing and Baracke 38 where Jewish prisoners were kept. You'll also learn about the organization of the Nazi concentration camp system, whose cynicism is epitomized by the slogan above the entrance gates: *"Arbeit macht frei"* (Work brings Freedom).

Frankfurt an der Oder

90km/56mi E via ① on plan.
This former Hanseatic city has been been home to the **European University Viadrina** since 1991. A third of its student body commutes across the Oder River from the Polish town of Slubice. Predominantly rebuilt in Socialist style after World War II, Frankfurt nevertheless has a number of worthwhile sights: the Rathaus (Town Hall), the Marienkirche and the Carl Philipp Emanuel Bach concert hall in a converted Franciscan abbey. There is also a museum (at FaberStraße 7) devoted to the life and work of author and poet **Heinrich von Kleist** (1777–1811), the town's most famous son.

Kloster Chorin★★ (Chorin Abbey)

71km/44mi north of Berlin.
Open year-round, daily 9am–6pm (Nov–Mar 4pm). 3€. (033366) 703 77. www.kloster-chorin.com.
Romantically ruined Chorin Abbey, near the Amtssee lake and surrounded by a lush park, was originally constructed in the 13C by Cistercian monks. The abbey was dissolved in 1542 and, after centuries of neglect, was saved by the architect Karl Friedrich Schinkel and the King of Prussia. Now partially restored, it is one of the finest Gothic red-brick structures in northern Germany. This peaceful site hosts a festival of classical music during the summer.

Schloss Rheinsberg★

87km/54mi northwest of Berlin.
Open year-round, Tue–Sun 10am–6pm (Nov–Mar 5pm). 6€ (Nov–Mar 4€). Closed Dec 24–25. Guided tour of park. 2.50€. (033931) 72 60. www.spsg.de.
Frederick the Great spent four years living in this palace, calling them happiest of his life. Small wonder, then, that the place is forever linked to him. Purchased by Frederick's father in 1734 it was remodeled—in Rococo-style—to meet the future king's needs. The architect Knobelsdorff, the painter Pesne and the sculptor Glume collaborated in this effort. Until German reunification, the palace was used as a sanatorium.

Niederfinow

70km/43.5mi northeast of Berlin.
Open Mar–Oct, daily 9am–6pm; Nov–Feb 9am–4pm. 1€. (033362) 215. www.schiffshebewerk-niederfinow.info.
About 20km/12.4mi southeast of Chorin, one of the greatest technological wonders in Germany rises from the flat Brandenburg countryside: an enormous **ships' lift** (Schiffshebewerk) that helps cargo barges overcome the height difference of 36m/118ft between the Oder River and the Oder-Havel Canal.
The massive steel structure was built in 1934 and is 60m/196.8ft high, 27m/88.5ft wide and 94m/308.4ft long. Visitors can experience the slow lift ride aboard cruise boats operating throughout the day (6€).

BODENSEE★★

LAKE CONSTANCE

With its expansive horizons and a climate mild enough for tropical vegetation, Lake Constance (*Bodensee* in German) attracts a multitude of German vacationers who regard it as their local "Riviera". In addition to the vistas, which encompass the Alps to the south in clear weather, tourists love the lake's clear waters, medieval towns and boat cruises.

Information: HafenStraße 6, 78462 Konstanz. ☎ (07531) 90 94 90. www.bodenseeferien.de.

▶ **Orient Yourself:** The Bodensee is filled by the Rhine as it empties out of the Alps and borders Switzerland and Austria. Due to its size (53 000ha/210sq mi with a maximum depth of 252m/827ft, only slightly smaller than Lake Geneva, the largest Alpine lake), the Bodensee creates its own microclimate especially conducive to fruit cultivation. Boat services ply the lake's waters, frequently linking Constance, Überlingen, Meersburg, Friedrichshafen, Lindau and Bregenz (in Austria). The islands of **Reichenau**★, on the Untersee, and **Mainau**★★, on the Überlingersee, are described under *KONSTANZ: Excursions*.

Don't Miss: Lake cruises from Constance or Friedrichshafen.

Organizing Your Time: Allow half a day for a leisurely boat cruise, possibly including lunch. The entire region easily warrants a full day or two.

Especially for Kids: Swimming or cruising on Lake Constance.

Also See: KONSTANZ, SALEM, SCHWÄBISCHE ALB.

Driving Tour

From Überlingen to Lindau *56km/35mi – allow 4hr*

Überlingen★ (*see ÜBERLINGEN*)

Birnau

An important stop on the Upper Swabian Baroque Route, this 18C pilgrimage church overlooks the Bodensee and was an exuberant collaboration of master artists of the day. Peter Thumb designed the building, Gottfried Bernard Göz was responsible for the richly detailed frescoes, while Joseph Anton Feuchtmayr carved the altars, stucco ornamentation and sculptures.

The church's most famous sculpture is the adorable "Honey Sucker", a cheeky cherub caught with his fingers inside a beehive.

Boats on the lake with Überlingen in the background

T. Krieger/MICHELIN

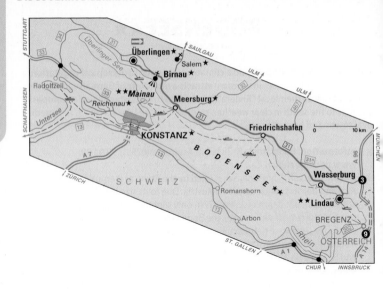

Meersburg★

This former residence of prince-arch-bishops Meersburg is now a picturesque village on a rocky outcrop overlooking the lake and surrounded by vineyards and orchards. The historic upper town (*Oberstadt*) is centered on the **Marktplatz**★, from which the **Steigstraße**★, bordered by half-timbered houses, offers delightful views.

Dominating the Unterstadt (lower town) from its perky perch is the massive medieval **Altes Schloss** (*Old Castle;* ◷*open Mar–Oct, daily 9am–6.30pm; Nov–Feb, daily 10am–6pm.* ◉*6.50€;* ☎*(07532) 800 00; www.meersburg.com*). For 7 years until her death in 1848, this was the home of **Annette von Droste-Hülshoff**, a poet born in Westphalia in 1797 and famous for the 1842 novella *Die Judenbuche* (*The Jew's beech*). The two tower rooms where Annette lived

and worked are part of the tour that also takes you to the prison, the torture chamber and the treasury.

▶ *The itinerary continues along the Grüne Straße (the Green Route), famous for its apple orchards, whose fruit is exported throughout Europe.*

Friedrichshafen

Friedrichshafen is a lively if industrial port town and the birthplace of the dirigible at the turn of the 20C.

Aside from the Zeppelin-Museum described below, the Baroque **church** (*Schlosskirche*) near the castle (still occupied by the ducal family of Württemberg) is worth a visit. Designed by Christian Thumb between 1695 and 1701, it features a richly detailed ceiling and fanciful choir stalls.

The Bodensee from a Zeppelin

Dirigibles are again floating in the skies above the Bodensee, having been reintroduced in 1997 by Zeppelin Luftschifftechnik (ZLT). The new Zeppelin NT flies at speeds up to 130kmh/78mph but at 75m/240ft long is only about one third the length of the first-generation airships. From March to September, the modern 12-seater is available for 1hr flights over the Bodensee. Prices start at 220€ for a 30-minute flight and 540€ for a 90-minute flight. Book ahead by calling ☎ (08704) 79 83 73 or through www.zeppelintours.com.

Friedrichshafen is the departure point for boat excursions to the Rhine falls in Schaffhausen, to the "flower island" of Mainau and to the stilt houses in Unteruhldingen (*see Überlingen*).

Zeppelin Museum `Kids`
Seestraße 22.
Open May–Oct, Tue–Sun 9am–5pm; Nov–Apr, Tue–Sun 10am–5pm; also open Mon in Jul, Aug, Sept; last entry 30min before closing. Closed Nov–Jun, Dec 24, 25 & 31. 7.50€ (child 3€). (07541) 380 10. www.zeppelin-museum.de.
In a converted railway station on the eastern promenade of Lake Constance, the Zeppelin Museum is a must-see for technology buffs. In six major departments, it presents the entire history of airships—the giants of the air—first developed in Friedrichshafen by Count Ferdinand Zeppelin at the turn of the 20C. Among the museum's main attractions is a 33m/108ft-long reconstructed walk-through section of the *LZ 129 Hindenburg* that tragically crashed in New Jersey in 1937.

Upstairs, an art exhibit demonstrates regional works from the Middle Ages to today. Look for works by Otto Dix, Max Ackermann and Karl Caspar.

Lindau★★ (*see LINDAU IM BODENSEE*)

Address Book

For coin ranges, see the Legend on the cover flap.

WHERE TO STAY

Gasthof Auer – *Stockacher Straße 62, 78359 Orsingen-Nenzingen. (07771) 24 97. www.auer-nenzingen. de. Closed 1 week in late July. 5 rooms. Restaurant.* Simple but welcoming, this inn combines a rustic restaurant serving seasonal, regional cuisine with a few basic but nicely decorated rooms.

Bodensee-Hotel Kreuz– *Grasbeurer Straße 2, 88690 Uhldingen-Mühlhofen. (07556) 92 88 90. www. bodensee-hotel-kreuz.de. 43 rooms. Restaurant.* This family-run hotel on a quiet side street offers rooms in a historic main building and a modern annexe. In either, the interior is warm and traditional with spacious, homey rooms, many with balcony.

Landgasthof Sternen – *Schienerbergstraße 23, 78345 Bankholzen-Moos. (07732) 24 22. www.zum-sternen.de. 18 rooms. Restaurant.* This congenial country inn is a great place to lay low in well-proportioned, charmingly furnished rooms. The restaurant is justly popular for its fresh fish and meat dishes sourced from regional suppliers.

Gästehaus Schmäh – *Kapellenstraße 7, 88709 Hagnau. (07532) 62 10. www.gaestehaus-schmaeh.de. 17 rooms.* This well-maintained guesthouse is situated in a quiet residential area and sports spotless, balconied rooms furnished in simple, rustic oak. Sun-worshippers will love relaxing with a book on the lawn behind the house.

Villa Seeschau – *Von-Laßberg-Straße, 88709 Meersburg. (07532) 43 44 90. www.hotel-seeschau.de. 18 rooms.* This pretty villa is surrounded by lush gardens and has elegant, good-sized rooms in neutral hues and with balcony views of the lake. The panorama terrace is the perfect spot for breakfast.

TAKING A BREAK

Strandcafé – *Strandbadstraße 102 78315 Radolfzell. (07732) 16 50. www. strandcafe-mettnau.de.* This modern glass pavilion has an enviable lakeside location with first-rate views from all tables. Come for coffee or pre-dinner sunset drinks.

WHERE TO EAT

Winzerstube zum Becher – *Höllgasse 4, 88709 Meersburg. (07532) 90 09. www.winzerstube-zum-becher.de. Closed 3 weeks in Jan and Mon.* This rustic establishment has been welcoming thirsty visitors since 1610 and run by the same family for the past 120 years. The kitchen specializes in regional cuisine with international accents.

BONN★

POPULATION: 312 000

In 1949, Bonn beat Frankfurt am Main to become the capital of the newly created Federal Republic of Germany. The decision surprised many people given the town's modest size and provincial character. Bonn, however, rose to the occasion and has maintained an international, cosmopolitan flair even since the capital was moved back to Berlin in 1991. There's plenty to see and do for visitors in the birth town of Ludwig van Beethoven, which has a lovely river location and a wealth of first-rate museums.

- **Information:** Windeckstraße 1, 53103 Bonn. ☎(0228) 77 50 00. www.bonn.de.
- ▶ **Orient Yourself:** Bonn is on the left bank of the Rhine River and easily accessible from Cologne by the A555 or A59 autobahns. Historic sights cluster in the old town while Museum Row is along the Adenauerallee south of here.
- **Parking:** Garages are located throughout the city: near the train station, near Beethoven's birth house, and near the Old Cemetery on Oxfordstraße.
- **Don't Miss:** Beethoven's birth house, House of History of the Federal Republic of Germany, Bonn Museum of Art and the Rhenish Regional Museum.
- **Organizing Your Time:** Allow one day for Bonn and another half day for the Siebengebirge.
- **Especially for Kids:** House of History of the FRG, Museum Alexander Koenig and the Siebengebirge (♿*see Excursions),* especially the funicular.
- ♿ **Also See:** KÖLN.

A Bit of History

Origins – Bonn has been inhabited since Roman times but only achieved importance in the 16C as a residence of the electors and archbishops of Cologne.

Capital of the Federal Republic of Germany – After **Konrad Adenauer** became West Germany's first chancellor in 1949, he pushed for Bonn (near his home town of Bad Honnef) to become the country's provisional capital. Bonn fulfilled that role for 50 years and

became in the process a well-respected seat of government. Since reunification and the transfer of government offices to Berlin in 1999, huge sums of money have been spent redefining the nature of the city. Several United Nations offices have opened here, along with the headquarters of international corporations.

Beethoven's formative years – Precursor of the Romantic music movement, **Ludwig van Beethoven** (1770–1827) was born in Bonn and grew up near the Church of St Remigius. At 13, Beethoven was already an accomplished musician, playing violin, viola and harpsichord in the Court of the Elector. At 22 the fervent admirer of Mozart and Haydn left Bonn for Vienna to follow in their footsteps. The **Beethovenhalle** hosts the annual international Beethoven Festival.

Walking Tour

Historic Center★★

Beethovenhaus (Beethoven's Birthplace)

Bonngasse 20.

○Open Apr–Oct, Mon–Sat 10am–6pm, Sun 11am–6pm (Nov–Mar 5pm). ○Closed Jan 1, Mon before Shrove Tue, Good Fri, Easter Sun, Dec 24–26 & 31. ◦5€. ☎(0228) 98 17 50. www.beethoven-haus-bonn.de.

Visit the room where Beethoven was born in 1770 in this modest town house that now chronicles the life and achievements of this great composer. You get to peruse portraits, original documents, musical instruments, listening horns and his life and death masks. Tickets also include admission to the **Digitales Beethoven-Haus**, a multimedia 3D experience next door.

▶ *Go south on Bonngasse toward the Markt.*

Altes Rathaus (Old Town Hall)

This charming Rococo building (1738) with its frilly pink and silver façade dominates the triangular market square.

▶ *Head east on StockenStraße.*

Kurfürstliche Residenz (Electoral Palace)

The lawns of the Hofgarten make a fine backdrop for this imposing Baroque building, built by Enrico Zucalli between 1697 and 1702 as a residence for the prince electors. Since 1818 the palace has been part of the university.

▶ *From the south end of the Kurfürstliche Residenz, take a right on Am Neutor and walk toward Münsterplatz.*

Münster★ (Cathedral)

The former Stiftskirche Sts Cassius and Florentius beautifully melds 11C–13C Romanesque and Gothic architectural features. The Romanesque baptismal font and stone carvings are noteworthy, as are the drawings (c. 1200), and fresco (c. 1200) depicting Mary.

The quiet **cloister★** (c. 1150) is considered one of the best preserved from the Romanesque period.

Sights

Rheinisches Landesmuseum★★ (Rhenish Regional Museum)

Colmanstraße 14–18.

○Open year-round, Tue–Sun 10am–6pm (Wed 9pm). ○Closed Jan 1, Thu before Shrove Tue, Dec 24 & 31. ◦5€. ☎(0228) 207 00. www.rlmb.lvr.de.

This museum offers an overview of the history, culture and art of the Middle

Bonn

M. Sondermann, Stadt Bonn

BONN					
		Fritz-Schroeder-Ufer	CY 15	Poststr.	BZ 34
		Gerhard-von-Are-Str.	BZ 16	Rathausgasse	CZ 36
Am Alten Friedhof	BZ 2	Kasernenstr.	BY 20	Remigiuspl.	CZ 38
Am Hof	CZ	Markt	CZ 23	Remigiusstr.	CZ 40
Am Neutor	CZ 3	Martinspl.	CZ 24	Sternstr.	BCZ 43
Belderberg	CY 7	Mülheimer Pl.	BZ 27	Sterntorbrücke	BY 45
Bertha-von-Suttner-Pl.	CY 9	Münsterpl.	BZ 28	Thomas-Mann-Str.	BYZ 46
Bottlerpl.	BZ 10	Münsterstr.	BZ 29	Welschnonnenstr.	CY 48
Brüdergasse	CY 12	Oxfordstr.	BY 31	Wenzelgasse	CY 49
Budapester Str.	BYZ 14	Poppelsdorfer Allee	BZ 32	Wilhelmstr.	BY 50

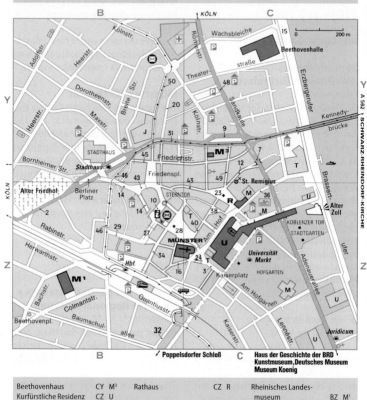

| Beethovenhaus | CY M³ | Rathaus | CZ R | Rheinisches Landes- | |
| Kurfürstliche Residenz | CZ U | | | museum | BZ M¹ |

and Lower Rhine from prehistory to the present.

Pride of place of the **Neanderthal** section goes to the skull and partial skeleton of a 42 000-year-old locally found hominid. **From Gods to God** (*Von Göttern bis Gott*) boasts plenty of treasures, most notably the Pieta Roettgen, a heart-wrenching wooden Madonna sculpture (c. 1360). The stag masks used in prehistoric rituals around 7 700 BC are also captivating. Celtic gold jewelry from BC 1C is a highlight of **Power and Powers** (*Macht und Mächte*), along with a Celtic bronze helmet and the tombstone of Marcus Caelius from AD 10.

Haus der Geschichte der Bundesrepublik Deutschland★ (House of History of the Federal Republic of Germany) [Kids]

Willy-Brandt-Allee 14.

⚲*Open year-round, Tue–Sun 9am–7pm.* ♿☏*(0228) 916 50. www.hdg.de.*

Germany's first museum of post-World War II history is an intriguing display of original objects, multimedia screens and interactive stations. Older visitors can retrace the historical events they experienced in their youth, while older children can watch the past unfold before their eyes. Highlights include a 1951 Mercedes that belonged to Adenauer, Germany first chancellor, an original 1950s ice cream shop and a section of a *Rosinenbomber* (candy bomber) plane used during the 1948/9 Berlin Airlift. About 40 percent of the exhibits are devoted to the history of the GDR, the former East Germany.

Kunstmuseum Bonn★
(Bonn Museum of Art)
Friedrich-Ebert-Allee 2.
Open year-round, Tue–Sun 11am–6pm (Wed 9pm). Closed Thu and Mon before Shrove Tue, Dec 24, 25 & 31. 5€. (0228) 77 62 60. www.bonn.de/kunstmuseum.

Expressionism forms the core collection of this excellent art museum which has a particularly strong reputation for its works by one-time Bonn resident August Macke. Other rooms emphasize German art since 1945, with works by Richter, Kiefer, Baselitz, Penck, Lüpertz, Beuys and other top artists. The neighboring **National Art Gallery and Exhibition Hall** (*Kunst- und Ausstellungshalle der Bundesrepublik Deutschland;* open year-round, Tue–Wed 10am–9pm, Thu–Sun 10am–7pm; closed Dec 24 & 31; 8€; 917 12 00; www.bundeskunsthalle.de) houses temporary exhibitions of international caliber.

Museum Alexander Koenig★ Kids
Adenauerallee 160.
Open year-round, Tue–Sun 10am–6pm (Wed 9pm). Closed Dec 24, 25 & 31. 3€. (0228) 912 20. www.museum-koenig.de.

This prestigious natural history museum combines old-fashioned dioramas and glass display cases with imaginative recreations of complete habitats, including the African savannah, the tropical rainforest, and the Arctic and Antarctica.

Deutsches Museum Bonn
(German Museum Bonn)
Ahrstraße 45.
Open year-round, Tue–Sun 10am–6pm. Closed Thu before Shrove Tue & Shrove Tue, Good Fri, May 1, Dec 24, 25 & 31. 4€. (0228) 30 22 55. www.deutsches-museum-bonn.de.

This museum, which is an offshoot of Munich's famous museum of the same name, emphasizes research and tech-

nology in Germany since 1945. Did you know that Germany invented the air bag, the atomic clock and the superfast Transrapid train?

Poppelsdorfer Schloss
(Poppelsdorf Palace)
Meckenheimer Allee 171.
About 1km/0.6mi south of the Altstadt, this palace was designed in the early 18C by Enrico Zucalli for the prince-electors of Cologne and completed by Balthasar Neumann in 1756. In 1818, it became part of the university; the extensive park was turned into a **botanical garden**.

Alter Friedhof (Old Cemetery)
Bornheimer Straße.
Northwest of the historic center, artists, scholars and celebrities are buried in this leafy old cemetery, including Robert and Clara Schumann, Beethoven's mother, Ernst Moritz Arndt and August Wilhelm von Schlegel.

August Macke Haus
(August Macke House)
Bornheimer Straße 96.
Open year-round, Tue–Fri 2.30pm–6pm, Sat–Sun 11am–5pm. 4€. (0228) 65 55 31. www.august-macke-haus.de.

Expressionist painter August Macke (1887–1914) lived in this neoclassical villa from 1910 until 1914. Inside are his recreated studio, examples of Macke's work and a survey of Rhenish Expressionism.

Excursions

Schwarz-Rheindorf★
Leave by the Kennedy bridge.
This suburb across the Rhine River is home to a rare double church, a Romanesque beauty consecrated in 1151. The upper chapel was used by the nobility, the lower by commoners. The latter boasts elaborate frescoes depicting scenes from the Book of Ezekiel.

Bad Godesberg
7km/4.3mi south of Bonn.
This residential suburb was the seat of foreign embassies until most of the federal government relocated to Berlin.

The **riverside walk** makes for a lovely stroll and offers views of the Petersberg Hotel and the Drachenfels ruins on the right bank of the Rhine River. **Views**★ are even better from the 13C Godesburg castle, now a restaurant.

Siebengebirge★ `Kids`
15km/9.3mi south on the right bank of the Rhine.
Cogwheel train: ⏰*operates May–Sept, daily 9am–7pm (every 30min); Jan, Feb & early Nov, Mon–Fri noon–5pm, Sat–Sun 11am–6pm (hourly); Mar & Oct 10am–6pm (every 30min); Apr 10am–7pm (every 30min).* ⊚*9€ (chlidren 5€).* ☎*(02223) 920 90. www.drachenfelsbahn-koenig-swinter.de/siebengebirge.*

The forested hills opposite Bad Godesberg are steeped in legend and lore. Since 1883, a creaky cogwheel train, the **Drachenbahn**, has delivered millions of visitors to the top of the 321m/1 050ft-high **Drachenfels** with its romantically ruined castle. Legend has it that Siegfried slew the dragon here and bathed in its blood to become invincible.

Remagen
21km/13mi south of Bonn, left bank.
Founded as Roman camp, Remagen is best known for its **bridge** that fell into American hands in 1945—the first time the Americans were able to establish operations east of the river. Days later, the bridge collapsed under the weight of armored vehicles. The remaining towers are today the site of **Friedensmuseum Brücke von Remagen**, the so-called Peace Museum (⏰*open Mar–Oct, daily 10am–6pm; Nov–Feb 10am–5pm;* ⊚*3.50€;* ☎*(02642) 201 59; www.bruecke-remagen.de*) with historical exhibits about World War II.

PARK & SCHLOSS BRANITZ

The gardens at Branitz Palace were the crowning achievement of Hermann Fürst von Pückler-Muskau (1785–1871)—a nobleman, travel writer and one of the most distinguished landscape architects of the 19C. Branitz had been in his family's possession since 1696 but it wasn't until the prince moved here in 1845 that it was transformed into the glorious park and garden you see today.

- 🄸 **Information:** Kastanienallee 11. 03042 Cottbus. ☎(0355) 751 52 21. www.pueckler-museum.de.
- ▶ **Orient Yourself:** Branitz is less than 5km/3mi east of Cottbus.
- 🄿 **Parking:** Parking is available near the park.
- ⏰ **Organizing Your Time:** Schloss Branitz and its park can be seen in half a day.
- 👣 **Also See:** SPREEWALD, BAUTZEN.

Visit

Park & Schloss Branitz
Schloss and Gutshof: ⏰*Open Apr–Oct, daily 10am–6pm; Nov–Mar, Tue–Sun 11am–5pm.* ⊚*4.50€. Marstall: Mar–Nov, Tue–Sun 11am–5pm.* ⊚*3.50€.* ⏰*Closed Dec 24 & 31.* ☎*(0355) 751 52 25. www.pueckler-museum.de.*

Hermann, Prince von Pückler-Muskau was born in Muskau Palace, but in 1845 he sold the estate and moved to Schloss Branitz, about 37km/23mi to the northwest. He used the proceeds from the sale to transform the surroundings into an exquisite **landscape park**. Covering 90ha/222 acres, it is divided into several zones, including a sculpture-studded flower garden adjacent to the Schloss itself. Soil from the excavation of lakes was used to shape hills and pyramids. Pückler placed particular emphasis on the alternation between open spaces, tree groupings, sculpture and pools. He and his wife, Lucie, are buried in the 11m/36ft high pyramid—called **Tumulus**—that rises from one of the lakes. Approaching the compound, the first building you get to is the **Gutshof**, which served as Pückler's office and now

Terrace and park of the luxurious Branitz estate, laid out by the extravagant Hermann, Prince of Pückler-Muskau

harbors the visitor center with an interactive, **multimedia exhibit** on the man, his peers, his life and achievements. Further on, in the center of park, the **palace** itself was completed 1772 and contains period furnishings and paintings by Carl Blechen, the Romantic painter born in Cottbus.

Nearby, the Tudor-style **royal stables** (*Marstall*) are used for temporary exhibitions, while the **Cavalier's House** (*Kavalierhaus*) is now a restaurant.

Between the two buildings lies the "**Pergola**" with reliefs by the Danish sculptor Berthel Thorwaldsen, zinc copies of antique sculpture and a bronze casting of the Venus Italica by Canova.

On the garden side is a terrace featuring two bronze griffins.

BRAUNSCHWEIG

BRUNSWICK

POPULATION: 245 000

Brunswick (Braunschweig) is the second largest city in Lower Saxony and has always been a thriving industrial town, which is why it was an attractive target for Allied bombers during World War II. Nearly obliterated in October 1944, it was rebuilt according to modern urban concepts, but some historic sights as well as a superb art collection survived and make up its touristic appeal today.

- **Information:** Vor der Burg 1, 38100 Braunschweig. ☎ (0531) 470 20 40. www.braunschweig.de.
- ▸ **Orient Yourself:** South of the Lüneburger Heath, Brunswick is on the A2 autobahn linking Hannover and Berlin.
- **Parking:** Garages are scattered throughout the town; a large one is on Wilhelmstraße at the corner of Neue Güldenklinke.
- **Don't Miss:** Altstadtmarkt, Herzog-Anton-Ulrich-Museum, and, if you're a car buff, Autostadt (◔see Excursions).
- **Especially for Kids:** Volkswagen's automotive theme park, Autostadt (◔see Excursions).
- **Also See:** WOLFENBÜTTEL, CELLE, HANNOVER.

A Bit of History

The Lion of Brunswick – In 1166, having boosted the House of Guelph to political power in Germany, Henry the Lion, Duke of Bavaria and Saxony, settled in Brunswick. Frederick I (aka Barbarossa), jealous of his rise, ultimately stripped Henry of nearly all his personal and public possessions. The lion sculpture on Burgplatz is Brunswick's symbol.

Sights

Town Center

Altstadtmarkt

Brunswick grew up around 5 distinct districts (**Altstadtmarkt, Hagen, Alteweik, Neustadt and Sack**), each with its own Town Hall and market. Altstadtmarkt is the oldest and anchored by the step-gabled Gothic **old Town Hall**. In the middle of the Poststraße is the **Drapers' Hall** (*Gewandhaus*), featuring the town's most decorated gable dating back to the late Renaissance.

Dom★ (Cathedral)

The original Romanesque cathedral was built in the 12C under Henry the Lion who is buried in its crypt alongside his wife Matilda. The most important works of art are the 12C carved wooden **Imervard Cross★**, the seven-branched 12C **candelabrum★**, the 12C **Marian Altar** and the medieval frescoes.

Herzog-Anton-Ulrich-Museum★

Museumstraße 1.
Open year-round, Tue–Sat 10am–5pm (Wed 1pm–8pm). Closed May 1 & Pentecost. 3€. (0531) 122 50. www. museum-braunschweig.de.
Established in 1754, this art museum features a priceless collection of German, Flemish and Dutch masters, including Rembrandt, Rubens, Vermeer, Cranach the Elder and Holbein. Other treats include extensive holdings of Italian majolica and porcelain from the Fürstenberg manufactory. Medieval art

is displayed in Henry the Lion's rebuilt palace, **Burg Dankwartsrode** (*Burgplatz 4; open Tue, Thu–Sun 11am–5pm, Wed 1pm–2.30pm, 4pm–8pm*). Upon the opening of a modern extension in 2010, the original Herzog-Anton-Ulrich-Museum will undergo a thorough renovation that may last through 2013.

Excursions

Autostadt★★ [Kids]

40km/25mi northeast in Wolfsburg.
Open year-round, daily 9am–6pm.
Closed Dec 24 & 31. 15€. (0800) 288 67 82 38. www.autostadt.de.
This 25ha/62 acre **Volkswagen theme park** next to the VW headquarters attracts over one million visitors a year. Landscaped parkland forms a pleasant backdrop for modernist pavilions, each dedicated to different VW brands, from Audi to Seat. You can ride the elevator to the top of the 48m/157ft **Autotürme** (car towers) where the new cars are stored, take a guided **factory tour** (45min) or drive an off-road Touareg along an **obstacle track**. *Combination tickets with the interactive science center* **Phaeno** (*23€; (0180) 106 06 00; www.phaeno.de*), opposite Autostadt, are available as well. Restaurants, cafes and a hotel are also on-site.

Helmstedt

47km/29mi east of Brunswick.
Helmstedt-Marienborn was once the most important border crossing between West and East Germany. Learn about border history at the **Zonengrenz-Museum** in Helmstedt (*Südertor 6; open year-round, Tue & Fri 3pm–5pm, Wed 10am–noon, 3pm–5pm, Thu 3pm–6.30pm, Sat–Sun 10am–5pm; (05351) 121 11 33; www.helmstedt. de*) or at the crossing itself, now the **Gedenkstätte Deutsche Teilung Marienborn★** (*exit Marienborn off A2 autobahn; open Tue–Sat 10am–5pm; 0394 06- 920 90; www.grenzdenkmaeler.de) and* an archive and documentation center.

BREMEN★★

POPULATION: 546 000

Bremen, Germany's oldest maritime city, is famous for Beck's beer and the Town Musicians of the eponymous Brothers Grimm' fairytale, the Town Musicians of Bremen. Enjoying trade rights from 965, it has a long and proud history of civic independence, joining the Hanseatic League in 1358 and beginning trading directly with America in 1783. Today, Bremen is a lively, compact, congenial city with a charming old town and bustling nightlife districts.

- 🛈 **Information:** Am Bahnhofsplatz, 28195 Bremen. ☎(0421) 308 00 10. www.bremen-tourismus.de.
- ▸ **Orient Yourself:** Bremen is at the southern end of the Weser estuary, while its sea port Bremerhaven is 59km/37mi downstream.
- 🅿 **Parking:** Look for garages near the Hauptbahnhof and throughout the inner city, including a large 24hr one on Pelzerstraße (enter on Knochenhauerstraße).
- 🅐 **Don't Miss:** Marktplatz, Böttcherstraße, German Emigration Center
- **Kids Especially for Kids:** Universum Bremen, German Emigration Center, Deutsches Schiffahrtsmuseum.
- 🕐 **Organizing Your Time:** Budget at least one full day to see Bremen and another half day for Bremerhaven.
- 🕭 **Also See:** OLDENBURG, LÜNEBURGER HEIDE.

A Bit of History

Bremen Ports – The twin ports in Bremen and Bremerhaven directly or indirectly employ about a third of the city-state's population and are Germany's second-busiest after Hamburg. Each year more than five million containers and 1.4 million vehicles pass through the port's terminals.

🕐*River and port tours (75min) leave from the quay by the St. Martinikirche. Departures Mar–Oct, daily 10.15am, 11.45am, 1.30pm, 3.15pm and 4.45pm (Mar, Apr and Oct no 10.15am and 4.45pm tours); Feb, Nov and Dec, Sat–Sun 1.30pm and 3.15pm.* ⚫*9€.* 🕭☎*(0421) 33 89 89; www. hal-oever.de).*

The market place in the heart of the old town, dominated by an immense statue of Roland

Bremer Touristik-Zentrale

Sights

Old Bremen

Marktplatz★★

Bremen's market square is one of the most beautiful in Germany. At its center is the 5.5m/18ft-high canopied statue of the knight **Roland** (1404), a symbol for freedom and civic autonomy. Together with the **Rathaus** (Town Hall), the statue is on UNESCO's list of World Heritage Sites.

Perhaps even more beloved is Gerhard Marcks' bronze sculpture (1951) on the Town Hall's west side. This pyramid formed by a donkey, dog, cat and rooster represents the characters from the popular Grimm fairy tale, the **Town Musicians of Bremen** (Bremer Stadtmusikanten).

The **Schütting**, an elegant 16C building, used to house Bremen's Guild of Merchants.

Rathaus★

Am Markt 21.

Visits by guided tour (1hr) only, Mon–Sat 11am, noon, 3pm and 4pm, Sun 11am and noon. No tours during official receptions. 5€. (01805) 10 10 30. www. bremen-tourism.de.

The original Town Hall was built in Gothic style in the 15C, shortly after Bremen joined the Hanseatic League. A renovation in Weser Renaissance style in the 17C added its decorative gables and a three-story façade rising above an arcaded gallery. Above this, tall windows

Richly-decorated Town Hall

Bremer Touristik-Zentrale

alternate with statues of Charlemagne and the Seven Electors (note that these are copies; the Gothic originals are in the Focke-Museum).

Inside, a splendid spiral **staircase**★★ (Wendeltreppe) in carved wood (1620) is worth taking a closer look at.

The Bremer Rathauskeller (entrance on the west side) serves 650 different German wines.

St. Petri-Dom★

SandStraße 10–12.

Open year-round, Mon–Fri 10am–5pm, Sat 10am–2pm, Sun 2pm–5pm. Closed May 1 & Oct 3. Tower 1€; Bleikeller (lead basement) 1.40€. (0421) 36 50 40. www.stpetridom.de.

St. Peter's Cathedral (Lutheran) was constructed in the 11C, and updated in the 16C and 19C. Notable religious artworks include a 16C **Virgin and Child**★ and, along the organ ballustrade, 16C carvings of Charlemagne and Willehad, the first Bishop of Bremen. Beneath the organ loft, the 11C western crypt houses Romanesque capitals and a magnificent bronze **baptismal font**★★ (Taufbecken, c. 1220).

A separate entrance just south of the main portal leads to the hugely popular—if macabre—**lead cellar** (Bleikeller; open Easter–Oct, same hours as church; 1.40€), which contains eight perfectly preserved, centuries-old mummified corpses in open coffins.

Pfarrkirche Unser Lieben Frauen (Church of Our Lady)

The interior of this 13C hall church, bare of decoration except for the 1709 chancel, is relieved by rounded ogive vaulting dating to its construction. The four main stained-glass windows, on biblical themes, were executed between 1966 and 1979. The church's simple **crypt** dates from the preceding church (St Veit), which has been traced to 1020, making it the oldest extant building in Bremen.

Stadtwaage (Weigh-House)

This simple 16C building features alternating layers of brick and embossed stone.

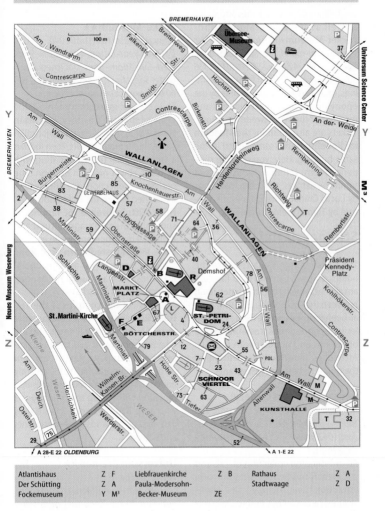

Böttcherstraße★

Running only 110m/121yd from the Marktplatz to the Weser, this narrow street is an architectural gem commissioned in the 1920s by coffee mogul Ludwig Roselius and designed primarily by architect Bernhard Hoetger. Expressionist in style, with Art Nouveau and Art Deco overtones, buildings feature whimsical design elements, such as façades buttressed by stone sculptures, a spiral staircase and a golden entrance

Coffee bean city

Bremen's close links with coffee date back over three centuries. The first ever coffee house in German-speaking countries was built here in 1673, before those in Vienna and Hamburg. Half of all the cups of coffee drunk in Germany are brewed from beans imported via the port at Bremen.

relief. A carillon made of Meissen porcelain chimes hourly between noon and 6pm (Jan-Mar at noon, 3pm and 6pm). The buildings house galleries and shops as well as the **Paula-Modersohn-Becker-Museum**★ *(Böttcherstraße 6–10; open year-round, Tue–Sun 11am–6pm; closed Dec 24 & 31; 5€; (0421) 336 50 66; www.pmbm.de)*. It features paintings, drawings and graphic works by the eponymous modern art pioneer and member of the Worpswede art colony. Tickets are also good for the **Museum im Roseliushaus** *(same hours)* in the same building. Here you can tour nine period rooms brimming with precious furniture, carpets, porcelain, paintings by Lucas Cranach the Elder and sculpture by Tilman Riemenschneider.

Schnoorviertel★

The cottages in this quarter, once the homes of fishermen and their families, are all that remains of Old Bremen. Built between the 15C and the 19C, they have all been restored and are used as art galleries, antique shops, restaurants and boutiques and popular with tourists. After dark, night owls descend upon the quarter's bars and restaurants.

Kunsthalle★ (Art Gallery)

Am Wall 207. Open year-round, Tue 10am–9pm, Wed–Sun 10am–5pm. 5€. (0421) 32 90 80. www.kunsthalle-bremen.de.

An outstanding collection of 19C and 20C French and German art is the main attraction here. The many fine works includes canvasses by Courbet, Delacroix and the Barbizon School; Menzel, Leibl, Beckmann; French and German Impressionists; and artists of the Worpswede School. Earlier periods of European art are illustrated by 15C Old Masters, such as Rubens, Rembrandt and Tiepolo. The graphics room *(Kupferstichkabinett)* includes over 230 000 prints and drawings of exceptional quality from Dürer's day to the present.

Focke-Museum★★

Schwachhauser Heerstraße 240. Open year-round, Tue 10am–9pm, Wed–Sun 10am–5pm. Closed Jan 1, Easter Sun, May 1. 4€. (0421) 699 60 00. www.focke-museum.de.

This regional museum presents 1 200 years of Bremen's history. The **Main House** *(Haupthaus)* covers major milestones in themed exhibits, then follows a chronological trail culminating with displays about modern Bremen. The prehistoric collections are displayed in a thatched annex, the Eichenhof.

Haus Mittelsbüren, a 16C farmhouse spotlights Bremen's agricultural and industrial development, while exhibits in the 1803 **Tarnstedt Barn** *(Tarnstedter Scheune)* zero in on various agricultural activities, such as animal husbandry, haymaking and dairy farming.

Also part of the complex is the 18C **Haus Riensberg**, a one-time summer residence for wealthy Bremen families where decorative arts, Fürstenberg porcelain and European glass art are now on display. Kids gravitate to the recently added Kids **Children's Museum** *(Kindermuseum)* with its big toy collection as well as to **Studio Focke**, where they can engage in hands-on experiments and activities.

Universum Bremen★★ Kids

Wiener Straße 1a. Open year-round, Mon–Fri 9am–6pm, Sat–Sun 10am–7pm; last admission 90min before closing. 9.50€ (child 7€). (0421) 334 60. www.universum-bremen.de.

Science gets a fun and entertaining twist at this state-of-the-art park. Visits start at the **SchauBox**, a rust-colored cube containing special exhibits, a restau-

Address Book

🪙*For coin ranges, see the Legend on the cover flap.*

WHERE TO STAY

🛏🛏 **Bölts am Park** – *Slevogtstraße 23.* ☎*(0421) 34 61 10. www.hotel-boelts. de. 16 rooms.* Quiet and family run, this classic Bremen townhouse offers well-tended rooms and a breakfast nook overlooking the small garden.

🛏🛏 **Hotel Buthmann**– *Löning-straße 29.* ☎*(0421) 32 63 97. www. hotel-buthmann.de. 9 rooms.* This little inn within walking distance of the train station and the old town has clean and spacious if fairly nondescript rooms.

🛏🛏🛏🛏 **Park Hotel** – *Im Bürgerpark.* ☎*(0421) 340 80. www.park-hotel-bremen.de. 177 rooms. Restaurant* 🛏🛏🛏. A sense of luxury embraces you the moment you enter the domed lobby of this elegant manor house near the park. Restaurant choices include fine dining in the winter garden or Mediter-ranean cuisine in the bistro.

WHERE TO EAT

🍴 **Paulaner's** – *Schlachte 30.* ☎*(0421) 169 06 91. www.paulaners.de.* At this pleasant, riverside Bavarian-style beer hall and beer garden you will find efficient, friendly service and a long menu that mixes north-ern and southern German specialities.

🍴🍴 **John Benton Restaurant** – *Am Markt 1.* ☎*(0421) 32 30 33.* Delicious cuts of aged steak are the main draw at this bi-level restaurant whose terrace offers beautiful cathedral views.

🍴🍴🍴 **Jürgenshof** – *Pauliner Marsch 1 (near Weserstadion).* ☎*(0421) 44 10 37. www.juergenshof.com. Reservations recommended.* Enjoy top-notch Bremen culinary delights and authentic northern German ambience at this reed-covered former shepherd's farm. The pleasant garden terrace is a bonus.

TAKING A BREAK

F. L. Bodes – *Bischofsnadel 1–2 (alley-way leading from Wallanlagen to Dom-shof).* ☎*(0421) 32 41 44. www.bodes. de. Closed Sun, Mon.* This fish shop and snack bar is a mere stone's throw from the town center. Try seafood and fish à la carte, choose from the blackboard menus or make your selection directly from the stalls. Lines are longest at lunchtime.

Konditorei Knigge – *Sögestraße 42–44.* ☎*(0421) 137 13. www.knigge-shop.de.* Bremen's classic café is the place to try such local specialties as the "Bremer Klaben", a hearty fruitcake.

NIGHTLIFE

Useful tip – Cafés, bars, restaurants and shops cluster in the historic Schnoor district, south of the cathedral. The riverside Schlachte promenade, on the right river bank, is chockfull of trendy restaurants and bars, many with river terraces.

Café Freitag – *Böttcherstraße 3–5.* ☎*(0421) 32 09 95.* Chic décor, a superb location in the Robinson-Crusoe House on lovely Böttcherstraße and a good-value menu give this all-day café an edge with locals and tourists alike. The terrace is perfect for people-watching.

Pannekoekschip Admiral Nelson – *Schlachte Anleger 1.* ☎*(0421) 3 64 99 84. www.admiral-nelson.de.* Ahoy there! Friendly "pirates" serve sweet or savory pancakes on this three-masted ship.

Salomon's – *Ostertorstr. 11–13.* ☎*(0421) 2 44 17 71. www.salomons-bremen.de. Closed Mon.* The trendy restaurant-lounge in a wing of the 19C courthouse serves reasonably-priced salads, pasta,

Pannekoekschip Admiral Nelson

M. Hertlein/MICHELIN

and meat dishes named for famous detectives, prisons or outlaws.

SHOPPING

The elegant shopping arcades of Lloydpassage, Domshof Passage and Katharinen-Viertel in the heart of town make for a fun browse. Independent boutiques are located in the historic Schnoor district and along Böttcher-straße.

---

rant and a multimedia theater. A bridge leads to the **Science Center**, housed in a silvery building shaped like a closed clam. Inside are 250 experiment and interactive stations divided into three themes: Earth, Humanity and the Cosmos. You can take a virtual journey into space, experience an earthquake, or dive 2km/1.2mi below the sea. The fun continues outdoors in the **EntdeckerPark** (Explorer Park), which counts a climbing wall and a water playground among its many attractions.

Überseemuseum Bremen★★ (Overseas Museum)

Bahnhofsplatz 13.
○*Open year-round, Tue–Fri 9am-6pm, Sat–Sun 10am-6pm.* ○*Closed jan 1, Easter Mon, May 1, Pentecost Sun, Dec 24, 25 & 31.* ✆*6.50€.* ♿✆ *(0421)16 03 81 01. www.uebersee-museum.de.*
History, ethnology, culture and trade combine into an exciting journey of discovery back in time and around the world. Learn about colonial trading, admire exotic artefacts from the South Seas or inspect shiny Samurai armor. Founded in 1896, the museum's vast collections have recently been dusted up and are now engagingly presented by continent, Oceania to Africa, America to Asia.

Excursions

Worpswede

24km/15mi north.
In the late 19C, the isolated village of Worpswede became one of northern Germany's most celebrated artist colonies. Among those who settled here were proto-expressionist Paula Modersohn-Becker, her husband Otto Modersohn and the poet Rainer Maria

Rilke. Numerous galleries, studios and workshops have sprung up since then. Asymmetrical buildings like the Worpswede Café and the Niedersachsenstein First World War Memorial represent the avant-garde ideas held by the group.

Bremerhaven

58km/36mi north.
Founded in 1827, half of the German fishing fleet is based at this vast sea port, but Bremerhaven is first and foremost a container port (✆*see Bremen Ports, above*).
The town's maritime history is given its due at the [Kids]**German Maritime Museum**★ (*Deutsches Schiffahrtsmuseum; Hans-Scharoun-Platz 1;* ○*open Mar–Oct, daily 10am–6pm,* ○*closed Mon Nov–Feb, Dec 24, 25 & 31;* ✆*6€; www. dsm.museum*), whose 500 historic boats could keep salty types busy for hours.
Bremerhaven's newest draw, though, is the **German Emigration Cente**★★★ (*Deutsches Auswandererhaus; ColumbusStraße 65;* ○ *open Mar–Oct, daily 10am–6pm, Nov–Feb 10am–5pm;* ✆*10.50€;* ♿✆*0421- 90 22 00; www.dah-bremerhaven.de*). Since late 2005, this vast center has told the moving story of those of brave European emigrants who traded poverty and persecution for hopes of a better life in the New World. Around seven million embarked from this very spot in Bremerhaven between 1830 and 1974.
A tour recreates every phase of the emigration process, from the teary-eyed quayside farewell to conditions aboard the vessel to the arrival at Ellis Island. Especially moving is the **Gallery of the 7 Millions** that lets you explore the biographies of individuals and learn what prompted them to leave their homelands.

BURGHAUSEN★★

POPULATION: 18 250

Right on the border with Austria, Burghausen has a lovely, well-preserved old town crowned by the longest hilltop fortress in Germany. The dukes of Bavaria, who became rulers of Burghausen in the 12C, converted its medieval castle into this formidable defense system that stretches for an impressive 1 043m/3 420ft atop a narrow, rocky spur.

- **Information:** Stadtplatz 112, 84489 Burghausen. ☎(08677) 88 71 40. www.tourismus.burghausen.de.
- ▶ **Orient Yourself:** Burghausen lies within a curve of the River Salzach, which forms the border between Germany and Austria.
- ☺ **Don't Miss:** The Burg from which Burghausen takes its name.
- ◷ **Organizing Your Time:** Allow two to three hours to visit the Burg.
- ◔ **Also See:** CHIEMSEE, BERCHTESGADEN.

Sights

Burg★★ (Castle)

Leave your car in the Stadtplatz and walk along the circular cliff road. Beneath the Wöhrenseeturm and beyond the lake, a steep path leads to the outer fortifications. From here, the ramparts are visible, stepped up the Eggenberg hill. The *Georgstor*, or **St. George's Gate**, is set in the innermost ring of battlements, which protect the last small medieval courtyard at the castle's center. Inside are two museums worth visiting.

Staatsgalerie (Bavarian Picture Gallery)

◷*Open Apr–Sept, daily 9am–6pm, Oct–Mar, daily 10am–4pm.* ◉*3€.* ☎*(08677) 46 59. www.pinakothek.de/zweiggalerien/burghausen.*

The former ducal apartments in the main castle building house this small branch of the famous Munich Pinakothek art museum. The focus is on original 15C–17C furniture, paintings, sculpture and tapestries made in Austria and Bavaria. From the observation **platform** *(62 steps, access from the second floor)*, enjoy splendid panoramic **views**★ of

Burghausen, dominated by its castle, for many years the largest fortress in Germany

©Jan Minea/iStockphoto.com

Address Book

For coin ranges, see the Legend on the cover flap.

WHERE TO STAY

Bayerische Alm – *Robert-Koch-Straße 211.* (08677) 98 20. www.bayerischealm.de. 23 rooms. Restaurant. Enjoy views of the Burg from your private balcony at this family-run inn on the town outskirts. The bi-level restaurant and beer garden serve fresh, light and healthy fare.

Hotel Post – *Stadtplatz 39.* (08677) 98 20. www.hotelpost.de. 24 rooms. Restaurant. This central inn has rooms that range from rustic to elegant and a restaurant serving upscale Bavarian home-cooking.

WHERE TO EAT

Fuchsstuben – *Mautnerstraße 271.* (08677) 627 24. *Closed Sun evenings and Mon.* Set in the heart of the old town, this tastefully decorated restaurant is filled with antiques.

Burghausen, the Salzach and the surrounding hills. The Gothic **chapel** *(in the same wing)* has elegant star vaulting.

Stadtmuseum (Municipal Museum)

Open mid-Mar–Apr & Oct, daily 10am–4pm; May–Sept, daily 9am–6pm. 2€. (08677) 651 98. www.burghausen.de/stadtmuseum.

The duchess' former private quarters *(west side of the main block)* now tells the history of Burghausen through an eclectic collection of tools, weapons, folk art, furniture, town models, paintings and sculpture.

Excursions

Raitenhaslach

6km/3.7mi south.

Red marble tombstones commemorating 15C–18C abbots are a key feature in this 12C Cistercian church, modified in the Baroque style in the late 17C. The life of St. Bernard of Clairvaux is illustrated in the fine **ceiling frescoes** (1739) by Johannes Zick of Lachen.

Tittmoning

16km/10mi south.

On the west bank of the Salzach, Tittmoning preserves the remains of its medieval fortifications and a castle, a former residence of the prince-bishops of Salzburg. Two fortified gateways give access to the broad **Stadtplatz**.

Brightly painted façades, some decorated with gilded figures, wrought iron signs, oriel windows and emblazoned fountains make this town a charming place to stop.

Altötting

21km/13mi northwest.

Each year, Altötting draws more than a million pilgrims who come to see the "Miraculous Virgin", a black Madonna, housed in the tiny, octagonal 8C **Gnadenkapelle**★ (Chapel of Mercy). Its walls are decorated with silver urns containing the hearts of Bavarian rulers.

The most famous item in the treasury of the **Gothic Collegiate Church** (Stiftskirche) across Kapellplatz square is the 15C **Goldenes Rössl**★★ (Golden Horse), an exquisitely-detailed portable gold altar given to Charles VI of France by his wife, Isabella of Bavaria.

Marktl am Inn

10km/6.2mi north.

This riverside village was thrust into the world's spotlight when its most famous son, Joseph Ratzinger (b. 1927), became Pope Benedict XVI in 2005. The pontiff's modest's **Birth House** *(Marktplatz; open mid-Mar–Oct, Tue–Fri 2pm–6pm, Sat–Sun 10am–6pm;* 3.50€; (08678) 747 680) has been turned into a small museum. It is opposite the church, **Pfarrkirche St. Oswald**, where he was baptized.

CELLE★★
POPULATION: 71 300

The former residence of the dukes of Brunswick-Lüneburg, Celle retains the vaunted air of an aristocratic retreat. Its carefully preserved center of half-timbered houses miraculously escaped war damage and is a joy to explore along with the restored ducal castle and the folklore museum.

- **Information:** Markt 14, 29221 Celle. ☎(05141) 12 12. www.region-celle.com.
- ▶ **Orient Yourself:** Celle is part of the Lüneburg Heath, a region filled with charming villages and lots of opportunities to immerse yourself in nature.
- **Don't Miss:** Celle's old town and its 13C castle.
- **Organizing Your Time:** An extensive wander would take about half a day.
- **Also See:** HANNOVER, BRAUNSCHWEIG.

Sights

Old Town
Celle's largely car-free old town boasts some of Germany's most elaborate half-timbered houses, especially along Neue Straße, Zöllnerstraße, Poststraße (note the richly carved Hoppener Haus, dating from 1532) and romantic Kalandgasse, near the church.

Altes Rathaus (Old Town Hall)
The heavily scrolled and pinnacled north gable (1579) of Celle's imposing Town Hall is a masterpiece of the Weser Renaissance. The *Ratskeller* (council cellar) has original Gothic vaulting.

Schloss★
Visit by guided tour (50min) only, Apr–Oct Tue–Sun 11am–3pm; Nov–Mar Tue–Sun, 11am and 1pm, Sat–Sun 3pm. Closed Dec 24 and 25. 3.50€. ☎(05141) 123 73.
Begun in 1292, Celle's castle initially doubled as the town's fortification and is flanked by massive corner towers. The eastern façade overlooks the town and features dormer windows topped by rounded pediments, as is characteristic of the Weser Renaissance style.
Tour highlights include the private rooms of exiled Queen Caroline-Matilde of Denmark (1751–1775), the last royal to live at the palace, and the **chapel★** (*Hofkapelle*) that is Gothic at its core but was modified in the 16C in magnificent Renaissance style. Nearby, the 17C Baroque Schlosstheater is said to be the oldest court theater in Germany still in use. An exhibition from the Bomann Museum in the eastern wing documents the history of the kingdom of Hanover.

Kunstmuseum★ (Art Museum)
Schloßplatz 7.
Open year-round, Tue–Sun 10am–5pm. 3€. ☎(05141) 123 55. www.kunst.celle.de.
Opposite the palace is what's billed as the world's first 24hr museum. In daytime, you can stroll through the galleries stocked with German contemporary art,

sculpture and graphic works. At night, the outdoor light installations are the main draw.

Bomann-Museum★

Schloßplatz 7.
Open year-round, Tue–Sun 10am–5pm. 5€. (05141) 123 72. www.bomann-museum.de.
Next to the Kunstmuseum, this collection presents a comprehensive survey of the cultural history of Lower Saxony and Celle. Pride of place goes to heavily detailed period rooms, including the kitchen of a wealthy family and a restored farmhouse.

Stadtkirche★ (Church)

An der Stadtkirche 8. Open year-round, Tue–Sat. www.stadtkirche-celle.de.
Originally Gothic, this church got a Baroque makeover in the 17C and is noteworthy for its 1613 altar, the 16C *Fürstenstuhl* (Prince's Seat) beneath the organ and the 1610 baptismal font. The tower can be climbed.

Excursion

Kloster Wienhausen★

10km/6.2mi south.
Visit by guided tour (75min) only, Apr–mid-Oct, Tue–Sat 10am, 11am, 2pm, 3pm, 4pm and 5pm, Sun hourly noon–5pm. 4€. (05149) 186 60.
Run by Protestant cannonesses since the Reformation, this 13C abbey counts wooden sculptures of the Virgin and Christ Resurrected among its treasures. The Nuns' Choir is embellished with early 14C **frescoes**★

CHIEMSEE★

Known as the "Bavarian Sea," the Chiemsee is the largest of the province's lakes. Its calm waters offer plenty of recreation options, including swimming, boating and windsurfing. The lake's two islands are both worth a visit: steer toward Herreninsel (Gentlemen's Isle) to tour King Ludwig II extraordinary palace and to the Fraueninsel (Ladies' Isle) to view its ancient Benedictine abbey. In the background are the Chiemgau Alps, a popular winter sports area.

- **Information:** Felden 10, 83233 Bernau. (08051) 96 55 50. www.chiemsee.de.
- **Orient Yourself:** Prien, on the western shore, is the busiest and most convenient among the resorts ringing the Chiemsee. The A8 autobahn (Munich to Salzburg) skirts the lake's southern shore.
- **Don't Miss:** Schloss Herrenchiemsee, quiet walks or a picnic on Fraueninsel.
- **Organizing Your Time:** Allow at least half a day to visit Schloss Herrenchiemsee and a couple of days to enjoy all the lake has to offer.
- **Especially for Kids:** Lake activities.
- **Also See:** WASSERBURG, BURGHAUSEN.

Sights

The Islands

Ferries to Herreninsel and Fraueninsel leave from the docks in Prien-Stock (exit the A8 at Bernau).
The trip to Herreninsel takes about 15min, round-trips cost 6.30€; combination tickets for Herreninsel and Fraueninsel (25min) are 7.40€.

Boat tours around the lake are 12.50€. (08051) 60 90. www.chiemsee-schifffahrt.de.

Herreninsel

The parks, woods and forests of the "Gentlemen's Isle" are ideal for a leisurely amble. King Ludwig II of Bavaria bought this island in 1873 to save it from deforestation and ended up building a sumptuous palace.

Boats with the village of Seebruck in the background

Schloss Herrenchiemsee★★

20min walk from the dock.

👁️Visit by guided tour (30min) only, Apr–mid-Oct, daily 9am–6pm; mid-Oct–Mar 9.40am–4.15pm. ⊘Closed Jan 1, Shrove Tue, Dec 24, 25 & 31. ⊜7€. ♿⊠(080 51) 688 70. www.herrenchiemsee.de.

It was to be the grandest of Ludwig II's palaces: a glorious edifice modeled on Versailles in honor of his idol, the French monarch Louis XIV.

Ludwig poured considerable funds into the construction of the **Neues Schloss** (New Palace) on Herreninsel but when he died in 1886 it was still only partly finished.

The resemblance to Versailles is quite striking: the Latona fountain stands amid formal French gardens, while the façade is adorned with columns and crowned by a flat roof in the Italian style.

Tours of the apartments start in the entrance hall with its splendid **double state staircase** *(Prunktreppenhaus)* and proceed to a succession of lavish and pompous rooms. The **state bedroom**★ and the 77m/252ft-long **Hall of Mirrors**★ are especially dazzling.

Address Book

🪙 *For coin ranges, see cover flap.*

WHERE TO EAT

⊜⊜⊜**Kloster-Wirt** –
Frauenchiemsee 50, Frauensinsel. Access by boat from Gstadt or Prien. ☎(08054) 77 65. www.klosterwirt-chiemsee.de✉. Part of the island's Benedictine Abbey, this dockside restaurant is nice spot for a hearty meal or just coffee and cake.

WHERE TO STAY

⊜⊜**Gruber-Alm** – *Almweg 18, 83370 Seeon-Seebruck.* ☎(08667) 696. www.gruber-alm.de. 20 rooms. Restaurant⊜⊜⊜. This pleasant hotel on a little hill affords views of the Chiemgau Alps. The "Wedding Room" has a handpainted ceiling, while others brim with rustic Bavarian hospitality. The restaurant serves tummy-filling regional dishes.

⊜⊜⊜**Alter Wirt-Bonnschlößl** –
Kirchplatz 9, 83233 Bernau am Chiemsee. ☎(08051) 965 69 90. www.alter-wirt-bernau.de. 41 rooms. Restaurant⊜⊜. Match your mood or comfort needs to these twin properties. The half-timbered Alter Wirt inn has rustic charm and country furnishings, while the Bonnschlössl offers modern rooms in a turreted 15C miniature palace with its own park.

⊜⊜⊜**Inselhotel Zur Linde** –
on the Fraueninsel. ☎(08054) 903 66. www.linde-frauenchiemsee.de. 14 rooms. Restaurant ⊜⊜⊜. A romantic island getaway, this inn dates from 1396 and was once the haunt of artists and writers. Rooms and public areas ooze unhurried charm, while the dining room, still with its original layout, adds yet more character to the place.

The south wing houses the **König Ludwig II Museum** *(entrance included in Schloss ticket)*, which documents the fairytale king's life through portraits, busts, historical photographs and original clothing. Spend some time here before the start of the guided tour.

Museum im Augustiner Chorherrenstift (Augustinian Canonry Museum)

Also known as Altes Schloss (Old Palace), this Baroque canonry (or monastery) was built in the 17C and is now partly a **museum** tracing 1 200 years of Bavarian history. Highlights include the Baroque

library designed by Johann Baptist Zimmermann and King Ludwig II's private quarters, including the blue bedroom.

Fraueninsel

This small islet is home to the Benedictine **Frauenwörth Monastery**, founded in 766 by Duke Tassilo III. The three-aisled church is Romanesque at its core but received Gothic touches in the 15C. Copies of its ceiling frescoes now grace the upper chapel of the nearby **Torhalle** (gatehouse), which presents changing art exhibits during the summer months.

DARMSTADT

POPULATION: 139 700

Darmstadt has a pedigree as an intellectual and cultural center thanks to a succession of art-loving princes but was practically obliterated by Allied bombs during World War II. During reconstruction, function often won out over aesthetics, although the former artists' colony of Mathildenhöhe continues to delight fans of Art Nouveau design and architecture.

▯ **Information:** Luisen-Center, Luisenplatz 5, 64283 Darmstadt. ☎(06151) 279 99 99. www.darmstadt.de.

▶ **Orient Yourself:** The former capital of the grand duchy of Hesse-Darmstadt is located near the Odenwald forest, 30km/18.6mi south of Frankfurt on the A5.

ⓟ **Parking:** Garages and lots are located throughout central Darmstadt, including near the main train station, along Zeughausstraße and south of Luisenplatz.

🌲 **Don't Miss:** Mathildenhöhe.

👓 **Also See:** FRANKFURT, MAINZ, WIESBADEN, HEIDELBERG.

Sights

Mathildenhöhe★★

Olbrichweg 13. ☎(06151) 13 33 85. *www.mathildenhoehe.info.*
In 1899 Grand Duke Ernst Ludwig invited seven artists, inlcuding Peter Behrens and Joseph Maria Olbrich, to build an **artists' colony** *(Künstlerkolonie)* on the eastern edge of the city. The result: one of the world's finest Jugendstil (Art Nouveau) architectural ensembles.

Studios and villas were grouped around a **Russian Orthodox Chapel** built between 1897 and 1899 at the behest of the last Russian tsar Nicholas II whose wife Alexandra was a member of the ducal family.

Olbrich's Ernst-Ludwig-Haus, which opened in 1901, today houses the **Museum Künstlerkolonie** *(Ⓒopen year-round, Tue–Sun 10am–5pm; ⚇3€).* Fronted by monumental sculptures of Adam and Eve, it showcases products designed by colony artists—silverware, furniture, jewelry—along with temporary exhibits.

There are also changing displays in the **Ausstellungsgebäude** *(Exhibition Hall; Ⓒopen year-round, Tue–Sun 10am–6pm, Thu 9pm; ⚇8€),* completed in 1908 and newly renovated in 2008. Next to this spacious hall looms the 48m/157ft-high **Hochzeitsturm** *(Wedding Tower; Ⓒ open March–Oct, Tue–Sun 10am–6pm; ⚇1.50€).* Its distinctive roofline resembles the outline of a hand and has become the city's emblem. There's a viewing platform on top.

Schlossmuseum

🎫 *Visit by guided tour (1hr) only, hourly, Mon–Thu 10am–1pm, 2pm–5pm, Sat–Sun 10am–1pm.* 🕐 *Closed major holidays.* 2.50€. ☎ (06151) 240 35. www.schloss-museum-darmstadt.de.

Like most of central Darmstadt, the former residence of the local landgraves was laid to ruins by Second World War bombing raids. Though faithfully restored on the outside, much of the interior is now used by the university. One section is taken up by the **palace museum** *(Schlossmuseum)*, where 22 furnished and decorated rooms provide a glimpse of life at court.

Prinz-Georg-Palais

Schlossgartenstraße 10.
🕐 *Open year-round, Mon–Thu 10am–1pm and 2pm–5pm, Sat–Sun 10am–1pm.* 🕐 *Closed major holidays.* 2.50€. ☎ (06151) 71 32 33. www.porzellanmuseum-darmstadt.de.

A petite Baroque palace built in 1701 by a local landgrave provides a suitably elegant setting for the priceless grand-ducal porcelain **collection**★, almost all gifts from the royal and imperial families of Europe. The table services and ornaments constitute one of the largest collections of porcelain from the Kelsterbach manufactory, as well as from German and Russian manufactories.

The Rococo **Prinz-Georg-Garten** is a rare example of a historical garden laid out in formal geometric patterns following late 18C principles of landscape gardening. Roughly 2ha/5 acres in size, it features scores of charming elements (including a summer house, a tea pavilion, ponds) as well as an orangery.

Hessisches Landesmuseum★

Friedensplatz 1.
🕐 *Closed for renovation until 2011.*
www.hlmd.de.

Grand Duke Ludwig I's private collection of paintings forms the core of this museum, including works by Rembrandt, Dürer and Cranach.

Russian chapel

Excursions

Grube Messel

11.6km/7.2mi north east.
Albert-Schweitzer-Straße 4a. 🕐 *Open Apr–Oct, Tue–Sat 2pm–5pm, Sun 10am–noon; Nov–Mar, Sat 2pm–4pm, Sun 10am–noon, 2pm–4pm.* ☎ (06159) 51 19. www.messel-museum.de.

A UNESCO World Heritage Site, the Messel open-pit is packed with fossilized critters and plants that lived roughly 50 million years ago during the Eocene era. Some 40 animal species have been excavated, most famously a type of primitive horse. Select fossils are displayed at the museum and there's also a platform overlooking the pit.

Jagdschloß Kranichstein

5km/3mi north east.
🕐 *Open Apr–Oct, Wed–Sat 1pm–6pm, Sun 10am–6pm; Nov -Mar, Wed–Sat 2pm–5pm, Sun 10am–5pm.* 🕐 *Closed Dec 24–Jan 6.* 2.70€. ☎ (061 51) 71 86 13. www.jagdschloss-kranichstein.de.

This small hunting lodge, built in 1578 for Landgrave Georg I, now contains an old-school **hunting museum** packed with exhibits ranging from prehistory to today. Rooms brim with trophies, paintings, artefacts as well as a prized collection of guns from four centuries.

DESSAU

POPULATION: 78 500

Dessau is famous as the birthplace of the Bauhaus, for which it was awarded UNESCO World Heritage Site status in 1996. The town was heavily bombed during World War II and, being trapped in East Germany, largely rebuilt in the socialist architectural style, with rather austere results. It is not, however, devoid of charm. Along with the Bauhaus buildings, Prince Leopold III's landscaped gardens are especially enjoyable.

- **Information:** Zerbster Straße 2c, 06844 Dessau. ☎(0340) 204 14 42. www.dessau-tourismus.de.
- ▶ **Orient Yourself:** Flanked by the Elbe and the Mulde rivers, Dessau is just off the A9 autobahn linking Berlin and Munich.
- **Don't Miss:** The Bauhaus buildings that put the city on the cultural map.
- **Organizing Your Time:** Allow three hours to explore the Bauhaus sites.
- **Also See:** WÖRLITZER PARK, WITTENBERG, MAGDEBURG.

Sights

Bauhausgebäude (Bauhaus Building)

Open year-round, daily 10am–6pm. Closed Dec 24 & 31. 4€. Guided tours (1hr) daily 11am and 2pm, Sat–Sun noon and 4pm. 4€. ☎(0340) 650 82 51. www.bauhaus-dessau.de.

The "Design Academy," built according to plans by Walter Gropius, opened in 1926 and displays key features of the Bauhaus style: cubic

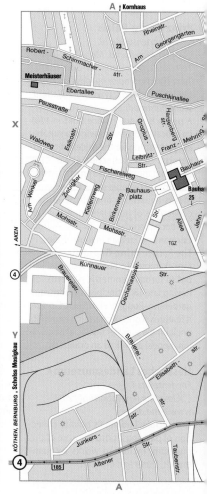

DESSAU		
Akazienwäldchen	BY	2
Bertolt-Brecht-Str.	CX	3
Carl-Maria-von-Weber-Str.	CX	5
Eisenbahnstr.	BY	8
Erdmannsdorffstr.	BY	10
Ferdinand-von-Schill-Str.	BCX	12
Flössergasse	CX	14
Friedrich-Naumann-Str.	CY	15
Friedrich-Schneider-Str.	CX	16
Hausmannstr.	BX	18
Humboldtstr.	CX	20
Johannisstr.	CX	
Kleiststr.	BX	21
Kornhausstr.	AX	23
Liebknechtstr.	ABX	25
Marktstr.	CY	26
Mendelssohnstr.	CX	28
Mozartstr.	CX	29
Richard-Wagner-Str.	CX	30
Schwabestr.	BX	32
Steinstr.	CX	33
Wallstr.	CY	34
Wörlitzer Str.	CX	37
Zerbster Str.	CXY	

blocks, lack of visible supports and glazed façades.

Meisterhäuser (Master Houses)

Ebertallee 59–71.

🕐*Open mid-Feb–Oct, Tue–Sun 10am–
6pm; Nov–mid-Feb, Tue–Sun 10am–5pm.*
5€. *Guided tours (1hr) Tue–Sun
12.30pm and 3.30pm, Sat–Sun 1.30pm.*
*4€. (0340) 661 09 34. www.bauhaus-
dessau.de.*

Walter Gropius masterplanned this small
development of houses for himself and
his Bauhaus professors, built 1925–26.
The **Kandinsky-Klee-Haus** and the **Fei-
ningerhaus** and are open to the public.
The latter houses a center dedicated to
the Dessau-born composer Kurt Weill.

Törtenensiedlung

The Bauhaus-designed Törten housing
estate south of Dessau was built between
1926 and 1928 to relieve a housing shortage
and to give workers a shot at owning their
own homes. Although few of the 314 terraced houses have remained unchanged, the
unmistakable Bauhaus style is still clearly
in evidence.

Other Bauhaus Buildings

Other important Bauhaus structures
include the **Arbeitsamt** *(August-Bebel-
Platz 16)*, a semicircular flat-roofed building designed by Walter Gropius in 1928;
the 1929 **Kornhaus** *(Kornhausstraße 146)*,
a restaurant on the banks of the Elbe
designed by Hermann Baethe and Carl

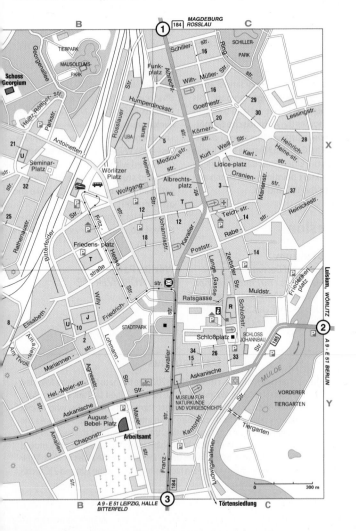

Address Book

For coin ranges, see cover flap.

WHERE TO STAY

City-Pension – *Ackerstraße 3a. (0340) 882 30 76. Fax (0340) 8825017. www.city-pension-dessau.de. 24 rooms.* This central hotel has functionally furnished, light and airy rooms. The generous breakfast buffet is great for getting the day kick-started.

WHERE TO EAT

Das Pächterhaus – *Kirchstraße 1, 06846 Dessau-Ziebigk. (0340) 650 14 47. www.paechterhaus-dessau.de. Closed Mon.* This nicely restored 1743 half-timbered house delivers seasonal dishes and excellent wines in its cozy rooms or the lovely garden in back.

Fieger; **Stahlhaus (***Südstraße 5),* **Haus Fieger** *(Südstraße 6),* **Konsumgebäude** *(Am Dreieck 1)* and **Laubenganghäuser** *(Peterholzstraße 40).*

Georgium

Open year-round, Tue–Sun 10am–5pm. Closed Dec 24 & 31. 3 €. (0340) 61 38 74. www.georgium.de.2 Surrounded by the richly landscaped English-style Georgengarten park, this palace built for Prince Johann Georg in the 18C houses the **Anhaltische Gemäldegalerie**, a prized collection of paintings by Old German Masters (e.g. Lucas Cranach the Elder, Hans Baldung Grien), 18C Frankfurt paintings and Dutch artists from the 16C and 17C.

Excursions

Schloss Luisium

4km/2.5mi east of Dessau. Guided tours (1hr) mid-Mar–Apr, Oct–Nov, Tue–Sun 10am–5pm; May–Sept, Tue–Sun 10am–6pm. 4.50€. (0340) 218 37 11. www.gartenreich.com.

This pint-sized 18C Neoclassical residence was designed by Friedrich Wilhelm von Erdmannsdorff for Princess Luise von Anhalt-Dessau.

Rooms exude refinement with delicate stucco ornamentation and murals, while the idyllic park makes for a fine stroll.

Schloss Mosigkau★

5km/3mi south west of Dessau. tours and fees same as Schloss Luisium. (0340) 52 11 39. www.garten reich.com.

The Rococo summer residence of Princess Anna Wilhelmine is richly furnished, decorated with silk and damask hangings and stucco ceilings and endowed with paintings by Rubens, Van Dyke and other masters.

The surrounding gardens have a romantic feel; don't miss the wonderful leafy labyrinth.

Wörlitz Park★★

see WÖRLITZER PAR

Das Bauhaus

One of the seminal aesthetic movements of the 20C, the Bauhaus School was founded by architect Walter Gropius in Weimar in 1919. He was joined by Paul Klee, Ludwig Mies van der Rohe, Wassily Kandinsky and other top talents of the day who taught architecture, design, painting and sculpture in an interdisciplinary approach. As the political climate in Weimar turned conservative, the school moved to Dessau in 1924 where they molded a new style of living in Bauhaus workshops. In 1932, they moved again, this time to Berlin, only to be closed down for good by the Nazis in 1933. Their design concepts, however, survived, and in fact it is hard to imagine 20C and 21C architecture without the Bauhaus.

BAD DOBERAN

POPULATION: 11 500

Doberan was put on the map in 1793 as the summer residence of Grand Duke Friedrich Franz I, who also founded Germany's first seaside resort in nearby Heiligendamm. Today, the town's principal sight is its superb Gothic brick cathedral. It is also the terminus of a historic narrow gauge train that has delighted young and old since 1886 and hosts international thoroughbred horse races in July and August.

- **Information:** Severinstraße 6, 18209 Bad Doberan. ☎(038203) 621 54. www.bad-doberan-heiligendamm.de.
- ▶ **Orient Yourself:** Bad Doberan is just a short drive west of Rostock via the B105., while Heiligendamm is another 5km/3mi farther northwest on the coast.
- **Don't Miss:** The Münster
- **Also See:** ROSTOCK.

Visit

Münster★★

🕐Open May–Sept, Mon–Sat 9am–6pm, Sun 11am–6pm; Mar, Apr and Oct, Mon–Sat 10am–5pm, Sun 11am–5pm; Nov–Feb, Mon–Sat 10am–4pm, Sun 11am–4pm. 🕐Closed Good Fri and Dec 24. ⊙2€. ⌒Guided tours available. ⌖☎(038203) 627 16. www.doberanermuenster.de.
Consecrated in 1368, this former Cistercian monastery church is a prime example of northern German red-brick Gothic style. Having been spared wartime ravages, it is one of the best preserved Cistercian churches in Germany. The design follows the strict order's architectural mandates with such features as mighty window on the towerless western façade and friezes below the roof line. Inside, the Münster's sumptuous décor reflects its significance as the burial place of the dukes of Mecklenburg.
The church is filled with 13C–14C art worth closer inspection. The magnificent wood-carved **high altar**★ from 1300 is considered the oldest winged altar in existence. Also note the rood altar (1370), embellished with a **triumphal cross**★ (depicted as the Tree of Life). The 11.6m/38ft-high tower-like carved oak **tabernacle**★, the oldest in Germany, dates back to roughly the same period.

Excursions

Molli-Bahn★★ 〔Kids〕

Departs from Bad Doberan Bahnhof (train station) May-Oct, daily 8.30am–6.45pm; Nov–Apr, daily 8.30am–4.45pm. ⊙6.40€ round-trip. ☎(038203) 41 50. www.molli-bahn.de.
Kids and nostalgia buffs love this 1886 steam-powered narrow-gauge railway affectionately known as "**Molli**". It chugs for 15.4km/9.5mi from Bad Doberan to Heiligendamm (20min) and on to Kühlungsborn (35min).

Heiligendamm

6.5km/4mi norwest.
Germany's oldest coastal playground was fashionable with the rich, famous and aristocratic throughout the 19C. In 2007 it again captured the international spotlight when hosting the G8 summit. The architecture is typical of period spa resorts with elegant 19C villas, especially along Professor-Vogel-Straße, attesting to the town's illustrious past.

Kühlungsborn★

14km/8.7mi northwest.
A coastal resort and spa, Kühlungsborn is one of the most popular vacation destinations on the Baltic Sea, thanks to miles of beaches backed by a fragrant pine forest.

DONAUESCHINGEN

POPULATION: 21 300

Owned by the counts (later princes) of Fürstenberg from 1448 until 1806, this tiny town is home to the source of the mighty Danube. Since 1921, the Festival of Contemporary Music has brought avant-garde musicians and music-lovers from around the world to town each October.

- **Information:** Karlstraße 58, 78166 Donaueschingen. ☎(0771) 85 72 21. www.donaueschingen.de.
- ▶ **Orient Yourself:** Donaueschingen is surrounded by the fertile Baar basin and wedged between the Black Forest and the Swabian Jura.
- **Don't Miss:** Source of the Danube.
- **Also See:** ROTTWEIL, FREIBURG IM BREISGAU.

Sights

Source of the Danube

The monumental fountain *(Donauquelle)* was built in the palace park in the 19C. It is considered the official source of the Danube, which travels 2 840km/1 775mi through 13 countries – Germany, Austria, Slovakia, Slovenia, Hungary, Croatia, Bosnia, Serbia and Montenegro, Bulgaria, Romania, Moldova and the Ukraine – on its way east to the Black Sea.

Fürstenberg-Sammlungen (Princely Collections)

Am Karlsplatz 7. ◷*Open Apr–Nov, Tue–Sat 10am–1pm, 2pm–5pm, Sun 10am–5pm.* ◉5€. ☎(0771) 865 63. www.fuerstenberg -kultur.de.

The Fürstenberg family enjoyed collecting precious and unusual objects, which are now displayed at this museum. There are robes and uniforms, goblets made of gold and ivory and a global menagerie of 'taxidermied' animals, but surely the oddest item is Napoléon's travel urinal.

Schloss (Palace)

By prearranged tours only, requiring a minimum of ten people. ◉*10€;* ☎(0771) 8 65 63.

The elegant Fürstenberg palace (1723) retains the luxurious amenities of the period, enriched with gold and silver plate, porcelain and fine Beauvais and Brussels Gobelins (tapestries).

The source of the Danube

R. Chéret/MICHELIN

DORTMUND ★

POPULATION: 587 624

Bye bye collieries and steel mills, hello high-tech and culture! Founded in the 9C, Dortmund has successfully mastered the transition from powerhouse of the industrial Revolution to future-oriented metropolis. Still famous for its beer and soccer team, the city has also extensive parks and hosts major trade shows.

- **Information:** Königswall 18a, 44137 Dortmund. ☎(0231) 18 99 92 22. www.dortmund-tourismus.de.
- ▶ **Orient Yourself:** Dortmund is on the eastern edge of the Ruhr region and is its largest city. A ring road following the course of the medieval town wall encircles the center where most of the museums and churches are located. The Westfalenpark, football stadium and trade fair grounds are in the southern town.
- **Parking:** Abundant garages include a huge one at the main train station.
- **Don't Miss:** Marienkirche, Petrikirche, Museum am Ostwall
- **Especially for Kids:** Westfalenpark
- **Also See:** ESSEN, SAUERLAND, MÜNSTER.

A Bit of History

Dortmund was reborn in the mid-19C with the Industrial Revolution, notably coal, steel and beer. Today, innovation and research, along with trade, insurance and the service sector buttress the local economy.

Sights

Westfalenpark★

Enter from Florianstraße.
🕐*Open year-round, daily 9am–11pm (automatic ticket booths).* ✆*2€.* ☎*(0231) 502 61 00. www.westfalenpark. dortmund.de.*
Dortmund's "green heart", this 70ha/ 173-acre park was created for the 1959 *Bundesgartenschau* (Federal Horticultural Show), which it hosted twice more,

in 1969 and 1991. Its most prominent feature is the Florianturm television tower but the vast park also harbors an open-air stage, a puppet theater, a gallery, a planetarium and the unique German Cookbook Museum. Another highlight is the **Rose Garden** *(Deutsches Rosarium)*, a fragrant oasis with 3 200 varieties from all over the world.

Florianturm

🕐*Open year-round, daily 10am–11pm.* ✆*1.70€.* ☎*(0231) www.fernmeldeturm-dortmund.de.*
Dortmund's television tower stands 220m/722ft tall and was named for the patron saint of gardeners. At 141m/462ft, it features a restaurant and a terrace with superb **panoramas**★ extending as far as the Sauerland on clear days.

Borussia Dortmund

Football (soccer) and Dortmund are practically synonymous thanks to its famous club, the BV Borussia Dortmund. Founded in 1909, it is one of the most successful in the Bundesliga (German Football League) having won six German championships (the last time in 2002). The club also won the UEFA Champions League in 1997. Home games are played at the venerable Westfalenstadion, currently known as Signal Iduna Park thanks to a sponsorship agreement with a local insurance company. One of the largest stadiums in Germany, it has more than 80 000 seats and hosted several matches during the 2006 FIFA World Cup.

St. Petrikirche

Reinoldikirche★

Ostenhellweg 2.

🕐*Open year-round, Mon–Sat 10am–6pm, Sun 1pm–6pm.* ☎*(0231) 52 37 33. www.sanktreinoldi.de.*

Right in the heart of town, this three-nave basilica was first consecrated in 1280 and was repeatedly damaged and rebuilt in subsequent centuries, the last time after World War II. It houses some outstanding 14C and 15C religious works: a sculpted reredos, probably Burgundian work; the bronze eagle pulpit (Adlerpult); a wood statue of St. Reynold, patron saint of the town; and a statue of Charlemagne. The church tower can be climbed for great city views.

Marienkirche★
(Church of St. Mary)

Kleppingstraße 5.

🕐*Open year-round, Tue–Fri 10am–noon, 2pm–4pm, Sat 10am–1pm.* ☎*(0231) 52 65 48. www.st-marien-dortmund.de.*

Blending Romanesque and Gothic elements, this 13C church houses two altars of great artistic merit. The main altar is the 15C **Marienaltar**★★, a triptych by Conrad von Soest noted for its harmonious composition and bright, evocative colors. In the northern side aisle, the **Berswordt Altar**★★ by an anonymous artist depicts the Passion of Christ. Other prized treasures include a 12C painted oak Madonna and Child and the intricately carved choir stalls (1523).

St. Petrikirche
(St. Peter's Church)

Petrikirchhof 7.

🕐*Open year-round, Tue–Fri noon–5pm, Sat–Sun 11am–4pm.* ☎*(0231) 721 541 73. www.stpetrido.de.*

The star exhibit of this 14C Gothic hall church near the main train station is its enormous **main altar**★★ (1521) depicting the Easter story in 48 scenes and 633 gilt carved oak figures. Carved by Master Gilles of Antwerp, it is known as the "Golden Miracle of Dortmund".

Museum für Kunst und Kulturgeschichte (Museum of Art and Cultural History)

Hansastraße 31.

🕐*Open year-round, Tue–Sun 10am–5pm, Thu 8pm, Sat noon–5pm.* 🕐*Closed Jan 1, Dec 24, 25 & 31.* ⊜*3€.* ♿☎*(0231) 502 55 22. www.mkk.dortmund.de.*

Delve into Dortmund history by perusing the paintings, sculptures, furnishings and crafts engagingly displayed inside a converted Art Deco bank building. Keep an eye out for the **Dortmund Treasure**★ *(Dortmunder Goldschatz)*, consisting of 444 gold coins, most from the 4C.

The emotive quality of Conrad von Soest's Madonna sculptures is striking, as is the craftsmanship of the Romanesque triumphal cross. Other rooms feature paintings by Spitzweg, Liebermann, Slevogt, Corinth and other 18C and 19C masters.

Museum am Ostwall

Ostwall 7.
🕐*Open year-round, Tue–Sun 10am–5pm, Thu 8pm, Sat noon–5pm.* 🕐*Closed Jan 1, Dec 24, 25 & 31.* 👓*3€.* 👟☎*(0231) 50 23 247. www.museendortmund.de.*
Fans of 20C and 21C art will be drawn to this fine museum where works by German Expressionists, most notably members of the Blue Rider and Bridge artist groups (Schmidt-Rottluf, Marc, Macke), form the core of the collection.
There are also edgy works by the Fluxus and Group ZERO art movements and contemporary photography, for instance by Jochen Gerz or Anna and Bernhard Blume.

Naturkundemuseum (Museum of Natural History)

Münsterstraße 271.
🕐*Open year-round, Tue–Sun 10am–5pm.* 🕐*Closed Jan 1, Dec 24, 25 & 31.* 👟☎*(0231) 502 48 56. www.museendortmund.de.*
Showstoppers at this classic natural history museum include a 55-million-year-old prehistoric horse, lifesize dinosaur models, a 650kg/1433lb rock crystal and the tropical South Seas aquarium.

Brauereimuseum (Brewery Museum)

Steigerstraße 16. 🕐*Open year-round, Tue–Sun 10am–5pm, Thu 8pm, Sat noon–5pm.* 👓*1.50€, Sat free.* 👟☎*(0231) 840 02 00. brauereimuseum.dortmund.de.*
Dortmund's beer history is creatively chronicled in the machine hall of the now defunct Hansa brewery.

Address Book

👟*For coin ranges, see the Legend on the cover flap.*

WHERE TO STAY

🍴🍴**Haus Überacker** – *Wittbräucker Straße 504 (B234), Dortmund-Höchsten.* ☎*(02304) 98 28 50. www.haus-ueber acker.de. Closed 3 weeks in Aug/Sept. 17 rooms. Restaurant* 🍴🍴🍴. Good family-run hotel in a neat half-timbered house with partly paneled rooms with solid wooden furnishings. The restaurant extends onto a heated winter garden and a pleasant terrace.

🍴🍴🍴**Parkhotel Wittekindshof** – *Westfalendamm 270 (B1).* ☎*(0231) 519 30. 65 rooms. Restaurant* 🍴🍴🍴. The neutral-toned décor is a meditation in understatement at this upscale hotel catering both to leisure and business travelers. The restaurant has an elegant touch, the Stube is more rustic.

WHERE TO EAT

🍴🍴**Hövels Hausbrauerei** – *Hoher Wall 5.* ☎*(0231) 914 54 70. www. hoevels-hausbrauerei.de.* Enjoy robust regional and German cuisine among the shiny copper vats and whimsical décor of this micro-brewery founded in 1854. A most charming ambassador of Dortmund's beer tradition.

🍴🍴🍴**Pfefferkorn** – *Hoher Wall 38.* ☎*(0231) 14 36 44. www.pfefferkorn-dort mund.de. Reservations recommended.* The old German-style décor, friendly service and pleasant atmosphere make this restaurant a good address for juicy steaks, fresh salads and such seasonal specialities as white asparagus, wild mushrooms and game.

ENTERTAINMENT

Borussia Dortmund – *Strobelallee 50. Tickets* ☎*(01805) 30 90 00. www.bvg.de.* Dortmund's famous football team plays home games at the Signal Iduna Park.

Konzerthaus Dortmund – *Brückstraße 21.* ☎*(01805) 44 80 44. www. konzerthaus-dortmund.de.* Philharmonic concerts, jazz and chansons provide entertainment at the city's architecturally distinguished concert hall.

Casino Hohensyburg – *Hohensyburgstraße 200.* ☎*(0231) 7 74 00. www.casino-hohensyburg.de.* Challenge Lady Luck at this chic casino below a ruined medieval castle about 13km/8mi south of the city center.

DRESDEN★★★

POPULATION: 504 795

Risen from the ashes of World War II and relative neglect during the Cold War years, Dresden has made a full-on comeback and can rightly reclaim its seat in the pantheon of European capitals of arts, culture and architecture. One night of fire carpet bombing in February 1945, just weeks before the armistice, laid waste to centuries of vision and cash expended by a series of Saxon rulers, most notably August the Strong. At least 35 000 people died in the conflagration. Since reunification, reconstruction has proceeded at a steady pace, culminating in the reopening of the landmark Frauenkirche in 2006.

- **Information:** Prager Straße 2, 01069 Dresden. ☎(0351) 49 19 21 00. www.dresden-tourist.de.
- **Orient Yourself:** Dresden sits in the heart of Saxony, on the banks of the Elbe and and is served by the A4, A13 and A14 autobahns.
- **Parking:** Garages abound, especially near the Frauenkirche and the Zwinger.
- **Don't Miss:** The Old Town, Frauenkirche, Zwinger, Grünes Gewölbe.
- **Organizing Your Time:** Budget at least a couple of days for this amazing city.
- **Also See:** MEISSEN, BAUTZEN, GÖRLITZ.

A Bit of History

"Florence on the Elbe" – Dresden's major development took place in the early 18C during the reigns of Electors **August the Strong** and his son Augustus III. These powerful patrons of the arts enticed scores of craftsmen and artists from Italy to build such magnificent Baroque edifices as the Zwinger, the Japanese Palace and the Hofkirche (court church). They also amassed outstanding collections of paintings and objets d'art.

The Night of the Apocalypse – A few months before the end of World War II, on the night of 13–14 February, 1945, Dresden was the target of one of the Allies' most destructive air raids. Three successive waves of Lancaster bombers left the blackened skeletons of the city's monuments emerging from a waste of smoking ruins, and a death toll of between 35 000 and 135 000. In all, 75 percent of the city was destroyed. Restoration of Dresden's historic sites and the rebuilding of residential quarters have given the town a special quality that marries urbanism with heritage.

Walking Tours

The Elbe divides Dresden into two distinct parts. South of the river, the old town (Altstadt) is dominated by the Zwinger, Semperoper and Frauenkirche; in the north, the new town (Neustadt) is anchored by Albertplatz.

Historic Center★★★ (Altstadt)

Semperoper★★ (Semper Opera House)

Numerous operas premiered at this famous venue, including Der Rosenkavalier by Richard Strauss. Designed by Gottfried Semper in Italian Renaissance style, it first opened in 1841 but had to be rebuilt a mere three decades later after a fire. Six sculptures surviving from the original structure were incorporated into this modern replica, open since 1985. They represent Schiller and Goethe (above the entrance), Shakespeare and Sophocles (on the left) and Molière and Euripides (on the right). Tours are only available on rehearsal- and performance-free days. Enquire at the tourist office or call ☎(0351) 491 14 96.

- Cross Theaterplatz and head to the Hofkirche.

Ehemalige Katholische Hofkirche★★ (Former Court Cathedral)

○Open year-round, Mon–Tue 9am–6pm, Wed–Thu 9am–5pm, Fri 1pm–5pm, Sat 10am–5pm, Sun noon–4pm. ☎(0351) 484 4712.

This enormous 18C basilica is the largest church in Saxony and was strongly influenced by the Italian Baroque. It is dominated by an 86m/282ft bell tower and decorated with statues of the saints and apostles. Above the high altar, a painting (1765) by Anton Raphael Mengs depicts the Ascension. The Baroque pulpit was executed by Balthasar Permoser in 1722, while the organ was the last work (1750–55) of the master craftsman **Gottfried Silbermann**. Several kings and princes of Saxony are buried in the crypt, as is the heart of August the Strong, whose body lies in Cracow cathedral.

▶ *Head east of the cathedral along Augustusstraße.*

Fürstenzug★ (Procession of the Princes)

Augustusstraße is paralleled by a stunningly detailed 102m/335ft-long ceramic mural hand-painted onto 24 000 Meissen porcelain tiles. It depicts Saxon rulers from 1123 to 1904.

A Line of Organ Builders

Gottfried Silbermann (1683–1753) apprenticed in Strasbourg with his brother Andreas, famous for creating Alsace organs of Ebersmunster. In 1710, Gottfried settled in Freiberg, designing instruments with remarkable tone. Of the 51 organs attributed to him, those in Freiberg are the best. Gottfried's nephew Johann Andreas followed suit, and designed 54 organs in the Upper Rhine region.

▶ *Turn left onto Brühlsche Gasse and follow it to the river.*

Brühlsche Terrasse

The so-called "Balcony of Europe", this riverside promenade was built onto the ancient fortifications and offers fantastic **views★** of the Elbe and the Neustadt.

▶ *Follow the promenade east, turn right onto Münzgasse and head to Neumarkt.*

Johanneum

Augustusstraße 1. ○Open year-round, Tue–Sun 10am–5pm. ○Closed Jan 1, Dec 24–25 & 31. ◌3€. ☎(0351) 864 40. www.verkehrsmuseum-dresden.de.

J. Bouraly/MICHELIN

Procession of Dukes of Saxe-Wettin, an immense mosaic covering one of the palace façades

DRESDEN

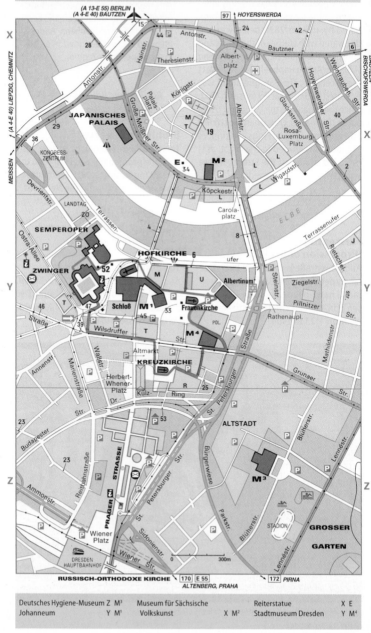

Address Book

👛 *For coin ranges, see the Legend on the cover flap.*

BASIC INFORMATION

Getting There – Drivers coming from Leipzig should take the A14 east to the A4 *(114km/70mi)*; from Berlin, follow the A113 south to the A13 *(190km/118mi)*.

Dresden Airport *(DRS; ☎(0351) 881 33 60; www.dresden-airport.de)* is less than 10km/6.2mi north of the city center. S-Bahn trains (S2) run into town from the airport throughout the day.

There is also direct **Deutsche Bahn** train service to and from Leipzig, Berlin, Meissen, Frankfurt and other cities. Note that Dresden has two railway stations: *Dresden-Hauptbahnhof* south of the Old Town and *Dresden-Neustadt* (Schlesischer Platz 1). Most trains stop at both stations.

Getting Around – Dresden's largely pedestrianized historic center contains most sights and museums and is compact enough for walking. The city is served by a network of trams and buses operated by Dresdner Verkehrsbetriebe (DVB; ☎(0351) 857 10 11; www.dv-bag. de). There are service centers at the Hauptbahnhof, *Mon–Fri 7am–7pm, Sat 8am–6pm, Sun 9am–6pm*; Postplatz, *Mon–Fri 7am–8pm, Sat 8am–6pm, Sun 9am–6pm*; Pirnaischer Platz and Albertplatz, *Mon–Fri 7am–6pm, Sat 9am–4pm*. Tickets are available at station vending machines, aboard, and at service centers. The basic fare is 1.80€. One-day passes *(Tageskarte)* cost 4.50€ and are worthwhile if you plan on multiple trips. One-day family/group tickets *(Familientageskarte)* start at 6€.

The DVB is integrated into the Verkehrsverbund Oberelbe *(VVO; ☎(0180) 22 66 22 66, Mon–Fri 9am–6pm, Sat 9am–4pm; www.vvo-online.de)*, which also covers "Swiss Saxony" *(Sächsische Schweiz)*, the eastern Erzgebirge mountains and parts of the Oberlausitz area

VISITOR INFORMATION

For **ticket reservations**, call Dresden Tourism at ☎(0351) 49 19 22 33; for room reservations the number is ☎(0351) 49 19 22 22 and for general information, dial ☎(0351) 49 19 21 00. Staff is standing by Mon–Fri 8am–6pm,

Sat 9am–4pm, Sun 9am–2pm. Or visit www.dresden.de.

Dresden Tourism also has two information offices: one across from the Hauptbahnhof (main train station) at Prager Straße 2, *Mon–Sat 10am–7pm*; the other at Schinkelwache on Theaterplatz near the Semperoper, *Mon–Thu 10am–6pm, Fri 10am–7pm, Sat–Sun 10am–5pm*.

City magazines *SAX* (www.cybersax. de) and the freebies *BLITZ!* (www.blitz-stadtmagazin.com) and *Frizz* (www. frizz-magazin.de) provide complete listings information. *SAX* is sold at newspaper kiosks and in bookstores, while the other two are usually found in bars, boutiques and the tourist offices as is the monthly *Dresdner Kulturmagazin* (www.dresdner.nu).

POST OFFICES WITH LATE HOURS

Altmarkt-Galerie Webergasse 2, inside mall; Mon–Sat 9.30am–9pm

Königsbrücker Straße 21–29, Mon–Fri 9am–7pm, Sat 10am–1pm.

DAILY PAPERS

Sächsische Zeitung (www.sz-online.de); *Dresdner Neueste Nachrichten* (www.dnn-online.de).

INTERNET

www.dresden-tourist.de; www.dresden-online.de; www.dresden.de.

TOURIST CARDS

These are available at tourist offices and DVB service centers.

Dresden-City-Card for 21€ (valid 48hr) lets an adult (plus any children under 6) use all buses, trams and Elbe ferries, plus free entry to 12 museums of the State Art Collections and discounts for other museums.

Dresden-Regio-Card for 32€ (valid 72hr) includes free rides on the S-Bahn trains along the Elbe to e.g. Meissen, Pirna and Königstein, discounts for rides on various narrow-gauge trains, and discounts at the region's main museums.

SIGHTSEEING

CITY TOURS BY COACH

Stadtrundfahrt Dresden – ☎(0351) 99 56 50, www.stadtrundfahrt.com, 1hr 30min tours, every 15 to 30min. First departure 9:30am, last one 5pm.

Day tickets cost 20€ and are valid for unlimited stops, basic tours around the Zwinger, Frauenkirche, Pfunds Molkerei and the Fürstenzug, an evening city tour, and admission to Schloss Pillnitz. Departure Augustusbrücke/Schloßplatz and 21 other stops such as Königstraße, Dr. Külz-Straße and the Frauenkirche. *Combination tickets with the Grünes Gewölbe cost 35€.*

WALKING TOURS

Themed walking tours are organized by igeltours—Dresdens andere Stadtführung; *(0351) 804 45 57; www.igeltour-dresden.de.*

BOAT TOURS

Sächsische Dampfschiffahrt, (0351) 86 60 90, *www.saechsische-dampf-schiffahrt.de,* offers 90min Elbe cruises in faux paddle-wheel steamers for 11€. Trips depart daily at 11am, 1pm, 3pm and 5pm from the Terrassenufer. Other otpions include trips to Schloss Pillnit, Meißen and "Swiss Saxony."

TRABI SAFARI

(0351) 899 00 60, www.trabi-safari.de, from 20€. Climb behind the wheel of an authentic GDR Trabant car and follow your guide who narrates the tour while driving a separate vehicle,

WHERE TO STAY

Gästehaus Mezcalero – *Königsbrücker Straße 64.* (0351) 81 07 70. *www.mezcalero.de. 23 rooms.* 6€. Artistically decorated with a Mexican-Aztec theme, this upscale hostel-hotel puts you equally close to nightlife and the sights. The cheapest beds are in dorms and some rooms share baths.

Hotel Privat – *Forststraße 22.* (0351) 81 17 70. *www.das-nichtraucher-hotel.de. 30 rooms. Restaurant.* On a quiet residential street, this small hotel has modern, spic-and-span rooms, a homey ambience and an generous breakfast buffet served in the wintergarten restaurant with terrace.

Gasthof Coschütz – *Kleinnaundorfer Straße 1.* (0351) 401 03 58. *www.gasthof-coschuetz.de. 11 rooms. Restaurant.* Four generations have run this well-furnished, comfortable hotel on the city outskirts. The restaurant features regional cuisine, select wines and seating on two terraces in summer.

Hotel Goldener Apfel – *Schulweg 3, 01326 Dresden-Pillnitz.* (0351) 26 16 60. www.goldener-apfel. de. *19 rooms.* Neart Pillnitz Palace, a 19C village school has morphed into a modern hotel with integrated health facilities, including saunas, steam rooms and hydro-massages. Breakfast is served in the historic tea tavern.

Hotel Zum Nußbaum – *Wirtschaftsweg 13.* (0351) 427 36 90. *www.hotel-nussbaum-dresden.de. 13 rooms. Restaurant.* This pleasant, intimate hotel on the city outskirts has well-kept rooms with no-nonsense furniture, and a restaurant with terrace. Bike rentals are available.

Landhaus Lockwitzgrund – *Lockwitzgrund 100.* (0351) 271 00 10. *www.landhaus-lockwitzgrund.de. 9 rooms. Restaurant.* The former stables of a noodle factory have been ingeniously converted into a romantic country estate. Rooms pair modern conveniences with historic features and the upscale restaurant enjoys a fine reputation with guests and locals alike.

Hotel Schloss Eckberg – *Bautzner Straße 134.* (0351) 809 90. *www.hotel-schloss-eckberg.de. 84 rooms. Restaurant.* A dreamy riverside park filled with art pieces surrounds this unique estate. Choose from antique-filled rooms in a Neo-Gothic palace or modern ones in the Kavaliershaus, which also has three saunas. All guests enjoy breakfast at the palace which also has a superb restaurant with views of the city silhouette across the river.

Martha Hospiz – *Nieritzstraße 11.* (0351) 817 60. *www.martha-hospiz.de. Closed Dec 22–27. 50 rooms. Restaurant.* Affiliated with a non-profit Christian organization, this hotel has a superbly central location, nice new rooms with classic furniture, some in Biedermeier style, and a cozy restaurant specialized in potato-based dishes in the vaulted cellars.

Hotel Bayerischer Hof – *Antonstraße 33.* (0351) 82 93 70. *www.bayerischer-hof-dresden.de. 50 rooms. Restaurant. Closed Sun.* This classy hotel offers spacious, elegant rooms with beautiful cherrywood furniture, ultra-comfy beds and a restaurant serving Bavarian and Saxon specialties.

WHERE TO EAT

Alte Meister – *Theaterplatz 1a.* ☎ *(0351) 481 04 26. www.altemeister.net.* This restaurant has bright, high-ceilinged and partly frescoed rooms. The atmosphere is casual; the terrace takes in the opera house and square.

Historisches Fischhaus – *Fischhausstraße 14 (5km/3mi north east of city center via Bautzner Str.)* ☎ *(0351) 89 91 00. www.fischhaus-dresden.de.* In business since 1573, this ambience-laden restaurant in a leafy setting on the city outskirts specializes in the fresh catch of the day. It is also a great place to try local beer and wine.

Kurhaus Kleinschachwitz – *Berthold-Haupt-Straße 128, 01259 Dresden-Kleinschachwitz.* ☎ *(0351) 200 19 96. www.kurhaus.net.* Right next to the ferry landing for Pillnitz Palace, this restaurant is noted for its beautiful architecture and good food. With its riverside beer garden, it makes a perfect refreshment break, especially if you're cycling along the Elbe River.

Le Maréchal de Saxe – *Königstraße 15.* ☎ *(0351) 810 58 80.* Elegant without being stuffy, this café-bar-restaurant is a good spot to indulge in fine French and fish specialities. Dark wood, gleaming tables and friendly service all contribute to a delightful evening.

Luisenhof – *Bergbahnstraße 8, 01324 Dresden-Weißer Hirsch.* ☎ *(0351) 214 99 60. www.luisenhof.org.* Set in a historic 19C building, this restaurant is called "Dresden's balcony" for its sweeping town views. Only fresh, seasonal ingredients are used and the cakes are homemade and delicious.

Opernrestaurant – *Theaterplatz 2.* ☎ *(0351) 491 15 21.* Set in an cube-shaped annex to the Semperoper, this restaurant is great for a glass of bubbly or a nibble before or after the opera. Choose from the ground-floor café or the classic dining rooms upstairs.

Pattis – *Merbitzer straße 53.* ☎ *(0351) 425 50. www.pattis.de. Closed*

2 weeks in Jan and Aug and Sun. Reservations recommended. Part of the Romantik-Hotel Pattis, this restaurant does a great job at resurrecting recipes once served at the Saxon court. If you just want a light meal, head to the bistro, otherwise book a table in the gourmet dining room.

Villandry – *Jordanstraße 8.* ☎ *(0351) 899 67 46. www.villandry.de. Closed Sun. Reservations recommended.* A bistro look and an accomplished Mediterranean menu characterize this relaxed restaurant which serves delicious international cuisine with a charming side of live music.

Caroussel – *Rähnitzgasse 19.* ☎ *(0351) 800 30. www.buelow-residenz. de. Closed Mon–Tue. Reservations recommended.* Meals are celebrations in this elegant dining room presided over by chef Dirk Schröer. His contemporary culinary concoctions use the best the region has to offer – from venison to lamb to mushrooms and fruit. In fine weather, enjoy your meal alfresco in the glass-covered inner courtyard.

Bean & Beluga – *Bautzner Landstraße 32.* ☎ *(0351) 44 00 88 00. www.bean-and-beluga.de. Closed Sun–Mon.* Stefan Herrmann's gourmet outpost has critics and patrons swooning. His modern cuisine weaves together global flavors, textures and ingredients into innovative dishes that get little competition from the restaurant's purist décor. Bistro downstairs.

TAKING A BREAK

Café Schinkelwache – *Theaterplatz 2.* ☎ *(0351) 490 39 09. www.restaurant-dresden.de.* A stately old guardhouse designed by Karl Friedrich Schinkel has been reborn as a classic café where you can relax from sightseeing over fresh pastries or a light meal.

Café Toscana – *Schillerplatz 7 (5km/3mi east of old town on the Elbe).* ☎ *(0351) 310 07 44.* This popular coffeehouse with winter garden and terrace boasts views of the *Blaues Wunder* bridge and a 12m/39ft-long cake buffet.

Dresdner Molkerei Gebrüder Pfund – *Bautzner Straße 79.* ☎ *(0351) 810 59 48.* Possibly the world's most famous dairy shop, Pfunds is decorated with a kaleidoscope of hand-painted tiles and comes with a café and restaurant specialized in cheese-based dishes. It is hugely popular with coach tourists.

ENTERTAINMENT

Cafés, bistros and restaurants abound in the Old Town around the Frauen-kirche and on Weisse Gasse near Alt-markt. In the Neustadt, upscale places concentrate on Königstraße, while a lively, more youthful scene dominates north of Albertplatz, especially on Alaunstraße and Louisenstraße.

Ballhaus Watzke – *Kötzschenbroder Straße 1 (corner of Leipziger Straße). ☎(0351) 85 29 20. www.watzke.de.* This brew-pub is set in a former dance hall with picture-perfect views of the Old Town from the riverside beer garden. Enjoy them while quaffing a mug of cold unfiltered house lager and tucking into a plate of hearty *Haxe* (roasted pork knuckle).

Brauhaus am Waldschlösschen – *Am Brauhaus 8b (2km/1.2mi east of Albertplatz; follow Bautzner Straße). ☎(0351) 652 39 00. www.waldschloess-chen.de.* At this attractive brew-pub you can enjoy a delicious *Dunkel* or a refreshing *Hefeweizen* along with cocktails and traditional dishes. There's live music Mon–Sat and splendid views across the Elbe from the beer garden anchored by a seven-tiered bronze fountain.**Italienisches Dörfchen** – *Theaterplatz 3. ☎(0351) 498 160. www.italienisches-doerfchen.de.* This gastro complex includes a fine Italian restaurant, a café, a beer garden and a riverside terrace. Some rooms have magnificent exposed beams, stucco-work and ceiling frescoes.

Winzerstube Zum Rebstock – *Hauptstraße 17. ☎(0351) 5 63 35 44. www.winzerstube-zum-rebstock.de.* This sweet little wine tavern overlooks a quiet courtyard accented with a fountain and herb garden. Glasses of wine from Saxony and the Nahe region can be paired with nibbles or a full meal.

Fährgarten Johannstadt– *Käthe-Kollwitz-Ufer 23b. ☎(0351) 459 62 62. www.faehrgarten.de. Closed Nov–Mar.* Kick back in this leafy beer garden and watch the Elbe steamers pass by, preferably at sunset. If the aroma of wood-fired steaks doesn't tempt you, perhaps the delicious beers and wines will. Children have a big playground to burn off excess energy.

Semperoper – *Theaterplatz. ☎(0351) 491 17 05. www.semperoper.de.* An evening at this illustrious opera house will not be soon forgotten. The busy performance schedules includes not only full-length operas but also ballet, jazz, classical concerts and contemporary dance. Book early or hope for last-minute cancellations.

SHOPPING

Dresden's main shopping streets are Prager Straße (department stores) and Wilsdruffer Straße. The best and most central all-purpose mall is the Altmarkt-Galerie. In the New Town, steer toward Königstraße (elegant boutiques), Hauptstraße (chains) and Alaunstraße (funky boutiques),

Kunsthofpassage – *enter from Alaunstraße 70 or Görlitzer Straße 21). www.kunsthof-dresden.de.* This series of five courtyards, each designed by a different local artist, brims with inde-pendent boutiques selling everything from ceramics to jewelry, fashion to home accessories.

Neustädter Markthalle – *Metzer Straße 1. ☎(0351) 810 54 45. www.markthalle-dresden.de.* This sensitively restored 1899 market hall has been reborn as a gourmet shoppers's nirvana. Pick up fresh produce and local specialities along with toys and teas, flowers and Freiberg porcelain on the ground floor and in the basement, or check out the fashions on the upper floor.

Markets – Altmarkt, Mon–Sat from 8am. The Spring Market *(Frühlings-markt)* is held here in May, the Autumn Market *(Herbstmarkt)* in September and the *Striezelmarkt* in December.

The Elbe and the brilliantly reconstructed Baroque town

The Renaissance-era **Johanneum** once housed the royal stables and is now the city's **Transport Museum** *(Verkehrsmuseum)*. An impressive collection of vintage cars, model trains and original planes illustrate the evolution of public transport.

▸ *Leaving the Johanneum, turn right and walk to the Frauenkirche.*

Frauenkirche★ (Church of Our Lady)

ⓒ*Open year-round, daily 10am–noon, 1pm–6pm.* ☜*Guided tours (50min) available.* ♿☎*(0351) 6560 6100. www. frauenkirche-dresden.de.*

Designed by Georg Bähr and first consecrated in 1726, this Dresden landmark was left as a postwar ruin for decades. After reunification, funds poured in from around the world to finance the resurrection of this stunning church. An exact replica of the original reopened in 2005, once again topped by the striking 95m/312ft-high 23.5m/77ft-wide dome that so characterizes the town silhouette. **Views★★** from the top are stupendous *(ⓒopen Mar–Oct, Mon–Sat 10am–6pm, Sun 12.30pm–7pm (Nov–Feb daily to 4pm).*

▸ *Head east on Landhausstraße, make a right on Wilsdruffer Straße and a left on pedestrianized Weisse Gasse.*

Neues Rathaus (New Town Hall)

This early 20C neo-Renaissance building is surmounted by a golden statue of Hercules. Trips up the 100m/328ft **tower** *(partly by elevator)* are available *(ⓒopen May–Oct, daily 10am–6pm; ☞2.50€).*

Kreuzkirche★

ⓒ*Open Mon–Sat 10am–6pm, Sun 10am–6pm (Nov–Mar 4pm).* ☎*(0351) 439 39 20. www.dresdner-kreuzkirche.de.*

Just west of the Town Hall, Dresden's oldest church has origins in the early 13C and has been home to the famous Kreuzchor boys' choir for nearly as long. The current structure is a Neo-Baroque beauty from 1900 with more than 3 600 seats, making it one of the largest Protestant churches in Germany.

Neustadt★ (New Town)

Reached via Augustusbrücke, Dresden's Neustadt spreads across an ancient city quarter destroyed by fire in 1685 and subsequently rebuilt in stone. It was spared from total devastation in 1945. Just beyond the bridge, Neustädter Markt is dominated by the gilded **equestrian statue★** of August the Strong. Stroll along the pedestrianized **Hauptstraße** to reach Albertplatz square, which is graced by two fountains.

Königstraße, which radiates southeast from Albertplatz, is one of Dresden's most elegant streets and lined with beautifully restored Baroque, neoclassical and Gründerzeit town houses.

From Albertplatz, follow Alaunstraße north into the lively student quarter teeming with bars, cafes, pubs, clubs and restaurants and accented by the **Kunsthofpassage**.

Sights

Zwinger★★★

Commissioned by August the Strong, master architect **Matthäus Daniel Pöppelmann** (1682–1737) designed and realized this stunning Baroque palace between 1711 and 1728. Sculpture was provided by Balthasar Perlmoser.

Painstakingly reconstructed, the complex now houses several museums (most famously the Old Masters Picture Gallery), and is one of Dresden's key attractions.

Note that several galleries are being reorganized and others closed in the coming years.

The huge rectangular courtyard is bookended by the **Wallpavillon**★★ (Rampart Pavilion) to the north and the **Glockenspielpavillon** (Carillon Pavilion) on the opposite end. It is in the former that the Zwinger's harmonious marriage of sculpture and architecture best expresses itself. Crowning the pavilion is August the Strong's idol, **Hercules,** carrying the world on his back. The Wallpavillon leads to a terrace and the **Nymphenbad**★★ (Bath of the Nymphs).

The southwest side of the complex, the elegant **Zwinger Gallery**, is best seen from the outside passing beneath the **Kronentor** (Crown Gate). Opposite, the **Semperbau** (Semper Building) is a 1847 work of Gottfried Semper with sculpture by Ernst Rietschel.

Gemäldegalerie Alte Meister★★★ (Old Masters Picture Gallery)

Semperbau, west wing.
Open year-round, Tue–Sun 10am–6pm.
Closed Dec 25. 7€. (0351) 491 420 00. www.skd-dresden.de.

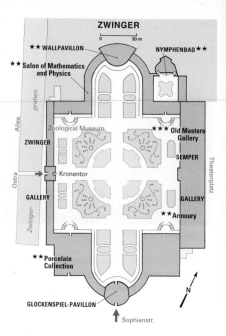

ZWINGER

★★ WALLPAVILLON
NYMPHENBAD ★★
★★ Salon of Mathematics and Physics
Zoological Museum
★★★ Old Masters Gallery
ZWINGER
SEMPER
Kronentor
GALLERY
GALLERY
★★ Armoury
★★ Porcelain Collection
GLOCKENSPIEL-PAVILLON
Sophienstr.

This collection of paintings is one of the best of its kind in the world. The most important masters from the Italian Renaissance and the Baroque period are represented, as are Dutch and Flemish painters from the 17C.

The admission ticket also includes access to the **Armory** as well as selections from the Sculpture Collection and the New Masters Gallery (*moved to the Semperbau until at least 2009 while their usual home, the Albertinum, is undergoing renovation*).

The reorganization may affect the presentation of the permanent collection of Old Masters outlined in the diagram.

Ground floor:
Galleries 1–4 contain tapestries after sketches by Raphael and numerous townscapes by Bernardo Bellotto, otherwise known as Canaletto, who painted Dresden and Pirna with such extraordinary precision that many were used as blueprints during the postwar reconstruction.

Galleries 5–6 house paintings by Dresden masters.

1st floor:

Galleries 101–102: Works by Silvestre and Canaletto.

Galleries 104–106 and 108–111: Flemish and Dutch painting from the 16C–17C. Rembrandt's *Self-portrait with Saskia* (**Gallery 106**), Rubens' *Bathsheba*, and Vermeer's *Girl Reading a Letter by the Window* (**Gallery 108**).

Gallery 107: Paintings by the Early Netherlandish (Jan van Eyck) and Early German (masterpieces by Holbein, Cranach the Elder and Dürer) schools.

Gallery 112: 17C French painting (Claude Lorrain, Nicolas Poussin).

Galleries 113–121: 16C Italian painting. Works by Veronese, Tintoretto, Giorgione *(Sleeping Venus)*, Titian, in **galleries 117–119**. A highlight is Raphael's portrayal of the Virgin and Child, the *Sistine Madonna*, in **gallery 117**.

Gallery 116: Paintings by Botticelli, Mantegna and Pintoricchio *(Portrait of a Boy)*.

2nd floor:

Gallery 201: Pastel painting. Jean-Étienne Liotard's *Chocolate Girl*, world's largest collection of works by Rosalba Carriera (75 pastels).

Gallery 202: 18C French painting.

Galleries 203–207: 18C Italian painting with works by Tiepolo and Crespi.

Galleries 208–210: Spanish painting (El Greco, Murillo, Zurbarán, Velázquez).

Galleries 211–216: 17C and 18C German painting.

Porzellansammlung★★ (Porcelain Collection)

East Asia Gallery, via Glockenspielpavillon. ⓒ*Open year-round, Tue–Sun 10am–6pm.* ⓒ*Closed Dec 25.* ⊙6€. ♿⚑*(0351) 491 420 00. www.skd-dresden.de.*

This gallery displays porcelain from the famous manufactory at **Meißen**, as well as rare and precious imports from Japan and China. Do not miss the "dragoon vases" for which the elector paid with 600 dragoon soldiers in 1717, or the life-size porcelain figures from Meißen on the upper floor (early 18C).

GEMÄLDEGALERIE

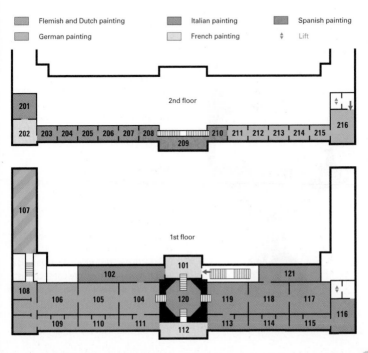

- Flemish and Dutch painting
- German painting
- Italian painting
- French painting
- Spanish painting
- ↕ Lift

2nd floor

201 · 202 · 203 · 204 · 205 · 206 · 207 · 208 · 209 · 210 · 211 · 212 · 213 · 214 · 215 · 216

1st floor

107 · 108 · 102 · 101 · 121 · 106 · 105 · 104 · 120 · 119 · 118 · 117 · 116 · 109 · 110 · 111 · 112 · 113 · 114 · 115

Dresden-Hellerau: Germany's first garden city

Ebenezer Howard's late 19C "Garden City Movement" inspired German entrepreneur Karl Camillo Schmidt to found a similarly progressive community in Hellerau in 1909 (www.dresden-hellerau.de). Top architects Heinrich Tessenow, Hermann Muthesius and Curt Frick collaborated on what would become Germany's first Garden City. The community and its annual festival attracted artists and visionaries from throughout Europe. Under the National Socialists and in the postwar years it served military purposes but is slowly being returned to its former glory.

Rüstkammer★★ (Armory)

Semperbau, east wing.
◎*Open year-round, Tue–Sun 10am–6pm.*
◎*Closed Dec 25.* ⊜*3€.* ☎ *(0351) 491 420 00. www.skd-dresden.de.*
Even dedicated pacifists should be able to appreciate the artistry of this precious collection of hand-crafted ceremonial weapons. The inventory includes 1 300 objects from the 15C to 19C and hailing from places throughout Europe and the Middle East. Only a selection is currently on view until the opening of a more extensive exhibit on the first and second floors of the Residenzschloss.

Mathematisch-Physikalischer Salon★★ (Salon of Mathematics and Physic)

◎*Closed until spring 2010.* ☎*(0351) 491 420 00. www.skd-dresden.de.*

*Green Vault Collections –
Diana's Bath (1704)*

Staatl. Kunstsammlungen Dresden

The inventive genius of scientists is documented in the clocks and instruments of the 16C to 19C, including sun, sand, oil, artistic and automatic time pieces.

Albertinum

This majestic Neo-Renaissance building normally houses the New Masters Gallery and the Sculpture Collection but is closed for a long restoration expected to last until at least 2009. In the meantime, changing displays from the permanent collections are presented within the Old Masters Picture Gallery and the Porcelain Collection in the Semperbau.

Residenzschloss

After a top-to-bottom makeover, Dresden's Renaissance palace now houses the dazzling Historical Green Vault and the New Green Vault, both brimming with hand-crafted *objets d'art* assembled by August the Strong.
⊛*Note that admission to the* **Historical Green Vault** *is by timed ticket only and limited to 120 people per hour. Advance reservations are highly recommended and available online (www.sk-dresden. de—payment by MasterCard or Visa) or by calling* ☎*(0351) 49 19 22 85.*

Historisches Grünes Gewölbe★★★ (Historical Green Vault Collections)

Residenzschloss, enter via Sophienstraße.
◎*Open year-round, Wed-Mon 10am–7pm.* ⊜*10€.* ◎*Closed Dec 25.* ☎*(0351) 491 420 00. www.skd-dresden.de.*
The re-created Historical Green Vault is a veritable walk-in treasure chest consisting of nine opulent rooms sheathed in mirrors, ivory, amber, marble, gold and silver. They are a perfect setting for the unique items displayed without protec-

tive glass, just as they would have been during the times of August the Strong. Cut stone vessels, rhinoceros horn goblets and astronomical table clocks are among the more unique treasures to be admired.

Neues Grünes Gewölbe★★★ (New Green Vault Collections)

Residenzschloss, enter via Sophienstraße. ◐*Open year-round, Wed-Mon 10am–6pm.* ◐*Closed Dec 25.* ⬙6€. ☎(0351) 491 420 00. www.skd-dresden.de.

In a modern setting on the palace upper floor, the New Green Vault features some of the collection's most stunning objects. Highlights include a cherry pit engraved with 185 faces (16C), a boat fashioned entirely from ivory (1620), a sculpture of a moor carrying a plate of emeralds by Balthasar Perlmoser (1724) and a hat clasp with a 41 carat green diamond (1769).

Museum für Sächsische Volkskunst★ (Museum of Saxon Folk Art)

Köpckestraße 1. ◐*Open year-round, Tue–Sun 10am–6pm.* ⬙3€. ⬙☎(0351) 491 420 00. www.skd-dresden.de

In the city's oldest Renaissance building, the 1568 Jägerhof (Hunters Court), this museum presents a wealth of regional art, furniture, pottery, sculpture, textiles, costumes, lacework, toys and carvings.

Museum für Völkerkunde★ (Museum of Ethnology)

Palaisplatz 11. ◐*Open year-round, Tue–Sun 10am–6pm.* ◐*Closed Jan 1, Dec 24, 25 & 31.* ⬙4€. ⬙ ☎(0351) 814 48 14. www.voelkerkunde-dresden.de.

The 18C **Japanese Palais** houses this huge and valuable repository of items from around the world, with an emphasis on Oceania. One wing houses the Museum of Prehistory.

Excursions

Schloss Moritzburg★

14km/8.7mi northwest, via Hansastraße. ◐*Open Apr–Oct, daily 10am–5.30pm; Feb-Mar and Nov–Dec visit by guided tour*

(1hr) only, hourly, Tue–Sun 10am–4pm; Jan, tours Sat–Sun 10am–4pm. ◐*Closed Dec 24.* ⬙6€. ☎(03207) 87 30. www.schloss-moritzburg.de.

Built in the 16C by Duke Moritz of Saxony, this hunting lodge has an idyllic island location and was turned into a Baroque pleasure palace under August the Strong in the 18C.

Schloss & Park Pillnitz★

10km/6.2mi southeast. ◐*Open Apr–Oct, Tue–Sun 10am–5pm; Nov–Mar visit by guided tour only, Sat–Sun 11am, noon, 1pm and 2pm.* ◐*Closed Dec 24 and 25.* ☎(0351) 261 32 60; www.schloesser-dresden.de.

This Baroque riverside summer palace with Chinese flourishes is surrounded by a lush garden and vine-covered slopes. It's a popular day trip from Dresden and easily reached by boat or bike.

Aside from strolling and picnicking, you can gain insight into daily court life by touring the New Palace. August the Strong's throne and decorative arts are displayed in the Bergpalais and Wasserpalais outbuildings (◐*open May–Oct, Tue–Sun 10am–6pm;* ⬙3€).

Freiberg★

37km/23mi south.

At the foot of the Erzgebirge mountain range (⬙*see ERZGEBIRGE*), Freiberg once pegged its considerable wealth to the nearby abundance of silver, copper and various minerals. The key sight is the 15C **Cathedral**★★ (⬙*visit by guided 45min tours, May-Oct, Mon–Sat 10am, daily 11am, 2pm, 3pm and 4pm; Nov–Apr, daily 11am, 2pm and 3pm;* ⬙3.50€; ⬙☎(03731) 225 98. www.freiberger-dom.de). It is filled with important religious artworks, including the **tulip pulpit**★★, a masterpiece by sculptor Hans Witten (c. 1505); the **Gottfried Silbermann organ**★★ (usually played during tours); and the Romanesque **golden entrance portal**★★ from 1230.

Swiss Saxony★★★ (⬙*see SÄCHSISCHE SCHWEIZ*)

Meißen★ (⬙*see MEISSEN*)

DÜSSELDORF★

POPULATION: 573 000

Finance, fashion and fun are the hallmarks of this modern Rhineland city and capital of the German state of Rhineland-Westphalia. Shopping is a major pastime here and the Old Town is nicknamed the 'world's longest bar' for good reason, while a long tradition in the arts is reflected in a multitude of first-rate museums and cultural institutions.

- **Information:** Immermannstraße 65b. 40210 Düsseldorf. ☎(0211) 17 20 20. www.duesseldorf-tourismus.de.
- ▶ **Orient Yourself:** Düsseldorf straddles the Rhine River and is served by an international airport, long-distance trains and several autobahns. Most of the sights and action concentrate along the river, especially in the Altstadt (Old Town).
- **Parking:** Garages are plentiful, notably around the Hauptbahnhof and near the Königsallee.
- **Don't Miss:** Quaff local Altbier in a traditional brew-pub, K20 art museum.
- **Organizing Your Time:** You'll want to devote an entire day to seeing the city.
- **Also See:** ESSEN *(37km/23mi north)*, KÖLN *(39km/24mi south)*, AACHEN *(81km/50.3mi south west)*.

A Bit of History

City of the arts – Düsseldorf has been an artistic mecca since the reign of Elector **Johann Wilhelm** (1679–1716, also known as Jan Wellem) who surrounded himself with brilliant musicians, painters and architects. Elector Carl Theodor provided another artistic impetus when founding a prestigious art academy in 1773. Now directed by Markus Lüpertz, its faculty has also included Paul Klee and Joseph Beuys. Of late, Düsseldorf has also added a few architectural gems by Frank Gehry and other stars of the genre, most notably in the revamped old harbor called the Mediahafen (Media Harbor)

The World of Fashion – Exhibitions, fairs and collections of haute couture secure Düsseldorf's reputation as a "mini-Paris" and German fashion capital. The city hosts several fashion trade shows throughout the year, including the CPD (Collections Premiere Düsseldorf), one of Europe's largest with over 1 400 exhibitors from over 40 countries.

Düsseldorf Marketing & Tourismus GmbH

Düsseldorf and the Rhine

Address Book

For coin ranges, see the Legend on the cover flap.

WHERE TO STAY

Airport Fashion Hotel – *Am Hain 44. ☎(0211) 439 50. www.fashion-duesseldorf.de. 39 rooms. Closed Dec 24–31. 38 rooms. Restaurant.* Close to the Trade Fairgrounds and Congress Center as well as the airport, this hotel is a peaceful retreat with appealingly furnished, modern rooms and two restaurants, one serving Chinese food, the other regional specialties.

Hotel Orangerie – *Bäckergasse 1. ☎(0211) 86 68 00. www.hotel-orangerie.de. 27 rooms.* This pretty hotel within a 19C town palace sits in a quiet corner of the Altstadt. The bright rooms are minimalist but comfortable and each is named after a different artist.

Sir Astor – *Kurfürstenstraße 18 & 23. ☎(0211) 173 370. www.sir-astor.de. 20 rooms.* The décor has been aptly described as "Scotland meets Africa" in this utterly charming boutique hotel near the main train station. Rooms reflect the owner's passion for design and detail. If they're fully booked, ask for a room at their sister property Lady Astor across the street, which are even more flamboyant.

WHERE TO EAT

Op de Eck – *Grabbeplatz 5 (in the K 20 Kunstsammlung building). ☎(0211) 32 88 38. www.op-de-eck.de.* This café-restaurant has a concave glass façade and modern design interior. On the menu: international specialities, home-made cakes and sorbets, and a good selection of wines and cocktails. A fine place for a light meal any time of day.

Berens am Kai – *Kaistraße 16. ☎(0211) 300 67 50. www.berensamkai.de. Closed Jan 1–8, Sat lunchtime, Sun, public holidays.* Catering to business folks and discerning hipsters, this Medienhafen restaurant affords splendid views of the Rhine through the panoramic glass front. The décor – concrete walls, chrome chairs, black cushions – is as contemporary as the international cuisine.

Rheinturm Top 180 – *Stromstraße 20. ☎(0211) 863 20 00. www.guennewig.de.* An elevator whisks you up Düsseldorf's television tower where you can enjoy superb views of the city from this slowly rotating restaurant at a lofty 172m/564ft.

Zum Schiffchen – *Hafenstraße 5. ☎(0211) 13 24 21. www.brauerei-zum-schiffchen.de.* This classic Rhenish brew-pub has had a loyal following for more than 350 years. Grab a seat at a polished wooden table, order a hearty meal and wash it down with the Altbier house brew. Nice beer garden, too.

TAKING A BREAK

Eis-Café Pia – *Kasernenstraße 1. ☎(0211) 326 233. Closed mid-Oct–mid-Feb.* Expect lines to snake out the door at what is quite possibly the best Italian ice cream parlor in town. The café also serves hot and cold drinks.

NIGHTLIFE

USEFUL TIPS

A warren of car-free lanes wedged between the Rhine River and the Königsallee boulevard, the Altstadt is known as "the longest bar in the world." With all sorts of drinking dens—historic brew-pubs to sleek bars—it can get packed and a little raucous at weekends.

Uerige – *Bergerstraße 1. ☎(0211) 86 69 90. www.uerige.de.* There's no better place to try Altbier than at this friendly brew-pub with old-world atmosphere. Casks serve as tables, and in summer everyone from business folk to students gathers outside chatting and quaffing.

Brauerei Schumacher – *Oststraße 123. ☎(0211) 828 90 20. www.schumacher-alt.de.* A tantalizing aroma of hops wafts out from the city's oldest privately owned brewhouse in town. Ultra-authentic and genial, it is a great place to sample Rhenish hospitality and the house brew.

Siam Cocktailbar – *Kurze Straße 13. ☎(0211) 836 94 21. www.siam-cocktailbar.de.* Choose from over 180 concoctions at this Asian-themed Altstadt bar that is the darling of the in-crowd.

DÜSSELDORF

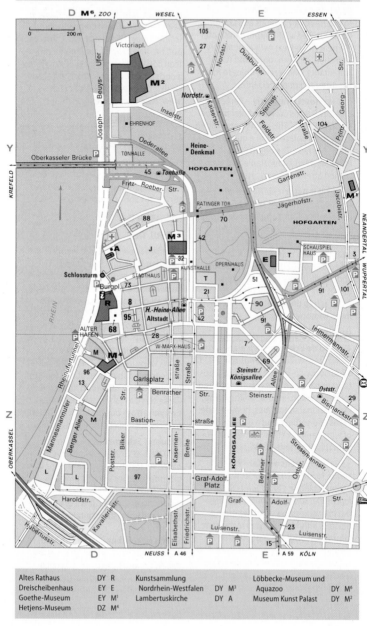

Poetry and Music in the 19C

Heinrich Heine (1797–1856), son of a Bolkerstraße merchant, spent his youth in Düsseldorf, deeply impressed with the French and Napoléon. A poet, pamphleteer, traveler, defender of liberalism and a Francophile, Heine described himself as "a German nightingale which would have liked to make its nest in Voltaire's wig."

Among the musicians who have given Düsseldorf its reputation as an artistic centre are Robert Schumann and Felix Mendelssohn-Bartholdy. **Schumann** (1810–56) was appointed conductor of the municipal orchestra in 1850 and lived on Bilkerstraße for four years. In 1854, he suffered a nervous breakdown and attempted to drown himself in the Rhine. His friend **Mendelssohn** (1809–47) brilliantly directed the city's Rhine Festival. He made his first journey to England in 1829, conducting his own *Symphony in C Minor* at the London Philharmonic Society.

Everything elegant centers on the graceful **Königsallee**★, with boutiques and arcades on either side of the old moat.

East Asian Connection– Düsseldorf plays an increasingly important role in economic relations linking Germany with East Asia, Japan in particular. More than 500 Japanese firms are based here, including banks, insurance companies, transport firms, advertising agencies, retailers, medical companies, hotels and restaurants.

Sights

Altstadt (Old Town)

This largely car-free riverside quarter is jam-packed with pubs, bars and shops. One of the busiest thoroughfares is **Bolkerstraße**, where the poet Heinrich Heine was born in the house at no 53. The area is also linked with the story of the tailor Wibbel, who attended his own funeral after switching identities to escape a prison sentence. This legend is recalled by the figures of the Schneider-Wibbel-Gasse carillon clock, which operates at 11am, 1pm, 3pm, 6pm and 9pm.

The Altstadt is paralleled by a pleasant **riverside promenade** *(Rheinuferpromenade)*. It allows you to stroll from Burgplatz square, where the medieval castle tower houses a shipping museum, all the way to the 234m/767ft-high **Rheinturm**, a TV tower with a revolving restaurant.

Marktplatz (Market Square)

Separated from the Rhine by the 16C Renaissance **Altes Rathaus** (Town Hall), this square is embellished by the bronze equestrian statue (18C) of Elector Jan Wellem. He is buried in the Baroque **Andreaskirche** (Church of St. Andrew) a short walk north of here.

Hofgarten and Schloss Jägerhof★ (Court Garden and Jägerhof Palace)

Hofgarten park is a shady continuation of the Königsallee. Its Napoléon Hill is crowned with a small bronze titled *Harmony,* a modest monument to Heinrich Heine. At the nearby pink Jägerhof palace, the **Goethe-Museum**★ *(Jacobistraße 2; ⏱open year-round, Tue–Sun 11am–5pm, Sat 1pm–5pm; ⊜3€; ☎0211-899 62 62; www.goethe-museum-kippenberg-stiftung.de)* takes you on a journey through the life, times and work of this much-revered poet and playwright.

☺ A Bit of Advice ☺

Local Gastronomy: The Altstadt taverns ooze Rhenish earthiness and are perfect for sampling such regional culinary specialties as *Himmel und Erde* (literally, Heaven & Earth this is black pudding with onions) and *Halve Hahn* (rye roll with cheese). On Friday evenings, there is a tradition of eating *Reibekuchen* (potato cake). Indigenous to Düsseldorf is the *Altbier*, a copper-colored, heavily hopped ale served in cylindrical 0.2l/0.4pint-size glasses.

Museum Kunst Palast★ (Fine Arts Museum)

Ehrenhof 4–5.
🕐*Open year-round, Tue–Sun 11am–6pm.*
💶*10€.* ♿☎ *(0211) 899 24 60. www. museum-kunst-palast.de.*

This encyclopedic art gallery touches on all genres from the Middle Ages to the present. Works by the Düsseldorf School dominate but you'll also find large-scale paintings by Rubens, moody landscapes by Caspar David Friedrich and warped Expressionism by Max Beckmann. The museum also houses a collection of medieval sculpture, and outstanding **glassware★★** from Roman times via Jugendstil to the present day.

K20 Kunstsammlung★★ (20C Art Collection)

Grabbeplatz 5; ⚲ *Closed for renovation until at least Oct 2009.* ☎ *(0211) 838 11 30. www.kunstsammlung.de.*

Designed by Danish architects Dissing and Weitling, this modern building houses a top-rated art collection with an emphasis on western European and American 20C works. Top paintings by Picasso, Chagall, Ernst and Beuys are complemented by nearly 100 works by Paul Klee who was a professor at the Düsseldorf Arts Academy from 1930 to 1933.

K21 Kunstsammlung★ (21C Art Collection)

Ständehausstraße 1; 🕐*Open year-round, Tue–Fri 10am–6pm, Sat–Sun 11am–6pm.* 💶*6.50€.* ♿☎ *(0211) 838 16 00; www. kunstsammlung.de.*

Truly cutting-edge art created since 1980 is the focus of the K20's sister museum, housed in a 19C state parliament building with its own little park. A spacious foyer with a giant pendulum gives way to three floors of galleries presenting works by Andreas Gursky, Candida Höfer, Thomas Ruff and Jeff Wall as well as video installations by Eija-Liisa Athila and sculpture by Thomas Schütte.

Medienhafen★ (Media Harbor)

South of the Altstadt, an old-time river port has been reborn as a high-tech, office and entertainment complex that doubles as a showcase of postmodern architecture. The overall design cleverly integrates the old with the new, the industrial with the edgy. Red-brick silos and warehouses have been converted, while new buildings have sprung up, most notably the **Neuer Zollhof** (New Customs Court). Designed by Frank Gehry, this three-part complex is a classic example of his undulating, organic style. Claude Vasconi's nautically-inspired **Grand Bateau** (Big Ship) is another stand-out. The tallest building is the **Colorium** by London-based William Alsop with its random color-patterned façade.

Excursions

Schloss Benrath★

10km/6.2mi south east.
🕐*Open mid-Apr–Oct, Tue–Sun 10am– 6pm; Nov–mid-Apr, Tue–Sun 11am–5pm.* 🕐*Closed Dec 24, 25 & 31 Dec.* 💶*5€ per museum, 10.50€ for all three.* ☎ *(0211) 899 38 32. www.schloss-benrath.de.*

This 18C Late Baroque palace designed by Nicolas de Pigage for Elector Carl Theodor offers a look at the lavish lifestyle enjoyed by the period's rulers. The west wing contains a natural history museum, the east wing has exhibits on European gardens.

Neandertal

14km/8.7mi east, via A46 autobahn, exit Haan-West, follow signs

This deep, steep valley carved by the little Düssel creek owes its name to Calvinist poet Joachim Neander (1650–80), who used it as a retreat. It was here that 60 000-year-old skeletal parts of Neanderthal Man were first discovered in 1856. The bones are the star exhibit of the multimedia **Neanderthal Museum** *(Talstraße 300;* 🕐 *open year-round, Tue–Sun 10am–6pm;* 🕐 *closed Dec 24, 25 & 31;* 💶*7€;* ♿☎*(02104) 7 97 97; www. neanderthal.de)*. Take a virtual journey through the stages of human evolution broken down into such themes as "daily life and survival", "tools and knowledge" and "myth and religion". Staff can also provide directions to the spot where Neanderthal Man was found.

KLOSTER EBERBACH★★

Founded by Bernard of Clairvau in 1136, this former Cistercian abbey existed for nearly 700 years until becoming secularized by the state in 1803. During the Middle Ages, it evolved into one of the region's finest wine estates and at one time even had its own fleet of ships plying the Rhine and is still a famous wine producer today.

- 🛈 **Information:** ☎(06723) 917 81 00. www.kloster-eberbach.de.
- ▶ **Orient Yourself:** The abbey is in the heart of the Rheingau wine region, about 20km/12mi northeast of the town of Rüdesheim on the Rhine.
- 🕓 **Organizing Your Time:** Allow two hours to tour the abbey.
- 👜 **Also See:** WIESBADEN, MAINZ, RHEINTAL.

Visit

🕓 *Open Apr–Oct, daily 10am–6pm; Nov–Mar, daily 11am–5pm.* 🕓*Closed Mon before Shrove Tue, Dec 24–25.* ⊜*3.50€.* 🎧Audio-guides ⊜*3.50€.* ♿☎*(06723) 917 81 00; www.klostereberbach.de*

Abbey Church

Built in two stages, in 1145–60 and in 1170–86, this three-nave Romanesque basilica reflects the understated and elegant austerity typical of Cistercian architecture. Gothic side chapels with tracery windows were added in the 14C, and there are remarkably elaborate **tombs**★ dating from the 14C to the 18C.

Abbey Buildings

Outlying 13C–14C buildings wrap around the **cloister**★ which, on the north side, gives access to the **monk's refectory**★★. Only the Romanesque portal remains of the original dining room, the rest was rebuilt in Baroque style and lidded by a magnificent stucco ceiling by Daniel Schenk, a court artist from Mainz.

The refectory is flanked by the **abbey museum** *(Abteimuseum)* on the left and the **monks' dormitory**★ to the right. Dating to c. 1250–70, the double-naved, ribbed vaulted room was built with a slightly rising floor and shortened pillars to create the illusion of length.

Monks usually gathered in the adjacent **chapterhouse**★ *(Kapitelsaal),* which was built prior to 1186 but got its beautiful star-ribbed vaulting in the middle of the 14C and stylized plant ornamentation around 1500.

The lay brothers slept and ate in the area west of the cloister. Their old refectory now contains a collection of mighty **wine presses**★, documenting the 800-year-old wine-producing tradition of the abbey. The oldest press dates from 1668.

Wine tastings are available. The complex also harbors a restaurant and guestrooms in the abbey's old mill.

The Name of the Rose

The cameras began rolling at Eberbach in 1986 for the filming of the monastic whodunnit *The Name of the Rose.* Director Jean-Jacques Annaud allegedly chose the Cistercian abbey of Eberbach from a list of 300 abbeys as the primary setting for Umberto Eco's novel. The dispute between the papal envoy and the Franciscan monk William of Baskerville, played by Sean Connery, was filmed in the chapterhouse, where monastic law was once laid down.

The scriptorium was reconstructed in the monks' dormitory. In the film, sentences were passed by the Holy Inquisition where people now gather to taste wine, in the monastery cellar. The abbey church and hospice also feature in the film.

EICHSTÄTT★★

POPULATION: 13 100

Eichstätt, a small episcopal town and seat of a Catholic university, owes its Baroque character to its reconstruction after the Thirty Years' War; only the cathedral survived the burning of the town by the Swedish army. But Eichstätt is also a center of contemporary architecture with dazzling buildings designed by Karljosef Schattner, Karl Frey and Günther Benisch.

- **Information:** Domplatz 8, 85072 Eichstätt. ☎(08421) 600 14 00. www.eichstaett.info.
- ▶ **Orient Yourself:** Eichstätt lies in the midst of the Altmühl Valley natural park.
- **Don't Miss:** The cathedral and the Residenzplatz.
- **Organizing Your Time:** Half a day is sufficient to take in Eichstätt's highlights
- **Also See:** ROMANTISCHE STRASSE, NÖRDLINGEN, NUREMBERG, REGENSBURG.

Sights

Dom★

The 14C cathedral is characterized by a mix of architectural styles. The east tower is Romanesque, the Gothic main portal is decorated with Biblical figures and scenes, while the west face was crafted by Baroque masters Jakob Engel and Gabriel de Gabrieli.

The *Gothic* **cloister★** was a 15C addition to the cathedral.

As you enter, turn left toward the late 15C **Pappenheim Altar★★** in the north transept. Carved from Jura limestone, it rises almost 9m/29.5ft high. On the other end, in the Gothic west choir, is a famous 1514 statue by Loy Hering depicting Eichstätt's first 8C bishop **St. Willibald**. Willibald's relics are housed in the elaborate canopied Baroque altar by Matthias Seynold behind the statue.

Leaving the cathedral via the eastern exit takes you to the **Mortuarium★**,

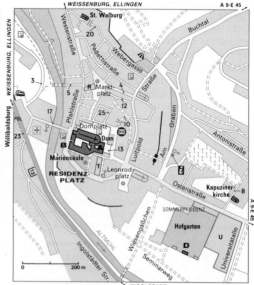

EICHSTÄTT

Dompl.	
Freiwasserstr.	3
Gabrielstr.	4
Herzoggasse	5
Kapuzinergasse	8
Loy-Hering-Gasse	10
Luitpoldstr.	
Marktgasse	12
Marktpl.	
Ostenstr.	
Pater-Philipp-Jeningen-Pl.	13
Spitalbrücke	17
Walburgiberg	20
Weißenburgerstr.	23
Westenstr.	
Widmanngasse	25

Fürstbischöfliche Residenz	B
Kreuzgang	A
Muschelpavillon	D

a Late Gothic funerary chapel paved with elaborate **tombstones**. The four stained-glass **windows** on the east wall depicting the Last Judgment are by Hans Holbein the Elder (c. 1500).

The **Domschatz- und Diözesanmuseum** (*Cathedral Treasury and Museum;* Ⓞ*open Apr–Oct, Wed-Fri 10.30am–5pm, Sat–Sun, 10am–5pm;* ☞*2€, no charge Sun;* ☎ *(08421) 507 42; www.bistum-eichstaett.de*) is filled with outstanding examples of ecclesiastical art. Highlights include a gold and jewel-encrusted finger reliquary of St. Jacob (12C), intricately woven Baroque tapestries, lavish monstrances and late medieval sculpture.

Residenzplatz★

Next to the cathedral, Residenzplatz is framed by lavish Rococo town houses, including the bishop's palace, that are the legacy of master builders Gabriel de Gabrieli and Maurizio Pedetti. An 18m/59ft-high column of the Virgin Mary rises from a cherub-festooned fountain in front of the bishop's palace.

Willibaldsburg (Willibald Castle)

Burgstraße 19.

This 14C hilltop castle is largely the work of Augsburg Renaissance architect Elias Holl. Within its confines are two museums, a garden with fantastic **views**★★ of the river and town, and a hand-carved **well** (*Tiefer Brunnen*) that is an astonishing 76m/249.3ft deep.

The **Jura-Museum**★ (Ⓞ*open Apr–Sept, Tue–Sun 9am–6pm; Oct–Mar, Tue–Sun 10am–4pm;* Ⓞ *closed Jan 1, Shrove Tue, Dec 24, 25 & 31;* ☞*4€;* ♿☎*(08421) 29 56*) has a fabulous collection of locally found fossils that should even get amateurs excited. Pride of place goes to an extremely rare fossilized skeleton of an archeopteryx, the creature that constitutes the evolutionary link between reptiles and birds.

Upstairs, the **Museum of Pre-History and Early History** (Ⓞ*see Jura-Museum;* ☞*4€*) chronicles regional history from the Stone Age to the early Middle Ages and counts a mammoth skeleton, Celtic weapons and Roman measuring devices among its possessions.

Excursion

Ellingen

29km/18mi northwest of Eichstätt.

☞*Visit by guided tour only, hourly, Apr–Sept, Tue–Sun 9am–5pm; Oct–Mar, Tue–Sun 10am–3pm.* Ⓞ *Closed Jan 1, Shrove Tue, Dec 24, 25 & 31.* ☞*4€.* ☎*(09141) 974 790.*

Ellingen served as the regional seat of the Teutonic Knights from the 13C until Napoléon's dissolution of the order in 1806. The **palace** (*Schloss*) was designed by Franz Keller (1718–25) and is largely Baroque infused with Neoclassical elements. The chapel has frescoes by Cosmas Damian Asam and stucco work by Franz Roth. The huge twin-flight **main staircase**★ is worth seeing, as is the small museum on the history of the Teutonic Order.

EIFEL★

This volcanic central highland region near the Belgian border has lots in store for travelers wishing to get off the beaten path. Roman ruins, a world-class race track, sparkling blue crater lakes, medieval castles and large swaths of quiet and unspoiled countryside await. Take your time: the Eifel's charms need to be sipped and savored like the fine red wine it produces, not gulped in haste.

🏛 **Information:** Kavalrienbergstraße 1, 54595 Prüm. ☎(06551) 965 60. www.eifel.info.

▶ **Orient Yourself:** The Eifel is near the border with Belgium and straddles the German states of Rhineland-Palatinate and North Rhine-Westphalia. It is roughly bounded by Aachen, Koblenz, Trier and Cologne.

👁 **Don't Miss:** The volcanic lakes called "Maare".

🕐 **Organizing Your Time:** Allow one day for the driving tour from Bad Münstereifel to Manderscheid.

🚶 **Also See:** BONN, KÖLN, AACHEN, RHEINTAL, MOSELTAL.

Driving Tour

From Bad Münstereifel to Manderscheid

145km/90mi
This leisurely drive follows the valley of the Ahr with its popular resorts, climbs to the forested Upper Eifel, and then meanders between the volcanic lakes of the Maare.

Bad Münstereifel
Hemmed in by massive **ramparts**★, this quaint town is littered with historic houses and monuments.
The **Stiftskirche St. Chrysanthus und Daria** is an outstanding twin-towered

---

Address Book

WHERE TO STAY

⊜**Pension Oos** – *Lieserstraße 16, 54550 Daun-Gemünden.* ☎*(06592) 29 09. www.pension-oos.de. Closed Nov–mid-Mar.* 🚗 *6 rooms.* This simple little B&B near the volcanic lakes has well-kept rooms sleeping two or three as well as a guest kitchen with fridge and coffeemaker.

⊜⊜**Hotel Seemöwe** – *Am Obersee 10, 52152 Simmerath-Einruhr.* ☎*(02485) 271. www.hotel-seemoewe.de. Closed Jan-Feb. 50 rooms. Restaurant* ⊜. Good hotel on the edge of the Obersee lake, with clean and well-cared for guestrooms and a lakeview terrace. The country-style restaurant offers traditional cuisine.

⊜⊜⊜**Burg Adenbach** – *Adenbachhutstraße 1, 53474 Bad Neuenahr-Ahrweiler.* ☎*(02641) 389 20. www. burghotel-adenbach.com. Restaurant closed Wed. 7 rooms. Restaurant* ⊜⊜⊜. Romance rules at this medieval castle in Ahrweiler. Beautiful, comfortable rooms come with canopy beds, pleasing color schemes and large bathrooms. The stout home-cooking served in the restaurant pairs well with the red wines from the property's own vineyard.

WHERE TO EAT

⊜⊜⊜**Historisches Weinhaus an der Rausch** – *Heisterbacher Straße 1, 53902 Bad Münstereifel.* ☎*(02253) 84 25. www.weinhaus-an-der-rausch. de. Closed Mon.* 🚗 This central half-timbered 1553 house next to a little waterfall puts a premium on fresh food, especially fish. The ambience is feel-good homey with décor accented by crisp tablecloths and frilly curtains.

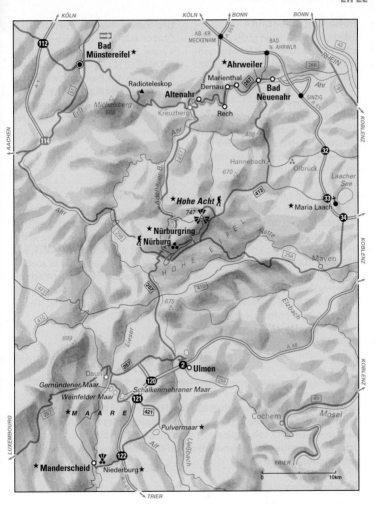

abbey church with an 11C Romanesque front.

A few miles east of Münstereifel, the road passes a giant **radio-telescope**, rejoins the Ahr at Kreuzberg and continues along the winding valley. The telescope is 100m/328ft in diameter and its parabolic depth is 21m/69ft.

Altenahr

In a rocky valley between two bends in the river, charming Altenahr is dominated by the scattered ruins of the 12C hilltop **Burg Are** castle. Catch the chairlift up the Ditschardhöhe hill for sweeping views.

Following the valley, with steep vineyards wedged in among rocky outcrops, takes you to a string of pretty, wine-pro-

ducing villages: Rech with its Roman bridge, Dernau and its "wine fountain" and Marienthal and its ruined convent.

Bad Neuenahr-Ahrweiler   Spa

This twin town has a delightfully split personality. At **Ahrweiler**★, which is still encircled by medieval fortifications, half-timbered houses line narrow, pedestrian-only streets. Study its Roman roots at the **Museum Roemervilla**. By contrast, Bad Neuenahr is a bubbly spa town with celebrated mineral springs, a casino and elegant 19C architecture.

▶ *Leaving Ahrweiler, the road climbs toward the forest before reaching the highlands.*

213

Hohe Acht Mountain★

Take in sweeping views of deep valleys, rolling hills and the ruined Nürburg castle from the tower atop the Eifel's highest mountain (747m/2 451ft).

Nürburgring★

☎(02691) 30 20. www.nuerburgring.de. This legendary **Formula 1 racing track** is home to the feared North Loop (Nordschleife), nicknamed "Green Hell" by Jackie Stewart. On certain days, you can take your own car along the track or hop aboard a BMW or Viper and let a professional do the driving. Car and motorcycle races take place during the warmer months.

Maare★ (Crater Lakes)

Eons ago, volcanic activity engulfed the upper reaches of the Eifel, resulting in a series of bright blue crater lakes. To learn more about this phenomenon, visit the

Eifel-Vulkan Museum (Leopoldstraße 9; ○ open Mar–mid-Nov, Tue–Fri 1pm–4.30pm, Sat–Sun 11am–4.30pm; ∞3€; ☎(06592) 98 53 53)) in Daun and the lakes themselves: the **Gemündener Maar**, the **Weinfelder Maar** (also known as Totenmaar), the **Schalkenmehrer Maar** and the almost perfectly circular **Pulver Maar★**.

▶ Follow the brown "Maare" route signs.

Manderscheid★

From atop the castle keep of the ruined Niederburg, **views★** extend to the Oberburg ruins and the Lieser Valley. in the parking lot at Pension Burgenblick, you can catch a trail leading up to another great **viewpoint★★**, the so-called Kaisertempelchen (little imperial temple). overlooking the Oberburg and Niederburg ruins.

EINBECK★

POPULATION: 28 200

In the Middle Ages, no fewer than 600 small breweries in this former Hanseatic town supplied the whole of Germany with "Einpöckisches Bier" (forerunner of Bock beer). Einbeck still retains part of its medieval fortifications, but a more attractive heritage are the hundreds of half-timbered houses, richly decorated with multicolored carvings.

🛈 **Information:** Marktstraße 13, 37574 Einbeck. ☎(05561) 313 19 10. www.einbeck-online.de.

▶ **Orient Yourself:** Einbeck is on the B3, about halfway between Göttingen and Hildesheim.

⊙ **Don't Miss:** The Old Town.

🕐 **Organizing Your Time:** Allow at least one hour to see Einbeck's Old Town.

👣 **Also See:** HILDESHEIM, HANN. MÜNDEN, GÖTTINGEN.

Walking Tour

Old Town★

There is a remarkable collection of half-timbered houses in the town center of Einbeck, most near the market square.

Marktplatz★★

The most distinctive building on Einbeck's historic market square is the **Old Town** (Rathaus), which was completed in 1606 and is fronted by a trio of

whimsical miniature towers reminiscent of witches' hats.

Also looming over the square is the 14C **Marktkirche** (market church) whose 65m/213ft-high tower is 1.5m/5ft off kilter, giving it the nickname "Leaning Tower of Einbeck." The church is filled a panoply of treasures, including a 12C Romanesque baptismal font and 14C Gothic altar.

Of special note are the two houses on the corner of Münsterstraße. The

Brodhaus (1552) with its jutting upper story was once owned by the baker's guild. Like most of the old houses, the impressive **Ratsapotheke** (1590) has ventilated attics that served as storage lofts for hops and barley.

▸ *Follow Tiedexerstraße,*
  west of the square.

Tiedexerstraße★★

This little lane is lined with especially ornate and beautifully restored half-timbered houses. The one at No 31 abuts the old town fortifications.

▸ *Turn left on Maschenstraße and*
  follow it to Marktstraße.

Marktstraße

The tourist office is housed in the fabulous **Eickesches Haus**★★ (1612–14) at the corner of Knochenhauer Straße. Closely examine the richly decorated façade and see if you can spot the female figures representing the five senses, the four Evangelists and four of the apostles.

Excursion

Bad Gandersheim

20km/12.4mi northeast.
The birthplace of Roswitha von Gandersheim, Germany's first (10C) poetess, is best known as a hot spring and saltwater spa. The twin octagonal towers of the **cathedral**★ overlook the town center. Inside are two altars, one 15C and the other 16C. The well-preserved half-timbered houses around the market square date from the 16C.

EISENACH★★

POPULATION: 44 100

The history of Eisenach is closely linked with the Reformer Martin Luther who went to school here and later translated the New Testament into German while in hiding at Wartburg castle. Eisenach is also the birthplace of the composer Johann Sebastian Bach and a gateway to the Thuringian Forest.

- **Information:** Markt 9, 99817 Eisenach. ☎(03691) 792 30. www.eisenach.de.
- ▸ **Orient Yourself:** Eisenach is on the northwestern edge of the Thuringian forest, just off the A4 autobahn.
- **Don't Miss:** The Wartburg.
- **Organizing Your Time:** Allow at least three hours for the Wartburg.
- **Also See:** ERFURT, WEIMAR, HANN. MÜNDEN.

A Bit of History

At the Heart of Germany – At the beginning of the 13C, the *Minnesänger* (*see INTRODUCTION: Music)* held legendary singing contests in the Wartburg, a custom that inspired Wagner's opera *Tannhäuser.*
Martin Luther attended school in Eisenach and sought refuge at the Wartburg in 1521/22 while under papal ban. This is where he translated the New Testament from the Greek into the German vernacular (*see INTRODUCTION: History).* Eisenach is also the 1685 birthplace of composer **Johann Sebastian Bach**.

Sights

Wartburg★★

Park in the pay lot below the castle and walk about 500m/547yd uphill.
Visit by guided tour (1hr) only; Mar–Oct, daily 8.30am–5pm; Nov–Feb, daily

EISENACH

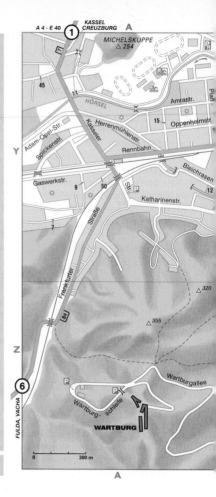

Wartburg Fortress, where memories of the Minnesänger mix with those of Luther

J. Bouraly/MICHELIN

9am–3.30pm. ⊘7€. ☎(036 91) 25 00. www.wartburg-eisenach.de.
Built between 1155 and 1180, Wartburg castle is one of the best preserved and most imposing Romanesque structures, despite later alterations in other architectural styles. Since 2000, it has been included on UNESCO's list of World Heritage Sites.
Perched on a rocky spur, the castle welcomes visitors through a 12C entrance leading into a 15C–16C **outer courtyard** *(Erster Burghof)* of half-timbered buildings. Inside the fortified complex is the **Palais**★, where the landgraves resided. Enjoy sweeping **views**★ of Eisenach, the Thuringian Forest and the Rhön foothills from the fortified wall and south tower.

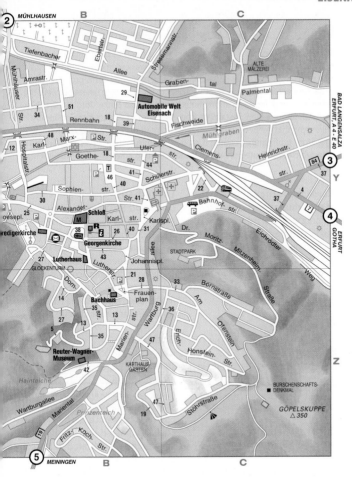

Address Book

🪙 *For coin ranges, see cover flap.*

WHERE TO STAY

🍽️ **Hotel St. Peter** – *Am Petersberg 7.*
☎(03691) 87 28 30. *www.stpeter-eisenach.de.*
14 rooms. Restaurant 🍽️🍽️. This little
hotel offers well-kept, modern rooms
along with a charmingly woodsy restaurant specialized in Thuringian cuisine.
🍽️🍽️🍽️ **Hotel Auf der Wartburg**
☎(03691) 79 70. *www.wartburghotel.*
de. 35 rooms. Restaurant 🍽️🍽️🍽️.
Fancy yourself knight and damsel while
staying in this landmark castle where
rooms lack no creature comforts and
the service is impeccable. The Landgraf-
enstube restaurant has a rustic feel.

WHERE TO EAT

🍽️🍽️ **Brunnenkeller** – *Markt 10.*
☎(03691) 21 23 58. *www.brunnenkel-*
ler-eisenach.de. Soak up centuries of
history in the vaulted cellars or enjoy
breezy views of the market square. The
food tends toward feel-good local specialities, including Thuringian sausages.
🍽️🍽️🍽️ **Turmschänke** – *Markt 10.*
Closed Sun. ☎(03691) 21 35 33. *www.*
turmschaenke-eisenach.de. Closed Sun.
Fine dine means scoring a table at this
elegant restaurant inside a fortification
tower from 1070. A hand-selected wine
list pairs well with richly nuanced and
expertly prepared seasonal cuisine.

Martin Luther in the Wartburg

After refusing to renounce his reformist views at the Diet of Worms on April 18, 1521, Martin Luther (&see INTRODUCTION: History) was excommunicated, declared an outlaw and placed under papal ban. To prevent his arrest, his protector Frederick III, the Elector of Saxony, spirited Luther to the Wartburg where he spent the next ten months living as an anonymous knight named Junker Jörg. He spent his days translating the New Testament from Greek into German: A major linguistic achievement that helped unify the many German dialects into a common language. More profoundly, though, it made the Bible more accessible to ordinary people, which contributed greatly to the success of the Reformation movement.

Tours *(available in English)* take in the **Hall of the Troubadours** *(Sängersaal)* where Moritz von Schwind's monumental fresco illustrates the Minnesänger contest. Tours end in the **museum** from where a narrow parapet leads to the **Lutherstube**, the austerely furnished room where Martin Luther stayed and worked on his translation.

The Old Town★

Markt
The market place is bordered by administrative buildings and townhouses surrounding a fountain with a statue of Eisenach's patron saint, St. George.

Thüringer Museum (Thuringian Museum)
Markt 24.
◯Open year-round, Tue–Sun 11am–5pm. ⊛2€. ☎(036 91) 67 04 50.
The former residence of the local dukes houses a collection of porcelain, paintings and folk art from the 18C–20C.

Georgenkirche
Markt.
◯Open year-round, daily 10am–noon, 2pm to 4pm. ☎(03691) 21 31 26.
This triple-aisled 16C church contains the tombs of several landgraves of Thuringia. Luther preached here in 1521 despite his being officially banned from the Holy Roman Empire. Johann Sebastian Bach was baptized here in 1685.

Predigerkirche
The late 13C Early Gothic church houses the **wooden sculpture collection**★ formerly in the Thuringian Museum. Carvings date from the 12C–16C.

Lutherhaus
Lutherplatz 8. ◯Open year-round, daily 10am–5pm. ⊛3.50€. ☎(03691) 298 30. www.lutherhaus-eisenach.de.
Martin Luther lived in this half-timbered house between 1498 and 1501 while studying at the Latin School. A modern exhibit uses paintings, documents and multimedia terminals to tell the story of his life and accomplishments.

Bachhaus
Frauenplan 21. ◯Open year-round, daily 10am–6pm. ⊛6€. &☎(03691) 793 40. www.bachhaus.de.
The house where Johann Sebastian Bach first saw the light of day no longer exists but it was very much like the 600-year-old half-timbered structure now holding a museum dedicated to the composer and his accomplishments. Peruse manuscripts, scores and portraits of the prolific Bach family. Visits include a live concert played on period instruments.

Automobile Welt Eisenach
Friedrich-Naumann-Straße 10.
◯Open year-round, Tue–Sun 11am–5pm. ⊛3€. &☎(03691) 772 12.
Vehicle manufacturing has been part of Eisenach's history since 1896 and car buffs and nostalgic types should make a beeline to this automobile museum housed in the original 1935 plant. A 1907 Wartburg Dixi, boxy GDR-era vehicles, cool sports cars and eccentric prototypes are all part of the extensive exhibit.

Excursion

Thuringian Forest★★
(&see THÜRINGER WALD)

EMDEN

POPULATION: 51 500

Emden is an easy-going and pleasant town with remarkable museums, most notably the Kunsthalle gallery of contemporary art. It traces its history back to the 8C and was an important trading place until the 16C. Completely flattened during World War II, Emden was rebuilt in modern but aesthetic fashion with a picturesque harbor, little canals and red-brick houses. Today, the driving force behind its economy is the huge Volkswagen factory.

- **Information:** Bahnhofsplatz 11, 26721 Emden. ☎(04921) 974 00. www.emden-touristik.de
- ▶ **Orient Yourself:** Emden sits on the mouth of the Ems River across from the Dutch border. Thanks to the Dortmund-Ems canals, the town has regained its position as Lower Saxony's chief maritime port.
- **Don't Miss:** Kunsthalle art museum.
- **Also See:** OLDENBOURG, BREMEN, OSTFRIESISCHE INSELN.

Sights

Ostfriesisches Landesmuseum★ (East Frisian Regional Museum)

Rathaus am Delft, Neutorstraße 7–9.
Open year-round, Tue–Sat 10am–6pm.
6€. ☎(04921) 87 20 58. www.landesmuseum-emden.de.

This recently modernized museum is a comprehensive treasure trove of all things East Frisian going back to the Stone Age. Pride of place goes to the **Rüstkammer**★★ (armory), one of Germany's largest collections of 16C and 17C weapons and armor once used by the local militia for defensive purposes. The **mummified body**★ of a young man who lived during the early Middle Ages and who was unearthed in a local peat bog always gets good crowds as well. A fine sampling of Dutch paintings, mostly from the 17C, and graphics arts, including works by Alfred Rethel and Max Liebermann, shows off Emden's artistic heritage.

Port

Ratsdelft.
The oldest section is the **harbor gateway** *(Hafentor)* built in 1635 and bearing the Latin inscription *"God is Emden's bridge, harbor and sailing wind"*.
In the historical harbor basin are several **museum ships** *(Museumsschiffe)*.

Pelzerhäuser

Open year-round, Tue–Wed and Fri-Sun 11am–6pm. ☎(04921) 253 35.
The steeply gabled, red-brick town houses at Pelzerstraße 11 and 12 are the only surviving examples of the 16C Dutch-Flemish Renaissance style that once dominated Emden. One contains period rooms that shed light on how an upper middle class family might have

lived in the 17C and 18C. The other house hosts changing exhibits.

Kunsthalle Emden★★ (Art Museum Emden)

Hinter dem Rahmen 13; northwest of town.

◑Open year-round, Tue 10am–8pm, Wed–Fri 10am–5pm, Sat–Sun 11am–6pm. ◎10€. ⬥⬤(04921) 97 50 50. www.kunst halle-emden.de.

This postmodern red-brick museum houses the sizeable private collection of *Stern* magazine founder and local boy Henri Nannen. A major emphasis is on **German Expressionist** art, with major household names brightening the spacious galleries.

Look for works by *Brücke* (Bridge) artists Kirchner, Heckel and Schmidt-Rottluff along with *Blue Rider* members Marc, Macke, Münter and Jawlensky. Contemporary creativity is represented by the 1980s **Neue Wilde** group (New Wild Ones) that included Hödicke, Zimmer, Richter and Damisch—less familiar names, perhaps, but all seminal post-1980 artists.

Excursions

Suurhusen

6km/3.7mi north, via the B70.

According to the Guinness World Records 2009, the tower (15C) of the 13C church in tiny Suurhusen tilts at a steeper angle (5.17º) than the tower of Pisa (3.97º), making it the world's "most leaning tower". Recent evidence, however, suggests this may be rivalled by a 12C church tower in Bedum, Holland.

Jever

60km/37mi northeast, via the B210.

This petite outpost is where the famous *Jever Pilsner* is brewed.

Sneak a peek into the hallowed brewery halls on a guided tour of the **Friesisches Brauhaus** *(Elisabethufer 18; ⌖tours by prior arrangement; ◎7€; ⬤(04461) 137 11; www.jever.de).*

Jever's most prominent historical landmark is the fortified 14C **Schloss** *(palace,* ◑open year round, Tue–Sun 10am–6pm; ◎3.50€; ⬥⬤(04461) 96 93 50)*, which now serves as a cultural history museum with period rooms, historical workshops and an audience hall with elaborate coffered oak ceiling.

ERFURT★★

POPULATION: 200 800

Erfurt, the state capital of Thuringia, is a peaceful, captivating university town with an enchanting silhouette of steeples and bell-towers. The cobbled lanes of its lively Old Town are lined with carefully restored centuries-old buildings. It is the main city closest to the geographical center of reunified Germany.

- **Information:** Benediktsplatz 1, 99084 Erfurt. ⬤(0361) 664 00. www.erfurt-tourismus.de.
- ▶ **Orient Yourself:** Erfurt is off the A4 autobahn, between Gotha and Weimar.
- P **Parking:** Garages near the Dom, the main train station and throughout town.
- ⊚ **Don't Miss:** Mariendom, Severikirche
- ◑ **Organizing Your Time:** Spend about one day seeing the main sights.
- ⬥ **Also See:** WEIMAR, EISENACH, THÜRINGER WALD.

A Bit of History

A trading town – Erfurt was founded as a bishopric by the English missionary St Boniface in 742.

Its strategic location along the important trade route linking the Rhineland with Russia—the Via Regia—greatly contributed to the town's prosperity in the Middle Ages. So did the production of a much sought-after blue pigment derived from the woad plant. In the 15C, Erfurt joined the Hanseatic League.

Spirituality and Humanism – Nicknamed "Thuringian Rome" because of its roughly 90 churches and chapels, Erfurt has long attracted religious thinkers. The influential Christian mystic **Master Eckhart** was born in nearby Gotha and in 1298 became prior of Erfurt's Dominican convent and vicar-provincial of Thuringia. Two centuries later **Martin Luther** further shook the religious world with his 95 theses protesting church corruption. He studied philosophy at Erfurt university between 1501 and 1505, then entered the Augustinian monastery before setting off for Wittenberg.

Walking Tour

Around the Domplatz

The Domplatz is dominated by two imposing houses of worship: the Mariendom (St. Mary's Cathedral) and the Severikirche (Church of St. Severus). In the square's center, an obelisk commemorates a visit in 1777 by the Archbishop of Mainz.

Dom St. Marien★★

Erfurt's most prominent landmark, the cathedral was completed in the 14C and stands on top of several predecessors dating back to the 8C.

Its richly ornamented **triangular portals**★★ at the north entrance consist of two doors set obliquely and supporting elegant statuary groups depicting the Apostles and the Wise and Foolish Virgins.

The church's **interior** boasts several important artworks: the Romanesque altar of the Virgin (1160); the **bronze candelabrum**★ shaped like a man and known as "Wolfram" (1160); the melodious Gloriosa bell (1497); and the intricately worked choir stalls (14C). The stained-glass **windows**★ above the choir (c. 1370–1420) depict episodes from the Old and New Testament as well as from the lives of various saints. Luther was ordained a priest here in 1507 and held his first lectures in *Auditorium Coelicum* below the church.

Severi-Kirche★ (Church of St. Severus)

Linked to the cathedral by a sprawling, 70-step open staircase, St. Severi is a five-nave Early Gothic hall church that also harbors its share of treasures.

Address Book

🪙 *For coin ranges, see cover flap.*

WHERE TO STAY

⊝⊜**Hotel Erfurtblick** – Nibelungenweg 20. ☎(0361) 22 06 60. www.hotel-erfurtblick.de. 10 rooms. This private, spotless hotel has light, airy rooms. Relax in the garden or enjoy views of the town from the breakfast room and terrace.

⊝⊜**Hotel Nikolai** – Augustinerstraße 30. ☎(0361) 59 81 71 19. www.hotel-nikolai-erfurt.de. 17 rooms. Restaurant ⊝⊜. In the heart of the old town, between the cathedral and the Augustinian monastery, this small hotel has timelessly elegant rooms The restaurant serves inspired home cooking.

WHERE TO EAT

⊝⊜⊜**Alboth's Restaurant** – Futterstraße 15. ☎(0361) 568 82 07. Closed Sun and Mon, late Jan to mid-Feb and 3 weeks in Jul /Aug. This chic restaurant is an historic town house has dark wood ceilings and serves meticuously prepared and creative international dishes with a regional touch.

⊝⊜⊜**Köstritzer "Zum güldenen Rade"** – Marktstraße 50. ☎(0361) 561 35 06. www.zum-gueldenen-rade.de. Stone walls, wood and paintings belie this stylish eateries origin as a tobacco mill dating back to 1551. Thuringian specialties dominate the menu, including excellent potato dumplings. In fine weather, tables in the garden and interior courtyard are the most coveted.

ERFURT							
		Fischmarkt	A		Regierungsstr.	A	34
		Löberstr.	B	22	Schlösserstr.	AB	36
Anger	B	Mainzerhofstr.	A	24	Schlüterstr.	A	37
Bahnhofstr.	B	Marktstr.	A		Walkmühlstr.	A	40
Dalbergsweg	A 13	Meienbergstr.	B	27	Wenigemarkt	B	42
Domstr.	A 15	Moritzwallstr.	A	28	Willy-Brandt-Pl.	B	43
Angermuseum	B M¹	Rathaus	A	R			

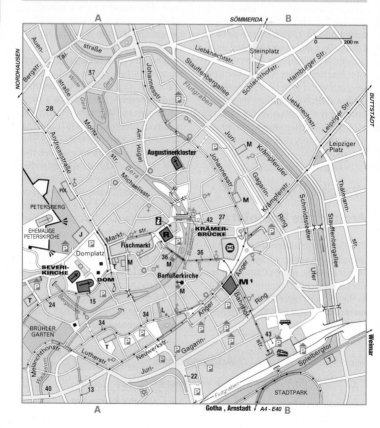

The saint's remains were brought to Erfurt from Ravenna, where he served as a bishop, in 836 and have been enshrined in an elaborate **sarcophagus**★ since the 14C. Also note the stone Madonna (1345) and the 15m/45ft-high baptismal font (1467)

▶ *Cross the Domplatz and follow Marktstraße.*

Around the Fischmarkt

Fischmarkt (Fish Market)
Inside the imposing Neo-Gothic **Rathaus** *(Town Hall;* ○*open year-round,* *Mon, Tue, Thu 8am–6pm, Wed 4pm, Fri 2pm, Sat–Sun 10am–5pm)* are **frescoes**★ illustrating the lives of Luther, Faust and Tannhäuser. The square is framed by magnificent townhouses that reflect the wealth of the one-time woad traders. Standouts include the buildings known as *"Zum Breiten Herd"* and *"Zum Roten Ochsen".*

Krämerbrücke★ (Merchants' Bridge)
This bridge across the little Gera River, built in 1325, is the only one north of the Alps with houses built on it. Most are narrow, half-timbered structures dating

from the 16C to the 19C. The bridge is 18m/59ft wide and 120m/393.7ft long.

Angermuseum★

Anger 18. ◦━Closed for restoration until at least 2009. ☎(0361) 554 56 11. www. angermuseum.de.

This museum presents medieval art from Thuringia in a Baroque building from 1706. Among its highlights are 14C and 15C **altarpieces**★★; a **Pietà**★★ by the Master of St. Severinus; and sarcophagai and paintings by Hans Baldung Grien. In the gallery is a collection of 18C–19C German landscape painting.

Augustinerkloster (Augustinian Monastery)

━Visit by guided tour hourly year round: Mon–Sat 10am–noon, 2pm–5pm, Sun 11am, 2pm and 4pm; until 4pm Mon–Sat in Nov–Apr; ≈5€; ☎(0361) 576 600. www.augustinerkloster.de.

This austere monastery is an important stop for Martin Luther pilgrims. The Reformer stayed here as an Augustinian Monk from 1505–1511. Tours take in the room where Luther lived and exhibits about his life and accomplishments. Admission to the church, where he held his first mass, is free.

Zitadelle Petersberg (Petersberg Citadel)

Open Apr–Oct, daily 11am–6pm; Nov–Dec, 11am–4pm. Closed Jan 1, Dec 24, 25 & 31. ≈3.50€. ━Guided tours (1hr) Apr–Dec several times daily; ≈3.50€) ☎(0361) 601 53 84.

One of the best-preserved Baroque fortifications in central Europe, this citadel was built between 1665 and 1707 atop the foundations of a Benedictine monastery. It contains a museum on military history, but to explore the subterranean defensive tunnels you must join a guided tour.

Excursions

Gotha★

25km/15.5mi west via the B7.

One of the oldest settlements in Thuringia, Gotha can trace its history back to 775 and prospered as an important trade route stop in the Middle Ages. After the Thirty Years' War, the local dukes built the first and largest Baroque palace in Thuringia: the U-shaped **Schloss Friedenstein** (*open year-round, Tue–Sun 10am–5pm; ≈5€; ☎(03621) 82 34 51; www.stiftungfriedenstein.de*), now home to several museums. If you have limited time, focus on the **Schloss-museum**, whose extravagant rooms are like a 3D textbook in the lifestyles of the rich and noble of the 17C and 18C. The opulent setting is the perfect backdrop for an eclectic collection of coins, sculpture, antiques, etchings and even objects from ancient Egypt. Walls are graced with paintings by such masters as Cranach the Elder and Rubens, although top billing actually goes to the famous *Gotha Lovers* by an anonymous artist. The **Kunstkammer** (art chamber) boasts such exotic items as engraved ostrich eggs, carved ivory and decorated coconut shells.

The other museums deal with local folk art and nature, but considerably more unique is the Baroque **Ekhof-Theater** (*separate admission ≈2.50€*). It has lavish décor and ingenious mechanics

Bad Frankenhausen

60km/37mi north via A71 autobahn.

Known as the **Kyffhäuser**, the dense forests to the north of Erfurt are steeped in legend and history. In 1525, the area was engulfed in the final battle of the German Peasants' War that ended with the peasants' bloody defeat by the allied princes of Saxony and Hesse. In the 1980s, East German artist Werner Tübke impressively depicted the event as a 14m/46ft-high and 123m /403ft-long circular oil painting. Featuring 3 000 figures in dozens of scenes, it is inside the custom-built **Panorama Museum** (*open Apr–Oct, Tue–Sun 10am–6pm, Nov–Mar 5pm; ≈5€; ☎(034671) 6190; www.panorama-museum.de*) on a hilltop about 3km/1.8mi north of Bad Frankenhausen.

Equally epic is the 81m/266ft-high **monument** (*open year-round, daily 9am–7pm; ≈5€*) atop the Kyffhäuser Mountain. Built in the 1890s, it commemorates the founding of the German Empire in 1871.

ERZGEBIRGE★

For centuries, the Ore Mountains coughed up silver, tin, cobalt, nickel and iron in sumptuous proportions, bringing great prosperity to this remote region of Saxony. When the mines petered out, locals turned to craftmaking as a source of income. Many of Germany's finest Christmas ornaments and decorations are still produced here, often by hand, to this day.

▯ **Information:** Adam-Ries-Straße 16, 09456 Annaberg-Buchholz. ☎(03733) 18 80 00. www.erzgebirge-tourismus.de.

▸ **Orient Yourself:** The mountains follow the border of Germany and the Czech Republic for about 150km.

◔ **Organizing Your Time:** Allow at least three hours for the suggested driving tour.

Driving Tour

From Annaberg-Buchholz to Klingenthal

81km/50.3mi (93km/57.7mi via Schwarzenberg). Follow the B95 from Annaberg-Buchholz (⌕see ANNABERG-BUCHHOLZ) to Oberwiesenthal.

Fichtelberg★

The highest peak of the Erzgebirge, the Fichtelberg soars 1 214m/3 983ft above the ski resort of Oberwiesenthal. Ride the chair-lift to the top for a sweeping **panorama**★.

▸ *A pretty forest road winds from Oberwiesenthal to Ehrenzipfel. Optional detour to Schwarzenberg.*

Schwarzenberg

Resting on a crag, this historic town boasts a 12C fortress that became the elector's hunting lodge in 1555–58 and the adjacent Baroque **St. Georgenkirche**★ (1690–99).

▸ *The road reaches the Sosa Talsperre, a pretty reservoir and a nice spot to stretch your legs. The route then climbs along the winding valley of the Zwickauer Mulde to Klingenthal.*

Klingenthal

This former mining community is best known for the musical instruments made here since the mid-17C. The Baroque church **Zum Friedenfürsten** makes a pleasant stop.

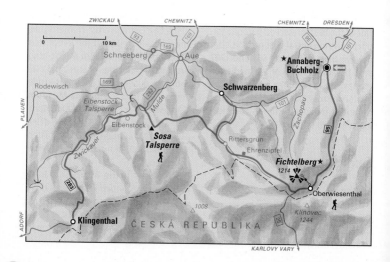

ESSEN ★

POPULATION: 589 500

Essen traces it pedigree back to the 8C but made its biggest mark on history during the Industrial Age. Closely associated with the Krupp family dynasty, Its steel works and collieries were the engines driving the German economy until well into the 1960s. Since then, Essen has been a city in transition, replacing its smokestacks with "clean-air" industries such as finance, administration, a university and plenty of business, commerce and culture. It has been named European Cultural Capital of 2010, along with the rest of the Ruhr region.

- **Information:** Am Hauptbahnhof 2, 45127 Essen. ☎(0201) 194 33. www.essen.de.
- **Orient Yourself:** Essen is one of the largest cities in the Ruhr region, wedged between Bochum and Duisburg along the A40 autobahn.
- **Parking:** Garages abound throughout the city center, including large ones at the train station and near the Town Hall (via Ribbeckstraße).
- **Don't Miss:** Zollverein, Münster, Museum Folkwang
- **Also See:** *DÜSSELDORF (35km/22mi southwest) DORTMUND (38km/23mi east), COLOGNE (74km/45mi south)*

Sights

Museum Folkwang★★

Kahrstraße 16D.
Open year-round, Tue–Sun 10am–6pm, Fri 9pm. Closed Jan 1, May 1, Easter Mon, Pentecost Mon, Dec 24 & 31. 5€. ☎(0201) 884 53 01; www.museum-folkwang.de.
An Aladdin's cave of paintings, sculpture, graphic art and photography stretching across the 19C and 20C, this museum is one of Germany's premier repositories of fine art with particular emphasis on German and French artists. Galleries are filled with a veritable who's who of famous names, from Romantic artist Caspar David Friedrich and modern trailblazers Cézanne, Gauguin and van Gogh to German Expressionists Heckel, Kirchner, Schmidt-Rottluff and postwar bigshots like Baselitz, Kiefer and Pollock.

Construction is underway on a new museum building designed by David Chipperfield. Until its completion in 2010, the old museum hosts temporary exhibits, while 80 masterpieces from the permanent collection are on view at Villa Hügel until August 2009.

Villa Hügel★

Open year-round, Tue–Sun 10am–6pm, park daily 8am–8pm. Closed Jan 1 and Dec 24–26. 3€. ☎(0201) 188 48 23. www.villahuegel.de.
This imposing Gründerzeit mansion stands in an attractive park on the north shore of **Lake Baldeney**. Three generations of the industrialist Krupp family lived here from 1873 to 1945. You can tour their private quarters, study company history and stroll around the lovely park. The biggest crowds turn out for the periodic special art exhibits.

Address Book

🪙 *For coin ranges, see the Legend on the cover flap.*

TOURS

CITY TOURS

The **tourist office** *(Am Hauptbahnhof 2; ☎(0201) 194 33; 🍴10€)* organizes 2hr bus tours taking in the major sights as well as the historic suburbs of Kettwig and Werden. Tours leave from the bus stop outside Haus der Technik on Hollestraße.

WHERE TO STAY

🛏️🛏️**Hotel Europa** – *Hindenburgstraße 35. ☎(0201) 23 20 41. www.hotel-europa-essen.de. Closed Christmas and Easter. 49 rooms.* This central city hotel above a parking garage radiates old-fashioned hospitality in well-kept rooms, some of them with more up-to-date décor.

🛏️🛏️**Landhaus Knappmann** – *Ringstraße 198, 45219 Essen-Kettwig. ☎(02054) 78 09. www.hotel-landhaus-knappmann.de. Closed Dec 22–Jan 4. 16 rooms. Restaurant 🍴🍴.* Run by the same family since 1919, this country inn has warmly furnished, large and modern accommodations, some with exposed half-timbered beams, others with whirlpool tub. Regional home-cooking dominates in the earthy, brewpub-style restaurant.

🛏️🛏️🛏️🛏️**Mintrops Stadt Hotel Margarethenhöhe** – *Steile Straße 46, 45149 Essen-Margarethenhöhe. ☎(0201) 438 60. www.hotel-margarethenhoehe.de. 30 rooms. Restaurant 🍴🍴🍴.* A former guesthouse of the industrial Krupp family has taken on new life as a chic, design-minded hotels with modern, artsy rooms with such extra touches as heated bathroom floors. The restaurant is known for its innovative dishes.

WHERE TO EAT

🍴🍴**Schote** – *Emmastraße 25. ☎(0201) 78 01 07. www.schote.de. Closed Mon and 3 weeks in Aug.* Behind large picture windows awaits this modern, brightly colored bistro with service that is all smiles. A lively locals' spot, it puts you close to the cafés and bars of Rüttenscheider Straße.

🍴🍴🍴**La Grappa** – *Rellinghauser Straße 4. ☎(0201) 23 17 66. www.la-grappa.de. Closed Sat lunch and Sun. Reservations recommended.* This candle-lit cove embellished with paintings, plates, bottles and mirrors is a fine place for an Italian dinner.

🍴🍴🍴**Casino Zollverein** – *Gelsenkirchner Straße 181. ☎(0201) 83 02 40. www.casino-zollverein.de. Closed Dec 26-Jan 10 and Mon.* The New World Cuisine is as creative as the design of this unique restaurant inside the former compressor hall of the Zollverein colliery. In summer a beer garden beckons.

🍴🍴🍴**Schloss Hugenpoet** – *August-Thyssen-Straße 51, 45219 Essen-Kettwig. ☎(02054) 12 04 50. www.hugenpoet.de. Restaurants.* Surrounded by a park, this gorgeous 1647 palace is filled with period pieces that give it a timeless elegance. For dinner, book a table in the fine dining Restaurant Nesselrode or the more casual Hugenpöttchen, which specializes in modern international cuisine with Italian inflections.

ENTERTAINMENT

Aalto Theater – *Opernplatz 10. ☎(0201) 812 22 00. www.theater-essen.de.* In a stunning building designed by Alvar Aalto, one of the seminal architects of the 20C, Essen's main cultural venue presents opera, light opera, musicals, ballet and classical concerts. With its flowing floorplan, the structure is meant to evoke the landscape of Aalto's home country, Finland.

Grillo Theater – *Theaterplatz. ☎(0201) 812 22 00. www.theater-essen.de.* Essen's main stage for live theater enjoys a fine reputation for its innovative productions of classic plays and for also taking on works by promising contemporary playwrights.

Philharmonie Essen – *Huyssenallee 53. ☎(0180) 595 95 98. www.philharmonie-essen.de.* The city's esteemed philharmonic orchestra is based in the gorgeous and completely modernized historic Saalbau concert hall. Opened by Richard Strauss in 1904, it enjoys superb acoustics and also hosts guest performers, artists-in-residence and jazz groups.

©Ulrike Hammerich/Dreamstime.com

Zollverein

Zollverein★★

Gelsenkirchner Straße 181.

🕐*Open year-round, daily 10am–5pm, Fri 7pm.* ☎*(0201) 83 03 60. www.zollverein.de.* Once one of the Ruhr region's most productive collieries, Zollverein has been rebooted as a cultural and arts center and included on UNESCO's prestigious list of World Heritage Sites.

The boiler house of the Bauhaus-style complex was ingeniously converted by Lord Norman Foster into the **Red Dot Design Museum** (🕐*open year-round, Tue–Thu 11am–6pm, Fri-Sun 11am–8pm;* 🕐*closed Jan 1, Dec 24, 25 & 31.* ⊜*5€;* ☎*(0201) 301 04 25; www.red-dot.de).*

It presents award-winning contemporary product design.

Scheduled to open in late 2009 in the former coal wash house, the **Ruhr Museum** *(www.ruhrmuseum.de)* uses state-of-the-art technology to trace the history of the Ruhr region from the pre-industrial era to today. Until then, you can see the free temporary exhibits at the **Visitor Center**, which also runs guided tours throughout the day.

Münster (Cathedral)★★

🕐*Open year-round, Mon–Fri 6.30am–6.30pm, Sat 9am–7.30pm, Sun 9am–8pm.* 🕐*Closed Mon, Fri 8am–10am.* ♿☎*(0201) 220 42 06. www.dom-essen.de.* Just off the main pedestrian shopping strip, Essen's medieval cathedral offers peaceful respite and a bonanza of art treasures, including some from the

Ottonian period. The undisputed highlights are the **Golden Madonna**★★★ (AD 980), one of the oldest surviving sculptures from the early Middle Ages, and a massive **seven-branch candelabrum**★ (c. 1000). The **cathedral treasury**★★ *(Domschatzkammer;* 🕐*open year-round, Tue–Sat 10am–5pm, Sun 11.30am–5pm;* 🕐*closed Oct 2008 to Feb 2009, major religious and public holidays;* ⊜*3€;* ☎*(0201) 220 42 06; www. domschatz-essen.de)* holds among other items four splendid **processional crosses**★★★ (10C and 11C) and a reliquary said to contain a nail from Jesus' cross.

Alte Synagoge (Old Synagogue)

Steeler Straße 29.

🕐*Open year-round, Tue–Sun 10am–6pm.* ☎*(0201) 884 5218. www.alte-synagoge. essen.de.*

Essen's 1913 synagogue features a memorial exhibit on Jewish life from Emancipation to today and another on the years of Nazi persecution from 1933–1945.

Werden

The suburb of Werden was largely spared wartime destruction and still exudes medieval charm. The sight not to miss is the **Abteikirche St. Liudger** (Abbey Church of St. Ludger), a harmoniously proportioned Late Romanesque church with an important treasury.

FRANKFURT AM MAIN★★

POPULATION: 643 000

Germany's financial and commercial capital, Frankfurt's center is a forest of skyscrapers filled with international companies, government organizations and banks. Some of the world's biggest trade shows, including the famous Frankfurt Book Fair, take place in high-tech halls near the airport, the largest and busiest on the continent. But Frankfurt isn't all business. Join the locals in the traditional apple cider taverns, visit Goethe's birth house or take in the stellar exhibits in the string of museums hugging the south bank of the Main River.

- ⓘ **Information:** Hauptbahnhof, 60329 Frankfurt am Main. ☎(069) 21 23 88 49. www. frankfurt.de.
- ▸ **Orient Yourself:** Frankfurt stands at Germany's crossroads, both literally and figuratively. Two major autobahns join here: The A3 (Köln–Nürnberg) and the A5 (Karlsruhe). The city is 2hr from Köln and 2hr 30 from Nürnberg.
- 🅿 **Parking:** Garages are located throughout the city. Visit http://wap.parkinfo.com for specific locations and fees.
- ⊘ **Don't Miss:** Städelsches Kunstinstitut, Römerberg and the cathedral.
- 🕐 **Organizing Your Time:** Allow a day to take in the major sights.
- 🄺🄸🄳🅂 **Especially for Kids:** Zoo, Senckenberg Natural History Museum.
- ⓒ **Also See:** DARMSTADT, WIESBADEN, MAINZ, RHEINTAL.

A Bit of History

The second coronation city – Built in the 8C on the site of a Roman military camp, Frankfurt rose to prominence in 1152 with the election of Frederick I Barbarossa as German king. All subsequent royal elections until 1796 took place here, a status officially confirmed in 1362 by the Golden Bull issued by Emperor Charles IV. In 1562 Frankfurt even replaced Aachen as the **coronation place** of the Holy Roman emperors – a privilege it retained until the dissolution of the Reich in 1806.

©Goesta A. C. Ruehl/Tourism + Congress GmbH Frankfurt a. M.

Frankfurt skyline

The Young Goethe – Johann Wolfgang von Goethe was born in Frankfurt in 1749. Between 1772 and 1775, he penned many of his classics here, including *The Sorrows of Young Werther*, which allegedly took him only four weeks.

Capital of Finance and Economy – In the 16C Frankfurt was granted the right to mint money. The money market flourished and the **stock exchange** followed. German banks dominated the economy in the 18C; in the 19C they acquired a worldwide reputation thanks to financiers such as **Bethmann** and above all, **Rothschild**, whose sons, "the Five Frankfurters", established branches throughout Europe. Industry quickly followed in the wake of such a favorable climate. Frankfurt has always been a trade show city, starting in 1240 with the first Autumn Fair. Since the 20C, the Fur Fair *(Pelzmesse)*, the Motor Show *(Automobilausstellung)* and the famous Book Fair *(Buchmesse)* have underscored Frankfurt's role as Germany's capital of commerce and finance as did the EU's decision to base the European Central Bank here.

City Life – Despite its cosmopolitan character, this metropolis on the

Address Book

♦For coin ranges, see the Legend on the cover flap.

BASIC INFORMATION

TELEPHONE PREFIX: 069

VISITOR INFORMATION

Tourismus + Congress GmbH can help with room reservations (☎21 23 88 00; *www.frankfurt-tourismus.de; open Mon–Fri 8am–9pm, Sat–Sun 9am–6pm*). Walk-in tourist office branches: Hauptbahnhof, central station entrance hall, *open Mon–Fri 8am–9pm, Sat–Sun 9am–6pm*; Römer, Römerberg 27, *open Mon–Fri 9.30am–5.30pm, Sat–Sun 10am–4pm*.

For listings and calendar of events, consult the city magazines *Journal Frankfurt* and *Prinz* (available at newsstands) or *Frizz* and *Strandgut* (free at bars, shops, tourist offices). *Welcome to Frankfurt* (in German) is another source.

POST OFFICES WITH LATE HOURS

Zeil 90 branch *(Mon–Wed 9.30am–8pm, Thu–Sat 9.30am–9pm)*; main train station—Hauptbahnhof, 1st floor *(Mon–Fri 7am–7.30pm, Sat 8am–4pm)*; airport branch *(daily 7am–10pm)*.

NEWSPAPERS

Frankfurter Allgemeine Zeitung, Frankfurter Rundschau, Frankfurter Neue Presse.

INTERNET

www.frankfurt.de
www.rhein-main.net
www.frankfurt-online.net
www.frankfurt-tourismus.de

GETTING AROUND

Much of the city center is a pedestrian zone, meaning the best way to get around is on foot.

PUBLIC TRANSPORTATION

The **RMV** (Rhein-Main-Verkehrsbund) is responsible for all public transportation services: Trams, buses, U-Bahn and S-Bahn, and regional trains in the greater Frankfurt region: ☎ (01805) 768 46 36 (0.14€/min) daily, 6am–midnight. The **VGF** (Verkehrsgesellschaft Frankfurt am Main) manages the local public trans-

portation of the city of Frankfurt: ☎194 49, Mon–Thu 8am–5pm, Fri 8am–1pm. Information kiosks are in the arcade of the Hauptwache, Mon–Fri 9am–8pm, Sat 9.30am–4pm; the arcades at Konstablerwache, Passage B level, Mon–Fri 9am–8pm, Sat 9.30am–4pm. The tariff rate 3 is valid for all rides within Frankfurt. Single tickets are 2.20€, day tickets 5.90€ (also valid for travel to the airport). Tickets are available at vending machines and from bus drivers but not aboard trams and U-Bahn and S-Bahn trains.

Internet: www.rmv.de; www.vgf-ffm.de

The **Frankfurt Card** costs 8.70€ (valid for 24hr) and 12.50€ (valid for 72hr) for travel within the VGF network (Tariff rate 3, plus to the airport). It also entitles you to a 50% discount on admission to 15 museums and other attractions, such as the zoo and the airport visitor terraces, and 20–25% off selected boat and coach tours. The Frankfurt Card is available at www.frankfurt-tourismus. de, selected hotels, Hauptbahnhof and Römerberg tourist information offices and Frankfurt airport.

Tip: For S-Bahn rides to the airport you need a ticket at tariff rate 4.

WHERE TO STAY

⊜⊜**A Casa Bed & Breakfast** – *Varrentrappstraße 49.* ☎*(069) 97 98 88 21. www.hotel-acasa.de. Closed end of Dec to beginning of Jan. 6 rooms. This*

Ebbelwei-Express

small English-style B&B in an old villa has tasteful, individually decorated rooms reflecting the theme of their names: Miami, Goethe, Rose Garden, Montparnasse, Bahama and Piccolo.

⊜⊜**Hotel-Pension Gölz** – Beethoven-straße 44. ☎(069) 74 67 35. www.hotel-goelz.de. Closed Dec. 12 rooms. A stone's throw from the city center and trade fair grounds, this family-run hotel in a 19C villa has spacious doubles rooms and basic singles. All rooms are nonsmoking.

⊜⊜**Hotel Wiesbaden** – Basler Straße 52. ☎(069) 36 50 75 80. www.hotelwiesbaden.net. 39 rooms. Small, simple, clean and comfortable, this hotel near the station is popular with backpackers and others traveling on a budget. Good value for money.

⊜⊜**Kolping Hotel Frankfurt** – Lange Straße 26. ☎(069) 29 90 60. www.kolpinghotel-frankfurt.de. 50 rooms Restaurant⊜. This simple, functional hotel is in the heart of the city center, near the Allerheiligentor and under the same roof as the Kolping youth training institute. The trade show grounds, airport and central station are within easy reach by public transport.

⊜⊜⊜**Hotel Hamburger Hof** – Poststraße 10. ☎(069) 27 13 96 90. www.hamburgerhof.com. 66 rooms. Light and airy rooms with stylish con-temporary touches make this business hotel opposite the Hauptbahnhof north exit a good base of operation.

⊜⊜⊜**Hotel Liebig** – Liebigstraße 45. ☎(069) 24 18 29 90. www.hotelliebig.de. Closed Dec22–Jan 2. 20 rooms. ⊡14€. Small hotel in a villa in the bank district with charming and luxurious rooms sporting Italian- and English-style furniture and beautiful fabrics.

⊜⊜⊜⊜**Hilton** – Hochstraße 4. ☎(069) 133 80 00. www.hilton.com. 342 rooms. ⊡29€. Restaurant⊜⊜. A spacious, open atrium-style lobby provides access to rooms that lack no modern conveniences and are reached via a glass elevator. Bonus: the fitness club with a 25m/82ft-long swimming pool. The restaurant serves American and international fare.

⊜⊜⊜⊜**Steigenberger Frankfurter Hof** – Am Kaiserplatz. ☎(069) 215 02. www.frankfurter-hof.steigenberger.de. 321 rooms. ⊡28€. Restaurants⊜⊜⊜, closed Sun. This 1876 grand hotel was once the ancestral residence of the Stei-genberg family and has been perfectly renovated. Luxury reigns throughout, from the elegant lobby to the rooms. Dining options are the bistro-style Oscar, the pan-Asian Iroha and gourmet restaurant Français.

WHERE TO EAT

⊜⊜**Bauer** – Sandweg 113. ☎(069) 40 59 27 44. www.gebrueder-bauer.de. Closed Sat lunchtime. ⊠ This fashion-able establishment, in a residential quarter near the city center, attracts people of all ages. The Bauer brothers serve varied dishes in a bistro-style setting.

⊜⊜**Steinernes Haus** – Braubach-straße 35. ☎(069) 28 34 91. www.stein-ernes-haus.de. Reservation necessary. This pleasant, rustic establishment is some 500 years old, making it one of the oldest in Frankfurt. It is surrounded by art galleries. Typical Frankfurt cuisine and specialities grilled on lava stone can be sampled here.

⊜⊜**Toan** – Friedberger Anlage 14. ☎(069) 44 98 44. Closed Mon and late Jun–mid-Jul. Right by the zoo and Frankfurt's green belt, this modern, streamlined restaurant serves excellent Vietnamese food and also has a garden terrace.

⊜⊜⊜**Meyer's Restaurant** – Große Bockenheimer Straße 54. ☎(069) 91 39 70 70 www.meyer-frankfurt.de. Closed Sun and public holidays. Reservations recommended. At this wee bistro-res-taurant on the edge of the pedestrian zone near the old opera house you can see the chefs bustling about in the open kitchen in back.

⊜⊜⊜**Restaurant-Café Zum Schwarzen Stern** – Römerberg 6. ☎(069) 29 19 79. www.schwarzerstern. de. Reservations recommended. Goethe once opined that one could study Frankfurt's diverse architectural styles simply by looking at this half-timbered house. The same is true today, since the restaurant was painstakingly rebuilt after the war and again sports pleasant, rustic décor. Upscale seasonal German cuisine dominates the menu.

Ernos Bistro – *Liebigstraße 15. ☎(069) 72 19 97. www.ernosbistro.de. Closed Sat, Sun and holidays (except during fair days), Dec 22–Jan 8, March 21-Apr 1, three weeks in Jul.* A comfortable ambience reigns at this Westend restaurant that delivers classic cuisine infused with a creative, personal touch. The list of French wines is superb.

Tiger-Restaurant – *Heiligkreuzgasse 20. ☎(069) 92 00 22 25. www.tigerpalast.com. Closed Sun and Mon, Feb 2–5, Jul 13–Aug 12.* This modern restaurant shares space with the Tigerpalast variety theater and serves classic cuisine with Mediterranean inflection. Candlelight and brick vaulting create a relaxed atmosphere.

Apple cider served in a jug

Krüger/Tourism + Congress GmbH Frankfurt a. M.

Zarges – *Kalbächer Gasse 10. ☎(069) 29 90 30. www.zarges-frankfurt.com.* This famous Fressgasse deli has to-die-for cakes and pastries, freshly made sandwiches and delicacies from around the world. A gourmet restaurant and a bistro serving breakfast and lunch are also part of the premises.

TAKING A BREAK

USEFUL TIPS

The section of Große Bockenheimer Straße between Opernplatz and Börsenstraße (nicknamed the *Fressgasse* or "eating alley") is lined with casual eateries and a good place to grab a quick bite to eat.

Kleinmarkthalle – *Hasengasse 5–7. www.kleinmarkthalle.de. Closed Sun.* It's hard to resist all the regional and international specialties on offer in the stalls of this two-story covered market.

Sandwicher Fastgoodfood – *Feldbergstraße 28. ☎(069) 71 03 40 67 www.sandwicher.de. Closed Sun.* If this contemporary sandwich shop is any indication, "healthy" and "fast food" do not have to be mutually exclusive. Everything's made to order. There are additional outlets at Reuterweg 63, Baseler Straße 10, Mainzer Landstraße 15–17 and Beethovenstraße 3.

Wacker's Kaffee – *Kornmarkt 9 (south of the crossroads between Kleiner Hirschgraben and Bleidenstraße). ☎(069) 28 78 10. www.wackers-kaffee.de. Closed Sun.* Over 30 roasted coffees and 60 teas are available at this traditional establishment in business since 1914. Pastries and light dishes are also available.

NIGHTLIFE

USEFUL TIPS

After dark, Frankfurt's liveliest quarter is Sachsenhausen on the left bank of the Main. It is laced with olde-world cobble-stoned streets lined with traditional taverns serving *Äppelwoi*, the dry cider that is a local specialty. To keep it cool, it is usually served in grey-blue earthenware jugs called *Bembel*. Look for taverns along Große Rittergasse (one block south of Deutschherrnufer) and along Schweizer Straße.

Café Hauptwache – *An der Hauptwache 15. ☎(069) 21 99 86 27. www.cafe-hauptwache.de.* A Baroque 18C guardhouse and prison has been rebooted as a chic, cosmopolitan café with a lovely terrace.

Harry's New-York Bar – *Walther-von-Cronberg-Platz 1 (in the Lindner Hotel) ☎(069) 66 40 10. www.lindner.de.* Grab a clubby leather armchair and unwind in style at this classic, elegant bar where a piano player usually tickles the ivories. It's famous for its seemingly endless cocktail menu.

Jazzkeller – *Kleine Bockenheimer Straße 18a. ☎(069) 28 85 37. www.jazzkeller. com. Closed Mon–Tue.* Louis Armstrong, Dizzy Gillespie, Chet Baker—all the masters of jazz have played in this red-brick cellar, a German institution since 1952.

Tigerpalast Varieté Theater– *Heiligkreuzgasse 16–20.* ☎ *(069) 920 02 20. www.tigerpalast.de.* Enjoy an entertaining line-up of magicians, musicians, clowns and acrobats from around the world at this intimate midnight-blue theater.

SHOPPING

Frankfurt's **main shopping street** (department stores, mainstream chains) is the Zeil. More exclusive boutiques have set up along Große Bockenheimer Straße and Goethestraße, while indie stores line the streets of Sachsenhausen, Schweizer Straße in particular.
A fun **flea market** is held along Museumsufer on Saturdays.

Mainhas preserved an easy-going Hessian flair. It is around the **Hauptwache**, a square dating from 1729, that Frankfurt is busiest. The **Zeil** is said to be Germany's busiest shopping strip. To the north, the Westend quarter is losing the fight to stave off office blocks encroaching from the commercial center. Cafés, cabarets, bars and restaurants are grouped around the central station, while the taverns of the olde-worlde Sachsenhausen quarter, on the south bank of the Main, specialize in the celebrated **Äppelwoi** or **Ebbelwei** (slightly bitter cider), and *Handkäse mit Musik* (a small yellow cheese served with onions and vinegar sauce).

A General View – Frankfurt suffered tremendous destruction in World War II and was rebuilt as a modern city. Its distinctive skyline of skyscrapers has even garnered it the nickname "Mainhattan". The silhouette is most striking from the **Untermainbrücke** bridge. For the best birds-eye view, take the elevator up the **Main Tower** (*Neue Mainzer Straße*), which has an open-air platform at 200m/656ft.

Sights

Römer and Römerberg

The Römerberg is Frankfurt's historical central square and ringed by a collection of step-gabled, half-timbered houses, built in the 15C by rich merchants. What you see today, however, are faithful postwar reconstructions.

The most imposing building is the Römer itself, on the western side of the square, which is a jumble of three joined buildings. The block has served as Town Hall since 1405. After 1562, its banquet hall was used to celebrate the election and coronation of the emperors. The hall where the coronation itself took place— the **Kaisersaal** (Ⓒ*open year-round, daily 10am–1pm, 2pm–5pm;* Ⓒ*closed during official functions;* ⬮*2€;* ♿☎*(069)21 23 88 00)*—doubles as a gallery of oil portraits depicting all 52 emperors—Charlemagne to Franz II (1806).

Other buildings ringing the Römerberg include the 13C **Alte Nikolaikirche**, the half-timbered **Haus Wertheim**, the 1464 Italianate **Steinernes Haus** and a row of half-timbered 15C–18C mansions (all reconstructed). In the center of the square is the **Gerechtigkeitsbrunnen** (Fountain of Justice, 1543). Contrasting with the historical architecture is the

Election of the Emperors

In the Holy Roman Empire, the emperor was elected, which is why the crown passed between such dynasties as the Franconians (Salians), Saxons (Ottonians), Bavarians and Swabians (Hohenstaufens). Emperors granted privileges to dukes, counts and high prelates in order to keep the title in their family. In 1356, the Golden Bull limited the number of Electors to seven, three from the clergy (the Archbishops of Mainz, Cologne and Trier) and four laymen (Duke of Saxony, Margrave of Brandenburg, Count Palatine, King of Bohemia).

postmodern starkness of the **Schirn Kunsthalle**, a contemporary art gallery on the south side of Römerberg.

Kaiserdom St. Bartholomäus★ (Cathedral St. Bartholomew)

◷ *Open year-round, daily 9am–noon, 2.30pm–6pm.* ◷ *Closed Fri morning. www.dommuseum-frankfurt.de.*

Though technically not a cathedral (it is not a bishop's seat), Frankfurt's Dom played a key role in German history. The elections of all German kings from 1356 onward took place in what is called the *Wahlkapelle*, an austere chapel attached of the south end of the choir. Between 1562 and 1792, the church also hosted 10 imperial coronations.

The Dom's outstanding feature is the tall **west tower★★** *(Westturm)*, ornamented with a gabled polygonal crown and lantern. Inside are several artworks worth noting: the 16C sandstone **Crucifixion** by Mainz artist Hans Backoffen; the 14C finely worked **choir stalls★** crafted in the Upper Rhine; and **mural paintings** from 1427 of the Cologne School illustrating the legend of St Bartholomew. In the north chancel is the **Altar of Mary Sleeping** *(Maria-Schlaf Altar)*, from 1434, also of the Cologne School and the sole surviving altar from the original church. The large **Descent from the Cross** on the west wall was painted by Anthony van Dyck in 1627.

Dommuseum★ (Cathedral Museum)

◷ *Open year-round, Tue–Fri 10am–5pm, Sat–Sun 11am–5pm.* ◷ *Closed Jan 1, Dec 24, 25 & 31.* ⊚2€. ♿☎(069) 13 37 61 86. *www.dommuseum-frankfurt.de.*

This small museum is accessed from the cathedral cloister. Besides the treasury *(Domschatz)*, preserving precious gold works and vestments from the high Middle Ages, the Late Merovingian tomb of a young girl merits special attention. West of the cathedral is an **Archeological Garden** *(Historischer Garten)*, with remains of Roman, Carolingian and Baroque fortifications.

Museum für Moderne Kunst★ (Modern Art Museum)

Domstraße 10.

◷ *Open year-round, Tue–Sun 10am–5pm (Wed 8pm).* ◷ *Closed Ascension Day, Pentecost, Corpus Christi Day.* ⊚7€, *free admission last Sat of month.* ♿☎(069) 21 23 04 47. *www.mmk-frankfurt.de.*

Viennese architect Hans Hollein designed this triangle-shaped museum dubbed a "slice of cake" by locals. It is a suitably edgy setting for an impressive collection of 20C art with particular emphasis on the New York School (Claes Oldenburg, Andy Warhol) and German contemporary artists (Joseph Beuys, Mario Merz, Katharina Fritsch, and Gerhard Richter). Displays from the permanent collection rotate every few months.

Leonhardskirche

The exterior of this 15C Gothic church conceals its Romanesque origins. Two octagonal towers remain at the east end, along with a doorway embellished with fine carvings by **Master Engelbert**. The central nave is surrounded on three sides by a gallery. Fine stained-glass windows illuminate the chancel. To the left of the chancel are a superbly carved reredos representing scenes from the life of the Virgin and a painting by Holbein the Elder depicting the Last Supper. The baptismal chapel is in the north aisle.

Paulskirche

It was in this circular building that the German National Assembly, elected after the revolution of March, met from 1848 to 1849. Originally a church, it now houses an exhibition devoted to the history of the German democratic movement.

Goethe-Haus★ and Goethe-Museum

Grosser Hirschgraben 23–25.

◷ *Open year-round, daily 10am–6pm (Sun 5.30pm).* ◷ *Closed Jan 1, Good Fri, Dec 24, 25 & 31.* ⊚5€. ☎(069) 13 88 00. *www.goethehaus-frankfurt.de.*

Fans of the poet, playwright, diplomat and scientist Johann Wolfgang von Goethe (1749–1832) flock to this large town house where the great man first saw the light of day. You can see the study on the top floor where he penned many of his early works—usually standing at a high desk. It has been recreated

FRANKFURT

Allerheiligenstr.	HY	3
An der Hauptwache	GHY	
Bethmannstr.	GZ	7
Bleidenstr.	HY	9
Bockenheimer Landstr.	GY	10
Domstr.	HZ	13
Elisabethenstr.	HZ	16
Friedberger Anlage	HY	20
Friedberger Landstr.	HY	22

Friedensstr.	GZ	24
Goethestr.	G	
Gr. Bockenheimer Str.	GY	27
Große Friedbergerstr.	HY	29
Großer Hirschgraben	GZ	30
Kaiserstr.	GZ	
Kalbächer Gasse	GY	32
Kleiner Hirschgraben	GY	35
Limpurgergasse	HZ	36
Münchener Str.	GZ	
Münzgasse	GZ	40

Rechneigrabenstr.	HZ	50
Roßmarkt	GY	
Schillerstr.	GY	54
Stoltzestr.	HY	58
Taunusstr.	GZ	62
Untermainanlage	GZ	65
Weißfrauenstr.	GZ	68
Weserstr.	GZ	69
Zeil	HY	

Alte Nikolaikirche	HZ	A
Deutsches Architektur-Museum	GZ	M6
Deutsches Filmmuseum	GZ	M7
Goethe-Museum	GZ	M2
Haus Wertheim	HZ	B
Historisches Museum	HZ	M1

Jüdisches Museum	GZ	M3
Kunsthalle Schim	HZ	M12
Liebfrauenkirche	HY	E
Museum für Moderne Kunst	HY	M10
Museum für Post und Kommunikation	GZ	M5

Museum für Völkerkunde	GZ	M8
Naturmuseum Senckenberg	GY	M9
Römer und Römerberg	HZ	R
Städtische Galerie Liebieghaus	GZ	M4
Steinernes Haus	HZ	C

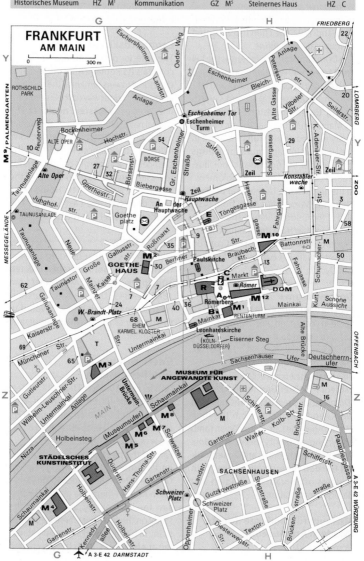

as it was in his lifetime. Right by the door hangs a silhouette portrait of Charlotte Buff, the object of his youthful passion and the inspiration for the character of Lotte in *The Sorrows of Young Werther*. A separate exhibition examines the lives of the Goethe family in 18C Frankfurt.

The adjoining **museum** is in fact a picture gallery dedicated to works by Goethe's contemporaries, including Tischbein, Graff, Hackert and Friedrich.

Museumsufer (Museum Bank)

Frankfurt's delightful "Museum Row" extends along the Schaumainkai between the Eiserner Steg and Friedens-brücke bridges.

Städel Museum★★

Schaumainkai 63.

⏰*Open year-round, Tue–Sun 10am–6pm (Wed–Thu 9pm).* ⏰*Closed Dec 24 & 31.* 🚪*10€.* ♿🕿*(069) 605 09 80. www.staedel museum.de.*

This stronghold of art houses 700 years' worth of European masters, making it one of the biggest and most important such collections in Germany. All the heavy hitters are there, from Old Masters such as Holbein the Elder, Grünewald, Altdorfer, Dürer, Vermeer, Rembrandt, Rubens and Tiepolo to French and German Impressionism, German Expressionism, Fauvism, Cubism, Surrealism, the Bauhaus and contemporary art. Part of the collection is in a stately 19C Neo-Renaissance building, the rest in a modern annex.

Museum für Angewandte Kunst★ (Museum of Applied Arts)

Schaumainkai 17.

⏰*Open year-round, Tue–Sun 10am–5pm (Wed 9pm).* 🚪*5€.* ♿🕿*(069) 21 23 85 30. www.angewandtekunst-frankfurt.de.*

The museum (1985) was designed by New York architect Richard Meier and consists of a modern building wrapped around a Neoclassical villa from 1803. Artifacts include furniture from the Middle Ages, Renaissance, Baroque and Jugendstil periods; 15C and 16C glassware; Islamic porcelain and carpets; and a book and calligraphy section.

Liebieghaus Skulpturen-Sammlung★ (Liebieg Sculpture Collection)

Schaumainkai 71.

⏰*Open year-round, Tue & Fri–Sun 10am–5pm, Wed–Thu 8pm.* 🚪*7€.* 🕿*(069) 650 04 90. www.liebieghaus.de.*

This museum is a fine place to trace the evolution of sculpture through the ages. The oldest works are from ancient Egypt, Greece and Rome, but there are also fine examples from the Middle Ages *(Tilmann Riemenschneider)*, the Renaissance *(Giambologna)* and Rococo and neoclassical *(Thorvaldsen)* periods. A sprinkling of Asian works provides an interesting contrast.

Deutsches Filmmuseum★ (German Film Museum)

Schaumainkai 41.

⏰*Open year-round, Tue, Thu–Fri 10am–5pm, Wed & Sun 10am–7pm, Sat 2pm–7pm.* 🚪*2.50€, free admission last Sat of month.* ♿🕿*(069) 961 220 220. www. deutschesfilmmuseum.de.*

The permanent exhibit of this museum is divided into two sections: one illustrates the origins of the cinema and displays such early inventions as a laterna magica and Edison's Kinetoscope (1889). The other zeroes in on the magic of movie making and the many steps involved in the production of both silent movies and talkies. This is supplemented by special exhibits and daily screenings of rare movies in the onsite cinema.

Zoo★★ 🔲Kids

⏰*Open year-round, Apr–Sept, daily 9am–7pm; Oct–Mar, 9am–5pm.* 🚪*8€ (child 4€).* ♿🕿*(069) 21 23 37 35. www.zoo-frank furt.de.*

Germany's second-oldest animal park (since 1858) is home to 4 800 denizens representing 565 species, including such endangered critters as black rhinos and okapis. The bird section with its huge free-flight aviary is also quite impressive. Penguins, reptiles, fish and insects inhabit the Exotarium while nocturnal animals such as koalas and the desert fox can be observed In the artificially darkened Grzimek-Haus. Kids especially love the simulated tropical storm in the crocodile enclosure.

Senckenberg Naturmuseum★ (Senckenberg Natural History Museum) `Kids`

Senckenberganlage 25,
via Bockenheimer Landstraße.
🕐*Open Tue, Thu–Fri 9am–5pm, Wed 8pm, Sat–Sun 6pm.* 💶*6€ (child 6–15yrs 3€).* ♿☎*(069) 754 20. www.senckenberg.de.*
Germany's largest natural history museum takes visitors on an eye-opening trip back in time and around the world. It is especially famous for its extensive **dinosaur collection**★★ (nearly 20 specimen) that includes a triceratops skull and a complete *Edmontosaurus* skeleton with preserved sections of scaled skin. Other highlights you will stumble upon include the 50-million-year-old fossils of a primitive horse★★ and other prehistoric animals dug up in the UNESCO-recognized pit mine of Messel. The shrunken head from the Ecuadorean Shuar Indian culture and the mummified bodies of two boys from Ancient Egypt are among the more macabre (and memorable!) objects on display.

Palmengarten★

Siesmayerstraße 61,
via Bockenheimer Landstraße.
🕐*Open Feb-Oct, daily 9am–6pm, Nov–Jan 4pm.* 💶*5€.* ♿☎*(069) 21 23 39 39.*
www.palmengarten-frankfurt.de.
If you need a break from the city bustle,, make a beeline to these lovely gardens that put on a dazzling display of plants and flowers throughout the year. The eponymous subtropical palms are housed in the 1869 **Palmenhaus**, one of the oldest greenhouses in Germany. The gardens are part of the Westend green belt and segue into the city's botanical garden and the vast Grüneburgpark, popular with joggers.

Excursions

Offenbach

7km/4.3mi east. Leave from the Deutschherrn-Ufer.
This town on the south bank of the Main is the center of the German leather industry and hosts an International Leather Fair twice yearly.

DLM Ledermuseum★★ (DLM Leather Museum)

Frankfurter Straße 86.
🕐*Open year-round, Sun–Fri 10am–5pm, Sat 10am–10pm.* 🕐*Closed Jan 1, Dec 24, 25 & 31.* 💶*4€.* ♿☎*(069) 829 79 80. www. ledermuseum.de.*
This museum unites three collections under a single roof: the **Shoe Museum** featuring four millennia of foot fashion from around the world; the **Museum of Applied Arts** with crafts and design from the Middle Ages onward, leather in particular; and the **Ethnological Museum** with objects from Africa, America and Asia.

Friedberg★

28km/17.4mi north via Friedberger Landstraße.
Friedberg is an attractive example of a medieval community with two distinct centers: the town enclosed within the Imperial castle and the bourgeois town grouped at the foot of the church, at either end of the main street (*Kaiserstraße*).
The **castle** (*Stauferburg*) erected by Frederick Barbarossa in 1180 together with its outbuildings follows the pattern of a Roman camp and still has the air of a small, self-sufficient town. The ramparts, now a promenade, have been made even more attractive with the addition of bays of greenery and look-out points. The 54m/177ft-high **Adolf's Tower**★ (*Adolphsturm, 1347*) with its four watch towers overlooks the assembled buildings and contains a local history museum.
The **Jewish Baths**★ (*Judenbad*, 13C) at Judengasse 20 in the bourgeois sector, consist of a 26m/85ft-deep domed well used by Jewish women for ritual ablutions required by Jewish law.
The **church** (*Stadtkirche*) is a 13C–14C building with a typically Hessian exterior: transverse attics with separate gables jutting from the roof above the aisles. Inside, an unusually tall **ciborium**★ (a chalice-like vessel that contains the sacrament) from 1462 looms in the chancel. On the left of the Late Gothic rood screen is the **Friedberg Madonna** (c. 1280), expressively carved from sandstone.

FREIBURG IM BREISGAU ★★
POPULATION: 212 500

Sunny Freiburg is one of the most attractive cities in southern Germany. Its five-hundred year-old university, the old town's cobbled lanes lined by half-timbered houses, a majestic cathedral and an easy-going Mediterranean flair make it a perfect base for exploring the Black Forest.

- **Information:** Rathausplatz 2–4, 79098 Freiburg. ☎(0761) 388 18 80; www.freiburg.de.
- **Orient Yourself:** Mid-way between Basel and Strasbourg, on the Rhine plain, Freiburg is on the A5 (Frankfurt–Basel) and the B294 which meanders through the Black Forest.
- **Parking:** Garages are located throughout the city, including several near the Old Town.
- **Don't Miss:** The Münster and the Augustinermuseum
- **Organizing Your Time:** Allow a day to appreciate the cathedral and the old town's charms.
- **Also See:** BADENWEILER, SCHWARZWALD.

A Bit of History

Freiburg was founded in the 12C by the dukes of Zähringen who conferred upon it a number of special privileges, hence the town's name which literally means "free town". From 1368 to 1798 the city was under Habsburg rule. In the second half of the 19C, Freiburg won renewed importance as a place of research and learning thanks to its university.

Sights

Münster★★
Pick up an English-language brochure in the foyer.
🕓*Open year-round, Mon–Sat 10am–5pm, Sun 1pm–7.30pm.* &.☎ (0761) 20 27 90. www.freiburger-muenster.info.
Work on Freiburg's magnificent cathedral began around 1200 in Romanesque style, but today all that remains from this period is the transept crossing and the two "Cockerel Towers" flanking it. In 1354, work started on a Gothic chancel. The grand design and severity of the times meant that construction was not finished until 1513.
The cathedral's **north side** features an interesting 14C tympanum above the door illustrating the theme of Original Sin. The **West Tower★★★** is surmounted

by a delicate spire. Four sharply jutting projections form a star at the foot of the tower house. On the **south side,** statues of the Apostles and the Old Testament kings stand on the buttresses of this richly ornate façade.
The cathedral's **west porch and doorway** feature late 13C figures. On the left wall, Satan, disguised as a knight, leads a procession.
The doorway itself, guarded by statues representing the Church (left) and the

S. Ollivier/MICHELIN

The cathedral tower and the finely worked masonry of its spire.

Synagogue (with eyes covered, right) deals with the mystery of the Redemption.

The **nave** is embellished with graceful galleries and statuary: **(1)** the Virgin at the pillar (1270–80); **(2)** a Late Gothic pulpit (1560); **(3)** a statue of Berthold V, last of the dukes of Zähringen and founder of Freiburg; **(4)** the Holy Sepulchre, from c. 1330; **(5)** 13C stained-glass medallions in the windows; and **(6)** a 1505 group sculpture, the Adoration of the Magi.

The **chancel** includes many more works of note, including **(a)** a Rococo baptismal font and **(b)** a 1521 Oberried altarpiece in the University Chapel. The two side panels, the *Nativity* and *Adoration of the Magi*, are by Hans Holbein the Younger. Also worth closer inspection are: **(c)** in the second Imperial Chapel *(Kaiserkapelle)*; an altarpiece depicting *Rest during the Flight to Egypt* by Hans Wydyz on the central panel; **(d)** a painting of the Crucifixion, in back of the large Hans Baldung Grien altarpiece; **(e)** the Romanesque Locherer Crucifix in beaten silver by Böcklin; and **(f)** an altarpiece in the Locherer Chapel by Sixt von Staufen (1521–24). The carved portion depicts the Virgin. The central panel of the **Hochalter**★★ (high altar) by **Hans Baldung Grien** (1512–16) portrays the Coronation of the Virgin.

Ascend the **West Tower** (○ *open year-round, Tue–Sat 9.30am–5pm, Sun 1pm–5pm; ∞1.50€; ☎(0761) 290 74 47)* along the stairway leading to the tower room. The upper platform beneath the beautiful spire offers **views**★ over the city, with the Kaiserstuhl and the Vosges visible in the distance.

Münsterplatz

The buildings facing the cathedral across this central square were all designed with municipal or ecclesiastical prestige in mind. They include: the **Erzbischöfliches Palais** (Archbishop's Palace from 1756; the **Historisches Kaufhaus**★ (Historical House of Trade) the center of commercial life in the Middle Ages; and the **Wentzingerhaus** (1761) with a splendid Rococo staircase. Originally the private residence of renowned local artist Johann Christian Wentzinger, it

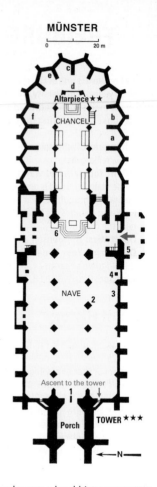

MÜNSTER

0   20 m

Altarpiece ★★

CHANCEL

NAVE

Ascent to the tower

Porch   TOWER ★★★

←— N —→

now houses a local history museum, the **Museum für Stadtgeschichte** (○ *open year-round, Tue–Sun 10am–5pm; ○ closed Jan 1, Dec 24, 25 & 31; ∞2€ (includes Augustinermuseum); ☎(0761) 201 25 15; www.museen.freiburg.de).*

Rathausplatz★

The pleasant Town Hall square has flowered balconies and a fountain featuring Berthold Schwarz, said to have invented gunpowder in Freiburg in 1350.

Augustinermuseum★★

Gerberau 15.
○*Open year-round, Tue–Sun 10am–5pm.*
○*Closed Jan 1, Dec 24, 25 & 31. ☎(0761) 201 25 31. www.museen.freiburg.de.*
In a former monastery, this museum contains a small but exquisite collection of medieval art. Among the spe-

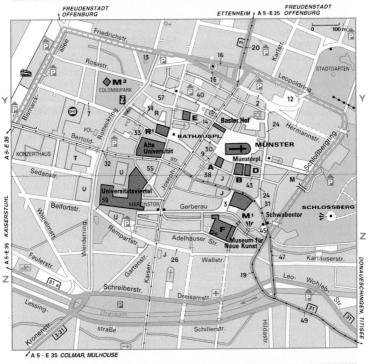

cial treasures are the altarpiece panel (once at Aschaffenburg) depicting the miracle of the Virgin Mary and the Snow, painted in 1519 by Matthias Grünewald, and works by Lucas Cranach the Elder and Hans Baldung Grien. Also of interest are fine furniture, fayences and watches from the 18C and paintings of the Black Forest dating from the 19C.

Museum für Neue Kunst★ (Museum of Modern Art)

Marienstraße 10a.

🕐*Open year-round, Tue–Sun 10am–5pm.* 🕐*Closed Jan 1, Dec 24, 25 & 31.*

⊛*2€.* ☏*(0761) 201 25 83. www.museen. freiburg.de.*

Paintings at this 19C former schoolhouse pick up where the Augustinermuseum leaves off. All major 20C movements—from German Expressionism to abstract art—are represented.

Schlossberg★   Kids

On this last foothill of the Black Forest (456m/1 500ft), woods have almost completely enshrouded Zähringen Castle.

A trail leads from the Schwabentor to the summit where you can enjoy pano-

Address Book

For coin ranges, see the Legend on the cover flap.

WHERE TO STAY

Hotel Oberkirchs Weinstuben – *Münsterplatz 22.* ☎ *(0761) 202 68 68. www.hotel-oberkirch.de. Closed Dec 30-Jan 6. 26 rooms. Restaurant.* Good service is taken very seriously at this venerable hotel in a completely updated 1738 building near the cathedral. Rooms are individually decorated and exude homey flair. The restaurant, furnished in dark wood, is particularly warm and welcoming.

Hotel Zum Roten Bären – *Oberlinden 12.* ☎ *(0761) 38 78 70. www.roter-baeren.de. 25 rooms. Restaurant.* If you want bragging rights for staying in Germany oldest hotel, book one of the cosy rooms in this gem near the Schwabentor. Don't worry, rooms have all the mod-cons you'd expect, while the cozy restaurant is a fine place to enjoy Swiss-influenced cusine.

WHERE TO EAT

Hausbrauerei Feierling – *Gerberau 46.* ☎ *(0761) 24 34 80. www.feierling.de.* This micro-brewery brews its own organic beer in copper vats still visible from the gallery. Regional cuisine is served here and in the biergarten across the road.

Schlossbergrestaurant Dattler – *Am Schlossberg 1 (follow Wintererstraße or take the Schlossberg cable-car).* ☎ *(0761) 317 29. www.dattler. de. Closed Tue.* Enjoy fabulous views over Freiburg's rooftops from this hilltop fine dining restaurant. Ask about their value-priced lunch specials.

Drexlers – *Rosastraße 9.* ☎ *(0761) 595 7203. www.drexlers-restaurant.de. Closed Sun and holidays.* Contemporary, seasonal fare is the name of the game at this crisp modern restaurant near the Columbi Park.

TAKING A BREAK

Markthalle – *Kaiser-Joseph-Str. 233 (via Grünwälderstr. and Fressgässle).* ☎ *(0761) 38 70 00. www.markthalle-freiburg.de. Closed Sun.* Piles of fruit and vegetables, mountains of bread, buckets of olives—Freiburg's market is a smorgasbord of culinary delights from around the world. Stock up, eat in, take out.

NIGHTLIFE

Kagan – *Bismarckallee 9 (in the building beside the central station; take the lift).* ☎ *(0761) 7 67 27 66. www.kagan-lounge. de.* At German-American designer Vladimir Kagan's posh party palace, you can sip your cocktails with a view from the 17th floor, then hit the dance floor on the 18th.

UC Café – *Niemensstr. 7 (between Bertoldstr. and Kaiser-Joseph-Str.).* ☎ *(0761) 38 33 55.* Sit below a shady maple tree at this popular café in Freiburg's pedestrian zone, where visitors stop for coffee and snacks.

---

ramic views from the lookout tower. *Cable-car service.*

Excursions

Kaiserstuhl★

Around 31km/19mi northwest of Freiburg. Leave Freiburg on Lessingstraße and go to Breisach via Gottenheim.

A small volcanic massif rising from the Baden plain, the Kaiserstuhl (the Emperor's Throne; 557m/1 828ft) enjoys a warm, dry climate particularly suitable for orchards and vineyards. In fact, the wines of Achkarren, Ihringen, Bickensohl and Oberrotweil are considered among the finest in the region. Villages worth a stop include **Endingen**★, with its fine old market square, and **Burkheim**★, in its picturesque spot on the southwest slope of the Kaiserstuhl.

Upper Black Forest★★★
See SCHWARZWALD

FULDA

POPULATION: 63 500

Fulda's name is closely linked to Christian history in Germany. But the town is not so much dominated by its medieval buildings as by its Baroque core, with the cathedral, palace and mansions of the nobility recalling a time when prince-bishops guarded the tomb of English missionary St. Boniface.

🗎 **Information:** Bonifatiusplatz 1, 36037 Fulda. ☎(0661) 102 18 14. www.tourismus-fulda.de.

▶ **Orient Yourself:** Fulda is the economic and cultural center of eastern Hessen and close to Thuringia and Bavaria.

😊 **Don't Miss:** The cathedral and St. Michaelskirche.

ბ **Also See:** EISENACH, FRANKFURT AM MAIN, WÜRZBURG, THÜRINGER WALD.

Sights

Dom (Cathedral)

Fulda's cathedral was remodeled in 1704 by Johann Dientzenhofer in a style inspired by the Italian Baroque. Pilgrims flock to the crypt beneath the high altar to visit the tomb of St Boniface. At the base of the **funerary monument★**, an 18C alabaster bas-relief represents the saint. His reliquaries are among the exhibits of the **Dommuseum** (Ⓞopen Apr–Oct, Tue–Sat 10am–5.30pm, Sun 12.30pm–5.30pm; Nov–Mar, Tue–Sat 10am–12.30pm, 1.30pm–4pm, Sun 12.30pm–4pm; Ⓞclosed mid-Jan–mid-Feb. ✺2.10€; ♿☎(0661) 872 07; www.bistum-fulda.de).

Michaelskirche★

Built around an eight-columned 9C rotunda with a stout, square tower, this church overlooks the cathedral forecourt. The vaulted crypt is Carolingian.

Excursions

Probsteikirche St. Peter

4km/2.5mi, allow 30min for walking and sightseeing. Leave Fulda via Petersberger Straße and the B458.

In an impressive hilltop location, this Romanesque sanctuary was largely remodeled in the 15C and contains five 12C **low-relief sculptures★★**: Christ in Glory and the Virgin flanking a triumphal arch, St Boniface, Carloman and Pepin the Short (Charlemagne's brother and father). Mural paintings from the 9C decorate the Carolingian crypt.

The sweeping **panorama★** takes in the Rhön massif to the east (Ⓒ*see below*), the Milseburg spur and the rounded dome of the Wasserkuppe.

The Rhön

104km/65mi southeast of Fulda.

The remnants of an enormous extinct volcano, the Rhön massif's craggy summits rise up to 1 000m/3 280ft above bleak moorlands. Strong winds make the area popular with gliders.

Gersfeld

31.5km southeast of Fulda.

The most central resort in the Rhön, Gersfeld has a Protestant **church** (1785) where the placement of organ, altar and pulpit liturgically symbolizes the Lutheran reform.

The Kreuzberg★

After a steep climb up this second-highest peak in the Rhön mountains (Calvary; 928m/3 045ft), you will be rewarded with a splendid **view★** of the massif. The Wasserkuppe (Ⓒ*see below*) can be seen to the north.

Wasserkuppe★★

Wasserkuppe is the highest peak in the Rhön mountains. From the gliding center, climb to the summit (950m/ 3 117ft) along a fence.

The **panorama★★** extends as far as Fulda and the Vogelsberg.

FÜSSEN

POPULATION: 13 900

The historic town of Füssen is like the dot of the exclamation mark at the end of the Romantic Road (Romantische Strasse) and enjoys a spectacular setting in the Alpine foothills. Most visitors use it as a base for Ludwig II's fairytale palace of Neuschwanstein and his ancestral home of Hohenschwangau, but the town is actually worth a stop in its own right. Attractions include an ancient abbey, art museums and the surrounding lakes.

- **Information:** Kaiser-Maximilian-Platz 1, 87629 Füssen. ☎(08362) 938 50. www.tourismus-fuessen.de.
- ▶ **Orient Yourself:** Tucked into the Königswinkel ("royal corner") in the Allgäu mountains, Füssen is surrounded by the lakes of Forggensee, Hopfensee and Weißensee.
- **Don't Miss:** Kloster St. Mang, Tegelbergbahn.
- **Organizing Your Time:** Half a day is sufficient to explore the town. Allow more time if enjoying outdoor activities.
- **Especially for Kids:** Lech Gorge, splashing in the Forggensee.
- **Also See:** SCHLOSS NEUSCHWANSTEIN, DEUTSCHE ALPENSTRASSE, ROMANTISCHE STRASSE, WIESKIRCHE.

Sights

Kloster St. Mang★ (Abbey of St. Mang)

This ancient Benedictine abbey looks back on more than 1 000 years of history. It honors the work of St. Magnus, an 8C missionary who founded a monk's cell here; he is buried in the church's crypt. In the 18C, the medieval complex got a complete Baroque makeover reflecting the skill and vision of Johann Jakob Herkomer who had learned his craft in Venice. The monastery was secularized in 1802.

Stadtpfarrkirche (Parish Church)

🕐 *Open year-round, daily 8.30am–6pm.*
Herkomer's Baroque design displays astonishing harmony and rich décor that encompasses an elaborate fresco cycle with scenes from the life of St. Magnus. An artistic and spiritual highlight is the high altar with statues by Anton Sturm. Various reliquaries of the saint, including his staff, are dotted around the church.

Museum der Stadt Füssen

🕐 *Open Apr–Oct, Tue–Sun 11am–5pm; Nov–Mar, Fri–Sun 1pm–4pm. ☜2.50€. ☎(08362) 90 31 46.*

The southern wing of the former abbey buildings, with trompe l'oeil paintings in the cloister, now house a modern museum containing exhibits on the history of the abbey, Füssen's violinmaking tradition and milestones from the town's past. Perhaps even more impressive are the richly decorated rooms themselves, most notably the festive **Kaisersaal**★★ (Imperial Hall), a large banquet hall embellished with fanciful frescoes and stucco ornamentation. In summer it hosts classical concerts. Also of note is the **Annakapelle**★ (St. Anna Chapel) from 850 with its macabre Dance of Death fresco from 1602, which vividly depicts the ravages of the Black Plague.

Hohes Schloss

The ramp up to the castle entrance starts behind the parish church.
🕐 *Open mid-Mar–Oct, Tue–Sun 11am–5pm; Nov–mid-Mar, Fri–Sun 1pm–4pm.*
🕐 *Closed Dec 24 & 31. ☜2.50€. ☎(08362) 90 31 64.*

Looming above the town, the fortified Late Gothic palace became the summer residence of the prince-bishops of Augsburg in the late 15C. Today, the former apartments house two collections: the focus of the **Bavarian Staatsgemäldesammlung** (Bavarian Picture

Address Book

🪙 *For coin ranges, see the Legend on the cover flap.*

WHERE TO STAY

🛏️🛏️**Hotel Eiskristall** – *Birkstraße 3.* ☎(08362) 50 78 12. *www.hotel-eiskristall.de. 32 rooms. Restaurant* 🍴🍴. Expect a hearty welcome when checking into this family-run hotel on the town outskirts, close to the ice stating rink. The Alpine décor with lots of wood, thick carpets and carved crafts are inviting, the rooms spacious and pleasantly rustic and the restaurant top notch.

🛏️🛏️🛏️**Hotel Geiger** – *Uferstraße 18, 87629 Füssen-Hopfen am See.* Spa ☎(08362) 70 74. *www.hotel-geiger.de. Closed Nov–mid-Dec. 24 rooms. Restaurant* 🍴🍴🍴. Newly renovated, this long-standing family hotel on the lakeside promenade features chic designer décor, a small spa with Finnish sauna and mint steam room and two restaurants, one rustic, one à la carte.

🛏️🛏️🛏️**Hotel Sonne** – *Reichenstraße 37.* ☎(08362) 90 80. *www.hotel-sonne.de. 50 rooms.* Champagne breakfast and free fitness center passes are among the extra perks at this central hotel with cheerful, spacious and modern rooms, many with balconies.

🛏️🛏️🛏️**Kurcafé** – *Prinzregentenplatz 4.* ☎(08362) 93 01 80. *www.kurcafe.com. 31 rooms. Restaurant.* This central family hotel has comfortable, modern rooms and a good restaurant.

WHERE TO EAT

🍴🍴**Zum Schwanen** – *Brotmarkt 4. Closed Mon, Sun dinner, mid-Jan–mid-Mar.* ☎(08362) 61 74. The welcoming hosts serve specialties from the Allgäu in a well-kept setting with a muted rustic flair.

Collection) is on Swabian art from the 15C and 16C. The most impressive room is the octagonal **Rittersaal**★ (Knights' Hall), which is lidded by a sumptuous coffered ceiling.

On the lower floor, the **Städtische Gemäldegalerie** (Municipal Picture Gallery) presents paintings by Spitzweg, Lier, Defregger and other Munich School members working around 1900. This is supplemented by a rotating selection of graphics by Franz Graf von Pocci (1807–76). For a dazzling **panorama**★ climb up the clocktower which is accessible via the gallery. Surrounding the castle is a public park called the Baumgarten.

Lechfall (Lech Gorge)   Kids
500m/547yd south.

The river Lech leaves the Alps in Füssen and cascades down a small, rocky gorge spanned by a footbridge.

Forggensee (Lake Forggen)   Kids
Boats depart from Füssen landing docks, Jun–mid-Oct, daily 10am–5.30pm. Commentary. ⊕8€ (50min tour), ⊕11€ (2hr tour). Forggensee Schifffahrt ☎(08362) 92 13 63. *www.schifffahrt.fuessen.de*

The Forggensee is a 12km/7.4mi long and up to 3km/1.8mi wide reservoir created in 1954 to regulate the waterflow of the Lech River. In summer it is swarmed by watersports enthusiasts and bicyclists enjoying the paved trails around its perimeter. Cruise boats ply its waters, allowing breathtaking views of the mountains, Neuschwanstein Castle and historic Füssen. In winter, the lake is drained and you can walk on the dry bottom to look for remnants of Stone Age and Roman settlements.

Tegelbergbahn★
Tegelbergstraße 33, operates year-round, daily 9am–5pm. ⊕15–20€. ☎(08362) 983 60. *www.tegel bergbahn.de.*

On clear days, **views**★★ don't get much grander than from the top of the 1730m Tegelberg, easily reached by gentle cable-car ride. Count the number of peaks and emerald lakes or watch hang gliders and parasailers hurl themselves over the mountain's ledge.

A trail leads to Neuschwanstein in about two or three hours, and in winter there's downhill and cross-country skiing.

GARMISCH-PARTENKIRCHEN★★★

POPULATION: 26 000

Germany's most famous winter sports resort snuggles against the massive peaks of the Wetterstein chain, most notably the Zugspitze which soars to a lofty 2 962m/9 717 and is the highest mountain in the country. The twin town hosted the fourth Winter Olympics in 1936 and the World Alpine Ski Championships in 1978.

- **Information:** Richard-Strauß-Platz 2, 82467 Garmisch-Partenkirchen. ☏(08821) 18 07 00. www.garmisch-partenkirchen.de.
- ▶ **Orient Yourself:** Garmisch-Partenkirchen is a highlight on the Deutsche Alpenstraße and less than 15km/9.3mi from the Austrian border.
- **Don't Miss:** Partnachklamm, view from Wank mountain, skiing.
- **Especially for Kids:** Snow sports, cable-car ride up the Wank, Leutasch Ghost Gorge
- **Also See:** Deutsche ALPENSRASSE, SCHLOSS LINDERHOF, WIESKIRCHE.

Sights

Alte St. Martin-Kirche (Old Church of St. Martin)

Garmisch's original parish church is a 13C Gothic pile in a picturesque neighborhood with carefully preserved chalets on the west bank of the River Loisach. Several of its medieval murals have been uncovered and restored, most notably a 7m/22ft-high image of St. Christopherus and scenes depicting the Crucifixion and the Last Judgment.

Neue St. Martin Kirche (New Church of St. Martin)

Garmisch's "new" parish church is an 18C work by the famous Wessobrunn architect Josef Schmuzer with ceiling

frescoes by Matthias Günther and a chancel carved by Frank Hosp.

Philosophenweg (Philosophers' Way) 🚶

The early 18C church of St. Anton is the departure point for this easy and panoramic walk along the icy Loisach River. Enjoy clear **views**★ of the surrounding massifs, including the Zugspitze looming behind the Waxenstein.

Excursions

Zugspitze★★★ (👈for access and description, see ZUGSPITZE)

Wank★★ Kids

20min cable-car ride, operates May–Oct, daily 8.45am–5pm at least half-hourly. ☏16€ round-trip. ①(08821) 79 70. www.zugspitze.de.
From the summit (1 780m/5 840ft) of sunny Wank mountain **views**★★ open up across the entire Wetterstein range and the Zugspitze peak, extending all the way to Munich on clear days. Enjoy varied vistas while following the two easy and bench-lined panoramic trails along the top.

Partnachklamm★★

About 90min round-trip. Bring raingear. 🕐Open year-round, daily 9am–5pm. ☏2€. ☏(08821) 31 67).

Neue St. Martin Kirche

Markt Garmisch-Partenkirchen

Address Book

For coin ranges, see the Legend on the cover flap.

WHERE TO STAY

Gästehaus Brigitte – *St. Martin-Straße 40.* ☎(08821) 739 38. www.hotelbrigitte.de. *11 rooms*. This spotless guesthouse is near the cable-car station and just around the corner from trails and the Olympic skating rink.

Hotel Garni Edlhuber – *Innsbrucker Straße 33, 82481 Mittenwald.* ☎(08823) 13 89. www.edlhuber-mittenwald.de. *16 rooms*. This friendly, family-run hotel at the foot of the Karwendel massif is an ideal getaway. Tots will appreciate the playground and big lawn.

WHERE TO EAT

Postkeller und Alte Braustub'n – *Innsbrucker Straße 13, 82481 Mittenwald.* ☎(08823) 17 29. www.postkeller-mittenwald.de. *Closed Mon.* The taps never run dry in this rustic brew-pub where rib-sticking regional cuisine is the name of the game.

Zur Schranne – *Griesstraße 4.* ☎(08821) 16 99. *Closed Tue.* Sample feel-good Bavarian food, served in particularly belt-loosening portions, at this typical regional eatery. Sit inside or on the covered terrace.

Joseph-Naus Stubn – *Klammstraße 19.* ☎(08821) 90 10. For a more refined, modern take on local cuisine, grab a table at this graciously rustic restaurant named for the man who first reached the Zugspitze summit in 1820.

TAKING A BREAK

Konditorei-Café Thron – *Marienplatz 13.* ☎(08821) 522 60. www.konditorei-thron.de. The delectable presentation alone of the cakes, tarts and chocolates at this pastry shop-cum-coffeehouse will get your mouth watering.

GARMISCH-PARTENKIRCHEN						
Am Kurpark	X 7	Hauptstr.	X	Rießerseestr.	X 38
Bahnhofstr.	X 10	Hindenburgstr.	X 18	Von-Burg-Str.	X 46
Ferdinand-Barth-Str.	X 15	Mittenwalder Str.	X 27	Wildenauer Str.	X 48
		Münchner Str.	X 30	Zugspitzstr.	X
		Parkstr.	X 32		
		Promenadestr.	X 35		

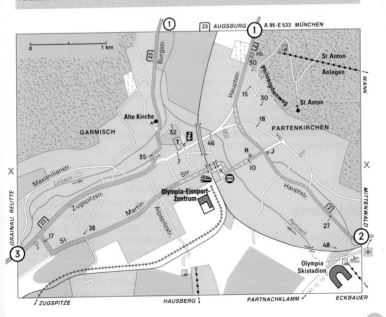

The splendor of this 800m/2 624ft-long deep narrow gorge carved by a rushing creek into solid rock will likely etch itself into your memory forever. The route passes two spectacular bottlenecks amid the thunder of falling water and clouds of frothy spray. In winter the route is decorated with icicles. The trailhead is about 2km south of the Olympic ski stadium.

Eibsee★

8km/5mi west.
The calm waters of this lake occupy a superb forest site. It lies at the foot of the Zugspitze, at an altitude of 1 000m/3 280ft and is encircled by a trail (⏱2hr walk).

Mittenwald★

20km/11.8mi east.
Mittenwald is intensely popular thanks to its gorgeous location below the Kranzberg and Karwendel massifs and because of the beauty of the town itself. Its biggest claim to fame is its abundance of intricately frescoed **house façades**★★ in a style called *Lüftlmalerei* (fresco house paintings, mostly seen in rural locations). The ones on Obermarkt are especially spectular.

Mittenwald has been a center of violin-making since the 17C, as is recalled in the **Geigenbaumuseum** *(Violin-making Museum; Ballenhausgasse 3;* 🕐*open Feb–mid-Mar, mid-May–mid-Oct, mid-Dec–Jan, Tue–Sun 10am–5pm; rest of the year, Tue–Sun 11am–4pm;* 🕐*closed Nov 5-Dec 12, Dec 24 & 31;* 🎫*2.50€;* ☎*(08823) 25 11; www.geigenbaumuseum-mitt enwald.de)*, which sheds light on the mysteries of the production process. There's still a violin-making school in town today.

Kids get a kick out of exploring the **Leutascher Geisterklamm** *(Leutasch Ghost Gorge;* 🕐*open mid-May–late Oct, daily 9am–6pm)*, a steep and craggy canyon accessed by metal bridges. Along the way, endearing "ghosts" reveal the gorge's many secrets.

GÖRLITZ★

POPULATION: 58 500

Germany's easternmost city became prosperous during the 15C and 16C through textile manufacture and trade in woad (blue dye). World War II miraculously spared the town's more than 4 000 historic houses and today it is a veritable 3D textbook of architecture through the ages.

- 🚹 **Information:** Brüderstraße 1, 02826 Görlitz. ☎(03581) 475 70. www.europastadt-goerlitz.de.
- ▶ **Orient Yourself:** Görlitz stretches along the west bank of the Neiße River, which has formed the border with Poland since 1945.
- 😊 **Don't Miss:** The Old Town.
- 🕐 **Organizing Your Time:** Görlitz can be seen in a day.
- 🧒 **Especially for Kids:** Outdoor recreation in the Zittauer Gebirge (⏱*see Excursions).*
- 👤 **Also See:** BAUTZEN, DRESDEN, SÄCHSISCHE SCHWEIZ.

Sights

Old Town★

Most of Görlitz's sights are concentrated in the historic town, which is anchored by two central squares, the Obermarkt and the Untermarkt.

Obermarkt

Fine Baroque houses line up along the north side of Görlitz' largest square, while its western flank is punctuated by the **Reichenbacher Turm** (🕐*open May–Oct, Tue–Sun 10am–5pm, Fri 8pm;* 🎫*3.50€;* ☎ *(03581) 67 13 55; www. museum-goerlitz.de)*, a fortified 52m/ 170.6ft-high tower first mentioned in

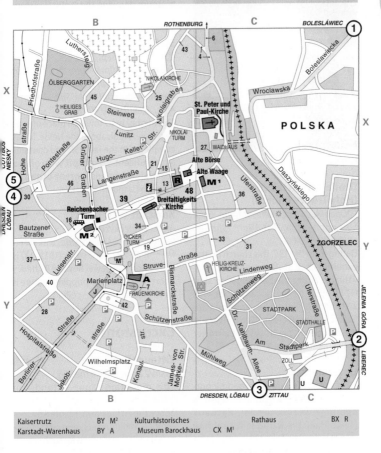

1376. 165 steps lead to a viewing platform for wonderful **views**★.

Admission here is also good at the nearby **Kaisertrutz** (⏰*open year-round, Tue–Sun 10am–5pm; ☎(03581) 67 13 55; www.museum-goerlitz.de*), a massive Late Gothic keep (1490) that was once part of the medieval town fortifications. It now houses local history exhibits but because of extensive restoration these are limited to the ground floor for the foreseeable future.

Barockhaus (Baroque House)
Neißstraße 30.

⏰*Open year-round, Tue–Sun 10am–5pm.* ≈*3.50€, includes admission to Reichenbacher Turm and Kaisertrutz.* ☎*(03581) 67 13 55. www.museum-goerlitz.de.*

This imposing Baroque mansion with lavish stucco-ornamented ceilings houses an interesting collection of furniture, paintings, sculpture, ceramics and glass from the Renaissance and Baroque periods. Highlights include fanciful 18C **cupboards and cabinets**★.

Karstadt-Warenhaus, Görlitz

R. Chéret/MICHELIN

Dreifaltigkeitskirche
(Holy Trinity Church)

⏱*Open May–Sept, Mon–Sat 10am–6pm, Sun noon–6pm; Oct 10am–5pm.* ♿ ✆*(03581) 64 34 60.*

Dating from the 13C, this church boasts exquisite choir **stalls**★ (1484) and two valuable altars: the Baroque high altar (1713) by Caspar Gottlob von Rodewitz, a student of Permoser, and the Late Gothic winged **Golden Maria altar**★ in the Barbara chapel. Its skinny bell tower is nicknamed *"Mönch"* (monk).

Untermarkt★

This historic square is framed by gorgeous buildings attesting to Görlitz's one-time wealth: the 14C **Rathaus** (Town Hall); the Baroque **Alte Börse** (old stock exchange; 1706–14), now a hotel; and the 1706 **Alte Waage** (weighhouse).

"Silesian Heaven"

"He who doesn't know "heaven" hasn't lived," goes a Silesian saying. Perhaps that is why their national dish is the *Schlesisches Himmelreich*. Prepared from pickled pork and dried fruit, it is served with a light lemon sauce and white bread dumplings.

Schlesisches Museum★★
(Silesian Museum)

Brüderstrassse 8. ⏱*Open year-round, Tue–Sun 10am–5pm.* ⬚*4€.* ✆*(03581) 879 10. www.schlesisches-museum.de.*

Since 2006, the Schönhof, the town's most imposing Renaissance building, has been home to this state-of-the-art museum detailing the cultural history of the region of Silesia.

St. Peterskirche★

⏱*Open May-Sept, Tue–Sat 10.30am–5pm, Sun 12.30pm–5pm; Oct, Tue–Sat 10.30am–4pm, Sun 12.30pm–4pm; Nov–Apr, Tue–Sat 10am–4pm, Sun 12.30pm–4pm.* ♿✆*(035 81) 40 28 58.*

This mighty twin-towered place of worship towers high above the Neiße. It was completed in the late 15C and contains a magnificent 17C **pulpit** with gilded acanthus leaves and a **great organ** by Eugenio Casparini (1703).

Karstadt-Warenhaus

An der Frauenkirche 5–7.

Fairly plain on the outside, this steel-framed department store (1912–13) is an Art Nouveau jewel beyond its heavy doors. The most eye-popping feature is its kaleidoscopic glass ceiling.

Excursions

Zittauer Gebirge★   <small>Kids</small>

35km/22mi south via the B66.

This mountain range extends for 20km/11.8mi, forming a towering ridge above the Zittau Basin. Favored by rock climbers, mountaineers and cross-country skiers, it is also noted for such spas as Lückendorf, Oybin and Jonsdorf.

St. Marienthal★

15km/9.3mi south via B66 in Ostritz.

Queen Kunigunde of Bohemia founded this still active Cistercian convent in 1234. In a pretty setting on a bend in the Neiße River, it bears unmistakable Bohemian influences, such as the west façade with its central projection. The church's interior was painted in 1850 in the narrative Romanesque style by Nazarene artists. The estate features Germany's most easterly vineyard.

GOSLAR★★

POPULATION: 43 750

Goslar is often deluged by day-trippers and for good reason: Its historic center is a wonderful maze of narrow cobbled lanes lined with some of the most richly decorated half-timbered houses in Germany. In 1992, the old town, along with the 1 000-year-old Rammelsberg mines, became a UNESCO World Heritage Site.

- **Information:** Markt 7, 38640 Goslar. ☎ (05321) 780 60. www.goslar.de.
- ▶ **Orient Yourself:** Goslar lies on the northern edge of the Harz National Park and makes a good base of operation for exploring this mountainous forest region.
- **Don't Miss:** The Old Town.
- **Organizing Your Time:** Allow three hours for a walking tour of the Old City and another half day if visiting the Rammelsberg Mine.
- **Especially for Kids:** Rammelsberg Mine.
- **Also See:** WOLFENBÜTTEL, BRAUNSCHWEIG, HILDESHEIM.

A Bit of History

The mines – Goslar's fortunes have always been pegged to the abundance of silver in the nearby Rammelsberg mines. They were the main reason Emperor Heinrich II made the town an imperial residence in the 11C. Goslar remained a home of the German kings and emperors until 1253 when it became a Free Imperial City and member of the Hanseatic League. Its prosperity peaked during the 15C and 16C, as is reflected in the abundance of the lavish half-timbered town houses still gracing the town center.

Restaurant opposite the Marktkirche

J. Bouraly/MICHELIN

Walking Tour

The Old Town★★★ (Altstadt)

The old town of Goslar is largely a pedestrian zone, making it a pleasant place to wander round.

▶ *Begin on Marktplatz (see map).*

Marktplatz★★
The market square is surrounded by slate-clad houses.
Two Gothic buildings, the Kaiserworth and the Rathaus, stand before the spires of the 12C **Marktkirche**. In the center of the square is a **fountain** *(Marktbrunnen)* with two bronze basins (1230). The square also features a chiming **animated clock** with four different scenes *(at 9am, noon, 3pm and 6pm)* representing the history of mining in the Harz mountains.

Rathaus★ (Town Hall)
Following the medieval custom, this 15C building was designed with an open hall at street level, an arcaded gallery opening onto the Marktplatz. On the south side, an exterior staircase leads to the first floor **State Room** *(Diele)*.

Huldigungssaal★★ (Hall of Homage)
◷*Open mid-Mar–Oct and Nov 26–Dec 31, Mon–Fri 11am–3pm, Sat–Sun 10am–*

Address Book

For coin ranges, see cover flap.

WHERE TO STAY

⊜⊜⊜ **Hotel Die Tanne** –
Bäringer Straße 10. ☎*(05321) 343 90.*
www.die-tanne.de. 22 rooms. Behind the
shale façade of this cozy hotel in a listed
building await bright, modern rooms
fitted with all major comforts.
The Finnish sauna and hotel bar make
good spots to unwind.

WHERE TO EAT

⊜⊜⊜ **Aubergine** – *Marktstraße 4.*
☎*(05321) 421 36. www.aubergine-goslar.
de.* Modern and sophisticated, yet warm
and welcoming, this restaurant will
charm you with candlelight, fresh flowers and a trickling fountain and tempt
you with cleverly composed Mediterranean cuisine. Great wines and romantic
summer terrace, too.

4pm. ⏱*Closed Dec 24.* ⊜*3.50€.* ☎*(053
21) 780 60.*
This room, transformed into the **city
council assembly hall** in 1490, was
magnificently decorated c. 1520.
The wall decorations feature Roman
emperors alternating with sibyls in
Renaissance costume, while the ceiling
depicts biblical figures, including Christ,
the prophets and the Evangelists. A tiny
side chapel contains an arm bone reliquary (c. 1300) of St Margaret.

Hotel Kaiserworth

Opposite the Rathaus, this Gothic edifice
(1494) is decorated with statues of eight
German emperors along with the irrev-
erent **Ducat Man** *(Dukatenmännchen)*
who is depicted as excreting a gold
coin—an allusion to Goslar's ancient
right to mint coins.

Fachwerkhäuser★★
(Half-timbered Houses)

The Schuhhof, a small square northwest
of the Rathaus, is entirely surrounded by
half-timbered buildings. Farther on, a
passageway on the left leads to the narrow Münzstraße, which in turn passes
an old inn, **Am Weißen Schwan**, and
then the **Alte Münze** (Old Mint). Now a
restaurant, this timbered building dates
from 1500. The fine house on the corner
of the Münzstraße and the Marktstraße
was constructed in 1526.
Facing the Marktkirche is the **Brusttuch**
(1521), built for a rich mine owner and
decorated with biblical, mythological
and legendary characters. It is now a
hotel and restaurant. Not far away looms

the tall gable of the **Bäckergildehaus**
(Bakers' Guild Hall, 1501–1557).
The **Renaissance houses** at the Markt-
straße-Bäckerstraße intersection are
adorned with friezes of the fan motif,
typical of Lower Saxony (e.g., Bäckerstraße 2).

▶ *Turn into Bergstraße which leads
to the Marktkirche.*

Siemenshaus★★

Schreiberstraße 12.
⏱*Open year-round, Tue and Thu 10am–
noon.* ☎*(05321) 78 06 20.*
One of Goslar's most spectacular houses
is the ancestral home of the industrial
Siemens family, built in 1693. Note the
tiled entrance *(Däle)* and picturesque
inner courtyard.

Sights

Neuwerkkirche★

⏱*Open Mar–Dec, Mon–Sat 10am–noon,
2.30pm–4.30pm, Sun 2.30pm–4.30pm.*
☎*(05321) 228 39. www.neuwerkkirche-
goslar.de.*
This former Cistercian collegiate church
(12C) is a three-aisled basilica whose
tall polygonal towers are exceptionally
elegant for a Romanesque church. Heavily ribbed, pointed vaulting characterizes the interior. Of particular artistic
merit is the former 13C **choir screen**★
festooned with sculptures of Christ,
the Virgin Mary, the apostles Peter and
Paul and two saints; it now serves as the
organ loft. The frescoes in the choir date

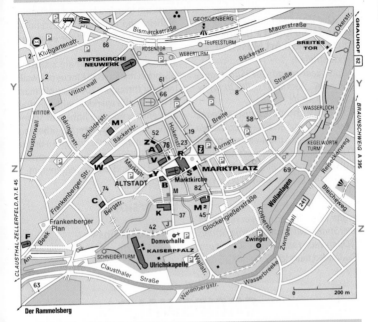

Der Rammelsberg

back to the early 13C and depict Mary on the throne and Old Testament scenes.

Frankenberger Kirche★

Enter on Frankenberger Plan. ○*Open Apr–Oct, daily 9am–6pm.* ☎*(05321) 224 64. www.frankenberg-goslar.de.*
Formerly the principal church of the local miners, the Frankenberger Kirche (1108) crowns Goslar's highest point. A three-nave basilica, it beautifully preserves its Romanesque features despite Gothic alterations in the choir and southern transept and a lavish Baroque altarpiece. Pillars and vaults are richly decorated with stone carvings, while the murals above the choir and upper loft were painted in the early 13C. The 12C altar bears a splendid Baroque

retable dating to 1675, which, like the 1698 chancel, originated in the Goslar woodcarving workshop of Heinrich and Jobst Lessen.

Kaiserpfalz (Imperial Palace)

○*Open Apr–Oct, daily 10am–5pm; Nov–Mar, 10am–4pm.* ○*Closed Dec 24 & 31.* ◉*4.50€.* ☎*(05321) 311 96 93.*
One of best-preserved Romanesque palaces in Germany, the Kaiserpfalz was built in the 11C under Emperor Henry III and for two centuries hosted several imperial diets. It was heavily restored in a Historicist style in the late 19C. At that time, the gigantic **Reichssaal** *(on the first floor)* was swathed in romanticized paintings depicting significant moments from Goslar's medieval glory days.

Beyond the Reichssaal is the early 12C **Palatine Chapel of St. Ulrich**, where the floorplan transitions from a Greek cross into an octagon. Inside is a tomb holding the heart of Heinrich III (the body is buried in the cathedral at Speyer).

Mönche Haus Museum für Moderne Kunst★ (Monks' House Modern Art Museum)

Mönchestraße 1.
🕐*Open year-round, Tue–Sun 10am–5pm.* ⌫*3€.* ♿⌕*(05321) 295 70. www. moenchehaus.de.*
A roll call of such top 20C artists as Beuys, Hundertwasser, Serra, Baselitz, Chilida and de Kooning is the bread and butter of this museum set up in a stately 1528 patrician mansion, adjacent half-timbered buildings and vaulted cellars.

Rammelsberg★ Kids

Bergtal 19, southwest of town via Clausthaler Straße and Rammelsberger Straße.
🕐*Open year-round, daily 9am–6pm.* ⌫*Guided tours (60–75min).* 🕐*Closed*

Dec 24 & 31. ⌫*11€, incl museum and one guided tour.* ☎*(05321) 75 00. www.ram melsberg.de.*
The source of Goslar's prosperity, the 1 000-year-old Rammelsberg mines are now a major tourist attraction. Spend a little time above ground at the **museum** to gain a better appreciation of their importance before descending deep into the bowels of the earth on a guided tour.

Two types of tours run are available. Historical mining is the focus of a walking tour through a 200-year-old maze of mine shafts sparkling with minerals and enhanced by a light and sound show. Kids usually prefer the other tour because it involves a ride on an underground railway and noisy demonstrations of old and modern equipment.

Excursion

Harz Mountains★★ – ♿*See HARZ.*

GREIFSWALD★

POPULATION: 53 000

There is evidence that Greifswald was granted municipal rights as early as 1250. Once it joined the Hanseatic League in 1281, the town flourished and continued to prosper for the next four centuries. The city boasts a decidedly Scandinavian flavor and a number of historic buildings largely spared destruction during World War II.

- ℹ **Information:** Rathaus am Markt, 17489 Greifswald. ☎(03834) 52 13 80. www.greifswald.de.
- ▸ **Orient Yourself:** This Baltic Sea town is about 30km/18.6mi east of Stralsund and bisected by the little Ryck River.
- ⊘ **Don't Miss:** The Marktplatz, Marienkirche, Museum of Pomerania
- 🕐 **Organizing Your Time:** Devote about half a day to take in the main sights.
- ♿ **Also See:** STRALSUND, ROSTOCK.

A Bit of History

Swedish Rule – After the Thirty Years' War, Greifswald became part of the Kingdom of Sweden in 1648. The Swedes exercised leniency for some 200 years, granting the town an unusual degree of autonomy. From 1815, when West

Pomerania became absorbed into Prussia, a busy period of construction began, to which the numerous well-preserved burghers' houses testify.

The Greatest German Romantic Painter – Highly influential landscape painter **Caspar David Friedrich** was born in Greifswald in 1774. Although he left town at the age of 20, he remained deeply attached to it and often includes its features in his work.

Sights

Marktplatz★

Greifswald's central square is dominated by the arcaded **Rathaus** (1738) and framed by several architecturally distinguished houses. Standouts include the one at **no 11**★ from the 15C with its jauntily decorated gable.

Marienkirche★

🕐*Open Jun–Sept, Mon–Fri 11am–4pm, Sat–Sun 10am–noon; shorter hours the rest of the year.* ♿☎*(038 34) 22 63.*
This red-brick hall-church has an elegantly structured east gable from the 14C whose ornate tracery contrasts with the stocky tower built a century earlier. Inside, the 1587 **pulpit**★, richly carved and adorned with inlaid wood, merits a closer look, as do the faded 15C frescoes in the southern tower.

Dom St. Nikolai★

🕐*Open May–Oct, Mon–Sat 10am–4pm, Sun 11.30am–1pm; Nov–Apr, Mon–Sat 11am–3pm, Sun 11.30am–1pm.* ☎*(03834) 26 27. www.dom-greifswald.de.*
Caspar David Friedrich was baptized in this 13C Gothic hall church whose nearly 100m/328ft-high tower, topped by an onion-domed Baroque spire, dominates the town silhouette. The interior is rather plain thanks to a 19C remodel, although some Late Gothic frescoes can still be seen in chapels 19 and 20.

Klosterruine Eldena (Eldena Abbey)

Wolgaster Landstraße.
The Cistercian abbey was founded in 1199, reached its height in the mid 14C but was badly damaged during the Thirty Years' War. The picturesque ruins were a favorite subject of Caspar David Friedrich.

Wieck★

The thatched fishermen's cottages, idyllic harbor and 19C **wooden swing bridge**★ *(Zugbrücke)* of this historic fishing village at the mouth of the River Ryck present a delightful scene.

Pommersches Landesmuseum★ (Museum of Pomerania)

🕐*Open Tue–Sun 10am–6pm (Nov–Mar 5pm).* 🕐*Closed Dec 24 & 31.* 💶*4.50€.* ♿☎*(03834) 22 63. www.pommersches-landesmuseum.de.*
This new museum in a converted Franciscan friary has exhibits on the cultural history of the Pommern region but is more notable for its picture gallery. Paintings by Friedrich, Runge and Liebermann are among the stars of the show.

Swing bridge at Wieck

M. Buffard/MICHELIN

HALLE

POPULATION: 240 000

Halle must balance its heritage as an old university town and birthplace of Georg Friedrich Händel with its legacy as the center of the chemical industry in GDR days. Since 1990, the town has progressed and cleaned up in leaps and bounds and is again ready for its close-up—and not only during the biannual Händel Festival!

- **Information:** Marktplatz 13, 06108 Halle. ☎(0345) 122 99 84. www.halle-tourist.de. Contact or visit the tourist office for a **Halle Welcome Card**.
- **Orient Yourself:** Halle is on the Saale River, some 30km/18.6mi northwest of Leipzig.
- **Parking:** Händelhauskarree garage on Hallorenring.
- **Don't Miss:** Moritzburg Art Museum, Händel-Haus.
- **Organizing Your Time:** Budget about half a day for Halle.
- **Also See:** LEIPZIG, NAUMBURG, DESSAU.

Sights

Marktplatz★

This huge square is dominated by the belfries of the Marktkirche and by the **Roter Turm** (red tower), built in the 15C and almost 80m/262.4ft high. An 1859 statue of Händel surveys the square.

Marktkirche★

◷Open Jan–Feb, Mon–Sat 12.30pm–5pm, Sun 3pm–5pm; Mar–Dec, Mon–Sat 10am–5pm, Sun 3pm–5pm. ☎(0345) 517 08 94. www.marktkirche-halle.de.
This three-aisled 16C Gothic hall church was wedged between two existing towers belonging to different Romanesque churches whose naves had been torn down. The **reredos**★ of the high altar carries a Virgin and Child painted by a pupil of the Cranach School. The most important exhibit, though, is Luther's death mask on display in its own room in the northwest tower.

Kunstmuseum Moritzburg★★ (Moritzburg Art Museum)

Friedemann-Bach-Platz 5.
◷Open year-round, Tue 11am–8.30pm, Wed–Sun 10am–6pm. ◷Closed Dec 24 & 31. ⊛5€, half-price after 5pm, free last Sun of the month. ☎(0345) 21 25 90. www.kunstmuseum-moritzburg.de.
Moritzburg castle was built in the 15C as a residence of the archbishops of Magdeburg and partly converted into a museum in the early 20C. It now houses the most significant art collection in Sachsen-Anhalt. Curatorial emphasis has been placed on **19C and 20C German painting**, presenting a sweeping survey of various periods, including Romanticism, Impressionism and Expressionism. The museum also offers a rare chance to view paintings created by artists from East Germany between 1949 and 1990, most notably Werner Tübke.

Händel-Haus★

Grosse Nikolaistraße 5.
◷Open Apr–Oct, Tue–Sun 10am–6pm. ☎(0345) 50 09 01 03. www.haendelhaus.de.
One of the world's most famous composers, **Georg Friedrich Händel** (1685–1759) was born in this big half-timbered house in 1685. Exhibits trace major stations in his life and career as well as regional music history. An adjacent building presents two floors of precious historical musical instruments.

Excursions

Doppelkapelle Landsberg (Double Chapel)

In Landsberg, 19km/12mi east of Halle.
⟿Visit by guided tour (1hr) only, May–Oct, Sat 3pm, Sun 11am and 3pm. ⊛2€. ☎(0346 02) 206 90.
The Romanesque double chapel of **St. Crucis** tops a rocky spur and is easily

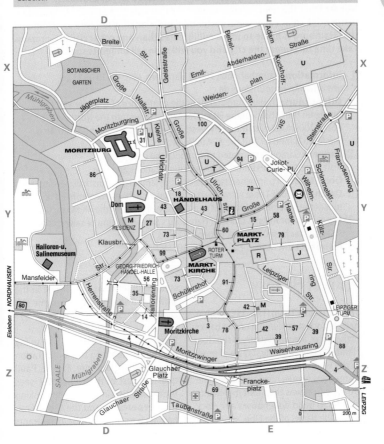

spotted from afar. It is one of only 30 such chapels in Germany where common people celebrated Mass in the lower chapel while the nobility sat upstairs. The **capitals**★ on the columns are adorned with extraordinarily rich figures and plant and animal motifs. From the balcony, there is a superb **view**★.

Eisleben
34km/21mi west.
Memories of **Martin Luther**, who was born—and died—in this small mining town are evoked at a number of sites. Both his **birthplace** (*Luther-Geburtshaus, Seminarstraße 16*) and the house where he died (**Luther-Sterbehaus**, *Andreaskirchplatz 7*) are now museums and included on UNESCO's list of World Heritage Sites.

Luther pilgrims might also want to stop by the church of St. Peter and St. Paul where he was baptized, St. Andreas Church where he gave his last sermon, and Marktplatz, anchored by a 1883 Luther statue.

HAMBURG★★★

POPULATION: 1 754 182

Germany's second largest city after Berlin, Hamburg is one of the most important ports in Europe. Its historic title of "Free and Hanseatic Town" and its status as a "city state" (Stadtstaat) testify to its eminence and influence through the centuries. Germany's publishing and media capital, renowned for its commercial dynamism and cosmopolitan atmosphere, is a city of contrasts.
Not far from the lively—and sometimes rowdy—St. Pauli district, upscale residential areas such as Harvestehude and Blankenese serve as reminders that Hamburg is home to more millionaires than any other city in Germany. Take time to explore the city and you will soon fall under its spell.

🄸 **Information:** Hauptbahnhof, 20099 Hamburg. ☎(040) 30 05 13 00. www.hamburg-tourismus.de.

▶ **Orient Yourself:** Hamburg stands at the confluence of the Bille and the Alster, on the estuary of the Elbe river, which flows into the North Sea about 100km/62mi to the northwest. The A1 autobahn links it to Bremen, the A7 to Hannover and the A24 to Berlin.

🅿 **Parking:** Garages are located throughout the city. Visit http://wap.parkinfo.com for specific locations and fees.

⊗ **Don't Miss:** Port, Speicherstadt, HafenCity, Hamburger Kunsthalle, Ballinstadt.

🄾 **Organizing Your Time:** Allow one day for exploring the city center; half a day for a tour of the port (including a boat cruise); and half a day for the Altona Excursion.

Kids **Especially for Kids:** A cruise of Hamburg's port, canoeing or sailing the Außenalster basin, Tierpark Hagenbeck Zoo.

ॐ **Also See:** LÜNEBURG, LÜBECK, KIEL, BREMEN).

A Bit of History

The Hanseatic Town (13C–15C) – Originally a modest settlement on the banks of the Alster, a small tributary of the Elbe, Hamburg enjoyed its first taste of prosperity when it became a member of the Hanseatic League, headed at that time by Lübeck. It was then that merchants started to build warehouses and dock along the banks of the Elbe.

Liberty and Neutrality – The geographic discoveries of the 16C and the sea routes they opened up destroyed the Hanseatic monopoly, so Hamburg traders set their sights on warehousing and distribution. The foundation of the first German Stock Exchange (Börse) in 1558 reflected the intense business activity in Hamburg, a situation helped by the city's policy of strict neutrality, which kept it out of the Thirty Years' War. North- and Latin-American development helped greatly to expand the city. By 1913, the Hamburg-Amerika steamship line was the largest in the world and shipbuilding became the city's key industry.

Business and Leisure – Like many big ports, Hamburg has a reputation for unbridled nightlife. The St. Pauli quarter, west of the city center, sees the most action in side streets flanking the **Reeperbahn** and the Große Freiheit. Its bars, dance clubs, restaurants and erotic establishments go strong and lurid 24/7. But there is much more to Hamburg leisure pursuits than the garish Reeperbahn district. The Alster Lake lies like a sparkling jewel in the heart of the city.

Between the Staatsoper (Opera House) and the Rathaus (Town Hall), pedestrian precincts and covered shopping arcades form an almost uninterrupted labyrinth of galleries, boutiques and restaurants. The Mönckebergstraße, which links the Rathaus with the railway station, is another major commercial artery.

Hamburg Tourismus GmbH

The Alster basin right in the heart of the city

Antique shops around the Gänsemarkt specialize in Asian art. Between the Rathaus and the station, an impressive variety of old maps, prints and travel works can be found in booksellers' shops, while philatelists and tobacco fiends frequent the small shops in the printing and counting house quarter.

The people of Hamburg are said to be very "British" Germans: they tend to be more reserved and serious than their lively southern compatriots. For visitors, Hamburg is among the most welcoming of German cities, and English is spoken in many of the restaurants, stores and wine cellars.

Culinary Specialities – Local dishes often mix local produce with Asian spices, sometimes combining meat, fruit and sweet-and-sour sauces all in one dish. Typical are *Aalsuppe*—eel soup—and *Labskaus*, a seaman's dish of minced meat, herring, chopped gherkins, beetroot and mashed potato, topped with fried eggs.

Sights

The Port★★

Exploring the port of Hamburg is one of the highlights of any trip to the city. Apart from the tower of the St.Michaelis Kirche, the best **viewpoint**★ from which to see the port is the Stintfang—a raised terrace below the youth hostel (*U/S-Bahn St. Pauli Landungsbrücken*).

Boat Trip Around the Port   Kids

Boats depart from the dock near the Baumwall U-Bahn station Apr–Oct, daily 10am–6pm every 30min; Nov–Mar, Mon–Fri noon and 2pm, Sat–Sun 10.30am–4pm, every 30min. Duration 1hr. Commentary. ☎10€. ☎(040) 37 31 68. www.barkassen-centrale.de. Visitors will be astonished by the sheer size of the dockyards and by the extraordinary activity in the shipyards on either side of the Elbe, where every type of vessel is constructed. Motorized ferries ply back and forth all day long, transporting south bank workers back to the city during the rush hour.

The Port of Hamburg

The Hamburg docks comprise 60 basins and more than 68km/42.3mi of quays. The overall surface area is more than 75sq km/29sq mi. Thanks to a relatively small tidefall (3m/9.8ft average), no locks are necessary in the basins accessible to ocean-going traffic able to navigate the Elbe. Some 320 shipping lines call regularly (about 650 departures a month) to transport goods to a thousand ports all over the world.

Address Book

For coin ranges, see the Legend on the cover flap.

BASIC INFORMATION

TELEPHONE PREFIX: 040

VISITOR INFORMATION

For general information or room and ticket reservations: *Tourismus-Zentrale Hamburg GmbH,* ☎*(040) 30 05 13 00, www.hamburg-tourism.de. Open Mon–Sat 9am–7pm.* **Information offices:** Main Train Station (Hauptbahnhof), main entrance Kirchenallee, *Mon–Sat 8am–9pm, Sun 10am–6pm;* Harbor, St Pauli Landungsbrücken between piers 4 and 5, *daily 8am–6pm (Nov–Mar 10am–6pm);* Airport, arrival hall terminals 1 and 2, *daily 6am–11pm.* All branches distribute the free monthly cultural listings magazine *Vorschau…* (followed by the month), which can also be picked up in many hotels. Newsstands sell the magazines *Prinz* (biweekly) or *Szene Hamburg* (monthly).

POST OFFICES WITH LATE HOURS

The post office at Mönckebergstraße 7 is open Mon–Fri 9am–7pm and Sat 9am–3pm.

NEWSPAPERS

Hamburger Morgenpost, Hamburger Abendblatt.

INTERNET

www.hamburg.de; www.hamburg-intern.de; www.hamburg-web.de; www.hamburg-information.de

PUBLIC TRANSPORTATION

Hamburg is best explored using the buses and underground trains (U-Bahn) of the **HVV** (Hamburger Verkehrsverbund; ☎194 49; www.hvv.de), whose service extends into the surrounding countryside. The central information office is at the Hauptbahnhof (Kirchenallee entrance) Mon–Fri 6am–9pm, Sat–Sun 7am–9pm, and in many U- and S-Bahn stations. Tickets are available from orange vending machines and bus drivers. Single tickets for rides in the city center start at 1.30€; a day ticket for one person costs 6€, a group day ticket for up to five people costs 8.60€ but is valid only after 9am. A 3-day pass costs 14.40€.

The one-day **Hamburg Card** costs 8€ and is valid for one adult and up to three children under 15; the group version (11.80€) is good for up to five people of any age on the issue date and after 6pm the day before. The 3-day version costs 18€ (29.80€ for a group) and the 5-day is 33/51€. Benefits include free travel on all public transport in the Greater Hamburg region; free or discounted entrance to Hamburg museums and discounts for over 110 places of interest and attractions, including sightseeing tours, restaurants and shops. The Hamburg Card is available at tourist offices, in many hotels, at vending machines, in the HVV customer offices and online at www.hamburg-tourism.de.

SIGHTSEEING

CITY TOURS

All tours described below depart from the Hauptbahnhof/Kirchenallee exit.

Options include a hop-on, hop-off tour by double-decker buses, which stop at eight major landmarks, including St. Michaelskirche and St. Pauli Landungsbrücken. It operates Apr–Oct, daily every 30min, 9.30am–5pm; Nov–Mar, Fri–Sun half-hourly 10am–4pm, Mon–Thu hourly 10am–4pm. The entire loop takes about 90min and costs 14€ for adults, 7€ for children. An alternative is a classic narrated 2hr 30min city tour departing daily at 10am and 2pm; it costs 19€ for adults, 9.50€ for children. Details from **Top Tour Hamburg** (☎*(040) 641 37 31; www.top-tour-hamburg.de)* or Hamburger Stadtrundfahrt (☎*(040) 792 89 79; www.hummelbahn.de)*

The Hamburg tourist office organizes a variety of **walking tours** Apr–Oct, for instance of the Speicherstadt/HafenCity or the Counting House District. Stattreisen Hamburg also runs thematic walks, including one of the red light district (☎*040- 430 34 81; www.stattreisen-hamburg.de).*

BOAT TOURS

Several companies offer boat tours of the Inner and Outer Alster, the Hamburg port and the Speicherstadt. See individual listings under Sights for details.

WHERE TO STAY

Hotel Etap Hamburg-City – *Holstenkamp 3, 22525 Hamburg-Eimsbüttel* (040) 85 37 98 20. *www.etaphotel.com. 180 rooms.* 5.50€. No surprises at this no-nonsense French chain hotel which provides inexpensive accommodation in the city center. Rooms are small but well-kept and sport all the modern conveniences.

Hotel Schwanenwik – *Schwanenwik 29.* (040) 220 09 18. *www.hotel-schwanenwik.de. 18 rooms.* This charming boarding house (completely smoke-free) occupies a magnificent 18C white bourgeois house on the Alster. The simple, modern rooms face the lake or the back garden.

Hotel Stephan – *Schmarjestraße 31.* (040) 389 51 08. *www.hotel-stephan.de. 29 rooms.* Oozing plenty of character in its woodsy public areas and well-kept homey rooms, this hotel puts you close to Altona train station. In summer, enjoy breakfast on the terrace.

Hotel Yoho – *Moorkamp 5.* (040) 28 41 91 91. *www.yoho-hamburg.de. 30 rooms.* 12.50€. *Restaurant* . Youthful and hip, this stately white Art Nouveau villa was completely redesigned by a team of architects and now houses a hotel for "young" people of all ages. Rooms are rather small but stylishly minimalist. Special rates apply to those under 26. The restaurant serves Middle Eastern food.

Hotel Am Elbufer – *Focksweg 40a, 21129 Hamburg-Finkenwerder* (040) 742 19 10. *www.hotel-am-elbufer.de. 14 rooms.* At this pleasant little hotel on the Elbe, only passing boats might disturb your peace and quiet. Rooms are dressed in bright reds and orange and come in a variety of sizes. Some have river views, as does the breakfast room.

Hotel Schmidt – *Reventlowstraße 60, 22605 Hamburg-Othmarschen* (040) 88 90 70. *www.hotel-schmidt.de. 50 rooms.* This hotel in a leafy neighborhood has a wide range of rooms—from very basic to quite deluxe—spread over several buildings. Table service at breakfast.

Fairmont Hotel Vier Jahreszeiten – *Neuer Jungfernstieg 9.* (040) 349 40. *www.hvj.de. 157 rooms.* 25€. *Restaurant* . Unpretentious luxury characterizes this lakeside grand hotel with luxurious Gründerzeit décor and charming, modern, comfortable rooms. Upscale cuisine is served in the Haerlin, Doc Cheng's and Jahreszeiten Grill restaurants.

WHERE TO EAT

Atlas – *Schützenstraße 9a.* (040) 851 78 10. *www.atlas.at. Closed Saturday lunch.* A former fish smokehouse has been recast as an upbeat bistro/restaurant-cum-cocktail bar with an ivy-covered terrace. It is somewhat hidden away in Phönixhof.

Café Paris – *Rathausstraße 4.* (040) 32 52 77 77. *www.cafeparis.net.* This classic brasserie feels so fantastically French, you half expect to see the Eiffel Tower through the window. Mirrors and framed prints line the walls, the servers wear crisp white shirts and the menu features salad Niçoise and Côte de boeuf. Très Gallic, très charming.

Gröninger Haus – *Ost-West-Straße 47.* (040) 33 13 83. *www.groeninger-hamburg.de. Closed Sat lunchtime and Sun. Reservations recommended.* A private brewery inside the city's oldest hotel (first documented in 1260) is a lovely spot to allow the day to wind down. Meals are hearty and come in belt-loosening portions. Wash them down with the in-house brew.

Warsteiner Elbspeicher – *Große Elbstraße 39.* (040) 38 22 42. *www.warsteiner-elbspeicher.de.* Ingeniously converted from an old riverside warehouse, this friendly bi-level establishment is divided into a casual downstairs bistro and a rustic restaurant upstairs where meals come with splendid harbor views. Overall, a fine place for fresh fish and typical Hanseatic dishes.

�🍺🍺🍺**Old Commercial Room** – *Englische Planke 10. ☎(040) 36 63 19. www.oldcommercialroom.de. Reservations recommended.* A Hamburg institution since 1795, the Old Commercial Room was founded by an English ship owner, which might explain the pub décor with mahogany, copper and maritime pictures. Traditional sailors' dishes dominate the menu *(Labskaus)*, but also lobster, sole and pork knuckle.

◑🍺🍺🍺**Louis C. Jacob** – *Elbchaussee 401, Hamburg-Nienstedten. ☎(040) 82 25 50. www.hotel-jacob.de. Reservations recommended.* Fine dining does not get much more refined than at this elegant hotel restaurant overlooking the Elbe. The delicious French cuisine is a delight. In fine weather, the most coveted tables are on the terrace with its lime trees; it was immortalized in a painting by Max Liebermann in 1902.

◑🍺🍺🍺**Le Canard** – *Elbchaussee 139, 2763 Hamburg-Altona. ☎(040) 88 12 95 31. Closed Sun and Mon. Reservations necessary.* Chef Ali Güngormüs is a magician when it comes to coaxing maximum flavor out of fresh quality ingredients. His dishes are light and Mediterranean, occasionally infused with an exotic Middle Eastern touch. Budget gourmets should come at lunchtime.

TAKING A BREAK

Destille – *Steintorplatz 1 (enter from Brockesstraße). ☎(040) 280 33 54. Closed Mon and Dec 24–Jan 1. Free admission if visiting the museum, otherwise 1€.* On the first floor of the Museum of Arts & Crafts, this little café is an excellent lunch stop, and not only for museum goers. Restful views of the leafy courtyard are gratis.

NIGHTLIFE

USEFUL TIPS

Hamburg's night-life has been synonymous with St. Pauli since time immemorial. In addition to its established temples of eroticism, the area around the Reeperbahn and Große Freiheit has become a rather trendy spot of late with more than 400 restaurants squeezing into these quarters. The inner city, too, between the Gänsemarkt and Millerntor (especially around Großneumarkt) offers plenty of opportunities to eat and drink; the passage quarter between Jungfernstieg and Stadthausbrücke is pleasant. The young, alternative crowd gathers in the "Schanzenviertel" west and southwest of the television tower (between Juliusstraße and Neuer Pferdemarkt).

Alex im Alsterpavillon – *Jungfernstieg 54. ☎(040) 35 01 87 15. www.alexgastro. de.* People of all ages gather throughout the day for a drink or a snack on what may well be Hamburg's finest waterfront terrace.

Amphore – *Hafenstraße 140 (follows the Elbe toward the west from Landungsbrücken). ☎(040) 31 79 38 80. www.cafe-amphore.de.* Friendly little café with a lovely harbor view from the terrace above old blockhouses (blankets available). Breakfast served until 3pm.

Christiansen's Fine Drinks & Cocktails – *Pinnasberg 60 (in St. Pauli, near the Fischmarkt). ☎(040) 317 28 63. www.christiansens.de. Closed Sun.* 250 cocktails, 160 brands of rum and 150 varieties of whisky on offer.

Cotton Club – *Alter Steinweg 10. ☎(040) 34 38 78. www.cotton-club.org.* Hamburg's local jazz institution was founded 1959, renamed the "Cotton Club" in 1963 and moved to this location in 1971. Performances most nights.

Grosse Freiheit 36 & Kaiserkeller – *Grosse Freiheit 36. ☎(040) 31 77 78 11. www.grossefreiheit36.de.* The Beatles rocked the Kaiserkeller back in 1960 and this venue is still going strong. The upstairs Grosse Freiheit 36 hosts dance parties, while alternative rock bands hold forth in the basement.

Laeiszhalle – *Johannes-Brahms-Platz 1. ☎(040) 34 69 20. www.laeiszhalle.de.* Hamburg's premier venue for classical music, this Neo-Baroque brick pile from 1908 hosts concerts by local and regional orchestras, including the State Philharmonic Orchestra, as well as international guest performers.

Staatsoper Hamburg – *Grosse Theaterstraße 25. ☎ (040) 35 68 68. www. hamburgische-staatsoper.de.* One of the world's most renowned opera houses.

SHOPPING

USEFUL TIPS

Department stores and mainstream chain stores line Mönckebergstraße and Spitalerstraße west of the main train station. Deeper pockets are required in the 9 exclusive shopping arcades around Jungfernstieg and Neuer Wall, which are the haunts of international designer boutiques and specialty stores. Steer toward the suburb of Eppendorf (Klosterstern to Eppendorfer Markt) to browse through independent boutiques selling trendy fashions, home accessories and gift items.

Harry's Hamburger Hafenbasar – *Balduinstraße 18 (corner of Erichstraße, in St. Pauli). ☎ (040) 31 24 82. www. hafenbasar.de. Open Tue–Sun noon–6pm. Admission 2.50€ (refunded with purchase).* A jumble of objects brought back by sailors from the four corners of the world, labyrinthine Harry's has been around for half a century and is really more a museum than a shop. Great for browsing for unique gifts.

Antique dealers – Mainly in the *Quartier Satin* on ABC-Straße and the *Antik-Center* of the covered arcade at Klosterwall 9–21; the latter has more than 60 stalls selling the best of yesteryear's collectibles.

Flea markets – The best regular flea markets are the Flohschanze markt in an old slaughterhouse in St. Pauli (every Sat 8am-4pm) and the monthly Kulturflohmarkt at the Museum of Work (Sat or Sun 9am-5pm).

Markets – The Fish Market *(www.fischmarkt-hamburg.de)* is the most famous market in Hamburg, held in the wee hours of every Sun (summer 5.30am–9.30am, winter 7am–10am). Weekly markets are held in all the city's districts, including a particularly nice one on Mon. A typical market is held on Mon and Fri under the U-Bahn bridge at Eppendorf.

Shoes, shoes, shoes! – Hamburg has some of the best shoe stores in Germany, with department stores seemingly overflowing with shoes!

St. Pauli District

North of the port and west of the new town.

St. Pauli had its golden age in the 1960s when the Beatles played the Star Club and Kaiserkeller in **Große Freiheit**. Its image was later considerably tarnished by prostitution and drug trafficking, but over the last few years this district, which has the city's biggest police station **(Davidwache)**, has undergone a renaissance. Although the sex industry is still in full swing, the area is also teeming with trendy bars, cafés and restaurants, many with a genuinely warm atmosphere and popular with locals and non-locals alike. St. Pauli spreads out around the **Reeperbahn**, the main thoroughfare, which runs parallel to the port.

Walking Tour

City Center

Allow one day

Binnenalster and Außenalster★★★ (Inner & Outer Alster Lakes) Kids

Departures from the Jungfernstieg pier. Alster-Rundfahrt (50min): late Mar–Sept daily 10am–6pm, half-hourly; Oct 10am, 11am–4pm half-hourly, 5pm; Nov–Mar 10.30am, noon, 1.30pm & 3pm. ☎ 10€ (child 5€). Alster-Kreuz-Fahrt (hop-on, hop-off at 9 stops): late Mar–Sept daily 10.15am–5.15pm. ☎ 1.30€ (child 0.65€) per dock or 8.50€ (child 4.25€) round-trip. ☎ (040) 35 74 24 19. www.alstertouristik.de.

The Alster Lake, north of the old town, is a beautiful stretch of water. It consists of two basins, the Binnenalster and the Außenalster, the latter (the larger of the two) offering sailing and canoeing. A fleet of motorboats ferries passengers regularly between nine landing docks. It is also possible to sail on the Alster canals (past beautifully kept parks and villas interspersed with undeveloped areas) and on the canals in the old town and port (two locks allow access to the port area from the Binnenalster).

Those with transportation can drive clockwise around the Alster, bordered by luxury apartments on one side and immaculate parks on the other.

Jungfernstieg★

Bordering the southern end of the Binnenalster (Inner Alster), the Jungfernstieg is among Hamburg's most cosmopolitan thoroughfares. The crowded terraces of the waterfront Alsterpavillon café-restaurant, the boats crossing the basin, the presence nearby of one of the world's most famous hotels (Vier Jahreszeiten), and the imposing new office blocks lining the Ballindamm all contribute to the spirited ambience.

▸ *Leave Jungfernstieg and walk along the Alsterfleet to the Town Hall.*

Rathausmarkt

Hamburg's majestic **Town Hall** (👁visit by guided tour only, year-round, Mon–Thu 10am–3pm, Fri 10am–1pm, Sat 10am–6pm, Sun 10am–5pm; 1.50€) with its 112m/367ft-high clock tower dominates this central square. Rebuilt after the fire of 1842 in Neo-Renaissance style and completed in 1887, it contains a veritable maze of 647 rooms and boasts a façade adorned with statues of 20 German emperors.

The bridge (*Schleusenbrücke*), which forms part of the Alster's lock system, crosses the Alsterfleet, a relic of the city's former canal system. On the far bank the colonnade of the Alsterarkaden shelters elegant shops and cafés.

▸ *Turn into Mönckebergstraße.*

St. Petri Kirche (Church of St. Peter)

Mönckebergstraße.
🕐*Open year-round, Mon–Thu 10am-6.30pm, Fri 10am-7pm, Sat 10am-5pm, Sun 9am-9pm.* ☎*(040) 325 74 00.*
This 12C church was rebuilt in Neo-Gothic style after the great fire of 1842. The **lion's head door handles**★ (1342) on the left west portal are regarded as Hamburg's oldest suriving work of art.

St. Jakobi-Kirche (Church of St. Jacob)

Jacobikirchhof 22.
🕐*Open year-round, Mon–Sat 10am-5pm.* ☎*(040) 303 73 70.*
Among the treasures of this 14C–15C hall church are the **reredos**★ of St. Luke and the Fishers' Guild; a triptych of the Coopers' Guild on the high altar; Georg Bauman's alabaster and marble pulpit (1610); and the famous 1693 **organ by Arp Schnitger**★.

▸ *Cross Steinstraße heading south to Burchardplatz.*

Kontorhäuser (Counting House Buildings)

These imposing brick buidlings dominate the printing, press and business quarter around Burchardplatz square. Of particular interest is the **Chilehaus** (*between Burgstraße and Meßberg*). Designed by Expressionist architect Fritz Höger, this 1924 building looms against the sky like the prow of a ship.

The Fish Market

The Hamburg fish market originated in the early 18C and has become a veritable institution. It is held every Sunday morning in the south of the St. Pauli district along the Elbe from 5.30am–9.30am (from 7am Oct–Mar). The cheerful fishmongers, crowds of people of all ages who come to buy or browse and musical entertainment in the *Fischauktionshalle* have made it part of living Hamburg folklore.

Speicherstadt warehouses

It was built for a rich local merchant who made his fortune mainly through trade relations with Chile, hence the name. The **Sprinkenhof** (1931) is a town within the town, an office complex complete with roadways open to vehicles.

▶ *Continue southwards and cross the Auf dem Sande canal to explore Speicherstadt.*

Speicherstadt★ (Warehouse Quarter)

After Hamburg joined the German Customs Federation in 1871, it became necessary to create a free trade zone. An entire district along the Zoll Canal and its side channels was flattened to make room for the Speicherstadt warehouses, set up between 1885 and 1927. Still the world's largest continuous warehouse complex, they store coffee, tobacco, spices, raw silk, oriental carpets and other goods. With its rows of gabled brick buildings topped with green copper roofs, Speicherstadt is an appealing quarter for a stroll or a **boat cruise** *(departs from Jungfernstieg, late Mar–Oct daily 10.45am, 1.45pm, 4.45pm; 2hr; 15€; (040) 5 74 24 19; www.alster touristik.de).* For a birds-eye view, catch a flight aboard the **HighFlyer hot-air balloon** *(Deichtorstraße 1; year-round, daily 10am–10pm, weather permitting; 15min; every 15min; 15€; (040) 30 08 69 68; www.highflyer-hamburg.de)*

HafenCity★★

Information Center: Sandtorkai 30.
Open year-round, Tue–Sun 10am–6pm (May–Sept, Thu 10am–8pm). (040) 36 90 17 99. www.hafencity.com.
Just beyond the Speicherstadt, Europe's **largest urban construction project** is taking shape on 155ha/383 acres of abandoned industrial wasteland: Hafen-City. Hamburg's newest district will be divided into 12 *Quartiere* (quarters), and will include a mix of shops, offices, leisure and cultural facilities along with living space for up to 12 000 people. One of its key features is the **Elbphilharmonie** (Elbe Philharmonic Hall), designed by the Swiss firm of Herzog & de Meuron. Set to open in 2010, it combines the classical brick architecture of a historic warehouse with the bold sweep of glass façades and a wavelike roof line.
To help you visualize this enormous building project, which will remain a work in progress until 2020, visit the HafenCity information center. A great overview of the vast construction site can be enjoyed from the bright orange **Viewpoint**, a 13m/42.6ft-high tower.

Altstadt (Old Town)

Hamburg's old town is bounded by the Nikolaifleet, the Binnenhafen (docks reserved for river craft and tugboats) and the Zoll Canal.
Highlights of the old town begin with the **St. Katharinen Kirche**, a 14C–15C

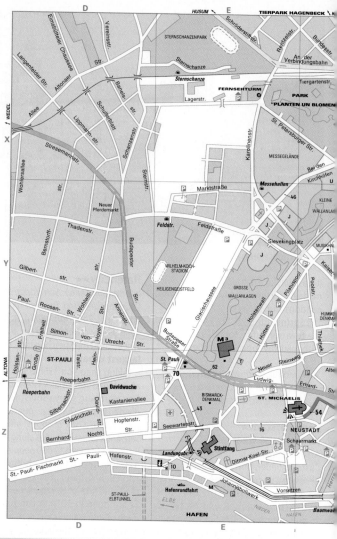

HAMBURG

Adenauerallee	HY 2	Graskeller	FZ 31	Poststr.	FY		
Alsterarkaden	GY 3	Große Bleichen	FY 33	Pumpen	HZ 68		
Bei dem Neuen Krahn	FZ 9	Große Burstah	FZ 35	Rathausstr.	GZ 69		
Bei den St. Pauli-		Große Johannisstr.	GZ 34	Reeperbahn	EZ 70		
Landungsbrücken	EZ 1	Große Reichenstr.	GZ 37	Reesendamm	GY 71		
Bergstr.	GY	Hachmannpl.	HY 39	Rothenbaumchaussee	FX 72		
Böhmkenstr.	EZ 16	Helgoländer Allee	EZ 43	Schleusenbrücke	GY 75		
Börsenbrücke	GZ 18	Holstenglacis	EY 46	Schmiedestr.	GZ 76		
Colonnaden	FY	Jungfernstieg	GY	Spitalerstr.	GHY		
Cremon	FZ 21	Kleine Reichenstr.	GZ 50	Stadthausbrücke	FY 77		
Dammtordamm	FX 23	Klingberg	GZ 51	Steintordamm	HY 79		
Dammtorstr.	FY	Krayenkamp	FZ 54	Steintorpl.	HY 80		
Gerhofstr.	FY 29	Millerntordamm	EZ 62	Zippelhaus	GZ 88		
		Mönckebergstr.	GHY				
		Neuer Wall	FYZ				

Hamburger Kunsthalle	HY M¹	Museum für		Museum für Völkerkunde	
Museum für Hamburgische		Kommunikation	FY M⁴	Hamburg	FX M⁵
Geschichte	EYZ M³	Museum für Kunst und		Rathaus	GZ R
		Gewerbe	HY M²		

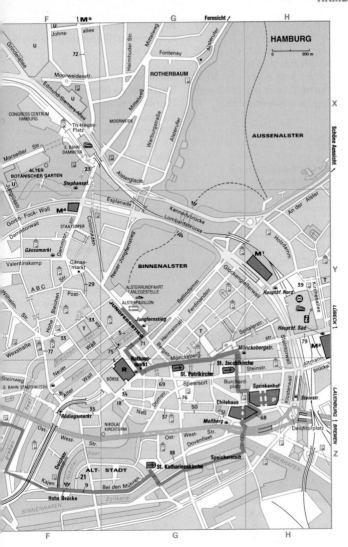

Gothic brick church featuring a bulbous openwork tower.

It was on **Deichstraße** that the great fire of 1842 erupted. Many of the 17C–18C merchants' houses have today been converted into bars and taverns.

The restored façades of warehouses opposite, lining the curve of the Nikolaifleet Canal, recall the Hamburg of yesteryear. The best view is from the **Hohe Brücke**, which crosses the Nikolaifleet and parallels the Binnenhafen.

St. Michaelis Kirche★ (Church of St. Michael)

◉*Open May-Oct, daily 9am–8pm, Nov–Apr 10am–6pm.* ⊛*2.50€ tower, 3€ tower & crypt.* ☎*(040) 37 67 81 00. www. st-michaelis.de.*

Designed in 1762 by Ernst Georg Sonnin, this church is one of the finest examples of the Baroque tradition in northern Germany. Its landmark tower (1786) rises high above the Elbe and offers sweeping **views**★ from the platform at 132m/433ft. Another level features **HamburgHIStory** *(every 30min, 12.30pm–3.30pm),* a multimedia show explaining high- and low points of the city's past 1 000 years.

Near the east end of the church, a blind alley off Am Krayenkamp 10 is lined with 17C brick and timber houses, built as **almshouses** (*Krameramtswohnungen*); today they are mostly art galleries.

Sights

Hamburger Kunsthalle★★ (Fine Arts Museum)

Glockengiesserwall.

🕐*Open year-round, Tue–Sun 10am–6pm (Thu 9pm).* 🕐 *Closed Dec 24.* 🚷 *8.50€.* ♿🕿*(040) 428 13 12 00. www.hamburger-kunsthalle.de.*

Consisting of three buildings, the Kunsthalle is one of Germany's largest art museums. From medieval religious artworks to 17C Dutch Masters and land- and seascapes by Rembrandt, Van Goyen and Ruysdael, you will find it here.

A particular strength of the collection is the section of 19C–20C German painting with works by Caspar David Friedrich, Philipp Otto Runge, Feuerbach, Von Marées, Böcklin, Menzel and Wilhelm Leibl (*Three Women in Church*). There is a dazzling display of work by Max Liebermann, Lovis Corinth and Edvard Munch as well as ground-breaking canvases by Max Beckmann, Oskar Kokoschka, Paul Klee and other members of the early 20C *Brücke* and *Blaue Reiter* artist groups.

The **Galerie der Gegenwart** is devoted to post-1960 art. Look for works by Richard Serra, Claes Oldenburg, Jenny Holzer, Bruce Naumann and Andy Warhol. German art is also well represented by artists like Sigmar Polke, Georg Baselitz, Markus Lüpertz, Mario Merz, Gerhard Richter, Rosemarie Trockel and Joseph Beuys.

Museum für Kunst und Gewerbe★ (Museum of Decorative Arts)

Steintorplatz 1.

🕐*Open year-round, Tue–Sun 10am–6pm (Thu 9pm).* 🕐*Closed May 1, Dec 24 & 31.* 🚷*8€.* ♿🕿*(040) 428 134 27 32. www.mkg-hamburg.de.*

In a 19C Neo-Renaissance palace, this vast museum houses collections of sculptures, ceramics, furniture, jewelry and musical instruments from antiquity to the present. The Jugendstil gallery is a knock-out.

Museum für Hamburgische Geschichte★ (Museum of Hamburg History)

Holstenwall 24.

🕐*Open year-round, Tue–Sat 10am–5pm, Sun 6pm.* 🚷*7.50€.* ♿🕿*(040) 428 132 23 80. www.hamburgmuseum.de.*

Hamburg's fascinating history gets the full treatment at this engaging museum through city models and numerous themed sections (emigration, Jewish Hamburg, the Hanseatic period, etc.).

Tierpark Hagenbeck★★   Kids

Leave via Grindelallee.

🕐*Open Mar–Jun and Sept–Oct, daily 9am–5pm; Jul–Aug 7pm; Nov–Mar 4.30pm.* 🚷*15€.* ♿🕿*(040) 530 03 30. www.hagenbeck.de.*

This delightful park (1907) boasts ancient trees, artificial lakes and hillocks and is a delightful place for a stroll. Some 2 500 creatures representing 360 species from five continents live in spacious, open enclosures. Since 2007, the vast **Tropen-Aquarium** (*Tropical Aquarium;* 🕐*9am–6pm;* 🚷*13€*), has brought visitors face to fin with more than 14 000 creatures in a fun undersea expedition.

BallinStadt Emigration Museum★★

Veddeler Bogen 2.

🕐*Open year-round, daily 10am–6pm.* 🚷*9.80€.* 🕿*(040) 31 97 91 60. www.ballinstadt.de.*

On the Elbe Island of Veddel, BallinStadt was the embarkation center for five million Europeans headed for America between 1850 and 1939.

Three recreated structures now house Hamburg's newest museum (open since 2007). Curators have dug deep into the bag of multimedia tricks to vividly portray all phases of emigration—packing to settling—and to bring to life people's hopes and hardships, dreams and realities. You can even trace your own roots in the Family Research Center.

Excursions

Altona
3.2km/2mi southwest

Altonaer Museum in Hamburg★★
(Altona Cultural History Museum)
Museumstraße 23. By car: Leave via Reeperbahn; by S-Bahn: station Hamburg-Altona). ○*Open year-round, Tue–Sun 10am–6pm (Thu 10pm).* ○*Closed Jan 1, Ascension Day, May 1, Dec 24 & 31.* ⊜*6€.* ♿⊞*(040) 428 11 35 82. www.altonaer-museum.de.*

Art, culture and day-to-day life in the lower Elbe valley and Schleswig-Holstein are illustrated here. Note the exceptional collection of ships' figureheads from the 18C–19C, the models of North Sea boats, the ceramics, fine Frisian embroidery and old toys. There is also a gallery with paintings of north German landscapes.

Altonaer Balkon (Altona Balcony)
The terrace south of Altona's Town Hall affords a **view**★ of the Köhlbrandbrücke and confluence of the two branches of the Elbe. Follow the **Elbchaussee**★, a spacious avenue bordered by fabulous mansions since the early 19C.

Klein Flottbek
10.2km/6.3mi west.

Jenischpark
Baron-Voght-Straße 50.
This landscaped park with exotic trees harbors two interesting spaces. The **Jenischhaus** (○*open year-round, Tue–Sun 11am–6pm;* ○*closed Jan 1, Dec 24 & 31.* ⊜*4€;* ⊞*(040) 82 87 90)* is a stately 19C Neoclassical villa whose luxurious rooms illustrate bourgeois lifestyles from the Late Renaissance to the beginning of the Jugendstil period.

Nearby, the **Ernst-Barlach-Haus** (○*open year-round, Tue–Sun 11am–6pm;* ○*closed Dec 24 & 31;* ⊜*5€;* ⊞*(040) 82 60 85; www.barlach-haus.de)* contains sculptures, wood engravings and drawings by this expressionist artist (1870–1938) who was born in Wedel. Visit his **birthhouse** (*Mühlenstraße 1;* ○*open year-round, Mon–Fri 10am–5pm;* ⊜*5€;* ⊞*(04103) 91 82 91; www.ernst-barlach. de)* to see more of his works.

Old windmill in Stade

Stade★
74.3km/46mi southwest.

More than 1 000 years old, Stade hugs a navigable stretch of the Schwinge, which flows into the Elbe. In the Middle Ages, it had a port the size of Hamburg's. During the Thirty Years' War, Swedish occupation troops transformed it into a garrison stronghold and administrative center.

Most buildings in the beautiful **old town**★★ were built after 1659, the date of a great fire. Among the picturesque half-timbered houses, note Hökerhaus (*Hökerstraße 27*), Doppelhaus (*Bäckerstraße 1–3*) and Haus Knechthausen (*Bungenstraße 20*).

The most magnificent home is the **Bürgermeister-Hintze-Haus** (*Wasser West*) in the old port.

Schwedenspeicher-Museum★
Wasser West 43. ○*Open year-round, Tue–Fri 10am–5pm, Sat–Sun 10am–6pm.* ○*Closed Jan 1, Dec 25 & 31.* ⊜*1€.* ⊞*(041 41) 32 22. www.schwedenspeicher.de.*

Built between 1692 and 1705, this Swedish brick granary (1692–1705) now houses the local history museum.

The most interesting items on display are four prehistoric **bronze wheels**★ (c. 700 BC) from a funerary carriage, as well as antique jewelry, weapons and pots.

HAMELN★

POPULATION: 58 500

This town is the setting for the Tale of the Pied Piper, as told by the Brothers Grimm in the 19C. Hameln glories in fine old houses, most of them in ornate Weser-Renaissance style.

🛈 **Information:** Deisterallee 1, 31785 Hameln. ☎(05151) 95 78 23. www.hameln.de.

▸ **Orient Yourself:** Hameln hugs the banks of the Weser and is located just south of the A2, about halfway between Bielefeld and Hannover. It extends into the Weserbergland, a hilly expanse that becomes a nature park.

🕲 **Don't Miss:** The unique Weser-Renaissance architecture, best seen on foot.

🕘 **Organizing Your Time:** Allow a couple of hours to see the Altstadt.

🧒 **Especially for Kids:** Weekly fairytale reenactments.

👶 **Also See:** LEMGO, HILDESHEIM, HANNOVER.

A Bit of History

A Jewel of the Weser-Renaissance – The Weser-Renaissance style (late 16-early 17C) so well displayed in Hameln is distinguished architecturally by ram's-horn scrollwork and pinnacled gables. Other characteristics include delicately worked stone bands encircling the building, jutting bay windows *(Utluchten)*, and large, well-developed dormers *(Zwerchhäuser)* with decorated gables.

The Pied Piper of Hameln – In 1284, a mysterious man in multicolored clothes promised the townspeople that, for a substantial reward, he would free Hameln from a plague of rats and mice. He played his pipe, and all the rodents emerged to follow him to the banks of the Weser, where they drowned.

When the townspeople didn't pay him, the piper returned and played again in revenge. This time it was the children who emerged from their houses. There were 130 of them, and they too followed him, never to be seen again. Only two escaped; one was mute, the other blind. The rather less romantic but more accurate version of this tale is that 13C overpopulation led to a troop of young people being sent by the authorities to colonize territories to the east. But it is the former 🧒**Grimm fairytale** that is acted out every Sunday at midday on the terrace of the Hochzeitshaus.

Walking Tour

Altstadt★ (Old Town)

Rattenfängerhaus★ (The Rat Catcher's House)

This large 1603 building has little to do with rats but it combines all the major elements of the Weser-Renaissance architectural style. The symmetrical façade features sculpted bands of stonework, adorned with carved busts and masks. The two-story projecting oriel used to feature a crown.

▸ *Take the Osterstraße, one of the most well-known streets in Hameln. It was here on July 26, 1284, that the children followed the Pied Piper. Stop at the top of the Kleine Straße to look at the splendid Renaissance houses (Haus Osterstraße 12, Leisthaus and Stiftsherrenhaus).*

Stiftsherrenhaus (Canons' House)

Osterstraße 8.

🕘*Open year-round, Tue–Sun 10am–4.30pm.* 🕘*Closed Jan 1, Good Fri, Dec 24 & 31.* ⊚*3€.* ☎*(05151) 202 12 15.*

Another remarkable house, this one half-timbered and built in 1558, is the only one in Hameln featuring figurative decorations. Represented are Greek and Roman as well as numerous biblical characters, including Christ, the apostles, David, and Cain and Abel. The Stiftsherrenhaus is

Address Book

WHERE TO STAY

♨♨♨**An der Altstadt** –
*Deisterallee 16. ☎(05151) 402 40. www.
hotel-an-der-altstadt.de. Closed Dec
21–Jan 6.* 20 rooms. This small Jugendstil
hotel in the heart of town is a nice place
to unpack your suitcase in comfortably
appointed guestrooms furnished in
cherrywood.

WHERE TO EAT

♨♨**Grüner Reiter** – *Kastanienwall 62.
☎(05151) 92 62 00. www.gruenerreiter.de.*
This building was built in 1713 as a
chapel for the soldiers of the Hameln
Fortress. The bistro-style restaurant in a
glass extension in the courtyard serves
breakfast, light lunches, afternoon
cakes and Italian dinners.

TAKING A BREAK

Museumscafé – *Osterstraße 8.
☎(05151) 215 53. www.museumscafe.de.*
If you have a sweeth tooth, you must try
the marzipan-filled Rat Catcher's Cake
(Rattenfängertorte) in this charming
café inside the Stiftsherrenhaus. More
substantial meals, often featuring seasonal ingredients, are also on the menu.

joined with the adjacent **Leisthaus** via
a bridge on the first floor. Rooms in both
rambling buildings now harbor the **local
history museum**, which counts the
world's largest collection of Pied Piper
memorabilia among its exhibits.

Dempterhaus
In the market square.
An outstanding building from 1607;
note its fine Weser-Renaissance projecting oriel.

Hochzeitshaus (Marriage House)★
◷*The Hochzeitshaus itself has closed
down, but the building can be admired
from the outside.*
The Weser-Renaissance-style building,
constructed between 1610 and 1617,
was used as a reception hall for burghers'
weddings. Three elegant gables break the
horizontals of the façade. A **carrillon**
from 1964 plays the Rattenfängerlied
(Rat Catcher song) at 9.35am, the Weser-
lied (by Gustav Pressel) at 11.35am, and
the Rattenfängerlied again at 13.05pm,
3.35pm and 5.35pm.

▶ *Take Fischpfortenstraße and pass
in front of Wilhelm-Busch-Haus,
then continue to the Weser.
Retrace your steps until you reach
the Wendenstraße.*

Haus Lücking
Wendenstraße 8.
This rich, half-timbered house of 1638
features a rounded doorway and is lavishly adorned with inscriptions and ornamentation.

▶ *At the end of the road, turn right
into Bäckerstraße.*

Rattenkrug
Bäckerstraße 16.
A projecting bay window and a five-floor-
tall gable distinguish this 1568 building.

▶ *Continue until the Münsterkirchhof.*

Münsterkirchhof (Collegiate Church)
From the gardens to the south, the church
appears to cower beneath its massive
polygonal tower, once part of a 12C
Romanesque basilica. Inside, the layout
of the columns and their capitals draws
attention to the raised transept.

▶ *Finish the tour by coming back
along Alte Markt-Straße, noticing
the Kürie Jerusalem passageway.*

HANNOVER

POPULATION: 516 000

Hannover is one of northern Germany's main economic hubs and a host of important trade shows such as the annual Cebit computer fair. But the city is not all buttoned-down business: Visitors will find a wealth of pleasant pastimes, most notably by exploring its grand gardens.

- **Information:** Ernst-August-Platz 8, 30159 Hannover. ☎(0511) 12 34 51 11. www.hannover.de.
- **Orient Yourself:** Set on a plain on the banks of the Leine and the Mittelandkanal, Hannover is halfway between the Baltic Sea and the North Sea. The A2 (Dortmund–Berlin) and A7 (Kassel–Hamburg) autobahns intersect here.
- **Parking:** Garages are located throughout Hannover. The ones around the Hauptbahnhof are easiest to find.
- **Don't Miss:** Hannover's terrific gardens.
- **Organizing Your Time:** Allow at least two hours to see the Herrenhäuser Gardens.
- **Especially for Kids:** Hannover Zoo.
- **Also See:** HILDESHEIM CELLE, HAMELN, BRAUNSCHWEIG.

Sights

Herrenhäuser Gärten★★ (Herrenhausen Gardens)

Begun in the 17C, one of Europe's most beautiful public parks comprises four separate and varied gardens linked by the Herrenhäuser Allee.

Großer Garten★★

⏱Open May–Aug 9am–8pm; Sept–Apr, 9am–sunset. ☞3€.

Creation of this splendid 50ha/123.5-acre Baroque garden started in 1666 but it didn't get its finishing touches until Electress Sophie turned her attention to it between 1696 and 1714. The oldest section, a French pleasure garden, features statues of allegorical figures and Roman gods. The paths in the southern section wrap around water features.

The first thing you will likely see is the huge **fountain** with its 80m/262.4ft-high plume. An exciting modern highlight is the whimsical **grotto** (⏱open May–Aug, 9am–7.30pm; Mar and Sept 6.30pm, Oct 5.30pm, Nov–Feb, Sun 12.30pm–3.30pm) decorated by the late French artist Niki de Saint Phalle. Illustrating the theme of human life, the octagonal foyer and two adjacent rooms sparkle with colored glass mosaics, mirrors, pebbles and painted fiberglass figurines.

Georgengarten

⏱Open 24hr.

Inspired by English landscape gardens, this romantic patch was laid out between 1835 and 1841 and is distinguished by great expanses of lawn.

Enjoy fabulous views from the **Leibniztempel**, a memorial dedicated to the philosopher and scientist, Wilhelm Gottfried Leibniz (1646–1716), on a raised peninsula.

The Wallmodenschlößchen is a pavilion housing the **Wilhelm-Busch-Museum** (⏱open Apr–Oct, Tue–Sat 11am–5pm; Sun 11am–6pm; Nov–Mar, Tue–Sat 11am–4pm, Sun 11am–6pm; ⏱closed Dec 24 & 31; ☞4.50€; ☎(0511) 16 99 99 11; www.wilhelm-busch-museum.de) dedicated to the famous poet, illustrator and humorist (1832–1908) who launched the advent of comic strips with such stories as "Max und Moritz".

Berggarten★

⏱Open May–Aug, daily 9am–7pm; Apr and Sept, 9am–6.30pm; Mar and Oct, 9am–5.30pm; Nov–Jan, 9am–4pm. ☞2€.

One of the oldest botanical gardens in Germany, Berggarten is a charming and colorful riot of 11 000 plant species, including cacti, orchids and flora native to the Canary Islands. There are

Address Book

For coin ranges, see the Legend on the cover flap.

WHERE TO STAY

City Hotel Hannover – *Limburgstraße 3* ☎ *(0511) 360 70. www.cityhotelhannover.de. 47 rooms.* Rooms are functional and comfortable at this impeccably run hotel in the pedestrian zone. The breakfast room exudes a cheerful Mediterranean mood.

Kastens Hotel Luisenhof – *Luisenstraße 1.* ☎ *(0511) 304 40. www.kastens-luisenhof.de. 145 rooms. Restaurant.* Comfort reigns supreme in Hannover's oldest hotel (1856), centrally located near the main train station. Rooms are elegantly furnished and the rooftop spa and leisure area are wonderful relaxation stations with a view.

WHERE TO EAT

Der Gartensaal – *Trammplatz 2.* ☎ *(0511) 16 84 88 88. www.gartensaal-hannover.de.* This bistro has an unusual location in the south entrance of the Neues Rathaus. Enjoy superb views of the Maschsee lake from the terrace or through the floor-to-ceiling windows.

Broyhan-Haus – *Kramerstraße 24.* ☎ *(0511) 32 39 19. www.broyhanhaus.de. Reservations necessary.* This 14C building, one of the city's oldest town houses, was bought in 1537 by master brewer Cord Broyhan. Today it offers three floors of timeless coziness along with hearty German cuisine (schnitzel, roast lamb) best washed down with a cold house brew.

TAKING A BREAK

Holländische Kakao-Stube – *Ständehausstraße 2–3 (Luisenstraße to the south west).* ☎ *(0511) 30 41 00. www.hollaendische-kakao-stube.de. Closed Sun and public holidays.* If you lust for thick and steamy hot chocolate, check out this charming café decorated with Dutch ceramics. Homemade pastries also figure prominently on the menu.

NIGHTLIFE

heimW – *Theaterstraße 6.* ☎ *(0511) 235 23 03. www.heim-w.de.* The white couches and red leather banquettes signal style and cool at this café-bar-lounge combination. Breakfast is served until 6pm, lunches are a bargain and the cocktail menu enormous.

Oscar's – *Georgstraße 54.* ☎ *(0511) 235 24 34. www.oscarsbar.de.* Wind down the day with a whisky or a cosmopolitan at this grown-up cocktail bar with dark wooden décor and jazz, swing and blues on the turntable. Sidewalk terrace. Happy hour 4pm–8pm.

---

some great greenhouses as well as the new **Sealife Hannover** (*open year-round, daily 10am–6pm; 13€; www.sealifehannover.com*), which takes you on a virtual journey from the local Leine River to the Caribbean and the Amazon rainforest. Along the way, visitors are introduced to 5 000 creatures residing in these aquatic habitats. A highlight is the 8m/26.2ft-long glass tunnel "through" the ocean.

At the far end of the garden's principal walk is the mausoleum of the Royal House of Hanover.

Welfengarten

The Welfenschloß (now part of the university) stands in the Welfengarten and is fronted by the trademark of the state of Niedersachsen, the Saxon Steed, created in 1876 by Friedrich Wolff.

Marktkirche

A four-gabled tower crowned by a sharp pinnacle presides over this Gothic brick church, rebuilt after 1945 to mimic the 14C original. The modern 1957 bronze doors by Gerhard Marcks contrast sharply with the overall style of the church. Inside, note the superb 15C sculpted polychrome **reredos**★★ representing the Passion.

Niedersächsisches Landesmuseum Hannover★ (Lower Saxony State Museum)

Willy-Brandt-Allee 5. *Open year-round, Tue, Wed, Fri–Sun 10am–5pm, Thu 7pm.*

Norbert Speicher / istockphoto.com

Southern facade of the Town Hall

🕐*Closed Jan 1, Good Fri, May 1, Dec 24, 25 & 31.* 💰*4€.* ♿🚞*(0511) 980 76 86. www.nlmh.de.*

This museum is divided into four departments. The **archeological department**★ *(Archäologie-Abteilung)* travels back in time half a million years and sheds light on the daily lives of our ancestors. One of the most memorable exhibits is a mummified male from AD 300, whose curly red hair has garnered him the nickname "Roter Franz" (Red Francis).

Fossils, dinosaurs, exhibits on tectonic plates and earthquakes are among the highlights of the **nature department** *(Naturkunde-Abteilung)*.

Living fish, amphibians, lizards, spiders and insects from around the world can be observed in recreated habitats in the attached Vivarium.

😊 A Bit of Advice 😊

The red line painted on the sidewalk throughout central Hannover is the **Roter Faden** *(Red Thread; www.roterfaden-hannover.de)*, a 4.2km/2.6mi self-guided city tour.

It kicks off at the tourist office and ticks off 36 sights, including the Neues Rathaus and the Nanas. Pick up the *Red Thread Guide (2€)* at the tourist office.

The **picture gallery** *(Landesgalerie)* is particularly proud of its extensive collection of German Impressionism and early Expressionism, with a healthy smattering of works by Liebermann, Slevogt, Corinth and Modersohn-Becker. Another emphasis is on German art from the Middle Ages to the Renaissance, periods associated with such names as Meister Bertram, Lucas Cranach, Tilman Riemenschneider, Sandro Botticelli und Jacopo Pontormo. Rubens, Rembrandt and Ruisdael represent the rococo.

Finally, there is the **ethnography department** *(Völkerkunde-Abteilung)*, which features exotic exhibits from New Guinea, Mexico, Indonesia and other non-European cultures.

Sprengel-Museum Hannover★
Kurt-Schwitters-Platz.

🕐*Open year-round, Tue 10am–8pm, Wed-Sun 10am–6pm.* 🕐*Closed Good Fri, Dec 24, 25 & 31.* 💰*7€.* ♿🚞*(0511) 16 84 38 75. www.sprengel-museum.de.*

A stabile by Calder, the *Hellebardier*, is an intriguing overture to this first-rate museum of 20C and 21C art. All the major household names are given wall space here, including Picasso, Klee, Nolde, Beckmann, the Hannover-born Kurt Schwitters, and Georg Baselitz. Works by members of the Brücke (Schmidt-Rottluff) and Blaue Reiter movements (Kandinsky, Jawlensky, Macke) are also exceptionally well represented. Fans of

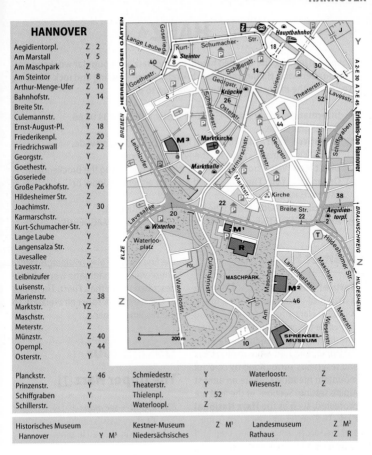

HANNOVER

Niki de St. Phalle will get their fill as will admirers of James Turrell's edgy light installations.

Zoologischer Garten★ (Zoological Garden) Kids

Adenauerallee 3.

🕒 *Open Mar–Oct, daily 9am–6pm; Nov–Feb, 10am–4pm.* 👁️*19.50€ (child 13.50€).* ☎ *(0511) 28 07 41 63. www.zoo-hannover.de.*

The Hannover Zoo is divided into five themed areas: the gorilla mountain with its waterfall; a 12 000sq m/120 000sq ft jungle palace for elephants, tigers and leopards; a Zambezi landscape with lions, giraffes and okapis; Meyer's Hof, a recreated Lower Saxony farm where chickens, pigs and ponies make their home, and Mullewapp, a fantasyland based on the illustrated children's book by Helme Heiner.

Neues Rathaus (New Town Hall)

🕒*Open Apr–Nov, daily 10am–6pm.* 👁️*2.50€.* ☎*(0511) 16 80.*

Anchored in the marshy soil by 6 026 beech poles, Hannover's new Town Hall was completed in 1913. Ride the unique slanted elevator to the dome to enjoy sweeping city views.

The Nanas

Leibnitzufer.

Niki de St. Phalle's colorful if grotesque female doll sculptures caused quite an uproar when first installed along the Leine banks in 1974, but they have since become a beloved landmark.

HARZ★★

Steeped in legend, the wooded heights of the Harz are a popular weekend get-away for Germans. Hiking, mountain biking, canoeing, skiing and rock-climbing are among the many activities the region has to offer.

- **Information:** Marktstraße 45, 38640 Goslar. ☎(05321) 34 04 66. www.harzinfo.de.
- **Orient Yourself:** At 110km/68.3mi long and 35km/21.7mi wide, the Harz is Germany's most northerly highland region.
- **Don't Miss:** Views from the Bodetal, Wernigerode, riding the Brockenbahn.
- **Organizing Your Time:** Allow half a day for either the Upper or Eastern Harz driving tours.
- **Especially for Kids:** Riding the Brockenbahn, Rübeland.
- **Also See:** WOLFENBÜTTEL, HILDESHEIM, BRUNSWICK, MAGDEBURG.

A Bit of History

Natural environment – The Harz is a quilt of varied landscapes. In the southern Harz you find gently rolling hills while the northern portion is characterized by wild, romantic valleys. In the Upper Harz, numerous mining lakes and reservoirs surrounded by colorful mountain meadows create an almost Alpine setting. Sections of the area are protected, such as the **Harz National Park**. The region was once rich in mineral resources; zinc, copper, lead and silver have all been mined here.

A place of legend – The highest point of the range, the **Brocken** (1 142m/3 746.7ft), attracts hikers to its windswept slopes. At the summit, according to legend, witches gather on the first night of May (Walpurgisnacht). These wild shenanigans were vividly described in Goethe's Faust. The shops of the Harz stock souvenirs relating to the Walpurgis legend.

Driving Tour

The Upper Harz ①

81km/50mi —see map.
This itinerary passes through vast tracts of rolling hills draped in pine.

Goslar★★ See GOSLAR.

Clausthal-Zellerfeld

This twin town is the former mining capital of the Harz. At Zellerfeld, the **Upper Harz Mine Museum** (Oberhar-

Harz countryside

J. Bouraly/MICHELIN

Address Book

WHERE TO STAY

�📧�📧**Hotel Zum Brockenbäcker** – Lindenwarte 20, 38875 Tanne. ☎(039457) 97 60. www.brockenbaecker. de. 16 rooms. A typical Harz region property, this family-run 1912 hotel offers adequate rooms oozing old-fashioned charm, fresh-baked bread at breakfast, a fitness room and bikes for active types and a sauna for relaxing.

�📧�📧📧📧**Michels Kurhotel Vier Jahreszeiten** – Herzog-Julius-Straße 64b, 38667 Bad Harzburg. ☎(05322) 78 70. www.kurhotelvierjahreszeiten.de. 74 rooms. Restaurant�📧�📧📧. In this former bath-house, historical architecture blends seamlessly with a modern interior. After dinner in the elegant restaurant, you can challenge Lady Luck at the inhouse casino.

zer Bergwerksmuseum; Bornhardstraße 16; ◐open year-round, daily 9am–5pm; ◐closed Dec 24; ◐5€; ☎(05323) 989 50; www.bergwerksmuseum.de) illustrates mining techniques used until 1930 and documents the history of the region. At Clausthal the **Pfarrkirche zum Heiligen Geist** (Hindenburgplatz) was built in the 17C and is one of the largest wooden churches in Europe. From the top of the **Oker Dam** (Okertalsperre) there is a fine **view**★ over the widely dispersed waters of the reservoir.

St. Andreasberg

👁Visit by guided tour (1hr), year-round, daily 11am and 2.30pm. ◐Closed Jan 1 and Dec 24. ◐4.50€. ☎(055 82) 12 49. The road leads first to an **old silver mine**★ (Silberbergwerk Samson, at the bottom of the valley), closed in 1910 but since reopened for tourists. The Fahrkunst, a machine of ingenious simplicity which sent down and brought back the miners, is still in functioning condition.

Braunlage

Served by the Brocken railway, this spa resort, prized for its climate and ski slopes, lies high up on a plateau overlooked by the wooded **Wurmberg** (971m/3 185.6ft).

Schierke

If you want to climb the summit of the **Brocken**—or at least have a go at it—the Schierke station on the **Brockenbahn** (Brocken narrow-gauge railway) is the place to start. Schierke is a lovely place in its own right and a gateway to the Harz National Park.

Wernigerode★

Wernigerode is one of the most delightful small towns in this region. Its **Rathaus**★★ (Town Hall, on Marktplatz) was first mentioned in 1277 and originally served as a courthouse and dance hall. The current model is mostly from the 16C and considered one of the finest half-timbered buildings in Germany. Breite Straße, as it leaves Marktplatz, is lined with more residential half-timbered beauties. The most admired building, though, is the **Krummelsches Haus** (1674) at no 74 whose timbered front has been covered up with a wooden façade so intricately carved that it resembles a copper-etching.

Schloss Wernigerode

◐Open May-Oct, daily 10am–6pm; Nov–Apr, Tue–Fri 10am–4pm, Sat–Sun 10am–6pm. ◐5€. ☎(03943) 55 30 30. www.schloss-wernigerode.de. Originally a medieval fortress built to protect the emperors while on hunting

😊 A Bit of Advice 😊

Nostalgia fans will love riding the narrow-gauge trains powered by steam locomotives that crisscross the eastern Harz. The Harzquerbahn, runs for 60km/37mi from Wernigerode to Nordhausen. The Brockenbahn chugs up Brocken mountain from Drei Annen Hohne. And the Selketalbahn runs from Quedlinburg to Hasselfelde.

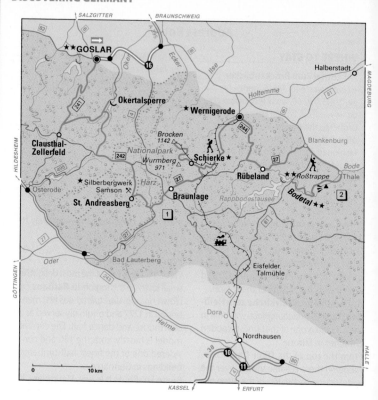

expeditions, this castle was repeatedly altered and given a romantic makeover in the 19C. Rooms are filled with original paintings and furniture and illustrate the exalted lifestyle once enjoyed by the German aristocracy.

The Eastern Harz ②
89km/55mi

Wernigerode★ (⟲see above)

Rübeland

◥₊₊Visit by guided tour (45min) only, Jul–Aug, daily 9am–5.30pm; Feb–Oct, 9am–4.30pm; Nov–Jan, 9am–3:30pm. ◓Closed Dec 24. ₷5€. ☎ (039454) 491 32.
Limestone caving is the chief draw of the Rübeland. In 🧒 **Hermann's Grotto★** *(Hermannshöhle)*, note particularly the Chamber of Crystals and the small pool inhabited by the sightless "cave fish" *(Grottenolmen)*.

▶ *Continue via Blankenburg and Thale to reach the Bode Valley.*

Bodetal★★
The river here has gouged a passage through a maze of rock masses and now flows along the foot of craggy cliffs. The most spectacular site is the **Roßtrappe★★** (charger's hoofmark), a 10min walk from the parking lot. From the look-out point, which juts out dizzyingly above the river far below, there is an incredible **view★★★** of the cliffs, the tumbling stream, a steep gorge and the distant woods. The place owes its name to the legend of a horse, ridden by a princess and chased by a giant, leapt with such force across the chasm that it left an imprint in the rock.
Following the course of the river, the scenic stretch of road twists and turns through the rugged forest landscape as far as the junction with the B81.

HEIDELBERG★★

POPULATION: 143 000

A source of inspiration for many a poet, each charmed by the town's natural beauty and its castle, Heidelberg symbolizes German Romanticism. Hölderlin wrote a famous ode to Heidelberg, and Brentano, Eichendorff and Von Arnim were among the Romantics who gathered here in the early 19C. But this jewel of the Neckar is also a lively university town with a vibrant cultural scene.

- **Information:** Willy-Brandt-Platz 1 (central station), 69115 Heidelberg. ☎(06221) 194 33. www.cvb-heidelberg.de.
- ▶ **Orient Yourself:** Heidelberg is 20km/12.4mi east of Mannheim and reached via the A5 autobahn (Frankfurt–Freiburg).
- P **Parking:** Heidelberg has several garages in the Old Town. Especially convenient are those on Neue Schloßstraße, near the castle, and below Karlsplatz, near the Rathaus.
- **Don't Miss:** Heidelberg Castle, a walking tour of the Old City and a panoramic stroll along the Philosophers' Walk.
- **Organizing Your Time:** Allow half a day for a tour of the castle and another half day for the rest of the city.
- **Also See:** MANNHEIM, SPEYER, WORMS, BAD WIMPFEN.

A Bit of History

The Political Capital of the Palatinate
– The *Pfalz* (Palatinate), of which Heidelberg was the political center, owes its name to the "palatines," the highest officers in the Holy Roman Empire. These functions no longer existed in the 14C, but their vestiges remained with the hereditary family. The governing prowess of these palatine-electors *(Kurfürsten)* made the Palatinate *(Kurpfalz)* one of the most advanced states of Europe.

The "Orléans War" (1688–97) – In the
16C, Elector Karl-Ludwig, hoping to ensure peace, married his daughter **Liselotte** (Elisabeth-Charlotte) to Duke Philip of Orléans, brother of Louis XIV. The marriage alliance proved disastrous to both the Palatinate and to Heidelberg: Political infighting resulted in the town's destruction and the sacking of the castle; total disaster followed in 1693, when it was completely destroyed by fire. Before long the electors abandoned the partly ruined castle, but today it is precisely this ivy-draped red-sandstone pile that gives Heidelberg its romantic flair.

Sights

Schloss★★★

⏱*Open Mar–Nov, daily 9.30am–6pm; Dec–Feb, daily 10am–5pm.* ☞ *3€.* ▰*audio-guide* ☞*4€.* ☎ *(06221) 65 44 29. www.heidelberg-schloss.de.*
Looming above the town, Heidelberg Castle is a superb example of a fortress with both Gothic and Renaissance features. For an **overview**★ of the town and the Neckar Valley, visit the Rondell promontory. Enter the castle through the **Elisabethentor**, a gate built by Friedrich V (allegedly in a single night in 1615) as a surprise for his wife Elizabeth Stuart. Two gates separated by a moat lead to the inner courtyard. The **gardens**★ were laid out under Friedrich V in the 17C. The east face of the castle, with its three towers, is visible from the Scheffel terrace.

Feudal Courtyard and Buildings
The courtyard is on the far side of a fortified bridge guarded by the **Torturm** (**7**; gate tower). The simple residential building, the **Ruprecht**, was built by Ruprecht III who became German king in 1400; above the crown are two little angels, thought to be the architect's

Heidelberg and its legendary castle

twins who died just before completion of the work. The 14C **Apothekerturm (1)** tower is even older and forms part of the **Deutsches Apothekenmuseum**★ *(German Pharmaceutical Museum; open Apr–Oct, daily 10.15am–6pm, Nov–Mar 10am–5.30pm; closed Dec 25; ⊛3€, including courtyard and Vat; ☎ (06221) 258 80)*, with 18C–19C apothecaries' equipment and an alchemist's laboratory complete with ancient instruments.

Gothic and Renaissance Additions

Immediately off the courtyard is the Gothic **Brunnenhalle** (Well Wing), whose granite Roman columns came from Charlemagne's palace at Ingelheim. The **Library (6)**, set back from the west wing, is awash with light and was once home to the royals' personal library, art collections and treasure. Only slightly more recent is the **Hall of Mirrors Wing** *(8; Gläserner Saalbau)*. Following a fire, only a shell remains of this tiered, Italian Renaissance building. The **Ottheinrich Wing** *(9; Ottheinrichsbau)*, built by Elector Otto-Heinrich, an enlightened Renaissance ruler, inaugurated the Late Renaissance period in German architecture.

Horizontals predominate in the façade, bearing biblical and mythological ornamentation. The famous sculptor, Alexander Colin of Mechelen (1526–1612), helped design the entrance, a triumphal arch festooned with the elector's coat of arms.

Transitional Renaissance-Baroque Additions

The **Friedrich Wing**★★ *(10; Friedrichsbau)*, whose façade retains the classical Renaissance design, also bears elements pointing toward the coming Baroque. The statues represent the ancestors of Friedrich IV who added the wing. The rear of the building and views over Heidelberg are best seen from the **Great Terrace** *(Altan)*, accessed via a passageway to the right of the Friedrich wing.

Großes Fass★ (Great Vat)

This colossal 18C cask, with a capacity of 221 726l/48 780gal, still serves up wine to visiting customers. The platform above the Fass hosts tastings and occasional dancing. The guardian of this extravagance, an enduring idol of local folklore, is a statue of the dwarf court jester **Perkeo**, celebrated for his astonishing drinking feats.

Views

From the right bank of the Neckar, which you reach either via he Alte Brücke or the Karl-Theodor Brücke bridges, are **views**★★ of the castle ruins and the old town clustered around the Heiliggeistkirche. Further views of the castle and the town can be seen from the Philosophenweg (Philosophers' Walk), reached

Address Book

For coin ranges, see the Legend on the cover flap.

WHERE TO STAY

Hotel-Restaurant Schnookeloch – *Haspelgasse 8.* (06221) 13 80 80. *www.schnookeloch.de. 11 rooms. Restaurant*. The Schnookeloch's history is intertwined with the history of this university town, the restaurant having been a traditional student hangout.

Hotel Backmulde – *Schiffgasse 11.* (06221) 536 60. *www.gasthaus-backmulde-hotel.de. 25 rooms. Restaurant*. This old sailors' lodging has pleasant rooms dressed in soothing browns and reds with crisp linen and brass chandeliers. Rustic dark wood beams and curtain give the dining room a rustic country flair.

Romantik Hotel Zum Ritter St. Georg – *Hauptstraße 178.* (06221) 13 50. *www.ritter-heidelberg. de. 39 rooms.* 11€. *Restaurant*. Behind the sandstone façade of this 1592 Renaissance building, visitors are welcomed with tradition and history. For fine dining, visit the Restaurant Belier, for an elbow-on-the-table atmosphere the Ritterstube.

WHERE TO EAT

Kulturbrauerei Heidelberg – *Leyergasse 6 (between Hauptstraße and Am Hachteufel).* (06221) 50 29 80. *www.heidelberger-kulturbrauerei.de. Closed Dec 24.* Though updated, this restaurant exudes old-style charm with coffered ceilings and cast iron chandeliers. Beer brewed on-site goes down well with the regional specialities. Rooms in the adjacent hotel are spacious and luxurious.

Schlossweinstube – *in Heidelberg Castle.* (06221) 979 70. *www.schoenmehl.de. Closed Dec 20–Jan 15 and Wed.* Modern black chairs provide a charming contrast to the traditional setting of shiny wooden floors, valuable etchings and ceramic-tile heating stoves.

TAKING A BREAK

Strohauer's Café Alt-Heidelberg – *Hauptstraße 49.* (06221) 18 90 24. *www.strohauer.de.* An unhurried ambience envelops this traditional café with its several-meter-long counter of homemade pastries complemented by an seasonal snack menu.

NIGHTLIFE

Zum Roten Ochsen – *Hauptstraße 217.* (06221) 209 77. *www.roterochsen.de. Closed Sun, public holidays and 3 weeks after Christmas.* Once frequented by such notables as Bismarck, Mark Twain and John Wayne, this student pub offers rib-sticking German fare served on tables carved with autographs. After 8pm, it becomes a piano-bar and a pleasant place to enjoy a beer or glass of wine.

---

by crossing the Alte Brücke and climbing the Schlangenweg.

Walking Tour

Old Town

Wedged between the Neckar and the hillside, Heidelberg's compact old town is bisected by the Hauptstraße, running parallel to the river.

▶ *Walk down from the castle via the western steps, then continue to Kornmarkt. Just beyond is Marktplatz with the Gothic Heiliggeistkirche.*

Heiliggeistkirche (Church of the Holy Spirit)

This Late Gothic church is distinguished by covered market stalls set up between the building's buttresses as they have been for centuries. The galleries in the apses were used for the Biblioteca Palatina, once Europe's finest library, which ended up as war booty at the Vaticanin 1623. The chancel was formerly the sepulchre of the palatine electors, but

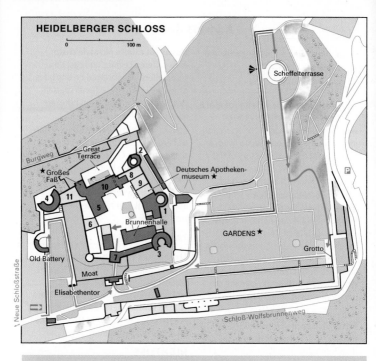

HEIDELBERGER SCHLOSS

0   100 m

Scheffelterrasse

Burgweg

Great Terrace

Großes Faß★

Deutsches Apotheken-museum ★

Brunnenhalle

GARDENS ★

Grotto

Old Battery

Moat

Elisabethentor

Neue Schloßstraße

Schloß-Wolfsbrunnenweg

End of Feudal Period (and subsequent altorations)

1) Apothekerturm (14c)   2) Glockenturm (14c)   3) Gesprengter Turm (15c)

Gothic-Renaissance Transitional Period (Ludwig V – 1508–1544)

4) Dicker Turm (1533)   5) Ladles' Wing   6) Library   7) Torturm

Renaissance

8) Hall of Mirrors Wing (1549)   9) Otto-Heinrich Wing (1566)

Renaissance-Baroque Transitional Period

10) Friedrich Wing (Friedrich IV – 1592–1610), and below, Great terrace (Altan)

11) English Wing (Friedrich V – 1610–1632)

only the tomb of Ruprecht III and his wife remains.

Haus zum Ritter★ (Knight's House)

This magnificent bourgeois house owes its name to a bust of St. George in knightly armor on a richly scrolled pediment. Built in 1592 for the Huguenot merchant Charles Bélier, it was the only Late Renaissance masterpiece to survive the devastating Orléans War.

▸ *Follow Hauptstraße to Universitätplatz and the Baroque Old University (Alte Universität).*

Studentenkarzer★
(Students' Prison)

Augustinergasse 2.

Open Apr–Oct, Tue–Sun 10am–6pm; Nov–Mar, Tue–Sat 10am–4pm. Closed public holidays. 2.50€. (06221) 54 35 54.

One of Heidelberg's most popular tourist attractions, the old student jail was in use from 1712 and 1914. A stint here was almost considered a rite of passage for male students. Walls are covered in inscriptions and graffiti.

Jesuitenkirche

This 18C Baroque church bears a façade based on the Gesù Church in Rome. The luminous triple nave is supported by pillars decorated with Rococo stuccowork. Accessed via the church is the **Museum of Sacred and Liturgical Art** (*Museum*

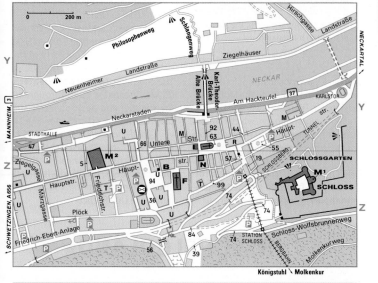

für sakrale Kunst und Liturgie; Richard-Hauser-Platz; ⏱*open Jul–Oct, Tue–Sat 11am–5pm, Sun 12.30pm–5pm; Nov–Jun, Sat 10am–5pm, Sun 12.30pm–5pm;* ⏱*closed Jan 1, Easter Mon, Pentecost, Dec 25–26;* ⬤*2€;* ☎*(06221) 16 63 91).* It houses religious artifacts from the 17C–19C, most notably an oversized silver Madonna by J. Ignaz Saller (1736).

▶ *Follow Hauptstraße west to the Palais Morass.*

Kurpfälzisches Museum★ (Electoral Palatinate Museum)

Hauptstraße 97.
⏱*Open year-round, Tue–Sun 10am–6pm.* ⏱*Closed Jan 1, Shrove Tue, Dec 24, 25 & 31.* ⬤*3€, Sun 1.80€.* ☎*(06221) 58 34 000. www.museum-heidelberg.de.*
A highlight of this museum is the jaw-bone of the prehistoric "Heidelberg Man" (500 000 BC). Other key displays are the **Altarpiece of the Twelve**

Apostles★★ *(Zwölfbotenaltar)* carved by Tilman Riemenschneider in 1509 and several **works from the Romantic Period**★★.

Excursions

Königstuhl

5km/3mi southeast, via Neue Schloßstraße, Molkenkurweg, and then Gaiberger Weg; or take the funicular: Molkenkurbahn funicular *(every 10min): late Mar–mid-Oct, daily 9am–8.20pm; mid-Oct–mid-Mar, 9am–5.10pm.* Königstuhlbahn funicular *(every 20min): late Mar–mid-Oct, daily 9.08am–7.48pm; mid-Oct–mid-Mar, 9.08am–5.18pm.* ⬤*8€ round-trip from Kornmarkt station.* ☎*(06221) 513 26 09. www.bergbahn-heidelberg.de.*
The 550m/1 804.4ft-high Königstuhl marks the highest point in Heidelberg and can be ascended by funicular. The

"Homo Heidelbergensis"

In 1907, the jaw of a man who lived some 500 000 years ago was found in Mauer near Heidelberg. Called **Heidelberg Man** (*Homo heidelbergensis*), this hominid is considered to be an ancestor of *Homo sapiens*, the species of modern humankind.

modern Molkenbahn travels from Kornmarkt via the Schloss to the Molkenkur viewpoint. There you switch to the nostalgic Königstuhlbahn, which rumbles to the top for even more sweeping views of the Neckar Valley. The total trip takes about 20min. Aside from hiking trails, kid-friendly diversions include a **falconry** and a **fairytale-themed amusement park** (🕐 open May–mid-Nov).

Schwetzingen★

10km/6.2mi west via the Friedrich-Ebert-Anlage.

During the spring asparagus season (*Spargelzeit*), gourmets flock to Schwetzingen, while music fans descend on this sweet little town during the May and June festival season.

Schwetzingen's **Schloss**★★, destroyed in the 17C, was rebuilt in 1700–1717 as a Baroque palace. About forty of the palace rooms are open to the public. The charming 18C **rococo theater**★ (*Rokokotheater*) is open throughout the summer and hosts concerts and plays during the Schwetzingen Festival (🕐 mid-Jun–early Sept; ☎ (06202) 12 88 28). The 72ha/178-acre **Schlossgarten**★★, which blends formal French and English gardens, is dotted with mock ancient temples and ruins so beloved during the Late Rococo.

INSEL HELGOLAND★

POPULATION: 1 700

Only 1sq km/0.38sq mi in size, the island of Helgoland is a mere blip in the North Sea, but its stark red-sandstone cliff silhouette exudes a timeless mystique. Home to unique flora and fauna, it draws thousands of tourists each year who come in pursuit of solitude, natural beauty and duty-free shopping bargains.

- 🗊 **Information:** Rathaus, Lung Wal 28, 27498 Helgoland. ☎ (04725) 813 70. www.helgoland.de.
- ▶ **Orient Yourself:** Helgoland is about 70km/43mi off the coast of Schleswig-Holstein. It is served by ferry from Cuxhaven, Hamburg and the Frisian Islands.
- 🚲 **Don't Miss:** Hiking, swimming and other outdoor pursuits.
- 🕐 **Organizing Your Time:** Helgoland can be visited on a day trip.
- 👶 **Especially for Kids:** The sea voyage to the island, beaches.
- 👣 **Also See:** NORDFRIESISCHE INSELN, INSEL SYLT, HUSUM.

A Bit of History

Helgoland was originally part of Denmark but ceded by the Danes to Britain in 1814 as part of the post-Napoléonic settlements. In 1890, it changed hands again as a result of the Zanzibar Treaty. This time Germany took possession in exchange for commercial rights in the East African island of Zanzibar. Helgoland was subsequently annexed to Schleswig-Holstein (at that time part of Prussia).

Getting there

Ferries leave from Hamburg, Wedel and Cuxhaven to Helgoland. *Katamaran "Halunder Jet"* departs Hamburg Mar–Oct, daily at 9am, calling at Wedel 9.40am and Cuxhaven 11.30am; return trip 4.30pm, arriving at Cuxhaven c. 5.45pm, Wedel c. 7.30pm, Hamburg c. 8.15pm. ☎ (0180) 320 20 25. www.helgoline.de. Reederei Cassen Eils also offers a ferry service from Cuxhaven to Helogland: www.helgolandreisen.de.

An Unusual Rock

Battered by the sea since time immemorial, tiny Helgoland is home to an aquarium, an ornithological observatory and a marine biology station. Blessed with natural beauty, it attracts leisure travelers eager to engage in **outdoor pursuits**★★: cliff walks, hiking, swimming, birding, biking and more. Shoppers can look forward to bargains on chocolates, cigarettes and spirits because neither duty nor VAT (currently 19 percent) are charged.

Lange Anna★ (Long Anna)

Helgoland's most famous natural landmark, this 80m/262.4ft-high bright red-rock column stands guard off its northwestern shore like some petrified sentinel. Nearby is the **Lummenfelsen**, Germany's smallest nature preserve (1.1ha/2.7 acres), which draws countless breeding bird species, most notably Helgoland's signature bird, the *Trottellumme* (common murre).

Düne

About 1km/0.6mi from the main island. Turquoise water lapping at white sandy beaches—no, this is not the Caribbean but a small islet that got separated from the main island during a stormy night on New Year's Eve 1720. Today, it is a swimmers' and nature-lovers' paradise. The southern beaches are particularly family-friendly, while sea lions can be observed lazing in the sand on the northern shore.

If all goes according to plan, Düne will be joined by an artificial land bridge in the coming years, thereby nearly doubling Helgoland's size.

HILDESHEIM★

POPULATION: 103 000

Founded as a bishopric in 815, Hildesheim managed to preserve its beautiful medieval buildings until an Allied air-raid laid waste to most of the city in 1945. In the 1980s, part of the old town was faithfully reconstructed, especially around the market square. The cathedral and the Church of St. Michael are both on the list of UNESCO World Heritage sites.

- **Information:** Rathausstraße 18–20, 31134 Hildesheim. ☎(05121) 179 80. www.hildesheim.com.
- **Orient Yourself:** Hildesheim is 34km/21mi south of Hannover, just off the A7 autobahn.
- **Don't Miss:** The Marktplatz, the Cathedral and the Pelizaeus-Museum.
- **Organizing Your Time:** Allow at least half a day to do Hildesheim justice.
- **Also See:** HANNOVER, HAMELN, GOSLAR, HARZ.

A Bit of History

The "Thousand-year-old" Rose Tree – Legend has it that in 815, Charlemagne's son, Emperor Ludwig the Pious, spotted a precious reliquary, which he had lost during a hunting expedition, lying amongst a rambling rose bush. In gratitude, he built a chapel next to the thorny shrub, around which grew the cathedral and town. The rose miraculously survived the 1945 air raid and still blooms every year.

Sights

Marktplatz★

The historical market square has been beautifully restored and is framed by buildings reflecting architectural styles in vogue over the course of the last eight centuries. The east side is flanked by Gothic buildings from the 13C, including the **Rathaus** (Town Hall), which underwent numerous modifications and extensions and was rebuilt in a simplified version after 1945. A carillon plays its merry tune daily at noon, 1pm and 5pm.

Medieval Architectural Gems

Housing the tourist office, the unusual early 14C **Tempelhaus** dominates the south side of the Marktplatz. Its most distinctive feature is the ornate 16C

Renaissance **oriel**★, which depicts the parable of the Prodigal Son. The nearby 16C half-timbered **Wedekindhaus** has bay windows spanning from ground level up to the roof, a typical feature of the Weser Renaissance style. Not far off is the **Lüntzelhaus** (1755), now a local bank, and the 14C Gothic **Rolandstift** with a Baroque porch (c. 1730).

The **Bakers' Guild Hall** (*Bäckeramtshaus, 1451*) and **Butchers' Guild Hall**★ (*Knochenhauer Amtshaus, 1529*) occupy the square's west side. The five upper floors house the **Stadtmuseum** (*local history museum;* ⏰*open year-round, Tue–Sun 10am–6pm;* ⏰*closed Dec 24 & 31;*

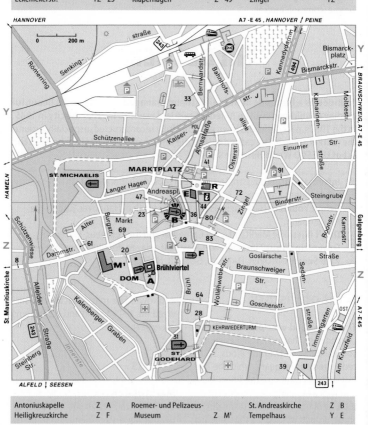

Address Book

For coin ranges, see cover flap.

WHERE TO STAY

Gästehaus Klocke –
Humboldtstraße 11. ☎(05121) 17 92 13.
Fax (05121) 1792140. www.gaestehaus-
klocke.de. 20 rooms.
Built over 100 years ago, this establishment is still run by the same family.
The guestrooms are individually
designed, but all are quiet, simply
and pleasantly decorated.

WHERE TO EAT

Kupferschmiede –
Am Steinberg 6 31139 Hildesheim-
Ochtersum (5km/3mi southwest via
Schützenwiese and the Kurt-Schumacher-
Straße, bear right 1km/0.5mi after
Ochtersum). ☎(05121) 26 30 25.
Closed Sun and Mon. This establishment
is located in the heart of the forest and
was built at the turn of the 19C. Various
dishes are served in the elegant
country-style house. Terrace.

2.50€; ☎(05121) 936 90; www.stadt-
museum-hildesheim.de).
The **Rokokohaus** on the north side
of the square is wedged between the
Stadtschänke, a local restaurant, and
the **Weavers' Guild Hall** (Wollenweber-
gildehaus).

Dom★ (Cathedral)

Open mid-Mar–Oct, Mon–Sat 9.30am–
5pm, Sun noon-5pm; Nov–mid-Mar,
Mon–Sat 10am–4.30pm, Sun noon–5pm.
Closed Good Fri & Dec 24. ☎(05121)
179 17 60. www.bistum-hildesheim.de.
Hildesheim's reconstructed 11C Romanesque cathedral is endowed with rare
and precious artworks. Two bronze casts
commissioned by Bishop Bernard in the
early 11C are worth closer inspection:
the **Christussäule**★ (Christ Column)
and the **Bernwardstüren**★★ (Bernward
doors), both depicting biblical scenes.
The doors stand almost 5m/16.4ft tall
and are 1m/3.28ft wide and were cast as
a single piece, an amazing achievement
for the time and one of the reasons they
are today a UNESCO World Heritage site.
Also note the massive 11C chandelier
and the 13C baptismal font supported
by figures representing the rivers of
Paradise. The **legendary rosebush** is
in the Romanesque **cloister**★ (open
10am–4pm Mon–Sat, noon–5pm Sun;
0.50€)

Roemer- und Pelizaeus-Museum★

Open year-round, Tue–Sun 10am–
6pm. 8€. ☎(05121) 936 90. www.
rpmuseum.de.
Named for its 19C benefactors, the law-
yer Hermann Roemer and the merchant
Wilhelm Pelizaeus, this museum houses
one of Germany's richest collections of
Egyptian antiquities. Highlights include
the life-size figure of Heimunu and the
statue of the scribe Heti from excavations near Giza. Rare items from ancient
Peru form another focal point.

Medieval Churches

Hildesheim is home to numerous
important medieval churches. Dating
from the 11C, the UNESCO-protected **St.
Michaelis-Kirche**★ exemplifies Ottonian architecture. Note the 13C painted
ceiling depicting the Tree of Jesse. The
12C **St. Godehardikirche**★ sports an
elegant silhouette marked by three slender spires. **St. Andreaskirche**, from the
14C and 15C, is a massive Gothic church
rebuilt post-war with the incorporation
of the west end of its 12C Romanesque
predecessor. Its tower, which rises
114m/374ft and is Lower Saxony's
highest, can be climbed. Fronted by a
Baroque façade, the **Heiligkreuzkirche**
is built on an 11C Early Romanesque
church but now has Gothic, Baroque
and Ottonian elements jostling for
attention. Finally, **St. Mauritiuskirche**,
an 11C church that was heavily stuccoed
in the 18C, lies in the Moritzberg quarter
in the western part of town.

BURG HOHENZOLLERN★

The ancestral home of the royal Hohenzollern family stands tall and turreted on a hill bordering the Swabian Jura; from any angle, it looks like a fortress plucked straight from a fairytale.

- **Information:** ☎ (07471) 92 07 87. www.preussen.de.
- ▶ **Orient Yourself:** 25km/16mi south of Tübingen, the castle is unmissable. Perched on the Zollern hill *(Zollernberg)*, it is reached via the B27 or the A81 (exit 31).
- **Don't Miss:** The panorama from atop the castle ramparts.
- **Organizing Your Time:** Allow two hours to tour the castle and its grounds.
- **Also See:** SCHWÄBISCHE ALB, SIGMARINGEN, OBERSCHWÄBISCHE BAROCKSTRASSE, TÜBINGEN.

A Bit of History

The Cradle of the Hohenzollerns – The Hohenzollern dynasty goes back to the counts of Zollern, rulers of Hechingen and subsequently divided into several branches. In 1415, the Hohenzollerns of Franconia became margraves, then prince-electors of Brandenburg. In 1618 they succeeded to the Duchy of Prussia. In the 18C the kingdom of Prussia became a leading power in Europe, and so it was a Hohenzollern, Wilhelm I, who became head of the German Empire, founded in 1871 at the instigation of Prussia. Less than 50 years later, military defeat in World War I ended the domination of the Hohenzollern dynasty: on November 9, 1918, Kaiser Wilhelm II was forced to abdicate.

Hohenzollern Castle

Visit

The Castle

Visit by guided tour (35min) only; mid-Mar–Oct, daily 9am–5.30pm; Nov–mid-Mar, 10am–4.30pm. ⊙*Closed Dec 24 & 31.* ⊛*4€ grounds only, 8€ with guided tour.*⚫*(07471) 92 07 87. www.burg-hohenzollern.com.*

Draped over a hillside, the massive castle projects medieval flair thanks to its many turrets and towers and crenelated walls but actually only dates to the 19C. Prussian architects Von Prittwitz and Stüler incorporated the Roman Catholic chapel of **St. Michael** *(Michaeliskapelle)*, the only remainder of the ancient fortress built by the counts of Zollern, into their design.

The church's stained-glass windows are said to be the oldest in southern Germany. In 1952, the US Army moved the coffins of Friedrich-Wilhelm I, the Prussian Soldier-King, and his son Frederick the Great from Potsdam to the neo-Gothic chapel where they stayed until being returned to Potsdam in 1991, following reunification.

*Guided tours provide access to the castle **treasury** *(Schatzkammer)*, a treasure chest of crowns and gowns, uniforms, snuff boxes, flutes and porcelain.

Before leaving the castle, tour the ramparts *(start on the left, after the drawbridge)* and enjoy the **panorama**★ of the Swabian Jura and the Upper Neckar Valley.

HUSUM

POPULATION: 21 000

The birthplace of writer Theodor Storm (1817–88) has survived the battering of the North Sea since time immemorial. Today, this "grey city on the sea," as Storm described it, is the commercial hub of North Friesland as well as a modern holiday region with abundant cultural offerings.

- **Information:** Großstraße 27, 25813 Husum. ☎(04841) 898 70. www.tourismus-husum.de.
- ▶ **Orient Yourself:** In the far northwestern corner of Germany, close to the Danish border, Husum is linked to the A7 autobahn via the B201 and B202.
- **Don't Miss:** The port and the North Frisian Museum.
- **Organizing Your Time:** Husum can be easily covered in a day.
- **Also See:** SCHLESWIG, KIEL.

Sights

Nordseemuseum Husum★ (North Sea Museum) Kids

Herzog-Adolf-Straße 25.
Open Apr–Oct, daily 10am–5pm; Nov–Mar, Tue–Sun 11am–5pm. Closed Jan 1, Dec 24, 25 & 31. 5€ (child 2€). ☎(04841) 25 45. www.museumsverbund-nordfriesland.de/nordseemuseum.
Completely redone and updated in 2007, this family-friendly museum illuminates various aspects of the North Sea region's cultural history in permanent and changing exhibits. The exhibits explore the variety of Germany's coastal landscapes as well as the flow of daily life among its inhabitants. The catastrophic consequences of floods are explored, as are the construction of dikes and the reclamation of land by polders.

Storm-Haus

Wasserreihe 31.
Open Apr–Oct, Tue–Fri 10am–5pm, Sat 11am–5pm, Sun & Mon 2pm–5pm; Nov–Mar, Tue, Thu & Sat 2pm–5pm. Closed Dec 24 & 31. 3€. ☎(04841) 66 62 70. www.storm-gesellschaft.de.
Theodor Storm lived in this typical 1730 merchant's house from 1866 to 1880. Its rooms provide a look at life during the Biedermeier age and include the writer's living room and the study where he penned more than 20 of his novellas. Paintings and documents from the writer's estate are also on view.

Schloss vor Husum (Castle at Husum)

König-Friedrich V.-Allee.
Open Mar–Oct, Tue–Sun 11am–5pm; Nov–Feb, Sat–Sun 11am–5pm. Closed Jan 1, Dec 24 & 25. 3.50€. ☎(04841) 897 31 30. www.museumsverbund-nordfriesland.de.
This 16C castle of Duke Adolf von Schleswig-Holstein-Gottdorf was originally built in Dutch Renaissance style and renovated in the Baroque style in the 18C.
It is now a popular venue for cultural events, including concerts, readings, lectures and contemporary art exhibits. The central tract is a museum where you can explore the palace's chapel, banquet hall and residential quarters.

Bust of Theodor Storm

Theodor Storm

Born in Husum in 1817, Storm regarded his birth town with great affection throughout his life.

A deeply sensitive character, Storm contributed to German literature such original works as *Immensee* (1849), a true poetic jewel that integrates song and narrative.

Excursions

Friedrichstadt
15km/9.3mi south.
Dutch religious refugees, the Remonstrants, were given sanctuary by Friedrich III of Schleswig-Holstein-Gottdorf and was founded as Friedrichstadt in 1621.
Canals lined by step-gabled houses still reflect the Dutch heritage.

Eidersperrwerk★ (Eider Dam)
35km/21.7mi south.
Skirting a bird sanctuary, the road arrives at the mouth of the River Eider, closed off by a **dam** built between 1967 and 1972. The five colossal steel sluice gates close when the coast is threatened by high seas.

Nolde-Museum★ at Seebüll
56km/34.7mi north.
Open Mar–Nov, daily 10am–6pm. 8€.
(04664) 364. www.nolde-museum.de.
In 1927, Expressionist painter **Emil Nolde**, who was actually born Emil Nansen (1867–1956), built his private residence in the solitude of the Seebüll marshes based on his own designs.
The stark, angular Bauhaus-style structure presents annually changing exhibits showing off all of Nolde's major creative phases. Works with a religious theme are displayed in his former studio and you can also catch glimpses of his living quarters.

IDAR-OBERSTEIN

POPULATION: 33 000

Since the Middle Ages, the history of Idar-Oberstein has been linked to the production and sale of gemstones. The abundance of agate, jasper, amethyst and other deposits here has made the town a center for cutting and polishing of the precious stones. The many jewelry museums and shops bear witness to this trade.

- **Information:** Hauptstraße 419, 55743 Idar-Oberstein. (06781) 563 90. www.idar-oberstein.de.
- **Orient Yourself:** Twin towns form this municipality: picturesque Oberstein at the foot of a gorge carved by the River Nahe, and Idar on the river's tributary.
- **Don't Miss:** The German Precious Stone Museum.
- **Organizing Your Time:** Allow five hours for the suggested excursion.
- **Also See:** BERNKASTEL-KUES, MOSELTAL, RHEINTAL, TRIER.

Sights

Deutsches Edelsteinmuseum★★ (German Precious Stone Museum)
In the Idar-Zentrum (Diamond Exchange), Hauptstraße 118.
Open mid-Feb–Apr, daily 10am–5pm; May–Oct, daily 9.30am–5.30pm; Nov–Jan 7, Tue–Sun 10am–5pm. Closed Dec 24, 25 & 31, Jan 8–mid-Feb. 4.20€. (06 781) 90 09 80. www.edelsteinmuseum.de.
The museum houses precious stones from around the world—agates through diamonds Its collection has grown to 10 000 glittering objects and includes raw rocks, crystals and cut stones.
Some of the treasures are presented in darkened rooms under black light making them phosphorescent. Elsewhere

you can admire replicas of famous gems, including the legendary Hope diamond.

Felsenkirche★

30min round-trip walk.
Access via stairs (214 steps) from Oberstein Marktplatz.
Open mid-Mar–Oct, daily 10am–6pm; Nov 1–15, daily 11am–4pm. 2€. www. felsenkirche-oberstein.de.

Framed by a rock overhang above the river, this church, restored several times, is worth a visit for the 15C winged altarpiece alone. The scenes of the Passion depict the event with a ferocious realism. According to legend, the church was built in atonement for a fraticide by the surviving brother.

Museum Idar-Oberstein

Hauptstraße 426 at Oberstein Marktplatz (below the Felsenkirche stairway).
Open Apr–Oct, daily 9am–5.30pm; Nov–Mar, daily 11am–4.30pm. Closed Jan 1, Dec 24, 25 & 31. 3.90€. (06781) 246 19. www.museum-idar-oberstein.de.

This museum emphasizes the region's minerals and precious stones. Aside from gemstones, you can get a close-up look at an old agate water mill as well as a 19C workshop of a goldsmith. A darkened room features fluorescent minerals sparkling in a rainbow of colors beneath ultraviolet light.

Historische Weiherschleife (Historical Stonecutting Mill)

Tiefensteiner Straße 87, in Tiefenstein district. Visit by guided tour (40min) only, mid-Mar–mid-Nov, daily 10am–6pm. 3€. (06781) 90 19 18. www.edel steinminen-idar-oberstein.de.

The faceting and polishing of gems is demonstrated by skilled craftsmen in the only surviving water-powered gemcutting mill in the Idar-Oberstein area. Recently added features are a multimedia show about "The Secrets of Gemstones", a special room that examines the esoteric uses of minerals, and a playground where children can dig for minerals in a big covered sand pit.

Edelsteinminen Steinkaulenberg [Kids]

Visit by guided tour (30min) only, mid-Mar–mid-Nov, daily 9am–5pm. 4€ child 2.50€. (06781) 474 00. www.edelsteinminen-idar-oberstein.de.

At the only gemstone mine in Europe open to the public, you can see first-hand how the precious minerals are harvested. If you want to dig up your own, head to the **Edelsteincamp** (*Gemstone Camp;* sessions by prior arrangement: Mon–Fri 9am–11am, noon–2pm, 3pm–5pm; 13€ (child 5€); sturdy footwear and comfortable clothes required). You get to keep whatever you dig up during the two-hour session.

Excursion

The Hunsrück

The Hunsrück, a low-mountain range, forms the southern rim of the Rhine schist massif, a region of low mountains and game-stocked forests slashed by steep valleys.

Erbeskopf

At 818m/2 683.7ft, this is the highest peak in the Hunsrück. Enjoy fine views from the wooden tower as well as the **Hunsrückhöhenstraße★**. The road passes the Stumpfer Turm, an old Roman watchtower.

Kirchberg

Clinging to a hillside, this village is filled with half-timbered houses, especially around the Marktplatz. Also note the pre-Romanesque St. Michaelskirche.

Simmern

The farming center of the Hunsrück, Simmern is home to the parish church of St. Stephan (15C). The church's **tombs★** of the Dukes of Pfalz-Simmern feature some of the finest Renaissance sculptures in the middle Rhineland.

Ravengiersburg

Tucked into the bottom of a valley, this village boasts a Romanesque church with an imposing west front. Above the porch: Christ in Majesty.

JENA

POPULATION: 102 500

Jena has developed steadily since the foundation of its university in 1548 and attracted numerous scientists and intellectuals over the centuries. Among them are political thinker Wilhelm von Humboldt, Goethe, Schiller and Hegel, who worked on his philosophical treatise while French and Prussian armies battled outside the gates in 1806. Jena is also famous for its optics, established in the mid-19C by Carl Zeiss and Ernst Abbe, inventors of the scientific microscope.

- **Information:** Johannisstraße 23, 07743 Jena. ☎(03641) 80 64 00. www.jena.de.
- **Orient Yourself:** Jena is northeast of the Thuringian Forest, just off the A4 autobahn and about 23km/14.3mi east of Weimar.
- **Don't Miss:** Zeiss Planetarium and Optical Museum.
- **Organizing Your Time:** Jena can be explored in a maximum of a day.
- **Especially for Kids:** Zeiss Planetarium.
- **Also See:** WEIMAR, NAUMBURG.

Sights

Stadtmuseum & Kunstsammlung (City Museum & Art Collection)

Open year-round, Tue, Wed & Fri 10am–5pm, Thu 2pm–10pm, Sat–Sun 11am–6pm. Closed Jan 1, Dec 24 & 31. ∞4€. ☎(03641) 359 80. www.stadtmuseum.jena.de.

This museum presents regional art and milestones in Jena's history in a beautiful, partially half-timbered building.

Stadtkirche St. Michaelis

This collegiate church of the Cistercians got a Gothic facelift in the 15C. Note the canopied porch on the south side.

Goethe-Gedenkstätte (Goethe Memorial)

Fürstengraben 26.

Open Apr–Oct, Tue–Sun 11am–3pm. Closed May 1, Ascension Day, Oct 3 & 31. ∞1€. ☎(03641) 93 11 88.

Exhibits in this former inspector's house at the Botanical Gardens, where Goethe stayed while in Jena, focus mostly on his accomplishments as a politician and natural scientist.

Schillers Gartenhaus (Schiller Museum)

Schillergässchen 2.

Open Apr–Oct, Tue–Sun 11am–5pm. Closed public holidays. ∞2.50€. ☎(03641) 93 11 88. www.uni-jena.de/Gartenhaus.html.

Schiller wrote several of his famous works (Wallenstein, Maria Stuart) while spending the summers of 1797 to 1799 in this garden house. Ground floor exhibts track his life in Jena, while upstairs are the family's private quarters, including his study and bedroom.

Address Book

For coin ranges, see cover flap.

WHERE TO STAY

☐☐ **Hotel Jenaer Hof** – Bachstraße 24. ☎(03641) 44 38 55 Fax (03641) 443866. Reservations recommended. 11 rooms. A simple, practical hotel in the heart of town in a Jugendstil building.

WHERE TO EAT

☐☐ **Ratzeise** – Markt 1. ☎(03641) 42 18 00. www.ratzeise.net. This restaurant, serving traditional cuisine, is in Jena's historic Town Hall. Its rustic interior matches the exterior. Enjoy views over the market place while dining.

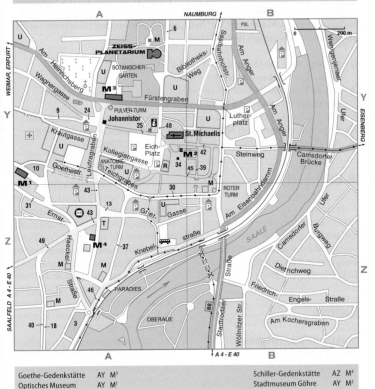

JENA		Goethestr.	AY		Oberlauengasse	BY	39
		Hainstr.	AZ	18	Rathenaustr.	AZ	40
Alexander-Puschkin-Pl.	AZ 3	Johannispl.	AY	24	Saalstr.	BY	42
Am Kochersgraben	BZ 4	Johannisstr.	AY	25	Schillerstr.	AZ	43
Am Planetarium	AY	Löbdergraben	AZ	30	Unterm Markt	ABY	45
Bachstr.	AY 9	Lutherstr.	AZ	31	Vor dem Neutor	AZ	46
Carl-Zeiss-Pl.	AY 10	Markt	AY	34	Weigelstr.	AY	48
Engelpl.	AZ 13	Neugasse	AZ	37	Westbahnhofstr.	AZ	49

Goethe-Gedenkstätte	AY M³		Schiller-Gedenkstätte	AZ M⁴
Optisches Museum	AY M¹		Stadtmuseum Göhre	AY M²

Zeiss Planetarium★ Kids

🕐*Open daily, showtimes vary.* ⌖*8€ (child 6.50€).* ♿☎*(036 41) 88 54 88. www. planetarium-jena.de.*

This state-of-the-art planetarium presents celestial shows geared toward both adults and children.

Optisches Museum★

Carl-Zeiss-Platz 12.

🕐*Open year-round, Tue–Fri 10am–4.30pm, Sat 11am–5pm.* 🕐*Closed Dec 24 & 31.* ⌖*5€.* ♿☎*(03641) 44 31 65.*

The museum retraces 500 years of the history of optics with a collection of spectacles, telescopes and photographic equipment. Also visit a workshop from 1866.

Statue of the Kurfürst on the Markt

KARLSRUHE ★

POPULATION: 282 500

Karlsruhe had its genesis in 1715 as the residential retreat of Margrave Karl Wilhelm of Baden-Durlach and evolved into a modern city with a grand palace and fine museums. It is home to the country's oldest school of technology (1825) whose graduates include Heinrich Hertz, discoverer of electromagnetic waves, and pioneering auto engineer Karl Benz, as well as the seat of the Bundesverfassungsgericht, Germany's highest court.

- **Information:** Bahnhofplatz 6, 76137 Karlsruhe. ☎ (0721) 37 20 53 83. www.karlsruhe-tourism.de.
- **Orient Yourself:** Karlsruhe is on the right side of the Rhine, close to the French border and served by the A5 and A65 autobahns.
- **Don't Miss:** Art lovers should head for the Fine Arts Museum and the ZKM.
- **Organizing Your Time:** Allow at least half a day for Karlsruhe's museums.
- **Also See:** KLOSTER MAULBRONN), SCHWARZWALD, PFALZ.

A Bit of History

A star is born – Karlsruhe is one of Germany's earliest master-planned cities, laid out in the 18C with the palace at its center and a network of streets radiating away from it. It became the capital of the Grand Duchy of Baden in 1806.

Sights

Staatliche Kunsthalle ★★ (Fine Arts Museum)

◷ *Open year-round, Tue–Fri 10am–5pm, Sat–Sun 10am–6pm.* ◷ *Closed Shrove Tue, Dec 24 & 31.* ⊛6€. ♿☎ *(0721) 926 33 59. www.kunsthalle-karlsruhe.de.*

This is one of Germany's finest and most comprehensive art museums and particularly famous for its **Old German Masters ★★**. Among the displays are an emotionally wrenching *Crucifixion* by Matthias Grünewald, a small tablet depicting *Maria and Child* by Lucas Cranach the Elder and several works by Dürer and his pupil Hans Baldung Grien. The Golden Age of Flemish and Dutch painting is represented by Rubens, Jordaens and Rembrandt.

The 19C collection on the ground floor showcases romantic landscapes by Caspar David Friedrich as well as bold ly pigmented canvases by Cézanne.

The adjacent **Orangery** focuses on Classical modern and contemporary art. Paintings by German Expressionists

---

Address Book

♿ *For coin ranges, see cover flap.*

WHERE TO EAT

🍽🍽 **Lehners Wirtshaus zum Goldenen Kreuz** – *Karlstraße 21a.* ☎ *(0721) 249 57 20.* If you are in the mood for solid German cuisine, make a beeline to this buzzy brasserie in the town center. The wooden tables and large bar exude a low-key feel which, in summer, extends to the lively, 300-seat beer garden.

WHERE TO STAY

🛏🛏 **Hotel Betzler** – *Amalienstraße 3.* ☎ *(0721) 91 33 60. www.hotel-betzler.de. 34 rooms.* In the heart of Karlsruhe, the Betzler is a good-value place to hang your hat, especially if you need easy access to public transport. Rooms are clean and functional. The pedestrian zone and most sights of interest are also within walking distance.

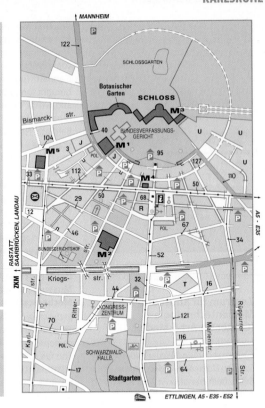

(Marc), Cubists (Léger, Delaunay) and works by Ernst and Dix stand alongside sculptures by Barlach, Lehmbruck and Henry Moore. Contemporary artists include Gerhard Richter, Yves Klein and Antoni Tàpies.

Schloss★ (Palace)

The palace served as the grand-ducal residence until 1918 and got a major drubbing in World War II. Only the tall **octagonal tower** (Schloßturm; ◷ open year-round, Tue–Thu 10am–5pm, Fri–Sun 10am–6pm; ◷4€; ☎ (0721)926 65 14) survived and can now be climbed for sweeping views of the city and the Black Forest. The palace park gives access to the **Botanical Garden** (Botanischer Garten; ◷ open year-round, Mon–Fri 8am–3.30pm; ☎ (0721) 926 30 08; www. rz.uni-karlsruhe.de), which is a fine place to relax among a profusion of flowers, trees and plants, many of them rare and exotic.

Badisches Landesmuseum★ (Baden Regional Museum)

◷ Open year-round, Tue–Thu 10am–5pm, Fri–Sun 10am–6pm. ◷ Closed Dec 24 & 31. ◷4€. ♿ ☎ (0721) 926 65 14. www. landesmuseum.de.

This palace museum covers all major historical periods from the last 2 000 years with paintings, furniture, uniforms, crowns and other jewelry, statues and other objects of cultural significance.

Museum beim Markt

Karl-Friedrich-Straße 6.

◷ Open year-round, Tue–Thu 11am–5pm, Fri–Sun 10am–6pm. ◷ Closed Dec 24 & 31. ◷2€. ♿ ☎ (0721) 926 65 78. www. landesmuseum.de.

Applied arts since 1900 are the main theme of this museum, which counts an exceptional collection of **Jugendstil★** (Art Nouveau) and Art Deco among its possessions.

The former seat of the grand dukes of Baden now houses Germany's supreme courts

Zentrum für Kunst und Medientechnologie★ (Center for Art & Media)

Lorenzstraße 19.

🕐*Open year-round, Wed–Fri 10am–6pm, Sat–Sun 11am–6pm.* ⬤*5€ per museum or 8€ for both, free after Fri 2pm.* &.🖂*(0721) 810 00. www.zkm.de.*

This early 20C weapons and ammunition factory now unites research, teaching, workshops and museums revolving around art and electronic media technologies under a single roof.

In the **Museum für Neue Kunst** (Museum for New Art), European and American work since 1960 take center stage with rotating shows featuring paintings, graphics, sculpture, photography and installations.

The **Medienmuseum** (Media Museum) is the world's first and only repository focused exclusively on interactive art. Many exhibits provide a snapshot of the technologies of the future. *Access at the level of the blue cube.*

Excursion

Schloss Bruchsal★★

20km/12.5mi north of Karlsruhe.

🕐*Open year-round, Tue–Sun 9.30am–5pm.* ⬤*5€ for palace and museums.* &.🖂*(07251) 74 26 61. www.schloesser-und-gaerten.de.*

Bruchsal was the residence of the last four prince-bishops of Speyer.

Their humungous Baroque palace was commissioned in 1720 by Prince-Bishop Damian Hugo von Schönborn, who brought some of the finest architectural and artistic talent to the Rhine.

Most notable among these was Balthasar Neumann whose magnificent **staircase**★★ (1731), lidded by elaborate stucco ornamentation, is a true rococo masterpiece. The **state apartments** are filled with original furnishings as well as silver, porcelain and portraits.

The vaulted Gartensaal (Garden Room) with its marble floor opens onto the park that used to extend all the way to the Rhine River 16km/10mi away.

Deutsches Musikautomaten Museum (German Museum of Mechanical Instruments) 🇰ids

In the main building.

🗣*Guided tours (1hr) with musical demonstrations 11am, 2pm & 3.30pm.*

This fun collection includes 200 musical instruments from the 18C to the 20C, most of them worked by cylinders or perforated, cardboard or rolls of paper. It is well worth taking the guided tour to experience the musical recitals. Cinema organs, "Barbary organs", and pianolas (mechanical pianos operated by perforated "piano rolls) are also on view.

Note the "household" organs and orchestrations (in 19C England Aeolian Orchestrelles, machines resembling oversize, upright pianos with manual keyboards and stops). Many instruments hail from Leipzig and the Black Forest.

Museum der Stadt Bruchsal (Local History Museum)

Southern part of the main block.

This palace museum presents the city's paleontological collection, including minerals from Bruchsal and the surrounding area.

The prehistoric department brims with fossil finds and excavations from the Stone Age to the Middle Ages.

Finally, there's a sparkling collection of coins and medals, many of them ancient and rare, that is sure to delight numismatists.

KASSEL★

Once the seat of landgraves, Kassel is renowned for the Wilhelmshöhe park, with its grottoes, waterfalls and palace. Kassel's post-war reconstruction has not always been done in the best taste, but the town's various sights make it an interesting stop nonetheless.

- **Information:** Obere Königstraße 8, 34131 Kassel. ☎(0561) 70 77 07. www.kassel-tourist.de.
- ▶ **Orient Yourself:** Kassel hugs the Fulda River *(boat tours from Fuldabrücke)* and is surrounded by two nature parks, the Habichtswald and the Naturpark Meißner-Kaufungen Wald. The town is also at the crossroads of the A7 (Fulda–Hannover) and the A44 (to Dortmund) autobahns.
- ◐ **Organizing Your Time:** Allow half a day for a visit of the Wilhelmshöhe park.

A Bit of History

The Brothers Grimm – Jakob (1785–1863) and Wilhelm Grimm (1786–1859) lived in Kassel from 1805 to 1830, working as court librarians. Fascinated by legends and folklore, the brothers collected a wealth of stories published under the title *Kinder und Hausmärchen*, known in English as *Grimms' Fairy Tales*.

Documenta – Kassel is associated best of all with the Documenta, an international exhibition of contemporary art held for 100 days every five years since 1955. The next one is in 2012.

Wilhelmshöhe★★

Park★★

This sprawling Baroque park boasts nearly 800 tree species and, in the late 18C, was transformed into an English style garden. **Löwenburg**, a mock medieval castle built around 1800, is a fine example of the period's Romanticism. The park is lorded over by the 72m/236ft-tall **Hercules**★ *(Herkules)*, emblem of Kassel and highlight of the park. **Views**★★ from up here are predictably fabulous. Below here, a **water staircase** *(Kaskadentreppe)* shoots an enormous **cascade**★ of water into the Neptune and Fountain pools.

Vast – and still very romantic – Wilhelmshöhe park

Ch. Bastin & J. Evrard/MICHELIN

KASSEL

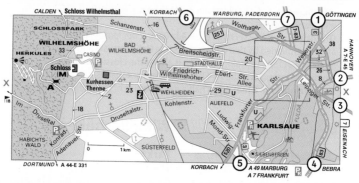

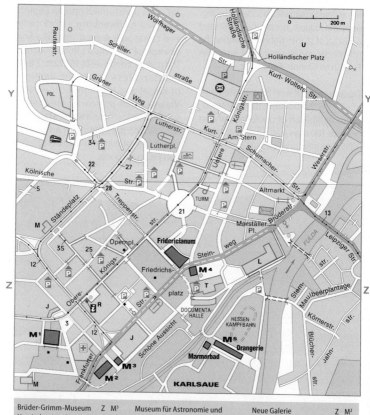

Schloss Wilhelmshöhe (Palace)

Open year-round, Tue–Sun 10am–5pm. Closed Dec 24, 25 & 31. 6€. (0561) 31 68 00. www.museum-kassel.de.

Completed in 1803, the palace now houses a prized **Antikensammlung**★ (collection of antiquities) from Greece and Rome. There are plenty of Greek vases, the 2C **Kassel Apollo**, a series of busts, a sarcophagus, urns and other precious objects.

if time is limited, head straight to the outstanding **Gemäldegalerie Alter Meister**★★★ (Old Masters Picture Gallery). Important works by German painters include Altdorfer's *Crucifixion*, a triptych *(Reisealtar)* by Cranach the Elder, Dürer's *Portrait of Elizabeth Tucher* and *Hercules at Antioch* by Hans Baldung Grien. The Dutch and Flemish Schools are represented by Rembrandt's *Portrait of Saskia van Uylenburgh*; Rubens' *Crowning of a Hero*, and Jordaens' *The Painter's Betrothal*. Also on display here are landscapes by Jan Brueghel, Jacob van Ruisdael, and Jan Steen. Works by Italians (Tintoretto, Titian, Bassano), Spanish (Ribera, Murillo) and French (Poussin) artists complete the collection.

Sights

Karlsaue Park★

The most popular sections of this 18C riverside park are the gardens below the Schöne Aussicht terrace, and the Siebenbergen Fulda island. The Baroque orangery is home to the **Astronomisch-Physikalisches Kabinet** (*open year-round, Tue–Sun 10am–5pm; closed Dec 24, 25 & 31; 3€; (0561) 31 68 05 00*) with a rich collection of astronomical instruments and clocks as well as an attached planetarium. Models demonstrate observable scientific phenomena and there area displays explains the evolution of technology since antiquity.

Excursions

Göttingen

47km/29.2mi north on the A7

Along with Heidelberg, Tübingen and Marburg, Göttingen is a town defined by its university, which was founded in 1734. Some 45 Nobel Prize winners have either studied, taught or conducted research here.

The charming old town bustles with students on bicycles and is filled with Gothic churches and Neoclassical university buildings.

The 13C–15C **Altes Rathaus** (Old Town Hall) harbors the tourist office but is perhaps best known for what lies beneath it: the **Ratskeller** (wine cellar), a rustic tavern that is probably the most fun and lively spot in Göttingen. Out front is the **Gänselieselbrunnen** (Goosegirl Fountain), the city's emblem. Newly anointed PhDs must give her a kiss.

One of the city's most impressive views is the **Vierkirchenblick**, with a church on each point of the compass if viewed from the south-east corner of the market: east, St. Albanikirche; south, St. Michaelskirche; west, St Johannis; and north, St. Jakobi with the tallest tower in town.

The eastern part of the old town is dotted with **half-timbered houses**. One of the biggest beauties is the **Junkernschänke**★ *(Barfüßerstraße 5)*, a 16C Renaissance inn with a stunning multicolored façade.

Finally, a visit to Göttingen should include a stop at the 🔟**Städtisches Museum** (*Municipal Museum; Ritterplan 7/8; open year-round, Tue–Fri 10am–5pm, Sat–Sun 11am–5pm; closed major public holidays; 1.50€ (child 1€) (0551) 400 28 43. www.museum. goettingen.de*), housed in a well-preserved, half-timberd Renaissance building. It contains comprehensive exhibits highlighting various aspects of historical and cultural development of Göttingen, both as a town and as a university.

Art fans are drawn to the rooms housing religious works and paintings by regional artists. There is also a section dedicated to contemporary glass art. There is also a **Museum für Kinder** (Museum for Children) within the museum with special child-orientated tours and an exhibition of old toys from as far back as the 19C.

KIEL★

POPULATION: 233 000

A key German naval base since 1860, Kiel was obliterated in World War II and post-war reconstruction was largely in a functional, modern style. Today it has recaptured its role as gateway to Scandinavia and celebrates its maritime tradition with the world's largest sailing event, the annual Kiel Week.

- **Information:** Andreas-Gayk-Straße 31, 24103 Kiel. ☎ (0431) 67 91 00. www.kiel-tourist.de.
- ▶ **Orient Yourself:** Kiel is at the end of a 17km/10.5mi deep inlet in the Baltic Sea at the eastern end of the North Sea-Baltic Sea canal (Kiel Canal).
- **Don't Miss:** A leisurely stroll along the picturesque Hindenburgufer.
- **Organizing Your Time:** Allow a day for Kiel and environs.
- **Especially for Kids:** The U-Boat at Laboe, Schleswig-Holstein Open-Air Museum (☉ *see Excursions*)
- **Also See:** SCHLESWIG.

A Bit of History

A maritime city – Kiel, founded in the 13C, was always a seafaring town, even if it never achieved more than regional importance as a Hanseatic city. For centuries Kiel led a tranquil existence, until 1871 when it became Germany's main naval base. Within a few years, the little harbor city grew into an industrial metropolis. Every year, during the last week in June, it hosts one of the world's largest boat festivals and sailing regattas, the Kieler Woche (Kiel Week).

Walking Tour

Hindenburgufer★★

This promenade extends for almost 4km/2.5mi along the shore, with shady parks on one side and extended **views**★ on the other.

Rathaus (Town Hall)

Fleethörn 18–24. ☎ *(0431) 90 10.*
Completed in 1911, the Rathaus is dominated by its 106m/347.7ft tower inspired by the Campanile in Venice. An elevator takes you to the top for splendid **views**★ and a carillon chimes hourly.

Parade of sailing ships during Kiel Week

©Imagebroker.net/Photoshot

Address Book

For coin ranges, see the Legend on the cover flap.

WHERE TO STAY

Consul – *Walkerdamm 11.* ☎*(0431) 53 53 70. www.hotel-consul-kiel. de. 40 rooms. Restaurant.*
Close to Kiel's port and the railway station, this hotel is well-served by public transport and has been run by the same family for three generations. Rooms are individually decorated, clean and well equipped.

Parkhotel Kieler Kaufmann – *Niemannsweg 102.* ☎*(0431) 881 10. www.kieler-kaufmann.de. 37 rooms. Restaurant.* This historical, ivy-draped hotel sits in a small park upstream from the port. Rooms in the main building, a former banker's villa, are particularly elegant and spacious. Bright and cheerful, the restaurant serves upscale international cuisine and affords lovely views of the firth.

WHERE TO EAT

Alte Mühle – *An der Holsatiamühle 8 (east bank of the Kieler Förde, follow signs for "Schwentinetal").* ☎*(0431) 205 90 01. www.altemuehle-kiel.de.* In a former 19C mill on the banks of the river Schwentine, this lovely restaurant-café combination serves modern German cuisine, including some creatively updated regional dishes and vegetarian selections. Reasonably priced set lunch menus are available Mon to Fri.

Lüneburg-Haus – Zum Hirschen – *Dänische Straße 22.* ☎*(0431) 982 60 00. www.lueneburghaus.com. Closed Sun.* In a historical town house, above a wine and delicatessen shop, modern regional fare is served in a relaxed bistro ambience.
A hand-selected wine list and attentive staff are bonuses.

TAKING A BREAK

Werkstatt-Café – *Falckstr. 16 (in the town center).* ☎*(0431) 918 65. Closed Sun. www.werkstattcafe-kiel.de.* Try the delicious homemade cakes or one of the dishes of the day at this congenial café with a charming garden. It is right next to a goldsmith's workshop ("Werkstatt") and also showcases the work of local artists.

NIGHTLIFE

Café-Restaurant Schöne Aussichten – *Düsternbrooker Weg 16 (north of the town center, west bank of the Kieler Förde).* ☎*(0431) 210 85 85. www. schoene-aussichten-kiel.de.* Living up to its name (beautiful views), this establishment offers views over the firth, especially from the summer terrace. Mediterranean-inspired food (mainly fish) dominates the menu but you are welcome to just stop for cake or a beer.

Kieler Brauerei – *Alter Markt 9 (town center).* ☎*(0431) 90 62 90. www.kielerbrauerei.de.* This sociable micro-brewery has a salad bar, lunch specials and an all-you-can-eat buffet on Sun.

Excursions

Schleswig-Holsteinisches Freilichtmuseum★★ (Schleswig-Holstein Open-Air Museum) Kids

Hamburger Landstraße 97. 6km/3.7mi south in Molfsee.
Open Apr–Oct, daily 9am–6pm. 6€ (child 2€); Nov–Mar, Sun 11am–4pm (only some houses open; 3€ (child 1.50€). ☎(0431) 65 96 60. www.freilichtmuseum-sh.de.
Sixty traditional buildings typical of the north Elbe countryside have been relocated to this charming open-air museum. Watch craftspeople operate the forge, the potter's workshop, the old-fashioned bakehouse and the weavers' looms in the old-fashioned ways.

Laboe★ Kids

20km/12.4mi north.
This Baltic resort has a pretty harbor and is popular with families for its sandy dunes and calm waters. Overlooking the mouth of the Kiel Firth is the **Marine-Ehrenmal** (German Naval War Memorial; *open Apr–Oct, daily*

9.30am–7pm; Nov–Mar, daily 9.30am–5pm; ≈4€; ⚐⚐(04343) 42 70 62; www.deutscher-marinebund.de/ehrenmal), built between 1927 and 1936 in honor of the 35 000 German navymen who lost their lives during World War I. Today it serves as a memorial for naval war casualties of all nations and also contains a hall filled with historic ship models. **Views**★★ from the 85m/279ft-high tower extends as far Denmark on clear days. Adjacent to the tower is an original Second World War submarine, the **U 995** (🕒same hours as Marine-Ehrenmal, ≈2.50€), whose cramped quarters can be explored. ≈Combination tickets 5.50€.

Nord-Ostsee-Kanal (Kiel Canal)

This 100km/62mi-long link between the Baltic Sea and the North Sea was inaugurated by Wilhelm II in 1895 and is one of the world's busiest waterways. From the second viaduct between Kiel

and Holtenau (Olympiabrücke, reached via Holtenauer Straße and Prinz-Heinrich-Straße) you have a good view of the **Holtenau** locks. Also worth seeing are the **Rendsburg Railway Viaduct**★, the **Grünental Bridge** on the B204, and the **Hochdonn Railway Bridge**.

Holsteinische Schweiz★ (Holstein's "Little Switzerland")

51km/31.7mi.

Between Kiel and Lübeck Bay, Holstein's "Little Switzerland" is sprinkled with lakes among wooded hills of glacial moraine. Its highest point is the Bungsberg at 168m/550ft. Worthwhile stops in this region include the town of **Plön** and the largest of the lakes, **Großer Plöner See**; **Eutin**, birthplace of the composer Carl Maria von Weber, with its 17C town center; and **Malente-Gremsmühlen**, a small isthmus resort and departure point for boating trips.

KOBLENZ★

POPULATION: 107 500

In a strategic location at the confluence of the Rhine and the Moselle rivers, Koblenz was established in 9 BC as a Roman camp and has grown into a mid-size, modern town dotted with historic buildings and charming wine taverns. The departure point for river excursions, Koblenz is also one of the town hosting the "Rhine in Flames" summer festival, a celebration of music, fireworks and illuminated boats.

- **Information:** Bahnhofplatz 17, 56068 Koblenz. ☎(0261) 313 04. Or at the Rathaus, Jesuitenplatz 2. ☎(0261) 13 09 20. www.touristik-koblenz.de.
- ▶ **Orient Yourself:** At the confluence of Rhine and Moselle, Koblenz is also at the junction of the Hunsrück, Eifel and Westerwald mountain ranges.
- **Don't Miss:** Deutsches Eck, wine taverns, Ehrenbreitstein Fortress.
- 🕒 **Organizing Your Time:** it takes half a day to explore the town and the fortress.
- **Also See:** MOSELTAL, RHEINTAL, LIMBURG AN DER LAHN, BONN.

A Bit of History

A refuge for French aristocracy – Koblenz came under French influence after the 1789 French Revolution when it welcomed scores of refugees. Over the coming decades France and Prussia fought repeatedly over this region, alternating control until 1815 when the defeat of Napoleon returned the land to Prussia. The impressive **Rheinanlagen**, a splendid riverside promenade, dates from the 19C French occupation.

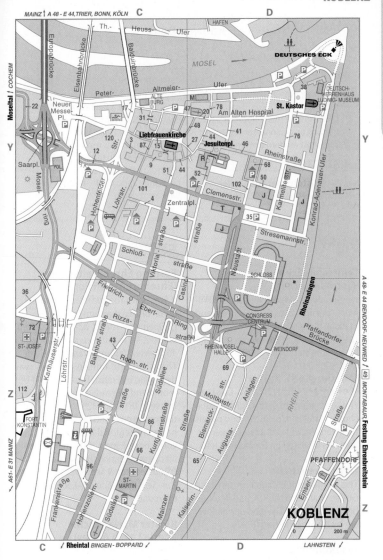

Address Book

For coin ranges, see cover flap.

WHERE TO STAY

Trierer Hof – *Clementstr 1.* (0261) 100 60. www.triererhof.de. Closed Dec 21–28. 36 rooms. This central hotel puts a premium on personal service; rooms feature most modern conveniences.

WHERE TO EAT

Historischer Weinkeller – *Mehlgasse 14.* (0261) 973 89 87. Closed 2 weeks in Feb and Sun. Classical cuisine with Mediterranean inflections dominates the menu in this 13C vaulted wine cellar in the old town.

Schiller's Restaurant – *Mayener Str. 126.* (0261) 963 53 30. Closed Jan 1–21 and Sun. A sophisticated ambience rules this restaurant with winter garden and terrace. Rooms in the attached hotel are modern and pleasantly appointed—those in the back are quieter.

Sights

Deutsches Eck★ (German Corner)

A monumental equestrian statue of Wilhelm I presides over this tongue of land marking the confluence of the Rhine and the Moselle. Enjoy fine views from the base of the statue *(107 steps)*.

Stiftskirche St. Kastor (Collegiate Church of St. Castor)

The south transept of this Romanesque church features 16 painted wood panels that were once part of a rood screen. St. Castor is depicted on the bottom left.

Liebfrauenkirche

This Romanesque church got its Late Gothic chancel in the 15C and Baroque belfries in the 17C. The modern windows are by HG Stockhausen (1992).

Jesuitenplatz

In the courtyard of a 17C Jesuit College (now the Town Hall), the *Schängelbrunnen* (fountain) evokes the mischief perpetrated by the city's street urchins.

Mittelrheinmuseum

Florinsmarkt 15–17. Open year-round, Tue–Sat 10.30am–5pm, Sun 11am–6pm. Closed Jan 1, Shrove Tue, Good Fri, Easter Mon, Dec 24, 25 & 31. 2.50€. (0261) 129 25 20. www.mittelrhein-museum.de. This museum retraces the history of the town and environs through paintings, religious artifacts and everyday items dating as far back as the Middle Ages.

Excursions

Festung Ehrenbreitstein★ (Ehrenbreitstein Fortress)

4.5km/3mi. Cross the Rhine on Pfaffendorfer Brücke then turn left.

Open year-round, daily 10am–5pm. 1.50€, 4€ with museum. (0261) 60 75 40 00. www.festungehrenbreitstein.de. This strategic hilltop fortress was destroyed by French troops in 1801 but rebuilt and expanded by the Prussians between 1817 and 1828. **Views**★★ from the top are great and the compound also harbors a regional history museum, a youth hostel and a restaurant. A chairlift operates during the warmer months *(Easter–May & Sept–Oct 10am–5pm, Jun–Sept 9am–6pm;* 4.50€ one way, 6€ round-trip*)*.

Kloster Maria Laach★ (Maria Laach Abbey)

20km/12.4mi west.

Near a volcanic lake, this well-preserved 12C Romanesque basilica is part of a Benedictine abbey. The cloister-style **entrance portico**★ has intricately worked capitals and the hexagonal baldaquin over the altar suggests a possible Moorish influence.

Rheintal★★★ (*see RHEINTAL*)

Moseltal★★★ (*see MOSELTAL*)

KÖLN★★★

COLOGNE

POPULATION: 976 000

The city of Cologne likes to have a good time. Case in point: Kölsch – a word synonymous for the local dialect and the local beer. This pleasant Rhineland city did, however, go through a bleak period after nearly being leveled during World War II. But it has managed to rebuild itself with remarkable vigor. Visitors will enjoy the city's elegant churches, colorful riverside houses and numerous museums.

- **Information:** Kardinal-Höffner-Platz 1 (opposite the cathedral), 50667 Köln. ☎ (0221) 22 13 04 00. www.koelntourismus.de.
- ▸ **Orient Yourself:** Cologne is surrounded by a ring road linking up with ten autobahns, the A3 (Frankfurt–Essen), A4 (Aachen), the A59 (Düsseldorf) and the A555 (Bonn) chief among them.
- **Don't Miss:** Cologne's Cathedral, the Roman-Germanic Museum, Museum Ludwig, Schnütgen-Museum.
- **Organizing Your Time:** Cologne warrants a couple of days of exploration. Allow a minimum of one hour for the cathedral, three hours to get round the rest of the sights, and the remainder for the museums, boat cruises and beer halls.
- **Especially for Kids:** Chocolate Museum
- **Also See:** BONN, DÜSSELDORF, EIFEL.

A Bit of History

Cologne in Roman Times – Once the Roman legions extended the Empire as far as the Rhine, General Agrippa, colonizer of the region, named the local settlement Oppidum Ubiorum, after the Germanic Ubii who lived there. But by AD 50, the town had adopted the name which would stick, at least in part: *Colonia Claudia Ara Agrippinensium* and "Colonia's" first defensive walls were built. Roman ruins still exist in the Zeughausstraße, outside the cathedral, and at the Praetorium, beneath the present Town Hall. From its official recognition onwards, the town flourished: it was the start of an era, rich in craftwork,

Cologne at night with the cathedral in the background

© www.koelntourismus.de

Address Book

PUBLIC TRANSPORTATION

The main local transportation network in Cologne is the **Kölner Verkehrsbetriebe** (KVB; 24hr hotline ☎ (01803) 50 40 30), which operates buses, subways (U-Bahn) and trams (Straßenbahn). The KVB is linked with the regional Rhein-Sieg transport authority (VRS), which extends as far as Bonn.

The city is divided into price zones. Short trips costs 1.90€, longer ones are 2.30€. A *Tageskarte* (Day Pass) costs 5.20€ or 6.70€, respectively, for one person and 7.60€ and 9.80€ for up to five people traveling together. Both are valid for unlimited trips between 9am and 3am the following day. A one-week pass is 14.70€ or 18.90€. The most central service center is in the Neumarkt U-Bahn station, open Mon–Fri 8am–8pm, Sat 8.30am–5pm.

Internet – www.kvb-koeln.de

The **Köln Welcome Card**, available at the tourist office and in hotels, entitles you to unlimited public transportation and discounts at museums, attractions, entertainment venues, tours, restaurants, bars and other places. Single cards cost 9€ for 24hr, 14€ for 48hr and 19€ for 72hr. Group cards are good for three adults or families (2 adults, up to 3 children) and costs 18€, 28€ and 38€, respectively.

SIGHTSEEING

CITY TOURS

A hop-on, hop off tour bus with recorded commentary operates Wed-Sun 10.30am–4.30pm (18€). Buses depart every 45min from outside the tourist office and stop at 13 major attractions. Without getting off, the loop takes 90min. Live commentary tours (15€, 90min) depart daily 11am, noon and 2pm, Fri-Sat also 4pm (Nov–Mar, 11am and 2pm only) from outside the tourist office. For self-guided walking tours (in English), the staff here rents i-guides (8€ for 4hr), a small hand-held device that takes you to 47 sights in 100min.

BOAT TOURS

KD Köln has the largest fleet of excursion boats on the Rhine (☎ (0221) 208 83 18; www.k-d.com). Other companies include Dampfschiffahrt Colonia (☎ (0221) 257 42 25; www.dampfschiffahrt-colonia.de) and Köln-Tourist Personenschifffahrt (☎ (0221) 12 16 00; www.koelntourist.net).

EVENTS

Carnival turns Cologne into a giant party city with costumed revelers crowding streets and pubs during Carnival Week, which starts on the Thu before Ash Wed (when Lent begins). A highlight is the big parade on Rose Monday. November brings art connoisseurs from around the world to town for **Art Cologne**.

PUBLICATIONS

Cultural calendars of events can be found in the monthly publication *Köln im...* (followed by the month) at tourist information offices (1€). Other monthly magazines like *StadtRevue* and *Prinz* are sold at news kiosks.

WHERE TO STAY

☺Hotel Im Kupferkessel – *Probsteigasse 6 (north of Christophstraße near St. Gereon's Church).* ☎ (0221) 270 79 60. www.im-kupferkessel.de. 13 rooms. This well-kept hotel on the edge of the old town is a fine budget pick even if rooms are small and some must share the bathroom down the hall. The sunny breakfast room is anchored by a wooden spiraling staircase.

☺☺Hotel Brandenburger Hof – *Brandenburger Straße 2* ☎ (0221) 12

Cologne Central Station

© www.koelntourismus.de

28 89. www.brandenburgerhof.de. ⚲
31 rooms. North of the old town, this
reasonably priced hotel has small but
functional rooms and a petite garden
for relaxing. It is close to the main train
station and cathedral.

⚲⚲**Haus an den Sieben Wegen**
– Grafenmühlenweg 220, 51069 Köln-
Dellbrück. ☎(0221) 689 30 00. www.
hotel-7-wege.de. Closed Christmas to
early Jan. 15 rooms. Days start with an
opulent breakfast buffet at this neat,
well-appointed and well-run hotel near
a wooded area. Welcome perks such
as an electric kettle and minibar await
in the rooms, some of which are quite
spacious.

⚲⚲**Hotel Trost** – Vogelsanger
Straße 60–62, 50823 Köln-Ehrenfeld.
☎(0221) 952 91 00. www.hotel-trost.de.
⚲ 18 rooms. Rooms are good-sized,
modern and reflect a personal attention
to detail at this well-kept family-run
hotel in a renovated historic building.

⚲⚲⚲**Das kleine Hotel** – Wich-
heimer Straße 200, 51067 Köln-Holweide.
☎(0221) 691 05 91. daskleinehotelkoeln.
de. 7 rooms. Small but beautiful, this
privately-run property has snug rooms
with heavy pine furniture and wooden
floors. A tram station is nearby.

⚲⚲⚲**Hopper Hotel et cetera** –
Brüsseler Straße 26. ☎(0221) 92 44 00.
www.hopper.de. 49 rooms. Restaurant
⚲⚲⚲. Behind the thick walls of a
former monastery from 1894 await
trendy, streamlined rooms with parquet
floors and marble baths. A modern
altar-painting dominates the bistro-
style restaurant.

⚲⚲⚲⚲**Hotel Im Wasserturm**
– Kaygasse 2. ☎(0221) 200 80. 88 rooms
⚲22€. Restaurant ⚲⚲⚲⚲. A listed
19C brick water tower has been ingeniously converted into a chic designer
hotel with a soaring lobby and rooms
boasting the full complement of creature comforts. Enjoy magnificent views
from the 11th-floor restaurant.

⚲⚲⚲⚲**Excelsior Hotel Ernst**
– Domplatz. ☎(0221) 27 01. www.excel-
siorhotelernst.de. 122 rooms. ⚲25€.
Cologne's most illustrious defender
of the grand tradition sits directly opposite the towering cathedral.

A sumptuous marble lobby leads to
refined rooms and grand suites, along
with a sauna and fitness facilities.

WHERE TO EAT

⚲**Brauhaus Goldener Pflug** –
Olpener Straße 421, 51109 Köln-Merheim.
☎(0221) 310 56 31. www.brauhaus-
goldener-pflug.de. This classic Cologne
brewpub tickles palates with hearty
Rhenish fare as well as fresh and light
bistro-style cuisine. In summer, relax in
the beer garden.

⚲⚲**Hase** – St. Apern-Straße 17. ☎(0221)
25 43 75. Closed Sun. Quality ingredients
are woven into dishes that are creative
without getting too tricky. The chic dining room with its pale wooden tables
is great for kicking back at the end of
the day.

⚲⚲**Heising und Adelmann** –
Friesenstraße 58. ☎(0221) 130 94 24.
www.heising-und-adelmann.de. Closed
Sun and public holidays. A lively restaurant in fashionable bistro style delivers
relaxed flair and modern, international
cuisine. 50 cocktails to choose from at
the bar. Lovely terrace out back.

⚲⚲⚲**Em Krützche** – Am Franken-
turm 1. ☎(0221) 258 08 39. www.em-
kruetzche.de. Closed Mon. This traditional brewpub has fed tummies and
souls for over 400 years with hearty
regional specialties.

⚲⚲⚲**L'escalier** – Brüsseler Straße
11. ☎(0221) 205 29 98. Closed Sun.
Reservations required. A haze of good
aromas greets you at this intimate cellar
restaurant which serves palate-teas-
ing modern international cuisine and
"surprise menus" for adventurous types.

⚲⚲⚲⚲**Le Moissonnier** – Krefelder
Straße 25. ☎(0221) 72 94 79. Closed Dec
24–Jan 3, 1 week at Easter and 3 weeks
in July, Sun, Mon. Reservations required.
Great ambience and handsome Art
Nouveau (Jugendstil) décor characterize
this bistro that would not look out of
place in Paris. Creative French cuisine.

⚲⚲⚲⚲**Hanse Stube** – Trankgasse 1,
at Excelsior Hotel Ernst. ☎(0221) 270
34 02. www.excelsiorhotelernst.de.
French food fanciers crowd around the
crisply draped tables at this sophisticated restaurant in one of Cologne's top

hotels. Service is impeccable and the wine list inspired.

⊜⊜⊜⊜⊜**La Vision** – *Kaygasse 2, at Hotel im Wasserturm.* ☎ *(0221) 200 80. www.hotel-im-wasserturm.de. Closed 4 weeks in Jul-Aug, Sun, Mon.* You feel as though floating above the city while dining in this circular 11th-floor restaurant with its glass front. On the menu is modern, international cuisine with flavors woven together like fine tapestry.

TAKING A BREAK

Café Eigel – *Brückenstraße 1–3 (Glock-engasse to the east).* ☎ *(0221) 257 58 58.* This traditional yet modern café serves homemade confections, cakes and pastries and exhibits and sells works by local artists.

Café Reichard – *Unter Fettenhennen 11 (opposite the cathedral).* ☎ *(0221) 257 85 42. www.cafe-reichard.de.* Enjoy this cafe's classic interior, a winter garden and a large terrace with great views of the cathedral. Come for a meal, a snack, a coffee or a drink.

Käse-Pavillon – *Breite Straße 29 (access via Opernpassagen or Neue Langgasse).* ☎ *(0221) 270 68 07. Closed Sun.* This "temple to cheese" has hundreds of tempting choices. Make your own sandwich or choose from the menu. Hot casseroles, desserts and a small wine selection are also available.

NIGHTLIFE

USEFUL TIPS

The old city offers a wealth of tempting options when it comes to drinking, dining or finding entertainment. Bars cluster in the Belgian Quarter (between Aachener and Venloer Straße), the university district (around Zülpicher Straße), around Chlodwigplatz and the area around Friesenstraße. The traditional beer is "Kölsch," served in 0.2l glasses.

Früh am Dom – *Am Hof 12–14.* ☎ *(0221) 2 61 32 13. www.frueh.de.* This old-time beer hall and restaurant gets good marks from both locals and tourists. No need to order your Kölsch – it will be already waiting for you. The restaurant

on the first floor is a bit quieter than the raucous beer hall downstairs.

Päffgen – *Friesenstraße 64–66 (between Friesenplatz and Römerturm).* ☎ *(0221) 13 54 61. www.paeffgen-koelsch.de.* This traditional beer hall serves cold Kölsch, regional dishes and plenty of local color, in summer in the beer garden.

Papa Joe's Biersalon "Klimperkasten" *Alter Markt 50–52.* ☎ *(0221) 258 21 32. www.papajoes.de.* Retro rules in this 1920s pub with walls swathed in old photos and film projectors and mechanical instruments (cranked up hourly) constituting part of the décor. An enjoyable trip down memory lane.

Papa Joe's Jazzlokal "Em Streckstrump" – *Buttermarkt 37.* ☎ *(0221) 257 79 31 www.papajoes.de.* Jazz reigns supreme here as it has every evening for around 30 years. Drinks are a bit pricey but the concerts are free and the atmosphere bustling. "Four O'Clock Jazz" Sun often brings the house down.

Hyatt-Biergarten – *Kennedyufer 2a (across the Hohenzollernbrücke from the cathedral).* ☎ *(0221) 828 12 34. www. cologne.regency.hyatt.de. Open Apr–Oct in good weather.* The beer garden of this luxury hotel on the Rhine's east bank offers magnificent views of the cathedral and historic center. In summer, crowds gather for jazz on Sunday (noon–3pm, free).

SHOPPING

USEFUL TIPS

Cologne's main shopping street is the pedestrianized Hohe Straße, which runs south from the Cathedral and is lined with chain and department stores. It is crossed by Schildergasse, which has smaller shops. Not far from the Neumarkt are shopping arcades, such as Neumarktpassage and Neumarktgalerie. Exclusive boutiques line Breite Straße, Mittelstraße and Pfeilstraße. There is also shopping around Chlodwigplatz, and in Bonnerstraße and Severinstraße. **Antique shops** and **art galleries** are concentrated in St. Apern-Straße; more galleries lie north of Neumarkt (Albertusstraße) and around the cathedral.

4711 Echt Kölnisch Wasser – *Glock-engasse 4711*. ☎*(0221) 925 04 50. www.4711.com.* At the traditional home of the famous Eau de Cologne, you can freshen up at a fountain of *aqua mirabile*, view a historical exhibition and pick up some souvenirs and beauty products. The carillon on the southern façade of the building plays the Marseillaise every hour from 9am to 9pm.

trade and architecture, which did not end until the time of the Great Invasions, in the 5C.

The Holy City beside the Rhine – Cologne's political power in the Middle Ages derived from the Church. Until 1288, the archbishops of Cologne exercized powers both spiritual and temporal. In the 13C and early 14C, the city became the religious, intellectual and artistic center of the Rhine Valley. Eminent men came to preach: the Dominican **Albertus Magnus** (teacher of Thomas Aquinas) and **Master Eckhart**, as well as the Scottish Franciscan **Duns Scotus**.

It was the work of such religious scholars that led in 1388 to the creation of Cologne University by local burghers.

Trade and Commerce – Because of its favorable position on the Rhine and along important trade routes, Cologne soon became a power in the commercial world, imposing its own system of weights and measures over the whole of northern Germany. The town's first fair was held in 1360. Its elevation to the status of Free Imperial City in 1475 did no more than set an official seal on the dominant role Cologne had in fact been playing since the 13C.

The Modern City – Industrialization in the late 19C quickly expanded Cologne. After World War II, **Konrad Adenauer** continued the process of modernization begun while he served as the city's mayor from 1917 to 1933. It was on the watch of the man destined to become the Federal Republic's first Chancellor that the university (shut down under French occupation in 1798) was reopened in 1919; that the Deutz exhibition halls *(Messehallen)* were built; and that green belts were added throughout the city.

Art and Culture – Diversity, above all, marks cultural life in Cologne today. Apart from music and drama, the fine arts hold pride of place: more than 100 galleries are devoted to contemporary art exhibitions alone. The *Kölner Kunstmesse* and Art Cologne are both highly regarded annual international art fairs. The Schnütgen Museum, the Museum Ludwig and the Josef-Haubrich-Halle are among venues mounting important temporary exhibitions.

Heinrich Böll (1917–85), one of the pre-eminent German post-war writers and winner of the Nobel Prize for Literature in 1972, was born in Cologne. His work, sparing neither the Church nor society, is inseparable from his birthplace.

Publishing houses and printers have been based in Cologne for centuries. Building on this history has been the post-war push into electronic media. Cologne, the media city, is currently Germany's TV capital, with eight television stations, recording studios, a media park and an Academy of Media Arts.

Town Life – There is a strong sense of neighborhood in Cologne. Each locality centers on its individual parish church, each of which preserves its own traditions. St Severin is the oldest and most typical. But all Cologne citizens appreciate the old town bordering the Rhine. Remodeled in the 1980s, the old town is now, night and day, one of the liveliest parts of the city.

Since the riverside highway has been diverted underground between the Hohenzollern and Deutzer bridges, land has been transformed into attractive gardens *(Rheingarten)* perfect for walking, relaxing and embarking on a leisurely boat cruise.

Inside the cathedral

© Vivalapenler/Dreamstime.com

lously, it survived World War II almost intact and was declared a UNESCO World Heritage Site in 1996.

Exterior

The twin-towered western façade marks a high point in the Flamboyant Gothic style. Embellished gables and slender buttresses burst ever upward, in line with tapering spires 157m/515ft high. The bronze doors **(1)** in the south transept entrance (1948–54) are by Ewald Mataré.

Interior

The building's colossal proportions are fully appreciated from the nave, 144m/472.4ft long, 45m/147.6ft wide, and 43.5m/142.7ft high. The five Late Gothic **stained-glass windows**★ in the north aisle (1507–08) depict the lives of the Virgin and St Peter.

The Cross Chapel *(Kreuzkapelle)* off the north ambulatory houses the rare **Gero★ Crucifix** *(Gerokreuz)* **(3)**, an early

Dom★★★ (Cathedral)

Self-guided tour pamphlets available in the foyer. ⏰*Open year-round, daily 6am–7.30pm.* 👥*Guided tours available.* ♿☏*(0221) 17 94 05 55. www. koelnerdom.de.*

It took over 600 years to complete this monumental cathedral. In 1164, when Frederick I Barbarossa donated the relics of the Three Magi to the city, an influx of pilgrims created the need for a larger church. Thus began construction of the first Gothic church in the Rhineland whose design was inspired by the cathedrals at Paris, Amiens and Reims. Builders first set to work in 1248 and by 1320 the chancel was completed. The south tower followed by 1410 but soon after building was suspended because of lack of funds and political turmoil. When it resumed in the 19C, the original plans were used, and in 1880 the cathedral was finally consecrated before Emperor Wilhelm I. Miracu-

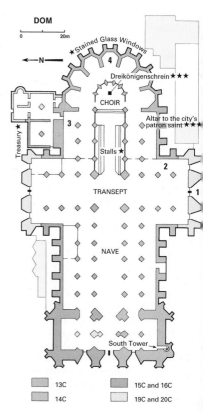

DOM

0   20m

★Stained Glass Windows★

Dreikönigenschrein ★★★

CHOIR

Altar to the city's patron saint ★★★

Treasury ★

Stalls ★

TRANSEPT

NAVE

South Tower

13C
14C
15C and 16C
19C and 20C

Carnival

Celebrations in Cologne start at 11 minutes past 11 on the 11th day of the 11th month, gradually climaxing during the three days preceding Ash Wednesday. Things get under way beforehand with Weiberfastnacht, the Women's Carnival (the Thursday before Shrove Tuesday—women throughout town indiscriminately cut off men's neckties). Then there is the People's Carnival the Sunday before Shrove Tuesday with the Veedelszöch and the Schullzöch; Rosenmontag, the day before Shrove Tuesday, features a procession with elaborately decorated floats, bands and a cavalcade of giant current events caricatures; and finally Shrove Tuesday (Fastnachtsdienstag), which ends at midnight with the burning of straw dolls ("Nubbel"). Carnival associations meet on the evening of Ash Wednesday for a meal of fish. During the carnival season, the inhabitants of Cologne and its visitors go wild, so don't expect any peace and quiet.

A brochure and leaflet detailing the procession routes and other important information, such as traffic direction and room reservation, are at the Cologne tourist office.

example of 10C Ottonian art. In the axial chapel (*Dreikönigskapelle*) the stained-glass window, the *Älteres Bibelfenster* **(4)**, was installed in 1265. The shrine behind the high altar contains the relics of the Three Magi. Called **Schrein der Heiligen Drei Könige**★★★, it is a 12C masterpiece in gold. The last chapel in the south ambulatory (*Marienkapelle*) contains the altar of the city's patrons, the **Altar der Stadtpatrone**★★★. Painted c. 1440 by **Stefan Lochner**, it illustrates

Stained glass window of the cathedral

© Philip Lange/Bigstockphoto.com

The Adoration of the Magi, St. Ursula and St Gereon.

The south transept houses a Flemish polyptych of 1521 with double side panels known as the **Altarpiece of the Five Moors (2)** (*Agilolphusaltar*). Finally, the finely carved **choir stalls**★ (14C) (*Chorgestühl*), the most extensive in Germany, contain 104 seats.

For a panorama of Cologne and the surrounding countryside, climb the 509 steps of the **South Tower** (*Südturm*) to a platform at 97m/318ft. The belfry (*Glockenstube*) houses the world's largest swinging church bell: **St Peter's Bell** (*Petersglocke*) was cast in 1923 and weighs 24t.

The **cathedral treasury**★ (*Domschatz kammer;* ◷open year-round, daily 10am –6pm; ⊜4€; ♿☎ (0221) 17 94 05 30) contains a wealth of religious art. Gold and silver liturgical plates, the shrine to St. Engelbert and a reliquary monstrance with St. Peter's chain are among the standouts.

Romanesque Churches

The High Middle Ages (1150–1250) saw the construction of numerous churches built in the Romanesque style. Certain design elements, like the clover-leaf (trefoil) chancel, originated in Cologne (◐see INTRODUCTION: Art).
Most were destroyed in World War II, but a dozen were subsequently rebuilt.

KÖLN

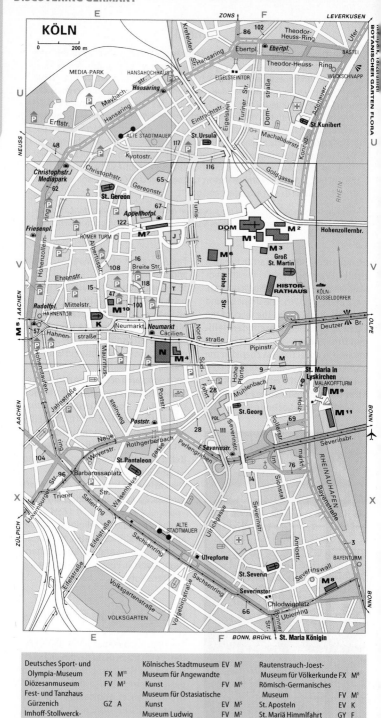

0   200 m

Deutsches Sport- und		
Olympia-Museum	FX	M¹¹
Diözesanmuseum	FV	M³
Fest- und Tanzhaus		
Gürzenich	GZ	A
Imhoff-Stollwerck-		
Museum	FX	M⁹
Josef-Haubrich-Halle	EV	N
Käthe-Kollwitz-Museum	EV	M¹⁰
Kölnisches Stadtmuseum	EV	M⁷
Museum für Angewandte		
Kunst	FV	M⁶
Museum für Ostasiatische		
Kunst	EV	M⁵
Museum Ludwig	FV	M²
Museum Schnütgen	FV	M⁴
Prätorium	GZ	C
Rautenstrauch-Joest-		
Museum für Völkerkunde	FX	M⁸
Römisch-Germanisches		
Museum	FV	M¹
St. Aposteln	EV	K
St. Mariä Himmlfahrt	GY	F
St. Maria im Kapitol	GZ	B
Wallraf-Richartz-Museum		
Fondation Corboud	GZ	M¹²

St. Maria-im-Kapitol★

Marienplatz 19. ☎(0211) 21 46 15.
www.maria-im-kapitol.de.
This late Ottonian church (11C) features the oldest **cloverleaf chancel**★ in Cologne. The crypt extends beneath almost the entire body of the chancel, the largest in Germany (exceeded only by the one in Speyer Cathedral). On the left side of the east clover-leaf is an altarpiece of the Madonna of St. Hermann-Joseph (c. 1180). The **Renaissance choir screen** is richly decorated with sculpture (c. 1525). At the west end of the south side aisle are the original wooden **church doors**★ from 1065.

St. Severin

Im Ferkulum 29. www.sankt-severin.de.
☎(0221) 931 84 20.

St. Severin is the oldest Christian foundation in Cologne, dating to the 4C and built on a Roman-Frankish burial ground. The present building dates from the 13C (chancel) and 15C (west tower and nave). The chancel in the fine Gothic

©Elke Wetzig/Wikimedia Commons

St. Maria-im-Kapitol

Eau de Cologne

The people of Cologne were familiar with Cologne's "aqua mirabile" as early as the 16C, although it did not become widely known until the 18C. Its success is due to the enterprising spirit of an Italian immigrant family, the Farinas, of whom the most famous is **Johann Maria Farina**. "Cologne water" *(Kölnisch Wasser)* was thought to have medicinal properties to cure a number of ills. In the wake of the Farina family's success, other producers of the wonder-water sprang up, making "Eau de Cologne" famous. The new wave of producers included **Wilhelm Mühlens**, who founded a company in Glockengasse in 1792.

Under Napoleon, the use of Eau de Cologne as medicine was banned, so manufacturers began marketing their cure-all as toilet water. Mühlens' business was located at no. 4711 Glockengasse, and in 1875 this number was registered as a trade mark for authentic Eau de Cologne *(Echt Kölnisch Wasser). The carillon in the gable of no 4711 Glockengasse plays the Marseillaise every hour from 9am to 9pm.*

nave features paintings by the Master of St Severinus. The tomb of St. Severinus, bishop of Cologne around 400 and one of the city's patron saints, is buried in the crypt.

St. Pantaleon★
Am Pantaleonsberg 2. ☎(0221) 31 66 55. www.pantaleon.webzeiten.info.
The nave and impressive Westwerk are examples of Ottonian architecture (10C). The **rood screen**★ at the chancel is Late Gothic.

St. Gereon★
Gereonsdriesch 2. ☎(0221) 13 49 22. www.stgereon.de.
The originality of this church lies in its elliptical floor plan and the addition, in 1220, of a **decagon**★ between its towers. The crypt with its 11C mosaic floor contains the tomb of St. Gereon. The frescoes date from the 13C.

St. Andreas
Komödienstraße 4–8. ☎(0221) 160 66 18. www.sankt-andreas.de.
Built in the early 13C with a trefoil apse, this church teems with remarkable architectural details. At the beginning of the 15C, the Romanesque chancel was replaced with a Gothic one modeled on that in Aachen.

St. Ursula
Ursulaplatz 24. ☎(0221) 13 34 00.
In the north aisle are 30 plates (1456) by Stefan Lochner depicting the martyrdom of St. Ursula. The daughter of a British king, the saint was murdered by Huns along with ten of her companions in the 5C.
In the south transept is the **Goldene Kammer**★ *(Golden Chamber; ∞1€)*, which contains 120 reliquary busts.

Sights

Museum Ludwig★★
Bischofsgartenstraße 1.
⊙*Open year-round, Tue–Sun 10am–6pm.*
⊙*Closed Jan 1, Carnival week, Dec 24, 25 & 31. ∞9€. ☎(0221) 22 12 61 65. www. museenkoeln.de.*
This spacious museum with its unusual roof houses an important collection of 20C art, with particular emphasis on the Expressionist movement and works by the Brücke and Blaue Reiter groups. There is also a good display of art from between the two world wars: Constructivism, the Bauhaus and New Objectivity.
Another strong point is a collection of **Russian Avant-Garde** art. The Surrealist department reveals Dadaism's birth in Cologne and includes a variety of works by **Max Ernst** (he was born nearby in Brühl), Miró, Dalí and Magritte.
Cubism is represented by Gris, Léger and Delaunay, and **Nouveau Réalisme** by Klein, Tàpies, Burri and Dubuffet. Curators are especially proud of their **Picasso** collection, which encompasses several hundred works.
German post-war and contemporary art includes works by the **Gruppe Zero**,

mainly by **Beuys**, Baselitz, Richter, Penck and Kiefer. American abstract painting is represented (Rothko, de Kooning), as is **Pop Art** (Rauschenberg, Warhol and Segal).

Canvasses, video, installations and other media by contemporary artists from Europe, America and Asia illustrate the most recent artistic trends.

Also integrated into the museum complex is the **Agfa Foto-Historama**, which presents a survey of over 150 years of photography, from the magic lantern and daguerreotype to calotype and spooled film all the way to microfilm and digital cameras.

Römisch-Germanisches Museum★★ (Roman-Germanic Museum)

Roncalliplatz 4.

Visit afternoons or weekends to avoid school groups. Open year-round, Tue–Sun 10am–5pm. Closed Jan 1, Carnival week, Dec 24, 25 & 31. 5€. (0221) 22 12 44 38. www.museenkoeln.de.

As capital of the Roman province of Lower Germania, Cologne enjoyed immense prosperity between the 1C and the 4C, due largely to trade between the Roman colonizers and the Germanic Ubii tribe. Evidence of these exchanges is displayed in this stellar museum.

In the basement is the **Dionysius Mosaic**★, an exceptionally well-preserved Roman mosaic made of one and a half million fragments of stone (measuring 14.5x7m/48x23ft). Belonging to a banqueting hall of a 3C Roman villa, it was uncovered during the construction of an air-raid bunker in 1941 and preserved on its original site. Adjacent rooms evoke funerary rites and the daily lives of the ancient Romans. Exhibits also include the enormous **Poblicius Tomb**★★ (AD 40), an officer of the Roman Legion; the **Philosophers' Mosaic**; and an array of Roman **glassware**★★.

Wallraf-Richartz-Museum & Fondation Corboud★★

Martinstraße 39.

Open year-round, Tue, Wed & Fri 10am–6pm, Thu 10am–10pm, Sat–Sun 11am–6pm. 9€. (0221) 276 93. www.museenkoeln.de.

Housed in an angular postmodern building designed by OM Ungers, this museum specializes in fine art from the 13C to the 19C, with a particular emphasis on local artists.

The Medieval Painters of Cologne collection culminates with the Late Gothic work of Stefan Lochner. Also of note are the **Master of St Veronica** and the **Master of Life of the Virgin**. Among the **German Old Masters** on view are **Dürer** and **Lucas Cranach the Elder** *(Virgin and Child)*.

Baroque art is represented by Rubens, Ruisdael, Hals and **Rembrandt**, including a famous late self-portrait. Spanish, Italian and French artists include Murillo, Tiepolo and Boucher. There are also canvasses by 18C–19C German artists Caspar David Friedrich and Cologne-born **Wilhelm Leibl**. French Impressionists Renoir, Monet, Sisley, Cézanne, Van Gogh and Gauguin rank among the perennial crowd-pleasers. Most are on permanent loan from the Switzerland-based Fondation Corboud.

Museum Schnütgen★★

Cäcilienstraße 29.

Open year-round, Tue–Fri 10am–5pm, Sat–Sun 11am–5pm. Closed Jan 1, Carnival, Dec 24, 25 & 31. 3.20€. (0221) 22 12 36 20. www.museenkoeln.de.

The 12C former Cäcilienkirche, one of the dozen Romanesque churches still standing in the city, makes a suitable site for this museum of sacred art from the 6C to the 19C. Numerous **Madonnas in wood** illustrate the local "tender" style in statuary. A collection of medieval items in ivory, most of them from Byzantium, France or other parts of Germany, displays particularly fine workmanship. Also note the works in gold, silver and bronze and medieval textiles.

Museum für Ostasiatische Kunst★★ (Museum of East Asian Art)

Universitätsstraße 100.

Open year-round, Tue–Sun 11am–5pm (Thu 8pm). Closed Jan 1, Carnival week, Dec 24, 25 & 31. 4.20€. (0221) 22 12 86 08. www.museenkoeln.de.

Germany's oldest museum of Asian art (founded in 1909) is surrounded by

Museum für Ostasiastische Kunst, Köln

Ceremonial urn, Museum für Ostasiastische Kunst

a Japanese garden laid out by Masa-yuki Nagare (b. 1923). The permanent exhibition displays works from China, Japan and Korea and covers all periods of artistic endeavor from the Neolithic Age to the present. Among the oldest items are Chinese vessels (16C–12C BC). Other highlights include Buddhist art from China and Japan; Chinese ceramics from all phases of its evolution; 17C Chinese furniture and writing equipment, as well as Japanese screens.

Kolumba★

Kolumbastraße 4.
Open year-round, Wed–Mon noon–5pm. Closed Carnival Mon, Dec 24 & 25. (0221) 933 19 30. www.kolumba.de.
The Archbishopric of Cologne possesses a stunning collection of 2 000 years of religious art, which it shares with the public in the evocative setting of the Late Gothic church of St. Kolumba. Ruined in World War II, it was recently converted into a museum by Swiss architect Peter Zumthor. Among the most famous works is Stephan Lochner's **Virgin with Violets**.

Museum für Angewandte Kunst★ (Museum of Applied Arts)

An der Rechtsschule.
Open year-round, Tue–Sun 11am–5pm. Closed Jan 1, Carnival week, Dec 24, 25 & 31. 6€. (0221) 22 12 67 35. www. museenkoeln.de.

This museum contains an extensive collection of furniture, ceramics, glassware, metalwork, jewelry and textiles from the Middle Ages through the present. Of particular interest are tapestries from Basel, a Venetian wedding goblet from the 15C, two life-size animal figures made from Meissen porcelain, and Baroque and Jugendstil glassware.

Rautenstrauch-Joest-Museum (Ethnographic Museum)

Ubierrring 45.
In summer 2009, the museum is expected to move to a new location at Josef-Haubrich-Hof in the Old Town. Until then, the permanent collection can only be seen on prearranged guided tours. (0221) 33 69 40. www.museenkoeln.de.
Founded in 1901, this museum is a veritable treasure-trove of non-European art and culture with such highlights as Thai and Khmer ceramics from the 8C to the 16C, ancient Egyptian art, and art by Native Americans.

Walking Tour

Old Town

The cultural heart of Cologne extends south of the central station and the Hohenzollernbrücke, the busiest railway bridge in the world, with a train crossing every two minutes, day and night. Several outstanding museums sit in the shadow of the Cathedral. The Römisch-Germanisches Museum and Diözesan-museum rub shoulders with the Museum Ludwig, a 1986 edifice whose distinctive saw-tooth roof contrasts with the Gothic spires of the cathedral. The complex also includes, at basement level, a concert hall, the **Kölner Philharmonie**. From Heinrich-Böll-Platz, behind the museums, a series of terraces leads down to the Rheingarten riverside promenade.

▶ *Head south along the riverside promenade (here called Frankenwerft) and take in lovely views of the Rhine. After about 0.5km/0.2mi the row of candy-colored houses of Fischmarkt appears on your right with the church of Groß St. Martin*

The School of Cologne

Manuscript illumination and altar ornamentation were blossoming arts in Cologne in the early 14C. Painting attained its summit in the early 15C, with the works of **The Master of St Veronica** and **Stefan Lochner**, a native of Meersburg (on Lake Constance). From 1450 on, under the influence of the Dutch schools, the artists of Cologne abandoned the idealistic mysticism of the Gothic period for the gracious realism of the Renaissance.

This later work is characterized by delicate colors and an emotional depiction of subjects. Religious sculpture in Cologne peaked between the 14C and 15C. Many **Madonnas** display this style of tenderness sweeping Europe around 1400: the hinted smile, draping fabrics and a relaxed stance.

towering behind it. Beyond the church the Martinsviertel quarter teems with tourist cafés and bars. Leave the river via Lintgasse, which leads to the Alter Markt square.

Altes Rathaus★ (Old Town Hall)

This building with its reconstructed 15C Gothic tower (carillon at noon and 5pm) and the Flemish Renaissance pavilion (1569–73) lies at the heart of the old Jewish quarter. In 1349, the ghetto was stormed, its inhabitants killed and their homes torched. Beneath the glass pyramid in the square outside the Town Hall is an 1170 Jewish ritual bath, called **Mikwe** (◐*open year-round, Mon–Fri 8am–4.45pm, Fri 8am–noon, Sat 10am–4pm, Sun 11am–1pm; pick up key at Rathaus, Sun at Praetorium*).

Praetorium

The entrance is hidden near the underground garage in Kleine Budengasse.
◐*Open year-round, Tue–Fri 10am–4pm, Sat–Sun 11am–4pm.* ☎*(0221) 221 23 04.*
The foundations of the Roman governor's palace (1C–4C) were excavated after World War II and are largely preserved. In the antechamber are small sculptures, bricks and receptacles from Roman times. Visitors can also view the Roman sewer, which was used as an air-raid shelter during World War II.

▸ *Head back toward the Alter Markt and follow Martinstraße to the dance hall.*

Gürzenich Dance Hall

This was one of the first secular Gothic buildings (1441–44) and served as a model for many townhouses. The "council's dance hall" was used for banquets in the Middle Ages and then again since the 19C when the modern carnival was born.

▸ *Follow Martinsstraße south to* **Heumarkt** *(hay market) dominated by an equestrian statue of Prussian king, Frederick William III (1770–1840). South of here, across Cäcilienstraße, is St. Maria-im-Kapitol. Walk toward the river, turn right and continue to the Rheinauhalbinsel (peninsula) and its* **Schokoladenmuseum**★ *(Chocolate Museum).*

Schokoladenmuseum★ (Chocolate Museum) [Kids]

Rheinauhafen.
◐*Open year-round, Tue–Fri 10am–6pm, Sat–Sun 11am–7pm.* ◐*Closed Jan 1, Carnival week, Dec 24, 25 & 31.* ∞*6.50€.*
♿☎*(0221) 931 88 80. www.schokoladen museum.de.*
This unusual museum takes as its subject the tastiest of foodstuffs, chocolate.
It is housed in a Gründerzeit customs warehouse and a modern glass annex and reached via a historical swing bridge. Inside are displays about the 3 000-year history and production of chocolate, a miniature chocolate factory and the history of the 19C Cologne-born chocolate firm Stollwerck.
A delicious treat from a chocolate fountain completes the visit.

Excursions

Altenberger Dom★

20km/12.4mi northeast.

This former Cistercian abbey church (known locally as the Bergischer Dom), lies in a lush green valley. The pure Gothic building (1255–1379) has celebrated Roman Catholic and Protestant services alternately since 1857. Its huge (18x8m/59x26ft) colored canopy (c. 1400) above the west entrance is considered the largest stained-glass window in Germany.

Brühl★★

18km/11mi south via the B51.

Brühl developed around a fortress, whose foundations, in the 18C, were used to built **Schloss Augustusburg**, a fantastic Rococo extravaganza commissioned by Cologne archbishop and prince elector Clemens August. Together with his hunting lodge, Jagdschloss Falkenschloss, it was entered on **UNESCO**'s World Heritage List in 1984. Below are some of the sights worth visiting in Brühl.

Schloss Augustusburg★★ (Augustusburg Palace)

⟜Visit by guided tour (1hr) only; Feb–Nov, Tue–Fri 9am–noon, 1.30pm–4pm, Sat–Sun 10am–5pm. ⊚5€. ♿⟨02232⟩ 440 00. www.schlossbruehl.de.

Clemens August, a member of the Bavarian Wittelsbach ruling family, hired François de Cuvilliés as chief architect of his palatial residence. Cuvilliés in turn drew some of the era's finest artists and craftmen from throughout Europe. Chief among them was **Balthasar Neumann,** the mastermind behind the magnificent **staircase★★**, a riot in greyish-green and yellowish-orange faux marble and elaborate stuccowork thoughout. Crane your neck to study the **ceiling fresco★**, a work of Carlo Carlone that celebrates the prince and the House of Wittelsbach. Tours take in about two dozen rooms, each one seemingly more lavish than the previous. Highlights include the **large new suite,** comprising a garden room with more Carlone frescoes; the **summer suite,** with floors covered in blue and white tiles from Rotterdam; and the **yellow suite,** used principally by Clemens August as his private quarter.

The **Schlosspark** (palace gardens) starts out as a French Baroque **garden★**. It was designed by Lenôtre student Dominique Girard in 1728 and is sprinkled with reflective ponds and elaborate flower beds. It gives way to an English-style park masterminded by Peter Joseph Lenné after 1840.

Jagdschloss Falkenlust★ (Hunting Palace Falkenlust)

⟨See Schloss Augustusburg. ⊚3.50€.

This captivating little two-story Rococo palace with its belvedere and lantern roof is designed in a perfectly symmetrical shape. It is just an easy stroll away from Augustusburg via the Schlosspark. Inside, the **Japan room★** with its lacquered paintings is among the most memorable. The staircase is covered with blue and white tiles up from floor to ceiling. Particularly remarkable is the small **mirrored room★**, a miniature masterpiece with its blue-edged panels and gilded carved frames.

Max Ernst Museum

Comesstraße 42.

⟨Open year-round, Tue–Sun 11am–6pm. ⟨Closed major public holidays. ⊚5€. ☎(02232) 579 31 10. www.maxernstmuseum.de.

Right behind Schloss Augustusburg, this new museum in a modern building is dedicated to Brühl-born Dadaist and Surrealist Max Ernst (1891–1976) and shows examples from all his phases of creativity.

Phantasialand★

Berggeiststraße 31–41.

⟨Open mid-Mar– Oct, daily 9am–6pm and select dates in winter. ⊚31€ (children 1m/3.28m–1.45m/4.7ft 27.50€; children up to 1m/3.28ft, free). ♿☎(02232) 362 00. www.phantasialand.de.

The sprawling amusement park offers thrill rides and attractions within seven themed areas. You can take a watery log flume ride, watch a Wild West stunt show or embark on a simulated space flight. Many adventures are geared toward small children, but there are also hair-raising thrill rides, including the Black Mamba roller coaster and the "Talocan Suspended Top Spin".

KONSTANZ★

CONSTANCE

POPULATION: 82 000

Probably founded by Roman emperor Constantius Chlorus (292–306), Konstanz (Constance) has an enviable location right on the shores of its namesake lake and a well-preserved Old Town made a lively and happening spot thanks to a large student population. It is also the gateway to the "flower island" of Mainau and charming Reichenau island with its ancient abbey.

- **Information:** Bahnhofplatz 13, 78462 Konstanz. ☏(07531) 13 30 30. www. konstanz.de.
- **Orient Yourself:** Bordering Switzerland, Konstanz sits at the point separating the lake proper (Bodensee in German) from its picturesque prolongation (Untersee). The islands of Mainau *(to the north)* and Reichenau *(to the west)* are linked to the town by a causeway.
- **Don't Miss:** The beautiful islands of Mainau and Reichenau.
- **Organizing Your Time:** Allow two hours to tour Mainau Island.
- **Especially for Kids:** Outdoor activities on Mainau and Reichenau Islands (*see Excursions*).
- **Also See:** BODENSEE, SALEM, SCHWARZWALD.

A Bit of History

Council of Constance – From 1414 to 1418, a council convened in Koblenz to resolve the Great Schism that had led to the simultaneous existence of three popes. The only conclave ever held north of the Alps concluded in 1417 with the election of Pope Martin V.

Two years earlier this same council had summoned before it the Bohemian religious reformer **Jan Hus**, rector of the University of Prague. Regarded as a threat to the Church's hold on power, his Reformist ideas were categorically rejected, Hus was declared a heretic and burned at the stake. A precursor of Protestantism, he was hailed as a national hero in his native Bohemia.

Sights

Lake Shore★ (Seeufer)

The easy-going, almost Italianate charm and ambience of Konstanz is particularly evident along its lakeside. Just beyond the boat dock *(near the tourist office)* is the **Konzilgebäude** (Council Building) a 14C warehouse where the Council of Constance convened in the 15C; it is now used as a concert and congress hall.

At the bottom of the jetty, the 10m/ 32.8ft-high **Imperia** is a slowly rotating monumental female sculpture created by artist Peter Lenk in 1993. It satirizes the influence the Italian courtesan Imperia wielded as the lover of members of the Council; she was immortalized by Honoré de Balzac in his novel *Ribald Tales (Contes drôlatiques)*.

Across the road, in the municipal gardens *(Stadtgarten)*, is a monument to Count Ferdinand von Zeppelin (1838–1917), the celebrated airship inventor. He was born in Constance on the Insel, a tiny island in the Stadtgarten and reached via a footbridge. Across the *Rheinbrücke* and along the *Rheinsteig* are the old **defensive towers** (*Rheintorturm, Pulverturm*). On the opposite bank, the Seestraße *(to the right)* is lined with Jugendstil villas.

The lake itself offers numerous opportunities for water sports, boating and excursions.

Münster★ (Minster)

Since its construction lasted from the 11C to the 17C, this former **cathedral** lacks any architectural unity. The **panels★** (*Türflügel*) of the porch doors in the main façade are decorated with bas-relief sculptures representing scenes

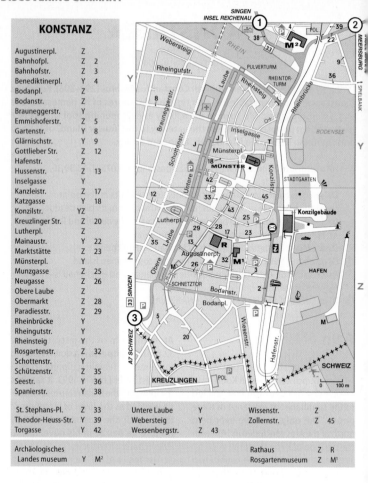

from the life of Christ (1470). The 13C
Mauritiuskapelle houses the minster's
most prized piece of sculpture, the **Holy
Tomb**★, a vaulted dodecagon containing three statuary groups. It is one of the
few examples of its kind from the High
Middle Ages, bearing a stylistic resemblance to the sculptures of Bamberg and
Naumburg.

In the crypt, four gilded 11C–13C plaques
represent Christ in Majesty, the Eagle of
St John, and St Conrad and St Pelagius,
patrons of the diocese. They are known
as the **Konstanzer Goldscheiben**
(gilded plaques of Constance). The
tower (○open Mon–Sat 10am–5pm,
Sun noon–5pm; ⊜2€) can be climbed
for sweeping city and lake views.

Rathaus (Town Hall)
The façade of this Renaissance building
is embellished with paintings illustrating
the history of Constance.

Archäologisches Landesmuseum (State Museum of Archeology)
Benediktinerplatz 5.
○*Open year-round, Tue–Sun, 10am–
6pm.* ○*Closed Jan 1, Dec 24, 25 & 31 Dec.*
⊜*3€, free 1st Sat of month.* ⬤⊜*(07531)
980 40. www.konstanz.alm-bw.de.*
This museum is housed in an old convent building of the Peterhausen Abbey.
History comes to life in 3 000sq m/
32 291sq ft of exhibition space, beginning with the buildings on stilts from
4000 BC and continuing to the recent
industrial past.

Address Book

⚓ *For coin ranges, see cover flap.*

WHERE TO STAY

⚐⚐⚐ **Buchner Hof** – *Buchnerstraße 6 (via Mainaustr.).* ☎(07531) 810 20. www.buchner-hof.de. *13 rooms.* In a quiet location, this little hideaway near the lake and the old town is run with a personal touch. Rooms are bright and cheerfully furnished in a pleasing palette of colors.

⚐⚐⚐⚐ **Hotel Barleben am See** – *Seestraße 15, 78464 Konstanz-Staad.* ☎(07531) 94 23 30. www.hotel-barleben. de. *8 rooms.* This 1872 villa turned boutique hotel draws lots of regulars to its lovely, personalized rooms. The location in the heart of parkland adjacent to the lakeside promenade boosts its appeal as a romantic getaway.

⚐⚐⚐⚐⚐ **Steigenberger Inselhotel** – *Auf der Insel 1.* ☎(07531) 12 50. www. konstanz.steigenberger.de. *102 rooms. Restaurant* ⚐⚐⚐⚐. Still boasting details of its former reincarnation as a monastery, this hotel envelops guests in a tasteful, upscale ambience that moves smoothly from the public areas to the rooms. Dine in the elegant restaurant or on the splendid terrace with lake views.

WHERE TO EAT

⚐⚐ **Konzil-Gaststätten** – *Hafenstraße 2.* ☎(07531) 212 21. Closed Dec 24-Feb 28. Housed in historic rooms with jaunty wooden ceilings, this restaurant is casual enough not to intimidate yet imbued with enough culinary creativity to keep foodies happy. Wherever possible, the chef uses fresh, organic and locally sourced ingredients.

Sea Life   Kids

HafenStraße 9.
🕐*Open May, Jun, mid-Sept–Oct, daily 10am–6pm; Jul–mid-Sept, 10am–7pm; Nov–Apr, Mon–Fri 10am–5pm, Sat–Sun 10am–6pm.* ⊛12.95€ child 9.50€. ☎(07 531) 12 82 70. www.sealifeeurope.com.
At this smallish aquarium you follow the flow of the Rhine from its source to the North Sea, encountering 3 700 aquatic creatures along the way. A 8m/24ft-long tunnel, where sharks, skates and turtles dart around you, is a highlight, as are touch pools where sea anemones and star fish welcome young visitors.

Excursions

Insel Mainau★★
(Mainau Island)   Kids

7km/4.3mi north. 🕐*Open sunrise–sunset. Oct–Mar* ⊛*14.90€ (child 7.50€); Mar– Nov* ⊛*6.50€ (child 3.20€).* ♿☎(07531) 30 30. www.mainau.de.
Friedrich I, the duke of Baden, quite literally sowed the seeds for this lavish garden island in 1853. Now owned by a Swedish aristocratic family, the Bernadottes, it is a lavish symphony of scent and color draped across 45ha/111 acres and one of the most popular destinations in the lake region. The palace, Baroque church and exotic and tropical flowers and plants contribute to the island's magic. The petting zoo, playground, pony rides and butterfly house are kids' magnets.

Insel Reichenau★
(Reichenau Island)

7km/4.3mi west.
Located in the Untersee, Reichenau traces its origins to 724 when St Pirmin founded the first Benedictine monastery in Germany on this petite Lake Constance island. For centuries, it was a renowned center of learning and arts. Reichenau monks were particlularly noted for producing outstanding illuminated manuscripts as well as brilliant frescoes during the Ottonian period. Thanks to its three ancient churches, Reichenau has enjoyed UNESCO World Heritage Site status since 2000. Note especially the 9C Carolingian church in Oberzell with its wall paintings from c. 1 000, and the Romanesque former abbey church in Mittelzell. Here, a wooden vaulted apse, a Gothic chancel and a 1477 altar with relics of St. Mark are among the treasures deserving closer inspection.

BAD KREUZNACH★

POPULATION: 44 000

Founded by the Romans, Bad Kreuznach is today celebrated both for the health-giving qualities of its mineral springs and for the equally refreshing wines of the Nahe region. The center of the thermal resort is on Badewörth Island, its downstream tip spanned by the Alte Nahebrücke.

- **Information:** Kurhausstraße 22–24, 55543 Bad Kreuznach. ☎(0671) 836 00 50. www.bad-kreuznach-tourist.de.
- ▶ **Orient Yourself:** Bad Kreuznach is in the Lower Nahe Valley, 15km/9.3mi from the Rhine, where the Nahe emerges from the Palatinate mountains to the north.
- **Don't Miss:** The Römerhalle.
- **Organizing Your Time:** Bad Kreuznach and surrounds can be toured in a day.
- **Also See:** IDAR-OBERSTEIN, WORMS, RÜDESHEIM, RHEINTAL.

Sights

Museen im Rittergut Bangert (Museums at Bangert Manor)
Hüffelsheimer Straße 11.
Open Jan, daily 10am–4pm; Mar–Jun & Sept–Dec, daily 10am–5pm; Jul–Aug, daily 10am–6pm. Closed Dec 24 & 31. 3.50€ each or 6€ combination ticket. ☎(0671) 920 78 77. www.museen-bad-kreuznach.de.

This large manor has roots in 1326 but the current Neoclassical structure only dates to the 18C. It is surrounded by lush gardens with a small lake, tropical trees and a museum.

Schlossparkmuseum
The former manor unites three collections under one roof: the **Pre- & Early History Collection** traces human evolution from the early Stone Age to the early Middle Ages and counts 1 000-year-old glass vessels among its prized possessions. The **local history exhibit** zeroes in on the discovery of the mineral springs and the town's subsequent development into a posh spa resort in the 19C. Finally, there is the **Art Collection**, which presents primarily sculpture created in the 19C and 20C by the local Cauer family.

Römerhalle and Römervilla★
This museum at the western end of the palace park features archeological findings unearthed in Bad Kreuznach and local environs. Exceptional exhibits include two 3C **mosaic floors**★★. One depicts the sea god Oceanus in his element. Even more epic is the Gladiator Mosaic, which shows wild animals and gladiators in combat; beneath is a Roman central heating system. Both mosaics were found during excavations at an adjacent Roman villa. Fragments of marble reliefs and painted walls are testament to the previous grandeur of this structure.

Excursion

Bad Münster am Stein-Ebernburg★
4.5km/3mi. Park near the Kurhaus, then 1hr round-trip walk.
Go into the **Kurpark**★ and walk through the gardens to the Nahe. On the far side of the river is **Rheingrafenstein**★★, an ancient castle draped across a 136m/446ft rock face.

▶ *Take the ferry across the Nahe and, from the Hüttental café-restaurant, climb to the panoramic platform.*

From here, there is a fine **view**★ of the Bad Münster basin and, downstream, the Rotenfels, whose sheer cliffs tower 214m/702ft above the river.

LAHNTAL

The winding course of the lower Lahn is characterized by wild scenery and steeply wooded banks. The valley makes a charming setting for excursions to a number of castles and the delightful historic towns of Weilburg and Limburg.

- **Information:** Brückenstraße 2, 35576 Wetzlar. ☎ (07000) 524 68 25. www.daslahntal.de.
- ▶ **Orient Yourself:** The Lahn valley cuts through the Taunus-Rhine massif and meanders through the forests of the Nassau Natural Park east of Koblenz.
- **Don't Miss:** The suggested driving tour, if you have a car.
- **Organizing Your Time:** Allow four hours for the driving tour.
- **Also See:** KOBLENZ, MARBURG.

Driving Tour

From Bad Ems to Wetzlar *89km/55.3mi*

Bad Ems

The Lahn valley, separating the Westerwald and the Taunus-Rhine massif, is rich in mineral springs. A flagstone bearing the date July 13, 1870, commemorates the Bad Ems meeting of Prussian King Wilhelm I and the French Ambassador to Prussia, Count Vincent de Benedetti, which precipitated the outbreak of the Franco-Prussian War of 1870–71.

Nassau

This health resort in the Lahn Valley was the cradle of the counts of Laurenburg, from whom Dutch royalty, including William of Orange, William III of England and the current Dutch royal family, are descended. Points of interest include the Adelsheimer Hof (Town Hall), the Stammburg (ancestral castle) and the Steinisches Schloss.

Kloster Arnstein

1km/0.6mi by a steep uphill road from the Obernhof bridge.
The Premonstratensian church bears one Romanesque chancel (west) and one Gothic (the east).

Balduinstein

These are the ruins of a 1320 castle of Baudouin of Luxembourg, a one-time archbishop of Trier. It was built to rival nearby **Schloss Schaumburg** (⊙*open*

Bad Ems

©Schaengel/Wikimedia Commons

May–Jun, Sat–Sun 10am–5pm; Jul–Aug, Tue–Sun 10am–5pm; ⊜2€; ☎(06432) 50 12 75; www.schloss-schaumburg.de), which has roots in the 9C but is now a Neo-Gothic pile reminiscent of castles in Scotland or Ireland.

Diez

Dominating this small town, the 17C **Schloss Oranienstein** is an early Baroque edifice that was the ancestral seat of the House of Nassau-Orange. It boasts stucco ornamentation by Castelli and Genone and ceiling frescoes by Jan van Dyck. In the 19C the palace served as barracks for Prussian cadets; today sections are used by the German army. Some rooms are taken up by the **Oranien-Nassau-Museum** (*visit by guided tour (1hr) only, Apr–Oct, Tue–Fri 9am, 10.30am, 2pm and 3.30pm, Sat–Sun 10.30am, 2pm and 3.30pm; Nov–Mar, Tue–Fri 9am, 10.30am, 2pm and 3.30pm; ⊜3€. ☎(06432) 940 16 66).* Tours take you inside the **Blue-Golden Hall** with its copper etchings and paintings. The Calvinist chapel is decorated with rich stucco ornamentation and frescoes.

Limburg an der Lahn★
See LIMBURG.

Burg Runkel★
The picturesque **setting**★★ of the castle, built into the rock face, and the ancient village below it can best be appreciated from the 15C bridge over the river.

Weilburg
Visit by guided tour (50min) only; Mar–Oct, Tue–Sun 10am–5pm (last tour 4pm); Nov–Feb, Tue–Sun 10am–4pm (last tour 3pm). Closed Jan 1, Dec 24–26 & 31. ⊜3.50€. ☎(06471) 22 36.
Weilburg is the former residence of the dukes of Nassau-Weilburg and later of the grand dukes of Luxemburg and almost completely encircled by the Lahn river. Its dominant feature is a 400m/312ft-long 16C Renaissance **castle** built on a rocky hillside. Thirty of its rooms are open for touring.

On Schlossplatz, the **Bergbau- und Stadtmuseum** (*Museum of Mining and City History;* open *Apr–Oct, Tue–Fri 10am–noon, 2pm–5pm, Sat–Sun 10am–5pm; Nov–Mar, Mon–Fri 10am–noon, 2pm–5pm; ⊜3€; ☎(06471) 37 94 47)* is devoted to the local mining industry. Kids especially enjoy exploring a 300m/984ft-long underground mine.

Braunfels
A small spa town, Braunfels is sprinkled with pretty half-timbered houses, especially around the Marktplatz. Approaching the village, the massive, heavily turreted **Schloss** (*castle;* visit by guided tour only, *Apr–Oct, daily 11am–5pm; Nov–Mar, Sat–Sun 11am–5pm; ⊜3€; ☎(06442) 50 02; www.schloss-braunfels. de)* looks as if plucked from the pages of a fairytale book. It has origins in the 13C but what you see today dates mostly to the 19C. Only the 15C tower, the Late Gothic hall and the early 18C kitchens are older. The perimeter wall encloses the entire village.

LANDSHUT★

POPULATION: 61 000

In an idyllic spot on the banks of the Isar, Landshut looks back on an illustrious history as the 13C ancestral seat of the House of Wittelsbach and later capital of Lower Bavaria. Its medieval center remains beautifully intact and provides the perfect backdrop for the "Landshuter Hochzeit" (Landshut Wedding), an elaborate festival staged by the townspeople every four years (next in 2009).

- **Information:** Altstadt 315, 84028 Landshut. ☎(0871) 92 20 50. www.landshut.de.
- ▶ **Orient Yourself:** Landshut is in the rolling countryside of the Isar, a tributary of the Danube, about 70km/43mi northeast of Munich.
- **P Parking:** Garages are located throughout the Altstadt, on Altstadtstr., Innere Münchener Str. and Bindergasse.
- **Don't Miss:** The Altstadt and St. Martinskirche.
- **Organizing Your Time:** Sights can easily be seen in one day.
- **Also See:** STRAUBING.

Sights

St. Martinskirche★ (Church of St. Martin)

Kirchgasse 232. ☎(0871) 922 17 80. www.st.martin-landshut.de.
Designed by Hans von Burghausen, this 14C–15C Gothic hall church is easily recognized by its **steeple**★★, which soars skyward for 131m/449.7ft and is considered the world's tallest brick construction. The church's three-nave interior with its nearly 30m/98.4ft-high net-vaulted ceiling is just as impressive and filled with artistic masterpieces. Most precious is the delicate *Virgin and Child* by Hans Leinberger (1518), although the

Triumphal Cross by Michael Erhard (1495) almost steals the show: at 8m/26ft high it is one of the largest crucifixes of the Late Gothic period and was carved from a single linden log.

Altstadt★

In Landshut, Altstadt does not refer to "old town" but to its main central artery, which is flanked by arcaded 15C and 16C buildings with a rich variety of gables. It was in the banquet hall of the triple-gabled Rathaus (Town Hall), that Ludwig and Hedwig held their wedding reception in 1475 (⟨see Infobox).

Address Book

⟨For coin ranges, see the Legend on the cover flap.

WHERE TO STAY

◔◔ **Gästehaus Elisabeth** – *Bernsteinstraße 40, 84032 Altdorf.* ☎(0871) 93 25 00. www.hotel-elisabeth-altdorf.de. 33 rooms. Restaurant ◔. This family-run property includes access to tennis courts and a sauna among its perks.

WHERE TO EAT

◔◔**Bernlochner** – *Ländtorstr. 3.* ☎(0871) 899 90. www.bernlochner.com. *Closed Sun.* This contemporary restaurant in the local theater serves modern, international cuisine.

TAKING A BREAK

Café Belstner – *Altstadt 295.* ☎(0871) 221 90. *Closed Sun.* www.cafe-belstner.de. Choose from a wide selection of homemade cakes, tarts and chocolates, or order a light lunch.

Princely marriage

Every four years, Landshut locals dress up in costume and re-enact with great pomp the marriage in 1475 of Georg, the son of Duke Ludwig the Rich, to Hedwig, daughter of the king of Poland. Don't miss it if you're in Bavaria in early summer 2009.

Stadtresidenz (Town Palace)
Altstadt 79.

Visit by guided tour (45min) only, Apr–Sept, Tue–Sun 9am–6pm; Oct–Mar, Tue–Sun 10am–4pm. Closed Jan 1, Shrove Tue, Dec 24, 25 & 31. 3€. (0871) 92 41 10.
Two main blocks linked by narrow wings comprise this charming palace (1536–43) arranged around an arcaded courtyard opposite the Town Hall. The **Deutscher Bau** (German building) faces the Altstadt (18C furniture, decorations, etc.); the 16C **Italienische Bau** (Italian

building) is considered the first Renaissance palace on German soil. Its most impressive room is the Italian Hall, with a coffered ceiling by Hans Bocksberger the Elder.

Burg Trausnitz
Visit by guided tour (45min) only, Apr–Sept, daily 9am–6pm; Oct–Mar 10am–4pm. 5€. (0871) 924 11 44. www.burg-trausnitz.de.
The fortress founded in 1204 was decorated during the Renaissance with fine arcaded galleries (1579). Interesting features include the chapel with its Early Gothic statuary and the Gothic hall known as the Alte Dürnitz. Note also the Jesters' Staircase *(Narrentreppe)*, painted in the 16C with scenes from the Commedia dell'Arte. Admission is also good for a spin around the **Kunst-und Wunderkammer**, which displays 750 exotic, bizarre, artistic and precious items collected by the local dukes.

LEIPZIG ★

POPULATION: 497 500

Leipzig has been renowned as a place of commerce since the Middle Ages, but the city can also be proud of its musical heritage. Bach, Wagner and Mendelssohn-Bartholdy all lived here, and its orchestras and musical institutions still enjoy a fine reputation throughout Europe. In the late 1980s, Leipzig was a leading center of the peaceful protests that led to the downfall of the socialist-led German Democratic Republic, paving the way for the reunification of the two Germanies in 1990 (see INTRODUCTION: History).

- **Information:** Richard-Wagner-Straße 1, 04109 Leipzig. (0341) 710 42 60. www.lts-leipzig.de.
- **Orient Yourself:** Leipzig is in the far west of Saxony, at the confluence of the Weiße Elster and Pleiße rivers.
- **Parking:** Garages are plentiful, especially near the main train station.
- **Don't Miss:** Bach Museum, St. Thomas Church and the Musical Instrument Museum; a concert at the Gewandhaus.
- **Organizing Your Time:** Allow a full day to explore Leipzig's musical and political heritage.
- **Also See:** HALLE, NAUMBURG.

A Bit of History

The Leipzig Fairs – The first mention of Leipzig was in the chronicle of Bishop Thietmar of Merseburg (975–1018), who noted the death of the Bishop of Meißen in "Urbs Lipzi". The township of "Lipzk" was granted a city charter around 1165, which was also roughly the year when it held its first trade fair. It is still held today, making it the oldest in the world.

City of Books and Music – One of the world's earliest books, the *Glossa Super Apocalipsim*, was printed in Leipzig in 1481. These days, Leipzig nurses its literary heritage with an annual book fair, Germany's second-largest after Frankfurt. It is also the location of several publishing houses, including Brockhaus and Insel Verlag. Leipzig also enjoys a fine reputation musically, thanks to the Choir of St. Thomas *(Thomanerchor)*, the Gewandhaus Orchestra, and the Mendelssohn-Bartholdy University of Music & Theater.

A prosperous city – The discovery in the 16C of silver in the Erzgebirge mountains ensured Leipzig's prosperity. Today the city is still an important economic center with corporate investors including Porsche and BMW.

J. Bouraly/MICHELIN

Statue of Leibniz, born in Leipzig in 1646.

Sights

Museum der Bildenden Künste★★ (Fine Arts Museum)

Katharinenstraße 10.
🕐*Open Tue, Thu–Sun 10am–6pm, Wed noon–8pm.* ⊛*5€.* ♿*☎(0341) 21 69 90. www.mdbk.de.*

One of Europe's most important art collections, with works from the Late Middle Ages to the present, moved to a modernistic, 34m/111.5ft-high glass cube in 2006.

Notable **German Old Masters** include works by Master Francke, Lucas Cranach the Elder and Hans Baldung Grien. **Flemish Old Masters** are represented by disciples of van Eyck and Rembrandt, van der Weyden, Frans Hals and van Ruisdael. **Italian Masters** include Conegliano, Francia and Tintoretto.

German 19C painters receive ample space, with works by Anton Graff, Tischbein, CD Friedrich, Spitzweg, Böcklin, Liebermann, Klinger and Leibl.

In the Sculpture Department there are works by, among others, Permoser, Thorvaldsen, Rodin and Klinger. The collection of prints and drawings offers a virtually unbroken survey of graphic art from medieval times to the present.

Museen im Grassi★

Johannisplatz 5–11.
www.grassimuseum.de.

The Grassi museum complex, one of Germany's cultural highlights, was built between 1925 and 1929 in the Expres-

Gewandhausorchester Leipzig

Many orchestras were founded as court orchestras, but not the Leipzig Gewandhaus Orchestra, which got its start in 1843 thanks to donations from wealthy burghers. The orchestra got its unusual name ("cloth-hall orchestra") because its first performance space in 1781 was in the converted Clothworkers' Guildhall. Famous composers and performers appeared here over the centuries, and Beethoven's *Triple Concerto*, Schubert's *Symphony in C major*, Mendelssohn's *"Scottish" Symphony*, and Brahms' *Violin Concerto in D major* all premiered here. In 1884, the orchestra finally got its own purpose-built concert hall. Bombed in 1944, it was rebuilt in modern fashion in 1981. Famous Gewandhaus directors have included Felix Mendelssohn-Bartholdy, Arthur Nikisch and Kurt Masur. Since 2005 it is helmed by Riccardo Chailly.

sionist style, with echoes of Art Deco, by architects Carl William Zweck and Hans Voigt. It recently emerged from an extensive renovation and shelters three museums organized around four inner courtyards.

Museum für Angewandte Kunst★ (Museum of Applied Arts)

Open year-round, Tue–Sun 10am–6pm. Closed Dec 24 & 31. 5€. (0341) 222 91 00.

This collection covers European arts and crafts from the Middle Ages to the early 20C. Exhibits include furniture (e.g., Nuremberg hall cabinet, 16C), porcelain (Meissen), glassware (Venetian, Bohemian), and valuable Jugendstil pieces (Gallé, Lalique).

Museum für Völkerkunde★ (Museum of Ethnography)

Open year-round, Tue–Sun 10am–6pm. Closed Dec 24 & 31. 4€. (0341) 973 19 00. www.mvl-grassimuseum.de.

One of the oldest and most important ethnographic museums in Europe, this institution explores the history and culture of the peoples of Asia, Africa, America and Oceania.

Museum für Musikinstrumente★ (Museum of Musical Instruments)

Open year-round, Tue–Sun 10am–6pm. Closed Dec 24 & 31. 4€. (0341) 973 07 50. www.mfm.uni-leipzig.de.

One of Europe's finest of its kind, this museum displays 5 000 instruments from five centuries and from around the world, as well as an interactive sound laboratory.

Völkerschlachtdenkmal (Battle of the Nations Monument)

Prager Straße.

Open Apr–Oct, daily 10am–6pm; Nov–Mar, 10am–4pm. Closed Jan 1, Dec 24, 25 & 31. 5€. (0341) 241 68 70. www.voelkerschlachtdenkmal.de.

This memorial commemorates the Allied victory over Napoleon in 1813. The 91m/298.5ft-high tower can be climbed (364 steps).

Zeitgeschichtliches Forum★ (Forum of Contemporary History)

Grimmaische Straße 6.

Open year-round, Tue–Fri 9am–6pm, Sat–Sun 10am–6pm. (0341) 222 20. www.hdg.de.

This modern and engaging museum chronicles the history of the GDR, the daily lives of its citizens and the peaceful movement that led to its downfall.

Deutsche Nationalbibliothek (German National Library)

Deutscher Platz 1.

Founded in 1912, this library stocks all known German language books, a collection currently comprising 14 million titles.

Arcades

Leipzig's glass-roofed arcades are remarkably well restored and now make an attractive setting for a great variety of shops, cafés and bars.

Mädlerpassage – *Opposite Naschmarkt*. This is the grandest and best known of the arcades, home to Auerbachs Keller, where Goethe set scenes in *Faust*.

Specks Hof – *Schuhmachergäßchen*. The restoration of this 1911 trade hall preserved its best old features while modernizing the whole.

Strohsack – This modern arcade links Nikolaistraße with Ritterstraße. Check the time on the glass-covered clock in the floor.

Steibs Hof – *Between Brühlstraße and Nikolaistraße*. This 1907 trade fair house appeals with its blue and white tiled courtyards.

Jägerhofpassage – *Between Hainstraße and Grosse Fleischergasse*. This 1914 Jugendstil arcade with ivory-tiled walls now houses a movie theater.

Address Book

For coin ranges, see the Legend on the cover flap.

WHERE TO STAY

Hotel Am Bayrischen Platz – *Paul-List-Straße 5. ☎(0341) 14 08 60. 32 rooms.* Karl Marx slept here in 1874, and if you wish you can bed down in the very room in this villa-style hotel. Others are rather small and less fancy but still tastefully furnished.

Hotel Michaelis – *Paul-Gruner-Straße 44. ☎(0341) 267 80. www.hotel. michaelis.de. 59 rooms. Restaurant , closed Sun.* Built in 1907 and now a listed building, this hotel has been renovated with an eye for detail. Rooms are harmonious, elegant and individually styled, while the restaurant is modern and tastefully decorated.

Hotel Fürstenhof – *Tröndlinring 8. ☎(0341) 14 00. www.starwoodhotels.com. 92 rooms. ⊡22€. Restaurant , closed Sun.* Behind the façade of this classic mansion (1770) awaits a luxuriously elegant interior. Service is impeccable and the Mediterranean-style spa complex an oasis of relaxation. Refined restaurant.

WHERE TO EAT

"Zill's Tunnel" Restaurant – *Barfußgässchen 9. ☎(0341) 960 20 78. www.zillstunnel.de.* This restaurant-cum-tavern has been doling out German and Saxon dishes since 1841.

Barthels Hof – *Hainstraße 1. ☎(0341) 14 13 10. www.barthels-hof.de.* At this carefully restored 18C restaurant you can match your mood to one of the three dining rooms: the elegant white-linen Webers Speisestube, the cross-vaulted Barthels wine tavern and the historical cellars. Two courtyards beckon in good weather. All in all, a fine establishment to sample classic Saxon cuisine.

Auerbachs Keller – Historische Weinstuben – *Grimmaische Straße 2 (Mädler-Passage). ☎(0341) 21 61 00. www.auerbachs-keller-leipzig.de. Closed Sun.* A Leipzig institution, this wine tavern and restaurant has been in business since 1525.

It was a favorite hangout of Goethe and reportedly provided inspiration for a scene from *Faust*. The cuisine is classic and traditional.

TAKING A BREAK

USEFUL TIPS

"Leipziger Lerchen" (Leipzig larks) are a local specialty found in all cake shops. The actual bird once contributed to the town's culinary reputation, but when the king of Saxony banned lark hunting in 1876, bakers transferred the name to a new pastry, made of shortbread and almond paste.

Kaffeehaus Riquet – *Schumachergässchen 1–3. ☎(0341) 961 00 00. www.riquethaus.de.* Easy to spot thanks to the two iron elephant heads flanking its entrance, this 1908 former trading house is now a classic Viennese coffee house.

Zum Arabischen Coffe Baum – *Kleine Fleischergasse 4. ☎(0341) 961 00 60. www.coffe-baum.de.* One of the oldest coffee houses in Europe, it has a café with terrace on the ground floor, a restaurant on the 1st floor, Arabian, Viennese- and Parisian-style cafés on the 2nd floor and a porcelain museum on the 3rd floor.

NIGHTLIFE

USEFUL TIPS

Lively bars cluster in the city center between the Brühl and the Neues Rathaus. The most animated lane is the Barfußgässchen in the pedestrian zone, which is chock-a-block with bars, restaurants and cafés. West of here, Gottschedstraße draws scores of night owls and students. For alternative flair, head south to Karl-Liebknecht-Straße, locally known as "Karli".

Gasthaus & Gosebrauerei Bayerischer Bahnhof – *Bayerischer Platz 1 (at Windmühlenstraße and Nürnberger Straße). ☎(0341) 124 57 60. www.bayerischer-bahnhof.de.* The traditional beer of Leipzig, Gose, is brewed in this former train station. In addition to the usual ingredients, it contains salt, lactic acid and coriander. Rustic setting, lovely self-serve beer garden and copious dishes.

Kümmel-Apotheke – *Grimmaische Straße 2–4 (in Mädlerpassage).* ☎*(0341) 960 87 05. www.kuemmel-apotheke.de.* Any time is a fine time to stop by this pleasant bistro. Order coffee, a light meal or a drink and watch the world on parade.

Vinothek 1770 – *Tröndlinring 8 (in the Fürstenhof hotel).* ☎*(0341) 140 33 33.* Gorbachev and Mick Jagger are among the famous folk who have sipped exquisite wines in this small bar at the Hotel Fürstenhof. More than 170 wines are available, many of them by the glass, along with cheese, antipasti and a few seasonal dishes.

PUBLICATIONS

The monthly calendar of events, *"Leipzig im…"* is available at the tourist office for 0.50€, while the monthly magazine *Prinz* can be bought at kiosks.

SHOPPING

USEFUL TIPS

Leipzig is a great place to shop. Many of the finest stores are in such glass-roofed arcades as the Mädlerpassage (AZ 24), Specks Hof (ABY 38), Strohsack (BY), Steibs Hof (BY 39) and Jägerhofpassage (AY). The biggest shopping mall is in the main train station.

Museum in der Runden Ecke (Stasi Museum)

Dittrichring 24.
◐*Open year-round, daily 10am–6pm.* ◑*Closed Jan 1, Dec 23–26 & 31.* ♿☎*(0341) 961 24 43. www.runde-ecke-leipzig.de.*
This contemporary exhibition reveals the methods used by the infamous East German Ministry for State Security, the *"Stasi,"* in the very quarters that once housed them.

Walking Tour

Old Town ★

The historic center of Leipzig, south of the impressive central station *(Hauptbahnhof)* with its huge shopping mall, is encircled by a ring road tracing the town's medieval fortifications.

Augustusplatz

This vast square is ringed by some of Leipzig's most important cultural institutions. The entire north side is taken up by the monumental opera house from the 1960s. Behind it is a pleasant park with a duck pond and a statue of Richard Wagner.
On the square's west end looms Leipzig's first skyscraper, the **Krochhaus** (1928–29), as well as Leipzig University. The most imposing building, though, is the **Neues Gewandhaus**, a concert hall inaugurated in 1981 and home of the

famous Gewandhausorchester. The massive auditorium has seats for up to 1 900 music fans. The bust of Beethoven (1902) in the foyer is a work by Leipzig-born Max Klinger.

▶ *Skirt the Neues Gewandhaus and turn into Schillerstraße. South of the university stands the **Leibniz monument**, a stone's throw from the Egyptian Museum.*

Ägyptisches Museum★ (Egyptian Museum)

Schillerstraße 6.
◐*Open year-round, Tue–Sat 1pm–5pm, Sun 10am–1pm.* ◑*Closed Jan 1, May 1, Dec 24 & 31.* ☎2€. ♿☎*(0341) 973 70 10. www.uni-leipzig.de/~egypt/.*
The 9 000 exhibits in this museum range from antiquity to the Christian era.

▶ *Continue west along Schillerstraße to the Neues Rathaus.*

Neues Rathaus (New Town Hall)

The 19C Town Hall was built on the foundations of Pleißenburg Castle, best known as the scene of a famous argument between Luther and Eck in 1519.

Thomaskirche★ (Church of St. Thomas)

First documented in 1212, this Late Gothic triple-aisle church took on its present appearance in the late 15C. **Johann Sebastian Bach** was cantor

It Started with Prayer Group on Mondays…

From 1982, Christians and non-Christians met at the Nikolaikirche every Monday to pray for peace. Members of the State Security (Stasi) began guarding the streets leading to the Nikolaikirche. Still a growing number attended, filling the 2 000-seat church to overflowing. Many were arrested following the prayer meetings, and tensions rose. After uniformed troops attacked unarmed civilians in Leipzig on October 7, 1989, people feared the worst: 1 000 members of the East German Socialist Unity Party (SED) had been summoned to the upcoming October 9 prayer meeting. But when the prayer meeting participants left the church, a crowd of at least 10 000 awaited them holding candles. The peaceful revolution worked; the Berlin Wall and East German regime collapsed the following month. "We were ready for anything," said an SED member, "But not for candles and prayers."

here for 27 years and is buried opposite the altar. The church is also renowned for the **St. Thomas boys' choir** (Thomanerchor) once directed by Bach. It performs Fridays at 6pm, Saturdays at 3pm (sacred choral music and Bach cantatas) and Sundays at 9.30am (main service).

Bachmuseum

Opposite the Thomaskirche,
Thomaskirchhof 16.
🕐*Closed until at least February 2009.*
Temporary exhibit next door 🕐*open daily*
11am–6pm. ♿☎*(0341) 913 72 00. www.*
bach-leipzig.de.
The museum occupies the 16C home of the Bose merchant family, who was good friends with Bach himself. Instruments, manuscripts and documents trace the life and legacy of the great composer,

with an emphasis on his years in Leipzig (1723–1750).

▶ *Head east on Thomasgasse.*

Altes Rathaus★ (Old Town Hall)

On Markt, this long, low building with its decorated façade and dwarf gables is a typical example of German Renaissance architecture. It was completed in 1556 after plans by architect and burgomaster Hieronymous Lotter. The tower features a balcony for town pipers or heralds. Today the building houses the local history museum, the **Stadtgeschichtliches Museum** (🕐*open year-round, Tue–Sun 10am–6pm;* 🕐*closed Dec 24, 25 & 31;* ⊚*4€;* ♿☎*(0341) 965 13 20; www.stadtgeschichtliches-museum-leipzig.de).*

Musicians in Leipzig

Johann Sebastian Bach worked and composed in Leipzig from 1723–1750 as cantor of St. Thomas and as music director for all the town's churches. Bach had faded into obscurity when **Felix Mendelssohn-Bartholdy** became director of the Gewandhaus orchestra in 1835. He turned Leipzig into a city of musical renown, established Germany's first musical conservatory and composed numerous original musical works. **Clara Wieck** and **Robert Schumann** lived in a Neoclassical house in Inselstraße 16, which now contains a memorial exhibit. The *Spring Symphony* was composed here.

Thomaskirche where Bach was cantor

J. Bouraly/MICHELIN

LEIPZIG

		Katharinenstr.	AY	18
		Klostergasse	AY	21
Am Hallisches Tor	AY 3	Kupfergasse	AZ	23
Böttchergäßchen	BY 5	Mädlerpassage	AZ	23
Grimmaische Str.	ABZ 13	Naschmarkt	AY	26
Grimmaischer Steinweg	BZ 12	Otto-Schill-Str.	AZ	27
Große Fleischergasse	AY 14	Preußergäßchen	AZ	29

Rastfreischulstr.	AZ	30
Reichsstr.	AY	31
Schloßgasse	AZ	33
Schuhmachergäßchen	ABY	34
Specks Hof	ABY	38
Steibs Hof	BY	39
Thomasgasse	BYZ	40

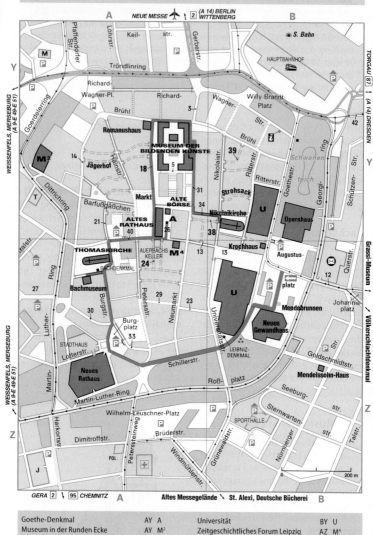

Goethe-Denkmal	AY A	Universität	BY U
Museum in der Runden Ecke	AY M²	Zeitgeschichtliches Forum Leipzig	AZ M⁴

Alte Börse★ (Old Exchange)

On the Naschmarkt.

This former commodity market (built 1678–87) was Leipzig's first Baroque edifice. Today it is a splendid venue for receptions, concerts and other events. The statue outside (Carl Seffner, 1903) shows Goethe as a student.

Katharinenstraße

North of the Alte Börse.

Of the Baroque houses on the west of Katharinenstraße, the finest is the **Romanushaus** *(at the Brühl)*, built in 1701 by Johann Gregor Fuchs. The neighboring houses *(nos 21 and 19)* were built in the mid-18C. The Fregehaus

Railway Station Renovation

Leipzig's main train station, which had deteriorated badly in spite of being Europe's largest railway terminus, was given a major facelift in the late 1990s and is now one of the most extravagant in Germany. Marrying the old with the new, the original 1915 building boast a 267m/876ft long by 32m/105ft wide hall, two entrance lobbies and incorporates an enormous shopping mall with more than 220 retail stores. Art is also prominently displayed, with Jean Tinguely's *Luminator* making a striking impression.

(no 11), also built by Fuchs, belonged to the wealthy banker Christian Gottlob Frege whose trade emporium stretched across Europe and to America.

▶ *Skirt Sachsenplatz and head back toward the Alte Börse via Reichsstraße passing the Fine Arts Museum on your right (see Sights, below).*

Nikolaikirche★
(Church of St. Nicholas)

Nikolaistraße.
🕐*Open year-round, daily 10am–6pm.*
☎*(0341) 960 5270.*
This 12C church played a key role in the peaceful revolution of 1989 *(see infobox)*. Dedicated to St. Nicholas, the patron saint of merchants, it was originally Romanesque in style but saw several Gothic modifications, including the 14C chancel and west towers and the 16C triple nave and central tower. Its impressive Neoclassical **interior**★, by Carl Dauthe, dates back to the late 18C. Pale, fluted pillars end in light green palm leaves, while the vaulting is coffered in rose with stucco flowers. 30 paintings hang in the narthex and chancel.

The Late Romanesque wooden crucifix in the chancel is believed to be the oldest work of art in town.

LEMGO★

POPULATION: 43 000

Lemgo was founded in the late 12C at the crossroads of two trading routes and surrounded in 1365 by a still extant town wall. Its Late Gothic and Renaissance town houses still testify to the prosperity of this former Hanseatic town.

▶ **Information:** Kramerstraße 1, 32657 Lemgo. ☎(05261) 988 70. www.lemgo.net.
▶ **Orient Yourself:** Lemgo is in rural eastern North Rhine-Westphalia, a short distance from the A2 (Hannover–Dortmund).
🕐 **Organizing Your Time:** Allow two hours for the Walking Tour.

Sights

Junkerhaus★

Hamelner Straße 36.
🕐*Open Apr–Oct, Tue–Sun 10am–5pm; Nov–Mar, Fri–Sun, 11am–5pm. ☎(05261) 21 32 76. www.junkerhaus.de.*
Karl Junker (1850–1912) was a painter, sculptor and architect with an eccentric streak, which explains the unusual design of his 1891 half-timbered home which he personally designed and crafted.

Organized around a spiral, it offers changing views from every perspective and is adorned with whimsical sculpture, carvings, imaginative furniture and other touches.

Witch-Hunting in Lemgo

During the Inquisition, death was the penalty for heresy and sorcery. Great waves of persecution ran through the country. The town of Lemgo became the focus of a "witch-hunt" by inquisitor J Sprenger. From 1564–1681, more than 200 women were persecuted as witches, most of them tortured to the point of false confessions.

The persecution finally came to an end when a young woman withstood the torture, was banished from the region and then sued her torturers before the Imperial supreme court.

Schloss Brake (Brake Palace)

Schloßstraße 18.

🕐*Open year-round, Tue–Sun 10am–6pm.*
🕐*Closed Jan 1, Dec 24, 25 & 31.* 🐾*3€.* ♿
☎*(05261) 945 00. www.wrm.lemgo.de.*
This mighty palace dates back to the 12C but was repeatedly tinkered with until the 19C, although its predominant style is Weser-Renaissance. Inside is the **Weserrenaissance-Museum**, which explores art and culture between the Reformation and the Thirty Years' War. Also stop by the palace chapel and climb up the seven-story tower to take in sweeping views over Lemgo.

Walking Tour

The Old Town★

▸ *Head east from the Ostertor gate toward Mittelstraße with its grand half-timbered houses. Note the fine façades of no 17 and no 36, the House of Planets (Planetenhaus).*

Rathaus★★ (Town Hall)

The Town Hall is a hodgepodge of eight joined buildings overlooking the market square. The elegant façade of the old apothecary's shop displays sculpted portraits of ten famous philosopher-physicians, from Aristotle to Paracelsus. Beneath the central arcades, witchcraft trials were held around 1670.

▸ *Bear left into Breite Straße.*

Hexenbürgermeisterhaus (Witch Hunter's House)

Breite Straße 19.

🕐*Open year-round, Tue–Sun 10am–5pm.*
☎*(05261) 21 32 76.*
This splendid 16C Weser-Renaissance building houses the **city museum** with exhibits on everyday culture, trade and witch-hunting. A creepy highlight is the collection of torture and execution instruments from the estate of an actual family of executioners.

Marienkirche (Church of St. Mary's)

A Renaissance 16C organ, among the oldest in German, adorns this triple-aisle Gothic church. Admire, too, the baptismal font (1592), the pulpit (1644) and the Triumphal Cross (c. 1500).

▸ *Backtrack to Papenstraße, then turn right.*

St. Nicolaikirche (Church of St. Nicholas)

Lemgo's oldest church (13C) is dedicated to the patron saint of merchants and combines Romanesque (three-figure tympanum), Gothic (frescoes) and Renaissance (pulpit) elements; it is often used as a concert venue.

▸ *Papenstraße leads back to the starting point.*

Excursions

Herford

20km/12.4mi west.

This former Hanseatic town between Teutoburger Wald and the Weser River sprouted around an 8C convent and has beautifully preserved half-timbered houses. The convent's Romanesque church, the **Münster** (1220–1280), is one of the oldest in Westphalia and sports a 16C Late Gothic baptismal font and Romanesque capitals. Nearby, the 14C **Johanniskirche** bears fine 17C **carvings**★, both sculpted and painted.

LIMBURG AN DER LAHN★

POPULATION: 34 000

The powerful yet elegant silhouette of the cathedral dominates the Limburg skyline. The town center consists largely of half-timbered houses dating from the 13C to the 18C.

- 🛈 **Information:** Hospitalstraße 2, 65549 Limburg. ☎(06431) 61 66. www.limburg.de.
- ▶ **Orient Yourself:** Bordering Hessen and Rheinland-Pfalz, Limburg is reached via the A3 linking the town to Wiesbaden and Frankfurt to the south and Koblenz to the north.
- **Don't Miss:** Limburg's cathedral.
- 🕔 **Organizing Your Time:** Allow about half a day to explore the town.
- **Also See:** WIESBADEN, LAHNTAL, KOBLENZ, FRANKFURT AM MAIN.

Dom★ (Cathedral)

Limburg's St. Georgsdom enjoys a picturesque **setting**★★ on a rocky spur and is especially noted for its striking architecture, which is a classic example of the Romanesque-Gothic transitional style. The exterior remains Romanesque and closely resembles the Rhineland Romanesque-style cathedrals (*see INTRODUCTION: Architecture*), but its interior is already Gothic. Look for Gothic hallmarks: galleries, arcades, a triforium and clerestory windows. Artistic highlights include the 13C stone rood screen and the frescoes in the nave. From the cemetery terrace is a good **view**★ of the Lahn river.

Staurothek Diözesanmuseum★

Domstraße 12.
🕔Open mid-Mar–mid-Nov, Tue–Sat 10am–1pm, 2pm–5pm, Sun 11am–5pm.

2€. ☎(06431) 29 54 82. www.stau rothek.de.

The 10C Byzantine reliquary cross known as the Limburger Staurothek is the jewel of the religious art collection displayed in this museum. The most precious exhibit, though, is the so-called 15C "Dernbacher Beweinung", a group of sculptures representing the lamentation over Christ's Passion and Death.

Sights

Old Town★ (Altstadt)

Take time to discover the beautiful old houses along Limburg's winding alleys and pretty squares, most notably Domplatz, Fischmarkt, Brückengasse, Römer, Rütsche and Bischofsplatz. Walderdorffer Hof (Fahrgasse) is an impressive Renaissance construction.

LINDAU IM BODENSEE★★

POPULATION: 24 000

Bavaria's westernmost town, Lindau's old town sits on an island in Lake Constance and exudes a casual, almost Mediterranean flair. Its lanes brim with fine gabled burghers' houses reflecting its past prosperity as a trading partner with Italy.

- **Information:** Ludwigstraße 68, opposite the train station, 88131 Lindau. ☎(08382) 26 00 30. www.lindau.de.
- ▶ **Orient Yourself:** Lindau is on the far eastern edge of Bodensee (Lake Constance). Ferries link the town to Konstanz and Bregenz (Austria) several times daily *(www.bsb-online.com).*
- **Don't Miss:** A stroll through the old town.
- **Organizing Your Time:** Allow one hour for a walking tour of the Old Town.
- **Also See:** BODENSEE, KONSTANZ, DEUTSCHE ALPENSTRASSE.

Walking Tour

Old Town★★

Marktplatz (Market Square)

A large circular fountain anchores Lindau's handsome market square, which is dominated by two churches. The Baroque **Haus zum Cavazzen**★, on the west side, houses the **town museum** *(Stadtmuseum;* ⊘*open year-round, Sun & Tue–Fri 11am–5pm, Sat 2pm–5pm;* ⊜*2.50€;* ☎*(08382) 775 65 14).*

- ▶ *Follow Maximilianstraße★★, the old town's picturesque main artery, then turn right into the Zeppelin straße.*

Schrannenplatz

The Brigands' Tower *(Diebsturm),* a well-known Lindau landmark, is part of the medieval fortifications. The nearby **Peterskirche**, the oldest church in town (AD 1 000), now serves as a war memorial. It is adorned with **frescoes** (15C) by Hans Holbein the Elder.

- ▶ *Backtrack on Zeppelinstraße toward the harbor.*

Hafen★ (Harbor)

Lindau's harbor is the departure point for trips on one of Lake Constance's pleasure boats. For **boat tours**, contact Bodensee-Schiffsbetriebe GmbH *(Schützingerweg 2;* ☎*(08382) 27584 10; www.bsb-online.com).*

Lindau harbor

©Gillet Luc/iStockphoto.com

Address Book

For coin ranges, see cover flap.

harbor channel are a major perk of the stylish restaurant.

WHERE TO STAY

Alte Post – *Fischergasse 3.* *(08382) 934 60. www.alte-post-lindau. de. 11 rooms. Restaurant*. This family-run hotel in the old town is attached to a rustic restaurant radiating old-world charm.

Hotel Lindauer Hof – *Seeprom- enade.* *(08382) 40 64. www.lindauer- hof.de. 30 rooms Restaurant*. This hotel is a winning marriage of history and modern sophistication and pleasantly close to the lake. Meals are served on the first floor or on the pretty terrace.

Hotel Bayerischer Hof – *Seepromenade.* *(08382) 91 50. www. bayerischerhof-lindau.de. 97 rooms. Restaurant*. Sporting a classical façade, this elegant hotel has plush yet traditional décor and flair. Views of the

WHERE TO EAT

Schachener Hof – *Schachener Straße 76, 88131 Lindau-Bad Schachen.* *(08382) 31 16. www.schachenerhof- lindau.de. Closed Jan, Tue–Wed.* The menu has few false notes at this well- run restaurant with bright and cheery ambience, carefully prepared regional and international dishes and competent service.

Hoyerberg Schlössle – *Hoy- erbergstraße 64 (on Hoyers hill), 88131 Lindau-Hoyren. Closed Feb.* *(08382) 252 95. www.hoyerbergschloessle.de. Reservations recommended.* Dream- ily located above the town, this little castle allows diners to dip into a pool of pleasurable gourmet fare while enjoy- ing sweeping views from the intimate dining rooms or the fabulous terrace.

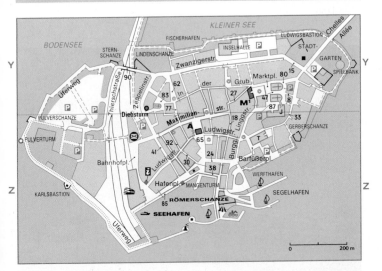

Altes Rathaus	Z A	Stadtmuseum	Y M¹

SCHLOSS LINDERHOF★★

Ludwig II's most whimsical palace is tucked deep into the forest in one of the most secluded valleys of the Ammergau Alps. Though not particularly large, it was the young king's favorite retreat and beautifully reflects his romantic fantasies.

▶ **Information:** ☏ (08822) 920 30. www.schlosslinderhof.de.
▶ **Orient Yourself:** Linderhof Palace is in the idyllic Ammer valley, about 13km/8mi southwest of Oberammergau.
🕐 **Organizing Your Time:** Allow half a day to visit the palace and its gardens; more in summer when lines may be long.
👓 **Also See:** DEUTSCHE ALPENSTRASSE, WIESKIRCHE, GARMISCH-PARTEN-KIRCHEN, SCHLOSS NEUSCHWANSTEIN.

Visit

Palace: 👣*Visit by guided tour only; Apr–Sept, daily 9am–6pm; Oct–Mar, 10am–4pm.* 🕐*Closed Jan 1, Shrove Tue, Dec 24, 25 & 31. Outbuildings closed Apr–Sept.* 🎟*Summer 7€, winter 6€.*

Schloss★★(Palace)

Ludwig II had this intimate palace built between 1874 and 1879 in a style blending Italian Renaissance and Baroque elements.

Drawing inspiration from his idol, French King Louis XIV, rooms reflect his extravagant tastes and fertile imagination. The lavish **state bedchamber** surpasses even the luxury of Versailles, while the dining room has a table that disappeared in the floor.

Park★★

The Italianate terraced gardens complement the landscape's natural slopes. Views from the **Temple of Venus** rotunda are especially enjoyable when the fountains are in action.

Do not miss the **Moorish Kiosk**, an exotic extravaganza of stained glass, feathers, painted wood and even an enamel throne. The **Venus Grotto** is just as lavish and features an artificial lake complete with waterfall and a shell-shaped boat that Ludwig was rowed around in by a servant.

Park designed by the architect Karl von Effner

F. Zaninotto/MICHELIN

LÜBECK★★★

POPULATION: 213 000

The "queen" of the Hanseatic League, Lübeck is a vivacious town that still retains much of its medieval character despite being badly damaged in World War II. In 1987, its entire Old Town was placed on the UNESCO World Heritage list. Its port, 20km/13mi north in Travemünde is one of the busiest on the Baltic Sea. Don't miss the marzipan herefis, one of the town's culinary specialties.

- **Information:** Holstentorplatz 1, 23552 Lübeck. ☎(01805) 88 22 33. www.luebeck-tourism.de.
- ▶ **Orient Yourself:** Lübeck is 60km/37mi northeast of Hamburg and reached via the A1 autobahn.
- **Parking:** Garages are plentiful in and around the Old Town.
- **Don't Miss:** A relaxed stroll through the Old Town.
- **Organizing Your Time:** Budget about a day to do this lovely town justice.
- **Also See:** WISMAR, HAMBURG.

A Bit of History

At the Head of the League – The 14C marked the peak of Lübeck's power as capital of the Hanseatic League. In the 16C, merchants and shipowners joined forces to revitalize the port by establishing relations with Holland and France. For a long time, Dutch architecture was the preferred style for the rich burghers on the banks of the Trave.

Walking Tour

Old Town★★★

Girdled with canals, crowned by belfries and towers, the old town of Lübeck is on a largely pedestrianized island. The nicest way to enter is through the **Holstentor**, a national symbol in Germany.

Holstentor★★(Holsten Gate)

This fortified gate was built between 1466 and 1478, before the construction of the city fortification, more as a matter of prestige than protection. Today it houses the **City History Museum** (*Stadtgeschichtliches Museum;* ◷open *Apr–Sept, Tue–Sun 10am–5pm; Oct–Mar, 10am–4pm;* ◷ *closed Dec 25, 26 & 31;* ☜*5€;* ☎*(0451) 122 41 29*).

▶ *Continue east of the gate via Holstenstraße to the Markt.*

Rathaus★ (Town Hall)

☞*Visit by guided tour only, year-round, Mon–Fri 11am, noon and 3pm.* ☎*(0451) 122 10 05)*

One of the most beautiful Town Halls in Germany, Lübeck's Rathaus flanks two sides of the Marktplatz. Construction began in 1250 and resulted in an elegant edifice in dark glazed brick and supported by a gallery of arcades. Note the high protective walls pierced with blind arcades. Pass beneath the arcades to see, on the Breite Straße, a stone staircase (1594) in Dutch Renaissance style.

Marienkirche★★ (Church of St. Mary)

The north side of Marktplatz is dominated by one of the finest red-brick Gothic churches in Germany. In the 17C, composer Dietrich Buxtehude

Rathaus at Lübeck

J. Bouraly/MICHELIN

Holstentor used to appear on the 50 Deutschmark note

was church organist here. The interior is audacious in design and grandiose in proportion. A fire in 1942 exposed the original 13C and 14C decoration.

▶ *Go through the arcade of the Chancellery (15C–16C) to Mengstraße.*

Buddenbrookhaus

Mengstraße 4.

🕐*Open Apr–Dec, daily 10am–6pm; Jan–Mar, 11am–5pm.* ⊕*5€.* ♿*☎(01805) 92 92 00. www.buddenbrookhaus.de.*

The name derives from Thomas Mann's 1901 novel *The Buddenbrooks*, which chronicles the decline of a patrician Lübeck family. No matter how attractive the concept, Heinrich and Thomas Mann were not born in the Buddenbrookhaus. However, it is true that in 1841 their grandfather Johann Siegmund Mann bought the 18C Baroque house, and the brothers were frequently guests there during their childhood and adolescence.

▶ *Follow Mengstraße to the Schabbelhaus, backtrack and turn left on Breite Straße.*

Haus der Schiffergesellschaft★ (House of the Seamen's Guild)

Breite Straße 2.

Behind the stepped Renaissance gable, awaits a handsomely decorated ancient seaman's tavern with rough wooden tables, copper lamps and model ships dangling from the beams. It is now a restaurant (*🕐see Address Book*).

Jakobikirche★ (Church of St. Jacob)

Opposite the Haus der Schiffergesellschaft.

The magnificent woodwork of the two organ **lofts**★★ (16C–17C) in this small Gothic hall-church is noteworthy. Larger than life-size representations of apostles and saints adorn the pillars of the central nave. The chapel north of the tower is now a memorial to the shipwrecked and displays a lifeboat from the *Pamir*, the full-rigged Lübeck ship lost with all hands aboard in 1957.

▶ *Follow the promenade to northern old town and the Burgtor gate.*

Burgtor★ (Castle Gate)

This fortified gateway defended the narrow isthmus, once the only land approach to Lübeck. The structure is a fine example of 13C–15C military architecture.

▶ *Head south on Große Burgstraße.*

Heiligen-Geist-Hospital★ (Hospice of the Holy Spirit)

Since the late 13C, the three turreted gables of this almshouse have stood above the Koberg. The chapel, a large Gothic hall embellished with 13C and

14C paintings, is just outside the even bigger Great Hall of the hospice.

Katharinenkirche★
(Church of St. Catherine)

🕐Open Apr–Sept, Tue–Sun 10am–5pm. ⚲1€. ♿☎(01805) 92 92 00. www.die-luebecker-museen.de.

Converted into a museum, the lower niches of the façade of this 14C church contain modern **statues**★, the first three on the left being by Ernst Barlach. As you enter, note on the right *The Resurrection of Lazarus* by Tintoretto.

The "Höfe und Gänge"

From St. Catherine's, turn left into the Glockengießerstraße with its open courtyards *(Höfe)*, set back from the street in typical Lübeck style. Note, successively, the delightful **Füchtingshof** *(no 25)* with its Baroque doorway; the **Glandorps-Gang**, a narrow alleyway, at no 41, and, from nos 49 to 51, the **Glandorps-Hof**. The building at no 21 is now the **Günter Grass-Haus** *(🕐open Jan–Mar, Tue–Sun 11am–5pm; Apr–Dec, daily 10am–5pm; ⚲5€; ♿☎(01805) 92 92 00; www.die-luebecker-museen.de),*

LÜBECK

		Holstenstr.	Y	36	Pferdemarkt	Y	59
		Hüxstr.	Y		Rehderbrücke	Y	61
Balauerfohr	Y	10	Klingenberg	Y		Rosengarten	Y	63
Beckergrube	Y		Kohlmarkt	Y	42	Sandstr.	Y	64
Breite Str.	Y		Königstr.	XY		Schlumacherstr.	Y	66
Fleischhauerstr.	Y		Langer Lohberg	X	48	Schmiedestr.	Y	67
Fünfhausen	Y	23	Marktpl.	Y	53	St. Annen-Str.	Z	65
Große Burgstr.	X	28	Mühlenstr.	Z		Tünkenhagen	Y	81
Große Petersgrube	Y	31	Mühlentorbrücke	Z	56	Wahmstr.	Y	

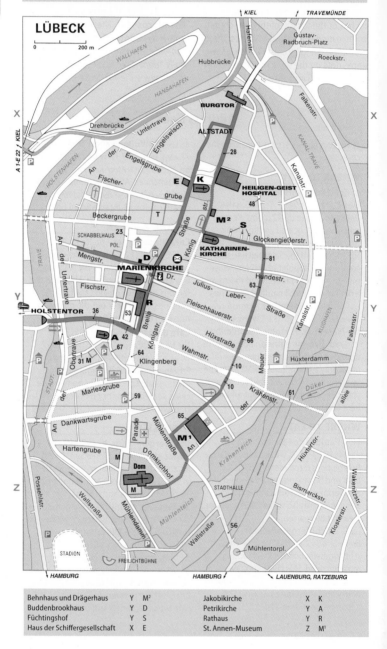

Behnhaus und Drägerhaus	Y	M²	Jakobikirche	X	K
Buddenbrookhaus	Y	D	Petrikirche	Y	A
Füchtingshof	Y	S	Rathaus	Y	R
Haus der Schiffergesellschaft	X	E	St. Annen-Museum	Z	M¹

with exhibits about the famed German contemporary writer and winner of the Nobel Prize for Literature in 1999.

▶ *Head south to the cathedral district.*

St. Annen-Museum★
St. Annen-Straße 15.
🕐*Open Apr–Sept, Tue–Sun 10am–5pm; Oct–Mar, 11am–4pm.* 🕐*Closed Dec 25, 26 & 31.* ☞*5€.* ☎*(0451) 122 41 37.* ☎*(01805) 92 92 00. www.die-luebecker-museen.de.*
Paintings and sculpture from Lübeck's churches are displayed in this museum alongside German modern art.

Dom
The 14C Gothic expansion transformed this Romanesque church. Inside are a monumental Late Gothic **Crucifix**★ by Bernt Notke and stone screen (early 14C) with a wooden tracery balustrade.

Excursions

Travemünde★
20km/12.4mi northeast.
This smart Baltic spa resort boasts a fine sandy beach, a 2.5km/1.5mi-long promenade and a casino. Ferries leave to Scandinavia and Estonia. In summer, it hosts **Travemünde Week**, an international yachting event. Explore the charming old town, with its half-timbered houses and the fishermen's church of St. Lorenz. The waterfront is lined with gabled houses from the 18C and 19C.

Ratzeburg★
23km/14.3mi southeast.
The island town of Ratzeburg is built in the middle of a **lake**★. The Schöne Aussicht viewpoint in Bäk on its east shore provides the best **view**★ of the town.

LÜNEBURG★★

POPULATION: 71 000

Lüneburg was quite literally built on salt, a coveted mineral and source of its prosperity since the 10C. The last salt mine closed in 1980, ending a 1 000-year tradition. Lüneburg was spared during World War II and today is a colorful university town and gateway to the Lüneburg Heath.

🛈 **Information:** Am Markt, 21335 Lüneburg. ☎(04131) 207 66 20. www.lueneburg.de.
▶ **Orient Yourself:** Lüneburg is about 56.5km/35mi southeast of Hamburg, east of the A7 autobahn (Hannover–Hamburg). Coming from Hamburg, though, the quickest route is via the A255 and A250. The Ilmenau river, a tributary of the Elbe, flows through town.
🅿 **Parking:** Garages are located near the main train station and the Rathaus on Graalwall.
👁 **Don't Miss:** The Rathaus and the rest of the old town.
🕐 **Organizing Your Time:** Exploring Lüneburg's charms takes about half a day.
👜 **Also See:** HAMBURG, LÜNEBURGER HEIDE.

Sights

Historisches Rathaus★★ (Historical Town Hall)
Am Markt 1.
👣*Visit by guided tour only, year-round, daily 10am, 11.30am, 1.30pm and 3pm.* 🕐*Closed Jan 1, Dec 24–26 & 31.* ☞*4.50€.* ☎*(04131) 30 92 30.*
Consisting of a cluster of eight buildings, Lüneburg's municipal headquarters is the largest surviving medieval Town Hall in northern Germany. The **Great Council Chamber**★★ *(Große Ratsstube)*, to the right of the entrance hall, is a Renaissance masterpiece (1566–84). Paneled throughout, it is adorned with intricate wood sculptures carved by Albert von Soest.
The **Fürstensaal** *(Princes' Apartment)* is equally striking. Gothic in style, it has lamps fashioned from stags' antlers

and a superbly beamed and painted ceiling.

Marktplatz (Market Square)

Aside from the Town Hall, other note-worthy buildings framing the market square include the Court of Justice, the former Ducal Palace and the **Heinrich-Heine-Haus**, where the parents of the famous 19C poet lived on the second floor.

Altstadt★ (Old Town)

The houses of the Old Town are char-acterized by traditional red brick archi-tecture and boast steeply stepped gables prevalent throughout northern Germany. The nicest ones line a long, narrow square known as **Am Sande★**. Note especially no 1, the 16C **Shwarze Haus**(Black House), which was once a brewery and now houses an interna-tional chamber of commerce.

At Große Bäckerstraße 10 you'll find the 1598 **Rathsapotheke** (pharmacy), with its fine twisted brick gables. The Reitende-Diener-Straße is another attractive lane with a double row of identical low houses, each embel-lished with medallions and curled brick cornices.

St. Johanniskirche (Church of St. John)

○Open mid-Mar–Dec, Mon–Thu 10am–5pm, Fri 10am–8pm, Sat 10am–6pm, Sun 11am–5pm. ○Closed Jan–mid-Mar, Mon–Thu. ☎(04131) 445 42. www.st-johanniskirche.de.

Am Sande culminates in this hulking 15C church, easily recognized by its leaning steeple. Inside all eyes are on the high altar with precious sculpted reredos by Heinrich Furnhoff. Its painted panels depict scenes from the lives of St. John the Baptist, St. Cecilia, St. Ursula and St. George (late 15C).

Nikolaikirche (Church of St. Nicholas)

Lüner Straße 15.

○Open Jan–Mar, daily 10am–5pm; Apr–Dec, 9am–5pm. ☎(04131) 243 0770.

The central nave of this triple-aisled 15C Gothic church soars an impressive 30/90ft high and ends in an intricate star-vaulted ceiling. Have a closer look at the gilded high altar by Hans Borne-mann, which depicts 20 carved scenes from the life of Jesus. There is also a bronze baptismal font dating back to 1325. The jaunty church steeple was not added until the 19C.

Address Book

ℰFor coin ranges, see the Legend on the cover flap.

WHERE TO STAY

⊜⊜ **Herz der Heide** – Ernst-August-Straße 7–9, 29614 Soltau. ☎(05191) 967 50. 14 rooms. This well-kept and reasonably quiet B&B with a garden is located in a residential district. Each room has its own character; some come with their own kitchenette.

⊜⊜⊜**Bargenturm** – Vor der Sülze 2. ☎(04131) 72 90. 40 rooms. Restaurant ⊜⊜⊜. Close to the pedestrian zone, this property exudes contemporary flair from the lobby to the rooms. The restaurant has a friendly, modern ambi-ence and a small inner courtyard.

⊜⊜⊜**Bergström** – Bei der Lüner Mühle. ☎(04131) 30 80. 125 rooms. ⊊15€. Restaurant ⊜⊜⊜. Hugging a particularly scenic stretch of the Ilmenau River, this hotel has tastefully appointed rooms and is well equipped with modern communication devices. Rooms in the ancient water tower are particularly appealing. The brasserie-style restaurant extends to a winter garden, and there is a wine bar as well.

WHERE TO EAT

⊜⊜**Zum Heidkrug** – Am Berge 5. ☎(04131) 241 60. www.zumheidkrug. de. Closed for 1 week in Jan, 1 week around Easter, 2 weeks in Jul/Aug and 1 week in Oct, Sun–Tue. This brick Gothic building was built in the 15C and now houses a comfortable, Michelin-starred, well-presented restaurant on two floors. Classic dishes show off the chef's considerable talent. Lunches are cheaper. A few country-style rooms are available as well.

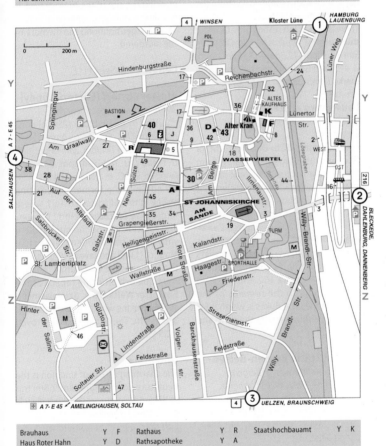

Wasserviertel★ (Old Port Quarter)

Enjoy a particularly fine view of this district from the bridge across the Ilmenau. On the left you will spot the *Alter Kran*, a crane dating from the 14C and in use until the 19C. Looking upstream, there is a good view of the *Lüner Mühle*, a grand 16C half-timbered mill.

Excursions

Kloster Lüne (Lüne Abbey)

2km/1.2mi via ① on the plan. Am Domänenhof. Visit by guided tour only (1hr), Apr–mid-Oct, Tue–Sun 10.30am (Sun 11.30am), 2.30pm and 3.30pm. 5€ (8€ with museum). ☎ (04131) 523 18. www.kloster-luene.de.

Founded in the 12C as a Benedictine convent, the complex welcomes you with a murmuring fountain surrounded by Gothic buildings on three sides and a Late Baroque guesthouse on the fourth. Particularly fine features include the stained glass windows from the 14C–17C, the frescoed refectory and the muraled nuns' cells. The church boasts a Baroque organ, a Gothic baptismal font and the nuns' choir with a *Lamentation* from the workshop of Lucas Cranach the Elder. There is also an interesting little tapestry **museum**★ (Open Apr–mid-Oct, Tue–Sun 10.30am–12.30am, 2.30pm–5pm; 4€) with Gothic tapestries and finely worked embroidery.

Lauenburg an der Elbe

25km/15.5mi north via ① (B209) on the plan.

Founded in the 13C by Duke Albrecht I of Saxony, Lauenburg grew wealthy from the salt trade because of being located at a strategic point where the ancient salt route from Lüneburg to Lübeck crossed the Elbe. Today it sits at the southern terminus of the Elbe-Lübeck Canal. At the foot of a steep, wooded slope is the lower town, whose narrow streets are lined with **half-timbered houses** built between the 16C and the 19C. A walk uphill to the remains of the palace of the local dukes is worth it for the sweeping views over the town and the river.

Gedenkstätte Bergen-Belsen

7km/4.3mi southwest of Bergen. Anne-Frank-Platz, 29303 Lohheide. Open Apr–Sept, daily 10am–6pm; Oct–Mar, 10am–5pm. Closed Jan 1, Dec 24–26 & 31. (05051) 475 90. www.bergenbelsen.de.

The **memorial** *(Gedenkstätte)* to the victims of Bergen-Belsen concentration camp was erected in 1946. The **Dokumentenhaus** (documentation center) near the entrance has a permanent exhibition chronicling the history of the camp and its victims. Bergen-Belsen started out as a POW camp but was turned into a concentration camp in 1943. After the war, it provided shelter and assistance to displaced persons fleeing to Germany from eastern Europe.

All in all, some 70 000 people were incarcerated here, including **Anne Frank** whose famous diary is a heart-wrenching personal account of the horrors of the Nazi period.

Along with her sister, she died at the camp in 1945 at age 15. There is a tombstone erected in their honor.

The **monument**, a 45min walk from the parking lot, is beyond the tumulus marking the site of the mass graves. It is a simple obelisk with inscriptions in 13 languages honoring the memory of the murdered.

Celle★★ – See CELLE.

Kloster Ebstorf (Ebstorf Abbey)

26km/16mi south of Lüneburg.

Visit by guided tour (75min) only, Apr–mid-Oct, Tue–Sat 10am–11am, 2pm–5pm, Sun 11.15am, 2pm–5pm; mid-Oct–end Oct, Tue–Sun 2pm. Closed Good Fri. 3€. (05822) 23 04.

Do not miss the former Benedictine abbey in the village of Ebstorf, where impressive features include the 14C and 15C cloister and the nuns' gallery with its life-size wooden statue of St. Maurice (1300) and several Virgins from the Romanesque and Gothic periods. A unique exhibit is the replica of the **Ebstorfer Weltkarte**★, a circular medieval map of the world with a diameter of 3.57m/11ft. The original was destroyed in 1943.

Undeloh★

The charming village of Undeloh is the departure point for the 4km/2.5mi trip to Wilsede, a nature reserve largely left untouched by civilization.
Cars are prohibited; horse-drawn service is available.

Kloster Wienhausen★
See CELLE: Excursions.

Wilseder Berg★

The highest elevation in the Lüneburg Heath rises to a modest 169m/554ft. From the top, a vast **panorama**★ of heath and woodlands unfolds. On clear days, you can even spot the spires of Hamburg's churches.

Denkmal Lönsstein

On the Wietzer Berg (mountain) in Oberohe area, 56.6km/35mi south of Lüneburg

This memorial stone is dedicated to the journalist and author, Hermann Löns (1866–1914), whose writing celebrated the people of the North German moors, especially **Lüneburger Heide★★**. His grave—**Das Hermann-Löns-Grab**—is to be found in the Tietlinger Wacholderhains near Walsrode.

Lüneburger Heide★★

38km/23.6mi west of Lüneberg.

This heathland region covers the area between Hannover, Hamburg and Bremen. It was on this heath that Germany finally surrendered to the Allied Forces on May 4, 1945.

Around the heath are many attractions, such as **Heidepark Soltau★** themepark, Serengeti Park Hodenhagen, the **Vogelpark Walsrode★**, and three wildlife parks, so it is a great area to visit with children. Spa There are also spa and health resorts and various accommodations in the vicinity *(go to www.lueneburger-heide.de and click on Übernachten).*

Vogelpark Walsrode★ Kids

Am Rieselbach, 29664 Walsrode.
Open Mar–Oct, daily 9am–7pm; Nov–Feb, 9am–6pm. 14€. (05161) 604 40. www.vogelpark-walsrode.de.

The Heath

In the Middle Ages, the name "Heide" signified the boundary of a village; only later did it come to mean the common heather *(Calluna vulgaris)*, which carpets the ground in August and September. The bell-heather *(Erica tetralix)* blooms in July, if rarely, preferring marshy areas.

The heath is actually a man-made shrubland. 5 000 years ago Lüneburg Heath was covered in forest which eventually was uprooted by farmers. To keep the forest at bay, farmers burned, grazed cattle and sheep or lifted the turf with hoes. Only then was the light-hungry heath able to spread.

Flora and Fauna – Juniper *(Juniperus communis)* thrives in the Lüneburg Heath as well, as do birch, mountain ash, pine and oak, gorse, broom, silver grass, crowberries, bilberries and cranberries.

Moorland sheep serve as living mowers. They maintain the heather at a height of 20cm/7.8in. Both genders have horns; those of the male are spectacularly coiled. There were one million moorland sheep on Lüneburg Heath around 1800, when it was much larger, but only a few thousand are left today.

Bees are also an intrinsic feature of the heath. They frequently come with traveling beekeepers who carry their swarms in baskets called "Lüneburg Bogenstülpern". The largest bird on the heath is the nearly extinct blackcock or capercaillie. There are plenty of buzzards, red kites, hobbies and kestrels, with herons and snipes in the lowlands and high moors. Fall sees flocks of fieldfares.

Boulders – Large and small granite boulders are scattered over Lüneburg Heath. They came from Scandinavia as boulder clay and were left behind when the glaciers of the last Ice Age retreated over 18 000 years ago.

Address Book

Kürzentrum Lüneburg – *Uelzener Straße 1–5, 21335 Lüneburg.* ☎*(041) 31 723 200. www.kurzentrum.de.*

Spa Spa treatments, saunas, physiotherapy and more relaxing treats are available here. There is also a "Kinderwelt" with childcare facilities and pools with waterslides.

Almost 4 000 feathered creatures live in this fun and family-friendly **bird park**, most of them in their natural habitat and at semi-liberty.

You can help feed playful penguins, walk through an exotic tropical jungle, visit owls in an abandoned castle and watch a bird show.

Wildpark Lüneburger Heide Kids

Am Wildpark, 21271 Nindorf-Hanstedt. ⏱*Open Mar–Oct, daily 8am–7pm (ticket office closes 5.30pm); Nov–Feb, 9am–4.30pm (ticket office closes 3.30pm).* ☞*8.50€ (child 6.50€).* ☎*(041) 84 89 39 0. www.wild-park.de.*

The whole family can enjoy a day at this wildlife park with animals including otters, buffalo, bears and birds of prey.

Heidepark Soltau Kids

Heidenhof, 29614 Soltau. ⏱*Open mid-Mar–Oct, daily 9am–6pm (Jul–Aug 8pm).* ☞*31.50€ (ages 12 and up); 24.50€ (4–11yrs); free under-4s.* ☎*(05191) 91 91 and (01805) 91 91 01. www2.heide-park.de.*

This small amusement park keeps kids entertained with dozens of rides and attractions centered around themes such as Little America. Thrills include roller-coasters, bird and dolphin shows and water log rides.

MAGDEBURG ★

POPULATION: 227 500

Magdeburg grew up on an important trade crossroads and was one of the key cities in the Middle Ages until the Thirty Years' War brought the glory years to an end. During World War II, Magdeburg was almost completely destroyed by fire bombing and in GDR days became a model city of socialist architecture. In 1990, it beat out Halle as capital of the federal state of Sachsen-Anhalt.

- **Information:** Ernst-Reuter-Allee 12, 39104 Magdeburg. ☎(0391) 540 49 00. www.magdeburg-tourist.de.
- ▶ **Orient Yourself:** Magdeburg is in the heart of Sachsen-Anhalt and served by the A2 (Berlin–Hannover) and A14 autobahns (Leipzig).
- P **Parking:** Garages are near the Johanniskirche and on the Elbuferpromenade.
- **Don't Miss:** A walk through the Old Town.
- Kids **Especially for Kids:** Elbauenpark.
- ⏱ **Organizing Your Time:** Magdeburg can be appreciated in one day.
- **Also See:** DESSAU, WÖRLITZER PARK.

A Bit of History

A steadfast merchant city – Magdeburg was founded by Emperor Otto I, who built his favorite palace here and raised the town to the status of archbishopric in 968. The early success of this commercial center, which declared its support for Martin Luther in 1524, was brought to an end in 1631 when imperial troops laid siege to the town before destroying it and killing most of its 20 000 inhabitants. Famous local figures include Baroque composer Georg Philipp Telemann (1681–1767).

Address Book

For coin ranges, see the Legend on the cover flap.

WHERE TO STAY

Hotel Bördehof – *Magdeburger Straße 42, 39179 Magdeburg-Ebendorf.* (039203) 515 10. www.boerdehof.de. *42 rooms.* Near the autobahn, this converted farmhouse has cheerful and modern rooms. Cap off a day on the tourist track with a relaxing session in the sauna or by watching the pretty birds fluttering around the onsite aviary.

Plaza Hotel – *Halberstädter Straße 146–150.* (0391) 605 10. www.12plaza.de. *104 rooms. Restaurant.* This hotel is on the outskirts of town and well served by public transport. Behind its modern, white façade await comfortable rooms tastefully decorated in English country style. The restaurant serves classic German food.

Residenz Joop – *Jean-Burger-Str. 16.* (0391) 626 20. www.residenzjoop.de. *25 rooms.* This villa hotel is in a quiet residential district. From 1903 until World War II it was the Swedish consulate. Rooms are spacious, comfortable and tastefully furnished.

Herrenkrug Parkhotel – *Herrenkrug 3.* (0391) 850 80. www.herrenkrug.de. *147 rooms.* A symbiosis of Jugendstil and modern accents characterize this delightful hotel in the middle of a park. Rooms are decked out in a pleasing palette of colors and ooze comfort and sophistication. See separate entry for the onsite restaurant Die Saison.

WHERE TO EAT

Die Saison – *Herrenkrug 3.* (0391) 850 87 30. www.herrenkrug.de. *Reservations recommended.* Flaunting playful retro-chic Jugendstil elements, this top-flight restaurant in the Herrenkrug Parkhotel is surrounded by a park designed by Peter Lenné. Dine on modern, seasonal cuisine in elegant rooms with high wooden ceilings and panoramic windows, or grab a table on the park-facing terrace.

NIGHTLIFE

Alex – *Ulrichplatz 2 (southeast of the roundabout btn. Ernst-Reuter-Allee and Otto-von-Guericke-Str.)* (0391) 59 74 90. www.alexgastro.de. This central hot spot for Madgeburg's young and young-at-heart bustles all day long. In the morning, crowds invade for the big breakfast buffet, at night for cocktails. It's a good place to watch the sun set over the Ulrichplatz fountain.

Le Frog – Brasserie am See – *Heinrich-Heine-Platz 1 (in the Rotehorn public park on the right bank of the Elbe).* (0391) 531 35 56. www.lefrog-md.de. This glass pavilion occupies a pretty lakeside spot in the sprawling Rotehorn park. Whether it's coffee and cake, a Mediterranean meal or a late-night cocktail, there's something for everyone here. If the weather permits, you can even quaff a cold one in the pleasant Biergarten.

Dom★★★ (Cathedral)

Open May–Sept, daily 10am–6pm; Apr & Oct, 10am–5pm; Nov–Mar, 10am–4pm. (0391) 541 04 26. www.magdeburgerdom.de.

Begun in 1209 and the burial site of Otto I, Magdeburg's Dom is considered the oldest Gothic house of worship in Germany and, at 120m/393.7ft long, is also one of the largest. The towers, though, were only completed in 1520. The light-flooded if rather austere interior is an artistic treasure trove. The most precious works are the famous Early Gothic sandstone sculptures of the Five Wise and Five Foolish Virgins (1250). Also of note are the intricately carved choir stalls (1363) and the emotional war memorial by 20C artist Ernst Barlach. Since 2005, the Dom has been juxtaposed by the **Grüne Zitadelle** (*Green Citadel;* *open year-round, daily 10am–6pm;* *guided tours (1hr) Mon–Fri 11am, 3pm and 5pm, Sat–Sun hourly 10am–5pm;* (0391) 620 96 55; www.gruene-zitadelle.de), a whimsical building by Swiss cult artist and architect Friedensreich Hundertwasser.

Since 1974 the Kloster Unser Lieben Frauen has been an art museum

M. Hertlein/MICHELIN

Sights

Old Town★

The historic center and cathedral of Magdeburg lie west of the Rver Elbe.

Kloster Unser Lieben Frauen★★ (Convent of Our Beloved Ladies)

Regierungstraße 4–6.
Open year-round, Tue–Sun 10am–5pm.
2€. (0391) 56 50 20. www.kunstmu-seum-magdeburg.de.

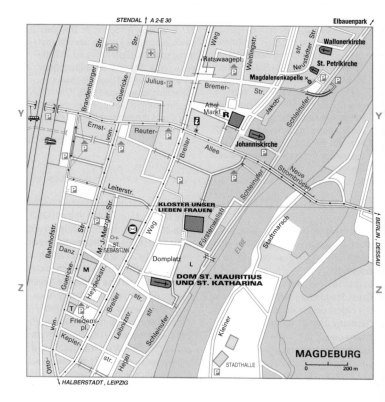

Magdeburg's oldest surviving building is a harmonious 12C Romanesque design convertd into a concert hall and an art museum.

On display are contemporary works by Giovanni Anselmo, Mario Merz, Siegfried Anzinger, Leiko Ikemura, Enrico Castellani and others, as well as a survey of sculpture from antiquity to the present.

Rathaus (Town Hall)

On Markt, outside the Italian Renaissance-style Town Hall, stands a gilded copy of the famous equestrian statue of the Magdeburg Knight (1240).

Johanniskirche
(Church of St. John)

◎Open Mar–Oct, daily 10am–6pm; Nov–Feb, 10am–5pm. ☎(0391) 593 45 48.

Magdeburg's oldest parish church (941), in which Martin Luther preached (see the memorial in front of the church), was all but destroyed during World War II. It

is now used as a venue for various events and exhibitions.

Elbauenpark★ Kids

Tessenowstraße 5a.

◎Open May–Sept, daily 9am–8pm; Mar–Apr 10am–6pm, Oct 9am–6pm, Nov–Feb 10am–4pm. ◎23€. ♿☎(0391) 59 34 50. www.elbauenpark.de.

This amusement park features 14 themed gardens, a butterfly house and numerous other attractions. A highlight is the conical **Jahrtausendturm**★★ (Millennium Tower), at 60m/196.8ft the world's tallest wooden tower. Inside, an exhibit traces 6 000 years of science and technology and includes lots of hands-on experiments. Kids also love the colorful **Spielhaus** (Playhouse), where they can let their imagination go wild. Other diversions incude schussing down a tobogganing track, tackling the 25m/82ft-high Angerfelsen climbing rock, and getting lost and found in a leafy labyrinth.

MAINZ★

POPULATION: 185 500

The capital of the federal state of Rheinland-Pfalz, Mainz is Germany's largest and most important wine market and birthplace of Johannes Gutenberg, the inventor of moveable type. Its historic center was nicely reconstructed after World War II and brims with handsome buildings housing atmospheric taverns.

- **Information:** Brückenturm am Rathaus, 55116 Mainz. ☎(06131) 28 62 10. www.info-mainz.de/tourist.
- ▶ **Orient Yourself:** Mainz is near the confluence of the Rhine and the Main, across the river from Wiesbaden and not far from Frankfurt. It is the eastern gateway to the Romantic Rhine wine region.
- P **Parking:** Garages are located throughout the city. Visit http://wap.parkinfo.com for fees and locations.
- **Don't Miss:** The Dom and Gutenberg Museum.
- **Organizing Your Time:** Allow up to a day to see Mainz's highlights.
- **Also See:** WIESBADEN, FRANKFURT AM MAIN, RHEINTAL.

Sights

Gutenberg-Museum★★★

Liebfrauenplatz 5.

◎Open year-round, Tue–Sat 9am–5pm, Sun 11am–3pm. ◎Closed public holidays. ◎5€. ♿☎(06131) 12 26 40.

The art of the printed word is revered in the Gutenberg Museum as in no other place. Exhibits trace the evolution of printing from the beginnings in Asia but focus primarily on the achievements of native son Johannes Gutenberg. The most prized items are two original **Gutenberg Bibles**★★★

(1452–55). Other interesting displays include incunabula and 16C–19C books, ancient presses and typesetting machines, and a section on modern book production and paper. Set up in the basement is Gutenberg's recreated work-shop, while at the **Druckladen** (printshop) you can learn how to print your own books using the ancient technology.

Römisch-Germanisches Zentralmuseum★ (Roman-Germanic Central Museum)

Ernst Ludwig Platz 2.
🕐*Open year-round, Tue–Sun 10am–6pm.* 🕐*Closed Jan 1, Shrove Tue, Easter Mon, Pentecost Mon, Dec 24, 25 & 31.*
☎*(06131) 912 40.*
http://web.rgzm.de.
In the former Electors' Palace (15C–17C), this rambling museum houses collec-tions on the pre-history of ancient Europe and the advanced Mediterranean civilizations, and Ancient Roman and early medieval archeology. Five original Roman ships discovered in the 1980s are displayed in the affiliated **Museum für Antike Schiffahrt** *(Museum of Ancient Shipping; Neutorstraße 2b; same hours).*

Landesmuseum Mainz★ (State Museum Mainz)

Große Bleiche 49–51.
🕐*Open year-round, Wed–Sun 10am–5pm, Tue 10am–8pm.* 🕐*Closed most public holidays.* 🎟3€, *free Sat.* ☎*(06131) 285 70.*
www.landesmuseum-mainz.rlp.de.
The Department of Antiquities traces the cultural history of the Rhineland from prehistory to the present. Of particular interest is the Steinhalle which houses some 300 stone memorials dating from the period of the Roman colonization of Germany, including **Jupitersäule** (Jupi-ter's Column). The museum's medieval and Baroque sections and its extensive collections of Höchst porcelain and Jugendstil glassware are also well worth seeing. The 20C Department houses the largest collection of works by Antoni Tàpies in Germany.

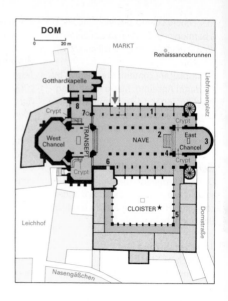

Walking Tour

Cathedral Quarter

▶ *From the Liebfrauenplatz, walk down Domstraße and turn left around the cathedral.*

Dom★★ (Cathedral)

Dedicated to Sts Martin and Stephen, Mainz' Romanesque cathedral is one of the most magnificent in Germany. There are lovely **views**★★ of its complex ridge roof and six towers from the Leichhof square. The adjoining square, the Höf-chen, segues into Gutenbergplatz on the south and Marktplatz to the northeast. The cathedral has a double choir linked by pillars affixed with **stone funeral monuments**★ honoring 44 of Mainz' 84 archbishops. In the second chapel **(1)** is a moving 15C tomb, and a multi-colored Gothic funerary monument is attached to one of the main pillars **(2)**. In the east crypt, beneath the chancel, is a modern **gold reliquary (3)** of the saints of Mainz. A pillar **(4)** in the east chancel bears another funerary monument sur-rounded by statuettes of St. Benedict, St. Catherine, St. Maurice and St. Clare. A door in the south aisle leads to the Gothic **cloister**★ *(Kreuzgang).* Besides the tombstones, note the bas-relief **(5)**

MAINZ

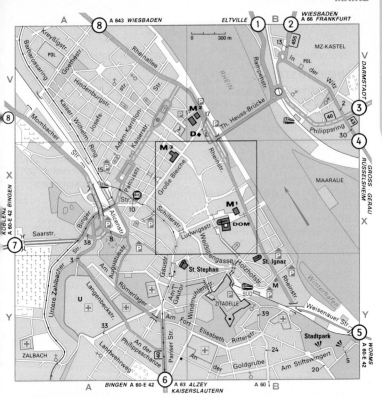

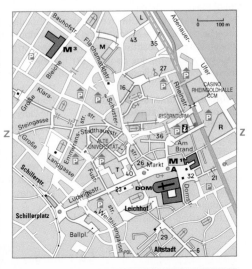

Address Book

🖢*For coin rangees, see cover flap.*

WHERE TO STAY

◖◗**Hammer** – *Bahnhofsplatz 6.*
☎*(06131) 96 52 80. Closed Dec 19-Jan4.*
40 rooms. Opposite the main train
station, this property offers modern
and functional rooms and ensures a
good night's sleep thanks to its thick,
soundproof windows.

◖◗◗ **Stiftswingert** –
Am Stiftswingert 4 ☎*(061 31) 98 26 40*
Fax (061 31) 9826450 www.hotel-
stiftswingert.de. 🄿 *30 rooms* ☷.
Well managed hotel with cherrywood
furnished guestroooms and modern
bathrooms and facilities.

WHERE TO EAT

◖◗**Weinhaus Schreiner** – *Rhein-*
straße 38 ☎*(061 31) 22 57 20. Closed 2*
weeks in July and Aug, Sun and bank

holidays. A typical local wine bar with
plain, rustic décor and lively atmosphere.
Seasonal dishes with a regional flavour
are on the menu.

◖◗◗**Geberts Weinstuben** –
Frauenlobstraße 94. ☎*(06131) 61 16*
19. Closed 2 weeks Jul, Mon, Sat lunch.
Patrons share laughs over a glass of
wine or earthy regional fare at this cozy,
family-run wine tavern founded in 1887.
Sit inside or in the wine-draped inner
courtyard.

◖◗◗**Maus im Mollers** –
Gutenbergplatz 7. ☎*(06131) 627 92 11.*
Closed Jul, Mon & Tue. Reservations
recommended. This contemporary
restaurant on the 6th floor of the
state theater near the cathedral offers
sweeping views, impeccable service
and cuisine that delivers modern takes
on classic dishes.

---

of the 14C master-singer Heinrich von
Meißen. Fine statues adorn the doorway
(6) of the former chapter-house *(Kapitelsaal)*, built in the 15C in an elegant
Rhineland style. In the opposite wing is
a fine 1328 pewter baptismal font **(7)**.
Beyond, a Romanesque doorway **(8)**
leads to the Gotthardkapelle.

Dom- und Diözesanmuseum & Domschatz (Cathedral Museum & Treasury)

🕘*Open year-round, Tue–Sun 10am–5pm.*
💶*3€ museum, 3.50€ treasury, 5€ com-*
bination ticket. ☎*(06131) 25 33 44. www.*
dommuseum-mainz.de.
Religious art spanning 2 000 years can
be admired at this museum accessed
via the cathedral cloister. The vaulted

rooms in the basement are an evocative backdrop for priceless Early Gothic
sculpture, including fragments from a
13C rood screen created by the Master of
Naumburg with scenes of the *Last Judgment.* On the upper floor, take in the fine
views of the cathedral roof before turning your attention to 60 paintings from
the Late Middle Ages onward. Works
from the workshop of Lucas Cranach
the Elder are among those deserving
closer examination.

The cathedral treasury is housed in
the St. Nicholas Chapel, accessed from
the west side of the cloister. It displays
precious liturgical objects from ten
centuries.

Gutenberg

Johannes Gutenberg (c. 1394–1468), the father of modern printing, is Mainz' most
famous son. After honing his skills in Strasbourg as a young man, he returned to
Mainz where he devised a groundbreaking printing technique using moveable
type. It allowed large volumes of books to be printed at low cost. Gutenberg did not
profit from his invention, however. Unable to repay his creditors, he died in poverty
in 1468.

Old Town

Ignazkirche
(Church of St. Ignatius)
Kapuzinerstraße 36.

Open year-round, daily 9am–6pm.
This church is the work of Johann Peter Jäger, built in 1763–75 and illustrating the transition from Rococo to Neoclassicism. Outside the church stands an imposing 16C group of the **Crucifixion**★ *(Kreuzigungsgruppe)* by Mainz artist Hans Backoffen (1519), who designed it as his own funerary monument.

Stephanskirche★
(Church of St. Stephen)
Kleine Weissgasse 12.

Open year-round, Mon–Sat 10am–5pm, Sun noon–5pm.
This late 13C church is the oldest Gothic hall church on the Middle Rhine. Though severely damaged in World War II, it has been beautifully rebuilt and is one of Mainz' must-see sights thanks to Marc Chagall's remarkable **stained-glass windows**★★. Created between 1978–85, they illustrate biblical themes such as the salvation history of the Israelites and the Crucifixion. There are a further 18 colorful windows by Charles Marq, a close friend of Chagall's.

▶ *Follow Maria-Ward-Straße. Along the Ballplatz and the Schillerplatz note the lavish mansions.*

Schillerplatz and Schillerstraße
The Baroque mansions in this square and street house the ministries of the state of Rheinland-Pfalz.
The fountain In the center of Schillerplatz is decorated with carnival scenes.

MANNHEIM

POPULATION: 308 400

Mannheim's city layout is a rarity among European towns: its center is essentially a chessboard of 142 identical blocks (Quadratstadt), each identified by a letter and a number. But it would be wrong to think this is a staid, inflexible city. Local enthusiasm for the arts is and always has been strong. It was at Mannheim's theater where many of Schiller's plays premiered back in the 18C.

- **Information:** Willy-Brandt-Platz 3, 68161 Mannheim. ☎(0621) 10 10 11. www.tourist-mannheim.de.
- **Orient Yourself:** 23km/14.3mi southeast of Worms, Mannheim sits at the confluence of the Rhine and the Neckar rivers.
- **Parking:** Lots and garages are located throughout the city. Visit http://wap. parkinfo.com for fees and locations.
- **Don't Miss:** The Fine Arts Museum, Reiss-Engelhorn-Museen
- **Organizing Your Time:** Plan two hours to view the Fine Arts Museum.
- **Also See:** HEIDELBERG, SPEYER, WORMS.

Sights

Kunsthalle Mannheim★★
(Fine Arts Museum)
Friedrichsplatz 4.

Open year-round, Tue–Sun 11am–6pm. Closed Carnival, Good Fri, May 1, first Tue in May, Dec 24 & 31. ∞2.10€. ☎(0621) 293 64 30. www.kunsthalle-mannheim.com.

In a 1907 Jugendstil building, this acclaimed art museum concentrates on works of the 19C and 20C. The exceptional **sculpture collection** includes works by Rodin, Lehmbruck, Barlach, Brancusi, Giacometti, Moore, Nam June Paik, Richard Long, Mario Merz and other heavy hitters. Another focus belongs to such crowd-pleasing **French Impressionists** as Manet, Monet and Cézanne. **German Secession** artists

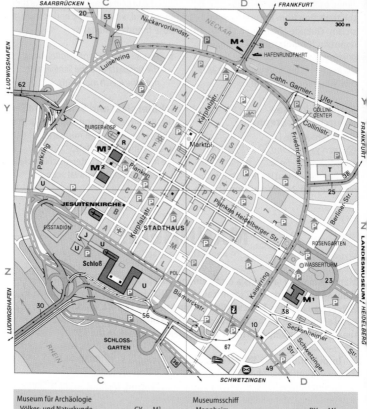

MANNHEIM			Kaiserring	DZ		Reichskanzler-		
			Konrad-Adenauer-			Müller-Str.	DZ	49
Bismarckpl.	DZ	10	Brücke	CZ	30	Schanzestr.	CY	53
Dalbergstr.	CY	15	Kurpfalzbrücke	DY	31	Schloßgartenstr.	CZ	56
Freherstr.	CY	20	Kurpfalzstr.	CDYZ		Seilerstr.	CY	61
Friedrichspl.	DZ	23	Moltkestr.	DZ	38	Spatzenbrücke	CY	62
Goethestr.	DY	25	Planken	CDYZ		Willy-Brandt-Pl.	DZ	67
Heidelberger Str.	DZ							

Museum für Archäologie			Museumsschiff		
Völker- und Naturkunde	CY	M³	Mannheim	DY	M⁴
Museum für Kunst-, Stadt- und			Städtische Kunsthalle	DZ	M¹
Theatergeschichte im Reiss-Museum	CY	M²			

are represented by Slevogt and Corinth, Beckman and Heckel are artists included among the **Expressionists**.

Reiss-Engelhorn Museen★★

🕐 *Open year-round, Tue–Sun 11am–6pm.*
🕐 *Closed Dec 24 & 31.* ✎*2.50€.* ☏*(0621) 293 31 51. www.rem-mannheim.de.*
This complex unites three separate museums. Housed in the former arsenal, the newly revamped **Museum im Zeughaus** takes you on a journey of discovery through the region's art and cultural history, theater and music history, natural history and international

photography in modern and playful yet substantive exhibits. There is an outstanding collection of **European porcelain and faience**★, with the highlight being a comprehensive display of Frankenthal porcelain from the Palatinate. The **local history collections** chronicle the development of the town.

The **Museum der Weltkulturen** (Museum of World Cultures) is in a modern cube by Carlfried Mutschler and Erwin Bechtold opposite the arsenal. Here the focus is on the archeology collections, which include important artifacts from the Paleolithic and Meso-

Address Book

For coin ranges, see cover flap.

WHERE TO STAY

Kurpfalzstuben – *L 14, 15* ☎*(0621) 150 39 20. www.kurpfalzstuben.de. 17 rooms. Restaurant* . This pretty turn-of-the-20C townhouse harbors a small hotel with contemporary and functional rooms. Those on the upper floors are more modern and brighter. The cozy restaurant serves Swabian specialties and exudes a convivial ambience thanks to warm décor and a historic tile oven.

Mack – *Mozartstraße 14* ☎*(0621) 124 20. www.hotelmack.de. 42 rooms.* Rooms at this welcoming property are spread among an Art Nouveau main building, a modern annex and an adjacent building. The well-kept, personalized rooms and a lavish breakfast buffet are among the assets likely to ensure a pleasant stay.

WHERE TO EAT

Henninger's Gutsschänke – *T6 28.* ☎*(0621) 149 12.* Earthy dishes paired with a side of local color are the name of the game at this woodsy wine tavern. **Doblers** – *Seckenheimer Straße 20.* ☎*(0621) 143 97. www.doblers. de. Closed Jan 1–10, Jun 24–Jul 8, Sun. Reservations recommended.* Chef Norbert Dobler's culinary lair is an inspired port of call where fresh, locally sourced ingredients are turned into creative classic and Mediterranean compositions.

Kopenhagen – *Friedrichsring 4.* ☎*(0621) 148 70. Closed Sun and holidays. Reservations recommended.* This culinary institution in the town center is often packed to the gills thanks to its excellent fresh fish dishes.

---

lithic eras, the Carolingian period, and from ancient Greece and Rome.

Schloss★ (Palace)

Bismarckstraße 1.

Open year-round, Tue–Sun 10am–5pm. 5€, including audio-guide. ☎*(0621) 292 28 91. www.schloss-mannheim.de.* Construction of this Baroque palace, the biggest in all of Germany (400 rooms, 2 000 windows), lasted from 1720 to 1760 and drew upon the talents of the period's finest artists, including Balthasar Neumann and Cosmas Damian Asam. Today, the building is largely used by the university but, following a recent restoration, the opulent living quarters are once again accessible to the public. Furniture, paintings, tapestries, porcelain and clocks are among the items reflecting the illustrious lifestyle of the prince-electors. A highlight on the ground floor is the Rococo library of Princess Elisabeth Augusta, which is the only room that has barely been altered.

Jesuitenkirche (Jesuit Church)

Open year-round, daily 9am–noon, 2pm–8pm. ☎*(0621) 12 70 90. www. jesuitenkirche.de.*

Built at the same time as the palace, this massive edifice is said to be the biggest Baroque church in southwest Germany. The façade, though, is Neoclassical.

Landesmuseum für Technik und Arbeit in Mannheim (Regional Museum for Technology & Labor)

Museumsstraße 1.

Open year-round, Tue, Thu-Fri 9am– 5pm, Wed 9am–8pm, Sat–Sun 10am– 6pm. Closed Good Fri, Dec 24, 25 & 31. 3€. ☎*(0621) 429 89. www.landes museum-mannheim.de.*

Two hundred and fifty years of industrial development in southwest Germany are retraced in this modernistic building, which impresses with the elegance, lightness and transparency of its architecture. The museum illustrates the effect of industrialization on people's lives. History is presented in a chronological spiral, from enlightened absolutism on the fifth floor to the 20C in the basement. Live demonstrations of historical machines and interactive stations complement the exhibits.

MARBURG★★

POPULATION: 78 000

Built on the side of a hill, this charming town was once a great pilgrimage center, with crowds drawn to venerate the relics of St. Elizabeth of Hungary. Since the Reformation, Marburg has become a center of Protestant scholarship and theology, largely due to its prestigious 16C university.

- **Information:** Pilgrimstein 26, 35037 Marburg. ☎(06421) 991 20. www.marburg.de.
- ▶ **Orient Yourself:** Marburg is on a rocky outcrop above the Lahn river and at the center of a triangle formed by Frankfurt, Kassel and Cologne.
- **Don't Miss:** Old Marburg walking tour, St. Elizabeth's Church.
- **Organizing Your Time:** Allow two to three hours for the sights.
- **Also See:** LAHNTAL, SAUERLAND.

A Bit of History

St. Elizabeth (1207–31) – Princess Elizabeth, daughter of the king of Hungary and intended bride of Landgrave Ludwig of Thuringia, was brought under the care of the Thuringian court to Wartburg Castle near Eisenach (see EISENACH) at the age of four. Early in her life she became known for her kindness toward the sick and unfortunate. She married Ludwig in 1221, but after he died of the plague in 1227 Elizabeth was heartbroken and withdrew to Marburg. Here she dedicated her life to helping the sick and the poor. She died, most likely of exhaustion or a disease, at the age of 24.

A place of pilgrimage – Elizabeth was canonized only four years after her death (1235). Her remains were exhumed the following year to be immortalized in the superb Gothic church built in her honor.

A steady stream of pilgrims flocked here to pay her respects and it became one of the largest centers of pilgrimage in Western Christianity.

Seat of the Reformation – In 1529 Elizabeth's descendant, **Philip the Magnanimous**, abolished the cult of relics and buried Elizabeth's remains in a local cemetery. Philip later invited Reformers Martin Luther and Hyldrych Zwingli to the famous "Marburg Religious Discussion" (1529).

Sights

Elisabethkirche★★ (Church of St. Elizabeth)
Open Apr–Sept, daily 9am–6pm; Oct 9am–5pm; Nov–Mar, 10am–4pm. Shrine: 2€. ☎(06421) 654 97. www.elisabethkirche.de.

The first truly Gothic church in Germany was built between 1235 and 1283. It is also considered the country's first hall church and is filled with important art treasures.

As you amble around, pay special attention to the following: **(1)** a statue of St. Elizabeth (c. 1470) wearing an elegant court gown, in the nave; **(2)** an openwork Gothic rood as well as a modern Crucifix by Ernst Barlach; **(3)** an altarpiece of the Pietà (1360); **(4)** the tomb of St. Elizabeth (after 1250); **(5)** the remains of 14C–15C frescoes in the niches; and **(6) St. Elizabeth's Shrine**★★ *(Elisabethschrein)* in the old sacristy. This masterpiece in gold was completed by craftsmen from the Rhineland c. 1250. Other highlights: **(7)** St. Elizabeth's Window assembled from 13C medallions; **(8)** a 1510 statue of St. Elizabeth personifying Charity by Ludwig Juppe; **(9)** *The Landgraves' Chancel*, the necropolis of the descendants of St. Elizabeth.

> ▶ *Leaving the church, climb up to the old town by way of the Steinweg—an unusual ramp with three levels. It continues as the Neustadt and then the Westergasse. Turn right into Marktgasse.*

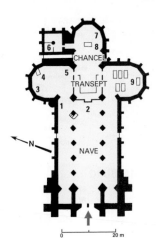

Marktplatz★ (Market Square)

The upper market *(Obermarkt)* is still framed by historic buildings. Particularly outstanding examples include nos 14 and 21, from 1560; no 23; and no 18, a stone house of 1323, the oldest preserved house still inhabited. The fountain, dedicated to St. George, is a popular meeting spot.

Rathaus (Town Hall)

Marburg's Town Hall is a 16C Gothic building much beloved for its mechanical rooster that crows reliably on the hour every hour. It sits in a lofty perch atop the Renaissance tower, which was added in 1581 by Eberhard Baldewein because the original building was considered too modest.

> ▶ *Nikolaistraße leads to the forecourt of the Marienkirche.*

Marienkirche (Church of St. Mary's)

This late 13C church sits adjacent to a Gothic former ossuary. From the terrace, there is a fine view over the roofs of the old town to the valley beyond. Past the church, you can glimpse the castle above. At the end of the esplanade, a passage leads down to the **Kugelkirche** *(end of the 15C;* ⊙*open year-round, daily 9am–6pm)*, a fine small church in the Late Gothic style.

> ▶ *Climb some more, this time to the top of the Kugelgasse. Before the Kalbstor fortified gate, turn right into Ritterstraße.*

Ritterstraße

The house at Ritterstraße 15 once belonged to legal historian Friedrich Karl von Savigny (1779–1861), one of the founders of the "historical school" of the study of law. He was also a key member of the group called "Marburg Romantics" that also included Clemens von Brentano, Achim and Bettina von Arnim and Jakob and Wilhelm Grimm.

Schloss★ (Palace)

⊙*Open Apr–Oct, Tue–Sun 10am–6pm; Nov–Mar, Tue–Sun 10am–4pm.* ⊙*Closed Jan 1, Dec 24, 25 & 31.* ⊛*3€.* ☎*(06421) 282 23 55. http://web.uni-marburg.de/ uni-museum.*

From the 13C to the 17C, the landgraves of Hessen resided in this hilltop castle,

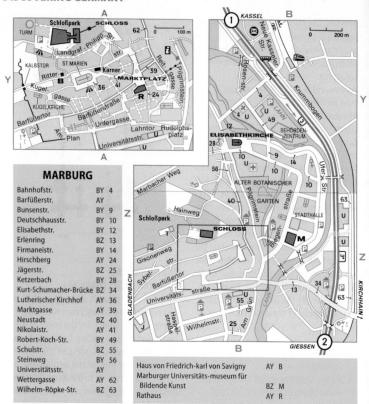

MARBURG

which treats you to sweeping views of the Lahn Valley from the terrace. Surviving buildings (13C–15C) include the Gothic Princes' Hall with its double nave, the west hall which reveals excavations of the previous fortress (9C and 11C), the south hall with its memorials of the founding of the university (1527) and of the religious debates that took place in Marburg in 1529, and finally the castle chapel with its medieval ceramic floor. After touring the historical palace rooms, proceed to the 15C Wilhelmsbau wing, which houses the **Universitätsmuseum für Kulturgeschichte**★ (University Museum of Cultural History). It has five floors of exhibits spanning the period from the Bronze Age to today. Of particular note are findings from a 5C Merovingian warriors' grave, Celtic coins, Romanesque crucifixes, fragments of stained glass from the St. Elisabethkirche, a 15C tapestry depicting the story of the Prodigal Son, and a collection of medieval shields and armor.

On the two top floors, the spotlight is on daily life in the 18C and 19C.
Assembled are a hodgepodge of glass, porcelain, doll houses and costumes as well as fully decked-out Biedermeier and Jugendstil period rooms.

Universitätsmuseum für Bildende Kunst (Fine Arts Museum)

Ernst-von-Hülsen-Haus, Blegenstraße 11 (next to the Stadthalle performance hall). ○*Open year-round, Tue–Sun 11am–1pm, 2pm–5pm.* ○*Closed Jan 1, Dec 24–25 & 31.* ☏ *(06421) 82 23 55. http://web.uni-marburg.de/uni-museum.*

Four centuries of paintings, graphics and sculpture grace the rooms of this museum. The collection is especially strong when it comes to Expressive Realists, which refers to art created by artists born in the first decade of the 20C. These include Ernst Hassebrauk, Joseph Mader, Willi Oltmanns und Alfred Wais.

KLOSTER MAULBRONN★★

One of the earliest Cistercian foundations in Germany, this enormous abbey remains well preserved with all its outbuildings inside a perimeter wall. The school established here in 1557 has seen the flowering of such diverse talents as Johannes Kepler, Friedrich Hölderlin, Justinus Kerner and Hermann Hesse. The abbey was added to the UNESCO World Heritage List in 1993.

- **Information:** ☎ (07043) 92 66 10. www.schloesser-und-gaerten.de.
- ▶ **Orient Yourself:** The abbey is in the heart of the Salzach valley, in a small, fortified medieval village, approached by a rampart walk.
- ⏱ **Organizing Your Time:** Allow two hours for your visit.
- 👝 **Also See:** BAD WIMPFEN, STUTTGART, KARLSRUHE.

A Bit of History

The Cistercians – This Benedictine order traces its name to the monastery of Cîteaux in Burgundy, France, which was founded by Robert of Molesmes in 1098. The order grew rapidly and by the 13C maintained 742 monasteries between Ireland and Syria.

In Germany, early foundations include the abbeys of Kamp in the Rhineland, Ebrach in Bavaria, Altenberg near Cologne and, well, Maulbronn.

Monasteries in Roman Catholic regions got Baroque makeovers in the 18C, while those in Protestant regions, such as Maulbronn, survived unaltered.

Visit

⏱ *Open Mar–Oct, 9am–5.30pm; Nov–Feb, Tue–Sun, 9.30am–5pm.* ⏱ *Closed 24, 25 and 31 Dec.* ⊛ *5€.*

Founded in 1147, Maulbronn is considered the most complete and best-preserved medieval monastery complex north of the Alps.

Surrounded by fortified walls, the main buildings were constructed between the 12C and 14C in transitional Romanesque-Gothic style. The structure was instrumental in paving the way for Gothic architecture throughout northern and central Europe.

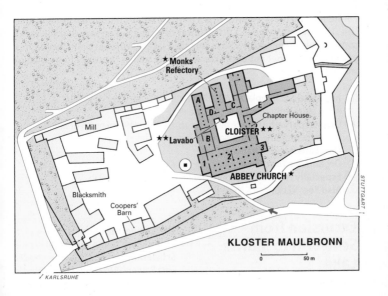

Scarlet Traces

The red crayon sketches on the vaulted ceilings of the monks' refectory are in fact the outlines of a fresco that was never painted. Jörg Ratgeb, the artist who sketched them, was captured and killed in 1526 for his role in the ill-fated Peasants' Revolt.

Abbey Church★

Consecrated in 1178, the church houses a 13C Paradise Porch (1), the first German example of the Romanesque-Gothic transition. Inside, a Romanesque rood screen (2) topped by a dog-tooth frieze divides the nave into separate sections for the monks and the lay brothers. A large Crucifix (1473), impressively sculpted from a single stone, stands before the screen. Note the richly carved choir stalls, made c. 1450, and the beautiful 14C **Virgin** (to the left of the high altar) (3), probably from the Cologne school.

Cloister★★

The west gallery leads to the **lay brothers' refectory (A)** (rebuilt 1869–70), and to the Romanesque **storeroom (B)**, now a lapidarium. The **monks' refectory**★, completed c. 1220–30 and perhaps the most impressive room in the complex, is flanked by the calefactory (C) and the kitchens (D).

Off the east gallery are the **chapterhouse** and **connecting building (E)**.

Monastery Buildings★

Behind the cloister stands a three-story Gothic palace. The picturesque **Faustturm** (Faust Tower), with its curved roof, dominates the southeast corner of the medieval fortifications. The famous Doctor Faust, who inspired Goethe, Wagner and many others, was supposedly summoned here in 1516 for alchemy experiments. Back in the monastery's main courtyard, the **museum** is housed in the Frühmesserhaus and on the first floor of the former cooperage (now an information center).

MECKLENBURGISCHE SEENPLATTE★★

Sprinkled with more than 1 000 lakes; the intensely rural Mecklenburg Lake District is also known as Land der Tausend Seen **(the land of the thousand lakes) Formed during the last Ice Age, it is a peaceful region, untouched by mass tourism. Time seems to move a little slower here, so plan on savoring the area's considerable charms slowly. Since only a few lakes have roads along their shores, you will need to get out of the car and onto a trail or the water to truly enjoy this area.**

- **Information:** Turnplatz 2, 17207 Röbel/Müritz. ☎(039931) 53 80. www.mecklenburgische-seenplatte.de.
- **Orient Yourself:** The lake district is about 80km/49.7mi north of Berlin and centers on the Müritz National Park.
- **Don't Miss:** Müritz National Park
- **Organizing Your Time:** Allow one full day for the suggested excursion.
- **Especially for Kids:** Outdoor activities at Müritz National Park.
- **Also See:** NEUBRANDENBURG.

Excursion from Schwerin to Müritz Lake

150km/94mi – allow one day.

The **Schweriner See** forms an idyllic backdrop to the provincial capital **Schwerin**★ and its castle. The novelist Fritz Reuter (1810–74), who was born in this region, found inspiration and solace

Address Book

For coin ranges, see the Legend on the cover flap.

WHERE TO STAY

Hotel Paulshöhe – *Falkenhäger Weg, 17192 Waren.* ☎ *(03991) 171 40. www.hotel-paulshoehe.de. 7 rooms, 7 bungalows. Restaurant.* In a pleasant location 200m from the Tiefwarensee lake you'll find lodging with all the mod-cons and a warm and well presented restaurant.

Hotel Seestern – *Müritzpromenade 12, 17207 Röbel.* ☎ *(039931) 580 30. Closed Jan–Feb. 29 rooms. Restaurant.* This hotel sits on a small tongue of land jutting into the lake. Ask for one of the bilevel rooms with superb views. The restaurant is in a welcoming annex and has a winter garden and a terrace.

Insel-Hotel – *An der Drehbrücke, 17213 Malchow.* ☎ *(039932) 86 00. www.inselhotel-malchow.de. 16 rooms.* This property in the old town, on the edge of a swinging bridge, has good-sized rooms with crisp, no-nonsense style; some have views of Malchow Lake.

Hotel Kleines Meer – *Alter Markt 7, 17192 Waren.* ☎ *(03991) 64 80. www.kleinesmeer.com. 30 rooms. Restaurant.* A central location near the harbor and friendly, modern rooms with a good range of communication devices, are among the assets of this hotel. The restaurant exudes contemporary flair and serves ambitious international cuisine.

on the peaceful wooded shores of **Krakower See**. Today, the lake is a paradise for bird-watchers.

The **Plauer See**, the third largest lake in Mecklenburg-Vorpommern, offers flat shores to the north and thick forest to the south. Together with the **Müritz**, it forms the heart of the Mecklenburg lake district.

Northeast of the lakes, **Mecklenburg's "Switzerland"** is a stretch of low mountains. The road leads through the town of **Malchin**, with its fine brick basilica, to the Kummerower See. To the west of the **Malchiner See** *(on the B108)* **Schlitz Castle** is set in a wonderful park.

The pearl of the district is **Müritz Lake** with **Waren** on its north shore being the main tourist center. In addition to the two parish churches of St. Georg and St. Maria, the old and new Town Halls and the Löwenapotheke (pharmacy) draw the eye. **Röbel** has a pretty marina with attractive boathouses. East of the lake, **Müritz Nationalpark**★ is the realm of hikers, cyclists and bird watchers. Keep an eye out for a rare osprey, the sea eagle *(near the fish pools at Boek)* and white storks *(near Kargow)*.

Lake Müritz with boathouses

©Dagmar Schneider/iStockphoto.com

MEISSEN

POPULATION: 28 500

Meissen is famous for its porcelain, distinguished by its logo showing a pair of crossed swords in blue. The heart of Germany's northernmost wine growing region, it also produces pleasantly fruity dry white wines. Meissen's historic center, which is remarkably well preserved, is dominated by the flamboyant Albrechtsburg and the cathedral.

- **Information:** Markt 3, 01662 Meissen. ☎(03521) 419 40. www.touristinfo-meissen.de.
- **Orient Yourself:** Meissen lies in the picturesque Elbe valley, near Dresden.
- **Don't Miss:** The Burgberg and the Porcelain Museum.
- **Organizing Your Time:** It takes about half a day to explore Meissen.
- **Also See:** DRESDEN.

A Bit of History

The porcelain of Saxony – It was in 1708, during the reign of Augustus the Strong, that **Johann Friedrich Böttger** (1682–1719) discovered the formula for creating the white hard-paste porcelain until then made only in China. It's based on kaolin (china clay), which is still mined near Meissen. In 1710 Augustus, Elector of Saxony and King of Poland, founded the Royal Saxon Porcelain Manufactory.

Sight

Porzellan-Museum★ (Porcelain Museum)

Talstraße 9. ⏱*Open May–Oct, daily 9am–6pm; Nov–Apr 9am–5pm.* ⏱*Closed Dec 24–26.* ⬤*8.50€.* ☎*(03521) 46 82 08. www.meissen.de.*

In 1865, the studios and workshops of the Meissen factory were transferred from the Albrechtsburg, where they had been for 150 years, to this site about 1km/0.6mi southwest of the town center. Start your visit by joining the guided tour of four **demonstration workshops★★**, where the processes of manufacturing, decorating and firing porcelain can be observed (*expect long lines*). This is followed by a spin around the **Schauhalle** (exhibition room), which displays the world's largest collection of Meissen porcelain from 1910 to today.

Walking Tour

Old Meissen

The old town has plenty of Gothic and Renaissance charm. **Marktplatz** is dominated by the Late Gothic **Rathaus** (Town Hall, 1470–86), the Bennohaus from the

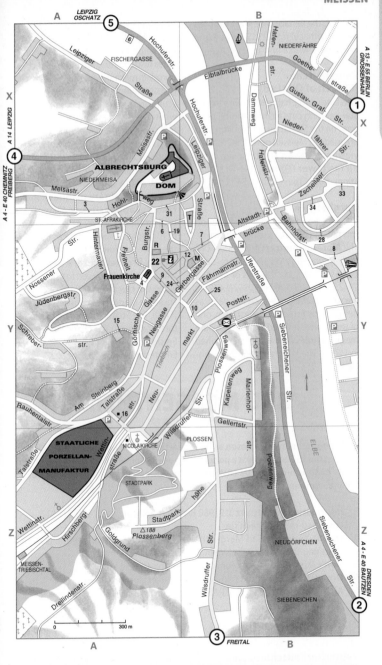

late 15C, the Renaissance **Marktapotheke** (pharmacy) from 1555–60, and the Hirschhaus with a fine 1642 doorway.

Frauenkirche (Church of Our Lady)

This Late Gothic hall-church with its fine star-vaulting cuts a commanding presence on the Marktplatz. Its carillon bells are made of Meissen porcelain. For nice views of the town and the river, climb up the **tower** (*open Apr–Oct, daily 10am–noon, 1pm–5pm; 2€*).

Burgberg★★

The castle and cathedral all cluster on this hill, the original site of the town. The **Albrechtsburg**★ (*open Mar–Oct, daily 10am–6pm; Nov–Feb, 10am–5pm; closed Jan 1, last 3 weeks of Jan, Dec 24, 25 & 31; 3.50€; (03521) 470 70; www.albrechtsburg-meissen.de*) was designed by Arnold von Westfalen, one of the most esteemed architects of late medieval times, who was commissioned in 1471 by the Margrave Albert. The fin-

ished work (1521–24) is one of the finest civic examples of the Late Gothic style. An exhibit on the ground floor illuminates historical and technical aspects of porcelain making, while the second floor boasts a stunning collection of medieval sculpture. Two rooms tell the story of when the castle was home to Europe's first porcelain manufactory.

Next door, the **Dom**★ is a Gothic hall church built from 1250 atop a Romanesque sanctuary but not completed until the late 15C. Early 16C sketches for bronze **funerary plaques**★ in the **Fürstenkapelle** (Dukes' Chapel) are said to be the work, at least partly, of Albrecht Dürer and Lucas Cranach the Elder. In front of the rood screen is the **Lay Brothers' Altar**★ (*Laienaltar*), which can also be traced to Cranach the Elder; the crucifix and the altar candlesticks are made from Meissen porcelain (1760). The **Stifterfiguren**★★ (Benefactors' Statues) in the chancel represent Emperor Otto I and his second wife, Empress Adelaide.

BAD MERGENTHEIM★

POPULATION: 22 300

Bad Mergentheim was chosen as headquarters for the Knights of the Teutonic Order in the 16C and today is a popular stop on the Romantic Road. It is celebrated for its historic old town, its castle and grounds and the healing qualities of its mineral springs.

- **Information:** Marktplatz 3, 97980 Bad Mergentheim. (07931) 571 31. www.bad-mergentheim.de.
- ▶ **Orient Yourself:** Bad Mergentheim is set among the forested hills of the charming Tauber valley between Würzburg and Rothenburg.
- **Don't Miss:** Castle & Museum of the Teutonic Order
- **Organizing Your Time:** Allow two hours to explore the town.
- **Also See:** ROMANTISCHE STRASSE, HOHENLOHER LAND.

Sights

Deutschordenschloss und Museum (Castle & Museum of the Teutonic Order)

Schloss 16.
Open Apr–Oct, Tue–Sun 10.30am–5pm; Nov–Mar, Tue–Sat 2pm–5pm, Sun 10.30am–5pm. 4.20€. (07931) 522 12. www.deutschordensmuseum.de.

This 12C castle was extended in the mid-16C to become the residence of the Teutonic Order and its Grand Master. The museum of the Teutonic Order occupies three floors and has an eclectic collection that ranges from historic dolls' houses to medieval sculpture and panel painting, faïences, alabaster and marble reliefs from the Renaissance and Baroque, as well as ivory carvings.

The Teutonic Order

The Teutonic Order was founded as a Germanic Hospitaller community in the Holy Land; it became a religious order in 1198 when the knights returned home after the fall of Jerusalem. They became princes of sizeable territories and estates, either by conquering them or by accepting them as gifts.

In 1525 the Grand Master of the order, Albrecht von Brandenburg-Ansbach, adopted Luther's teaching and suppressed the order's religious role. The community's territory of Prussia also became secular.

Dispossessed of its seat, the Teutonic Order elected as its new headquarters Schloss Mergentheim, which the order had controlled since 1219. The castle remained the Teutonic residence for three centuries. In 1809 Napoleon abolished the order.

Today it has reconstituted itself as a religious and charitable body and is headquartered in Vienna.

On the second floor, the **New State Rooms** take you through the audience chamber, the "State Bedroom" and the assembly hall *(Kapitelsaal)*. Exhibits on the third floor trace the history of the Teutonic Order.

Excursion

Stuppach
6km/3.7mi toward Schwäbisch Hall.
Open Mar–Apr, Tue–Sun 10am–5pm; May -Oct, Tue–Sun 9.30am–5.30pm; Nov, Tue–Sun 11am–4pm. 1.50€. (07931) 26 05.
The parish church of this village boasts the **Stuppacher Madonna**★★ (1519), considered one of the finest works of Matthias Grünewald. It forms the central panel of the celebrated altarpiece from the Chapel of Our Lady of the Snow in Aschaffenburg.

Deutschordenschloss

©Boardrx182/Wikimedia Commons

Address Book

For coin ranges, see cover flap.

WHERE TO STAY

Hotel Bundschu –
Milchlingstraße 24. (07931) 93 30. www.hotel-bundschu.de. 58 rooms. Restaurant , closed Mon.
This family-run hotel in a quiet residential district has attractive rooms with comfortable and modern furnishings. Mediterranean-style restaurant with garden terrace.

WHERE TO EAT

Zirbelstube –
Poststraße 2. (07931) 59 36 07. Closed Jan–mid-Feb, mid-Jul–Aug, Sun, holidays. Walls covered in dark pine and decorated with attractive paintings give this restaurant an air of elegance and comfort. The richly nuanced classical fare draws mostly upon regional ingredients.

MOSELTAL★★★
MOSELLE VALLEY

Scattered with picturesque villages and renowned for its wines, the Moselle Valley is an enchanting region best explored on a leisurely boat cruise. Castles, vineyards and romantic villages line both sides of the river.

- **Information:** Kordelweg 1, 54470 Bernkastel-Kues. ☎(06531) 973 30. www.mosellandtouristik.de.
- ▸ **Orient Yourself:** The peaceful Moselle River enters Germany near Trier and meanders to Koblenz where it flows into the Rhine.
- **Don't Miss:** Sampling the famous white wines, Bernkastel-Kues, Burg Eltz.
- **Organizing Your Time:** Allow at least one day for the suggested driving tour.
- **Also See:** EIFEL, IDAR-OBERSTEIN, RHEINTAL.

Driving Tour
From Trier to Koblenz
195km/121mi

Trier★★ – *See TRIER.*

Neumagen-Dhron
This town is known for its Roman discoveries, which can be admired at the Rhineland Museum in Trier. A copy of the famous stone-carved **wine ship** sits next to the chapel, opposite the Am Römerweinschiff café.

Bernkastel-Kues★
This double town straddles the Moselle about 50km/31mi east of Trier. Bernkastel is the prettier of the two towns with higgledy-piggledy half-timbered houses lining a warren of narrow, cobbled lanes. The nicest surround the **Markt★**, a

Cruise boat at Bernkastel-Kues

S. Ollivier/MICHELIN

small, sloping square centered on the 17C **Michaelsbrunnen** (St. Michael's fountain).

South of town, **Burg Landshut** (Landshut Castle) squats atop a rocky promontory. It was built in the 13C by the archbishops of Trier but has been in ruins since the 17C War of the Orléans Succession. From up here panoramic **views★★** take in a bend in the Moselle where even the steepest slopes are planted with vines.

The main draw of Kues across the river is the **St. Nikolaus-Hospital** *(chapel and cloisters ◷ open year-round, Sun–Fri 9am–6pm, Sat 9am–3pm; guided library tours Apr–Oct, Tue 10.30am, Fri 3pm; 4€; ☎(06531) 22 60; www.cusanus.de)*, a hospice founded in 1447 by humanist and theologian Nikolaus Cusanus. The number of lodgers was restricted to a symbolic 33—the age of Christ at his death—a tradition that is still respected to this day.

Admire the Late Gothic cloister, the chapel with its fine 15C reredos, and the bronze copy of the cardinal's tombstone (the original is in Rome, at San Pietro in Vincoli). Note the fresco depicting the *Last Judgement (to the left of the entrance)* and the **tombstone of Clara Cryftz**, the prelate's sister.

The **library** houses almost 400 manuscripts, in addition to astronomical instruments once used by Cusanus himself.

Finish your sightseeing with a wine tasting in the atmospheric cellars of the complex' **Vinothek**.

▶ *The road passes through typical wine-growing villages: Ürzig, Kröv, Enkirch and Pünderich among them. From Enkirch, make a 5km/3mi detour to Starkenburg. One magnificent vineyard follows another. Some 3km/1.8mi after the bridge at Zell, take the left turn toward Marienburg.*

Marienburg

The old convent here enjoyed an exceptional **setting**★★. From the restaurant terrace and the wooden "Prinzenkopf" look-out tower *(follow the trail; 45min round-trip)* there are impressive **views**★★ of the river and its environs.

Beilstein

This tiny fortified village is nicknamed "Sleeping Beauty of the Moselle" because of its compact shape and fairytale setting amid steeply sloping vineyards. A cluster of half-timbered houses huddles around a picturesque Marktplatz. Note especially the Zehnthaus, the church of St. Christopher and the 18C wine cellars. The village is lorded over by an enormous Baroque hall church (1635) and a romantically ruined castle. The latter is reached via a steep staircase *(30 min round-trip)* and will treat you to

sweeping views across the town and the meandering river valley.

Cochem

Cochem is presided over by the playfully turreted and pinnacled 11C **Reichsburg**★★ (*guided tours (40min) mid-Mar–Nov, daily 9am–5pm; 4.50€; (02671) 255; www.reichsburg-cochem. de*). Badly destroyed by French troops in the 17C, the castle was elaboratedly restored in the 19C and is one of the most celebrated sites in the region thanks to its spectacular setting atop a vine-clad hill.

Views are great from up here but even better from the **Pinner-Kreuz**★ hill, comfortably reached by **chairlift** (*open mid-Mar–Nov; 4.50€ one-way, 5.80€ round-trip; (02671) 98 90 65; www.cochemer-sesselbahn.de*).

Excursion

Burg Eltz★★

10km/6.2mi from Hatzenport, plus 15min walk or 5min by bus.
Guided tours (40min), mid-Mar–Oct, daily 9.30am–5.30pm. 8€. (02672) 95 05 00. www.burg-eltz.de.

Address Book

⚓For coin ranges, see the Legend on the cover flap.

CRUISES

Cruises run between Koblenz and Cochem. Departure Koblenz: May–mid-Jun, Fri–Mon 9.45am, mid-Jun–Sept, daily 9.45am, arrives Cochem 3pm. Departure Cochem: May–mid-Jun, Fri–Mon 3.40pm, mid-Jun–Sept daily 3.50pm, arrives Koblenz 8pm. No service Jun 11–19. ⚓24€ one way.
KD Deutsche Rheinschiffahrt
☎(0221) 208 83 18; www.k-d.com.

WHERE TO STAY

⚓**Wein- und Gästehaus Port** – *Weingartenstraße 57, 54470 Bernkastel-Kues. ☎(06531) 911 73. www.ferienweingut-port.de.* ⚓ *5 rooms, 4 aparements.* At this peaceful wine estate days start with a hearty breakfast in the winter garden and wrap up with a wine tasting, perhaps paired with a robust steak from the grill.

⚓⚓**Reichsschenke "Zum Ritter Götz"** – *Robert-Schuman-Straße 57, 54536 Kröv. ☎(06541) 816 60. www.reichsschenke.de. Closed 2 weeks in Feb and 3 weeks in Nov. 16 rooms. Restaurant* ⚓⚓. This historic inn has smart, uncluttered rooms and a woodsy low-ceilinged restaurant. The menu caters to all tastes with classic German fare, regional dishes and upscale French cuisine.

⚓⚓ **InterCity Hotel Hahn** – *At Hahn airport, Bldg 1380, 55483 Hahn. ☎(06543) 50 98 00. www.hahn.intercityhotel.com. 35 rooms.* ⚓9€. This hotel next to Hahn airport is convenient to travelers. Rooms are simple but well-equipped.

⚓⚓⚓**Hotel Bären** – *Schanzstraße 9, 54470 Bernkastel-Kues. ☎(06531) 95 04 40. www.hotel-baeren.de. Closed Nov–Mar Sun-Tue. 33 rooms. Restaurant* ⚓⚓. It's well worth spending a little extra for modern rooms with river-facing balconies at this family-owned hotel. The adjacent restaurant serves everything from snacks to rib-sticking meals.

This romantic 1 000-year-old **castle**★★ bristles with towers and turrets rising majestically from the thick forest at the far end of the Eltz Valley. Tours take you into fabulously decorated rooms with wooden and netvaulted ceilings, a bedroom with 15C frescoes, the splendid

Knights Hall and the still intact medieval kitchen. Tickets also give access to the **treasury**★, a feast of gold, silver, porcelain and fancy knick-knacks.

Koblenz★ – ⚓*see KOBLENZ.*

Cochem

©Anja Frost/istockphoto.com

MÜNCHEN★★★

MUNICH

POPULATION: 1 305 500

"Lederhosen and laptops" is the motto of Bavaria's vibrant and prosperous capital and it beautifully encapsulates the city's knack for blending tradition with innovation. Beer halls, gardens and Baroque churches, fantastic shopping, and world-class art and culture galore make it easy to fall in love with Munich.

Information: Bahnhofsplatz 2 & Marienplatz 8, 80335 München. ☎(089) 23 39 65 00. www.muenchen.de.

▸ **Orient Yourself:** Munich is the largest city in southern Germany and the third largest in Germany. Served by the A 9 (Berlin) and the A 8 (Salzburg) autobahns, it also has a huge and modern international airport.

Parking: Garages are located throughout this city. Visit http://wap.parkinfo.com for fees and locations.

Don't Miss: Pinakothek art museums, German Museum, English Garden, beer halls, Viktualienmarkt, Residenz, Marienplatz.

Organizing Your Time: You will want to spend at least two, preferably three or more days in this fascinating city.

Especially for Kids: German Museum, Museum of Human & Natural History, Hellabrunn Zoological Gardens, SeaLife Munich, Flugwerft Schleissheim

Also See: DEUTSCHE ALPENSTRASSE, ROMANTISCHE STRASSE.

A Bit of History

The Foundation of the Town – Munich's origins harken back to the 9C when a small village was established near a Benedictine abbey. The name München was derived from the German word for monk: *Mönch*. Ever since, the town's emblem has been a little monk *(Münchner Kindl)*. In 1158 Henry the Lion, Duke of Saxony, built a local bridge across the Isar River, forcing all traders to pass through Munich. This stratagem marked the beginning of the city's long and flourishing career as an economic power player.

The Rise of the Wittelsbachs – In 1180 Henry the Lion was stripped of his titles, banished from southern Germany and replaced with Count Otto von Wittelsbach. The House of Wittelsbach governed Bavaria without interruption until 1918.

The Kings of Bavaria – In 1806 Duke Max IV Joseph was promoted by Napoleon to King Maximilian I. His son, **Ludwig I** (1825–48), an enlightened and art-minded fellow, welcomed to his court

the best of Europe's architects and artists, eventually enriching Munich with the Alte Pinakothek, the university, the Glyptothek and the Propylaea. **Maximilian II** (1848–64) continued the artistic traditions of his father by founding the Bavarian National Museum in 1855.

In the history of the Wittelsbach dynasty, a special place must be reserved for **Ludwig II** (1864–86). This tormented romantic, a passionate admirer of Wagner, succeeded to the throne at the age of 18. Beloved by his subjects, he was a restless and emotional young man

"Simplicissimus"

A satirical literary journal created in Munich in 1896, *Simplicissimus* rapidly became famous throughout Germany for its caricatures and audacity. Writers such as Thomas Mann and Frank Wedekind took an active part in it, as did some avant-garde and Expressionist artists. In the 1930s, the Nazis took over this weekly publication and turned it into an instrument of propaganda. It disappeared, along with the Nazis, in 1945.

Address Book

🔖 *For coin ranges, see the Legend on the cover flap.*

BASIC INFORMATION

TELEPHONE PREFIX 089

VISITOR INFORMATION
Information points: *Bahnhofsplatz 2 (main train station); Neues Rathaus (Marienplatz 8).*

PUBLICATIONS

Several publications publish listings of current events. Check out the freebies *München im...* (followed by the month) and *In München* and the glossy for-purchase *Prinz*. Thursday *"SZ-extra"* supplement of the *Süddeutsche Zeitung"* newspaper also has listings.

TICKETS

Book tickets well in advance by phone, online or in person from the tourist offices or at commercial ticket vendors such www.muenchenticket.de and www.ticketbox.de.

POST OFFICES WITH LATE HOURS

Bahnhofsplatz 1, Mon–Fri 7.30am–8pm, Sat 9am–2pm; Postfiliale 24 at the airport (central area level 3) in McPaper, Mon–Sat 7.30am–9pm.

DAILY NEWSPAPERS

Süddeutsche Zeitung, Münchner Merkur.

INTERNET SITES

www.munich-online.de; www.munich-info.de; www.muenchen.de; www.munichfound.de; www.toytowngermany.com.

AIRPORT

☏ *(089) 975 00.* Munich International Airport, 34km/21mi north, is linked to the city by S-Bahn lines S1 and S8 *(departure every 20min from 3am to 12.30am, 8.80€)*, and by the Lufthansa Airport Bus *(departure every 20min from 5am to 9.40pm, 10€)*.

GETTING AROUND

Much of central Munich is a pedestrian and bicycle zone. Many sights are within walking distance; the city's main museums can be reached by tram from Karlsplatz. Munich's railway station *(Hauptbahnhof)*, a 10min walk from Marienplatz, is the main public transport hub.

Public Transport – Munich and its surroundings are divided into four ring-shaped price zones. The network consists of subways (U-Bahn), buses and trams (Straßenbahn), and light rail (S-Bahn). The main local transportation authority is **MVV** (Münchner Verkehrs-und Tarifverbund; ☏ (089) 41 42 43 44; www.mvv-muenchen.de). Information by phone, online or at the MVV office on the mezzanine level of the main train station, Mon–Sat 9am–6pm. Tickets are available from vending machines at any U-Bahn or S-Bahn rail station and in trams and from bus drivers. Single tickets must be stamped on the station platform or aboard buses and trams in order to be valid. The fine for riding without a valid ticket is 40€.

Tickets for the central zone (Münchner Innenraum), which includes Munich city center: Single tickets *(Einzelfahrt)* 2.20€; strip card *(Streifenkarte)* 10.50€ consists of 10 strips, stamp one strip for short trips, two strips for longer ones, can be used by more than one person and transfers are allowed. Single day tickets *(Single-Tageskarte)* 5€, and group day tickets for up to five people 9€, are valid from when they are stamped to 6am the following day. There is also a three-day ticket costing 12.30€ for one person, 21€ for up to five people.

CityTourCard – There are four versions: one-day single *(Single 1 Tag)* 9.80€, three-day single *(Single 3 Tage)* 18.80€, one-day "Partner" (for five adults—two children between 6 and 14 years old equal one adult) *(Partner 1 Tag)* 16€;

Nationaltheater

R. Cheret/MICHELIN

three-day "Partner" (Partner 3 Tage) 29€. The ticket entitles to unlimited use of public transportation in the city center and to discounts between 10% and 50% for about 30 sights, museums, castles, tourist attractions, city tours and bicycle hire. It is available from MVV offices, U-Bahn and S-Bahn tickets vending machines and in some hotels.

Bicycle rental – Munich is a very bicycle-friendly city. Radius Bike Tours (☎(089) 59 61 13; www.radiusmunich. com) rents bikes for 17€ per 24hr (50€ deposit) and also conducts bike and walking tours.

SIGHTSEEING

WALKING TOURS

The tourist office organizes tours with English-speaking guides for groups, on request (☎(089) 233 32 34). **Stattreisen** (☎(089) 54 40 42 30; www. stattreisen-muenchen.de) also offers dozens of themed walking tours (beer, architecture, via foot, tram or bike) in German. Regular guided tours in English are offered by **New Munich Tours** (www.newmunich.com), **Radius Tours** (see Bicycle Rental) and from **Munich Walk Tours** (☎(089) 24 23 17 67; www. munichwalktours.de).

BUS TOURS

SIGHTseeing Gray Line (Schützenstraße 9 ☎(089) 54 90 75 60, www. stadtrundfahrten-muenchen.de) – Hop-on, Hop-off Express Circle: Buses depart every 20 minutes and follow a 1hr loop taking in all major sights. You are free to get on and off as often as you wish. Tickets cost 13€ (child 7.50€). An extended route (Grand Circle) taking in Nymphenburg Palace and the Olympic Park is 19€. Buses depart from Bahnhofplatz (in front of Karstadt department store). Tickets available aboard.

FINDING YOUR WAY

The liveliest part of Munich is in the pedestrianized old town around Marienplatz and Karlsplatz (or "Stachus") via store-lined Neuhauser Straße and Kaufingerstraße. Elegant boutiques cluster in Maffeistraße, Pacellistraße, Maximilianstraße and Brienner Straße; antique dealers in Ottostraße near Maximilianplatz; art galleries under the arcades of Hofgartenstraße.

Schwabing, around Leopoldstraße, enjoyed its fame as the city's artistic and intellectual hub at the turn of the 20C and remains one of Germany's buzziest after-hours destinations.

REGIONAL SPECIALTIES

The most famous local specialties include the veal sausages known as Weißwurst, roast knuckle of pork (Schweinshaxe) and Leberkäs, a meat loaf. At beer festivals, a favorite offering is Steckerlfisch, which are small fish grilled on a skewer. Pretzels and white radishes (Radi) are often served with beer. And speaking of beer: Munich is Germany's beer capital. Five and a half million hectoliters (110 000 000 gal) of beer are brewed every year, most of it consumed in the beer halls and gardens (Biergarten) within Munich.

DATES FOR YOUR DIARY

Oktoberfest – The world's biggest public party is held on the Theresienwiese from mid-Sept to the first Sun in Oct. It originated in 1810 as part of the celebrations surrounding the marriage of Crown Prince Ludwig I of Bavaria to Princess Therese of Saxe-Hildburghausen. Each year, six or seven million locals and visitors flock to the huge beer halls and the thrill rides on the midway. The party kicks off on Sat with the Brewer's Parade, followed by the Costume Procession on Sun. But mostly Oktoberfest is about beer drinking: visitors consume around 7millon l/1 849gal of Wiesenbier, brewed especially for the event and delivered by horse-drawn drays. It is served in a 1l/0.2gal tankards called a Mass. For sustenance, revelers gorge on roast chicken and beef (two oxen are cooked on a spit each day). Hotels usually fill up, so book as early as a year in advance. If you show up during Oktoberfest, hope for cancellations but expect to pay top Euro.

Fasching – Carnival is celebrated with high spirits and much merriment and ends with the traditional market women's dance at the Viktualienmarkt.

Corpus Christi – The religious festival of Fronleichnam involves a procession of clergy, Roman Catholic personalities, Catholic student organizations and guild representatives through streets garlanded with young birch branches.

Other festivals – *Starkbierzeit* ("strong beer" festival) in March; *Auer Dult* (local festival) in late Apr/early May, late Jul and mid-Oct; *Tollwood Festival* (global music and theater) from late Jun to mid-Jul and in Nov; *Opernfestspiele* (opera festival) in Jul; and the *Christkindlmarkt* (Christmas market) in December.

All the cultural activities in Munich are listed in *Offizielles Monatsprogramm* (in German, 1.55€) and *Munich Found* (in English, 3€), both available from the tourist office.

WHERE TO STAY

◗◗ **Hotel Lutter** – *Eversbusch-straße 109, 80999 München-Allach.* ☎*(089) 812 70 04. www.hotel-lutter.com. Closed Dec 20–Jan 7. 28 rooms.* A very well-run, inexpensive hotel in the northwest of Munich. Rooms are functional and breakfast is served in a bright and charming winter garden.

◗◗◗ **Hotel Drei Löwen** – *Schiller-straße 8.* ☎*(089) 55 10 40. www.hotel 3loewen.de. 97 rooms. Restaurant*◗◗. This welcoming hotel near the main train station has bright, colorful and modern cozy rooms, whimsically decorated two-room suites and a wood-paneled lobby.

◗◗◗ **Hotel Platzl** – *Sparkassen-straße 10.* ☎*(089) 23 70 30. www. platzl.de. 167 rooms. Restaurants*◗◗ – ◗◗◗. Tradition marries modern comforts in this Bavarian-style hotel within staggering distance of the famous Hofbräuhaus and Munich's main historic sights. Dining options include the elegantly vaulted Pfister-mühle restaurant with its leafy terrace and the modern beer-hall-style Wirtshaus Ayinger.

◗◗◗ **Hotel Schlicker** – *Tal 8.* ☎*(089) 242 88 70. www.hotel-schlicker.de. Closed Dec 23–Jan 7. 69 rooms.* In the heart of the old quarter, this hotel in a 16C building offers personalized service and neat, well-kept and spotlessly clean rooms. Some have views of the new Town Hall with its world-famous carillon, but those in back are quieter.

◗◗◗ **Hotel Uhland** – *Uhlandstraße 1* ☎*(089) 54 33 50. www.hotel-uhland.de. 25 rooms.* Run by a multi-generational

family, this charming hotel is in a century-old Neo-Renaissance mansion on a quiet side street near the Oktober-fest grounds. It has rooms that suit all tastes, some with modern water beds, some with rustic furniture. Service is bend-over-backwards friendly.

◗◗◗ **Hotel Müller** – *Fliegenstraße 4* ☎*(089) 232 38 60. www.hotel-muel-ler-muenchen.de. Closed Dec 23–Jan 6. 44 rooms.* In a quiet spot in the happening Glockenbachviertel, steps from the historic center, this hotel includes such perks as free WiFi and a generous breakfast buffet in its room rates.

◗◗◗◗ **Hotel Bayerischer Hof** – *Promenadenplatz 2.* Spa ☎*(089) 212 00. www.bayerischerhof.de. 373 rooms.* ⌙*25.50€. Restaurant*◗◗◗. Hospitality doesn't get more luxurious than at this traditional grand hotel which has kept an illustrious guest list since 1841. The rooftop pool and spa offers the ultimate in relaxation with a view of the Frauenkirche.

◗◗◗◗ **Mandarin Oriental Hotel** – *Neuturmstraße 1.* ☎*(089) 29 09 80. www.mandarinoriental.com/munich 73 rooms.* ⌙*29€. Restaurant*◗◗◗. This ultra-posh boutique-sized contender counts smart rooms, personalized service, free minibar drinks and a rooftop pool among its assets. A marble staircase leads to the elegant Mark's restaurant serving classic-Mediterra-nean cuisine.

WHERE TO EAT

◗ **Dürnbräu** – *Dürnbräugasse 2.* ☎*(089) 22 21 95.* Oozing traditional Bavarian flair from every nook and cranny, this inn is a great spot for hearty meals and cool brews. Enjoy the terrace or court-yard garden in fine weather.

◗◗ **Bratwursthrezl** – *Dreifaltigkeit-splatz 1 (at Viktualienmarkt).* ☎*(089) 29 51 13. www.bratwursthrezl.de. Closed Sun.* This historical building has housed a sausage kitchen since 1901. The homemade sausages get their special smoky flavor from being grilled over beechwood.

◗◗ **Karawanserei** – *Pettenkofer-straße 1.* ☎*(089) 54 54 19 54. www. karawanserei-muenchen.de. Reserva-tions required.* No need to ride a camel through the desert to enjoy a fine meal

Arzmiller café and confectioner's

at this exotically decorated Persian restaurant in a little palace in the city center. The menu includes plenty of vegetarian options.

⊜⊜⊜**Bogenhauser Hof** – *Ismaninger Straße 85. ☎(089) 98 55 86. www. bogen-hauser-hof.de. Closed Dec 24–Jan 8, Sun and public holidays.* This former 19C hunting lodge is now a modern gourmet restaurant with inspired, seasonal cuisine. The idyllic summer garden is ideal for lounging over leisurely dinners on balmy summer nights.

⊜⊜⊜**Käfer Schänke** – *Prinzregentenstraße 73. ☎(089) 416 82 47. www.feinkost-kaefer.de. Closed Sun and public holidays.* This fine-food emporium blends a delicatessen shop, a catering service and a pleasant warren of a restaurant with stylish but relaxed décor. The globally inspired menu is likely to contain a favorite for everyone.

⊜⊜⊜**Lenbach** – *Ottostraße 6 ☎(089) 549 13 00. www.lenbach.de. Closed Sun. Reservations necessary.* Conceived by star designer Sir Terence Conran, this trendy restaurant's décor was inspired by the Seven Deadly Sins but the creative, contemporary food is considerably more down-to-earth.

⊜⊜⊜**Weinhaus Neuner** – *Herzogspitalstraße 8. ☎(089) 260 39 54. www.weinhaus-neuner.de. Closed Sun and public holidays.* Enjoy fine wines beneath the cross-vaulted ceilings of Munich's oldest wine tavern.

⊜⊜⊜**Tantris** – *Johann-Fichte-Straße 7. ☎(089) 361 95 90. www.tantris.de. Closed Sun–Mon and public holidays. Reservations essential.* Guarded by mythical monsters, this temple of

delight with its avant-garde black and orange decoration is one of the top restaurants in Munich. Hans Haas teases palates with his classical and innovative dishes.

TAKING A BREAK

Café Arzmiller – *Theatinerstraße 22 ☎(089) 29 42 73.* A good place to relax and forget the stress of the tourist track. Coffee, cakes and daily specials are served in the lovely, peaceful Theatinerhof. The house specialty, *Strudel*, is not to be missed.

Café Luitpold Palmengarten – *Brienner Straße 11. ☎(089) 242 87 50. www.cafe-luitpold.de. Closed public holidays.* This café offers a choice of more than 300 different cakes and tarts. The house specialty is *Luitpoldkuchen*, which can be enjoyed beneath a glass dome in the palm-filled inner courtyard or on the terrace facing Maximilianplatz.

Confiserie Rottenhöfer – *Residenzstraße 25/26. ☎(089) 22 29 15. www.rottenhoefer.de. Closed Sun and public holidays.* Founded in 1825, this chocolate shop was once official purveyor to the Bavarian court. It sells over 160 kinds of the sweet stuff and also operates a cafe.

Viktualienmarkt – *Viktualienmarkt. ☎(089) 23 39 65 00. www.viktualienmarkt.de. Closed Sun.* This traditional market dates back to 1807 and offers a wide variety of delectable victuals, including handmade sausages,

Viktualienmarkt

artesanal cheeses, smoked fish, fine olive oils and hearty loaves of bread.

NIGHTLIFE

USEFUL TIPS

Beer gardens are an integral part of Bavarian life, especially in Munich. Many of these chestnut tree-shaded gardens and terraces open at the slightest ray of spring sunshine. Although prices can be high and the service limited, people enjoy the unique atmosphere.

Munich's best-known café and bar scene is in **Schwabing**. Around the university is a plethora of student bars, while south of the Münchner Freiheit U-Bahn station, Leopoldstraße is lined by posh establishments where people go to "see and be seen". Other parts of town with good nightlife are Haidhausen (around Pariser and Weißenburger Platz) and the Gärtnerplatzviertel (quarter). For online information: www.munig.com, www.nightlife-munich.de and www.munichx.de.

Alter Simpl – *Türkenstraße 57.* ☎*(089) 272 30 83. www.altersimpl.de.* This casual pub with its nicotine-stained stuccoed ceilings has been a student haunt for over 100 years. Mainly Bavarian snacks and meals are served until 2am Mon–Thu and 3am Fri-Sat.

Tresznjewski – *Theresienstraße 72.* ☎*(089) 28 23 49. www.tresznjewski.de.* Opposite the Neue Pinakothek, this trendy eatery offers a wide choice of cocktails, hot drinks and uncomplicated food, from chicken burgers to pizza to schnitzel until well after midnight.

Hirschgarten – *Hirschgarten 1.* ☎*(089) 17 25 91. www.hirschgarten.de.* In a gorgeous spot in a former hunting preserve near Schloss Nymphenburg, this spirited beer garden can seat up to 8 000 people, making it one of the largest in Bavaria. *Augustiner* is the brew of choice.

Hofbräuhaus – *Am Platzl 9.* ☎*(089) 290 13 60. www.hofbraeuhaus.de.* Practically synonymous with Munich, this giant beer hall attracts scores of tourists from around the world but still manages to be a uniquely Bavarian experience. The action is at its most raucous on the ground floor *(Schwemme)* where a spirited brass band contributes to the

noise factor. The courtyard beer garden and the upstairs hall are quieter.

L-Opera – *Maximilianstraße 2.* ☎*(089) 54 44 46 44. www.l-opera.de.* Opposite the Residenz under the arcades of a stately 19C edifice, this place draws chatty clients from breakfast to late-night. An ideal spot on one of Munich's prettiest squares.

Seehaus – *Kleinhesselohe 3 (in the Englischer Garten).* ☎*(089) 381 61 30. www.kuffler-gastronomie.de.* This idyllic beer garden and restaurant has a dream location right on the shore of Lake Kleinhesselohe in the English Garden. Boat rentals are nearby.

SHOPPING

USEFUL TIPS

Many consider Munich Germany's best city for shopping. The old town has numerous arcades and boutiques catering to all budgets. *Beck am Rathauseck* and other department stores line Neuhauser Straße and Kaufingerstraße between Marienplatz and Karlsplatz (Stachus). Another good shopping district is Schwabing (along Leopoldstraße and smaller side streets such as Türkenstraße, which are home to small and funky boutiques. International labels are found in Residenzstraße, Brienner Straße and Maximilianstraße. The *Fünf Höfe* shopping center is a visual stunner in stylish Theatinerstraße and also filled with high-end boutiques and stores. Independent local and regional designers cluster in the charming Gärtnerplatzviertel along such streets as Reichenbachstraße and Hans-Sachs-Straße.

Art galleries – Most of Munich's key galleries are in Maximilianstraße and the nearby streets, in Residenzstraße and on Odeonsplatz. In the old artists' district of Schwabing, the most interesting drags are Türken-, Schelling- and Franz-Joseph-Straße.

Antiques – Munich antiques range from the elegant, exclusive dealers to bargain-basement bric-à-brac shops. Schwabing boasts a wealth of antique shops as does the city center around Maximiliansplatz, Lenbachplatz and Promenadenplatz.

prone to deep depression. Craving solitude and living in a fantasy world, Ludwig largely withdrew from society and dedicated himself to castle building: Neuschwanstein, Linderhof and Herrenchiemsee all sprang from his fevered brow. Declared mentally unstable, Ludwig II was deposed in 1886 and confined to Schloss Berg, on the shores of Lake Starnberg. He was found drowned there shortly afterwards. His uncle Luitpold was appointed prince regent. Luitpold's son, **Ludwig III**, was made the last king of Bavaria in 1912, but under pressure from a workers' revolutionary movement after World War I, he was forced to abdicate in 1918.

Between Two Wars – In 1919, **Adolf Hitler**'s German Workers' party was formed and its platform proclaimed at the Munich Hofbräuhaus. In 1923, Hitler fomented an uprising (the Munich Putsch, or Beer Hall Putsch). It was unsuccessful, the party was dissolved and Hitler imprisoned. Once released from prison, Hitler reorganized the group as the National Socialist (Nazi) Party and, by 1933, had risen to chancellor of Germany. In 1938, he chose Munich as the venue for a meeting with Chamberlain, Daladier and Mussolini at which the annexation of the Sudetenland was agreed.

Munich today – Munich was heavily bombed in World War II, but recovered rapidly to become the most important economic zone in southern Germany. It is now a prime purveyor of cars, electronics, insurance services, information technology and other industries. Microsoft, BMW and Siemens all have headquarters here and the trade fair grounds attract some two million visitors each years. Tourism is another key economic factor.

Sights

Central District

Schack-Galerie★
Prinzregentenstraße 9.
Open year-round, Wed–Sun 10am–5pm.

March Beer

The March "strong beer" season originated in the 17C when Franciscan monks began brewing high-alcohol beer to provide them with energy and sustenance during Lent. Although drinking was permitted during Lent, they still took a barrel to the Pope to make doubly sure. He readily assented, believing that such a "bad" beer (it was very strong and probably ruined during the journey) was punishment enough. These spring beers traditionally end in "ator".

Closed major public holidays. Closed until Sept 2009. 3€, Sun 1€. (089) 23 80 52 24. www.pinakothek.de/schack-galerie.
A nice complement to the Neue Pinakothek, the Schack-Galerie focuses on 19C German painting. Assembled by Count Adolf Friedrich von Schack (1815–94), it spans Early to Late Romanticism and includes works by such painters as Carl Rottmann, Moritz von Schwind, Carl Spitzweg, Arnold Böcklin and Anselm Feuerbach.

Münchner Stadtmuseum★ (City Historical Museum)
St. Jakobsplatz 1.
Open year-round, Tue–Sun 10am–6pm. 4€, Sun free. (089) 23 32 23 70. www.stadtmuseum-online.de.
In the stables of the old arsenal, this museum illuminates all aspects of the city's cultural history. Themes covered include musical instruments, puppetry, photography and film. A separate exhibit chronicles Munich during the Third Reich. The most important artistic item is a sculpture ensemble by Erasmus Grasser called the *Moriskentänzer* (Morris Dancers).

Jüdisches Museum★ (Jewish Museum)
St. Jacobsplatz 16.
Open year-round, Tue–Sun 10am–6pm. Closed Jan 1, Shrove Tue, Rosh Hashanah, Yom Kippur, Dec 24, 25 & 31. 8€. (089) 23 39 60 96. www.juedisches-museum-muenchen.de.

375

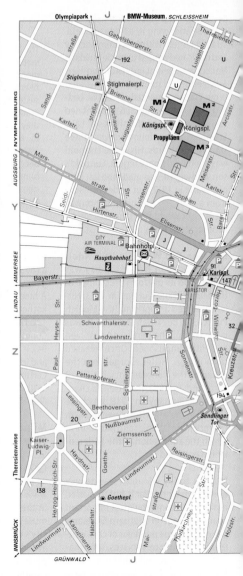

Munich's Jewish Museum (opened March 2007) is part of an architectural ensemble on St. Jakobs-Platz square that also includes a community center and a synagogue. The exhibit delivers impressions of the city's Jewish history and culture and highlights the contributions of outstanding members of the community in the past and today.

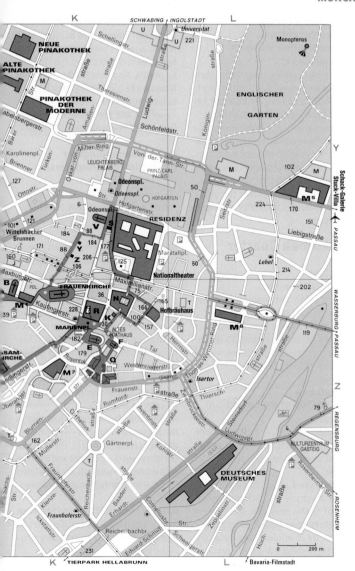

Deutsches Jagd- und Fischereimuseum (German Hunting and Fishing Museum)

Neuhauserstraße 2.
◷Open year-round, daily 9.30am–5pm (Thu 9pm). ◷Closed Shrove Tue, Dec 24 & 31. ◎3.50€. ☎(089) 22 05 22. www. jagd-fischerei-museum.de.

The museum, housed in a former Augustinian church, displays three floors of ancient and modern arms, trophies, paintings and drawings of hunting scenes, along with a veritable zoo's worth of stuffed animals.

Wittelsbacher Brunnen (Wittelsbach Fountain)

Lenbachplatz.
Designed by **Adolf Hildebrand,** this monumental classicist fountain was completed in 1895 to mark the completion of a water canal that for the first time provided Munich with clean drinking water.

Deutsches Museum – Verkehrszentrum (Transportation Museum)

Theresienhöhe 14a.

🕐 *Open year-round, daily 9am–5pm.* 🕐 *Closed Jan 1, Shrove Tue, Good Fri, May 1, Nov 1, Dec 24, 25 & 31.* 5€. 🅰(089) 500 80 65 00. www.deutsches-museum.de.

Housed in the former exhibition center near Theresienwiese, this museum traces the evolution of mobility in three large halls. Historical coaches and steam locomotives take you back to the beginning, while exhibits such as the ultraspeedy Transrapid train offer a glimpse of the future.

Pinakothek Quarter

Propyläen

West side of Königsplatz.

This imposing gateway by Leo von Klenze (1784–1864) was inspired by the Acropolis in Athens and completed two years before the architect's death. The frieze represents the Greek war of liberation against the Turks.

Glyptothek★ (Antique Sculpture Collection)

Königsplatz.

🕐 *Open year-round, Tue–Sun 10am–5pm (Thu 8pm).* 3.50€, *Sun 1€.* 🅰(089) 28 61 00. www.antike-am-koenigsplatz. mwn.de.

One thousand years of Greek and Roman sculpture are gathered under the roof of this museum, buttressed by a colonnaded Neoclassical porch. The scarcity of original Greek statues makes this exhibit even more remarkable. The **Tenea Apollo** *(Gallery I)*, with his handsome, smiling face, is among

the more memorable pieces, as is the **Barberini Faun** (c. 220 BC) *(Gallery II)*, which appears sated with drink and half asleep; it dates from the Hellenistic period. Also note the **bas-relief by Mnesarete** *(Gallery IV)*, which is said to have adorned the tomb of Socrates' daughter, and the statue of *Irene*, the Goddess of Peace *(Gallery V)*.

Antikensammlungen★ (Collection of Antiquities)

Opposite the Glyptothek.

🕐 *Open year-round, Tue–Sun 10am–5pm (Wed 8pm).* 3.50€, *Sun 1€.* 🅰 (089) 59 98 88 30. www.antike-am-koenig splatz.mwn.de.

Greek, Etruscan and Roman art is what you will find at this famous collection. Displays on the ground floor trace the evolution of pottery in Greece, which reached its zenith during the 6C and 5C BC. Geometric decoration was succeeded by the representation of black figures on a red background (illustrated by an amphora and a goblet by the painter Exekias). The transition toward the use of red figures against a background of varnished black can be seen on another amphora, where a single subject—Hercules' banquet in the presence of Athena—is treated in the two styles *(Gallery III, showcase 6)*. Certain vases (*loutrophora* and *lecythus* on a white background) were destined for funerary worship, others for domestic use.

Bronzes on the first floor and **Etruscan jewelry** in the basement *(Galleries VII and X)* testify to the enormous craftsmanship of these metalworkers.

Städtische Galerie im Lenbachhaus★ (Lenbach Collections)

Luisenstraße 33.

🕐 *Open year-round, Tue–Sun 10am–6pm.* 🕐 *Closed Shrove Tue, Dec 24.* ⚲ *Closed for three years starting February 2009.* 5– 10€, *depending on exhibit.* 🅰(089) 23 33 20 00. www.lenbachhaus.de.

Housed in a 19C villa, the Lenbach collections are devoted primarily to the works of **Munich painters of the 19C**. The landscapes of EB Morgenstern and portraits by FA von Kaulbach and F von

Defregger stand out, as do the powerful portraits created by **Franz von Lenbach** himself (*King Ludwig I, Bismarck, Wagner*).

But the gallery's international reputation is built, above all, on the avantgarde **Blaue Reiter** collection. Born in the tumultuous period just before World War I, the movement is represented by its founding members, Kandinsky and Marc, as well as by paintings of Jawlensky, Klee and Macke. **Contemporary art**, including works by Joseph Beuys and Anselm Kiefer, are usually shown in the Kunstbau annex.

Englischer Garten Quarter

Englischer Garten★ (English Garden)

Just north of the historic center, in the district of Schwabing, this vast park was designed in the late 18C and is characterized by broad, tree-bordered lawns, streams and lakes. It is particularly popular in summer for sunbathing, strolling, playing and picnicking. There are also several beer gardens, most notably the one below the **Chinese Tower** (*Chinesischer Turm*) which seats up to 7 000. Enjoy a view of Munich's old town from the **Monopteros**, a circular temple built by Klenze.

Bayerisches Nationalmuseum★★ (Bavarian National Museum)

Prinzregentenstraße 3.
Open year-round, Tue–Sun 10am–5pm (Thu 8pm). Closed Shrove Tue, May 1, Pentecost, Nov 1, Dec 24, 25 & 31. 5€. (089) 211 24 01. www.bayerisches-nationalmuseum.de.

Maximilian II created this museum in 1885 with the aim of preserving Bavaria's artistic and cultural heritage. The rooms on the ground floor offer a survey of Bavarian arts and crafts from **Romanesque to Renaissance** (*Galleries 1–19*), including silver and gold plate and religious statuary. The interior of an **Augsburg weaver**'s studio is in Gallery 9; the **Renaissance and Baroque** periods are represented by tapestries (*Gallery 22*), medieval town representations

A Little Exercise

The people of Munich enjoy all kinds of sports in the English Garden: jogging, cycling, basketball playing and... surfing. Yes, surfing! Just go to the bridge on Prinzregentenstraße at the southern tip of the park and see them 'hang ten' on an artificial wave.

and Italian bronzes (*Gallery 25*). The first floor houses musical instruments, board games, silverware and porcelain, while the basement is dedicated to folklore exhibits.

Museum Villa Stuck

Prinzregentenstraße 60.
Open year-round, Tue–Sun 11am–6pm. 4€. (089) 455 55 10. www.villastuck.de.

Franz Stuck (1863–1928) was a professor at the Munich Academy of Fine Arts from 1895 and a founding member of the Munich Secession. He personally drew up the plans for this exquisite Jugendstil villa along with its custom-made furniture, paneling, bas-reliefs, sculptures and coffered ceilings. Today the rooms house changing art exhibits.

Beer garden by the Chinese Tower in the English Garden

P. Scarlandis/Munich Tourist Office

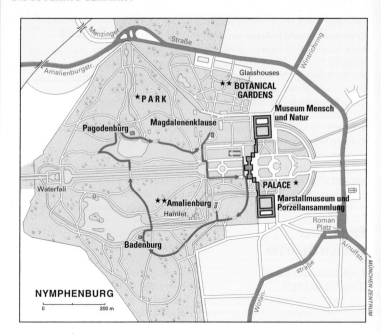

NYMPHENBURG

0 ————— 200 m

Schloss Nymphenburg★★ (Nymphenburg Palace)

🕐*Open Apr–mid-Oct, daily 9am–6pm; mid-Oct–Mar, 10am–4pm.* 🕐*Closed Jan 1, Shrove Tue, Dec 24, 25 & 31.* ⊜*5€.* ☎*(089) 17 90 80. www.schloesser.bay ern.de.*

The oldest part of this former summer residence of the Bavarian sovereigns is the 17C five-story central pavilion, built in the style of an Italian palazzo. Prince-Elector Max Emmanuel (1679–1726) added two side wings, while his successors Karl-Albrecht (1726–45) and Max III Josef (1745–77) commissioned various outbuildings.

From 1701 onward, the surrounding park was enlarged with formal French gardens and several park pavilions: the Pagodenburg (1719), Badenburg (1721), Magdalenenklause (1728) and Amalienburg (1739).

Schloss★★ (Palace)

The splendid **banqueting hall** *(Steinerner Saal, or Stone Hall)* is a symphony of white, gold and pale green and was richly adorned with colored stuccowork and frescoes by Johann Baptist Zimmer-

mann and his son, Franz. The rooms in the north wing are paneled and decorated with tapestries and paintings. One of the most fascinating rooms is the one devoted to **Chinese lacquer**. In the south pavilion, the apartments of Queen Caroline contain the famous **Schönheitengalerie** (Gallery of Beauties). King Ludwig I commissioned Joseph Karl Stieler (1781–1858) to immortalize the epoch's most beautiful women on canvas.

Park★

From the top of the palace steps you have a sweeping view over the formal flower gardens and the Grand Canal ending in a waterfall in the far distance.

Amalienburg★★

🕐*Same opening times as Schloss Nymphenburg.* ⊜*2€.* ☎*(089) 17 90 80.*

This charming Rococo hunting lodge is one of **Cuvilliés'** most accomplished designs. The simplicity and sobriety of the exterior contrasts vividly with the extraordinary richness inside. The **Hall of Mirrors** is a case in point: the combination of blue walls and ceiling, silver-plated stucco and wood-framed glass forms a marvelous ensemble.

Badenburg

🕐 Open mid-Apr–Oct, daily 9am–6pm.
2€. ☎(089) 17 90 80.
A luxurious heated swimming pool,
its ceiling decorated by mythological
motifs, is the centerpiece of this 18C
bathhouse.

Pagodenburg

🕐 Open mid-Apr–Oct, daily 9am–6pm.
2€. ☎(089) 17 90 80.
The 18C fascination with Asia is exemplified in the design of this octagonal
tea house where a drawing room, a
Chinese room and a boudoir occupy
the first floor.

Magdalenenklause

🕐 Open mid-Apr–Oct, daily 9am–6pm.
2€. ☎(089) 17 90 80.
A "hermitage" built in the popular mock
ruin style, this pavilion is dedicated to St.
Mary Magdalene.

Marstallmuseum und Porzellansammlung (Carriage Museum and Porcelain Collection)

🕐 Same opening times as Schloss
Nymphenburg. 4€. ☎(089) 17 90 80.
The museum is housed in the palace's
former stables. Besides superb 18C
and 19C harnesses, the Wittelsbachs'
broughams, coaches, sledges and sedan
chairs are on display. Note especially the
coronation coach of Emperor Karl VII,
and the state coach and personal sleigh
of Ludwig II.
Upstairs, a series of rooms houses the
**Bäuml Collection of Nymphenburg
Porcelain**. Painted figurines by Franz
Anton Bustelli, factory master from 1754
to 1763, are particularly stunning. The
reproductions in porcelain★—miniature copies of paintings in the Alte
Pinakothek—were commissioned by
King Ludwig I.

Museum Mensch und Natur (Museum of Human & Natural History) Kids

🕐 Open year-round, Tue–Sun 9am–5pm.
🕐 Closed Shrove Tue, Dec 24, 25 & 31.
2.50€, Sun 1€ (child 2.50€, Sun 1€).
&☎(089) 179 58 90. www.musmn.de.

Rarely is a natural history museum as
interesting and accessible, especially
to younger visitors. Exhibits shed light
on the origins and internal structure of
planet Earth, on the evolution of life
forms and much more. Informative
interactive games encourage visitors
large and small to get involved.

Botanischer Garten München-Nypmhenburg★★ (Botanical Gardens)

Menzinger Straße 65. 🕐 Open Jan, Nov,
Dec, daily 9am–4.30pm; Feb, Mar, Oct
until 5pm; Apr, Sept until 6pm; May–Aug,
until 7pm. 🕐 Closed Dec 24 & 31. 3€.
&☎(089) 17 86 13 10. www.botmuc.de.
Next to Schloss Nymphenburg, this is
one of Europe's finest botanical gardens
with over 14 000 plant species. The
Schmuckhof (opposite the main building), Spring Garden and Rose Garden
especially are particularly memorable,
even for the most casual of plant lovers. Rhododendrons brighten the Alpine
Garden; orchids and sub-tropical beauties bloom in the greenhouses.

Olympiapark Quarter

Olympiapark

Info Pavilion: 🕐 Open year-round, Mon–Fri
10am–6pm, 10am–3pm Sat. Guided
tours mid-Mar–Oct: Olympic stadium tour
at 11am (6€), park tour aboard miniature train at 2pm (8€). Olympic Stadium:
🕐 mid-Apr–mid-Oct, daily 8.30am–6pm,
mid-Oct–mid-Apr, 9am–4.30pm, closed
on events days. 2€. &☎(089) 30 67 24
14. www.olympiapark-muenchen.de.
Munich hosted the 20th Olympic Games
in 1972 and the grounds continue to be
used for sporting events, festivals and
concerts. They can be explored on
guided tours or by renting an audio
guide from the Info Pavilion (7€).
A highlight is the elevator ride up the
290m/951ft-high **Olympiaturm** (television tower; 🕐 open 9am–midnight;
4€) where you can take in a scenic
panorama★★ with views often extending as far as the Alps.
Your ticket also lets you take a spin
around the small and private **Rock 'n
Roll Museum** at the tower level. It features guitars, letters, fan mail and pho-

tographs of such giants as Jimi Hendrix and Jim Morrison.

SeaLife München `Kids`

🕒 *Open year-round, Mon–Fri 10am–6pm, Sat–Sun 10am–7pm.* ✆13.50€. ☎ (089) 45 00 00. www.sealifeeurope.com.

The latest addition to the Olympiapark, this child-oriented and partly interactive aquarium is home to some 10 000 marine and freshwater creatures.

The order of the tanks simulates the habitats encountered if following the flow of the Isar into the Danube, which itself flows into the Black Sea before spilling into the Mediterranean.

BMW-Museum `Kids`

Petuelring 130. Northeast corner of Olympiapark.

🕒 *Open year-round, Tue–Fri 9am–6pm, Sat–Sun 10am–8pm.* ✆12€ *(child 6€).* ♿☎(089) 38 22 56 57. www.bmw-museum.de.

Enlarged and revamped, the car maker's newly revamped flagship museum is housed in a giant silver bowl docked to a new pavilion. Inside, floating ramps lead visitors on a dynamic multimedia journey past shiny cars and motorcycles, from vintage wheels to concept cars and the latest production models.

The museum sits next to the BMW headquarters, plant and brand-new **BMW Welt** car pick-up center, which also has free exhibits that are open to the public.

Art Collections★★★

Munich's Alte Pinakothek (14C to 18C), Neue Pinakothek (19C) and Pinakothek der Moderne (20C) offer an all-encompassing survey of European painting.

Alte Pinakothek★★★

Barer Straße 15.

🕒 *Open year-round, Tue 10am–8pm, Wed–Sun 10am–6pm.* 🕒*Closed Shrove Tue, May 1, Dec 24, 25 & 31.* ✆5.50€, Sun 1€. ♿☎(089) 23 80 52 16. www.pinakothek.de.

The **Alte Pinakothek**, a colossal building designed by Leo von Klenze in the early 19C, houses paintings amassed by the House of Wittelsbach.

German School

The most extensive section is devoted to German Old Masters. Alongside sacred 15C paintings are works by painters inspired by the Italian Renaissance. Masterpieces include **Albrecht Dürer**'s *Four Apostles* (1526); **Albrecht Altdorfer's** *Landscape* (1528); and **Hans Holbein the Elder**'s *St. Sebastian Altarpiece* (1516).

Dutch and Flemish Schools

Among the most important works in this section are *The Land of Milk and Honey* (1566) by **Pieter Bruegel the Elder** and *The Last Judgment* (c. 1614–16) by **Peter Paul Rubens**. Early Dutch masterpieces

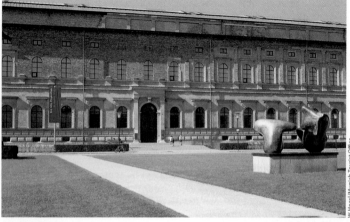

Alte Pinakothek

W.Hoesl/Munich Tourist Office

include the *Altarpiece of the Three Magi* (1455) by **Rogier Van der Weyden;** *Seven Joys of Mary* (c. 1480) by **Hans Memling;** and *Last Judgment* by **Hieronymus Bosch**. Finally, **Rembrandt**'s Passion cycle constitutes the heart of the collection of 17C Dutch paintings.

Italian School
Here the spotlight is on the great Renaissance masters: **Sandro Botticelli**'s *Lamentation of Christ* (post 1490); three major works by **Raphael** including the *Madonna Tempi* (1507); *The Crowning of Thorns* (1560) by **Titian**; **Tiepolo**'s the *Veneration of the Holy Trinity* by Pope Clemens (1739) and the *Adoration of the Magi* (1753); and several works by **Antonio Canaletto** and **Francesco Guardi**.

French School
French Classicism is represented by **Claude Lorrain**'s *Sea Port at Sunrise* (1674) and paintings by **Nicolas Poussin**, who takes his subjects from Ovid's *Metamorphoses* (1627). Among the 18C painters, **François Boucher**'s *Madame Pompadour* is on display, commissioned by her in 1756.

Spanish School
This school is notably represented by **Murillo**'s lively genre paintings alongside epic canvasses by **El Greco** and **Velázquez**.

Neue Pinakothek★★

Barer Straße 29, enter from Theresienstraße.
🕐*Open year-round, Wed 10am–8pm, Thu–Mon 10am–6pm.* 🕐*Closed May 1, Dec 24, 25 & 31.* 👁5.50€, Sun 1€. ♿☎(089) 23 80 51 95. *www.neue-pina kothek.de.*
The **Neue Pinakothek** is a well-proportioned postmodernist work by Alexander von Branca, completed in 1981. It replaced the original building by Friedrich von Gärtner that suffered irreparable damage during World War II. The collection focuses on works from the 19C and early 20C.

😊 A Bit of Advice 😊
Two other museums exhibit works by German Expressionists: The Lenbach Collections in Munich (*Blaue Reiter* movement) and the Buchheim Museum in Bernried (*Die Brücke* movement).
🕐*See INTRODUCTION: Art.*

Early 19C
Galleries **1, 2 and 2a** are devoted to European art from around 1800. Canvasses worth focusing on include: **Thomas Gainsborough**'s portraits and landscapes, works by **Jacques-Louis David**, including the *Marquise de Sorcy,* **Joshua Reynolds** *(Captain Pownall),* **William Turner** *(Ostend)* and **Francisco Goya** *(Marquesa de Caballero).*

Early 19C German painters
On display in Galleries **3 and 3a** are early Romantic works from Dresden, Berlin and Munich, including the highly spiritual landscapes of **Caspar David Friedrich**. Johann Christian **Dahl** (*Frederiksholm Canal in Copenhagen,* 1817) and Karl **Blechen** (*View of Assisi,* 1830) are also represented. Ludwig I of Bavaria was a great patron of the arts who commissioned many paintings, including those on display in Galleries **4 and 4a**. Galleries **5 and 5a** are devoted to the German Neoclassicists in Rome, including a well-known landscape by **Ludwig Richter**, *The Night-Watchman* (*Watzmann*, 1824).
The following galleries focus on two early 19C trends: the spiritual Nazarenes, who sought to reconcile northern and southern painting by harkening back to Raphael and Dürer; and artists of the **Biedermeier** style.

From Romanticism to Realism
Pride of place is given to French painters in Galleries **10 and 10a**.
The Romantics are represented by **Théodore Géricault** and his admirer **Eugène Delacroix**. In Galleries **11 and 11a**, **Andreas Achenbach** and **Carl Spitzweg** (*The Hussar, The Poor Poet,* 1839, *The Writer,* 1850) represent Late German Romanticism.

Late 19C German painters

Gallery **15** is entirely devoted to **Hans von Marées** (1837–87), a great portrait painter inspired by Renaissance art. Gallery **16** contains works by a group of German painters who went to live and work in Rome: Arnold Böcklin, Hans Thoma, **Anselm Feuerbach** and **Wilhelm Leibl**.

Impressionists, post-Impressionists and Symbolists

Galleries **18 and 19** contain paintings by German Impressionists, notably *Summer Holiday* by Friedrich von Uhde and *Portrait of the Writer Eduard Graf von Keyserling* (1901) by **Lovis Corinth**. Symbolism and Jugendstil provide the theme of Galleries **20 and 21a**. *Margarethe Stonborough-Wittgenstein*, the philosopher's sister, was the subject of a famous portrait by **Gustav Klimt** (1905). **Auguste Rodin**'s marble bust of *Helene von Nostitz* is surrounded by several works of Ferdinand Hodler (*Disappointed*), Egon Schiele (*Agony*, 1912) and Giovanni Segantini (*Ploughing*, 1890). Post-Impressionists Toulouse-Lautrec, Vuillard and Ensor share Gallery **21** with **Claude Monet**'s large-scale *Waterlilies* (1918). Galleries **22** and **22a** are devoted to such French Impressionists as **Paul Gauguin**, **Camille Pissarro**, **Edgar Degas**, and **Paul Cézanne**. Also on display is a painting from **Vincent Van Gogh**'s *Sunflowers* series (1888).

Pinakothek der Moderne★★

Barer Straße 40.
🕐*Open year-round, Tue–Sun 10am–6pm (Thu 8pm).* 🕐*Closed Shrove Tue, May 1, Dec 24, 25 & 31.* 9.50€, Sun 1€. ♿☎(089) 23 80 53 60. www.pinakothek.de.

The building, designed by Munich architect Stephan Braunfels, is known as the "Cathedral of Light" because of its glass rotunda and glazed saw-tooth roofs. It unites four museums with collections of 20C paintings, sculpture, graphics, design and architecture under a single roof.

Staatsgalerie Moderner Kunst (State Gallery of Modern Art)

3rd floor. The question of form and content in modern art is the underlying theme of the permanent exhibition, arranged in chronological order and by cross-influence.

"Classic" Modern Art (Galleries 1–17) – A large section is devoted to German Expressionism. The artist group "Die Brücke" *(The Bridge)*, which was led by **Ernst Ludwig Kirchner** and whose tortured subjects set them apart from the Fauves, is well represented. So are members of "Der Blaue Reiter" (*The Blue Rider*), who focused on abstraction and spiritualization of form; Franz Marc and **Wassily Kandinsky** were at the visionary helm of this group. Another Expressionist, **Max Beckmann**, is represented by the *Temptation of St. Anthony*.
The Cubists and Futurists moved toward autonomous art, as illustrated in numerous works by **Pablo Picasso** (including *Madame Soler*) and **Georges Braque**. Surrealism is represented by Max Ernst, René Magritte and Salvador Dali, and Bauhaus by Feininger and Paul Klee.

Modern Art (Galleries 20–36) – Important themes in art during the second half of the 20C— informal art, celebration of the trivial, rise of pop culture, etc.—are broached in artists' monographs. One can thus follow the works of **Joseph Beuys, Francis Bacon** (*Crucifixion*)

The Collection

The Pinakothek collection was started in the 16C by Duke Wilhelm IV, who commissioned historical scenes from the most eminent painters of his time, Altdorfer and Burgkmair. In the 17C, the Elector Maximilian I founded the Kammergalerie which, under King Ludwig I, developed into the finest exhibition of art in the whole of Europe. The building suffered severe damage in 1943, but the paintings had already been moved to a safe location.

and Willem de Kooning. The museum also displays some remarkable works by American artists, with paintings by **Andy Warhol**, photographs by Jeff Wall and videos by Bruce Nauman.

Other Departments

Neue Sammlung (New Design Collection, basement) – In addition to objects of industrial design, accessories, cars and computer equipment, the museum presents prototypes of items designed since the industrial revolution up to the 1960s.

Selections from the **Grafische Sammlung** (State Graphic Arts Collection) are shown in temporary exhibitions on the ground floor owing to their great sensitivity to light.

Finally, the **Architekturmuseum** (Architecture Museum) is the largest of its kind in Germany with a rich collection of models, photographs, blueprints and computer prints dating from the 16C to today. The focus is on architecture in Germany in the 19C and 20C with particular attention given to the genius of Leo von Klenze, Le Corbusier and Peter Zumthor.

Deutsches Museum★★★

Kids ⊙Open year-round, daily 9am–5pm. ⊙Closed Jan 1, Shrove Tue, Good Fri, May 1, Nov 1, Dec 24, 25 & 31. ⊛8.50€. ☎(08 9) 217 91. www.deutsches-museum.de.

Founded in 1903, this museum—one of the most important in the world for scientific and technical matters—is built on an isle in the Isar **(Museumsinsel)**. It traces the history of science and technology from the beginning of time to the present and explains physical processes and phenomena. Besides a large number of original items and reconstructions are dioramas and scale models. According to the wishes of founder and Bavarian electricity pioneer **Oskar von Miller**, the displays invite visitors to inquire, touch and discover.

⊛This is a huge museum, so be selective and don't expect to see everything on a single visit.

Ground Floor

Oil and gas, electricity, metallurgy and civil engineering are among subjects addressed on the ground floor.

The Aeronautical Section exhibits early planes, including the Messerschmitt Me-262—the first jet fighter made on a production line—helicopters, gliders and vertical take-off machines. The bulk of flying machines, though, is at the museum's branch in Schleissheim, the Flugwerft Schleissheim.

An Elbe sailing ship (1880) and an Italian steam tug (1931) stand at the entrance to the Navigation Department *(continued in the basement)*.

There's also a nifty collection of model trains, although to see the big engines, you have to visit the museum's new

Deutsches Museum

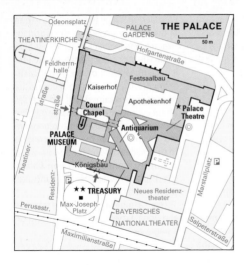

Verkehrszentrum branch near Theresienhöhe.

Basement

Among many other displays, the Navigation Section highlights naval construction, warships (including U-1, the first German submarine, built in 1906), methods of navigation, fishing techniques, and Jacques Picard's 1958 bathysphere. This is followed by an exhibit on mining techniques that includes a model salt mine.

Kids Kids aged 3 to 8 will be stimulated and entertained in the **Kinderreich**, an educational play zone.

First Floor

This floor is dominated by the Physical Science section (optics, mechanics, nuclear physics, electronics, etc.). The Old Aeronautics Hall presents pioneering flying machines, such as gliders built by Otto Lilienthal (c. 1885) and a 1917 Fokker Dr I Triplane, made famous by Baron von Richthofen's "circus" in World War I. Note also the Wright Brothers' Type-A Standard (USA, 1909), a Blériot Type XI (1909) and a Junkers F-13 (the first successful commercial airliner, 1919).

Second Floor

The main draw here is the re-created Altamira cave with its famous stone age paintings, but there is plenty more to keep your brain engaged: glass and ceramics, printing techniques, photography (Daguerre's apparatus, 1839), space travel, textiles and environmental science.

Third Floor

Exhibits on weights and measures, telecommunication, agriculture, microelectronics and computer science fill this floor.

Fourth to Sixth Floor

The upper floors are dedicated to astronomy and present everything from ancient equipment to solar system models. **Tickets** (€2€) for shows in the sixth-floor planetarium must be purchased at the information booth in the entrance foyer.

Residenz★★ (Palace)

Combined ticket for the Residenzmuseum and Schatzkammer €9€.

After the ruling Wittelsbachs had outgrown their original residence (*Alter Hof, on Burgstraße*), construction of a new royal palace began in 1385. The complex was expanded considerably in subsequent centuries and today consists of seven structures enclosing eight inner courtyards.

Schatzkammer★★ (Treasury)

Open Apr–mid-Oct, daily 9am–6pm; mid-Oct–Mar 10am–5pm; last entry 1hr before closing. Closed Jan 1, Shrove Tue, Dec 24, 25 & 31. €6€. (089) 29 06 71. www.residenz-muenchen.de.

Bavarian rulers had a passion for collecting precious things, as you will see on a tour of the treasury which brims with gold works, enamels, crystalware, carved ivories and other fanciful items. Among the highlights are an 11C cross made for Queen Gisela of Hungary, Heinrich's crown from 1280 and dazzling jewelry inlaid with precious stones.

Residenzmuseum★★

○*Open Apr–mid-Oct, daily 9am–6pm; mid-Oct–Mar, 10am–5pm.* ○*Closed Jan 1, Shrove Tue, Dec 24, 25 & 31.* ∞*6€.* ☎*(089) 29 06 71. www.residenz-muenchen.de.*

This museum is so huge that it is divided into two sections; one is open in the morning, the other in the afternoon. The most important rooms, such as the **Antiquarium** (c. 1570), can be seen all day. Inlaid with marble and embellished with ceiling frescoes, it is a treasure trove of original and copied statues from ancient Greece.

The **Morning Tour** leads you into the **Die Reichen Zimmer** (State Rooms, 1730–37), which illustrate early Rococo style. Highlights include the **königlichen Appartements** (Royal Apartments) in the **Königsbau** (King's Wing), which were built under Ludwig I between 1826 and 1835.

The **Afternoon Tour** takes you into the **Special Collections** with porcelain masterpieces from Meissen, Nymphenburg, Frankenthal and Sèvres.

The 17C **Hofkapelle** (Court Chapel) is dedicated to the Virgin Mary, patron saint of Bavaria.

The **Reiche Kapelle** (Ornate Chapel, 1607) was the private chapel of Duke Max I and is a lavish kaleidoscope of colored marble and gilded reliefs.

Altes Residenztheater (Cuvilliéstheater)★★

Enter via Brunnenhof courtyard. ○*Hours vary, usually daily 9am–6pm.* ○*Closed on rehearsal and performance days.* ∞*2€.*

This enchanting red and gold Rococo theater was masterminded by **François de Cuvilliés**, built in 1750s and recently restored. The prince-elector's box is set apart by the elegance of its hangings, marble and stuccowork.

Staatliches Museum Ägyptischer Kunst (Egyptian Art Museum)

Enter from Hofgartenstraße.
○*Open year-round, Tue 9am–9pm, Wed–Fri 9am–5pm, Sat–Sun 10am–5pm.* ∞*5€.* ☎*(089) 29 85 46. www.aegyptisches-museum-muenchen.de.*

Small but choice, this is the world's only museums focused exclusively on Egyptian art. All epochs from Ancient Egypt until the Coptic (Christian) era are represented, as are works from neighboring cultures in Nubia, Assyria and Babylon.

Walking Tour

Old Town★★ (Altstadt)

⌂*See itinerary on the city map.*

Marienplatz★ (St. Mary's Square)

This square is the heart of Munich and centers on the **Mariensäule**, a column

Frauenkirche and Neues Rathaus on Marienplatz

Office de Tourisme de Munich

erected in 1638 by Prince-Elector Maximilian in honor of Mary, patron saint of Bavaria. On the square's north side looms the fantastic Neo-Gothic **Neues Rathaus** (New Town Hall, 1867–1908) with the tourist office on the ground floor. Its enchanting **carillon** (*Glockenspiel*) has tourists craning their necks daily at 11am and noon (*Mar–Sept, also 5pm*) when brightly colored figurines emerge accompanied by merry chimes. Two scenes are represented: the upper level shows a knights' tournament held in 1568 in celebration of the marriage of Duke Wilhelm V to Renata of Lothringia; the lower half re-enacts the **Schäfflertanz** (Dance of the Coopers), first held to celebrate the end of the plague in the 16C.

The **Altes Rathaus** (Old Town Hall) on the square's eastern side is decorated with stepped gables and bell turrets and now houses the **Spielzeugmuseum** (toy museum).

Peterskirche (Church of St. Peter's)

This 13C three-aisle Gothic church acquired a Baroque look in the 17C and 18C. Note Erasmus Grasser's statue of St. Peter (1492) in the center section of the high altar. The bell-tower—affectionately nicknamed "Old Pete"—can be climbed (*306 steps, ∞1.50€*) for splendid city views.

Viktualienmarkt (Food Market)★

Fruit and vegetables, meat and fish have been sold on this market daily except Sunday since 1807. Stalls, kiosks and a

---

Karl Valentin

The comedic talent of Valentin Ludwig Fey (1882–1948), nurtured since his childhood in Munich's suburbs, rapidly brought him international acclaim. This nonconformist actor, author and friend of Brecht produced sketches that were both grotesque and tragic, earning him the nickname of "metaphysical clown". A trip to the **Valentin-Karlstadt museum** (*Tal 50, near the Isartor*) will take you into the world of this local star.

---

beer garden (*in suitable weather*) crowd around a colorful may pole, ensuring a lively atmosphere and making for a great lunch spot. Two of the six fountains recall local comedian Karl Valentin and his partner Liesl Karlstadt.

Heiliggeistkirche (Church of the Holy Spirit)

This Gothic hall church also went Baroque in the 1720s and got its Neo-Baroque façade in 1888. The mid-15C Virgin in the north aisle, said to be by Hammerthal, hails from the Benedictine abbey at Tegernsee.

▶ *Cross Talstraße, take the arcade through the old Town Hall and turn right into Burgstraße.*

Weinstadel

Burgstraße 5.
Munich's oldest surviving house (1552) used to be the office of the Clerk of the Court and sports a colorful *trompe-l'œil* façade.

▶ *At Burgstraße 10, opposite the Weinstadel, take the arcade to Ledererstraße, then cross diagonally into Orlandostraße.*

Hofbräuhaus

Munich's best-known beer hall has stood on Platzl square since 1589. Every day, servers deliver virtual rivers of beer in one-liter (1.75 pints) tankards (*Maßkrug*) to a thirsty crowd cheering on raucous brass bands performing popular songs. The huge vaulted **Bierschwemme**, on the ground floor, is the rowdiest section. Head to the beer garden if you like it quieter.

▶ *At the far end of Platzl square, turn left into Pfisterstraße.*

Alter Hof (Old Castle)

This building was the official Wittelsbach residence from 1253 to 1474. The south wing has an elegant tower with half-timbered corbelling (late 15C), known locally as the *Affenturm* (monkey tower). In recent times, sections of the building have been controversially turned into apartment and office buildings. The complex also contains a **central information office** about Bavarian castles and palaces and a free **multimedia exhibit** (⏱*open Mon–Fri 10am–6pm, Sat 10am–1pm*) about the Alter Hof and general Munich history.

▸ *The Hofgraben leads to Max-Joseph-Platz, flanked on the north and east by the Residenz palace.*

Nationaltheater (National Theater)

Built between 1811 and 1818 by Leo von Klenze, the national theater is home to the Bavarian State Opera and can seat up to 2 100 people.

Residenz★★ (⏱*See above*)

▸ *Follow Residenzstraße along the west side of the Residenz.*

Odeonsplatz

On the west side of this square stands the 19C Leuchtenberg-Palais, built for Eugène de Beauharnais, Count of Leuchtenberg, and now home to the Bavarian Finance Ministry. To the south, the **Feldherrnhalle** (1840–44) by Andreas Gärtner marks the southern terminus of grand Ludwigstraße built under Ludwig I; the northern end culminates in a triumphal arch *(Siegestor)*.

Theatinerkirche★

A fine example of Baroque architecture, this church was built between 1663 and 1688, first under the direction of the Italian Agostino Barelli and later by Enrico Zuccalli from Graubünden, Switzerland. The particularly lavish interior stucco ornamentation is primarily by Nicolo Petri. Several Bavarian rulers, including King Max I and Crown Prince Ruprecht are buried in the south transept.

▸ *From Salvatorstraße, go to Kardinal-Faulhaber-Straße.*

Erzbischöfliches Palais (Episcopal Palace)

Kardinal-Faulhaber-Straße 7.
Cuvilliés finest palace was built between 1733–37 and still serves as the residence of the local archbishop. It boasts a magnificent pink and white façade with a rounded balcony supported by cherubs.

Palais Portia

Kardinal-Faulhaber-Straße 12.
This pink and grey mansion was originally designed by Enrico **Zuccalli** (1694), with a façade by **Cuvilliés**, for one of Karl Albrecht's favorites, Countess Portia.

▸ *Take the alley at the end of Kardinal-Faulhaber-Straße.*

Frauenkirche★ (Church of Our Lady)

Altes Rathaus architect **Jörg von Halspach** also designed this vast Late Gothic hall church (1468–88). The two onion-domed towers were added in 1525 and are a symbol of the city.

In striking contrast to the austere, red-brick façade, the **interior** is brilliant white and makes a stunning impression. Eleven pairs of octagonal pillars support the reticulated vaulting. Seen from the entrance, the perspective of these columns forms a continuous line, effectively hiding the aisles.

In the south aisle is a monumental black marble **cenotaph**★ to Emperor Ludwig of Bavaria, by Hans Krumper (1619–22). All the chapels contain high quality paintings and altarpieces, and those off the ambulatory sport extraordinary 15C **stained-glass windows**. An elevator in the south tower whisks you to a **viewing platform**★ (⏱*open Apr–Oct, Mon–Sat 10am–5pm;* ✺*3€*).

▸ *Head west on Neuhauser Straße toward the Karlstor.*

Michaelskirche★ (Church of St. Michael's)

This 16C Jesuit sanctuary is considered the oldest Renaissance church north of the Alps. The façade is decorated with pilasters, bands of script and a statue of the church's patron, the Archangel Michael. The single nave inspired many Baroque builders in southern Germany. The pulpit and seven side altars date from 1697. Thirty of the Wittelsbach rulers, including King Ludwig II of Bavaria, are buried in the crypt *(Fürstengruft)*.

Richard-Strauss-Brunnen

Bas-relief sculptures on the central column of this **fountain** illustrate scenes from the opera *Salomé*, composed by the Munich-born Strauss in 1905.

▶ *Follow Eisenmannstraße which turns into Damenstiftstraße, then take the first alley on the left after Brunnstraße to Sendlingerstraße.*

Asamkirche★ (Church of St. Johannes Nepomuk)

The church, built in 1733, is usually referred to by the name of the men who constructed it, the **Asam Brothers**: the painter Cosmas Damian Asam and the sculptor Egid Quirin Asam. The church's remarkable unity of style is due to the fact that the brothers not only drew up the plans but also supervised every stage of the building process. The result is Rococo artistry run amok with color, stuccowork, gilding, statuary and embellishments of every sort covering every single square inch of wall space.

▶ *Return to Marienplatz via Sendlingerstraße and Rosenstraße.*

Driving Tours

Around Ammersee Lake

Round-trip of 116km/72mi.

Ammersee★

This glacial lake sits framed by wooded hills at an elevation of 533m/1 749ft and is popular for swimming, sailing and boating.

▶ *Follow the western lakeshore to Dießen.*

Dießen

Built in 1730 in exquisite Rococo style, Diessen's **Marienmünster**★ *(St. Mary's Minster)* is a collaboration between architect **Johann Michael Fischer**, the Asam brothers and Cuvilliés.

▶ *The road climbs from Fischen to Andechs, offering fine lake views.*

Kloster Andechs★ (Andechs Abbey)

Guided church tour (30min), mid-Apr–Oct, Mon–Sat noon, Sun 12.15pm. ☎*(08152) 37 60. www.andechs.de.*

Crowning the Heiliger Berg (Holy Mountain), this abbey overlooks the Ammersee and was founded in the 10C. Its **church**★★ is Gothic at its core but was remodeled in the 1750s in Rococo style by Johann Baptist Zimmermann. Bavarian composer Carl Orff (of *Carmina Burana* fame) is buried in the Chapel of Suffering. Still an active abbey, the monks run a brisk business as brewmasters. In fact, Kloster Andechs beer is considered among Bavaria's finest and can easily be sampled in the abbey's beer garden and Bräustüberl beer hall.

▶ *Return to Munich via Herrsching and Seefeld.*

Exploring the Foothills of the Bavarian Alps

172km/106.8mi round-trip.
This route links up with the German Alpine Road (⌖see DEUTSCHE ALPENSTRASSE) at Wallgau.

▶ *Head south on the A8 to exit 97, then join the B13 at Holzkirchen.*

Bad Tölz

The discovery of springs rich in iodine in 1845 transformed Tölz into a spa town famous throughout Europe.

The wide curve and steep slope of the **Marktstraße**★, bordered by colorful façades, gives the old town its special charm. Climb up **Kalvarienberg** (Calvary Hill) to a twin-towered church with the adjacent **Leonardikapelle** (Chapel of St. Leonard, 1743). The saint's anniversary, November 6, is celebrated each year by a pilgrimage of wagons and carts drawn by brilliantly harnessed horses. The **Blomberg peak** (1 248m/4 095ft) is a family-friendly destination with a chair lift, an Alpine Slide and, in winter, a tobogganing track.

▶ *Head west on the B472 for 13km/8mi, then take the left fork to join the B11.*

Kloster (Abbey) Benediktbeuern★

Founded in 739, this abbey has been run by St. John Bosco's Salesians since 1930. The Baroque **basilica** sports an elaborate ceiling fresco by Hans Georg Asam (father of the Asam Brothers), depicting the Birth, Baptism, Transfiguration and Resurrection of the Saviour, the Descent of the Holy Spirit and the Last Judgment. Elegant frescoes and stucco work make the attached **Anastasiakapelle**★ (1751–53) one of the most charming examples of Rococo art.

▶ *Follow the B11 south for 21km/13mi.*

Walchensee★

Framed by dense woods, this beautiful deep blue reservoir lake is popular with water sports fans. For a superb **view**★★, taking in the Walchensee, the Kochelsee, the Karwendel massif and Wetterstein range, take the **Herzogstandbahn** gondola (⬭7.50€).

▶ *Head north on the B11 and return to Munich via the A95 at Sindelsdorf.*

Excursions

Dachau Concentration Camp★

19km/11.8mi northwest.
Alte Römerstraße75, Dachau. Follow signposting "KZ-Gedenkstätte". ⏱*Open year-round, Tue–Sun 9am–5pm. Audio guide recommended (⬭3€).* ♿⌕*(08131) 66 99 70. www.kz-gedenkstaette-dachau.de.*
Nazi Germany's first concentration camp was organized near the pleasant town of Dachau on the orders of Heinrich Himmler in March 1933. Originally designed for the detention of German political opponents of the Nazi regime, the camp was soon flooded by tens of thousands of deportees, mostly Jews of diverse nationalities. More than 32 000 people died there, not even counting several thousand Russian prisoners-of-war killed on the nearby SS firing range. Whether on a guided tour or independent, visitors are sobered by the **ruins and commemorative monuments**. The original prisoner barracks were razed but two have been faithfully reconstructed and

the foundations of 32 others are still visible. They offer a glimpse of a camp which was designed for 5 000 prisoners of war but was crammed with 30 000 innocent people by 1944. At the rear camp entrance one can still read the inscription *"Arbeit macht frei"* ("Freedom Through Work"). A Jewish memorial, a Protestant commemorative sanctuary, and a Catholic chapel have been built within the precincts of the old camp. Just beyond its borders are the crematorium and a gas chamber, although the latter was apparently never used.

The **museum** in the former administration buildings presents *(in English and German)* a sobering and comprehensive look at life in the camp. Exhibits hone in on the organization of the KZ system throughout Europe; original statements, photographs and documents illustrate the camp's history, the prisoners' daily life, hard labor, medical experiments, mass executions, and its liberation.

Tierpark Hellabrunn★ (Hellabrunn Zoological Gardens) 〔Kids〕

6km/3.7mi south via Wittelsbacherstraße. Tierparkstr. 30.
⏱*Open Apr–Sept, daily 8am–6pm; Oct–Mar, 9am–5pm.* ⬭*9€ (child 4.50€, 4–14ys; free under-4s).* ♿⌕*(089) 62 50 80. www.zoo-munich.de.*
Munich's zoo was founded in 1911 and the first to combine a nature reserve and animal park. It sits in an idyllic spot on the banks of the Isar where generous enclosures house 5 000 animals. Highlights include the giant aviary, the elephant house, the jungle pavilion, the bat house (called Villa Dracula), the polar zone with penguins and polar bears, and a petting zoo.

Bavaria-Filmstadt (Bavaria Film Studios) 〔Kids〕

10km/6.2mi south via Hochstraße, Grünwalderstraße and Geiselgasteigstraße. Bavariafilmplatz 7.
⏱*Open mid-Mar–Oct, daily 9am–4pm; Nov–mid-Mar, 10am–3pm.* ◆*Guided tours (90min) continuously (1pm in English).* ⏱*Closed Dec 24–25.* ⬭*11€, 20€ with stunt show & 4D cinema.* ♿⌕*(089) 64 99 20 00. www.filmstadt.de.*

Munich has a long tradition of film and television production, as you will learn on a visit of these 1919 film studios where such famous movies as *The Boat* and *The Neverending Story* were produced. See some of the original sets and plenty of behind-the-scenes activity (maybe even a celebrity!) on the studio tour. Optional add-ons are a live-action stunt show and a 4D cinema.

Schloss Schleißheim★

15km/9.3mi north via Schleißheimer Straße. ⏰*Open Apr–Sept, Tue–Sun 9am–6pm; Oct–Mar, 10am–4pm.* ⏰*Closed Jan 1, Shrove Tue, Dec 24–25. Combined ticket to all three palaces ⬭6€.* ♿⬭*(089) 315 87 20. www.schloesser.bayern.de.*

The northern suburb of Schleissheim is home to a trio of palaces, most notably the **Neues Schloss** (New Palace; ⬭4€) built between 1701 and 1727 under Elector Max II Emanuel. The grand staircase leads to the **State Apartments** with a huge banqueting hall in dazzling white. The royal apartments and **galleries**, adorned with Baroque painting and works by 16C and 17C Dutch and Flemish masters, are also impressive.

The palace **grounds** were laid out in formal French style by Carbonet and Girard, with a central canal as their main axis.

At the far end of the park stands **Schloss Lustheim** (⬭3€), a 17C hunting lodge now housing precious Meissen porcelain. Also nearby is the Renaissance-style **Altes Schloss** (Old Palace; ⬭2.50€) where you can peruse religious art from around the world.

Flugwerft Schleißheim★ 〔Kids〕

Effnerstraße 18, 85764 Oberschleißheim, next to Schloss Schleißheim. ⏰*Open year-round, daily 9am–5pm.* ⏰*Closed Jan 1, Shrove Tue, Good Fri, May 1, Nov 1, Dec 24, 25 & 31.* ⬭6€ *(child 3€).* ♿⬭*(089) 315 71 40. www.deutsches-museum.de.*

A 1920s Bavarian air corps hangar now houses the aviation department of the Deutsches Museum. Aside from gliders, helicopters and small planes, it also has several military aircraft from the Cold War era, including a 1959 Lockheed F-104F Starfighter and a Soviet MiG-23BN from 1980. Behind a glass wall, engineers are busy restoring historical

craft. Children can even get their own "pilot's license".

Buchheim Museum★

45km/28mi southwest. Take the A95 to Seeshaupt, then follow the lakeside road. Am Hirschgarten 1, Bernried. ⏰*Open year-round, Apr–Oct, Tue–Sun 10am–6pm; Nov–Mar, 10am–5pm.* ⏰*Closed Dec 24 & 31.* ⬭8.50€. ♿⬭*(08158) 99 70 20. www.buchheimmuseum.de.*

Designed by Günter Behnisch, this museum on the shores of Lake Starnberg houses the vast private collection of German writer and painter Lothar-Günther Buchheim (author of *Das Boot*). Its main strength is in German Expressionism, with members of *Die Brücke*, such as Kirchner, Heckel, Pechstein and Schmidt-Rottluff, being particularly well represented. Other rooms display an eclectic collection of arts and crafts from around the world.

Landsberg am Lech★

62km/42.8mi east via the A96.

Landsberg sits on the old road from Salzburg to Memmingen and prospered through trade and toll collecting. Fortress gates, towers and perimeter walls still create an attractive medieval atmosphere. There is a fine **view**★ from the shady riverside promenade on the west bank of the Lech, where it meets the Karolinenbrücke.

Landsberg's triangular **Marktplatz** (market square) is surrounded by stately buildings with colorful exteriors. The most impressive is the elegant **Rathaus** (Town Hall) whose façade was executed c. 1720 by Dominikus Zimmermann, one of the greatest artists of the Wessobrunn School. Its gable is ornamented with finely worked stucco. In the far corner of Marktplatz stands the 14C **Schmalztor**, topped by a lantern turret roofed with glazed tiles. To reach another town gate, climb up Alte Bergstraße to the **Bayertor** (Bavarian Gate, 1425). With its projecting porch flanked by turrets and sculptures, it is one of the best preserved from its period in Germany. Outside the ramparts, the gateway is embellished with carved and painted coats of arms and a Crucifixion.

MÜNSTERLÄNDER WASSERBURGEN★

MOATED CASTLES OF THE MÜNSTER REGION

The rural, sparsely populated area surrounding the historic town of Münster (👆see below) is an attractive patchwork of flat fields, pastures and meadows dotted with some 100 moated fairytale castles. Most are privately-owned and can only be viewed from the outside, but some are open to visitors.

- 🗎 **Information:** An der Hohen Schule 13, 48565 Steinfurt. ☎(02551) 93 92 91. tollfree (0800) 939 29 19. www.muensterland-tourismus.de.
- ▸ **Orient Yourself:** The Münsterland is in the north-west of Germany, close to the Dutch border. Since public transportation is sparse, it is best explored by car or by bicycle.
- 👁 **Don't Miss:** Schloss Anholt.
- 🕐 **Organizing Your Time:** Allow one day to explore the Münsterland.
- 👆 **Also See:** MÜNSTER, SAUERLAND.

A Bit of History

Remains of medieval wars – The charming **Wasserburgen**—literally "water castles"—are found all over the Münster region. Witness to the incessant defensive battles between rival nobles, they are built on the sites of temporary encampments set up by the Teutonic tribes. The castles first appeared in the 12C in the form of wooden strongholds erected on artificial hills ("Motten") protected at the base by a surrounding defensive wall and a moat. The invention of firearms in the early 16C made this system of defense precarious, and it was replaced over time with proper fortifications isolated still more by moats or lagoons.

Many of these compounds are spread over two islands, joined by a bridge. The first isle, or "Vorburg", was used for outbuildings; the second, or "Hauptburg" for the main residence. Their defensive character became less distinct over the centuries, especially after the Thirty Years' War (1618–48). After that, palaces set in formal gardens began to appear.

Castles

Anholt★
Schloßplatz 1, **Isselburg-Anholt**.📷🎧 Visit by guided tour (1hr) only, May–Sept,

Tue–Sun 11am–5pm; Oct–Apr, Sun 1pm–5pm. 🕐Closed Jan 1, Dec 24–26 & 31. 🎧6€, combined ticket for guided tour and park, 🎧8€. ☎(02874) 453 53. www.fuerst-salm.de.
Surrounded by a landscaped park and restored Baroque garden, this moated castle (Hauptburg and Vorburg 12C–17C, converted into a Baroque palace c. 1700) is built around a square inner courtyard. The museum contains evidence of three centuries of royal home décor. There are paintings (Rembrandt, Brueghel, Murillo), tapestries, furniture, porcelain and weapons.

Gemen
Schloßplatz 1, **Borken**. 37km/23mi east of Anholt. This castle is a church-owned youth center (Jugendburg) and can only be visited by prior arrangement. ☎(028 61) 922 00.
The towers, battlements and buildings of this castle (15C, remodeled in the 17C) are grouped on a fortified islet arising from beautiful, shaded stretches of water.

Raesfeld
In **Raesfeld**. 11km/6.8mi south of Gemen. 📷🎧Visit by guided tour (1hr) only: ☎(028 65) 95 51 27. www.gemeinde-raesfeld.de/touristik.
Raesfeld castle, built between 1643 and 1658 by Alexander von Velen, now con-

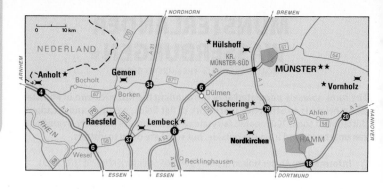

sists only of a building with two wings, the Vorburg and the castle chapel. It is used as a training center for various crafts and trades. Visible from afar is the 52.5m/ 172ft-high **onion-domed tower** the highest one of the region's moated castles.

Lembeck★

In **Lembeck**. *12.7km/7.9mi east of Raesfeld.* 👣*Visit to the castle museum by guided tour (45min—in German) only, Mar–Nov, Mon–Fri 1pm–5pm, Sat–Sun 11am–5pm. Park open 11am–6pm.* 👁*5€.* ☎*(02369) 71 67. www.schlosslembeck.de.*
The impressive approach to this castle follows a driveway punctuated by Baroque gateways and flanked by arched entrances. The monumental 17C palace features massive towers with onion-domed Baroque steeples protecting each corner. Guided tours take in splendidly furnished rooms reflecting the styles of the 17C and 18C. **Großer Saal**, the biggest one, is embellished with fine paneling and stuccowork.

Hülshoff★

Schonebeck 6, **Havixbeck**. *59.5km/37mi northeast of Lembeck* 🕐 *Open mid-Mar– Nov, daily 11am– 6pm.* 👁*5€.* ☎*(02534) 10 52. www.burg-huelshoff.de.*
The massive square towers of the outbuildings (first island) complement the residence (second island) built in 1545. This brick and stone manor features gable corners and a turret with a cupola and lantern. Admission to the park is free.
One of Germany's finest female poets, **Annette von Droste-Hülshoff** (1797–

1848) was born in this villa. Some fully furnished period rooms are open to the public, and there are also exhibits recalling her life and work.

Vischering★

Berenbrock 1, **Lüdinghausen**. *29.8km/18.5mi southwest of Hülshoff.* 🕐*Open Apr–Oct, Tue–Sun 10am–5.30pm; Nov–Mar, 10am–4.30pm.* 🕐*Closed Jan 1, Dec 24–26 & 31.* 👁*2.50€.* ☎*(02591) 799 00. http://burgvischering.luedinghausen.de.*
Built on two islands and protected by a double fortified wall, Vischering is the oldest and still one of the most formidable fortresses in the Münster region. It is essentially a Renaissance building constructed atop the foundations of a medieval castle. The fortress houses a museum with special emphasis on furniture from various eras. The wall and ceiling paintings and splendid sandstone fireplaces are particularly impressive. The Vorburg on a separate island once housed farm outbuildings. There is also a richly decorated carriage house.

Nordkirchen

9.5km/6mi southeast of Vischering. 👣*Visit by guided tour (1hr) only, May–Sept, Sun 11am–5pm; Oct–Apr, Sun 2pm–4pm; otherwise by prior arrangement daily 9am–6pm.* 👁*2€. Park free anytime, year-round.* ☎*(02596) 91 71 37.*
This 18C moated castle is the region's largest and known as "Westphalia's Versailles". The surrounding gardens are sprinkled with splendid sculptures.

Vornholz★ *– ⓒSee MÜNSTER: Excursions, Ostenfelde.*

MÜNSTER★★

POPULATION: 271 000

Münster, the historical capital of Westphalia, lies at the center of a wooded plain studded with moated castles and manor houses. The city's key moment in world history came in 1648 with the signing of the treaty that ended the Thirty Years' War. Today, it is a lively university city and Germany's secret "bicycle capital".

- **Information:** Heinrich-Brüning-Straße 9, 48127 Münster. ☎(0251) 492 27 10. www.tourismus.muenster.de.
- ▶ **Orient Yourself:** Münster can be reached via the A1 (Dortmund–Bremen), and is one hour by car from the big towns of the Ruhr.
- Ⓟ **Parking:** Garages are located throughout the Old City, near the main train station, near the Residenzschloß and near the theater on Wasserstraße.
- **Don't Miss:** The cathedral and the Prinzipalmarkt with the Peace Hall.
- **Organizing Your Time:** Allow one full day to see the sights of Münster.
- **Also See:** MÜNSTERLÄNDER WASSERBURGEN, OSNABRÜCK.

A Bit of History

The Peace of Westphalia – This twin treaty ended the Thirty Years' War and was signed in two towns: in Protestant Osnabrück on May 15, 1648, and in Catholic Münster on October 24, 1648. The treaties involved Emperor Ferdinand III, the kingdoms of Spain, France and Sweden, the Dutch Republic and their respective allies among the princes of the Holy Roman Empire.

It recognized and confirmed the cession to France of Alsace, guaranteed the independence of Switzerland and the Netherlands, and favored the development of Prussia. Protestants and Catholics were redefined as equal before the law, and Calvinism was given legal recognition.

Sights

St. Paulus-Dom★★

Domplatz 28. ⏲Open year-round, daily 6.30am–7.30pm (Sun 6pm). ☎(0251) 49 53 22. www.paulusdom.de.

Münster's squat twin-towered cathedral reflects the transitional style from Romanesque to Gothic prevalent in the 13C. The entrance is via the 16C south porch decorated with statues of the apostles and overlooked by Christ in Judgment. Inside, don't miss the 1540 **astronomical clock**★ in the southern ambulatory whose hours are struck by metal figurines wielding hammers. A carillon kicks into gear at noon Mon–Sat and 12.30pm Sun, and there is also a calendar that goes up to 2071 and a display of the moon phases and planet constellations. The **Chapel of the Holy Sacrament**★ is richly furnished (note especially the 18C silver tabernacle). The cathedral's modern **treasury**★★ *(Domkammer; ⏲open year-round, Tue–Sun 11am–4pm; ⏲closed Jan 1, Good Fri–Easter Sun, May 1 , Pentecost, Dec 24–26 & 31 Dec; ⊙1€; ☎(0251) 49 53 33)* is reached via the cloister. On the ground floor, 15C reliquary busts in copper and silver, the 11C head-reliquary of St. Paul, and a 13C Virgin surround a 13C **processional cross**.

The Anabaptists

Believed to have originated in Zurich, this radical religious reform movement endorsed adult baptism, polygamy and community of goods. In 1534, its followers attempted to establish a theocracy in Münster, deposing the magistrates and introducing its tenets. The era was brought to an end after a 16-month siege ending with the torture and execution of its leaders in the market square. The Anabaptists, or Rebaptists, were spiritual forerunners of the Mennonites and the Amish.

MÜNSTER			Hammer Str.	Z	30	Spiekerhof	Y	78
			Johannisstr.	Z	39	Steinfurter Str.	Y	80
Alter Fischmarkt	Y	2	Ludgeristr.	Z		Überwasserstr.	Y	83
Alter Steinweg	Y	5	Mauritzstr.	Y	48	Universitätsstr.	YZ	86
An der Apostelkirche	Y	8	Mauritztor	Y	51	Verspoel	Z	89
Bahnhofstr.	Z		Pferdegasse	Y	63	Wasserstr.	Y	92
Bogenstr.	Y	12	Prinzipalmarkt	YZ		Wolbecker Str.	Z	96
Drubbel	Y	16	Rothenburg	Z	69			
Eisenbahnstraße	Z	20	Salzstr.	YZ	72			

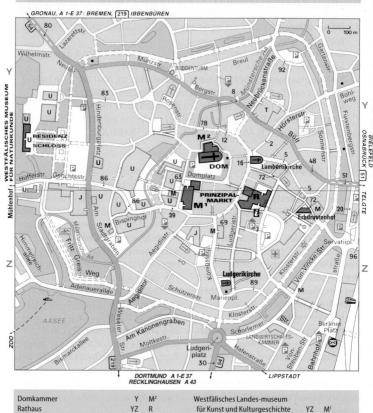

Domkammer	Y	M²	Westfälisches Landes-museum		
Rathaus	YZ	R	für Kunst und Kulturgeschichte	YZ	M¹

Westfälisches Landesmuseum für Kunst und Kulturgeschichte★ (Regional Art & History Museum)

Domplatz 10.

🕐 *Open year-round, Tue–Sun 10am–6pm (Thu 9pm).* 🕐 *Closed Dec 24, 25 & 31.* ⬤*3.50€.* ♿⬤*(0251) 59 07 01. www.landesmuseum-muenster.de.*

This museum's collections span the artistic arc from the Middle Ages to today. Particularly noteworthy are **altarpieces★★** by Conrad von Soest, Koerbecke and the Masters of Liesborn and Schöppingen.

Prinzipalmarkt★ (Principal Market)

The Principal Market is Münster's busiest and most historic street with elegant houses that were once the homes of rich burghers. Under the arcades, attractive shops jostle for attention with restaurants and cozy pubs.

Rathaus (Town Hall)

The dominant building on Prinzipalmarkt is the late 14C **Town Hall**, an impressive example of Gothic civic architecture. The diplomatic negotiations between 1644 and 1648 that brought an end to the Thirty Years' War were held in the **Friedensaal**★ *(Peace Hall;* 🕐*open year-round, Tue–Fri 10am–5pm, Sat–Sun 10am–4pm;* 💰*1.50€;* ♿*, ☎(0251) 492 27 24)*, a wood-paneled council chamber.

Lambertikirche (St. Lambert's Church)

Groined vaulting lidding the center nave and star vaults above the side aisles are the striking features of this Gothic hall church. Dangling from the tower are the iron cages that once held the dead bodies of the Anabaptist rebel leaders displayed to the public following the defeat of their uprising in 1535.

Residenzschloss (Palace)

This Baroque palace was once the residence of the prince-bishops and is now part of the university. The red brick of the elegant three-part façade designed by Johann Conrad Schlaun is variegated with sandstone facings. The park in the back segues into a botanical garden.

Excursions

Telgte

12km/8mi east on B51.

In the center of Telgte, next to the Baroque pilgrimage chapel with a Pietà from 1370, is the local museum, the Heimathaus Münsterland. One of its prize exhibits is a folk art textile, the **Lenten Veil**★ (1623), which measures 32sq m/344.4sq ft.

Freckenhorst

26km/16mi east on B51.

Freckenhorst's **Collegiate Church**★ *(Stiftskirche)* is a fine example of pre-Romanesque German architecture.

Ostenfelde

36km/22.3mi east on B51.

The graceful, privately owned **Schloss Vornholz**★ (Vornholz Castle, 1666) stands in a rolling landscape forested with ancient oaks. Built on two islets, it is a typical Münsterland "water castle". 🕐*See map in MÜNSTERLÄNDER WASSERBURGEN.*

Münsterländer Wasserburgen

– 🕐*See MÜNSTERLÄNDER WASSERBURGEN.*

Address Book

🕐*For coin ranges, see the Legend on the cover flap.*

WHERE TO STAY

🍷🍷 **Hotel Hiltruper Hof** – *Westfalenstraße 148, 48165 Münster-Hiltrup ☎(0251) 278 80. www.hiltruper-hof.de. 17 rooms.* For 150 years this little family-run hotel has welcomed guests into well-cared for rooms. Sports and leisure equipment are available locally.

🍷🍷🛏**Hotel Central** – *Aegidiistraße 1. ☎(0251) 51 01 50. www.central-hotel-muenster.de. 20 rooms. Closed second half of Aug, Dec 22–31.* Run by an art-loving couple, this small city hotel has works from Beuys to Warhol decorating the public areas and the modern and good-sized rooms.

WHERE TO EAT

🍷🍷 **Pinkus Müller** – *Kreuzstraße 4. ☎(0251) 451 51. Closed Sun.* 🍴
Right in the "Kuhviertel" student quarter, this typical Westphalian brew-pub exudes rustic ambience, pours its own beer and serves hearty meals to mixed crowds sitting around polished wooden tables. The same street has several other restaurants and cafes.

🍷🍷🛏 **Kleines Restaurant im Oer'schen Hof** – *Königsstraße 42. ☎(0251) 484 10 83. Closed Sun–Mon.* 🍴
This establishment is spread over three floors of an old glazed brick house. The ambience is pleasant thanks to a tasteful mix of rustic furniture with modern paintings.

NAUMBURG★

POPULATION: 30 000

Pretty Naumburg lies on the edge of the Thuringian basin, surrounded by terraced vineyards and wooded hillsides topped by castles. Lordly burgher houses, sturdy fortifications and, above all, the exceptional cathedral still reflect the town's heritage as a medieval trading center. The philosopher Friedrich Nietzsche spent a lot of time in the town at various stages of his life.

- **Information:** Markt 12, 06618 Naumburg. ☎(03445) 27 31 12. www.naumburg-tourismus.de.
- **Orient Yourself:** Naumburg is in the heart of the Saale-Unstrut wine-growing region, about 50km/31mi south of Halle.
- **Don't Miss:** Cathedral Sts Peter and Paul.
- **Organizing Your Time:** Allow half a day to see Naumburg.
- **Also See:** HALLE, WEIMAR, LEIPZIG.

A Bit of History

Important trading center – The seat of a bishopric since 1028, Naumburg started developing as a civic entity in the 12C and the city was an important trading center in the Late Middle Ages and Renaissance period. The "Peter-Pauls-Messe" held here was a serious rival to the trade fair in Leipzig.

A model town – Largely spared damage during World War II, in 1991 Naumburg was one of five cities in the nine new Federal German states to be selected as a model for restoring old city centers.

Sights

Dom Sts Peter und Paul★★ (Cathedral of Saints Peter and Paul)

Domplatz 16/17.

Open Mar–Oct, daily 9am–6pm (Sun from noon); Nov–Feb, 10am–4pm (Sun from noon). ☎(03445) 23 01 10.

This double-chancel cathedral is a perfect example of the stylistic evolution from Late Romanesque to Early Gothic. The Romanesque nave was built in the early 13C; by the late 13C the western section was completed with Early Gothic features. The eastern chancel is separated from the central nave by the only remaining hall-church rood screen in Germany.

The western chancel is bathed in ethereal light thanks to extraordinarily luminous stained-glass windows. It features another magnificent **rood screen★★**. This one is by the artist known only as the Master of Naumburg and depicts poignant, life-like scenes of the Passion. The splendid central portal shows a Crucifixion group, surmounted by the Majesty of God as a fresco in a quatrefoil. The same master also created the famous **statues★★★** of the cathedral's benefactors, Uta and Ekkehard.

View of Naumburg with the cathedral in the background

J. Bouraly/MICHELIN

Marktplatz (Market Square)

The large market square is framed by 16C–17C houses. The **Town Hall**, a Late Gothic building, has a beautiful portal from 1612 and boasts six transverse gables with tracery decoration. The same façade design is repeated on the *Schlößchen* (1543), behind which towers the church of St. Wenzel. The *Hohe Lilie* (municipal museum), with its Late Gothic corbie gable and traced transom, stands at the entrance to Herrenstraße.

St. Wenzel-Kirche★ (Church of St. Wenceslas)

A church on this site was first recorded in 1228. The present building was constructed in the 15C as a Late Gothic hall church with an unusual floor plan. Between 1610 and 1618, five Renaissance tribunes were added, and up to the mid-18C the interior was transformed into the Baroque style with a mirror-vaulted ceiling and a magnificent carved altar, and pulpit. The organ is one of the largest surviving works by **Zacharias Hildebrand** and was put through its paces by Johann Sebastian Bach, no less. Inside the church are also two fine paintings by **Lucas Cranach the Elder**: *The Adoration of the Magi* (1522) and *The Blessing of the Children* (1529).

Town houses

In Jakobstraße note the **Alte Post** (1574) with its three-story oriel. Houses in **Marienstraße** sport extravagantly ornate portals that reflect the burghers' one-time prosperity. **Herrenstraße** features some fine oriels, including the town's oldest at house no 1. The *Lorbeerapotheke*, an old pharmacy next door, also boasts a splendid oriel, as does the house at no 8 (1525).

Marientor (St. Mary's Gate)

This is the only one of the five original town gates to have survived. It is a rare example of a double gate with gatehouses, a curved courtyard to trap intruders, and a watchpath. It is 14C at its core but was extended in the 15C.

Nietzsche-Haus

Weingarten 18. ⏱*Open mid-Mar–Oct, Tue–Fri 2pm–5pm, Sat–Sun 10am–4pm.* ⊗*2€.* ☎*(03445) 20 16 38.*
From 1890 until 1897, during his collapse into mental and physical decline, Nietzsche was cared for in this house by his mother. Photos and documents (in German) evoke the intellectual life and works of the controversial philosopher.

Baroque Church Organ at the St. Wenzel Kirche

Joys of the Grape

Two lovely rivers give Germany's northernmost wine-growing region its name: The Saale and the Unstrut. Only 665ha/1 643 acres in size, this area has a viticultural heritage going back 1 000 years and considers Freyburg as its unofficial capital.

Some 30 grape varieties grow in these limestone and red sandstone soils, on vineyards clinging to steeply riverside terraces that are drenched by up to 1 600 hours of sunshine a year. Most varietals are dry, fresh and white, with Müller-Thurgau leading the pack, followed by Weissburgunder (pinot blanc), Silvaner and Riesling.

Only one quarter is dedicated to red wines, mostly Dornfelder and red Burgundy.

Excursions

Freyburg
7km/4.3mi north.
This wine-growing town hugs a picturesque stretch of the Unstrut River and is dominated by the hilltop Neuenburg castle. You can travel by steamer along the river as far as the Naumburg flower fields.

Schloss Neuenburg★
(Neuenburg Castle)
Open Apr–Oct, daily 10am–6pm; Nov–Mar, Tue–Sun 10am–5pm. 4€. (0344 64) 355 30. www.schloss-neuenburg.de.
Neuenburg castle was founded in 1090 by Ludwig der Springer, the landgrave of Thuringia as the eastern counterpart to the Wartburg fortress. The lower floor of the 13C double **chapel**★ was reserved for the common folk, while the nobility sat upstairs. The two floors are linked by a small grille in the ceiling. The castle houses an interesting and comprehensive museum with exhibits about the regional wine-making tradition, St. Elizabeth of Thuringia and a history of the castle and its owners.
The free-standing round tower behind the castle is the only surviving one of

three and is affectionately known as "**Dicker Wilhelm**" (Fat William; *open Apr–Oct, Tue–Sun 10am–6pm; 1.50€*). Dating back to the middle of the 12C, it is 23m/75.4ft high and has walls measuring 2.85m/9.3ft thick. Inside are historical exhibits and fabulous views from the top. *Combination tickets for both the tower and the castle are 5€.*

Schulpforta
On B87, just before Bad Kösen, 6km/3.7mi west. Cistercian abbey church and estate: open Apr–Aug, daily 10am–6pm; Sept–Mar, 10am–4pm. Closed Dec 24–Jan 6. Historic building: Visit by guided tour (75min) only, Apr–Sept, Sat 10.30am and 2pm. 2.50€. (034463) 351 10.
The **Cistercian monastery**, which was founded in 1137, was closed in 1540 and three years later became a prestigious boarding school for gifted students that still functions today. Its long list of famous alumni includes Schlegel, Fichte, Klopstock and Nietzsche. The **monastery church** has an imposing west façade from around 1300.

Bad Kösen★
On B87, around 7km/4.3mi west.
This attractive little health resort on the Saale boasts a unusual technical monument, the **brine extraction unit**★.
The **Romanisches Haus** (Romanesque House) is now a **local history museum** (*open Apr–Oct, Tue–Fri 10am–noon, 1pm–5pm, Sat–Sun 10am–5pm; Nov–Mar, Wed 10am–noon, 1pm–4pm, Sat–Sun 10am–4pm; closed mid-Dec–mid-Jan; 2€; (034463) 276 68).*
It was first recorded in 1138 as the Schulpforta monastery guesthouse and ranks among the oldest secular buildings in central Germany. A highlight of the museum is the collection of Käthe Kruse dolls which were produced here until 1964.

Rudelsburg and Burg Saaleck
These ruined fortresses, which were destroyed during the Thirty Years' War, lie in an attractive 12C **site**★ high above the Saale, about 3km/1.8mi to the south of Bad Kösen. Both are popular tourist destinations.

NEUBRANDENBURG

POPULATION: 68 600

This town, founded in 1248 at the behest of Margrave Johann von Brandenburg, is built on an almost circular ground plan, criss-crossed by a grid-like network of streets. When 80 percent of the old town was destroyed in 1945, the fortifications with their four unique gates were quite remarkably spared any damage, making them a principal tourist attraction.

🛈 **Information:** Marktplatz 1, 17033 Neubrandenburg, ☎ (0395) 194 33. www.neubrandenburg.de

▶ **Orient Yourself:** Midway between Berlin and the Baltic coast, Neubrandenburg is to the northeast of the pretty lake of Tollensesee.

🅿 **Parking:** Garages are in the heart of the old city, on Neutorstraße and on Stargarder Straße.

👁 **Don't Miss:** Neubrandenburg's medieval wall.

🕐 **Organizing Your Time:** Plan at least an hour to explore the town wall.

👶 **Especially for Kids:** Climbing the old wall and towers, and outdoor recreation in the Feldberger Seenlandschaft.

♿ **Also See:** MECKLEMBURGISCHE SEENPLATTE, GREIFSWALD.

Sights

Fortifications★★ 👶

Some 50 years after Neubrandenburg was founded in 1248, construction began on the town's defensive fortifications. In the end, the formidable wall was 2.3km/1.4mi-long, over 7m/23ft high and 1.4m/4ft 6in thick at the base. It was built using boulders from the vicinity and capped by several rows of bricks. The wall's four gates were closed every evening and only opened in return for payment. They remained the only access to the town right up to the mid-19C.

The gates are all of the same design, each an individual fortification. So that the town could be safely defended, three- to four-floor sentry posts were built into the wall every 30m/98ft. There were 56 of them in the 16C, 25 of which have been reconstructed. All able-bodied citizens were expected to maintain the posts, while defense of the gates was the duty of the four principal guilds: Bakers, Wool Weavers, Shoemakers and Blacksmiths.

The oldest gate, the **Friedländer Tor**, was built just after 1300. It is 19m/62.3ft high. On the outside it is possible to see the transition from the Romanesque to the Gothic period. The **Stargarder Tor**, built during the early 14C, is embellished with nine terracotta figures in long pleated robes, known as "Die Jungfrauen" *(the maids)*. The outer gate is especially sumptuously decorated. The **Treptower Tor**, built around 1400, stands 32m/105ft tall and is the highest of the gate towers. Both the main gate and the outer gate are richly decorated with brick tracery. The **Neues Tor** (New Gate), built after 1550 in the Late Gothic style, combines decorative elements of the other three gates.

Of the two towers that further reinforced the fortifications, only the 19m/62ft-high **Fangelturm** remains. It was used as a prison. The spire was added in 1845.

Konzertkirche (Concert Church)

Formerly the Church of St. Mary, this brick church was completed late in the 13C and was partly rebuilt in Neo-Gothic style in the mid-19C. In the 1990s, Finish architect Pekka Salminen converted the church into a state-of-the-art concert hall. Endowed with supreme acoustics, it is one of the main performance venues of the Neubrandenburg Philharmonic Orchestra (www.theater-und-orchester.de).

St. Johanniskirche (Church of St. John)

🕐 *Open year-round, Tue–Sat 10am–noon, 1pm–6pm, Sat 10am–4pm.* 🕐 *Closed public holidays.* &📞 *(0395) 582 22 88.*

The 13C–14C church of the former Franciscan monastery features a Renaissance **pulpit**★ supported by a figure of Moses, which dates from 1598. It is made of limestone and displays alabaster reliefs of Christ and the Evangelists.

Tollensesee ⟨Kids⟩

This lovely lake, which is 10.4km/6.5mi in length and almost 3km/1.8mi wide, lies to the south of the town, in the middle of an attractive landscape. The western bank slopes steeply up to Brodaer woods. In summer, locals and visitors flock to its shores for swimming, boating, tanning and picnicking. Boat rentals are available and it is also possible to explore the lake on a leisurely **boat cruise** (🕐 *May–Sept, Tue–Sun, 10am, 11am, 3pm; round-trip 1hr 30min, 2hr or 2hr 30min; 💶9–11€; Fahrgastschiff Mudder Schulten;* ☎ *0395 584 12 18)*

Excursions

Around the Feldberger Seenlandschaft★ (Feldberger 'Lake Country')

Burg Stargard

11km/6.8mi south of Neubrandenburg, via the E 251 and L33.

The castle ruins dominate their surroundings here.

Woldegk

20km/12.4mi farther on via the B104.

This town, with its five windmills, borders the Feldburger Seenlandscaft (🕐 *see below).*

Seenlandschaft

To the southwest of Woldegk, in the Mecklenburg-Strelit district, lies this lovely hilly lake region.

At 34 500ha/85 251 acres, the area is home to the rare European otter and also to the sea eagle, osprey and lesser spotted eagle. Woods, meadows, moors and lakes alternate attractively between **Fürstenwerder** and **Feldberg**. There are plenty of diving opportunities in the lakes here, such as Tauchcenter-Feldberg (www.tauchcenter-feldberg.de).

Carwitz

29.5km18.3mi southwest of Woldegk along the B198.

The former 1848 half-timbered home of the writer **Hans Fallada** (author of *Little Man, What Now?*, among many others) stands in an idyllic lakeside location and contains a museum about the man and his life.

Neustrelitz

39km/24.2mi northeast of Carwitz.

The former residence of the dukes of Mecklenburg-Strelitz still bears witness today to their proud past. Visitors can admire the **Schlossgarten**★ with its graceful buildings and monuments, part of which was laid out in the 19C as an English country park. The orangerie with its remarkable Pompeii-style **paintings**★, the Baroque town **church** (1768–78), the classical **Rathaus** dating from 1841, and the Neo-Gothic **Schloßkirche** (1855–59) are all worth seeing.

Ravensbrück

24km/15mi south of Neustrelitz on the E 251, 1km/0.6mi from Fürstenberg.

🕐 *Open year-round, Tue–Sun 9am–5pm.* 🕐 *Closed Dec 24–26 & 31.* ☎ *(033093) 60 80. www.ravensbrueck.de.*

Construction of Ravensbrück concentration camp on the shores of Schwedtsee lake began in 1938. It was the only major camp for women and by 1945 had seen 132 000 prisoners from over 40 nations. Tens of thousands died.

The camp is now a memorial site with a permanent exhibition in the old SS camp commander's headquarters that documents the history of the camp and the lives and deaths of its victims. The crematorium and a cell block can also be seen.

SCHLOSS NEUSCHWANSTEIN★★★

With its forest of playful towers and turrets, Neuschwanstein is the quintessential fairytale castle and a product of the imagination of King Ludwig II of Bavaria (1845–86). Set against a splendid backdrop of the Alps, it is the single most popular tourist attraction in Germany and deluged with visitors every day. A friend and sponsor of the composer Richard Wagner, Ludwig regarded this palace as a tribute to his operas and German heroic legends in general. Escape the crowds by hitting the forest trails surrounding the castle.

Information: Neuschwansteinstraße 20, 87645 Schwangau. ☎(08362) 93 98 80. www.neuschwanstein.com.

▶ **Orient Yourself:** About 5km/3mi east of Füssen, the castle is on a rocky ridge 200m/656ft above the Pöllat gorge, making an making an impressive site.

Don't Miss: The view of the castle from the Marienbrücke.

Organizing Your Time: Allow half a day for your visit, including waiting time.

Also See: ROMANTISCHE STRASSE, DEUTSCHE ALPENSTRASSE, FÜSSEN, WIESKIRCHE.

A Bit of History

The construction – King Ludwig II found the ideal location for "Neu-Hohen-schwangau" (the name "Neuschwanstein" only came in 1890) not far from Hohen-schwangau castle, where he had spent part of his childhood and youth. Ludwig came up with the design of the new palace himself. To a large extent it was inspired by the medieval Wartburg in Thuringia *(see EISENACH)*, which he had visited in 1867.

The end of a dream – Ludwig II only lived at Neuschwanstein for 170 days. The palace construction had put a seri-

ous strain on the royal coffers and the king's increasingly eccentric behavior led a government commission from Munich to bring him news of his dethronement on June 10, 1886. Just three days later, he was found floating dead in Lake Starnberg. The true circumstances of his death, and that of his doctor who had accompanied him on a walk that fateful evening, remain a mystery to this day.

Visit

Visit by guided tour (35min) only; Apr–Sept, daily 9am–6pm; Oct–Mar, 10am–4pm. Ticket booths open one

Wonderful Neuschwanstein castle of Ludwig II of Bavaria

F. Zaninotto/MICHELIN

Gothic with All Mod Cons

Ludwig II's plans for a home recreating Germanic mythology through Gothic architecture also took into account the latest scientific developments. The cranes used to build the castle were steam powered, a steel frame was used in the throne room, and the windows held broad panes of glass that were uncommon even in the 19C. Other features included a floor-based central heating system, flushing toilets, an elevator, electric bells to summon servants, and telephones on the third and fourth floors. Not so much the "Fairytale King" *(Märchenkönig)* as a man with his own private theme park.

hour prior. ⊙*Closed Jan 1, Shrove Tue, Dec 24, 25 & 31.* &*www.neuschwanstein. de.* ⊚*9€, same-day combination ticket with Schloss Hohenschwangau 17€. Buy tickets in Hohenschwangau village before embarking on the 30min walk up to the castle (horsedrawn carriage rides available, 5€ uphill, 2.50€ downhill). Advance tickets (1.80€ booking fee) available by phone and online from* **Ticketcenter** *(☎(08362) 93 08 30; www.ticket-center-hohenschwangau.de).*

The interior, with its profusion of gilded paneling and wall paintings, reflects Ludwig's fertile imagination and fantasies. The most distinctive chambers are on the third floor: the **throne room**★ (unfinished), the **bed chamber**★ furnished with Gothic pieces, the **living room**★ with its Lohengrin-inspired decorations, and the artificial stalactite cave with the adjacent winter garden, evoking the Tannhäuser legend. The design of the **Sändersaal** *(minstrels' hall)* is based on the Wartburg, where the legendary poetry contest featured in Wagner's opera, *Tannhäuser,* was said to have taken place in the early 13C.

For dreamy **views**★★ of the castle, take the short but steep ten-minute trail up to Marienbrücke bridge above the cascading Pöllat river.

Excursion

Schloss Hohenschwangau★

☛Visit by guided tour (35min) only; Apr–Sept, daily 9am–6pm; Oct–Mar, 10am–4pm. ⊙*Closed Jan 1, Shrove Tue, Dec 24, 25 & 31.* ⊚*9€, same-day combination ticket with Schloss Neuschwanstein 17€. For advance tickets, see Schloss Neuschwanstein.*

Maximilian II of Bavaria, who was at the time still the Crown Prince, commissioned this castle as the family's summer residence in the 1830s; it stands atop the foundations of a 12C fortress. The flamboyant Neo-Gothic style was in accordance with current taste and reflected Maximilian's predilection for chivalric romance. Ludwig II spent most of his largely unhappy youth in this castle, which stands in a picturesque setting on a wooded hill overlooking the pretty Alpsee. It is about a 15-minute walk to the castle from Hohenschwangau village.

In comparison with Neuschwanstein—and in spite of the almost compulsive repetition of the swan motif—Hohenschwangau has retained a romantic, comfortable feel. Queen Maria, Ludwig II's mother, spent much time here, which explains the welcoming, lived-in atmosphere.

After the maniacal decoration of Schloss Neuschwanstein, the clean lines of the maple and cherrywood Biedermeier furniture here may come as a relief. Still, some rooms also sport elaborate wall paintings, usually depicting scenes from German history or mythology.

One of Ludwig II's favorite rooms was the upstairs music room where he would listen to Richard Wagner playing the piano, still in situ today. Don't miss the king's bedchamber, where the ceiling is painted to represent night stars.

Follow your visit of the castle with a stroll to a beautiful **viewpoint**★ on a shaded rocky spur of the **Pindarplatz** on the Alpsee.

NÖRDLINGEN★

POPULATION: 20 000

The former Free Imperial City of Nördlingen lies in the middle of the Ries basin created by a giant meteorite about 15 million years ago. First recorded in 898, it is only one of three German towns still surrounded by a medieval town wall.

- **Information:** Marktplatz 2, 86720 Nördlingen. ☎ (09081) 841 16. www.noerdlingen.de.
- ▶ **Orient Yourself:** Nördlingen is at the center of the Ries basin, a meteorite crater with a diameter of 25km/15.5mi.
- **Don't Miss:** Rieskrater-Museum.
- **Organizing Your Time:** Allow half a day to explore the primary sights.
- **Especially for Kids:** Rieskrater-Museum.
- **Also See:** ROMANTISCHE STRASSE, EICHSTÄTT.

Sights

St. Georgskirche★ (St. George's Church)

This late 15C hall-church is surmounted by a majestic, 90m/295.3ft-high, copper-domed bell-tower, affectionately dubbed **"Daniel"** (�LJopen Apr–Oct, daily 9am–7pm; Nov–Mar, 9am–5pm; ☞1.50€). It is well worth braving the 350 steps to the top in order to fully appreciate Nördlingen's near circular shape and the crater within which it was built. A watchman still lives up here and calls out every half hour between 10am and midnight. Originally, this was intended to make contact with the guards holding watch on the town gates.

The church interior is canopied by graceful fan vaulting. The pulpit (1499) is reached via a corbelled staircase with only three steps. Note the curious little **organ** on the finely worked baldaquin (on the right side). The main altar is Baroque in style but incorporates five statues created in Gothic times. They depict Jesus on the cross, St. Mary, St. John and two angels and were created by Niclaus Gerhaert von Leyden.

Stadtmauer★ (Town Walls)

The Nördlingen town walls are completely preserved and fully accessible. The ramparts, which for the most part are covered, extend over a length of 2 632m/ 8 635ft and are punctuated by five gates and 14 towers.

One of the city gates in Nördlingen

©Andre Bienzeisler/istockphoto.com

Address Book

🪙 *For coin ranges, see cover flap.*

WHERE TO STAY

🍽️🍽️🛏️**Hotel Sonne** – *Marktplatz 3*
☎*(090 81) 50 67 Fax (090 81) 2 39 99*
www.kaiserhof-hotel-sonne.de. Closed
2 weeks in Nov. 29 rooms. Restaurant
🍽️🍽️. This traditional hotel in the
heart of Nördlingen dates from 1477.
It has comfortable rooms and a
countrystyle dining room with a neat
vaulted ceiling.

WHERE TO EAT

🍽️🍽️🍽️ **Meyer's Keller** – *Marien-*
höhe 8 (above Oskar-Mayer-Straße).
☎*(09081) 44 93. www.meyerskeller.*
de. Closed for 2 weeks in Jan, 1 week
in late May, Mon and Tue lunchtimes.
This pleasant brasserie serves tasty
regional dishes in a dining room
accented by parquet flooring,
modern artworks and contemporary
décor. In fine weather, sit outside
under a canopy of shady old trees.

One of the most attractive sections is
along the battlements from the Berger
Gate via the Alte Bastei, or old bastion,
to the Reimlinger Gate.

In order to learn more about the fortifications and their role in the history
of Nördlingen, swing by the small
but excellent **Stadtmauermuseum**
(🕐*open Apr–Oct, daily 10am–4.30pm;*
🪙*1€; ☎09081- 91 80)* in the Löpsinger
gate tower. Exhibits include canons and
uniforms from the Thirty Years' War.

Stadtmuseum★ (City Museum)

Vordere Gerberstraße 1.
🕐*Open Mar–Oct, Tue–Sun 1.30pm–*
4.30pm. 🕐*Closed Good Fri.* 🪙*3€.* ☎*(09*
081) 273 82 30. www.stadtmuseum-noerd
lingen.de.
Housed in a former hospital, this engaging museums has four floors of displays
covering the pre- and early history of the
Ries basin, along with the political and
economic influence Nördlingen enjoyed
as a free imperial city. Art fans will be
drawn to the collection of 19C painting
and altar panels by Old German masters.
A highlight here is the altar wings from

the St. Georgskirche painted by Friedrich
Herlin in 1462.

Not only kids will get a kick out of the
huge model featuring around 6 000 tin
figures in a recreation of a famous Thirty
Years' War battle that took place outside
the town walls.

Rieskrater-Museum★   Kids

Eugene-Shoemaker-Platz 1.
🕐*Open May-Oct, Tue–Sun 10am-*
4.30pm, Nov–Apr, Tue–Sun 10am–noon,
1.30pm–4.30pm. 🕐*Closed Jan 1, Good*
Fri, Dec 24–26 & 31. 🪙*4€.* ☎*(09081) 273*
82 20. www.rieskrater-museum.de.
The Ries meteorite crater was formed
approximately 15 million years ago.
Just imagine it—a giant stone sphere,
1km/0.6mi in diameter, hits the earth
at a speed of c. 70 000kph/43 496mph,
penetrating up to 1km/0.6mi into the
rock! The energy of 250 000 nuclear
atom bombs (such as that used in Hiro-
shima in Japan, 1945) is released, and a
wave of pressure and heat extinguishes
all life within a range of 100km/62mi.
A crater 14km/9mi in diameter forms,
which eventually extends to 25km/16mi
because of all the rock that eventually
caves in.

The crater, which was originally
4km/2.5mi deep, was gradually filled
in over the course of millions of years,
but later partially excavated and opened
up again.

The Rieskrater-Museum, which is housed
in a carefully restored barn (1503), does
a fine job of giving the layperson an
understanding of this mindboggling
phenomenon.

Excursion

Neresheim Abbey★

19km/12mi southwest.
👣*Guided tours Easter–Oct, Mon–Sat*
11am and 3pm, Sun 11.15am and 3.15pm.
☎*(07326) 8501. www.abtei-neresheim.de.*
The abbey church was the last major
commission designed by **Balthasar
Neumann** and built between 1745 and
1792. Inside, the seemingly weightless
ceiling decoration is a work of Martin
Knoller and was painted between 1771
and 1775.

NORDFRIESISCHE INSELN★

NORTHERN FRISIANS

This group of beautiful and wind-swept islands forms part of the Schleswig-Holsteinisches Wattenmeer (Wadden Sea) National Park, which was created in 1985. The islands' fragile environment, including tall dunes, is protected from the ravages of the North Sea by dykes and artificial banks.

- **Information:** Zingel 5, 25813 Husum. ☎(0180) 506 60 77. www.nordseetourismus.de.
- **Orient Yourself:** The North Frisian Islands are off the west coast of Schleswig-Holstein, in the North Sea, close to Denmark. Ferries for Föhr and Amrum leave from Dagebüll (43km/26.7mi north of Husum). For Pellworm, embark in Nordstrand (17km/10.5mi west of Husum). For the Halligen, catch a ferry from Husum or Nordstrand.
- **Don't Miss:** Amrum, mudflat hikes.
- **Organizing Your Time:** Spend at least a day relaxing on these islands.
- **Especially for Kids:** Island cruising and exploration.
- **Also See:** HUSUM, INSEL HELGOLAND.

Sights

Dägebull

Dägebull is a very small village and harbor on the northwesternmost point of Schleswig-Holstein.

Amrum

The smallest of the North Frisian islands, Amrum's west coast is home to sand dunes, heaths, woods, farmland and mudflats that provide a rich habitat for sea birds, making them a paradise for bird watchers. Its biggest natural asset is the **Kniepsand**, a gloriously white, fine beach that extends for nearly 12km/7.4mi and can get up to 1km/0.6mi wide. There is a 64m/210ft- high **lighthouse** in **Wittdün** from where you can enjoy sweeping views as far as the island of Sylt (see INSEL SYLT).

The village **Nebel** grew up around the medieval church of **St. Clemens** in the 16C. The town also features the **Öömrang-Hüs**, a 19C sea captain's house. The far north of the island, in the bird sanctuary **Amrum Odde**, is the departure point for guided walks across the mudflats to Föhr.

Föhr

Föhr is a peaceful island blessed with a mild climate. The landscape is largely marshland, dotted with pretty villages

Ferries

Dägebull–Föhr:
Eleven ferries daily. 45min.
Dägebull–Anrum: *Seven ferries daily. 60min; 90min via Föhr.*
Wyker Dampfschiffs-Reederei Föhr-Amrum GmbH: ☎(0180) 508 01 40. www.faehre.de.

(including Nieblum, Süderende and Oldsum). The beaches lie in the south; on the northern end is a windswept forest rich with birdlife.

The port of **Wyk** in the southeast is crisscrossed by well-tended narrow streets perfect for exploring at leisure. Those interested in local nature, history and culture should drop by the **Dr.-Carl-Häberlin-Friesen-Museums** (open Jul–Aug, daily 10am–5pm; mid-Mar–Oct, Tue–Sun, 10am–5pm; mid-Oct–Feb, Tue–Sun 2pm–5pm; closed Dec 24 & 31; 4.10€; ☎(04681) 25 71).

Dunsum is the departure point for a walk across the mudflats to Amrum.

Halligen★

These tiny islands are all that remain of mainland marshes once part of the coastal region. In 1600 there were more than 25 recorded islets, but all but ten of them have since been swallowed up by the fierce sea. Most of the Halligen are unprotected by sea dikes, resulting

Address Book

🪙*For coin ranges, see cover flap.*

WHERE TO STAY

⊜**Ekke Nekkepenn** – *Waasterstigh 19, Nebel, Amrum.* ☎*(04682) 945 60. www. ekkenekkepenn.de. 8 rooms.* Charming, petite hotel welcomes you with prettily decorated rooms. Mornings start with an ample breakfast featuring freshly baked bread and served in a cheerful room.

⊜⊜**Duus-Hotel** – *Hafenstraße 40, Wyk, Föhr.* ☎*(04681) 598 10. www. duus-hotel.de. Closed Jan 6-Feb 15, mid-Nov-Dec 24. 22 rooms. Restaurant*⊜⊜. A convenient location and well-kept, contemporary rooms (some with harbor views) are among the assets of this family-run hotel. The restaurant serves regional and international meals.

⊜⊜**Weiße Düne** – *Achtern Strand 6, Wittdün, Amrum.* ☎*(04682) 94 00 00. www.weisse-duene.de. 12 rooms. Closed late Nov–mid-Dec. Restaurant*⊜⊜.

Handsomely decorated rooms and self-catering apartments with modern amenities await at this delightful hotel. Enjoy local feel-good food with a rustic bent in the traditional restaurant.

WHERE TO EAT

⊜⊜**Friesenstube** – *Süderstraße 8, Wyk, Föhr.* ☎*(04681) 24 04. Closed mid-Jan–mid-Feb, Mon.* The Frisian décor, complete with cheerful wall tiles, gives this casual inn a winning ambience. The kitchen is known for its excellent fish dishes.

⊜⊜⊜**Landhotel Witt** – *Alkersumstieg 4, Nieblum, Föhr.* ☎*(04681) 587 70. www. landhotel-witt.de. Closed Jan 10–mid-Feb.* Handpicked antiques contribute to the stylishly elegant setting at this restaurant where imaginatively prepared regional dishes dominate the menu.

A Walk in the Sea

In the East Frisian islands, you can quite literally "walk on water"— well, at least on the bottom of the ocean floor. When the tide recedes, it leaves mudflats and shallow water channels, allowing you to trek between islands. This is more dangerous than it sounds, so never venture out without a local guide.

in temporary island submersions up to 50 times a year. At these times only a few reed-thatched houses perched on artificial mounds *(terps)* stay above the water. The prettiest Hallig is **Hooge**, but **Langeneß**, the largest with 18 mounds, is popular also, and Gröde also gets a fair number of visitors. Most are day-trippers but those with enough time will find an overnight stay a rewarding experience. Various shipping companies offer boat trips to the Halligen.

Pellworm

This island is enclosed by a 25km/15.5mi-long and 8m/26.2ft-high dike, without

which Pellworm would be inundated as it lies below sea level. Its main feature is the ruined tower of the **Alte Kirche St. Salvator**, whose origins date back to the 11C–12C. Nearby lies the **Friedhof der Heimatlosen** (Cemetery of the Homeless), where the bodies of strangers washed up on the island's shores are buried.

Nordstrand

Marshy Nordstrand is linked to the mainland by a 4km/2.5mi causeway and is formed of reclaimed farmland (polders) and villages sitting on terps.

🛳Ferries🛳

Nordstrand/Strucklahnung-shörn–Pellworm *(35mins).* *www.faehre-pellworm.de.*
Schlüttsiel–Hooge *(60min)*
Amrum–Hooge *(90min)*
Schlüttsiel–Langeneß *(90min via Hooge)*
Amrum–Langeneß *(30min).* *www.faehre.de.*

NÜRNBERG★★

NUREMBERG

POPULATION: 493 000

Thanks to being in the crosshairs of two major trade routes, Nuremberg prospered in the Middle Ages and also enjoyed political standing as the frequent host city of the imperial diets. In the 15C and 16C, it experienced a cultural flourishing that involved some of the finest artists of the day, including Albrecht Dürer. Although badly bombed in World War II, the city still preserves medieval flair, best experienced during the world's most famous Christmas market held every December. The Nazi leadership regarded Nuremberg as so quintessentially "Germanic" that they chose to stage their huge party rallies here.

- **Information:** Hauptmarkt 18, Königstraße 93 and Frauentorgraben 3, 90403 Nürnberg. ☎(0911) 233 61 35. www.tourismus.nuernberg.de.
- ▶ **Orient Yourself:** The second-largest city in Bavaria after Munich, Nuremberg is served by the A9 and A3 autobahns.
- **Parking:** Garages are located throughout the city. Visit http://wap.parkinfo.com for fees and locations.
- **Don't Miss:** The German National Museum and the old town.
- **Organizing Your Time:** Allow a day for the German National Museum and for taking in all the sights.
- **Especially for Kids:** A walk along the city's medieval ramparts.

A Bit of History

The Golden Age – Nuremberg reached its political and economic heyday during the 15C and 16C. On the crossroads of major trade routes and a mainstay for Franconian craftsmanship, the city once rivaled Augsburg in importance and wealth. The first German scientific university was founded in Nuremberg in 1526. Sculptors **Veit Stoß** (c. 1445–1533) and **Adam Krafft** (c. 1460–1508/09); bronze caster **Peter Vischer the Elder** (c. 1460–1529); **Michael Wolgemut** (1434–1519), painter of altarpieces, and above all, his pupil **Albrecht Dürer** (1471–1528) were all based in this city and profoundly influenced the artistic landscape throughout central Europe. From the 13C, **Hans Sachs** and the *Meistersänger* (*see INTRODUCTION: Music*) brought new life to a German

Pegnitz river and Heilig-Geist-Spital, in the heart of old Nuremberg

M. Hertlein/MICHELIN

Address Book

For coin ranges, see the Legend on the cover flap.

WHERE TO STAY

Hotel Am Jakobsmarkt – *Schottengasse 5.* (0911) 200 70. www. hotel-am–jakobsmarkt.de. *72 rooms.* Rooms here are either modern and functional or rustic and traditional and spread over the main building and a half-timbered annex reached via an inner courtyard.

Hotel-Restaurant Jägerheim – *Valznerweiherstraße 75, 90480 Nürnberg-Zerzabelshof.* (0911) 94 08 50. www.hotel-jaegerheim.de. *33 rooms. Restaurant*. This quiet hotel near the exhibition grounds is well served by public transport and has smart rooms with pale wooden furniture and a traditional restaurant.

Le Méridien Grand-Hotel – *Bahnhofstraße 1.* (0911) 232 20. www.grand-hotel.de. *186 rooms. 20€. Restaurant*. This palatial hotel has been an elegant home for guests since 1896. Next to the central train station, it has luxurious rooms, the nicest of which have Art Nouveau furnishings. The restaurant exudes refinement with marble floors and slender pillars.

WHERE TO EAT

USEFUL TIPS

The city's culinary specialty, *Nürnberger Rostbratwürste* is often offered as *Drei im Weckla* (three sausages in a roll) at stalls and in traditional restaurants.

Historische Bratwurstküche Zum Gulden Stern – *Zirkelschmiedsgasse 26.* (0911) 205 92 88. www.bratwurst kueche.de. The oldest sausage kitchen in town occupies a historic house of 1419, with woodsy, country-style wooden décor. Nuremberg sausage straight from the beech-wood grill is the specialty.

Sebald – *Weinmarkt 14.* (0911) 38 13 03. www.restaurant-sebald.de. *Closed Sun.* This charming house in the old town harbors a modern restaurant and bistro with a relaxed ambience. Sun-yellow walls and warm shades give it Tuscan flair.

Essigbrätlein – *Weinmarkt 3. Closed Dec 24–Jan 1, 2 weeks in Aug and Sun-Mon.* (0911) 22 51 31. Innovative and modern cooking in the elegant old-world style of a 1550 inn is what you will find at this top-rated restaurant near Hauptmarkt.

NIGHTLIFE

Altstadthof – Braustüberl "Schwarzer Bauer" – *Bergstraße 19–21.* (0911) 22 72 17. www.altstadthof.de. This old-style micro-brewery near the castle is a nice spot to kick back at the end of the day. Sit in the small bar or in the beer garden.

Blauer Adler – *Bahnhofsplatz 5 (in west wing of the central station).* (0911) 242 62 90. www.blaueradler.com. *Open daily from 9am.* Match your mood to one of five levels of this buzzy establishment that presents an interesting contrast to the station's historic architecture.

CULTURE

PUBLICATIONS

Events are listed in the monthly magazines *Plärrer* and *Prinz*, available at bookshops and newspaper kiosks. The free monthly listings magazine *Doppelpunkt* can be picked up in bars, restaurants and shops.

Online resources: www.kubiss.de, www.events-nuernberg.de, www. congressing.de.

SHOPPING

Karolinenstraße, Breite Gasse and Königsstraße are the city's busiest shopping streets, with department stores and a wide variety of specialist shops. If you're looking for small gifts, *Lebkuchen* are ideal. Traditionally made during Advent, these spicy gingerbread cookies are now available year round and often come packaged in attractive metal boxes.

Handwerkerhof – *Königstor (opposite central station, near the Frauentorturm).* (0911) 860 70. www.handwerkerhof. de. *Handwerkerhof shops closed Sun; some parts of the Handwerkerhof remain open.* Small crafts shops and traditional restaurants in a picturesque walled-in courtyard. Ideal for souvenir-hunting or taking a break from sightseeing.

poetic form and provided the inspiration for Richard Wagner's 1868 opera *Die Meistersänger von Nürnberg* (The Mastersingers of Nuremberg).

The Nuremberg Trials – It was in Hitler's "ideological capital" of the Third Reich that the notorious anti-Semitic laws were promulgated in 1935. And it was no coincidence that the Allies chose Nuremberg to bring high-ranking Nazi officials before an international military tribunal to face charges of war crimes. The trials took place between November 1945 and October 1946 in the **Justizpalast** (Palace of Justice) on Fürther Straße, now a Civil Court. About two dozen of the accused were condemned to death by hanging.

Germanisches Nationalmuseum★★★ (German National Museum)

Kartäusergasse 1.
🕐*Open year-round, Tue–Sun 10am–6pm (Wed 9pm).* 🕐*Closed Shrove Tue, Dec 24, 25 & 31.* ♿6€. ♿☎(0911) 133 10. *www.gnm.de.*
The museum, founded in 1852, possesses the largest collection of art and antiquities in Germany, although only 20 000 of its millions of items can be displayed at any given time. In fact, since the museum is so vast, keep the overwhelm factor at bay by studying the plan available upon entering and limiting your time to the sections that interest you most.

Upper Floors
The **picture gallery** (*first floor,* **Section B***, reopens in 2009*) displays works by **Albrecht Dürer**, Hans Baldung Grien, Hans Holbein the Elder, Albrecht Altdorfer and Lucas Cranach the Elder. There are also some later works, including a *Self-portrait* by Rembrandt. Works by **Veit Stoß**, Tilman Riemenschneider and Ignaz Günther stand out within the sculpture collection. The most noteworthy among the **scientific instruments** (**Section A**) is the so-called **Behaim**

Adam Krafft

Born in Nuremberg around 1460, Krafft left his mark on every church in the city. His early works – typical of the Late Gothic style – portrayed very expressive figures with tumultuous draperies, and rich decorative reliefs. He then moved toward greater clarity and his later, more monumental works, assume more rounded and restrained poses (see the Stations of the Cross from St. John's cemetery, dating from 1505, in the Germanisches Nationalmuseum).

terrestrial globe (c. 1493), the oldest surviving depiction of the earth in globe form. The second-floor galleries include an excellent exhibition of 19C and 20C art and design (**Section E**), notably Ernst Ludwig Kirchner's Expressionist *Self-portrait* (1914).
There are also three floors of folklore collections (**Section D**), including farmhouse furnishings, clothing and religious art.

Ground Floor
The impressive collection of medieval religious art (**Section C**) illustrates the work of craftsmen from the Carolingian period (9C) to the early Renaissance. Many types of decorative arts are represented, including glass, ceramics, furniture and textiles. The gold and silversmith's work should not be missed.
The section on ancient musical instruments (**Section D**) boasts the world's largest collection of historical pianos. There is also an extensive prints and drawings section and a numismatic collection (**Section F**).

Sights

Old Town★★

Hauptmarkt (Marketplace) and Schöner Brunnen★ (Beautiful Fountain)
The 14C Gothic four-tiered **fountain**, comprising 40 figures (*copies*) dominates the northwest corner of this cen-

tral square. At the top of the 19m/62.3ft-high pyramid-shaped structure, Moses is surrounded by the Prophets; depicted around the base are the seven Electors and nine Old Testament and medieval heroes: three forefathers, three Jews and three Christians. A seamless gold ring hangs from a railing *(on the upper part)*, where an apprentice locksmith is said to have placed it in the 17C. It has been polished by millions of hands touching it for good luck.

The hustle and bustle of the square, particularly during the Christmas market, masks its grisly origins: the Jewish quarter stood there until 1349, when it was razed to the ground and its occupants murdered by the locals.

Frauenkirche★

Hauptmarkt 14.

🕐*Open year-round, Mon & Thu 8am–6pm, Tue & Fri 9am–6pm, Wed 9am–7pm, Sat 9.30am–6.30pm, Sun 12.30pm–7pm.*
&.🖾.℡(0911) 20 83 37.

Dominating the Hauptmarkt, this Gothic church was built between 1355 and 1358 on the site of the synagogue destroyed in 1349. The main architect is believed to have been Peter Parler. The gable, with its pinnacles and niches, was designed by Adam Krafft (early 16C) and crowns the beautiful façade, one of the only original parts. The clock above the balcony, created in 1509 by Sebastian Lindenast and Georg Heuss, attracts visitors each day at noon for the *Männleinlaufen* (running of the little men). Colorful metal figurines representing the seven Electors are shown swearing allegiance to Emperor Karl IV after the Golden Bull was issued in Nuremberg in 1356.

Inside, the **Tucher Altar** in the chancel is a masterpiece of the pre-Albrecht Dürer Nuremberg school of painting: the triptych (c. 1445–50) represents the Crucifixion, Annunciation and Resurrection. Note the depiction of Jesus on his way to school, in the chancel.

Sebalduskirche★

Albrecht-Dürer-Platz 1.

🕐*Open Jan–Mar, daily 9.30am–4pm; Apr–May, 9.30am–6pm, Jun–mid-Sept 9.30am–8pm, mid-Sept–Dec 9.30am–6pm.* &.🖾.℡(0911) 214 25 00.

Nuremberg's oldest parish church was built around 1215 as a three-nave Late Romanesque basilica with two chancels, but was gothicized shortly thereafter. To the right of the entrance, at the far end of the first chancel, the **St. Peter Altarpiece** (1485) takes pride of place, painted on a gold background in Michael Wolgemut's studio. In the center, the richly decorated **baptismal font★** (c. 1430) is the oldest bronze religious work in Nuremberg. In the nave, on the inner side of the great left pillar, is the painted statue of St. Sebald (1390) and on the next column, the **Virgin Mary in Glory★** made of pear-tree wood.

The magnificent **reliquary shrine of St. Sebald★★** dominates the west chancel.

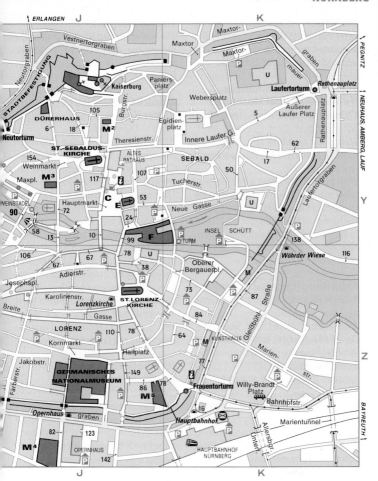

The Gothic tomb was cast in bronze by Peter Vischer (1519) and his sons and is supported by dolphins and snails and adorned with a host of statuettes.

Stadtmuseum Fembohaus (Fembo Municipal Museum)

Open year-round, Tue–Fri 10am–5pm, Sat–Sun 10am–6pm. Closed Jan 1, Shrove Tue, Good Fri, Dec 24–26 & 31. 5€. (0911) 231 25 95. www.fembo haus.de.

The museum occupies a 16C Renaissance mansion, the only patrician house to survive in its entirety. Exhibits cover the history of Nuremberg in traditional fashion and through a multimedia journey "narrated" by Albrecht Dürer and Hans Sachs (*4€*).

Kaiserburg (Imperial Castle)

Visit by guided tour (1hr 30min) only; Apr–Sept, daily 9am–6pm; Oct–Mar, 10am–4pm. Closed Jan 1, Shrove Tue, Dec 24, 25 & 31. 6€. (0911) 244 65 90.

Symbol of the city, the castle stands on a sandstone outcrop.

Between 1050 and 1571, all Holy Roman Emperors spent at least some time in residence here. Tours take in the **Palas** (main palace) with richly furnished rooms, the Romanesque double chapel, the Deep Well and an extensive collection of tools and weapons.

Tiergärtnerplatz

The half-timbered houses around the picturesque square by the Tiergärtnertor (gate) suffered the least damage during World War II.

Albrecht-Dürer-Haus★ (Dürer House)

Albrecht-Dürer-Straße 39.

Open year-round, Tue–Sun 10am–5pm (Thu 8pm). Also open Mon Jun–Sept & Dec. Closed Jan 1, Shrove Tue, Good Fri, Dec 24–26 & 31. 5€. (0911) 231 25 68.

The house where **Dürer** lived with his family from 1509 until his death in 1528 now houses a memorial exhibit shedding light on the life and times of this Renaissance giant. Watch a multimedia show to learn more about his work, then peruse original graphics and visit the recreated workshop where live printing demonstrations are held. Audio tours "narrated" by Agnes Dürer are spiked with personal anecdotes and provide insight into the family's daily life.

Stadtbefestigung★ (Fortifications)   Kids

Completed in the mid-15C, Nürnberg's fortifications have survived remarkably well. They consist of an inner and an outer ring (*Zwingermauer*), the ramparts of the former being topped by a covered parapet walk. A wide, dry moat (in which modern roads now run) was outside the

Imperial Castle, Nürnberg

©Milan Brunclik/istockphoto.com

The Magic of Albrecht Dürer

Nuremburg's most famous son, Albrecht Dürer (1471–1528) was the quintessenail Rennaisance man'. He was, at various points in his life, a woodcut and print maker, a revered painter, a mathematician, philosopher and a confident of the leading lights of his age, including Leonardo da Vinci. His brilliance in the arts was as revered in Italy, where he studied, as it was throughout northern Europe. Dürer was also a prolific author whose work profoundly affected other artists and thinkers of the time; he even wrote the first German textbook for adults on mathematics which was quoted by such giants as Kepler and Galileo. Other stand-out accomplishments: books on geometry and human proportions and a woodcut of a rhinoceros that was a true marvel of the age.

latter. No fewer than 67 defensive towers still exist, including the four 16C **Great Towers:** Frauentor, Spittlertor, Neutor and Laufertor.

The most interesting section extends between the Kaiserburg and the Spittlertor and is easily explored on a 30min walk starting in the castle garden *(Burggarten, below the Kaiserburg)*. From the ramparts walk to the watchpath, which can be followed as far as the Neutorzwinger. Continue inside the ramparts, then cross the suspension footbridge over the Pegnitz River before concluding the stroll.

Heilig-Geist-Spital
(Hospice of the Holy Spirit)

This 14C–15C building, spread over two wide arches, spans a branch of the Pegnitz. The covered part of the bridge, known as the **Crucifixion Courtyard** on account of Krafft's *Crucifixion Group*, used to be a home for the elderly.

Lorenzkirche★
Lorenzer Platz 10.
🕐*Open year-round, daily 9am–5pm. Suggested donation ⊜1€. ☎(0911) 244 69 90.*

This pretty church two Gothic choirs, one from the 13C, the other from the 15C. The most important element is the magnificent rose window that enlivens the west façade. Enter via the south door to admire Veit Stoß's 16C carved wooden masterpiece, **Annunciation★★**. Stoß also created the crucifix above the high altar. The **tabernacle★★** (1493–96), crafted from limestone by Adam Krafft, stands left of the main altar. It features more than a hundred figurines.

Driving Tour

Hersbrucker Alb

109km/67.7mi round-trip.
Follow Sulzbacher Straße, then take the A9 toward Bayreuth.

Neuhaus an der Pegnitz★

This charming locality, dominated by the tower of Burg Veldenstein, comes into view after a bend in the road.

▸ *Continue following the Pegnitz toward Hersbruck.*

Hersbruck

An attractive little town, Hersbruck has stately burghers' houses and the remains of medieval fortifications. The **Deutsche Hirtenmuseum** (German Shepherds' Museum, *Eishüttlein 7*) contains a folk art collection. Continue toward Happurg over the Pegnitz bridge, from which, looking back, there is a fine view of the Wassertor (fortified gate).

▸ *Return to Nuremberg via the B14.*

Erlangen

17km/10.5mi north.

This Baroque town became a haven for persecuted French Huguenots in the late 17C. The most striking building is the **Schloss** (palace), now part of the university. In the early 18C English **Schlossgarten** (garden) stands the **Fountain of the Huguenots**, built by the French in 1706 as a gesture of thanks to their protector, the Margrave of Bayreuth. Next door is a free **botanical garden** that is a delight throughout the year.

OBERSTDORF★★

POPULATION: 10 000

A well-known mountain, skiing and spa town in the Allgäu Alps of southern Germany, this charming resort is lorded over by the Fellhorn and Nebelhorn peaks and is the departure point for walking and hiking tours. Vehicles are banned from the center of town.

- **Information:** Prinzregenten-Platz 1, 87561 Oberstdorf. ☎(08322) 70 00. www.oberstdorf.de.
- ▶ **Orient Yourself:** Midway between Bodensee (Lake Constance) and the castles of Ludwig II, deeply incized into the Allgäu Alps, and seven other valleys, the town lies at the junction of the valley of the Iller River.
- **Don't Miss:** A trip to the Nebelhorn or the Fellhorn.
- ⏰ **Organizing Your Time:** Allow a full day to explore this Alpine resort.
- **Especially for Kids:** Riding the cable-car ride up the Nebelhorn or Fellhorn.
- **Also See:** DEUTSCHE ALPENSTRASSE, FÜSSEN.

Walking Tour

Nebelhorn★★

Take the Nebelhorn cable-car (45min) via three stations: Seealpe (1 280m/ 4 200ft), Höfatsblick (1 932m/6 338.5ft), Summit (2 224m/7 296.5ft).

⏰*Operates daily 8.30am–4.30pm, every 10min.* ⏰*Closed May 4–24 and Nov–mid-Dec. Round-trip summer* ⊙*15.50€ Seealpe, 21.50€ Höfatsblick, 25€ summit; ski day pass 33€.* ☎*(08322) 960 00.*

The highest cable railway in the Allgäu leads to the 2 224m/7 300ft-high summit of the Nebelhorn. In clear weather, the **panoramic view**★★ extends over more than 400 Alpine peaks, from the Zugspitze in the east to the Säntis in the west. Laced by numerous hiking trails, the Nebelhorn is also the departure point for the demanding "Hindelang climb". In winter, it morphs into a popular ski resort.

Address Book

For coin ranges, see the cover flap.

WHERE TO STAY

⊙⊙ **Hotel Traube** – *Hauptstraße 6.* ☎(08322) 80 99 40. www.hotel-traube. de. 20 rooms. Restaurant ⊙⊙. In the heart of town, this traditional hotel has comfortable rooms with country-style flourishes. A sauna and a solarium are popular relaxation zones, while the restaurant tempts you with a long menu of regional and international dishes. In summer, the pleasant Biergarten is the perfect spot for planning tomorrow's sightseeing schedule.

⊙⊙⊙ **Geldernhaus** – *Lorettostraße 16.* Spa ☎(08322) 95 75 70. www.geldern haus.de. Closed Nov. 11 rooms. Built in 1911, this is a handsome, petite hotel with pleasingly bright and comfortably furnished rooms. Staying here entitles

you to use the spa facilities at the nearby Parkhotel Frank.

WHERE TO EAT

⊙⊙ **Oberstdorfer Einkehr** – *Pfarrstraße 9* ☎(08322) 97 78 50. www. oberstdorf.net/einkehr. Reservations recommended. The Oberstdorfer Einkehr scores big on the popularity meter with both locals and visitors. The woodsy establishment is a fine place to try local specialties. Vegetarians are catered to as well, and there is even a kids' menu for pint-sized stomachs.

⊙⊙⊙ **Maximilians** – *Freibergstraße 21.* ☎(08322) 967 80. www.maxi milians-restaurant.de. Closed 2 weeks in Nov and Sun. Elegant restaurant furnished in country-house style typical of the region. Seasonal food is served with delicious refinement.

Fellhorn★★

*Take the Fellhorn cable-car in two stages
to the summit (2 037/6 683ft).*

🕐 *Operates mid-May–Oct, 8.30am–
4.50pm; mid-Dec–Apr (depending on
snow) 8.30am–4.30pm.Round-trip summer* ⊕*22€, ski day pass 35 €.* ☎ *(08322)
960 00.*

There is a wonderful **view**★★ over the
Allgäu, the Austrian and Swiss Alps, from
the 2 037m/6 683ft-high summit of the
Fellhorn. The mountain has an easily
accessible network of hiking paths,
including an interesting **Blumen- und
Wanderlehrpfad** (flower walk)with rare
Alpine blooms all the way to the peak.

Excursions

Breitachklamm★★

*6.5km/4mi southwest, plus 1hr 30min
round-trip walk.* 🕐*Open May-Sept, daily
8am–5pm; Oct–Apr, 9am–4pm.* 🕐*Closed*
Nov–mid-Dec. ⊕*3€.* ☎ *(08322) 48 87.
www.breitachklamm.de.*

In the lower gorge, galleries lead into
sheer, polished walls, where the turbulent mountain creek has carved a course
100m/328ft deep into the bedrock. You
can return via a series of stairways taking you to Walserschanze, on the Klein-
walsertal road, from where there is frequent bus service back into town.

Kleinwalsertal

17km/11mi.

A high valley of the Breitach River, this
mountain area was settled in the 13C by
the **Walsers**, Germanic emigrants from
the Upper Valais. Today the Kleinwalser-
tal has Austrian police, German customs,
a German postal service and Austrian
stamps. (Adopting the Euro simplified
money matters.) **Riezlern**, **Hirschegg**
and **Mittelberg** are the most popular
resorts.

OBERSCHWÄBISCHE BAROCKSTRASSE★★

The enormous prosperity and cultural influence of the Benedictine abbeys
of the 18C resulted in a flurry of beautiful Baroque churches throughout the
Upper Swabian Plateau. Some of the finest artists of the period were brought
in to create magnificent buildings whose fluid decorations harmonize with
the surroundings "so that God may be glorified in all things," according to the
inscription on the Weingarten façade.

- 🛈 **Information:** Klosterhof 1, 88427 Bad Schussenried. ☎ (07583) 33 10 60.
  www.oberschwaben-tourismus.de.
- ▶ **Orient Yourself:** Between Ulm and Bodensee (Lake Constance), this tour
  crosses the Upper Swabian Plateau through gentle hills and soft light.
- 🕑 **Don't Miss:** The abbey churches in Weingarten, Steingaden and
  Oberschwäbische Barockstraße.
- 🕯 **Also See:** SALEM, LINDAU IM BODENSEE, ULM, SCHWÄBISCHE ALB.

Driving Tour

85km/52.8mi

Ravensburg

This ancient Swabian town, and one-
time Free Imperial City, still shelters
behind a city wall of towers and fortified gateways. The road from Wangen
passes beneath the Obertor, a gateway
with stepped gables. At the end of
Marktstraße is a block of old buildings
comprising the Rathaus (14C–15C) and
the weigh-house with the Blaserturm,
a 15C–16C tower.

Another stone tower, the **Mehlsack**
(Sack of Flour), originally whitewashed,
towers 50m/164ft in the southern part
of the old town. A steep staircase (*240*

The Devil to Pay

Of the 66 stops (sets of pipes) of the Weingarten organ, the 46th is called Vox Humana. Joseph Gabler's ambition was to build an organ combining man and machine in resounding praise of God. After countless attempts to recreate a human sound, he is said to have sold his soul to the devil, who supplied him with a piece of metal which he melted down to make the pipes. The monks were so enthralled by the beauty of the organ's song that they were unable to pray, whereupon the abbot ordered an inquiry. Gabler was found out, confessed and sentenced to death. But since the only sounds produced by the organ now resembled wailing, Gabler was reprieved.

steps) leads up to the Veitsburg for even more spectacular views.

▶ *Follow the B30 toward Weingarten.*

Weingarten★★

🕐*Open year-round, Mon–Sat 9am–6pm, Sun noon–6pm.* ☏*(0751) 509 60. www. benediktinerkloster-weingarten.de.*
Consecrated in 1724, the abbey church in Weingarten rivals Ottobeuren as the largest Baroque sanctuary in Germany, 102m/334.6ft long and 44m/144.3ft wide at the transepts. Various architectural elements reflect an Italian influence transmitted by way of Salzburg. The interior is a collaboration of the masters of the day.

The frescoes on the vaulting ceiling by Cosmas Damien Asam are full of virtuosity, as are the choir stalls carved by Joseph Anton Feuchtmayer.

The **organ**★★ is due to Joseph Gabler (1700–71) and fits perfectly with the rest of the decoration: its 6 666 pipes follow the line of the windows and blend with the pink marble.

▶ *The tour continues along the Upper Swabian Baroque Road (signposted "Oberschwäbische Barockstraße") via the B30 until Bad Waldsee. Turn left onto the L275.*

Bad Schussenried

🕐*Museum & Church: Easter–Oct, daily 1.30pm–5.30pm. Library: Apr–Oct, Tue–Fri 10am–1pm, 2pm–5pm, Sat–Sun 10am–5pm; Nov–Mar, Sat–Sun 1pm–4pm.* 🕐*Closed Dec 24, 25 & 31.* ⊜*3€.* ☏*(07315) 502 89 75.*
This pleasant town's **abbey buildings** (now partly used as a psychiatric hospital and for art and cultural events) and abbey church owe their sumptuous Baroque appearance to Premonstratensian abbots. In the church, the upper panels of the intricately decorated choir stalls (1717) are separated by 28 statuettes representing men and women who founded religious orders.

The most spectacular part of the complex is the light-flooded Baroque **library**★ with two stories of bookcases canopied by a ceiling fresco by Franz Georg Herrmann depicting the Apocalypse, Scholarship, Education and Craft.

Steinhausen★

Designed by Dominikus and Johann Zimmermann, this hamlet's beautiful little pilgrimage church comprises a single nave and a small chancel, both oval. Capitals, cornices and window embrasures are adorned with birds, insects or flowers.

Zwiefalten church

▶ *Follow the L 275 until Riedlingen, then join the B312 to Zwiefalten.*

Zwiefalten★★

This village on the Danubian edge of the Swabian Jura has a remarkable **church**

that is considered a masterpiece of the Late Baroque. Like most edifices from this period, a comparatively plain façade conceals a lavishly decorated interior. Inside the 18C building by **Johann Michael Fischer** is a profusion of luminous colors, exuberant details and artistic virtuosity. The eye finally settles on the details: ceiling paintings of the Virgin Mary by Franz Joseph Spiegler, a pulpit decorated by Johann Michael Feuchtmayer (uncle of the sculptor and stuccoworker, Joseph Anton Feuchtmayer), angels and cherubs galore.

▶ *Go back to Riedlingen, then take the B311 to the left.*

Obermarchtal

🕊 *Tour on request.* ☎ *(07375) 95 91 00.* The 17C **abbey church** in this small town was one of the first completed by the Vorarlberg School. The rigidity of the architecture, an as yet undeveloped Baroque, and the church's heavy furnishings are lightened only by the Wessobrunn stuccowork.

OLDENBURG

POPULATION: 158 000

Steeped in tradition, this lively university city is the cultural and economic hub of the region. Seat of government for the Weser-Ems region, Oldenburg is becoming an increasingly popular commercial center.

🛈 **Information:** Kleine Kirchenstraße, 26122 Oldenburg.
☎ (0441) 36 16 13 66. www. oldenburg-tourist.de.

▶ **Orient Yourself:** Oldenburg is about 70km/43.5mi west of the Dutch border. Its river port is linked to the Weser and the North Sea by the Hunte, and to the Benelux countries by a coastal canal *(Küstenkanal)*.

🅿 **Parking:** You'll find parking on the Schloßplatz and near the main train station on Willy-Brandt-Platz.

🅐 **Don't Miss:** Schlossgarten

🕐 **Organizing Your Time:** Allow half a day to see the main sights of Oldenburg.

🕭 **Also See:** BREMEN, EMDEN.

Sights

Town Center

The old city embraces Germany's first pedestrian zone and buildings from five

centuries, generous parkland and the ancient ramparts.

Schloss (Palace)

Schlossplatz 1.
The Renaissance-Baroque Schloss provides a survey of the region's cultural

Landesmuseum Oldenburg

Oldenburg castle, former seat of the counts and dukes of Oldenburg, now home to the Regional Art and History Museum

history from the Middle Ages to the 19C. Exhibits are displayed in the lavish residential rooms that reflect the tastes and wealth of the grand dukes of Oldenburg who lived here until the end of World War I. The cycle of 40 miniature idyllic scenes by Tischbein (1751–1829) is particularly interesting.

Landesmuseum für Kunst und Kulturgeschichte (Regional Art and History Museum)

🕐*Open year-round, Tue–Fri 9am–5pm, Thu (8pm), Sat–Sun 10am–5pm.* 🕐*Closed Jan 1, Good Fri, Easter Sun, May 1, Pentecost, Dec 24, 25 & 31.* ≋*3€.* ♿☎*(0441) 220 73 00. www.landesmuseum-oldenburg.niedersachsen.de.*
Oldenburg castle has been transformed into an extraordinary museum with collections spread over three floors.

Augusteum
Elisabethstraße 1.
The grand ducal collection of paintings makes a perfect fit for this 19C Italian Renaissance-style edifice. The emphasis is on Italian and Dutch masters from the 16C to the 18C and on 18C–19C paintings by other Europeans. On the ground floor are changing exhibits about the history of painting and contemporary art.

Prinzenpalais
Damm 1.
This town house is filled with two floors of art from the 19c and 20C, starting with the Romantic period. Of particular interest are works by German Impressionists as well as by members of *Die Brücke Gruppe* (The Bridge) artist group. There is also a fine selection of canvasses by Franz Radziwill (1895–1955), a leading member of Magic Realism (a style related to Surrealism) that developed in the 1920s.

Stadtmuseum★
Am Stadtmuseum 4–8.
🕐*Open year-round, Tue–Sun 10am–6pm.* ≋*1.50€.* ♿☎*(0441) 235 28 81. http://stadtmuseum.oldenburg.de.*
Of interest are rooms from the villas Francksen (1877), Jürgens and Ballin, with paintings, furnishings and décor dating from the 17C to the early 20C. There are also departments on local history and an antiques collection.
Next door is the **Horst-Janssen-Museum** (🕐*open year-round, Tue–Sun 10am–6pm;* 🕐*closed May 1, Dec 24 & 31;* ≋*3.50€;* ♿☎*(0441) 235 28 91)* dedicated to the illustrator and graphic artist who was born and now buried in Oldenburg.

Schlossgarten★ (Castle Park)

A mild coastal climate favors the growth of magnificent trees and shrubs in this landscaped garden. A nice view of the Lambertikirche unfolds from the weeping willows on the lakeshore.

Landesmuseum für Natur und Mensch Oldenburg (State Museum of Natural and Human History)

Damm 38–44.

Open year-round, Tue–Fri 9am–5pm, Sat–Sun 10am–5pm. Closed Jan 1, May 1, Pentecost, Dec 24, 25 & 31. 3€. (0441) 924 43 00. www.naturund mensch.de.

These nature exhibits are focused on the northwest region of Germany with its varied landscapes and traces of pre- and early historic settlements. Natural, archeological and cultural aspects are presented in a display entitled "Neither sea nor land—the peat bogs, a lost landscape". A huge block of peat, in which ancient bodies were found buried, always attracts attention.

Excursion

Museumsdorf Cloppenburg★

31km/19mi south.

Open Mar–Oct, daily 9am–6pm; Nov–Feb, 9am–4.30pm. Closed Dec 24 & 31. 5€. (04471) 948 40. www.muse-umsdorf.de.

In an area of about 20ha/49 acres, 53 historic rural buildings from the 15C to the 19C have been moved and rebuilt here around a lake and a church. Most of the buildings come from the region between the Rivers Weser and Ems. Large farmsteads, mills, peasants' and tenants' houses illustrate various aspects of the history of Lower Saxony.

OSNABRÜCK

POPULATION: 165 500

The birthplace of writer Erich Maria Remarque *(All Quiet on the Western Front)*, Osnabrück made world history in 1648 with the co-signing of the treaty ending the Thirty Years' War; it was also signed in Münster. Its other famous native son is the painter Felix Nussbaum whose work is showcased in a new dramatic Libeskind-designed museum.

- **Information:** Bierstraße 22, 49074 Osnabrück. (0541) 323 22 02. www.osnabrueck-tourism.de.
- **Orient Yourself:** Osnabrück is at the northern end of the Teutoburg Forest, about 46km/28.5mi northeast of Münster and 85km/52.8mi north of the Ruhrgebiet cities.
- **Parking:** Garages are located throughout the city. The lot near the main train station is especially convenient.
- **Don't Miss:** Felix-Nussbaum-Haus
- **Organizing Your Time:** Allow half a day to see Osnabrück's sights.
- **Also See:** MÜNSTER, MÜNSTERLÄNDER WASSERBURGEN.

Sights

Rathaus (Town Hall)

Open year-round, Mon–Fri 8am–6pm, Sat 9am–4pm, Sun 10am–4pm. Closed Jan 1, Dec 24 & 31. (0541) 323 21 52.
This early 16C building had to be restored after World War II, but still retains its Gothic look. The Peace of Westphalia treaty of 1648 was announced from its steps. A statue of Charlemagne stands above the entrance.

Friedenssaal (Peace Chamber)

The hall in which the peace negotiations took place is adorned with portraits of

Before the Peace in 1648

Preliminaries to the **Peace of Westphalia** started in Osnabrück between the Emperor and the Protestant belligerents (Sweden and the Lutheran princes of Germany) five years before the end of the Thirty Years' War. On the other side, the Roman Catholic powers negotiated with the Emperor in Münster. News of the treaties' final signature was announced in Osnabrück on October 25, 1648, to a crowd, at first incredulous and then bursting into a spontaneous hymn of thanksgiving.

the heads of state and their delegates. The floor and ceiling have been rebuilt; the 16C wooden seats and chandelier are authentic. In the **treasury** is the priceless 14C *Kaiserpokal* (Imperial goblet).

Felix-Nussbaum-Haus★★

Lotter Straße 2.
🕐*Open year-round, Tue–Fri 11am–6pm, Sat–Sun 10am–6pm.* 🕐*Closed Jan 1, Dec 24 & 31.* ◉*5€.* ♿☎*(0541) 323 22 07.*

This Deconstructivist museum building (1998) was designed by **Daniel Libeskind** to house 160 works by native son Felix Nussbaum (1904–44). Its broken architectural lines and eccentric details are meant to be deliberately disorienting and are intended to reflect the emotional turmoil experienced by Nussbaum. His work places him under Neue Sachlichkeit (New Objectivity).

Excursion

Tecklenburg★

23km/14.3mi southwest. Park near the town entrance.
Tecklenburg, on the crest of the Teutoburg forest, is lined with lovely half-timbered houses. Head to the main square and then west, through the Legge gateway, to the oldest part, at the foot of the castle.

Address Book

🪙*For coin ranges, see cover flap.*

WHERE TO STAY

◉**Villa Antonia** – *Lessingstraße 1.* ☎*(03591) 50 10 20. www.hotel-villa-antonia.de. 16 rooms. Restaurant (◉◉).* This charming little hotel in a late 19C villa has bright and timelessly furnished rooms. The restaurant specializes in Austrian cuisine.

◉◉**Dom Eck** – *Breitengasse 2.* ☎*(03591) 50 13 30. www.wjelbik.de. 12 rooms.* Shadowed by the cathedral, this artist-decorated and family-owned hotel delivers Sorbian hospitality in modern and comfortable rooms.

◉◉◉**Goldener Adler** – *Hauptmarkt 4.* ☎*(03591) 486 60. www.goldeneradler. de. 30 rooms. Restaurant (◉◉).* Right in the heart of the historic center is this upscale hotel in lovingly restored 16C building. Rooms lack no modern conveniences, while the restaurant sports a romantic cross-vaulted ceiling.

WHERE TO EAT

◉**Mönchshof** – *Burglehn 1.* ☎*(03591) 49 01 41. www.moenchshof.de.* Time-travel back to the Middle Ages at this congenial inn where you'll be eating without utensils amid historical vaults or on the terrace with sweeping views. ◉◉**Schlossschänke** – *Burgplatz 5.* ☎*(03591) 30 49 90. www. schloss-schaenke.net.* Exposed brick walls, wooden beams and vaulted ceiling create a wonderfully cozy ambience in this 600-year-old tavern. The German and regional cuisine is light, modern, seasonal and fresh.

◉◉**Wjelbik** – *Kornstraße 7.* ☎*(03591) 420 60. www.wjelbik.de.* Come to this historic restaurant to sample Sorb culinary specialities such as elderberry soup or braised beef with horseradish. Dishes are mostly made with locally sourced ingredients.

OSTFRIESISCHE INSELN★

EASTERN FRISIAN ISLANDS

The East Frisian islands are part of the Wattenmeer (Wadden Sea) National Park, created in 1986. Due to the prevailing northwesterly tides and winds, the East Frisians are drifting ever farther southeast. The northern and eastern coasts of these islands are fringed by sandy beaches dotted with wicker-hooded deck chairs and windbreaks in summer.

- **Information:** Ledastraße 10, 26789 Leer. ☎(0491) 91 96 96 60. www.ostfriesland.de.
- ▶ **Orient Yourself:** The seven inhabited Eastern Frisian islands lie between the Ems and the Weser deltas off the North Sea coast of Germany. They are served by ferries whose timetables depend on the tides.
- **Don't Miss:** Quiet exploration of these islands. Take your time.
- **Organizing Your Time:** Allow 30min to two hours for ferry service, depending on the island.
- **Especially for Kids:** North Sea cruises and island exploration.
- **Also See:** BREMEN.

Sights

Borkum

Ferries depart from Emden. 2hr. 5 times daily. ☞*16.50€ day-return (child 8.25€). AG EMS:* ☎ *(04921) 890 70. www.ag-ems.de.*
The largest of the Eastern Frisians boasts an impressive beach promenade and good views of the mainland and a seal bank from the 60m/196.8ft **Neuer Leuchtturm**, a lighthouse from 1879 *(315 steps).*

Juist

Ferries depart from Norddeich. 1hr 30min. 1 ferry daily. ☞*17.50€ same-day return. Reederei Frisia:* ☎ *(04931) 98 70; www. reederei-frisia.de.*
This island (17km/10.5mi long) is home to an interesting **Küstenmuseum** *(Coastal Museum)* in the attractive village of Loog. It documents local coastal living, the history of lifeboat service and the importance of dyke building. Beyond the village is the **Bill** nature reserve.

Norderney

Ferries depart from Norddeich. 1hr. 9 ferries daily, 10 on Fri. ☞*16€ same-day return. Reederei Frisia:* ☎ *(04931) 98 70; www. reederei-frisia.de.*
The most urbanized of the East Frisian islands, Norderney is nicknamed "Queen

☺ Ferry Routes ☺

Emden–Borkum
Norddeich–Juist
Norddeich–Norderney
Neßmersiel–Baltrum
Bensersiel–Langoog
Neuharlingersiel–Spiekeroog
Harlesiel–Wangerooge

of the Frisian Islands" and was once the summer residence of the royal House of Hanover. Its main town still has much of its old charm with the spa rooms on the Kurplatz, well-tended spa gardens and 19C houses. In 2006, a state-of-the-art thalasso therapy center called **Bade: haus** opened in the historic ambience of the Art Nouveau sea water baths.

Baltrum

Ferries depart from Neßmersiel. 30min. Up to 3 ferries daily. ☞*16€ Oct–mid-Mar same-day return; 15€ rest of the year. Reederei Baltrum:* ☎ *(04933) 99 16 06; www.baltrum-linie.de.*
Around the smallest of the Eastern Frisians, the sea is usually calm. The main sight here is the **old church** in Westdorf, built one year after the great floods of 1826. The church bell was originally a ship's bell, washed up as jetsam. On the island's east side are impressive **sand dunes** *(Großes Dünental).*

©Martin Sach/istockphoto.com

Juist Island

Langeoog

Ferries depart from Bensersiel.
1hr. Up to 7 ferries daily. ☎18.50€ same-day return. Schiffahrt Langeoog, ☎(04972) 69 32 60 or (04971) 928 90, www.schiffahrt-langeoog.de.

The **Schiffahrtsmuseum** (Museum of Seafaring) on this island features Langeoog's first rescue ship, in service from 1945 to 1980. From the raised promenade along the chain of sand dunes, near Ebbe, there is a fine view of 14km/9mi of beach and sand banks.

Spiekeroog

Ferries depart from Neuharlingersiel.
45min. Up to 3 ferries daily. ☎19€ same-day return. ☎(04976) 919 31 01.

This car-free island combines state-of-the-art spa facilities with traditional village infrastructure. The **Alte Inselkirche**

of 1696 is the oldest surviving church in the Eastern Frisians. A Pietà made of wood and fragments of a pulpit are said to have come from a ship in the Spanish Armada that sank in 1588. One of the island's more unusual sights is the **Muschelmuseum** (Mussel Museum) in the basement of the seaside hall.

Wangerooge

Ferries depart from Harlesiel. 80min.
Up to 5 ferries daily. ☎26€ round-trip.
☎(04464) 94 94 11.

Over the course of history, this easternmost island has belonged to Holland, France, Russia (twice) and the Grand Duchy of Oldenburg. It is now a peaceful family vacation destination. The colorful island train runs from the isolated southwest point past lagoons rich in bird life straight to the village center.

The Local Brew

Tea-drinking is a way of life in the East Frisian islands whose inhabitants consume 14 times more tea per capita than people in the rest of Germany. The beverage was introduced to the region by the Dutch c. 1670 and soon caught on. Frederick the Great attempted to ban tea in 1777 but was forced to reconsider when so many disgruntled people left the region. Even during World War II the Eastern Frisians were allocated a more generous tea ration than others.

Eastern Frisian "tea ceremonies" are full of ritual. First warm the teapot. Then pour boiling water onto the tea leaves in the pot and leave to brew for 5min. Place a piece of white sugar crystal into a porcelain cup and pour on the strong, hot tea, which crackles pleasantly as it hits the sugar. Finally, add the merest splash of cream over the back of a special curved spoon made for this purpose. Stirring the tea, however, is a complete no-no and doing so a grave breach of local etiquette!

OTTOBEUREN★★

POPULATION: 8 000

The Benedictine abbey of Ottobeuren, founded in 764 under the patronage of Charlemagne, was transformed into the Baroque style in the 18C. The abbey church is undoubtedly one of the most stunning churches in Germany.

- **Information:** Marktplatz 14, 87724 Ottobeuren. ☎(08332) 92 19 50. www.ottobeuren.de.
- ▶ **Orient Yourself:** Ottobeuren is a charming village surrounded by forests and pastureland. The A96 autobahn (Memmingen–Munich) is 11km/6.8mi north.
- ☺ **Don't Miss:** The Abbey Church
- ◷ **Organizing Your Time:** Plan at least two hours to view the church and buildings.
- ◔ **Also See:** DEUTSCHE ALPENSTRASSE, ULM, WIESKIRCHE.

Sights

Abbey Church★★★
Brochure available at the entrance (2.50€).
◷*Open year-round, Fri–Wed 9am–sunset, 8.30pm latest, Thu 1pm–3pm.* ♿☎*(08332) 79 80. www.abtei-ottobeuren.de.*
In 1748, **Johann Michael Fischer**, the great architect of southern Germany, put the finishing touches on this jewel of German Baroque, which was to be his masterpiece. He was assisted by equally gifted Rococo masters when it came to the church's interior ornamentation: Johann Jakob Zeiller and Franz Anton Zeiller for the frescoes, Johann Michael Feichtmayr for the stuccowork, and Johann Joseph Christian for the figurative sculptures.

The church's astonishing dimensions are only evident once inside. The impression of space is enhanced by the unusual amount of light, a result of the church's north-south orientation. The architecture of the entire church is focused on the flattened central dome, amid a proliferation of paintings, stuccowork and sculptures with wonderfully depicted cherubs, draperies, and lighting.

The four altars, of St. Michael—patron saint of the Ottobeuren area and the Empire—of the Holy Guardian Angels, of St. Joseph and of St. John the Baptist, are remarkable features, as are the outstanding **pulpit** and, opposite, the representation of the **Baptism of Christ** in red and marble stucco.

On the altar of the Holy Sacrament stands a much venerated **crucifix** dating from 1220, the Ottobeurer Gnadenheiland

Abbey church

T. Krieger/MICHELIN

Interior view of Ottobeuren abbey church

F. Zaninotto/MICHELIN

(Merciful Redeemer). The **high altar**, with paintings of the Holy Trinity by Zeiller and larger than life figures of the Apostles and saints is outstanding. The walnut **choir stalls**★★ (1764) are masterpieces of the woodcarver's art. The high backs to the stalls are decorated with gilded lime-wood reliefs by Joseph Christian.

Karl Joseph Riepp, a pupil of the famous organ builder Silbermann, built both the **chancel organs**★★ in 1766.

Abbey buildings

◷*Open Palm Sun–Oct, daily 10am–noon, 2pm–5pm; limited hours rest of the year* ⊙*2.50€.* ☎*(08332) 79 80.*

The abbey's buildings were constructed between 1711 and 1725. Inside the **museum**★ admire the superb decoration of the rooms, in keeping with the architecture of the church. Note the **Prälatur** (abbatial palace) magnificent **library**, theater and **Kaisersaal** (Emperor's Hall), with a frescoed ceiling depicting the coronation of Emperor Charlemagne. The museum also houses interesting medieval artworks and 15C–17C paintings.

Excursion

Memmingen
11km/6.8mi northwest.

In the **old town**, surrounded by a preserved fortified wall, the characteristic appearance of a medieval trading center remains. On either side of the stream through the city center stand such ancient buildings as the **Siebendächerhaus** (House with Seven Roofs), once the tanners' headquarters. Interesting buildings also surround the **Marktplatz** (market square): the **Steuerhaus** (Taxation House, 1495), with its ground floor opened by arcades; and the 1589 **Rathaus** (Town Hall), which was remodeled in the Rococo style in 1765. A further highlight is the Late Gothic **Antonierhaus**, housing works by local painter Bernhard Strigel (1460–1528), and a museum on the Antonine Order. The 14C and 15C Gothic basilica **Martinskirche** has a fine chancel (1496–1500) by Matthias Böblinger, the architect of the Ulm Münster. The **choir stalls**★, dating from 1501 to 1507, are intricately carved with 68 figures of the Prophets, sibyls and church benefactors.

On Hallhof square, the 1617 belfry of the **Kreuzherrenkirche** surpasses the town's other towers in its beauty and ornamentation.

PADERBORN★

POPULATION: 144 258

Founded by Charlemagne in the 8C and situated in eastern Westphalia, modern Paderborn is commercial hub and a university town with about 15 000 students. Though badly pummeled during World War II, it boasts a good range of artistic, historical and architectural sights, plus the world's largest computer museum.

- 🛈 **Information:** Marienplatz 2a, 33098 Paderborn. ☎ (05251) 88 29 80. www.paderborn.de.
- ▶ **Orient Yourself:** Padernborn is in eastern Westphalia close to the Teutoburg Forest on the A33 autobahn, which connects with the A2 in the north and the A44 in the south.
- 🅿 **Parking:** Public garages abound in the town center and indicated through an electronic signpost system.
- 😤 **Don't Miss:** Dom, Heinz Nixdorf Museumsforum.
- 🕐 **Organizing Your Time:** Paderborn warrants about half a day.
- 🖔 **Also See:** SOEST, DORTMUND, KASSEL.

A Bit of History

Birthplace of the Holy Roman Empire

– Paderborn's beginnings are tied to Charlemagne who, in 776, established a power base here from which to defeat the Saxons and to oversee their Christianization. In 799, a deposed Pope Leo III fled to Paderborn to ask for Charlemagne's help in restoring him to the papal throne. In exchange, he was to be crowned emperor, thus laying the foundation for the Holy Roman Empire that lasted until 1806. The coronation took place in Rome on Christmas Day 800.

Sights

Dom★

Marktplatz.
🕐*Open year-round, daily 10am–6.30pm. www.erzbistum-paderborn.de.*
Paderborn's cathedral was built between 1225 and 1270 as a three-aisled Gothic hall church with a Romanesque west tower. The main entrance is through the south portal, which is also known as "Paradies".
It dates to 1250 and is richly festooned with sculptures of St. Mary, Christ, the Apostels and other biblical figures. Inside, the elaborate **tomb of Prince-**

Bishop Dietrich von Fürstenberg★ and the late Gothic high altar are artistic standouts. The crypt is the largest in Germany and shelters the relics of Paderborn's patron saint, St. Liborius (348–398) that were transferred to the city in 836.

Be sure to follow the signs to the cloister to have a look at the endearing **Drei-Hasen-Fenster**★ *(Three Hares' Window)*. It shows three hares chasing each other in a circle with each of the ears shared by two animals so that only three ears are shown in all.

Clocktower of the Cathedral, Paderborn

©Paul Rüsing/istockphoto.com

Libori Festival

Every year in late July, the people of Paderborn mix up religious tradition and worldly entertainment for one week of fun in honor of the city's patron St. Liborius. The largely pedestrianized center is transformed into a veritable drinking and partying zone where up to a million visitors let their hair down during live concerts, exhibitions, shows, even impromptu sing-alongs with local nuns!

Thrill seekers head to the midway with its carousels and roller coasters, shopaholics can indulge their addiction on the Pottmarkt arts and crafts market, while clubbers keep the city's dance floor hopping until dawn. See www.libori.de for the full run-down.

Diözesanmuseum (Cathedral Treasury)

Markt 17.
◷*Open year-round, Tue–Sun 10am–6pm.* ◉*2.50€.* ♿ ☎*(05251) 125 14 00. www. erzbistum-paderborn.de/museum.*
A modern building next to the cathedral houses religious treasures from 20 centuries, including such celebrated items as a Madonna from 1058 and the gilded silver shrine of Liborius from 1627.

Kaiserpfalzen★★ (Imperial Palaces)

In 1964 archeologists made a sensational find: just north of the cathedral they discovered the foundations of Charlemagne's 8C palace.

Continued excavations also unearthed the adjacent remnants of Heinrich II's palace from the early 11C. The latter has been meticulously reconstructed and now houses a modern **museum** *(◷open year-round, Tue–Sun 10am–6pm; ◷closed Dec 24, 25 & 31; ◉2.50€; ☎(05251) 10 51 10; www.kaiserpfalz-pad erborn.de).*
It houses displays that shed light on daily life in the early Middle Ages.

Bartholomäuskapelle (Chapel of St. Bartholomew)

◷*Open year-round, daily 10am–6pm.*
This tiny chapel next to the imperial palaces is the oldest hall church north of the Alps (1017). It has splendid acoustics and elaborate capitals.

Heinz Nixdorf Museumsforum★★ [Kids]

Fürstenallee 7.
◷*Open year-round, Tue–Fri 9am–6pm, Sat–Sun 10am–6pm.* ◷*Closed Jan 1, Nov 1,*

Dec 24, 25 & 31. ◉*5€.* ♿ ☎*(05251) 30 66 00. www.hnf.de.*
The evolution of communication technology gets the spotlight at this engaging and interactive museum. In one section you can travel back 5 000 years to the beginnings of writing in Mesopotamia, then fast-forward into cyberspace in another. In between you are all sorts of historic calculating machines, typewriters, telephone exchanges and even a full-scale replica of Eniac, a 1940s US Army computer that is the size of an entire room.

Museum für Stadtgeschichte (City History Museum)

Hathumarstraße 7–9.
◷*Open year-round, Tue–Sun 10am–6pm.* ☎*(05251) 882 35 01.*
City history is chronicled in this one of the oldest and prettiest half-timbered buildings in town, the 16C Adam-und-Eva-Haus. It is so named because sculptures on the façade depict the expulsion of Adam and Eve from the garden of Eden.

Rathaus (Town Hall)

This splendid example of Weser Renaissance architecture is one of the most beautiful Town Halls in the region. Completed in 1616, it sports a triple gable and arcades supported by Doric pillars. In front stands a Baroque fountain decorated with the city's coat of arms.

Paderquellen (Pader Springs)

Paderborn derives its name from the Pader, Germany's shortest river. It originates from 200 springs in a park just north of the cathedral and flows into the Lippe River after a mere 4km/2.5mi.

PASSAU★★

POPULATION: 50 000

Passau enjoys an enchanting setting at the confluence of the Inn, the Danube (Donau) and the little Ilz rivers. The old town, with its Baroque churches and patrician houses, lies crowded onto the narrow tongue of land separating the Inn and the Danube. The Oberhaus fortress looms above town on a wooded bluff on the northern bank of the Danube.

- **Information:** Rathausplatz 3, 94032 Passau. ☎ (0851) 95 59 80. www.passau.de.
- ▶ **Orient Yourself:** Passau is in eastern Bavaria, right on the border with Austria, and consists of three quarters: Ilzstadt to the north, Innstadt to the south, and the peninsula of Altstadt. The A3 passes near Passau.
- **Parking:** Find parking on the Domplatz and south of the Schanzlbrücke.
- **Don't Miss:** Views from the Veste Oberhaus, Dom St. Stephan, the Three Rivers Point.
- **Organizing Your Time:** Budget about a day to enjoy Passau's charm at leisure.
- **Also See:** BURGHAUSEN, STRAUBING.

A Bit of History

A Powerful Bishopric – The See was founded in the 8C by St. Boniface, the English-born "Apostle of Germany" (⚑ see FULDA). By the late 10C it had become extraordinarily powerful and, until the 15C, encompassed the entire Danube Valley, including Vienna.

A Commercial Base – From the Middle Ages, river trade (especially of salt, also called the "white gold") played an important role in the town's prosperity.

Today, it is an important river cruise stop en route to Vienna and Budapest.

Sights

Veste Oberhaus (Fortress)

This imposing citadel was built in 1219 as a refuge for the bishops against rebellious burghers. It is linked with the Veste Niederhaus by a fortified road. From the belvedere marked "Zur Aussicht", near the parking lot, and from atop the tower (142 steps), there are magnificent

Passau and its cathedral

M. Hertlein/MICHELIN

Address Book

♿ *For coin ranges, see the Legend on the cover flap.*

WHERE TO STAY

⌾**Rotel Inn** – *Donauufer, 50m/55yds from the main train station (Hauptbahnhof).* ☎*(0851) 951 60. www.rotel-inn.de. Closed Oct–Apr.* ⌷ *93 rooms.* This hotel on the bank of the Danube has single and double rooms, but bathrooms are down the hall.

⌾⌾**Euro-Hotel Passau** – *Neuburger Straße 128.* ☎*(0851) 98 84 20. www. euro-hotel-passau.de. 70 rooms.* This multi-storied hotel is close to the conference center and the A3 autobahn (Passau-Süd exit). Rooms are modern and functional.

⌾⌾⌾ **Hotel Passauer Wolf** – *Rindermarkt 6.* ☎*(0851) 931 51 10. 40 rooms. Restaurant* ⌾⌾⌾. This traditional establishment is mid-way between the Danube and the Altstadt's pedestrian zone. Each room is furnished uniquely and the restaurant delivers rustic meals with a side of beautiful river views.

WHERE TO EAT

⌾⌾**Heilig-Geist-Stift-Schenke** – *Heiliggeistgasse 4.* ☎*(0851) 26 07. Closed Jan 6–31 and Wed.* This establishment built in 1358 has a cozy, rustic atmosphere. Expect beautiful, vaulted ceilings, open fires and charming vine-covered garden.

TAKING A BREAK

Atelier Café – *Ort 2 (between Schaiblingsturm and Dreiflüsseeck).* ☎*(0851) 934 66 11. www.ort2.de. Closed Nov–Jan.* The Austrian proprietor of this cafe prepares cakes and cold dishes, many of which are Austrian specialties. In fine weather, it is all best enjoyed in the idyllic garden.

Café Greindl – *Wittgasse 8.* ☎*(0851) 356 77. Open Mon–Sat 6.30am–6pm, Sun 11am–6pm.* This classic café has delectable tarts, cakes, ice-creams, and home-made chocolates. In good weather, there is a little terrace outside. Another branch is in the pedestrian zone *(Theresienstr. 8).*

NIGHTLIFE

Café Duft – *Theresienstraße 22.* ☎*(0851) 346 66. www.cafeduft.de.* A former stable, this café also features a terrace on the pedestrian zone. Regional and *tapas* dishes also served, at night in cozy candlelight.

---

views★★ over the Inn, the Danube and Passau itself. The town's history, art and religious roots, including some paintings of the Danube School, are traced in the small **Oberhausmuseum**.

Dom St. Stephan

Most of this Late Gothic **cathedral** was destroyed by fire in the 17C and rebuilt in the Baroque style. The cavernous sanctuary is richly decorated with frescoes and stuccowork. Four **lateral chapels** feature paintings by the Austrian artist JM Rottmayr (1654–1730). From the Residenzplatz, visitors can admire the cathedral's **east end**★★, a remarkable Late Gothic work. The cathedral also houses the world's largest **organ**★★ with 17 774 pipes and 233 stops.

Residenzplatz

The square is bordered on the south by the early Neoclassical bishops' **New Palace**. The surrounding streets are still lined by arcaded houses with corbelling and concealed ridge roofs.

Rathausplatz

The 14C Rathaus (Town Hall) with its painted façade dominates this picturesque square. The tower dates to the late 18C.

Glasmuseum★★

Am Rathausplatz, in the Hotel "Wilder Mann".
⌾*Open year-round, daily 1pm–5pm.* ⌾*5€.* ☎*(0851) 350 71. www.glasmuseum.de.*

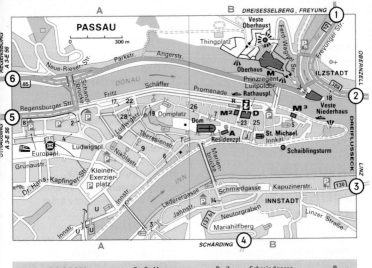

Glassware from Bohemia, Bavaria and Austria, from 1700 to 1950 makes up the bulk of this precious collection of 30 000 pieces. The most important display comes from **Bohemia** (Biedermeier, Historicism, Jugendstil); note especially the Lobmeyr state goblet depicting the *Marriage of Neptune with Amphitrite*, which is considered a key glass work of the 19C.

Dreiflüsseeck★ (Three Rivers Point)

From St. Michaels-Kirche, go down to the Inn quayside.
The fast-flowing Inn River runs past the Schaiblingsturm (1481), once used to store salt. At the confluence, the greenish current of the Inn can be seen running alongside the brown Danube waters and dark water of the Ilz before they mingle. From the Danube bank, on the far side of the promontory, there is a fine viewpoint.

Excursions

Dreisesselberg★

48km/30mi northeast, 3km/1.8mi from the Czech border.
The drive to this curious group of granite rocks, eroded into flat, saucer-like shapes, runs through some of the most remote regions of the Bavarian forest. Green triangles waymark the trail leading to the lowest rock outcrop. From there, steps rise to the summit of the **Hochstein** (1 332m/4 370ft) from where you can enjoy a splendid **panorama**★.

Asambasilica of Altenmarkt

In Osterhofen, 36km/22.3mi northwest. Leave Passau by ⑥ on the town plan.
Three great names of the Bavarian Baroque style left their mark on this opulent church: Johann Michael Fischer in the architecture and the brothers Cosmas and Damian Asam in the decoration. Note the monumental high altar with its wreathed columns and enraptured angels.

Danube School

The German painters working in the Danube Valley in the 16C were among the first to depict landscape for its own sake. The best masters of this so-called school were Albrecht Altdorfer, Lucas Cranach the Elder, Wolf Huber and Jörg Breu the Elder.

Driving Tour

Bayerischer Wald★ (Bavarian Forest)

Round-trip leaving from Bodenmais (70km/43.5mi north of Passau). About 65km/40.4mi. Budget about three hours. The Bavarian forest includes low, rounded mountains, wild rock bastions and isolated, river valleys and a protected national park area, founded in 1970. The natural woodland draws a wide variety of animal species. Together with the Bohemian Forest on the Czech side, it forms the largest contiguous forest in Europe. The area is known for its glass industry with many studios, factories and shops.

Bodenmais★

This town with a healing climate lies in a pastureland at the southern foot of the forest's highest mountain, the Großer Arber (1 456m/4 775ft).

▷ *Travel 23km/14.3mi toward* **Kötzting**, *where the road follows the pastoral* **Weißer Regen Valley** *within sight of the peaks of the* **Osser**. *Continue climbing as far as the* **Lamer Winkel**, *a hollow of woods and upland meadows at the head of the valley.*

Hindenburg-Kanzel★

A **look-out point**★ offers a fine view of the Lamer Winkel and the Arber.

Großer Arber★★

From the lower cable terminal, 1hr round-trip, including 20min walk.
🕐*Operates May–first snow, 9am–4.30pm, first snow–mid-Jan, 8.30am–4pm, mid-Jan–Apr 8.30am–4.30pm.* ⬤*9.50€ round-trip.* ☎*(09925) 941 40. www.arber.de.*
From the upper terminal, a path leads to two rocky crags, one overlooking the **Schwarzer Regen depression**★★, and another (surmounted by a cross) with views of the Lamer Winkel and the forest to the north.
The **Großer Arbersee**★ lake sits to the right as the road winds down through the forest. On the way are several **views**★ of the Zwiesel basin, the Falkenstein and the Großer Rachel.

PFALZ★

PALATINATE

The Palatinate is a lovely patchwork of forests (Pfälzer Wald), vineyards, hills crowned with castles and small towns where time seems to move a little slower. The German Wine Road runs through this region which is blessed with a mild climate that also encourages the growth of figs, lemons and exotic fruit.

- 🛈 **Information:** Hetzelplatz 1, 67433 Neustadt an der Weinstraße. ☎(06321) 926 80. www.neustadt.eu, www.deutsche-weinstrasse.de.
- ▷ **Orient Yourself:** The Palatinate mountains stretch from the Rhine plains to the Vosges. The main access route is the A65 autobahn from Mannheim or Karlsruhe. The German Wine Road starts 15km/9.3mi to the west of Worms, at Bockenheim *(B271)* and winds 80km/50mi south toward France.
- 😊 **Don't Miss:** The suggested driving tour, which meanders through some of Germany's finest wine country.
- 🕐 **Organizing Your Time:** Allow at least one day for the suggested excursion.
- 👁 **Also See:** MANNHEIM, HEIDELBERG, KARLSRUHE.

Address Book

For coin ranges, see the Legend on the cover flap.

WHERE TO STAY

⊝⊜⊜ **Hotel Zum Lam** – *Winzergasse 37, 76889 Bad Bergzabern. ☎(06343) 93 92 12. www.zum-lam.de. 11 rooms. Restaurant ⊝⊜⊜, closed Wed.* As well as being a charming resort town, Bad Bergzabern is known for its abundance of 18C half-timbered houses. This hotel is one of them. Enjoy the pleasant garden terrace and rooms lacking none of the major mod cons.

⊝⊜⊜⊜ **Hotel Deidesheimer Hof** – *Am Marktplatz 1, 67146 Deidesheim. ☎(06326) 968 70. www.deidesheimer hof.de. Closed Jan 7–18. 28 rooms.* This elegant inn has tastefully furnished rooms and a gourmet restaurant serving upscale regional specialties.

WHERE TO EAT

⊝⊜ **Weinstube Ester** – *Triftweg 21, 67098 Bad Dürkheim. ☎(06322) 98 90 65. www.ester24.de. Closed Mon and Tue.* Many regulars come to this rustic tavern typical of the Palatinate region. Regional dishes, mostly meat and sausage specialties, are on the menu and are a perfect fit with with the delicious local wines.

⊝⊜⊜ **Reuters Holzappel** – *Hauptstraße 11, 76889 Bad Bergzabern. ☎(06343) 42 45. www.reuters-holz appel.de. ✉ Closed Mon.* This traditional wine cellar occupies a 250-year-old farmhouse with courtyard. Wooden furniture and plenty of trinkets give it a cozy and comfortable ambience while the menu is dominated by local and international dishes.

A Bit of History

The Wines of the Palatinate – Germany's largest wine-growing region produces almost one-third of the country's total output. The most famous vintages come from the villages of Bad Dürkheim, Forst, Deidesheim and Wachenheim.

Excursion from Worms to Bad Bergzabern

151km/91mi – see map.

Worms★ – See WORMS

South of Worms, the Rhine plain becomes progressively devoted to viticulture.

Freinsheim

This large wine town is still encircled by its medieval ramparts. The Baroque Town Hall, beside a 15C church, has an overhanging roof that protects an outside staircase.

Bad Dürkheim

Sheltered by the Pfälzer Wald, this spa town has soothing thermal springs and enjoys a mild climate in which fig, almond and chestnut trees thrive. A couple of miles west *(via Schillerstraße and Luitpoldweg)* is the ruined Limburg abbey.

Deidesheim

This is one of the most prosperous and prettiest towns on the German Wine Road with its half-timbered houses, a wine museum and numerous galleries.

Neustadt an der Weinstraße

The commercial hub of the Wine Road, Neustadt has a pretty **old town**★ that boasts the largest number of historic houses in the region. Its narrow, picturesque lanes surround a pretty market with 18C Town Hall.

Hambacher Schloss

Neustadt.

Open Mar–Nov, daily 10am–6pm. 4.50€. ☎(06321) 308 81. www.ham bacher-schloss.de.

Founded by the Salian Franks in the 11C, this castle was the summer residence of the Speyer bishops before being destroyed in 1688.

The castle is also considered to be "the cradle of German democracy". In 1832,

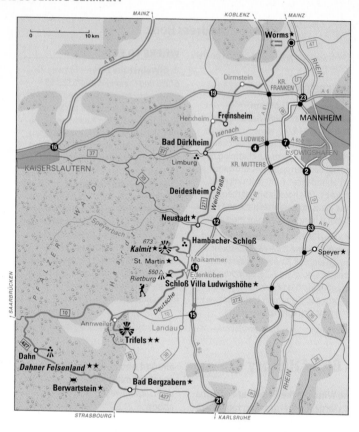

some 30 000 freedom-loving citizens from all parts of Germany demonstrated here for freedom and unity of Germany This was also when the black, red and gold flag, which was adopted as the German national emblem in 1919 and again in 1949, was first raised. An exhibit commemorates the event.

Kalmit
8km/5mi.
The Kalmit (673m/2 208ft) is the highest outcrop in the Rhineland Palatinate.

From the Kalmithaus terrace, there is a **view**★★ of the Rhine plain and Speyer cathedral. Return to the Wine Road via the charming village of **St. Martin**★.

Schloss-Villa Ludwigshöhe★
2km/1.2mi from Edenkoben. ↝ *Historic rooms visit by guided tour only, Apr–Sept, daily 9am–6pm; Oct–Nov and Jan–Mar, 9am–5pm. The Max-Slevogt-Galerie can be visited independently of the guided tour.* ✆2.60€. ✆ (06323) 930 16. www. max-slevogt-galerie.de.

Rhine-Main-Danube Canal

Ever since Roman times, emperors, kings, engineers and visionaries have dreamed of linking the Rhine and Danube rivers. Charlemagne took a first stab at this great enterprise, called Charlemagne's Ditch (Fossa Carolina). Bavaria's Ludwig I made another attempt 1000 years later with the building of the Ludwig Canal. But it would not be until the late 20C that the amazing feat of engineering would finally be completed. In 1992, the inauguration of the 177km/110mi Rhine-Main-Danube Canal created the final link between the North Sea and the Black Sea.

Built by Ludwig I of Bavaria, this stately Italianate villa houses a **gallery**★ devoted to the German Impressionist painter Max Slevogt (1868–1932). The apartments are also open to the public. A chair-lift goes up to the Rietburg (550m/1 804ft), departure point for forest walks.

Trifels★

7km/4.3mi from Annweiler. ◐*Open Easter–Sept, daily 9am–6pm; Oct–Easter 9am–5pm.* ●*2.60€.* ☎*(06346) 84 70.*
Trifels makes an imposing sight even from a distance.
The castle here was a former Hohenstaufen stronghold, and in the 12C and 13C, the temporary residence of the crown jewels.
The castle is best known as the place where **Richard the Lionheart** was imprisoned by Emperor Henry IV while returning from a crusade in 1193. Richard was eventually ransomed and returned to England in 1194.

Dahner Felsenland★★

The resort of **Dahn** is surrounded by one of the best hiking areas in Germany, with breathtaking mountains and outcroppings of red sandstone. The **castle ruins**★ of Altdahn dominate the town. Staircases and guard rooms hewn into the rocks add to the charm of the castle, the heart of which dates from c. 1100.

Burg Berwartstein★

Turn off toward Erlenbach (B427).
◐*Open Mar–Oct, daily 9am–6pm; Nov–Feb, Sat–Sun, 1pm–5pm.* ●*2.50€.* ☎*(06398) 210; www.burgberwartstein.de.*
This former robber baron's lair is sits 100m/328ft above the village of Erlenbach.
Much of the castle is open to the public, including subterranean passages.

Bad Bergzabern★

This charming health resort brims with half-timbered houses. The **Gasthaus zum Engel**★ (1579) is said to be the finest Renaissance building in the region.

POTSDAM★★★

POPULATION: 148 700

Just west of Berlin, Potsdam was chosen in the 17C as the residence of the electors of Brandenburg because of its ideal setting – a natural woodland dotted with lakes and crisscrossed by canals and the River Havel. It is to Frederick the Great that Potsdam owes its renown as "rococo jewel". In 1990, the city's palaces and parks garnered a spot on the list of UNESCO World Heritage Sites.

- **Information:** Am Neuen Markt 1, 14467 Potsdam. (0331) 27 55 80. www.potsdam.de.
- ▸ **Orient Yourself:** Potsam, the capital of the state of Brandenburg, is just west of Berlin, in the heart of the Havelland, an area of canals and lakes.
- ℙ **Parking:** Garages are located throughout the city, including one near Sanssouci Palace.
- **Don't Miss:** Sanssouci Palace.
- ◐ **Organizing Your Time:** Allow at least half a day for a tour of Sanssouci.
- **Also See:** BERLIN, WITTENBERG.

A Bit of History

A Prussian Versailles – Under Friedrich Wilhelm (1713–40), Potsdam became an administrative center and a garrison town. By contrast, the king's son, **Frederick the Great** (Friedrich II) was a great patron of the arts. Most of the blockbuster sights for which Potsdam is famous were built on his watch, notably Sanssouci and the Neues Palais. Frederick, as fluent in French as in German, welcomed many eminent Frenchmen to his court, among them **Voltaire**.

Sanssouci Palace and terraced gardens, dear to the heart of Frederick the Great

The Potsdam Conference – The treaty defining the occupation and future of Germany after World War II was signed at Cecilienhof Palace on August 2, 1945 by the leaders of the Allied powers (Atlee, Truman and Stalin).

Sanssouci Palace and Park★★★

▶ *Follow the itinerary suggested on the map.*

This huge complex marries architecture with landscape better than any of its kind in Germany.
Wandering around, it is easy to understand why Frederick the Great took such delight in coming here.

Friedenskirche (Peace Church)

Modeled on Rome's basilica of San Clemente, the church contains a fine **mosaic**★ made on the island of Murano in the 18C.
The mausoleum houses the recumbent statues of Emperor Friedrich III and his wife, and the sarcophagus of Friedrich Wilhelm I.

Bildergalerie★ (Picture Gallery)

○*Open Apr–mid-Oct, Tue–Sun 10am–6pm. ◎3€. ☎(0331) 969 41 81.*
Amid the rich 18C Rococo of the great rooms visitors can admire works mainly from the Italian (Bassano, Tintoretto and Caravaggio), Flemish (Van Dyck, Rubens and Terbrugghen) and French (Simon

Vouet and Van Loo) schools, all acquired by Friedrich II.

Schloss Sanssouci★★★

Tours are limited to 2000 visitors a day and often sell out before noon. Admission is by timed ticket. ◎▸Visit by guided tour (40min) only, Apr–Oct, Tue–Sun 10am–6pm; Nov–Mar, 10am–5pm. ○Closed Dec 24, 25 & 31. ◎8€. ☎(0331) 969 42 02. www.spsg.de.
It is impossible to remain unmoved by the majestic façade as one climbs the great staircase leading to the palace from the park side. Architect Knobelsdorff originally planned for the façade, adorned with 36 atlantes, to encompass the entire terrace area. But the king preferred a generous proportion of space which indeed became one of his favorite places for relaxing. On the far side of the palace the state entrance is flanked by an elegant semicircular colonnade.
Tours take in all 12 rooms and reveal the enormous skill and artistry of the Rococo craftsmen who decorated them. Highlights include the Concert Room, the domed Marble Hall, the king's study and bedchamber and the Music Room, his favorite.

Neue Kammern★ (New Chambers)

○*Open Apr, Sat–Sun 10am–8pm; May--Oct, Tue–Sun 10am–6pm; mid-May–mid-Oct, Tue–Sun 10am–5pm. ◎3€. ♿☎(0331) 969 42 06.*
Designed in 1747 by Knobelsdorff, this former orangery was soon transformed into the palace guesthouse.

The Rococo interior is captivating. Note the **Ovidsaal**★, decorated with scenes from Ovid's *Metamorphoses*.

Orangerie (Orangery)

👁️ *Visit by guided tour (30min) only, Apr, Sat–Sun 10am–6pm, May–Oct, Tue–Sun 10am–6pm.* ☜4€. ♿☎(0331) 969 42 80. The orangery was built in the style of an Italian Renaissance palace between 1851 and 1860, after plans by Friedrich Wilhelm IV. Among the magnificent apartments visited by Czar Nicolas I and his wife, the malachite hall is particularly impressive. Even better is the Raphael Hall★, which houses 47 copies of paintings by Raphael.

Neues Palais★★ (New Palace)

👁️ *Visit by guided tour (1hr) only, 10am–6pm Nov–Mar to 5pm).* ⏰*Closed Dec 24, 25 & 31, Tue.* ☜6€. ☎(0331) 969 43 61. This imposing building was commissioned by Frederick the Great to demonstrate Prussia's economic power after the Seven Years' War. Some 400 rooms, with excessively lavish decorations and a superabundance of sculpture, testify to the ambitious nature of the project—which was nevertheless completed in only six years. Tours lead through the Grotto Hall, decorated with shells and fossils; the elegant Marble Hall, and the theater in the south wing. Separate admission (☜5€) gives you access to

Ph. Gajic/MICHELIN

Neues Palais

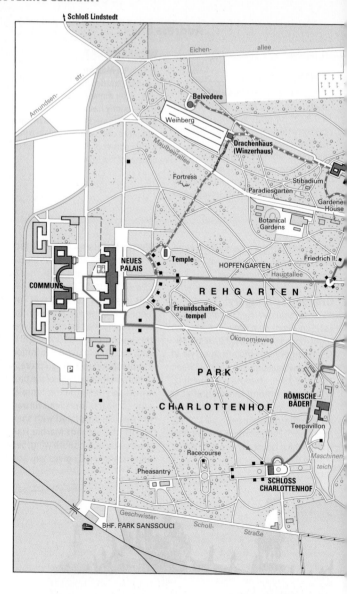

Frederick the Great's **private apartments**. Also here is the **Pesne-Galerie** (☜2€) with a broad survey of works by this French painter. The latter two are only open April to October.

Schloss Charlottenhof★

👣Visit by guided tour (45min) only, mid-May–mid-Oct, Tue–Sun 10am–5pm. ☜4€. ☎(0331) 969 42 28.

Karl-Friedrich Schinkel and his pupil, Ludwig Perseus, drew up the plans for this palace, built in the Classical Italian style between 1826 and 1829.

Tours include a stop in the bedchamber and in the office of Alexander von Humboldt.

Römische Bäder (Roman Baths)

Schinkel, Perseus and landscaper Lenné designed these baths with an eye toward harmonizing them with their natural setting. The **interior décor**★ of the baths is tastefully done.

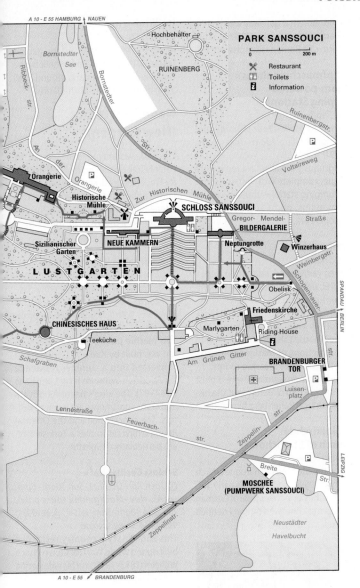

PARK SANSSOUCI

0   200 m

✕ Restaurant
🚻 Toilets
ℹ Information

A 10 - E 55 HAMBURG / NAUEN

Hochbehälter

RUINENBERG

Bornstedter See

Ruinenbergstr.

Voltaireweg

Orangerie

Historische Mühle

Zur Historischen Mühle

SCHLOSS SANSSOUCI

Gregor- Mendel- Straße

BILDERGALERIE

Neptungrotte

Winzerhaus

Weinbergstr.

Sizilianischer Garten

NEUE KAMMERN

L U S T G A R T E N

Schlögenhauer

SPANDAU / BERLIN

Obelisk

CHINESISCHES HAUS

Teeküche

Marlygarten

Friedenskirche

Riding House

Am Grünen Gitter

BRANDENBURGER TOR

str.

Schafgraben

Lennéstraße

Feuerbach-   str.

Zeppelin-   str.

Luisen- platz

LEIPZIG

Zeppelinstr.

Breite   Str.

MOSCHEE (PUMPWERK SANSSOUCI)

Neustädter Havelbucht

A 10 - E 55 / BRANDENBURG

A pergola leads to the Tea Pavilion, not unlike a temple, with a single room decorated all in blue, which has a good view of the lake and gardens.

Chinesisches Teehaus★★ (Chinese Tea House)

🕐 *Open mid-May–mid-Oct, Tue–Sun 10am–5pm.* 💶1€. ☎*(0331) 969 4222.*
A circular pavilion decorated with gilded statues, this structure arose from the "Sino-mania" so popular in 18C Germany. There is an exhibition of Chinese and Meissen porcelain inside.

Sights

The Town

Brandenburger Tor★
Luisenplatz.

This monumental gateway was built in the Baroque fashion in 1770 but takes the form of a Roman triumphal arch.

Dampfmaschinenhaus★ (Steam-powered Pumping Station)

Breite Straße 28.

Visit by guided tour (30min) only, May–Oct, Sat–Sun 10am–6pm. 2€. (0331) 969 42 25.

Incongruously installed in a replica of a mosque, complete with minarets, this 19C pumping station supplies water to the fountains, pools and cascades in Sanssouci Park.

Filmmuseum★

Breite Straße 1a.

Open year-round, daily 10am–6pm. 3.50€. (0331) 271 81 12. www.filmmuseum-potsdam.de.

Dating from 1685 and modified by Knobelsdorff in 1746, the former royal stables now house this small museum with reconstructions of Marlene Dietrich's and Lilian Harvey's dressing rooms. Exhibits focus on German Expressionist films, émigré film directors and the history of the local Babelsberg film studios.

Nikolaikirche★ (Church of St. Nicholas)

Am Alten Markt.

Built on the site of an old Baroque church destroyed by fire in 1795, this early 19C church is the perfect example of German Classicism as conceived by Karl Friedrich Schinkel.

Schloss Cecilienhof

Holländisches Viertel★ (Dutch Quarter)

Along the Mittelstraße are the gabled houses of the Dutch Quarter, built by the Dutch architect Boumann around 1740 for artisans from the Netherlands.

Neuer Garten★★ (New Garden)

This park was laid out in the late 18C by Peter Lenné on the shore of Heiliger See for Frederick the Great, who was a great fan of English-style landscaped gardens. Interesting features in the park include the orangery, the pyramid, the kitchens and the marble palace.

Marmorpalais (Marble Palace)

Open Apr–Oct, Tue–Sun 10am–6pm, 5€; Nov–Mar (guided tour only), Sat–Sun 10am–5pm. Closed Dec 24, 25 & 31. 5€. (0331) 969 42 046. www.spsg.de.

This marble palace in the Neuer Garten was built by Karl von Gontard and converted into a summer residence for Friedrich Wilhelm II by Langhans (1744–97). The king's beautiful private and state apartments are open to visitors. The concert hall and the Oriental Room, which resembles a Turkish tent, are particularly delightful.

Schloss Cecilienhof★

Open Apr–Oct, Tue–Sun 10am–6pm. 6€; Nov–Mar (guided tours only), Tue–Sun 10am–5pm. 5€. (0331) 969 42 44. www.spsg.de.

This English-style country residence built during World War I for Crown Prince Wilhelm (1882–1951) and his wife Cecilia of Mecklenburg-Schwerin (1886–1954) is worth seeing for its own sake. But it is the historic **meeting rooms of the Potsdam Conference** of 1945 that draw the most attention. Members of the Allied delegations signed the Potsdam Agreements here on August 2, 1945, outlining Germany's occupation and future development.

The luxury hotel **relaxa Schlosshotel Cecilienhof** also occupies space in this palace *(Neuer Garten 14669 Potsdam; (0331) 37 05 0; www.relaxa-hotel.de).*

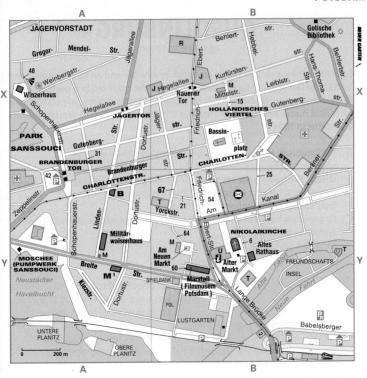

Excursions

Brandenburg

38km/23.6mi west.

It was in the 14C that this small town in the heart of the Havelland (an area of scattered lakes fed by the River Havel) began to prosper, mainly through the cloth trade.

The **Dom St. Peter und St. Paul**★, founded in 1165 and remodeled in the 14C, is furnished with several Gothic altarpieces. In the two-aisle crypt is a mausoleum memorializing the clergy murdered during the Nazi regime.

Rich exterior decoration distinguishes the 15C **St. Katharinenkirche**★, which boasts a hall chancel with an ambulatory typical of brick-built Gothic churches.

Kloster Lehnin★ (Lehnin Abbey)

28km/17.4m southwest.

Open Mon–Fri, 10am–4.15pm, Sat–Sun, 12.30pm–5.30pm. Closed Jan 1, Dec 24–26 & 31. (03382) 76 88 55. www.klosterkirche-lehnin.de.

This three-aisle brick basilica, commissioned by Margrave Otto I of Brandenburg and occupied in 1192 by the Cistercian Order, combines Romanesque and Early Gothic elements.

Worth seeing on the inside are a Triumphal Cross dating from 1225 and the funerary stone of the Margrave Otto IV.

QUEDLINBURG★

POPULATION: 23 000

Lorded over by a rock pinnacle crowned by a castle and an abbey church, the half-timbered town of Quedlinburg is one of the most picture-perfect towns in the Harz region. More than 700 houses in the historic center are classified as historical monuments, which elevated the town to UNESCO's World Heritage List status in 1994.

- **Information:** Markt 2, 06484 Quedlinburg, ☎ (03946) 90 56 24. www.quedlinburg.de.
- ▶ **Orient Yourself:** Quedlinburg is near the A14 autobahn (Leipzig–Magdeburg), and an ideal base for exploring the Harz mountains.
- **Don't Miss:** The Schloßberg, Old Town
- **Organizing Your Time:** Allow half a day for a leisurely tour of the Old Town and the Schloßberg.
- **Also See:** HARZ, HALLE, MAGDEBURG.

Old Town★

Markt★ (Market Place)

The early 17C Renaissance **Rathaus** borders the northern side of the market place. On the left of the façade is a statue of Roland (c. 1440). Houses built in the 17C and 18C line the other three sides of the square.

Old Streets★

Circle St. Benediktkirche via Marktstraße and Kornmarkt to explore the cobbled lanes behind the Rathaus (Town Hall), then return to the Markt along Breitstraße, with several picturesque alleyways opening off it. On the far side of the square, stroll toward the castle by way of Wordgasse, Hohe Straße and Blasiistraße. On one side of the charming **Schloßbergplatz**★, at no 12, stands the late 16C **Klopstockhaus** (◷open Apr–Oct, Wed–Sun 10am–5pm; Nov–Mar, Wed–Sun 10am–4pm; ◷closed Jan 1, Dec 24 & 31; ⊚3€; ☎(03946) 2610) in which

the poet Friedrich Gottlieb Klopstock was born in 1724. Today it contains exhibits recalling his life and work.

Lyonel-Feininger-Galerie★

Behind the Klopstock Museum, Finkenherd 5A.
◷Open Apr–Oct, Tue–Sun 10am–6pm; Nov–Mar, Tue–Sun 10am–5pm. ◷Closed Jan 1, Dec 24 & 31. ⊚6€. ⬥☎0394622 38. www.feininger-galerie.de.
This gallery houses works by Expressionist painter Lyonel Feininger. Born in New York City, Feininger trained in France and Germany, where he exhibited with the Blaue Reiter group in 1913. After World War I he joined the Bauhaus.

Schlossberg★

Stiftskirche★★ St. Servatius (Collegiate Church)

On the site of the original 9C church, the present basilica was begun in 1070 and ranks as one of the most impor-

---

Lyonel Feininger (1871–1956)

Born in New York to musicians, Feininger was fascinated from a young age by the visual universe of the American metropolis. At the age of 16 he was sent to Germany to study music, but quickly became interested in sculpture and started a career drawing picture books. Over time, Feininger became a painter known for melding Expressionism and Cubism, and focusing on apparently banal subjects (factories, boats, ports and buildings). In 1919 Walter Gropius invited Feininger to join the Bauhaus, where he taught until the closure of the school by the Nazis.

H. Champollion/MICHELIN

Interior of the Stiftskirche St. Servatius

tant Romanesque houses of worship in Germany. Beneath the chancel, the **crypt**★★ is divided by three aisles with diagonal rib-vaulting decorated by **frescoes**★ depicting scenes from the Bible. The **Domschatz**★★ (Treasury)— manuscripts, a 10C Gospel, and, above all, the **Quedlinburg Knotted Carpet**★—is kept in the sacristy.

Schloss (Palace)

The 16C–17C palace formed part of the abbey, and took on its irregular floor plan due to the rocky base on which the castle was built. The **Schloßmuseum**★ (Ⓞopen Apr–Oct, daily 10am–6pm, Nov–Mar, Sat-Thu 10am–4pm; Ⓞclosed Dec 24 & 31; ≈3.50€; ☎(03946) 90 56 81) presents the history of Quedlinburg. The Abbess' Reception Room, the Throne Room and the Princes' Hall (mid-18C) can be visited.

Excursion

Gernrode
7km/4.3mi south.
Gernrode's collegiate church of **St. Cyriacus**★, first documented in 961, is another fine example of Ottonian period Romanesque architecture with a typical three-aisle nave, flat ceiling and upper galleries.
The hall crypt is among the earliest of its type in Germany. Upstairs is the **Holy Sepulchre group**★, a rare example of Romanesque sculpture.

RASTATT ★

POPULATION: 47 500

In 1698, Margrave Ludwig of Baden (1665–1707), known as Ludwig the Turk, moved his seat from Baden-Baden to Rastatt. The town still retains traces of its prestigious past, which lasted until this line of margraves died out in 1771.

- **Information:** Herrenstraße 18, 76437 Rastatt. ☎ (07222) 97 24 62. www.rastatt.de.
- ▶ **Orient Yourself:** Less than 10km/6.2mi from the French border, Rastatt straddles the Murg River just before it flows into the Rhine.
- **Don't Miss:** A trip to Schloss Favorite (see Excursion).
- **Organizing Your Time:** Allow two hours for a tour of the Schloss.
- **Also See:** KARLSRUHE, BADEN-BADEN, SCHWARZWALD.

Sights

Schloss ★ (Palace)

Visit by guided tour (45min) only, Apr–Oct, Tue–Sun 10am–5pm; Nov–Mar, Tue–Sun 10am–4pm. Closed Dec 24, 25 & 31. 4.50€. ☎ (07222) 97 83 85. www.schloesser-und-gaerten.de.

This harmonious U-shaped palace was built 1698–1707 by Italian master architect Domenico Egidio Rossi who was replaced with **Michael Ludwig Rohrer** after Ludwig the Turk's death in 1707.

Royal Apartments

The margravial apartments are richly embellished with frescoes and stuccowork. The sumptuous **Ahnensaal** (Hall of Ancestors), whose column capitals are decorated with stucco figures representing Turkish prisoners, is especially noteworthy.

The Margraves

Germany's margraves began with Charlemagne, who set up border marches *(Mark)* as defensive measures, a contrast from the internal Carolingian counties. These hostile borders were overseen by a *marchione* (military governor), a term derived from the words **Markgraf** (margrave) and marquis. In time this title became honorific and hereditary.

Wehrgeschichtliches Museum (Military Museum)

Access via the south wing.

Open May–Oct, Tue–Sun 10am–5.30pm; Nov–Apr, Fri–Sun 10am–4.30pm. Closed Dec 24 & 31. 3€. ☎ (07222) 342 44. www.wgm-rastatt.de.

Weapons, uniforms and pictures illustrate German military and general history from 1500 to 1918.

German Freedom Movements Memorial Museum

Access via the north wing.

Open year-round, Sun–Thu 9.30am–5pm, to 2pm Fri. Closed Jan 1, Dec 24, 25 & 31. ☎ (07222) 77 13 90. www.erinnerungsstaette-rastatt.de.

Displays document German freedom movements from 1500 to the resistance in former East Germany up to 1990.

Excursions

Schloss Favorite ★★

5km/3mi southeast.

Visit by guided tour (1hr) only, mid-Mar–Sept, Tue–Sun 10am–6pm; Oct–mid-Nov, Tue–Sun 10am–5pm. 5.50€. ☎ (07222) 412 07.

The exterior of this charming 18C Baroque palace is coated with an unusual matrix of gravel and granite chips. The **interior ★★** is particularly fine, sporting floors of brilliant scagliola (stucco imitating encrusted marble); mirrors, mosaics and chinoiserie.

REGENSBURG★★

POPULATION: 129 000

Regensburg is among the most delightful towns in eastern Bavaria with a history going back 2000 years and a remarkably well preserved medieval center that includes a stunning cathedral, an ancient stone bridge and Italianate patrician towers. In 2006, it was placed on UNESCO's list of World Heritage Sites.

- **Information:** Altes Rathaus, 93047 Regensburg. ☎(0941) 507 44 10. www.regensburg.de.
- ▶ **Orient Yourself:** Regensburg is located in eastern Bavaria and spans the Danube at the crossroads of the A3 and A93.
- **Parking:** Garages are located throughout Regensburg. Visit http://wap.parkinfo.com for fees and locations.
- **Don't Miss:** The cathedral.
- **Organizing Your Time:** Budget at least a full day for this lovely city.
- **Also See:** STRAUBING.

A Bit of History

Preserved by time – Regensburg began in 179 AD as a Roman garrison guarding the natural frontier of the Danube at its most northerly point. The town was converted to Christianity in the 7C, and St. Boniface founded a bishopric there in 739, making it a center for religious life in the Middle Ages. As the seat of the Bavarian dukes (6C–13C), the town developed into an important trading post. It became part of Bavaria in the 19C and lost influence to Munich, which saved it from bombardment during World War II. Today its city center is one of the best preserved medieval towns in Germany.

The City of Diets – Once a Free Imperial City, Regensburg hosted plenary sessions of the Imperial Diet charged with responsibility for the internal peace and external security of the federation of the Holy Roman Empire. From 1663 to 1806 the city was the seat of a Permanent Diet—the first indication of a broad German government. The Diet drew representatives from 70 other states to Regensburg.

Sights

Kathedrale St. Peter★
Domplatz 1.
Open Apr–Oct, daily 6.30am–6pm; Nov–Mar, 6.30am–5pm. ☎(0941) 597 10 02. www.bistum-regensburg.de.
Construction on this cathedral began after 1260 but was essentially brought to a halt in 1525; the spires were not added until the 19C. The **Eselsturm** (Donkey Tower), above the northern transept is all that remains of the original Romanesque sanctuary. The **west front**, richly decorated, is the work of a local family of sculptors named Roritzer. The main entrance, flanked by two Neo-Gothic towers, is unusual, with a triangular, jutting porch. A statue of St. Peter can be seen on the pier.
Inside, the huge Late Gothic nave houses two 13C masterpieces of local

---

The Gorges of the "Donaudurchbruch"

Between Kelheim and Kloster Weltenburg, the Danube narrows as it "breaks through" steep, narrow limestone cliffs in a series of meanders. The best way to view this beautiful gorge is on a boat cruise. Up to 20 tours depart from Kelheim daily from mid-March to October. Drop by the tourist office or visit www.schiffahrt-kelheim.de for a timetable. The round-trip is 7.80€.

M. Hertlein/MICHELIN

Detail of Dom St. Peter

Gothic statuary: the Archangel Gabriel and, opposite, Mary at the Annunciation. The three chancel windows are adorned with beautiful 14C stained **glass**★★. The cathedral is home to a famous boys' choir, the Regensburger Domspatzen.

Domschatzmuseum (Cathedral Treasury)

Krauterermarkt 3. In the south wing of the bishops' residence (Bischofshof), entrance via the courtyard.

○*Open Dec–Oct, Tue–Sat 10am–5pm, Sun noon–5pm.* ○*Closed Jan 1, Dec 24.* ◈*2€.* ☎ *(0941) 576 45. www.bistumsmuseen-regensburg.de.*

The cathedral's treasury displays liturgical items, reliquaries and vestments from the 11C to the 18C.

Kreuzgang (Cloister)

Access via the cathedral garden.

○*Open Apr–Oct, daily 6.30am–6pm, Nov–Mar to 5pm.* ⬝⬝*Guided tours, May–Oct, Mon–Sat 10.30am and 2pm, Sun 2pm; Nov–Apr, daily 2pm.* ◈*3€.* ☎*(0941) 586 55 00.*

Inside the cloister, traces of ancient frescoes adorn the walls of the Romanesque **Allerheiligenkapelle** (All Saints Chapel). The Alter Dom, the old 11C Stefanskapelle, is another highlight with an altar reliquary thought to date from the 5C–8C.

Diözesanmuseum (Religious Art Museum)

○*Open Apr–Oct, Tue–Sun 10am–5pm.* ◈*2€.* ☎ *(0941) 516 88. www.bistumsmuseen-regensburg.de.*

The museum is installed in the **Ulrichskirche**, an Early Gothic 13C church with 1 571 murals. Among other exhibits, visitors can see antique bishops' crosses, reliquaries and religious paintings.

Alte Kapelle★ (Old Chapel)

St.-Kassians-Platz 7.

The Basilica of Our Lady associated with this chapel stands on the south side of Alter Kornmarkt. Originally Carolingian, the Alte Kapelle was completely transformed in the Rococo style in the 18C. The splendid reredos, the painted ceiling and the gilded stuccowork are beautifully accented by the light penetrating the tall windows. It is only open during services but there is a glass plane through which the interior can be admired.

St. Kassianskirche (Church of St. Cassian)

A Romanesque basilica with pillars and 18C Rococo decoration, this is Regensburg's oldest parish church; first mentioned in 885. The church's chief highlight is an altar (1498) in the south aisle. The wooden sculpture of the *Schöne Maria* (Lovely Mary) is by Hans Leinberger (1520) and was a major point

Address Book

For coin ranges, see the Legend on the cover flap.

WHERE TO EAT

Haus Heuport – *Domplatz 7* ☏*(0941) 599 92 97. www.heuport.de. Closed 2 weeks in Jan.* This 13C mansion is located in the center of the old town, opposite the cathedral. Behind the beautiful façade is a small restaurant and cocktail bar. Simple cuisine is served in the dining room or on the terrace.

David – *Watmarkt 5.* ☏*(0941) 56 18 58. Closed Carnival Week, 2 weeks in Aug, Sun and Mon.* Accessed by elevator, this 5th-floor restaurant is located in a historic mansion and serves Mediterranean cuisine in a romantic atmosphere. A beautiful covered terrace offers views of the town.

WHERE TO STAY

Hotel Wiendl – *Universitäts-straße 9.* ☏*(0941) 92 02 70. www.hotel wiendl.de. 35 rooms. Restaurant , closed Sat & Sun dinner.*

This small, unpretentious hotel has simple rooms furnished in pale chestnut wood. Country-style restaurant.

Hotel Kaiserhof – *Kramgasse 10.* ☏*(0941) 58 53 50. www.kaiserhof-am-dom.de. 30 rooms.* Welcoming guest-rooms all offer views of the cathedral's twin towers. The breakfast room is set in a former 14C chapel with a high vaulted ceiling.

TAKING A BREAK

Café Goldenes Kreuz – *Haidplatz 7* ☏*(0941) 5 72 32.* This elegant café is in a historic building with abundant Gothic design details. In summer enjoy the people-watching from the terrace facing vibrant Haidplatz.

NIGHTLIFE

Brauhaus Joh. Albrecht – *Schwarze-Bärenstraße 6.* ☏*(0941) 510 55. www. brauhaus-joh-albrecht.de.* This lively micro-brewery serves delicious beers that pair up exceptionally well with the hearty regional dishes dominating the menu.

---

of pilgrimage until the church became Protestant in 1542.

Haidplatz★

This square is surrounded by historic buildings, including the Zum Goldenen Kreuz inn (at no 7) with a stone tower and façade. In the center of the square is the 1656 **Justitiabrunnen** (Fountain of Justice).

Altes Rathaus★ (Old Town Hall)

Visit by guided tour (1hr) only, Apr–Oct 9.30am–noon, 1.30pm–4pm, every half hour; Nov–Jan 6 & Mar, 10am–3.30pm, every 90min, Jan 7-Feb 10am, 11.30am, 1.30pm, 3pm. Closed Jan 1, Dec 24 & 25. 7.50€. ☏*(0941) 507 34 40.* The eight-story tower of the old Town Hall dates from 1250. The Gothic western section was built c. 1360.
The façade includes a gabled doorway and a pedestal supporting a charming oriel window.

Tours include a stop in the *Reichssaal* (Imperial Hall) where the delegates of the Permanent Diet once gathered.

Fischmarkt (Fish Market)

This is one of Regensburg's oldest market squares, built in 1529 in Italian style.

Steinerne Brücke (Stone Bridge)

This 310m/1 017ft-long bridge from the 12C rests on 16 arches and for many centuries was the only crossing across the Danube for many miles. From the middle, there is a fine **view**★ of the old town. In the foreground is the 14C Brück-turm gateway, flanked by the huge roof of the 17C Salzstadel (salt loft). Beside this building, on the quayside, is the **Historische Wurstküche**, the oldest sausage kitchen in Germany.

Basilika St. Emmeram★

Emmeramsplatz 3. Open year-round, daily 10am–4.30pm.

This was once the abbey church of an 8C Benedictine monastery. A Gothic gateway on **Emmeramsplatz** leads to the huge Romanesque porch (12C) and the double doors at the church entrance. The 11C sculptures by these doors (Jesus Christ, St. Emmeram and St. Dionysius) are among the oldest in Germany.

Schloss Thurn und Taxis

Emmeramsplatz 5.

Visit by guided tour (90min) only, mid-Mar–Nov 7, Mon–Fri 11am, 2pm, 3pm, Sat–Sun also 10am and 1pm; Jan 5–mid-Mar & Nov 9–Dec Sat–Sun 10am, 11am, 2pm, 3pm; Nov 10–28, Mon–Fri 2.30pm. *Closed Dec 24 &25.* *11.50€.* *(0941) 504 81 33. www.thurnundtaxis.de.*

The Thurn and Taxis princes held the German postal monopoly until the 19C. As compensation for losing the monopoly, they were given the St. Emmeram abbey buildings, which the family has occupied since 1816. Tours take in the state apartments, lavishly decorated in Historicist style, as well as the cloister of the Basilica St. Emmeram.

Fürstliche Schatzkammer (Treasury)

Open mid-Mar–Nov 8, Mon–Fri 11am–5pm, 10am–5pm Sat–Sun; Nov 9–mid-Mar, Sat–Sun 10am–5pm. *4.50€.* *(0941) 504 81 33.*

The north wing of the Neoclassical former stables of Schloss Thurn und Taxis contains a branch of the Bavarian Nationalmuseum. Displays include fine furniture, porcelain, weapons and gold and silver trinkets from leading workshops in Europe.

Document Neupfarrplatz

Dachauplatz 2–4.

Visit by guided tour (45min) only, Sept–Jun, Thu–Sat 2.30pm; Jul–Aug, Thu–Mon 2.30pm. *5€.* *(0941) 507 14 42.*

Neupfarrplatz is a palimpcest of Regensburg history as excavations in the 1990s revealed. On top of a Roman camp was built, in the Middle Ages, the town's Jewish quarter. After it was razed in 1519, a pilgrimage chapel was built atop the old synagogue. Since 2000, a multimedia presentation brings to life the past.

Excursions

Walhalla★

11km/6.8mi east.

Open Apr–Sept, daily 9am–5.45pm; Oct 9am–4.45pm; Nov–Mar, 10am–11.45am, 1pm–3.45pm. *Closed Shrove Tue, Dec 24, 25 & 31.* *4€.* *(09403) 96 16 80. www.walhalla-regensburg.de.*

Built between 1830 and 1842 by Ludwig I of Bavaria, this Doric temple honors great German men and women. Inside are 127 marble busts and 64 commemorative plaques of famous soldiers, artists and scientists, politicians, musicians and other movers, shakers and thinkers.

Befreiungshalle★ (Liberation Hall)

28km/17.3mi southwest.

Open mid-Mar– Oct, daily 9am–6pm; Nov– mid-Mar, 9am–4pm. *3€.* *(09 441) 68 20 70.*

Celebrating Germany's liberation from Napoleonic rule, this cylindrical 19C

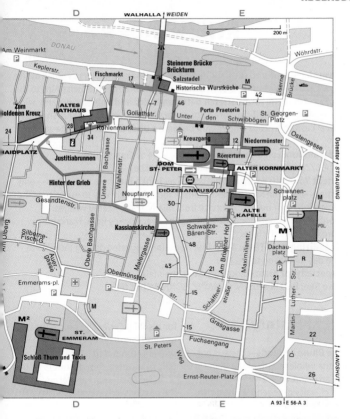

REGENSBURG		Haidpl.	D	Pfauengasse	E	30
		Königsstr.	E 21	Rathauspl.	D	34
Brückstr.	E 7	Landshuter Str.	E 22	Thundorfer Str.	E	42
Domgarten	E 12	Ludwigstr.	D 24	Viereimergasse	E	43
Fröhliche-Türken-Str.	E 15	Luitpoldstr.	E 26	Weiße-Hahnen-Gasse	E	46
Gesandtenstr.	D	Maximilianstr.	E	Weiße-Lilien-Str.	E	48
Goldene-Bären-Str.	D 17	Neue-Waag-Gasse	D 28			
Goliathstr.	DE	Neupfarrpl.	DE			

Historisches Museum	E M¹		Marstallmuseum Thurn und Taxis Museum	D M²

memorial was conceived by Ludwig I. Inspired by Greek architecture, its central hall bears allegorical statues representing the Germanic peoples.

Kloster Weltenburg★

33km/20.5mi southwest, on the banks of the Danube. ○*Open year-round, daily 8am–6pm.* ♿☎*(09441) 20 40.*
Weltenburg Abbey was built by Cosmas Damian Asam in 1718, with a narthex and a nave, both of them oval. A statue of St. George is the church's centerpiece; the dome bears a *trompe-l'œil* Asam composition on the theme of the Church Triumphant. The abbey operates the world's oldest monastic brewery and has an enchanting beer garden.

😊 A Bit of Advice 😊

Nothing goes better with Bavarian *Bratwurst* than *Händlmaier's süßer Hausmachersenf*, the sweet, smoky mustard: a Regensburg specialty concocted by Johanna Händlmaier in 1914 to sell in her butcher's shop as the perfect accompaniment to her husband's sausages.

RHEINTAL★★★

RHINE VALLEY

Few rivers have captured the imagination of artists and travelers as much as the Rhine, a 1 320km/820-mile ribbon rushing northward from the Swiss Alps to the North Sea. Along the nicest stretch between Mainz and Koblenz, dreamy wine villages with dainty half-timbered houses are lorded over by legend-shrouded medieval castles. In 2002, the region became a UNESCO World Heritage Site.

- **Information:** Loreley Besucherzentrum, 6346 St. Goarshausen. ☎(06771) 959 91 11. www.romantischer-rhein.de.
- ▸ **Orient Yourself:** Roads parallel both river banks, but there no bridges—only ferries—between Koblenz and Mainz. A more leisurely way to experience the region is by tour boat with service from nearly all the nearby villages.
- **Don't Miss:** A boat tour or drive along the river, Loreley Rock, Marksburg, Burg Rheinfels, Bacharach.
- **Organizing Your Time:** Allow four hours for suggested driving tour 1 and one day for driving tour 2.
- **Especially for Kids:** Marksburg, Burg Rheinfels.
- **Also See:** BAD KREUZNACH, MAINZ, BONN, MOSELTAL.

A Bit of History

The Rhine Legends – There is not, along the whole length of the Rhine, a castle, an island, even a rock without its tale of chivalry or legend. **Lohengrin**, the Knight of the Swan, appeared at the foot of the castle of Kleve (Cleves); at the **Loreley**, a beautiful enchantress bewitched boatmen with her song, leading their vessels to disaster.

But the single outstanding Rhine legend is the story of the Nibelungen (*see INTRODUCTION: Literature*), which provided Richard Wagner with inspiration for his *Ring Cycle*. The epic **Nibelungenlied** (Song of the Nibelungen) was probably composed late in the 12C and tells of murder, the splendors of the 5C Burgundian court at Worms, and of the passions inflaming the hearts of its heroes. The tribal treasure is rumored to be buried in the Rhine near Worms.

From the Alps to the North Sea – The Rhine rises in the Swiss Alps. Gushing down the mountains, it quickly reaches Bodensee (Lake Constance), which it crosses at a sluggish pace. After the exit from Lake Constance, rock outcrops

Burg Gutenfels and the fortified island of Pfalz on the Rhine

D. Scherf/MICHELIN

The Mäuseturm

According to legend, Hatto, Archbishop of Mainz, built this tower to collect tolls from boatmen. When famine hit the local peasants, they fled to Mainz to demand wheat. Hatto sent them to the granary, locked them inside and set fire to the building. Soon nothing remained but a few mice who managed to escape. They scampered to the archbishop's palace and ate everything they could find. Hatto headed to his Rhine tower for refuge, but the mice followed him, and when his boat landed, they polished him off.

from the Black Forest and the foothills of the Jura produce the famous Rhine Falls at Schaffhausen (*see Green Guide Switzerland*). Farther downstream, limestone strata cause *Laufen* (rapids). At Basel, the Rhine abruptly changes direction, veering north to fertilie the land of the Vosges and the Black Forest.

From Bingen to Neuwied, north of Koblenz, the Rhine cuts its way through the Rhineland schist massif, where the rock can foment dangerous whirlpools. This "romantic" stretch of river valley, with its alternation of steeply terraced vineyards, woods, escarpments and castle ruins, is the most picturesque part of the Rhine River. Later, having passed through the industrial region around Duisburg, the river turns west and curls slowly across the plain toward the sea.

An Exceptional Shipping Lane – The Rhine is navigable over almost 1 000km/620mi between Rotterdam and Rheinfelden and has always been an important European waterway. The world's largest river port is in Duisburg-Ruhrort.

Driving Tours

1 The Loreley★★ – from Rüdesheim to Koblenz

75km/47mi.

This route, following the Rhine's east bank, passes through the wildest and steepest part of the Rhine Gorge, with splendid views of the castles and fortresses lining the river.

After **Rüdesheim**★ (*see RUDESHEIM*), the road runs beneath terraced vine-

yards overlooked by the ruins of Burg Ehrenfels. This fortress was built by the archbishops of Mainz at the same time as the Mäuseturm on the opposite bank, which served as a toll booth.

After Assmannshausen, silhouetted high up on the opposite bank, the crenellated towers of Rheinstein, Reichenstein and Sooneck appear one after the other. The tower of Fürstenberg, on the wooded slopes facing Lorch, marks the start of an open stretch of vineyards and the towers of **Bacharach**, followed by the fortified isle of Pfalz.

Pfalz bei Kaub★ (Pfalzgrafenstein)
Opposite Kaub.

Open Apr–Sept, Tue–Sun 9am–1pm, 2pm–6pm; Oct–Mar, 9am–1pm, 2pm–5pm. Closed Dec. 4.50€.

The massive five-sided keep of this ship-like toll fortress rises from the center of the river, encircled by a turreted fortified wall. Before a sharp bend in the river, admire the **setting**★★ of the towers of Oberwesel at the foot of the Schönburg across the river. The sharp bend leads to the most untamed stretch on this part of the Rhine.

The Loreley★★

This legendary spur, 132m/433ft high, symbolizes the Romantic Rhine and enjoys a special place in German literature. The outcropping reduces the river's width by one quarter. According to legend, the Loreley was a water sprite who bewitched boatmen with her beauty and melodious songs at the river's most dangerous spot.

St. Goarshausen

The town, strung out along the river bank, is dominated by **Burg Katz** (Cat Castle), said to have been built to neu-

Address Book

🪙 *For coin ranges, see the Legend on the cover flap.*

WHERE TO STAY

⊖⊖**Altkölnischer Hof** – *Blücher-straße 2, 55422 Bacharach.* ☎*(06743) 13 39. www.altkoelnischer-hof.de. Closed Nov–Mar. 18 rooms. Restaurant* ⊖⊖. This family-run hotel is in an old, restored half-timbered building. Rooms ooze plenty of charm and history with their wooden furniture and tasteful décor. Rhenish specialties are served in the paneled dining room.

⊖⊖**Zum Goldenen Löwen** – *Heerstraße 82, 56329 St. Goar.* ☎*(06741) 16 74. www.goldener-loewe-stgoar. de. 12 rooms. Restaurant* ⊖⊖. This convenient little hotel with well-kept rooms of varying size and furnishings. Old German-style rustic restaurant.

⊖⊖**Hotel Landsknecht** – *Aussiedlung Landsknecht 6 (B9), 56329 St. Goar-Fellen.* ☎*(06741) 20 11. www. hotel-landsknecht.de. Closed Dec 23–27, Jan 2–31. 19 rooms. Restaurant* ⊖⊖, *closed Nov–mid-Mar, Tue and Wed.* This pleasant, modern family-run property with attached wine estate has comfortable rooms facing the Rhine or a lovely garden. The rustic restaurant also has river views from its terrace.

⊖⊖⊖**Park-Hotel** – *Marktstraße 8, 55422 Bacharach.* ☎*(06743) 14 22. www.park-hotel-bacharach.de. Open mid-Mar–mid-Nov. 25 rooms. Restaurant* ⊖⊖. This family-run establishment offers comfortable rooms, some with Rhine River views, and regional dishes in the *Pfalzgrafen* room.

⊖⊖⊖⊖**Schloß Rheinfels** – *Schloßberg 47, 56329 St. Goar.* Spa ☎*(06741) 80 20. www.schloss-rhein fels.de. 60 rooms. Restaurant* ⊖⊖. Across from the Loreley Rock, just outside the impressive castle, the hotel and villa offers an elegant ambience in comfortable rooms, as well as an extended spa center. There is a fine dining restaurant as well as a castle tavern with a panoramic terrace overlooking the Rhine Valley.

WHERE TO EAT

⊖⊖**Gasthaus Hirsch** – *Rheinstraße 17, 56154 Boppard-Hirzenach.* ☎*(06741) 26 01. www.gasthaus-hirsch.net. Closed Mon and Tue.* A tasteful, rustic establishment with a paneled dining room adorned with paintings. Tasty dishes are made with market-fresh and, wherever possible, locally sourced ingredients.

⊖⊖**Tannenheim** – *Bahnhof Buch-holz 3 (B327), 56154 Boppard-Buchholz.* ☎*(06742) 22 81. www.hotel-tannenheim. de. Closed Dec 22–Jan 19, Thu, Sat lunch, Sun dinner.* This charming restaurant has been run by the Fuchs family for four generations. It also has a few rooms and a pretty garden. Expect varied seasonal dishes.

⊖⊖⊖**Zum Turm** – *Zollstraße 50, 56349 Kaub.* ☎*(06774) 922 00. www.rhein-hotel-turm.com. Closed 1 week in early Jan, 1 week early Aug, 2 weeks early Nov and Tue.* This establishment near the old tower was founded over 300 years ago and has housed an upscale family-run restaurant for over a century. The menu ranges from tummy-fillers such as sage-laced roast pork to creative culinary temptations, including trout mousse and dove pot au feu.

---

tralize **Burg Maus** (Mouse Castle), a little farther downstream.

Loreley Viewpoint★★

From St. Goarshausen take the road signposted "Loreley-Burgenstraße". From April to October, shuttle buses leave from St. Goarshausen boat landing. There are impressive **views**★★ plunging down into the romantic gorge from several accessible spurs here. On the pla-teau a landscape garden with marked trails is laid out and a **visitor center** (🕐*open Mar–mid-Nov, daily 10am–6pm;* ⊘*2.50€;* ♿☎*(06771) 59 90 93; www.lore-ley-touristik.de)* has interactive displays covering the Loreley legend and local geology, flora and fauna.

▸ *At Kamp-Bornhofen, turn right toward Dahlheim, then right again at the sign "Zu den Burgen".*

Treacherous Loreley and the Goethe pleasure boat

The Rival Brothers

The hill slopes become wild again. Beyond Kestert there is a fine **panorama**★★; from the ruins of **Liebenstein Fortress**, the castle of **Sterrenberg** and the valley below come into view. The two castles are traditionally linked to a legend concerning two rival brothers. From Boppard on, where the Rhine swings into a huge double loop, the landscape becomes densely cultivated by vines. Soon the fortress of Marksburg emerges on its promontory above the town of Braubach.

▶ At Braubach, take the road to Nastätten.

Marksburg★   Kids

📷 *Visit by guided tour (50min) only, early Mar–Oct, daily 10am–5pm continuous departures; Nov–early Mar, 11am–4pm on the hour.* ◐*Closed Dec 24 & 25.* ⊜*5€.* ☎*(02627) 206. www.marksburg.de.*
The **castle**, the only one in the whole Rhine Valley never to have been destroyed, is spectacularly sited on a craggy hilltop. Tours take you inside a Gothic assembly hall, the medieval kitchen and the torture chamber. Noteworthy are the medieval garden and a collection of armor from 600 BC to the 15C.

Burg Lahneck

3km/1.8mi from Lahnstein, near the confluence of the Rhine and the Lahn.
📷 *Visit by guided tour (40min) only; Easter–Oct, daily 10am–5pm.*

⊜*4€.* ☎*(02621) 91 41 71. www.burg-lahneck.de.*
The ruins of this fortress, originally built in the 13C to protect neighboring silver mines, were reconstructed in Neo-Gothic style in the 19C. From the keep is a **view** of the junction of the two rivers and the troubadour castle of Stolzenfels, across the Rhine.

2 The Rhine Castles★★★ – from Koblenz to Bingen

63km/39mi.

This itinerary retraces the previous one, in the opposite direction, on the west bank of the river. Soon after leaving Koblenz, Lahneck comes into view again, its tower overlooking the river confluence. Above, on the right, is Stolzenfels.

Koblenz (↻see KOBLENZ)

Schloss Stolzenfels (Palace)

📷 *Visit by guided tour (45min) only; Apr–Sept, Tue–Sun 10am–6pm; Oct–Mar, 10am–5pm.* ⊜*2.60€.* ◐*Closed Dec.* ☎*(0261) 516 56. www.schloss-stolzenfels.de.*
This enormous **castle** was reconstructed in 1842. The style is now Neo-Gothic, and the sumptuous **interior**★ is a museum. From the slope against which Stolzenfels is built, the terrace offers a view of Koblenz and the citadel of Ehrenbreitstein.

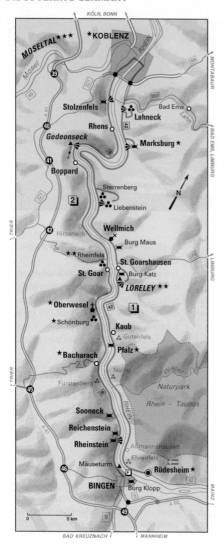

ing at four separate lakes rather than a continuous river.

Boppard

Originally a Roman camp, Boppard became a Free Imperial City in the Middle Ages. Interesting sights include the Late Romanesque Severuskirche and the Gothic Carmelite church with its rich interior fittings: 15C choir stalls and Renaissance tombs. The **museum** in the 14C fortress displays, among other things, wooden furniture by local artist Michael Thonet.

There is also a pleasant riverside walk and the Römerkastell where you can see a section of the 4C Roman town wall and graves from the Frankish period in the 7C.

The beginning of the "romantic" Rhine Gorge is marked by the two Rival Brothers fortresses (*see above*) on the opposite slopes. After Hirzenach, the Cat and Mouse castles are visible, standing above St. Goarshausen.

St. Goar

The village, clinging to the hillside at the foot of the impressive **Burg Rheinfels**★★ (*open mid-Mar–Oct, daily 9am–6pm; Nov–mid-Mar, Sat–Sun 11am–5pm, if weather permits; ₰4€; ☎(06741) 7753*) stands guard over the Loreley passage along with St. Goarshausen across the river. Rheinfels was, until it fell to the French in 1797, the most powerful fortress in the entire valley.

It is worth climbing the clock tower to get an overall view of the turbulent Rhine and the Cat and Mouse castles. Kids love exploring the maze of towers, gates and courts comprising Rheinfels. Bring or borrow a flashlight to go inside the underground defensive tunnel network.

Beyond St. Goar, the river banks are steep and heavily wooded until Oberwesel.

Gedeonseck★★

1hr round-trip, including 20min on a chair-lift.

Apr 1–10 & mid-end Oct, daily 10am–5pm; Apr 11–30 & Oct 1–15 to 5.30pm; May–Jun & Sept to 6pm; Jul & Aug 9.30am–6.30pm. ₰6.50€ round-trip. ☎(06742) 25 10. www.sesselbahn-boppard.de.

In fine weather, a trip up this 240m/787.4ft-high rock outcrop will treat you to superb **views**★ of the river's hairpin curve near Boppard. The **Four Lake View**★ gives you the illusion of look-

Oberwesel

Sixteen towers survive of the original town wall hemming in this appealing wine-growing village. It is possible to walk along sections of it, from where there is a good view of the Rhine. South of the town, the Gothic **Liebfrauen-kirche★** has a fine 14C altarpiece, one of the oldest in Germany, a Gothic rood screen and an unusual 1510 triptych illustrating the 15 cataclysms presaging the end of the world.

From the terrace of **Schönburg Castle★**, a little farther on, is a view of Kaub, on the far side of the river, and the fortified isle of Pfalz. Schönburg is a block of three forts sheltered by a common defensive wall.

Bacharach★

Once the property of the counts of the Palatinate, Bacharach, a town of vineyards and ancient towers, is one of the prettiest—and thus most popular—resorts in the Rhine Valley. The stately half-timbered houses on Marktplatz and along Oberstraße are a delight, especially when decked out with flowers during the warmer seasons. One of the last Romanesque naves built in Germany can be seen in Peterskirche. A trail behind the church leads up to the romantically ruined Gothic Wernerkapelle (chapel) and the medieval Burg Stahleck, now a youth hostel.

The ruined towers of Nollig and Fürstenberg mark the end of the valley's most grandiose stretch. The road passes below castles whose sites are ever more audacious, from Sooneck to Reichenstein and finally Rheinstein.

Burg Sooneck

◉*Visit by guided tour (45min) only, Apr–Sept, Tue–Sun 9am–6pm; Oct–Nov & Jan–Mar 9am–1pm and 2pm–5pm.* ◉*Closed Dec.* ◉2.60€. ☎*(06743) 60 64.*

This **fortress** is restored and tiered to suit the terrain with a maze of staircases, platforms and terraced gardens beneath the turrets. It clings to a steep slope of the Soonwald outcrop.

The Rhine Valley Castles

The Rhine Valley boasts an impressive number of castles. Stately residences, defensive forts, toll gates, travelers' refuges for travelers, each served a purpose. While many were severely damaged in fighting during the 17C and 18C, many castles were rebuilt in following the creation of the German Confederation in 1815.

Burg Reichenstein

◉*Open Mar–mid-Nov, daily 9am–6pm.* ◉*3.40€.* ☎*(06721) 61 17.*

Well-situated at the mouth of a rural valley, this 10C Neo-feudal **castle** has a collection of arms and hunting trophies. After serving as an imperial tollhouse, it was converted into a summer residence in the 19C.

Burg Rheinstein

◉*Open mid-Mar–mid-Nov, daily 9.30am–5.30pm; mid-Nov–mid-Mar, Mon–Thu 2pm–5pm, Sun 10am–5pm.* ◉*Closed Dec20–Jan 31.* ◉*4€.* ☎*(06721) 63 48. www.burg-rheinstein.de.*

The **castle** is perched on a perpendicular rock spur, in a commanding position above the Rhine. From the foremost watchtower there is a bird's-eye **view★★** of the valley. Rheinstein was the first of the Rhine castles to be rebuilt by the Hohenzollerns (after 1823).

Once past the **Mäuseturm**, balanced on its tiny islet in the middle of the river, the valley widens out and the east bank becomes covered with terraced vines.

Bingen

Bingen started out as a strategic Roman camp set up at the confluence of the Rhine and the Nahe *(Castel Bingium)*. Nowadays, tourism and wine-growing are the town's main sources of income. Sights include the landmark **Burg Klopp** and the **Historisches Museum am Strom** (◉*open year-round, Tue–Sun 10am–5pm;* ◉*3€;* ♿☎*(06721) 991 531)* with exhibits on local history and on the 12C abbess, artist, author and all-round genius Hildegard von Bingen.

ROMANTISCHE STRASSE★★

By way of river valleys and an idyllic, rolling countryside, the "Romantic Road" recalls at every stage some aspect of uniquely German history. As the route unfolds, it evokes medieval city life (Rothenburg), the religious sensibility of artists like Tilman Riemenschneider, German chivalry (Bad Mergentheim), Baroque episcopal courts and Imperial towns like Würzburg.

- **Information:** Marktplatz, Dinkelsbühl. ☎(09851) 902 71. www.romantischestrasse.com.
- ▸ **Orient Yourself:** Germany's most popular tourist route stretches from the Main Valley to the foot of the Bavarian Alps, passing river valleys, fields, forests, orchards and pretty little towns. The entire route is signposted "Romantische Straße." From April to October, the Europabus travels the route in both directions once a day. Deutsche Touring (☎01805) 79 03 03; www.deutsche-touring.com).
- **Don't Miss:** Rothenburg o.d. Tauber, Dinkelsbühl
- **Organizing Your Time:** Allow four hours for suggested driving tour ⒈; five hours for driving tour ⒉; and a full day for driving tour ⒊.
- **Also See:** DEUTSCHE ALPENSTRASSE, MÜNCHEN.

Driving Tours

⒈ From Würzburg to Rothenburg o. d. T.

91.5km/56.8mi

▸ Leaving **Würzburg**★★ (⚲see WÜRZBURG), the B27 descends toward the Tauber valley.

Bad Mergentheim★ –
49km/30.4mi south of Würzburg.
⚲See BAD MERGENTHEIM.

Weikersheim
12.8km/8mi east of Bad Mergentheim.
⚲Visit by guided tour (1hr) only; mid-Mar–Nov, daily 9am–6pm, Dec–mid-Mar, daily 10am–noon and 1pm–5pm. ⚲Closed Dec 24 & 31. ⚲5€. ⚲☎(07934) 99 29 50. www.schloss-weikersheim.de.
Once the seat of the counts of Hohenlohe, this town's castle (1580–1680) on the banks of the Tauber has scant Baroque influences. The magnificent **Rittersaal**★★ (Knights' Hall) is typical of the transition between the Renaissance and Baroque styles.

Dinkelsbühl

Address Book

For coin ranges, see the cover flap.

WHERE TO STAY

Zum Goldenen Anker – *Untere Schmiedgasse 22, 91550 Dinkelsbühl. (09851) 578 00. www.goldener-anker-dkb.de. 25 rooms. Restaurant.* This old inn has spacious country-style rooms and traditional cooking.

Hotel Kunst-Stuben – *Segringer Straße 52, 91550 Dinkelsbühl. (09851) 67 50. www.kunst-stuben.de. 6 rooms.* This small, homely property is managed by an artist couple happy to offer tours of their studio. Immaculate rooms and a library ensure a restful stay.

Laurentius – *Marktplatz 5, 97990 Weikersheim. (07934) 910 80. www.hotel-laurentius.de. 11 rooms. Restaurant*. Behind the cheerful yellow façade await immaculate rooms with Italian furnishings. The restaurant is in a beautiful vaulted cellar.

Hotel Blauer Hecht – *Schweinemarkt 1, 91550 Dinkelsbühl. (09851) 58 10. Closed Jan. 44 rooms. Restaurant*. This charming hotel in a former brewery inn of 1684 has beautifully furnished rooms with individual flair and a rustic old German restaurant.

Romantik Hotel Greifen-Post – *Marktplatz 8, 91555 Feuchtwangen. (09852) 68 00. www.greifen.de. 35 rooms. Closed Jan 1–7. Restaurant, closed Sun dinner, Mon.* This 600-year-old establishment knows the true meaning of hospitality. Rooms are elegantly furnished and the dining rooms drips with historic charm.

Formal gardens (1710), accented with grotesque statues in the Franconian style, end in a charming orangery.

▶ *The narrow Tauber Valley, begins above the town of Bieberehren. The road rises and falls over slopes covered alternately by woodland, orchards and willow-fringed riverbanks.*

Creglingen★

11.8km/7.3mi east of Weikersheim.
The isolated **Herrgottskirche** (open May–Nov, daily 9.15am–6.30pm; Nov–Mar Tue–Sun noon–4pm; Apr, daily 9.15am–5.30pm; 2€; www.herrgottskirche.de), 1.5km/1mi along the road to Blaufelden, contains the **Altarpiece of the Virgin Mary**★★ carved by Tilman Riemenschneider. The artist has channeled his own sensitivity into the expression of the Madonna at the Assumption. Opposite the church is a **Fingerhutmuseum** (thimble museum)—the only one of its kind in Germany.

Detwang

16km/10mi southeast of Creglinen.
In the church at Detwang another **Riemenschneider altarpiece**★ depicts the *Crucifixion*.

Rothenburg ob der Tauber★★★

– *1.7km/1mi from Detwang.*
See ROTHENBURG OB DER TAUBER.

② From Rothenburg o. d. T. to Donauwörth

117.5km/73mi

Feuchtwangen

35km/21.7mi southeast of Rothenburg ob der Tauber.
Once a Free Imperial City, this town was also the birthplace of medieval minstrel, Walther von der Vogelweide. An attractive market square sits surrounded by pretty houses and overlooked by a parish church with an Altarpiece of the Virgin by Michael Wolgemut. Installed in a 17C burgher's house is a **Fränkisches Museum** (Museum of Franconian Folklore) displaying a collection of furniture and regional pottery and costumes.

Dinkelsbühl★

12.2km/7.5mi south of Feuchtwangen.
Ramparts and watchtowers still surround this idyllic medieval town which, every July, hosts a colorful festival (*Kinderzeche*) commemorating how the town was spared destruction in the Thirty Years' War (*see Calendar of Events*). The

Georgskirche★ has retained its Romanesque tower. Other highlights include the **Deutsches Haus**★ *(Am Weinmarkt)* and the Hezelhof *(Segringer Straße 7).*

The undulating landscape is supplanted, after Nördlingen, by the bleak Ries basin, thought to have been caused millions of years ago by a meteorite.

Nördlingen★ – *32.4km/20mi southeast of Dinkelsbühl.* See NÖRDLINGEN

Schloss Harburg

17.6km/11mi southeast of Nördlingen. Visit by guided visit (50min) only, mid-Mar–Oct, Tue–Sun 10am–5pm. 5€. (09080) 968 60.

This large fortified castle looks down on the picturesque houses of a village along the banks of the Wörnitz. Tours take in the church, the water tower, the prison tower, the private quarters, the well and the festival hall.

▸ *Leave via Mündlingerstraße, to the left, and take the Romantic Road to Mündling for Kaisheim.*

Kaisheim

14km/8.7mi northeast of Harburg.
The former Cistercian abbey church was built at the end of the 14C in the full flower of the Gothic era. (The abbey itself is now a penal institution). Around the chancel is a 12-sided **ambulatory**★ *(to visit, apply at the presbytery.)* The 18C emperor's room in the Imperial foundation is open to the public *(on request).*

Donauwörth

6.3km/4mi south of Kaisheim.
This Free Imperial City is proud of its pastel historic buildings along the Reichsstraße; the most impressive are the Town Hall and *Fuggerhaus* (1543). The 18C Baroque pilgrimage church of Heilig Kreuz boasts Wessobrunn stuccowork. The Gothic Liebfrauenmünster has beautiful 15C murals. Parts of the town's fortifications still stand.

③ From Donauwörth to Füssen

148km/92mi.

This drive along the ancient *Via Claudia,* one of the main arteries of the old Holy Roman Empire, owes its interest less to the route (which follows the Lech Valley) than to the historical sites on the way. These include **Augsburg**★★, **Landsberg**★, **Neuschwanstein**★★★ and **Hohenschwangau**★, and *(well worth the price of a small detour)* the **Wieskirche**★★.

ROSTOCK★

POPULATION: 198 500

Rostock, once a member of the Hanseatic League, is the biggest city in the Mecklenburg-Vorpommern *Land* in northern Germany, and its strategic location on the wide Warnow estuary has always favored its development. Rostock's port, continues to play an important role in international maritime commerce. Though postwar reconstruction was not always pleasing, Rostock still has its charms, especially in its seaside suburb of Warnemünde.

▸ **Information:** Neuer Markt 3, 18055 Rostock. (0381) 381 22 22. www.rostock.de.

▸ **Orient Yourself:** A key Baltic port, Rostock is served by the A19 and A24 autobahn from Berlin (allow 2hr 30min); the A20 links the town to Lübeck.

P Parking: Garages situated throughout Rostock, also near the train station.

Don't Miss: The Baltic resorts of Warnemünde, Fischland, Darß and Zingst

Organizing Your Time: Allow half a day to see all the sights.

Kids Especially for Kids: Baltic resorts of Warnemünde, Fischland, Darß, Zingst.

Also See: BAD DOBERAN, STRALSUND, MECKLEMBURGISCHE SEENPLATTE.

Rathaus

A Bit of History

Object of Desire – By the 13C, Rostock was already a member of the Hanseatic League, minting its own money and asserting independence from the princes of Mecklenburg. The first Baltic university was founded here In 1419. Such an exalted position drew the envy of powerful neighbors and the town suffered substantial damage during the Thirty Years' War (1618–48), the Nordic struggle for supremacy (1700–21) and the Napoleonic Wars (1803–15). In more modern times, until German reunification, Rostock was East Germany's only significant outlet to the Baltic.

Sights

Old Town★

Marienkirche★★

The imposing 13C cross-shaped basilica is one of the biggest churches in northern Germany. The massive tower was not completed until the 18C. From the top is a **panorama**★ of the city and the docks. Inside the church, note the 1472 **astronomical clock**★★ (its face was remodeled in 1643), which comprises a calendar valid until 2017.

Rathaus (Town Hall)

Neuer Markt.
This Town Hall is composed of three 13C–14C gabled houses topped by a brick gallery supporting seven towers. The Baroque façade was added in 1727.

Schiffahrtsmuseum★   (Navigational Museum)

Liegeplatz-Schmarldorf, International Exhibit Garden Exhibit grounds.
◔Open Apr–Jun, Sept Tue–Sun 9am–6pm; Jul–Aug, daily 9am–6pm; Oct–Mar, Tue–Sun 10am–4pm. ✏4€ (child 2.50€). ☎(0381) 12 83 13 64. www.schifffahrtsmuseum-rostock.de.
Exhibits inside a decommissioned 10 000-ton freighter chart the history of maritime travel in the Baltic region from its earliest days to the present. Models of ships, paintings, navigational instruments and photographs document maritime life and work.

Kröpeliner Straße

This pedestrian zone is Rostock's shopping and commercial center.
It is bordered by gabled houses with façades from Baroque and Renaissance times. At no 82, the brick façade of the 15C Heilig-Geist-Spital has an unusual stepped gable.

Kulturhistorisches Museum (Cultural History Museum)

Klosterhof 7. ◔Open year-round, Tue–Sun 10am–6pm. ◔Closed Jan 1, Good Fri, Dec 24, 25 & 31. ✆☎(0381) 20 35 90. www.kulturhistorisches-museum-rostock.de.
This former 13C Cistercian convent, founded by Danish Queen Margarethe,

Old Port of Warnemünde

©Anja Frost/istockphoto.com

is the region's only completely preserved abbey complex. It houses medieval art, including the **Altarpiece of the Three Kings**★ (late 15C), crafts, toys, coins and Dutch paintings from the 16C to 19C.

Excursions

Warnemünde★   Kids
11km/6.8mi north.
This former fishing village, bought by its citizens from the Prince of Mecklenburg in 1323, has become Rostock's most popular beach resort, with charming little streets.

Fischland, Darß and Zingst   Kids
Northeast of Rostock.
The peninsular chain of Fischland-Darß-Zingst is an attractive coastal area alternating with woods, salt-marshes and moorland. The narrow tongue of land extends north and east, parallel to the mainland and separated from it by a lagoon of brackish Baltic seawater and fresh riverwater. The artists' village of **Ahrenshoop** in the slightly hilly **Fischland** is a popular vacation resort. **Darß** and **Zingst** form part of the Vorpommern Boddenlanschaft National Park. The little villages and seaside resorts feature attractive reed-covered houses and cottages.

Güstrow★
50km/31mi south of Rostock.
Güstrow became the residence of the dukes of Mecklenburg-Güstrow in the

16C and grew increasingly wealthy over the next centuries. The elegant burghers' houses around the **cathedral** and **market squares** and along surrounding streets are evidence of this period.
A highlight is the **Schloss**★ (Oopen mid-Apr–mid-Oct, daily 10am–6pm; mid-Oct–mid-Apr, Tue–Sun 10am–5pm; Oclosed Dec 24; 3€; (03843) 75 20; www.schloss-guestrow.de), a superb 16C Renaissance palace that blends Italian, French and German elements. The **Dom**★, a 14C Gothic brick basilica, is richly endowed with artworks, having been the court church of the dukes of Mecklenburg. Note the **Güstrow Apostles**★, 12 almost life-size oak figures by Claus Berg of Lübeck from c. 1530. A stark contrast to these is Ernst Barlach's modernist sculpture *Der Schwebende.*

Ernst-Barlach Stiftung★ (Barlach Museum)
OOpen Apr–Oct, Tue–Sun 10am–5pm; Nov–Mar, 11am–4pm, also Mon Jul-Aug. Atelierhaus, Ausstellungsforum & Graphics Cabinet 5€; Gertudenkapelle 4€, combination ticket 7€. (03843) 822 99. www.ernst-barlach-stiftung.de. This museum honoring Ernst Barlach (1870–1938) has two locations: his religious works are in the Late Gothic **Gertrudenkapelle**. Further works are presented at the artist's studio, the **Atelierhaus**, on the shores of the Inselsee. A new building, the **Ausstellungsforum** with attached Graphics Cabinet is just a few yards from the studio and presents rotating exhibitions.

ROTHENBURG ob der TAUBER★★★

POPULATION: 11 000

One of the oldest towns on the "Romantic Road," Rothenburg overlooks the winding course of the River Tauber from its rocky crag. Once behind the ramparts in the pedestrian-only medieval center, visitors revel in the 16C among ancient houses, fountains and narrow, cobbled lanes.

- **Information:** Marktplatz 2, 91541 Rothenburg. ☎(09861) 404 800. www.rothenburg.de.
- ▶ **Orient Yourself:** The old town stands on a steep promontory overlooking the Tauber River valley.
- **Don't Miss:** A stroll through the Old Town.
- **Organizing Your Time:** Allow four hours for the suggested walking tour.
- **Especially for Kids:** The mechanical clock on the Ratstrinkstube and a walk along the ramparts.
- **Also See:** ROMANTISCHE STRASSE.

A Bit of History

A Long Drink *(Meistertrunk)* – During the Thirty Years' War, Protestant Rothenburg was unable to withstand the Catholic siege by General Tilly's army. After 40 000 victorious mercenaries had pillaged the town for three months, Tilly decided to raze it unless, he declared, some local could empty in a single draught a tankard (a 6-pint/3.4liter tankard) of wine. The town mayor, a man named Georg Nusch, volunteered and

miraculously succeeded: Rothenburg was saved. Ever since Rothenburgers have re-created the event annually at Pentecost.

Saved again – Rothenburg stagnated throughout the 17C and 18C, too poor to expand beyond its own walls. In the 19C, however, the town's steep-roofed houses with their gables, staircase turrets and corner oriels were rediscovered by Romantic painters, and Rothenburg became a major tourist attraction.

Herrngasse in Rothenburg

©Angela Jones/Bigstockphoto.com

Rothenburg: a striking illustration of the Middle Ages

Walking Tour

▶ *Starting at Marktplatz, follow the itinerary marked on the town map.*

Rathaus★ (Town Hall)

This 14C structure in the **Old Town**★★★ has seen a number of architectural additions over the centuries. Visitors can inspect the **Historiengewölbe** (historic vaults), now a history museum, or climb the tower for a **view**★ of the fortified town. North of Marktplatz is the gable of the 1446 *Ratstrinkstube* (now the tourist office) with a **mechanical clock** from 1910 that re-enacts the Long Drink *(on the hour, 11am–3pm, 8pm–10pm)*.

Baumeisterhaus

With its elaborate Renaissance façade and pretty courtyard, this former private home is one of the most beautiful buildings in Rothenburg. Statues on the first floor represent the seven virtues, those on the second the seven deadly sins.

Mittelalterliches Kriminalmuseum (Museum of Medieval Justice)

Burggasse 3–5.
○*Open Apr–Oct, daily 9.30am–6pm; Nov & Jan–Feb, 2pm–4pm; Mar & Dec, 10am–4pm.* ∞*3.80€.* ☎*(09861) 53 59. www.kriminalmuseum.rothenburg.de.* Punishment was swift and brutal, as you will learn at this museum which displays documents and instruments of public humiliation, torture and execution.

Plönlein

A picturesque corner of half-timbered houses, often photographed: one street is level, another ascending to the Siebers tower, another descending. The fountain once supplied the fish stock used by Tauber fishermen.

▶ *Leave the old town through the Koboldzell gate, make a sharp right, and follow the path circling the spur some way below the ramparts for impressive* **views**★★ *of an arched, two-story viaduct (Doppelbrücke) in the valley below. Return to the old town via the Burggarten.*

Burggarten (Castle Garden)

All that remains of the double fortress erected on this promontory is a chapel, the Blasiuskapelle, which has been turned into a war memorial, and a fortified gateway, the Burgtor. The area is now a large public garden with magnificent **views**★.

▶ *Return to the town via the Burgtor; assailants unaware of the grimacing mask above the second gate risked being drenched in boiling oil here.*

Herrngasse★

The mansions of medieval burghers line this busy commercial street. In the **Franziskanerkirche**, note the 15C and 16C sculptures and the Creglingen Madonna (1400).

ROTHENBURG OB DER TAUBER		Hafengasse		Markt	15
		Herrngasse		Marktpl.	16
		Heugasse	8	Obere Schmiedgasse	18
Alter Stadtgraben	5	Kapellenpl.	9	Rödergasse	
Georgengasse	3	Kirchgasse	10	Untere Schmiedgasse	23
Grüner Markt	6	Kirchpl.	12	Vorm Würzburger Tor	24

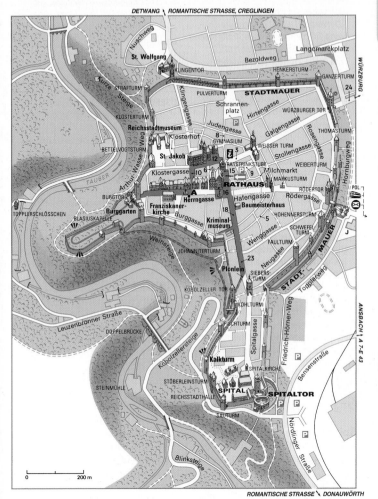

DETWANG ∖ ROMANTISCHE STRASSE, CREGLINGEN

ROMANTISCHE STRASSE ∖ DONAUWÖRTH

Back in Herrngasse, check out the hidden courtyards. Number 15 features a half-timbered gallery on embossed wooden pillars.

▸ *Turn left into Kirchgasse after the round fountain.*

St. Jakobskirche★
Klostergasse 15.

🕐*Open Apr–Oct, daily 9am–5.15pm; Nov, Jan-Mar 10am–noon, 2pm–4pm; Dec 10am–5pm.* ⊚2€.

This 14C Gothic church shelters Tilman Riemenschneider's masterful **Heilig-blutaltar ★★ (Altarpiece of the Holy Blood)** (1504). Note the tense, perplexed expressions conveyed in the scene, as well as Jesus' compassion. Also note the stained glass windows in the east chancel.

Address Book

& *For coin ranges, see the Legend on the cover flap.*

WHERE TO STAY

◎◎**Hotel-Gasthof Schwarzes Lamm** – *Detwang 21, 91541 Rothenburg-Detwang (follow Romantische Straße toward Bad Mergentheim). ☎(09861) 6727. www.hotelschwarzeslamm-rothenburg.de. Closed mid-Jan–mid-Feb. 30 rooms.Restaurant ◎◎.* This charming establishment with a long family tradition is located in the oldest part of Rothenburg. Rooms are quiet, modern and have balconies. In fine weather, the lime-tree garden is a pleasant hangout.

◎◎**Mittermeier** – *Vorm Würzburger Tor 9. ☎(09861) 945 40. www.mittermeier.rothenburg.de. 27 rooms. Restaurant ◎◎◎, closed 2 weeks in Jan & Aug, Sun and Mon.* Friendly and dedicated staff as well as individually decorated themed rooms (e.g. "Africa" or "Spain") give this pretty sandstone villa an edge. The restaurant serves an upscale menu with a youthful, fresh style.

◎◎**Hotel Spitzweg** – *Paradeisgasse 2. ☎(09861) 942 90. www.hotel-spitzweg.de. 9 rooms.* This little 16C hotel has comfortable, rustic rooms and plenty of memorabilia of the Romantic painter Carl Spitzweg who once lived in Rothenburg.

WHERE TO EAT

◎◎**Baumeisterhaus** – *Obere Schmiedgasse 3. ☎(09861) 947 00.* This 1596 Renaissance gem opposite the Town Hall serves hearty Bavarian cuisine on two floors adorned with beautiful old wall paintings. The courtyard is surrounded by half-timbered galleries.

TAKING A BREAK

USEFUL TIPS
Many cafés sell the locally famous *Schneeballen* (snowballs), which are cakes made with shortbread pastry and traditionally covered with icing or cinnamon.

Caféhaus – *Untere Schmiedgasse 18. ☎(09861) 939 85. Open 9.30am-6pm, terrace/winter garden closed Jan-Easter.* Over one hundred specialty coffees and a wide variety of *Schneeballen* are served here. The glass-fronted winter garden affords a magnificent view of the green Tauber valley.

NIGHTLIFE

Zur Höll – *Burggasse 8. ☎(09861) 42 29. www.romanticroad.com/hoell.* This picturesque half-timbered house now harbors a *Weinstube* serving mainly fine Franconian wines and brandies as well as traditional dishes.

Sights

Spitalkirche★
This hospital's Gothic chapel features notable works of religious art.

Spitalkirche★ (Ramparts) [Kids]
Constructed in the 13C and 14C, these ramparts, complete with gates and towers, are still perfectly preserved. Long stretches are open to the public.

St. Wolfgangskirche
⊙*Open Apr–Sept, daily 10am–1pm, 2.30pm–5pm; Oct Tue–Sun & weekends in Dec 11am–4pm. ◎1.50€.*
North of the Klingentor, this curious 15C Gothic church, fortified and incorporated into the barbican, doubled the defenses of the gateway.

Reichsstadtmuseum (Imperial City Museum)
⊙*Open Apr–Oct, daily 10am–5pm; Nov–Mar, 1pm–4pm. ◎Closed Shrove Tue, Dec 24 & 31. ◎3.50€. ☎(09861) 93 90 43. www.reichsstadtmuseum.rothenburg.de.*
A Dominican monastery from 1258 to 1554, this building is now a local museum showing, among other collections, the Rothenburg Stations of the Cross (1494).

Also on view is the tankard reportedly drained by Mayor Nusch in front of General Tilly. Its design depicts the emperor and the seven electors and was made in 1616.

ROTTWEIL★

POPULATION: 25 600

Rottweil is the oldest town in southwestern Germany and became a Free Imperial City in 1268. Traces of the Baroque era are still evident, especially in the church buildings. The town is also famous for its traditional carnival called Fasnet.

- **Information:** Hauptstraße 21, 78628 Rottweil. ☎(0741) 49 42 80. www.rottweil.de.
- ▸ **Orient Yourself:** Rottweil occupies a pleasant location on the Upper Neckar, between the Swabian Jura and the Black Forest and near the A81 autobahn.
- 🅿 Lots on Kriegsdamm or Nägelesgraben are 2min walk from the town center.
- **Don't Miss:** Rottweil's Old Town.
- **Organizing Your Time:** Allow three hours for the walking tour.
- **Also See:** DONAUESCHINGEN, TÜBINGEN, SCHWARZWALD, SCHWÄBISCHE ALB.

Walking Tour

Old Town★
The almost fully preserved late-medieval town center is fun to explore at leisure. The oriel-festooned burghers' houses along Hauptstraße are especially interesting. There is also a great **view**★ of the Swabian Alps.

▸ *Turn left at the Rathaus (Town Hall).*

Heiligkreuzmünster (Minster of the Holy Cross)
The 15C Late Gothic minster features a high altar adorned with a crucifix attributed to Nuremberg master Veit Stoß (1447/8–1533). Splendid 15C **altarpieces**★ decorate the side chapels, including St. Peter's altarpiece in the north side aisle, St. Nicholas' altarpiece in the south side aisle and the Virgin Mary and Apostles altarpieces.

▸ *Go through Pfarrgasse, left along Schulgasse to Kriegsdamm.*

Dominikanermuseum (Dominican Museum)
🕐*Open year-round, Tue–Sun 2pm–5pm.* 🎟*1.50€.* ♿☎*(0741) 7662.*
This modern museum exhibits a prized collection of 14C–16C **Swabian sculptures**★, including those by Hans Multscher and Michel Erhart, as well as important Roman excavations from the ancient settlement of *Arae Flaviae*. A key find is the **Orpheus Mosaic**★ from the 2C AD, composed of 570 000 pieces.

▸ *Take Lorenzgasse to Lorenzkapelle.*

Lorenzkapelle (Chapel of St. Lorence)
This 16C funerary chapel houses a collection of **stone sculpture** produced by the Rottweil stonemason's lodge in the late Middle Ages.

▸ *Turn left, and take Hauptstraße back to the town's central intersection.*

Kapellenkirche (Chapel Church)
The **tower**★ of this landmark Gothic church is a splendid example of the Flamboyant style. The lavish interior dates back to the Baroque period.

Excursions

Dreifaltigkeitsberg★ (Trinity Hill)
20km/12.4mi southeast.
A minor road leads to this lovely pilgrimage church from Spaichingen, on the edge of the Swabian Jura.
From the hill a sweeping **panorama**★ unfolds that takes in the Baar Depression and, in the distance, the dark outline of the Black Forest.

RÜDESHEIM AM RHEIN★

POPULATION: 10 000

The wine town of Rüdesheim lies at the gateway to the "Romantic Rhine" and is a key tourist center in the valley. Its narrow streets, most famously the Drosselgasse, are crammed with traditional wine taverns where you can sample the celebrated local Riesling and other varietals.

- **Information:** Geisenheimerstraße 22, 65385 Rüdesheim. ☎(06722) 29 62. www.ruedesheim.de.
- **Orient Yourself:** Rüdesheim lies at the southern end of the Rhine Gorge, where the river, deflected by the Taunus massif, turns north again.
- **Don't Miss:** A sampling of Rüdesheim's famous Riesling wine.
- **Organizing Your Time:** Allow two hours for the excursions.
- **Also See:** RHEINTAL, WIESBADEN, MAINZ, BAD KREUZNACH.

Sights

Rheingauer Weinmuseum Brömserburg (Wine Museum)

Rheinstraße 2.
Open mid-Mar–Oct, daily 10am–6pm. 5€. ☎(06722) 23 48. www.rheingauer-weinmuseum.de.

This museum is housed in a medieval castle that has seen stints as a 13C residence of the Mainz bishops, as a stronghold of the knights of Rüdesheim, and as a meeting place for brigands. Exhibits include old winepresses and Roman amphorae (vases and jars for storing or transporting wine).

Niederwalddenkmal (Niederwald Memorial)

Access on foot, by road (2km/1.2mi) or by cable-car (terminal on Oberstraße: 20min round-trip; 6€ round-trip). www.niederwalddenkmal.de.

Built in 1883 to commemorate the 1871 founding of the German Empire, this memorial comprises a massive statue of Germania sitting on a bronze plinth featuring Bismarck, Emperor Wilhelm I, German princes and their armies.

Excursions

The Rheingau

Southern exposure allows cultivation of vines high up on the foothills of the Taunus. Note the picturesque villages of Geisenheim, Winkel and Hattenheim, surrounded by vineyards, en route to Eberbach Abbey.

Kloster Eberbach★★ –

See Kloster EBERBACH

Address Book

For coin ranges, see cover flap.

WHERE TO STAY

Hotel Trapp – *Kirchstraße 7, 65385 Rüdesheim. ☎(06722) 911 40. www.ruedesheim-trapp.de. Closed Dec 24–mid-Mar. 35 rooms. Restaurant .* This family-run property has rooms in Mediterranean style. Enjoy sophisticated home-cooking in the prettily decorated restaurant.

Breuer's Rüdesheimer Schloss – *Steingasse 10, 65385 Rüdesheim. ☎(06722) 905 00. www.ruedesheimer-schloss.de. Closed Dec 23–Jan 7, Feb 1–5. 27 rooms. Restaurant .* This class act beautifully marries a historic building from 1729 with artsy, contemporary rooms. The gourmet restaurant extends into a lovely, flower-festooned courtyard. Be sure to taste the owners' own wine.

Kiedrich

3km/1.8mi east of Kloster Eberbach.

The 15C **church** in this wine-growers' market town still bears its original, rare Flamboyant elements: carved **pews**★★ and choir stalls are adorned with polychromatic embellishment and Gothic inscriptions. Gregorian chant in a Gothic German dialect has been practised in Kiedrich since 1333.

Look out for the ruins of **Burg Scharfenstein**, high above the town. This castle played an important defensive role in the Middle Ages before being put to ruin in the 16C; only the round keep remains.

Eltville am Rhein

3.2km/2mi southeast of Kiedrich.

The oldest town in the Rheingau makes for a pleasant stopover to explore the narrow streets, 16C–17C town houses and 14C castle. The Johannes Gutenberg memorial at the latter is testimony to the fame the inventor of moveable type enjoyed during his lifetime.

INSEL RÜGEN★

The Baltic island of Rügen, Germany's largest, offers a surprising variety of scenery. In the west, the straits widen toward the open sea. Fabled chalk cliffs and sandy beaches in the east attract summer crowds. The southern shores are wooded; and to the north is the deep, jagged Jasmunder Bodden (gulf).

- **Information:** Bahnhofstraße 15. 18528 Bergen auf Rügen. ☎ (03838) 80 77 80. www.ruegen.de.
- ▶ **Orient Yourself:** Rügen can be reached by train or car via a long bridge (2.5km/1.5mi) that straddles the straits at Stralsund. Ferries to Scandinavia leave from the port of Saßnitz.
- **Don't Miss:** Chalk cliffs of the Stubbenkammer, Hiddensee Island.
- **Organizing Your Time:** Allow half a day for the sights on the island and another half day to visit Hiddensee (*see Excursion*).
- **Especially for Kids:** Rügen's bathing resorts, Hiddensee Island.
- **Also See:** GREIFSWALD, ROSTOCK, INSEL USEDOM.

Sights

Putbus★

The "white town" in the southeast of the island was founded in 1810 by Prince William Malte of Putbus as a royal seat and bathing resort. The princely seat no longer remains, but the Neoclassical town does, most notably around a circular, central square—the **circus**★. It is surrounded by 16 mansions that are finished in dazzling white and stand out from the green of the oaks. Nearby, the 19C **Theater**★ (*Alleestraße*) bears a portico of four Tuscan columns and is endowed with fabulous acoustics.

The 75ha/185-acre **Schloßpark**★ with its orangery, royal stables and parish church, is laid out in the style of an English garden.

Jagdschloss Granitz (Granitz Hunting Palace)

12km/7.4mi east of Putbus, south of Binz. ○*Open May-Sept, daily 9am–6pm; Oct, 9am–4pm; Nov–Apr, Tue–Sun 10am–4pm.* ○*Closed Dec 25.* ☜*3€.* ☎*(038393) 22 63.*

In 1837 Prince William Malte I of Putbus built a Neo-Gothic Tudor hunting lodge atop the Tempelberg, the highest point in eastern Rügen. The four crenellated corner towers of the "castle" rise up in the middle of Granitz woods. A 19C viewing tower and platform are reached via a cast-iron **spiral staircase**. From the top, the **view**★★ of Rügen Island is breathtaking. The rooms inside the house are open to the public.

Störtebeker

Klaus Störtebeker was a notorious pirate said to have been born in Ruschwitz on Rügen in 1370. As a young man, he drank from his master's tankard at work, and, having been seen by his boss, was promptly chained and beaten. But Störtebeker's strength was such that he broke free and thrashed his tormentors. Then he took off in a fishing boat as far as the cape of Arkona. There he joined Michael Gödecke and his band of brigands whose reputation struck terror into all who sailed the coast. Störtebeker became one of the most feared buccaneers of his age, scouring the seas until eventually being captured in Hamburg and condemned to the guillotine. As a mark of the respect he commanded, his last request was granted: mMercy for the companions arrested with him.

Legend has it that Störtebeker hid his booty beneath the cliffs of the Stubbenkammer, and once a year a ship steered by phantom buccaneers is said to haunt this coast. Every summer, at Ralswiek, islanders put on a play commemorating the adventures of this anti-hero, scourge of the rich and benefactor of the poor.

Bathing Resorts★ 〔Kids〕

Binz, **Sellin**, **Baabe** and **Göhren** are in the southwest of the island, awaiting visitors with sandy beaches, beautiful resort architecture and a woodland backdrop. They can be reached via the **"Rasender Roland"** (Racing Roland), a nostalgic steam train shuttling between Putbus and Göhren.

Address Book

⚱For coin ranges, see cover flap.

WHERE TO STAY

⊜⊜▩**Strandhotel Lissek** – *Strandpromenade 33, 18609 Binz. ☎(038393) 38 10. www.strandhotel-lissek.de. 40 rooms.* Carefully restored spa architecture with great attention to detail, along with all major mod cons. Some rooms have fine views of the Baltic Sea. The restaurant specializes in fish and is often packed to the gills.

⊜⊜▩**Wreecher Hof** – *Kastanienallee, 18581 Putbus-Wreechen. ☎(038301) 850. www.wreecher-hof.de. 43 rooms. Restaurant ⊜⊜▩.* This off-the-beaten track resort consists of 7 reed-thatched buildings in an idyllic location. It is a good place for those needing plenty of elbow space since most are suites with separate bed and sitting quarters. The international restaurant has a winter garden and beautiful terrace.

Jasmund National Park★★

Germany's northernmost national park is famous for its stunning chalk cliffs that border the deep blue sea.

This postcard idyll greatly inspired Romantic painter Caspar David Friedrich, especially a spot called the **Stubbenkammer**.

The most famous cliff is the 117m/384ft-high **Königsstuhl** (*King's chair; ⚱1€*). For background and information, visit the **National Park Visitors Center** (🕓 *open Easter–Oct, daily 9am–7pm; Nov–Easter 10am–5pm; ⚱6€; ☎(038392) 66 17 66; www.koenigsstuhl.com*), where you can watch a multimedia film and peruse exhibits on the park's flora, fauna and geology.

Kap Arkona★

Kap Arkona, with its 50m/164ft-high chalk cliffs, is the northernmost point of the island. The **old lighthouse** (🕓*open Jul–Aug, daily 10am–7pm; May–Jun & Sept, 10am–6pm; Mar–Apr & Oct, 10am–5pm; Jan–Feb & Nov, 11am–4pm; ⚱3€*), a square, three-story brick building, was built in 1826–29 according to plans by Karl Friedrich Schinkel. There is a wonderful **view**★★ from here to the neighboring island of Hiddensee.

Excursion

Hiddensee Island★   Kids

Ferries depart from Wiek and Schaprode on Rügen and from Stralsund, duration 30min-2hr 30min, from ⊙13.70€ roundtip.
Reederei Hiddensee, Fährstraße 16, Stralsund, ☏(0180) 321 21 50, www. reederei-hiddensee.de.
No cars allowed on the island, bicycle rental recommended.

Hiddensee Island, the "pearl of the Baltic", is 17km/10mi off the west coast of Rügen and almost entirely within the Nationalpark Vorpommersche Boddenlandschaft. The island boasts a gorgeous landscape, with towering cliffs, land spits, lagoons and coastal inlets. The highest point is the **Dornbusch peak** (72m/236ft) in the north, site of the island's trademark **lighthouse** (1888). Hiddensee is crisscrossed by trails and bicycle paths. The village of **Grieben** is famous for its thatched houses. **Kloster** has developed into a bathing resort. The playwright **Gerhart Hauptmann** (1862–1946), best known for his Naturalist dramas, is buried in the churchyard. Hauptmann's summer residence, Haus Seedorn on Kirchweg, is open to the public. The island's administrative center is at **Vitte**, a fishing village turned tourist resort. South of Vitte are vast dunes interspersed with marshland *(Dünenheide)*. **Neuendorf**, the island's most southerly village, has fishermen's houses in such a way that living quarters face the sun.

RUHRGEBIET

RUHR REGION

Historically, the Ruhr Region is best known as one of the world's largest industrial areas, a conglomeration of 50 cities joined together by sweat, coal and steel. No more. The Ruhr has been reinventing itself at a steady clip, embracing its industrial past but focusing on a future filled with culture and the arts. Aspiring to undergo a model transformation from industrial to creative powerhouse, it could become a model for other cities worldwide. No wonder then that it was selected as the European Capital of Culture 2010.

- **Information:** Königswall 21, 44137 Dortmund. ☏(0231) 18 16 186. www.ruhrgebiettouristik.de.
- **Orient Yourself:** The Ruhr Basin (4 400sq km/1 700sq mi) lies along the Ruhr, Rhine and Lippe rivers and encompasses the cities of Duisburg, Essen and Dortmund plus scores of mid-size and smaller towns.
- **Don't Miss:** Religious art lovers will be impressed by Essen's cathedral and its artworks.
- **Organizing Your Time:** Allow two days to get a flavor of the Ruhr region.
- **Especially for Kids:** Warner Bros. Movie World, the Open Air Technical Museum and the Schwebebahn.
- **Also See:** KÖLN, MÜNSTER.

A Bit of History

Important Industrial Center – Although most of the furnaces and mines are no longer in operation, the Ruhr Region remains one of the world's most important industrial centers. Much of German steel is manufactured here; Duisburg is the largest inland port in Europe and the largest river port in the world. The landscape in the region's north is shaped by the chemical industry and modern mining operations.

A New Image – The legacy of heavy industry has become an opportunity to rework the Ruhr's "Black Country" image in favor of culture and leisure activities. Former industrial plants have been turned into cultural venues, shopping

German Mining Museum in Bochum

malls and adventure playgrounds. Old pits and factories have been converted into industrial museums, offering insight into the production methods and social history of the region. About two dozen of the biggest attractions are linked by a 400km/248mi-long **Industrial Heritage Trail**.

Sights

Bochum

Kunstmuseum Bochum (Fine Arts Museum)

Kortumstraße 147, opposite the Stadtpark. ○*Open year-round, Tue–Sun 10am–5pm (Wed 8pm).* ◉*3€.* ○*Closed Jan 1, Good Fri, May 1, Dec 24, 25 & 31.* &◉*(0234) 516 00 30. www.bochum.de/kunstmuseum.*
The collections in this spacious, airy modern building concentrate mainly on contemporary international art.

Deutsches Bergbau-Museum★★ (German Mining Museum)

Am Bergbaumuseum 28. ○*Open year-round, Tue–Fri 8.30am–5pm, Sat–Sun 10am–5pm.* ○*Closed Jan 1, May 1, Dec 24–26 & 31.* ◉*6.50€.* &◉*(02 34) 587 70. www.bergbaumuseum.de.*
Founded in 1930, this museum examines the evolution of mining from antiquity to the present. A miners' lift descends 20m/65.6ft underground, where the

2.5km/1.5mi of abandoned workings in the **Schaubergwerk** illustrate methods of coal extraction and transport. The tour ends with a trip up the 71m/233ft-high mining tower.

Eisenbahnmuseum★ (Railway Museum)

Dr-C-Otto-Straße 191, in northern Bochum-Dahlhausen surburb. ○*Open Mar–mid-Nov, Tue–Fri 8.30am–5pm, Sun 10am–5pm.* ◉*5.50€.* ◉*(02 34) 49 25 16. www.eisenbahnmuseubo chum.de.*
Founded by railway enthusiasts, this museum is installed in an abandoned station and repair shop on the north bank of the Ruhr. Equipment from as long ago as 1914 is for the most part still in working condition. More than 180 steam and electric locomotives trace the evolution of the railway as a form of transportation.

Bottrop

Josef Albers Museum

Im Stadtgarten 20 (near town center). ○*Open year-round, Tue–Sat 11am–5pm, Sun 10am–5pm.* ○*Closed Jan 1, Dec 24, 25 & 31.* &◉*(02041) 297 16. www.quadrat -bottrop.de.*
Bottrop-born Constructivist painter and Bauhaus theorist Josef Albers referred to his work as *Hommage an das Quadrat* (Homage to the Square). This ultra-modern museum displays a survey of his work and other Constructivists. The adjoining sculpture park contains works by Max Bill, Donald Judd, Norbert Kricke etc. The same complex also harbors a **museum of pre- and local history**. The **Ice Age Hall**★ houses Germany's largest Quaternary Era collection.

Movie Park Germany★ [Kids]

Warner Allee 1, in Bottrop-Kirchhellen, via A31, exit Kirchhellen. ○*Open mid-Mar–Oct, daily 10am–6pm, 8pm or 10pm, depending on the day. Call for specific opening times.* ◉*31€.* ◉*(02 045) 89 90. www.movieparkgermany.de.*
This movie film and amusement park features more than 35 attractions, thrill rides and live shows spread across such themed sections as Old West, Streets

of New York and Santa Monica Pier. Scream your head off on the MP Xpress roller coaster, join SpongeBob on a Back Splash water ride or take in the scene from the Ferris wheel. If you need a little peace and quiet, head for the **Museum of German Film History**★, examining over 100 years of celluloid history.

Duisburg

Wilhelm-Lehmbruck-Museum★★

Friedrich-Wilhelm-Straße 40,
in Duisburg town center.
◐*Open year-round, Tue–Sat 11am–5pm,*
Sun 10am–6pm. ◐*Closed Jan 1, 24, 25, 31*
Dec. ◉*5€.* ◐*(0231) 283 26 30. www.*
lehmbruckmuseum.de.

This museum is home to a prestigious collection of over 700 20C sculptures and objets d'art. Look for emotional works by Barlach and Kollwitz, Cubist and Constructivist sculpture by Archipenko, Duchamp and Brancusi and otherworldly Surrealist contributions by Arp and Dalí.

One museum wing showcases works by Duisberg sculptor **Wilhelm Lehmbruck** (1881–1919). The surrounding park (7ha/17.3 acres) contains outdoor sculptures by international artists against a wooded backdrop.

Museum der Deutschen Binnenschiffahrt★

Apostelstraße 84, in Duisburg-Ruhrort.
◐*Open Tue–Sun 10am–5pm.* ◐*Closed*
Jan 1, Dec 24–26 & 31. ◉*3€.* ◐*(0203) 80*
88 940. www.binnenschiffahrtsmuseum.de.

The former Art Nouveau swimming pool is one of the country's largest museums about the economic, technological, and social aspects of inland shipping. Visitors examine developments from dugouts to modern tug boats. Two museum ships (◉*2€, accessible May–Sept only*) from 1882 and 1922 are a 10min stroll through the port, near the maritime stock exchange.

Landschaftspark Duisburg Nord

Emscherstraße 71, In Duisburg-Meidrich.
◐*(0203) 429 19 42. www.landschafts*
park.de.

This enormous retired iron and steelworks has been ingeniously recycled into a adventure playground and cultural events venue. You can learn SCUBA diving in the old gas tank, go rock climbing on its ore bunkers, brave a high-wire parcours suspended between buildings or ascend to the top of the blast furnace for fine views. The cultural program includes movie screenings, theater productions and dance parties.

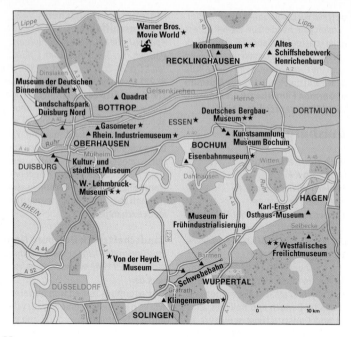

Hagen

Karl-Ernst-Osthaus-Museum

☛Closed until March 2009.
Hochstraße 73.

🕑Open year-round, Tue–Sun 11am–
6pm. 🕑Closed Jan 1, May 1, Dec 24, 25
& 31. ⌨3€. ☎(02331) 207 31 38. www.
keom.de.

Founded by industrialist Karl Ernst Osthaus, this museum is a beautiful space
designed by Belgian Art Nouveau artist
Henry van de Velde in the early 20C. It
was built to display Osthaus' collection
of art—the Museum Folkwang—which
was sold by his heirs to the city of Essen
following his early death in 1921. Since
reopening in 1992, the museum has
presented eclectic exhibits aimed at
treating the museum as a body, as a
diverse unit whose components, like
organs, complement and combine with
one another.

Westfälisches Freilicht-
museum★★   Kids
(Westphalian Open-Air
Museum)

At Hagen-Selbecke, in the valley of
Mäckingerbachtal. Leave Hagen heading south on the Frankfurt, then the
Eilpe road. At Eilpe, turn right toward
Breckerfeld-Halver and continue for just
over 1.5km/1mi to Selbecke. 10min walk
from the parking lot.

🕑Open mid-Mar–Oct, Tue–Sun 9am–
6pm. ⌨5€. ☎(02331) 780 70. www.
freilichtmuseum-hagen.de.

Along 2.5km/1.5mi of the Mäcking valley, more than 60 workshops and buildings illustrate the evolution of crafts and
trades from the late 18C through the
19C. A half-timbered 18C house is now
a **Blacksmith Museum** with a working
forge. There are also examples of James
Nasmyth's steam hammer (c. 1840) and
the zinc rolling mill of Hoesch (1841),
both of which were key inventions during early industrialization.

Higher up the valley an 18C **paper mill**
houses a printing museum.

Finally is a village of traditional craftspeople, where saddlers, smiths, rope
makers, bakers and brewers demonstrate and sell their crafts.

Oberhausen

Gasometer★

Am Grafenbusch 90, next to CentrO
shopping mall. 🕑Viewing platform:
year-round, Tue–Sun 10am–5pm (Wed

to 3pm). Interior (audio tours): *Sat–Sun 10am–5pm*. Special exhibits: *daily 10am–8pm, Fri to 10pm*.
♿☎*2€; exhibition prices vary*. ♿☎*(0208) 850 37 30. www.gasometer.de*.
The present exhibition hall used to be Europe's largest blast furnace gas storage tank in its heyday (68m/220ft in diameter, built in 1928–29). The space is so spectacular, it is worth a visit even when no exhibits are on. An elevator takes you to the viewing platform at 117m/350ft for sweeping views across the entire Ruhr region. Next door is the CentrO, one of the largest shopping malls in Germany.

Rheinisches Industriemuseum★ (Rhenish Industrial Museum)
Hansastraße 20, Oberhausen (behind the main train station).
🕐*Open year-round, Tue–Sun 10am–5pm.* 🕐*Closed Jan 1, Good Fri, May 1, Dec 25 & 31.* ☎*4€. ☎(0208) 857 92 81. www.rim. lvr.de.*
The Altenberg zinc works was in operation until 1981 and is a rare completely preserved factory site from the early days of industrialization. The "Heavy Industry" exhibit shows the 150-year history of the iron and steel industry in the Ruhr region and displays such objects as ingot moulds, mill rollers, a steam hammer and a steam locomotive.

Recklinghausen

Ikonen-Museum★★ (Icon Museum)
Kirchplatz 2a.
🕐*Open year-round, Tue–Sun 10am–6pm.* ☎*5€. ☎(02361) 50 19 41. www.ikonen-museum.com.*

Considered the most important museum of icons outside the orthodox world, this museum counts more than 1 000 works from Russia, Greece and the Balkan countries in its collection. Most are arranged by theme: the Holy Trinity and the Celestial Hierarchy); the Virgin Mary; the Saints and their Days.

Altes Schiffshebewerk Henrichenburg (Historic Ship Lift)
Am Hebewerk 2, Waltrop.
🕐*Open year-round, Tue–Sun 10am–6pm.* 🕐*Closed Dec 24-Jan 1.* ☎*3.50€.* ♿☎*(02363) 970 70. www.schiffshebe werk-henrichenburg.de.*
In 1899 Emperor Wilhelm II inaugurated this amazing construction, which lifted river barges traveling on the Dortmund-Ems-Canal 14m/46ft high, thereby opening up a direct waterway to the North Sea. It was in operation until being replaced with a larger, more modern ship lift in 1962. An exhibit illustrates the construction process and technical, political and economic aspects of canal building and river shipping. The museum ship **MS Franz Christian** gives insight into shipboard life.

Solingen

Deutsches Klingenmuseum★ (German Blade Museum)
Klosterhof 4, Solingen-Gräfrath.
🕐*Open year-round, Tue–Sun 10am–5pm (Fri from 2pm).* 🕐*Closed Jan 1, Dec 24, 25 & 31.* ☎*3.50€.* ♿☎*(0212) 25 83 60. www. klingenmuseum.de.*
Solingen is known the world over for its quality knives and other cutting instruments. In the former Gräfrath Abbey, an

---

Solingen – The Art of Steel

"Cutting edge" is a term that has defined Solingen for centuries, as it is here that steel has been turned into legendary cutting instruments. The town's first mention in history was in 1067 and by the 1600s local craftsmen were creating knives, swords and instruments that were unequaled in quality. Solingen's location near plentiful forests that provided charcoal and atop rich deposits of iron, along with its proximity to the key trading center of Cologne, guaranteed the prosperity of its skilled townspeople. Such tradition of excellence continues to this day, through firms such as Henkels and Wüsthof. And so it should come as no surprise that about 90 percent of all blades made in Germany still hail from this small town.

elegant Baroque building, this museum essentially presents the cultural history of cutting instruments and eating utensils, showcasing silverware from the Bronze Age to today. Another focal point is on weapons from around the world, bronze swords from Iran to ceremonial rapiers from France.

From the abbey, descend the steps to the historic **Marktplatz** where houses have been restored in the traditional half-timbered style of the Bergisches Land, with slate shingle roofs and walls and green wooden shutters.

Wuppertal

Von der Heydt-Museum★

Turmhof 8, Wuppertal-Elberfeld.
Open year-round, Tue–Sun 11am–6pm (Thu to 8pm. Closed Easter Mon, May 1, Pentecost Mon, Dec 24, 25 & 31. ⊚3€. &☎(0202) 563 62 31. www.von-der-heydt-museum.de.

This museum, housed in the old 19C Elberfeld Town Hall, has an interesting collection of paintings and sculpture, many donated by the Wuppertal banking family Von der Heydt. The collections include 16C and 17C Flemish and Dutch painting; French and German painting from the 19C to Impressionism, Expressionism (Kirchner, Beckmann), Fauvism, Cubism (Braque) all the way to the present. Sculptures from the 19C and 20C are also on display (Rodin, Maillol).

Schwebebahn (Suspended Railway) [Kids]

A unique mode of transport for getting around Wuppertal is the world's oldest suspended passenger railway (1898–1903) and one of the safest means of public transport. Completely non-polluting, the electric cars travel 12m/36ft above the Wupper River for just over 13km/8mi. Most of the station buildings date from the turn of the century.

OBERES SAALETAL★
UPPER SAALE VALLEY

The winding Saale River forms a natural link between towns like Jena and Halle, masterpieces of sacred architecture like Merseburg and Naumburg, and numerous riverside castles.

- ℹ **Information:** Teichgraben 5, 07743 Jena. ☎(03641) 59 06 21.
- ▶ **Orient Yourself:** Rising on high ground at the eastern extremity of the Thuringian Forest, the River Saale flows 427km/265mi to the north before joining the Elbe upstream of Magdeburg.
- ⊚ **Don't Miss:** The Fairy Grottoes
- ⊙ **Organizing Your Time:** Allow four hours for the suggested driving tour.
- [Kids] **Especially for Kids:** The Fairy Grottoes
- ⚲ **Also See:** WEIMAR, JENA, THÜRINGER WALD.

Driving Tour

From Rudolstadt to Saalburg

61km/38mi

Rudolstadt

Once the seat of the princes of Schwarzburg-Rudolstadt, this town is dominated by the fine silhouette of 18C **Schloss Heidecksburg**★(Oopen April-Oct, Tue–

Sun 10am–6pm, Nov–Mar 10am–5pm; ⊚6€; ☎(03672) 429 00; www.heidecksburg.de). Several magnificent Rococo **rooms**★★ are open to the public, and there's also a regional history museum. **Views**★ from up here are delightful.

Saalfeld

The façade of the Renaissance **Rathaus** (Town Hall) in Marktplatz (market square) centers on a stepped tower with two oriel windows. The historic rooms of a Franciscan abbey house the **Stadt-museum Saalfeld** (⊙*open year-round, Tue–Sun 10am–5pm;* ⊙*closed Dec 24 & 31;* ⊛*4€;* ♿☏ *(03671) 59 84 60; www. museumimkloster.de*), with collections on local history and folklore.

Feengrotten★ (Fairy Grottoes)

[Kids] *1km/0.6mi southeast of Saalfeld on B281.* ☛*Visit by guided tour (45min) only.* ⊙*Open Mar–Oct, daily 9.30am–5pm; Nov–Dec and Feb, 10.30am–3.30pm; Jan, Sat–Sun 10.30am–3.30pm.* ⊛*7€.* ☏*(03671) 550 40. www.feengrotten.de.* The subterranean grottoes of this abandoned slate mine are a whimsical wonderland with stalactite and stalagmite formations sparkling in a myriad of fantastic colors.

▶ *Leave Saalfeld on B85. Cross the Saale at the Hohenwarte Dam and follow the shores of the Hohenwarte reservoir (Talsperre) for 10km/6.2mi. Via Drognitz and Remptendorf,*

Saalfelder Feengrotten

Saalfeld Fairy Grottoes.

the route arrives at the Bleiloch reservoir, the largest between Saalfeld and Blankenstein. Driving across the dam, you arrive back at the river's east bank.

Saalburg

Now a lakeside town, Saalburg lost its outskirts when the valley was flooded. Note the remains of the 16C fortifications.

SAARBRÜCKEN★

POPULATION: 182 000

Although pummeled by bombs during World War II, the capital of the Saarland has developed into a regional metropolis infused with subtle French flair, a host of museums and a large number of beautifully restored Baroque buildings by master architect Friedrich Joachim Stengel.

▪ **Information:** Gerberstraße 4 (Rathaus-Carrée), 66111 Saarbrücken. ☏ (0681) 93 80 90. www.die-region-saarbruecken.de.

▶ **Orient Yourself:** Saarbrücken is in the Saar valley, on the French border and at the crossroads of the A6 autobahn to Mannheim and the A4 to Metz, France.

P **Parking:** Garages in the Old City are at Tal- and Reepersbergstraßen and at Roon- and Stengelstraßen.

☺ **Don't Miss:** The Ludwigsplatz and its yellow and red Ludwigskirche.

⊙ **Organizing Your Time:** Allow three to four hours for all the sights.

✦ **Also See:** UNTERES SAARTAL, PFALZ.

Sights

Alt-Saarbrücken

Schloss (Palace)

The medieval fortress was replaced in the 17C by a Renaissance castle, demolished in 1738 to make way for a Baroque palace designed by Stengel. Since then,

the palace has suffered various forms of destruction, including war and fire, but was completely renovated in 1989 by Gottfried Böhm. It now has a modern look and is used by the city administration and as a cultural venue.

The **Historisches Museum Saar** (⊙*open year-round, Tue–Sun 10am–6pm (Thu 8pm), Sat noon–6pm;* ⊛*4€;* ♿☏ *(0681)*

Address Book

WHERE TO EAT

🍴🍷🛏**Weismüller** – *Gersweiler Straße 43a.* ☎*(0681) 521 53. www.weissmueller-restaurant-quack.de. Closed Dec 27-Jan 6, Sat lunch, Sun dinner and Mon. Reservations recommended.* This 19C villa delivers modern fine dining on the 1st floor, more casual international fare in the downstairs brasserie and a bar in the basement. In summer, sit on the terrace beneath a canopy of old trees.

WHERE TO STAY

🍷🛏**Hotel Schlosskrug** – *Schmoller-straße 14.* ☎*(0681) 367 35. www.hotel-schlosskrug.de. Closed Dec 24-early Jan. 20 rooms. Restaurant* 🍴🛏This traditional guesthouse in an old town house has functional rooms, some with their own bath as well as larger family rooms with several beds. The restauant is a good place to try regional home-cooking paired with freshly poured pilsner.

506 45 01; *www.historisches-museum.org)* adjoins the right wing of the castle. Its permanent exhibition deals with World War I and National Socialism in the Saar region.

Museum für Vor- und Frühgeschichte (Museum of Early & Prehistory)

Schlossplatz 16.
🕐*Open year-round, Tue–Sun 10am–6pm (Wed to 8pm).* 🕐*Closed public holidays.* ♿ ☎*(0681) 95 40 50. www.vorgeschichte.de.* Housed in the Neo-Baroque former Parliament building, this museum imaginatively presents archeological items from the beginning of the Stone Age to the early Middle Ages. A highlight is the **Celtic princess's grave**★★ from Reinheim, which dates to 400 BC. The find is considered one of the most important in Central Europe from the Early Celtic period. The princess' jewelry and tomb furnishings, including a gilded bronze pitcher, are wonderfully preserved.

Museum in der Schlosskirche

Am Schlossberg 6.
🕐*Open Tue–Sun 10am–6pm (Wed to 8pm).* ☎*(0681) 950 76 38. www.saarland museum.de.*
The recently renovated palace church now houses a museum of religious art from the 13C to the 19C. Also of note are the three Baroque tombs of the Saarbrücken princes and the colorful stained-glass windows by Georg Meistermann (1950s).

Ludwigsplatz★★

The square is bordered in the north, south and west by eight magnificent townhouses of various sizes. All with three stories and mansard roofs, they illustrate the transition from the Late Baroque to the Neoclassical style. Their white and silver-grey coloring enhances the effect of the Ludwigskirche, built in yellow and red sandstone in the center of the square. The governor of the Saarland has his offices in Ludwigsplatz.

Ludwigskirche (Church of St. Louis)

🕐*Open year-round, Tue–Sun 10am–5pm.* 🕐*Often closed on Sat afternoons for weddings.* ♿☎*(0681) 525 24. www.ludwigs kirche.de.*
After a top-to-bottom restoration, this Baroque Protestant church—a Stengel masterpiece—once again radiates its former glory. The east end exhibits a degree of splendor unusual in a Protestant church, with statues of the Evangelists by Franziskus Bingh.

St. Johann

St. Johanner Markt★

The old town around the market square is the true heart of Saarbrücken. The focal point is the beautiful fountain (designed by Stengel), with its obelisk and cast-iron railing, built in 1759–60. Life pulses in the crooked, mostly car-free lanes and in the numerous pubs and bistros.

Political Ping-Pong

Today, the Saarland is the smallest and least populous of the 16 German states (not counting the city states of Berlin, Hamburg and Bremen) but long stretches of its 20C history have actually been spent in a veritable tug-of-war over its borders with France. Rich in natural resources, coal in particular, the region fell under French control in the 1920s as part of the reparation payments negotiated at the Treaty of Versailles. However, when the statute ran out in 1935, more than 90% of the local population voted in favor of returning to German rule. A similar situation occurred after World War II until another referendum in 1956 once again unified the Saarland with Germany. To this day, though, the French influence is still strongly felt in the local dialect and in the high quality of the regional cuisine.

Basilika St. Johann★

⏱ *Open year-round, daily 9.30am–5pm.* ☎ *(0681) 329 64.*

This Stengel-designed church with its onion tower and lantern is another jewel of the Late Baroque period.

Stadtgalerie (City Gallery)

St. Johanner Markt 24.

⏱ *Open Tue–Sun 11am–7pm (Wed noon–8pm).* ☎ *(0681) 936 83 21.*

This first-floor gallery displays contemporary and conceptual art, new media, installations, performances and video art. In summer, concerts and art exhibits take over the charming courtyard.

Sights

Saarland Museum – Alte Sammlung (Old Collection)

*Karlstraße 1
(opposite the Moderne Galerie).*

⏱ *Open year-round, Tue–Sun 10am–6pm, Wed 10am–10pm.* ⏱ *Closed Tue after Easter and Pentecost, Dec 24, 25 & 31.* 👁1.50€. ☎ *(0681) 996 40. www.saarlandmuseum.de.*

On display are paintings and decorative arts from southwestern Germany and Lorraine from the 16C to 19C. A highlight is the collection of portraits of the princes of Nassau-Saarbrücken as well as local tycoons of the Industrial Age. Some rooms are dedicated to coins, miniatures, silver, porcelain and furniture.

Saarland Museum – Moderne Galerie (Modern Gallery)

Bismarckstraße, on the banks of the Saar.

⏱ *Open year-round, Tue–Sun 10am–6pm, Wed 10am–10pm.* ⏱ *Closed Tue after Easter and Pentecost, Dec 24, 25 & 31.* 👁1.50€. ♿☎ *(0681) 996 40. www.saarlandmuseum.de.*

The diversity of European art from the late 19C to the 21C is featured in this museum. The collection's particular strengths lie with **German Impressionism**★ (Liebermann, Slevogt, Corinth) and **Expressionism**★ (Kirchner, Jawlensky). Other major artists include Picasso, Léger, Tàpies and Beuys. The museum also owns the estate of the sculptor Alexander Archipenko.

Stiftskirche St. Arnual★ (Collegiate Church of St. Arnual)

In the St. Arnual suburb, via Talstraße and Saargemünder Straße.

This 13C–14C Gothic church was given a Baroque dome in 1746 based on plans by Stengel. It was named after 7C Bishop Arnuald of Metz. As the burial place of the dukes of Nassau-Saarbrücken, the church houses 50 **tombs**★★ dating from the 13C to the 18C, some of which are veritable works of art.

Excursions

Völklinger Hütte★★   Kids

*Rathausstraße 75, Völklingen.
10km/6.2mi west of Saarbrücken.*

⏱*Open mid-Mar–Oct, daily 10am–7pm; Nov–Mar, 10am–6pm.* ⏱*Closed Dec 25 & 31.* 👁12€ (child 3€). ☎ *(06898) 910 00. www.voelklinger-huette.org.*

This iron- and steelworks was established in 1873 and at its peak employed 16 000 people. It remained in operation until 1986 and, in 1994, became the first industrial monument to be included on UNESCO's list of World Heritage Sites. Today it is essentially a giant adventure playground where guides take you on a tour through the labyrinths of blast furnaces and air heaters, coking gas pipes and suspended railways. You can climb to the top of the 30m/98.4ft-high charging platform where the blast furnace was once fed with coke and ore. High-caliber special exhibits take place in the blast furnace house, while kids gravitate toward the interactive **Ferrodrom** where exhibits de-mystify scientific principles.

Schlossberghöhlen

Homburg. 20km/12.4mi east on the A6 autobahn. Advance reservations recommended.

Open Apr–Oct, daily 9am–5pm; Nov, Feb & Mar 10am–4pm. 3€. (06841) 20 64. www.homburg.de.

The largest sandstone caves in Europe are man-made, 2km/1.2mi-long corridors which extend over 12 levels.

The caves were built between the 11C and 17C for defensive purposes. They served as munitions and food stores and were used as air raid shelters during World War II.

Römermuseum Schwarzenacker (Roman Museum)

2km/1.2mi east of Homburg, on the B423.

Open Apr–Oct, daily 9am–5pm; Nov, Feb & Mar, 10am–4pm. 3€. (068 48) 73 07 77. www.roemermuseum-sch warzenacker.de.

This **Roman settlement** was founded around the time of the birth of Christ and destroyed by the Alemanni in AD 275. Excavations revealed Roman roads and buildings, which are displayed in an open- air museum.

UNTERES SAARTAL

LOWER SAAR VALLEY

Far from the tourist routes, the Lower Saar Valley remains largely unspoiled. Between Mettlach and Konz, where it flows into the Moselle, the Saar River cuts its way through the Hunsrück massif. Grapes, predominantly Riesling, have been cultivated here since the 18C.

- **Information:** Freiherr-vom-Stein-Straße 64, 66693 Mettlach. (06864) 83 34. www.tourist-info.mettlach.de.
- **Orient Yourself:** South of the Moselle Valley, the Saar valley runs along the French and Belgian borders. The B51 road links the Saar to Saarburg and Trier.
- **Don't Miss:** The breathtaking scenery at Cloef.
- **Organizing Your Time:** Allow two hours for the suggested driving tour.
- **Especially for Kids:** The town of Saarburg with its waterfall in the heart of the city center.
- **Also See:** MOSELTAL, SAARBRÜCKEN, EIFEL.

Driving Tour

From Mettlach to Trier

57km/35mi.

Mettlach

The Baroque, red sandstone façade of the abbey, now headquarters of Villeroy & Boch ceramics, rises above the road to Merzig. In the abbey gardens stands the 10C "Alter Turm", a ruined octagonal funerary chapel for the Merovingian duke Lutwinus, the abbey's founder.

Cloef★★

6.4km/4mi northwest of Mettlach then 15min round-trip walk.

From a viewpoint high above the river is a breathtaking view of the Montclair loop, a hairpin curve of the Saar River

German wines

(Deutscher) Tafelwein – Table wine with no clearly defined region of origin, perhaps a blending of other Common Market wines or of purely German ones.

Landwein – Medium quality wine with an indication of origin (e.g. Pfälzer Landwein) and made from officially approved grapes. It can be dry or medium dry.

Qualitätswein bestimmter Anbaugebiete – Wine of superior quality with an allocated control number and from an officially recognized region (Gebiet), e.g. Moselle, Baden, Rhine.

Qualitätswein mit Prädikat – Strictly regulated wine of prime quality, grown and made in a clearly defined region. These wines will be designated: Kabinett (a reserve wine), Spätlese (a late-harvest wine), Auslese (wine from selected grapes), Beerenauslese and Trockenbeerenauslese (sweet wine) or Eiswein (wine produced from grapes harvested after a minimum -7°C frost).

enclosing a wide, densely wooded promontory. From Cloef or Orscholz, a detour (about 30km/18.6mi round-trip via L177 and B406) takes you toward the Moselle valley and the Roman villa in the town of **Nennig**, which is officially Germany's hottest place with very hot summers, in particular.

Römische Villa Nennig★★ (Roman Villa)

🕐Open Apr–Sept, Tue–Sun 8.30am–noon and 1pm–6pm; Mar, Oct & Nov, 9am–11.30pm, 1pm–4.30pm. ➁1.50€. ♿➁(06866) 13 29. www.nennig.de.
In 1852, a farmer accidentally discovered the remains of an enormous Roman villa thought to date from the 2C or 3C AD. A superb **floor mosaic** (16x10m/52x33ft) survives, consisting of eight medallions framed by intricate geometric designs and gladiator scenes.

▸ The road follows the valley from Mettlach to Saarburg past forested lower slopes, escarpments and vineyards.

Saarburg   Kids

This picturesque town on the banks of the Saar is dominated by a mighty ruined fortress. Dating from at least 964 and later property of the electoral princes of Trier, it was blown up by the French in 1705. There is a good view of the town and Saar valley from the site. The **old town**, with its charming medieval alleyways, half-timbered houses and a 20m/65ft **waterfall** in the town center, makes a delightful scene.

Amüseum am Wasserfall

Am Markt 29.
🕐Open Sun–Fri 11am–4pm. ➤Guided tours available. ➁065 81/99 46 42. www.saarburg.de.
The local museum shows the uses of waterfalls over the centuries.
Ask at the Amüseum for details of the **Hackenberger Mühle** (watermill).

▸ After Konz, where the Saar joins the Moselle, follow the river to Trier.

Trier★★ See TRIER.

Address Book

For coin ranges, see cover flap.

WHERE TO STAY

➁➁**Saarpark** – Bahnhofstraße 31 (B51), 66693 Mettlach. ➁(06864) 92 00. www.hotel-saarpark.de. 47 rooms. This contemporary hotel shelters travelers in homey and functional rooms. For sustenance, try the cheerful restaurant or the rustic beer pub.

WHERE TO EAT

➁➁➁**Schloss Berg** – Schlosshof 7, 66706 Perl-Nennig. ➁(06866) 791 18. www.victors-gourmet.de. Closed early–mid Jan, 3 weeks in Jul, 1 week late Oct. Culinary wunderkind Christian Baus treats food fanciers with deep pockets to exquisite classical cuisine in an exclusive palace setting.

SÄCHSISCHE SCHWEIZ★★★

SWISS SAXONY

Swiss Saxony is one of Germany's most striking natural wonders, an area of craggy sandstone cliffs, rock outcrops, whimsical pinnacles and deep gorges carved by the Elbe River. The valley can be explored by road, following the itinerary below, or by river on one of the "Weiße Flotte" boats linking Dresden and Bad Schandau.

- 🛈 **Information:** Bahnhofstraße 21, 01796 Pirna. ☎(03501) 470 147. www.saechsische-schweiz.de.
- ▶ **Orient Yourself:** Swiss Saxony lies along the Elbe River between Dresden and the Czech border.
- 😊 **Don't Miss:** Bastei and Festung Königstein.
- 🕐 **Organizing Your Time:** Allow one day for the suggested driving tour.
- 🧒 **Especially for Kids:** Festung Königstein.
- 👣 **Also See:** DRESDEN, MEISSEN, BAUTZEN.

Driving Tour

Round-trip from Dresden

78km/49mi

Dresden★★★ 👣*See DRESDEN.*

- ▶ *Leave the city to the east via Pillnitzer Landstraße.*

Schloss Pillnitz ★
👣*See DRESDEN: Excursions.*

Bastei★★★
Perched on a rocky outcrop, the Bastei was the site of a 13C wooden castle and today is most famous for its sweeping **views**★★ across the Elbe and the almost otherworldly rock formations that form the heart of the Saxon Switzerland National Park. Only a few foundations survive from the original castle, which is reached via the photogenic 76m/249.3ft-long stone **Basteibrücke** *(bridge)*. From here, a series of narrow footbridges *(not suitable for the vertigo-prone!)* takes you through the ruined fortress and to ever more spectacular views. To avoid the worst crowds, arrive early or late in the day. Sunset is especially nice.

- ▶ *Follow the S 165 (Basteistraße) east, then turn right onto the S 163 to Bad Schandau via Waltersdorf.*

Bad Schandau★
This spa town renowned for its iron-rich waters is the region's main tourist center. The new **Nationalparkhaus** *(Dresdner Straße 2b;* 🕐*open Apr–Oct, daily 9am-6pm; Nov–Mar, Tue–Sun 9am–5pm;* 💶*4€;* ☎ *(035022) 502 40; www.lanu.de)* has interpretive and interactive exhibits about the national park flora, fauna and history and makes for a good introduction to the region and its natural charms.

At the town exit, towards Schmilka, the **Personenaufzug** *(elevator;* 🕐*open*

Bastei viewpoint, Swiss Saxony

D. Scherf/MICHELIN

Apr & Oct, daily 9am–6pm, May–Sept, 9am–7pm, Nov–Mar, 9am–5pm; 2.50€) whisks you up a 50m/164ft-high tower for great views of the surrounding countryside. From here a trail takes you to another viewpoint over the Schrammsteine rock massif in about 1hr. These formations are especially popular with rock climbers. If you want less exertion, board the nostalgic **Kirnitzschtal-bahn**★ railway, which trundles through a canyon alongside a creek and eventually arrives at a waterfall.

▸ *Cross the Elbe at Bad Schandau and turn right along B172 to Königstein.*

Festung Königstein★★ (Königstein Fortress)

Open Apr–Sept, daily 9am–8pm; Oct, 9am–6pm, Nov–Mar, 9am–5pm. 5€. (035021) 646 07. www.festung-koenig stein.de.

A great sweep of the Elbe arrives at the tabletop mountain called **Königstein**

(360m/1 181ft) which is crowned by a formidable fortress. Built between the 13C and the 16C, it served at one time as a prison whose list of famous inmates included porcelain inventor JF Böttger (see MEISSEN); August Bebel, co-founder of the Social Democrat party; and Fritz Heckert, co-founder of the Spartacists and a prominent German Communist. From the rampart walk, you will have far-reaching **views**★★ of the Liliental tabletop mountain across the Elbe and as far as Bohemia.

Barockgarten Großsedlitz★

Open Apr–Aug, daily 8am–8pm; Sept–Mar, 8am–dusk. 3€. (03529) 563 90. www.barockgarten-grosssedlitz.de.

This French-style garden was commissioned in 1719 by Count Wackerbarth and is considered a prime example of Baroque landscape gardening.

▸ *Return to Dresden on B172.*

Nationalpark Saxon Switzerland

Saxony's only national park was created in 1990 and extends for 93.5sq km/36.1sq mi between Dresden and the Czech Republic border. Within its boundaries it protects a unique quilt of nature composed of thick forests, shaggy meadows, golden fields, deep valleys, tabletop mountains and, most famously, bizarre sandstone formations formed by erosion from the Elbe and her tributaries over a period of 100 million years. Naturally, such beauty has inspired numerous artists, most famous among them Romantic painter Caspar David Friedrich. More than 400km/248.5mi of hiking trails crisscross this gorgeous area whose natural towers and pinnacles are also popular with rock climbers.

BAD SÄCKINGEN★

POPULATION: 16 500

The warm springs at Bad Säckingen have cured weary bodies since the Middle Ages. Today the little spa is also known as "Trumpeter's Town" because of the 19C novel "The Trumpeter of Säckingen" by local lad Joseph Victor von Scheffel.

- **Information:** Waldshuter Straße 20, 79713 Bad Säckingen. ☎(07761) 568 30. www.bad-saeckingen-tourismus.de.
- ▶ **Orient Yourself:** The town sits on the southern edge of the Black Forest, across from the Swiss border.
- **Don't Miss:** The Fridolinsmünster and the Covered Bridge.
- **Organizing Your Time:** Allow three hours to explore Bad Säckingen.
- **Also See:** SCHWARZWALD.

Sights

Fridolinsmünster★

Münsterplatz 8.
Open year-round, daily 8am–8pm.
☎(07761) 568 190.
Named after St. Fridolin, the Irish missionary who converted the Alemanni and founded a missionary cell here in 522, this twin-towered church dominates the skyline of Bad Säckingen. Although its crypt dates back to the Carolingian era, the present building is a Gothic basilica built in the 14C and later embellished with Rococo features by JM Feuchtmayer. There is a statue of the saint above the porch alongside Count Ursi of Glarus, one of his converts. The saint's relics are kept in the Fridolinkapelle (chapel) on the right side of the choir in a superb 18C **silver shrine**★ made in Augsburg.

Gedeckte Brücke★ (Covered Bridge)

There has been a bridge in this spot since the 13C, but the stone pillars of this wooden bridge were not erected until 1575. The bridge is 200m/656ft long, the longest of its kind in Europe, and spans the Rhine, leading to Stein in the Swiss canton of Aargau.

Schloß Schönau

As the town that inspired Joseph Viktor von Scheffel's novel "The Trumpeter of Säckingen" (1854), it is quite appropriate that the local palace should harbor the unusual **Trompetenmuseum** (Trumpet Museum; *open year-round, Tue, Thu & Sun 2pm–5pm;* ☎(07761) 22 17; *www.trompetenmuseum.de*). It boasts the largest collection of these instruments in Europe, the oldest dating back to 1664. Also of interest is an original 1900 trumpet workshop brought here from the town of Oldenburg. From the corner of the park there is a good view of the covered bridge.

The palace itself was built c. 1600 by the lords of Schönau and is surrounded by pleasant gardens. It also contains the local history collection, pre- and early history exhibits and of several centuries' worth of Black Forest clocks.

Excursion

Waldshut

26km/16mi west.
Halfway up a wooded slope rising from the Rhine, this small town provided the spark plug for the Black Forest peasant revolt of 1524.

Today it retains two of its fortified 13C gateways: the Lower (or Basle) Gate to the west and the Upper (or Schaffhaus) Gate to the east.

The heart of the historic **old town**★ is **Kaiserstraße**, a street whose orderly line of houses is interrupted by overhanging eaves. Buildings of note include the 18C Late Baroque **Town Hall;** the **"Wilder Mann"**, a 16C town house; and the 16C **"Alte Metzig"** (Butcher's Gateway), now home to the **local museum** (*Heimatmuseum*).

SAUERLAND★

The meandering Lenne and Ruhr rivers cut through the forest-draped medium-range mountains of the Sauerland that is a popular getaway for residents of the heavily urbanized Ruhr Region. In winter, skiers converge on the town of Winterberg while in summer walkers, cyclists and water sports enthusiasts enjoy the area's many lakes, trails, limestone caverns and cute little hamlets.

- 🛈 **Information:** Johannes-Hummel-Weg 1, 57392 Schmallenberg. ☎ (02974) 969 80. www.sauerland.com.
- ▶ **Orient Yourself:** The Sauerland stretches from the southeastern Rhineland to eastern Westfalia. It is bisected north-south by the A45 autobahn (Hagen–Frankfurt) and also served by the A4 from Cologne.
- 👁 **Don't Miss:** The historic town of Soest and the outdoor pursuits at the Möhnesee.
- 🕐 **Organizing Your Time:** Allow one day for the suggested driving tour.
- 🧒 **Especially for Kids:** The Attahöhle caves and water sports throughout the region.
- 👶 **Also See:** MÜNSTER.

A Bit of Geology

Mountains, lakes and forests – The Sauerland is the most mountainous area of the Rhineland Schist Massif. It is crowned by the **Kahler Asten** (843m/2 766ft), near Winterberg. Lake reservoirs supply water and hydro-electric energy to the Ruhr towns and serve as water sports centers. The Upper Sauerland, especially the forested Rothaargebirge, is popular with Nordic walkers, hikers and mountain bikers.

Driving Tour

From Soest to Bad Berleburg *181km/112.4mi*

Soest★

A northern gateway to the Sauerland, the historic town of Soest is still amost entirely encircled by its 16C town wall and famous as the birthplace of German **Pumpernickel**, a dense black rye bread. The pious and fans of church architecture and religious art will find plenty to like about the town. Dominating its silhouette is the massive 11C–12C Romanesque **Patroklidom** (Propst-Nübel-Straße 2; 🕐 open year-round, daily 10am–6pm), noted for its elaborate **western façade**★★ and perfectly balanced square **tower**★★. The

Romanesque frescoes (c. 1165) in the choir are the originals, while those found elsewhere were restored in 1950.

The 14C Gothic hall-church **St. Maria zur Wiese**★ (Wiesenstraße; 🕐 open year-round, Mon–Sat 11am–4pm, Sun noon–4pm), better known as Wiesen-kirche, sports two filigree spires that were added in the 19C. Inside, note especially the 1520 **stained-glass window** depicting a "Westphalian Last Supper" showing Jesus and disciples sitting down for a meal of local food specialties (boar's head, ham, pitchers of beer and rye bread loaves).

Finally, there is **St. Maria zur Höhe** (Hohe Gasse; 🕐 open Mon–Fri 10am–5.30pm, Sat 10am–5pm, Sun noon–5pm; closes 4pm Oct–Mar), also known as Hoh-nekirche. It contains Romanesque wall paintings, a high altar with paintings of the Passion, and a circular Scandinavian-style cross, called a *Scheibenkreuz*.

- ▶ *Follow the L 670 (Hiddingser Weg) south for about 7km/4.3mi.*

Möhnesee★

This lake reservoir on the northern edge of the Sauerland is 10km/6.2mi long. The northern lakeshore is open to visitors and water sports enthusiasts. The south bank is a well-forested nature reserve known for its birdlife.

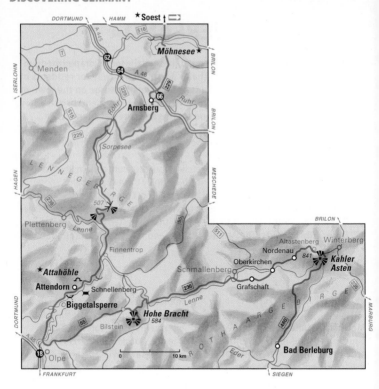

> Follow the B229 south for about
> 20km/12.4mi toward Arnsberg.

Arnsberg

The old town is built on a spur of the Ruhr. To the north, a clock tower commands the approach to the Schloßberg ruins; to the south is a hunting-themed Rococo gate.

> Beyond Arnsberg, the B229 skirts the
> right bank of the Sorpesee reservoir
> before crossing the Lennegebirge
> massif. There are many scenic
> viewpoints.

Attahöhle★ (Grotto)   [Kids]

Finnentroper Straße, Attendorn.
Look for signpost just before reaching
Attendorn.
Visit by guided tour (40min) only;
May–Aug 9.30am–4.30pm; mid-Mar–Apr
and Sept–mid-Oct, 10am–4pm; mid-
Oct–mid-Mar 10.30am–3.30pm. Closed
Dec 24 & 25. 6.50€ (child 4.50€).
(02722) 937 50. www.atta-hoehle.de.

This is one of Germany's largest and most impressive limestone caverns with a subterranean network of trails extending for 3km/1.8mi. Many stalactites and stalagmites are visible, as are stone "draperies," some of them translucent.

Attendorn

The old Town of Attendorn boasts a 14C Town Hall with stepped gable, the arcaded covered market (Alter Markt), and the **"Sauerland Cathedral"** (Sauerländer Dom). Southeast of Attendorn is the 17C **Burg Schnellenberg**.

Biggetalsperre

This dam, dating from 1964, forms with the **Lister barrage** the largest reservoir in Westphalia. It is a popular for swimming, sailing and windsurfing.

> About 2km/1.2mi before Olpe, fork
> left on the B55. Soon after Bilstein,
> on a small mountain road, turn
> right turn toward the Hohe Bracht.

Hohe Bracht

Alt 584m/1 916ft.
From the viewing tower (620m/2 034ft above sea level) is a fine panorama that includes the Rothaargebirge massif as far as the Kahler Asten.

▸ *After crossing the rural Lenne Valley, the route passes* **Grafschaft** *and* **Oberkirchen**, *with charming half-timbered houses, before the landscape becomes wilder and hillier. Beyond* **Nordenau**, *a typical slate-roofed Upper Sauerland village, is the ski station of Altastenberg. On the far side of a plateau, the road nears Kahler Asten.*

Kahler Asten

At 843m/2 765.7ft above sea level, this is the highest point of the Sauerland region. Views from the look-out tower are superb. To the northeast is the spa and winter-sports center of Winter-berg where diversions include skiing, snowboarding and tobogganning as well as an indoor skating rink and a 1 600m/5 249.3ft-long bobsled run. In summer, the 5km/3mi trek up the Kahler Asten get visitors' hearts pumping.

▸ *Slate quarries flank the road back down. There are many attractive views towards the south.*

Bad Berleburg   Spa

This Kneipp spa resort is dominated by **Schloss Berleburg** *(Berleburg Palace; ☛visit by guided tour only; May–Sept, daily 10.30am and 2.30pm, Oct–Apr, Tue, Thu, Sat–Sun 2.30pm; ☞4€; ☎(02751) 421),* which dominates the historic town center. Although it has origins in the 13C, the current Baroque structure was built in 1733 and is still owned by the ancestral local rulers, the family of Sayn-Wittgenstein.

SCHLESWIG ★

POPULATION: 27 000

Schleswig-Holstein's oldest town has origins as a Viking village first mentioned in 804. Today, it is a pleasant town on the Schlei, an inlet of the Baltic Sea, with interesting sights and a relaxing, easy-going atmosphere.

🛈 **Information:** Plessenstraße 7, 24837 Schleswig. ☎(04621) 98 16 16. www.schleswig.de.
▸ **Orient Yourself:** Schleswig was built on low-lying banks at the inner end of a Baltic fjord, the Schlei, which extends for 43km/26.7mi from the coast.
🎫 **Don't Miss:** The Viking Museum, the Nydam Boat and the Globushaus
🕐 **Organizing Your Time:** Allow at least half a day to explore Schleswig.
Kids **Especially for Kids:** The Viking Museum.
🕯 **Also See:** HUSUM, KIEL.

A Bit of History

The Vikings – Viking traders settled on the south bank of the Schlei by the 9C. Set on major crossroads, the settlement became an important northern European trade center.

The area, Haithabu, was encircled with a vast defense system of which a portion remains beside the Haddebyer Noor. In the 11C, Haithabu's residents, seeking better defenses, crossed to the north bank of the Schlei to found Schleswig.

Schloss Gottorf (Gottdorf Palace)

🕐*Open Apr & Oct, daily 10am-6pm; May–Sept, 10am-7pm; Nov–Mar, Tue–Fri 10am-4pm, Sat–Sun 10am-5pm. ☞6€. ♿☎(04621) 81 32 22. www.schloss-gottorf.de.*

Two large museums devoted to Schleswig-Holstein's cultural history are housed in this 16C–18C palace, once the seat of the Holstein-Gottorf ducal family. In 1762, some members married into the Imperial House of the Russian Tzars.

Landesmuseum für Kunst und Kulturgeschichte★★ (State Museum of Art and Cultural History)

This museum contains extensive cultural and historical collections (arts, crafts and traditions). Note the collection of paintings by **Lucas Cranach the Elder** and the **Renaissance chapel**★★ with its ducal loggia and oratory. Another memorable section contains exquisite **Jugendstil**★ pieces.

An adjacent building houses Rolf Horn's collection of 20C paintings – Expressionism to the present. Particularly striking are paintings by Emil Nolde and Alexei von Jawlensky and sculptures by Ernst Barlach.

Archäologisches Landesmuseum★

This museum offers a systematic presentation of Schleswig-Holstein's pre- and early history from the Paleolithic Age to the time of the Vikings. There are spectacular finds from the 4C (bodies found perfectly preserved, fragments of clothing, shoes, weapons) rescued from the peatbogs.

Housed in its own hall is the **Nydam Boot**★★, an oak-hulled longship from around 320 AD that is 23m/75.4ft long by 3m/9.8ft wide and was powered by 36 oarsmen. It is the oldest surviving Germanic longship, and was probably sunk in the peatbogs as a sacrifice in c. AD 350.

Globushaus★★

In a separate building, about a 5min walk from the palace through a Baroque garden, is the reconstructed **Gottdorfer Globus** (globe; Ⓞopen Apr–Oct, 10am–6pm; ⚫10–14€). At over 3m/9.8ft high, it can be entered. The original was created in the 17C and is now in the Lomonosov Museum in St. Petersburg.

Sights

Dom St. Peter★

Thanks to its graceful spire, this brick Gothic hall-church can be easily spotted from far away. The most remarkable work of art is the 1521 **Bordesholm Altarpiece**★★ in the chancel.

Holm★

This picturesque sailors' and fishermen's quarter with its 18C–19C houses is centered around a small cemetery and chapel.

Wikinger Museum Haithabu (Viking Museum)★ 🔟🔟🔟

Follow B76 towards Kiel.
Ⓞ*Open Apr & Oct, daily 9am–5pm; May–Sept, 9am–7pm; Nov–Mar, Tue–Sun 10am–4pm.* Ⓞ*Closed Dec 24 & 31.* ⚫*4€ (child 2.50€).* ♿ ☎*(04621) 81 30. www.schloss-gottdorf.de.*

Near the Haddebyer Noor lagoon, next to the original Viking settlement, this engaging museum sheds light on the daily lives of the Haithabu residents. It features recreated huts and displays jewels, weapons and domestic implements along with models of the Viking village. A highlight of the Boat Hall (*Schiffshalle*) is a Viking longship, reconstructed from fragments dredged from the ancient port.

Henrik Matzen/Schloß Gottorf

Viking longship, Wikinger Museum Haithabu

SCHWÄBISCHE ALB★

SWABIAN JURA

The Swabian Jura region is a paradise for walkers, cyclists and history buffs. From the highest point at Lemberg (1 015m/3 330ft), the Jura plateaux drop 400m/1 312.3ft to the Neckar Basin in the northwest. Mountain outcrops form natural fortresses; some were chosen as castle sites by such famous dynasties as the Hohenstaufens and Hohenzollerns.

- **Information:** Marktplatz 1, 72574 Bad Urach. ☎(07125) 94 81 06. www.schwaebischealb.de.
- ▶ **Orient Yourself:** East of the Black Forest, between Stuttgart and Lake Constance, the Swabian Jura is punctuated by caves, dry valleys and steep-sided gorges.
- **Don't Miss:** Burgruine Reußenstein and Burg Hohenzollern.
- **Organizing Your Time:** Allow one day for driving tour 1 and half a day for driving tour 2.
- **Especially for Kids:** Urwelt-Museum Hauff, Bärenhöhle caverns
- **Also See:** TÜBINGEN, STUTTGART, OBERSCHWÄBISCHE BAROCKSTRASSE, KONSTANZ, SIGMARINGEN.

Driving Tours

1 From Kirchheim unter Teck to Burg Hohenzollern

125km/77.6mi

Kirchheim unter Teck

The tower of the 18C half-timbered Rathaus (Town Hall) overlooks the central intersection in town.

Holzmaden   Kids
Urwelt-Museum Hauff★

(Prehistoric Museum; Aichelberger Straße 90; ☉open year-round, Tue–Sun 9am–5pm; ☉closed Jan 1, Dec 24, 25 & 31; ☜5€; ☎(07023) 28 73; www.urweltmuseum.de) displays fossilized dinosaurs, fish, sea lilies and ammonites found locally in the 180 million year old Jurassic slate strata.

Burgruine Reußenstein (Castle ruins)

45min round-trip walk.
Head for the edge of the escarpment to appreciate the **setting**★★ of Reußenstein as it dominates the Neidlingen valley. From the look-out point built into the castle ruins there is a **view**★ of the whole valley and, beyond it, the plain of Teck.

▶ *After Wiesenstein, with its half-timbered houses, the route follows the Schwäbische Albstraße, marked by blue-green arrows.*

Bad Urach

This is a pretty town, enclosed deep in the Erms Valley, with half-timbered houses surrounding the picturesque central Marktplatz (market square).

Uracher Wasserfall (Urach Falls)

15min round-trip walk. Leave from the parking area marked "Aussicht 350m".
At the end of the walk you will be rewarded with an Impressive **view**★ of the valley and the waterfall (flow reduced in summer).

Schloss Lichtenstein

Visit by guided tour (30min) only, Apr–Oct, daily 9am–5.30pm; Feb–Mar & Nov, Sat–Sun 9am–4pm. ☜5€. ☎(07129) 41 02.www.schloss-lichtenstein.de.
Built on a rock spur, Lichtenstein looks medieval but in fact only got its fairytale looks in the 19C.
Before crossing the entrance bridge, turn right for two viewpoints: one overlooks the Echaz Valley, the other the castle itself.

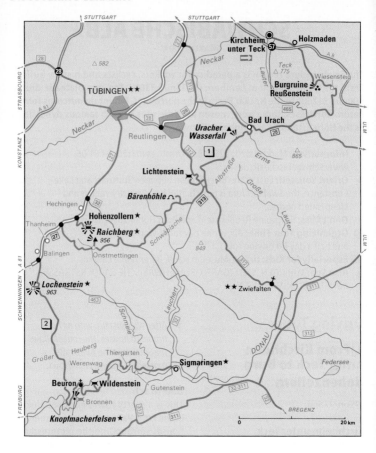

Bärenhöhle (Bear Grotto) 〔Kids〕

Near the town of Erpfingen.

☞*Visit by guided tour (30min) only; Apr–Oct, daily 9am–5.30pm. Mar & Nov, Sat–Sun 9am–5pm.* ✆*3€.* ☎ *(07128) 925 18.*

This popular cavern was once home to prehistoric bears and contains well-pre-served fossilized bones.

▶ *At Onstmettingen, follow the signs 'Nädelehaus' and 'Raichberg'.*

Raichberg★ 〔🚶〕

30min round-trip walk.

🅿Park at the hotel and walk past a stone tower, across the fields to the lip of the plateau. From here **views**★ extend over the downward sweep of the Jura. In the distance, you can spot the turrets of Burg Hohenzollern.

▶ *Continue to BURG HOHENZOLLERN (〔💰〕see BURG HOHENZOLLERN) via Tannheim and Hechingen.*

②From Hohenzollern to the Danube Gap★

89km/55.3mi

Burg Hohenzollern★ –
〔💰〕*See BURG HOHENZOLLERN.*

Lochenstein★ 〔🚶〕

30min round-trip walk.

🅿Park at the Lochenpaß saddle and climb to the Lochenstein summit (alt 963m/3 159.4ft) topped by an iron cross. From here a **view**★ of the Bal-ingen-Hechingen depression, and, in the distance, Hohenzollern Castle is possible.

▶ *Beyond the pass, the road corkscrews downhill and then crosses the bare, rolling uplands of the Großer Heuberg plateau.*

Knopfmacherfelsen★

Below the parking lot, make your way to a **viewpoint**★ of the Danube Valley as far as Beuron Abbey and, on the right, Schloss Bronnen.

Kloster Beuron (Beuron Abbey)

🕐 *Open year-round, daily 6am–8pm.* ♿ ☎ *(07466) 170. www.erzabtei-beuron.de.* This flourishing Benedictine congregation contributed to the revival of monastic life, the liturgy and the use of the Gregorian chant in Germany. The **Gnadenkapelle** *(Chapel of Mercy)*, added in 1898, is decorated in the so-called "Beuron style" inspired by a 19C Byzantium-influenced school of sacred art.

Burg Wildenstein

7km/4.3mi from Beuron via Leibertingen. This small citadel commanding the Danube has a defense system made up of two moats and two towers linked by a fortified wall.

▶ *Below Beuron, the road follows the **Danube Valley**★ past Wildenstein and Werenwag castle towards Sigmaringen. Approaching the town, the cliffs give way to whimsical rock pinnacles between Thiergarten and Gutenstein.*

Sigmaringen★ –
👉*See SIGMARINGEN.*

SCHWÄBISCH HALL★★

POPULATION: 36 500

This town, built in tiers up the steep flank of the Kocher Valley, grew up around salt springs already known in Celtic times. In the Middle Ages, it was famous for the Imperial silver coins, the Heller, minted here. The town's well-preserved half-timbered houses and tranquillity make this a pleasant stopping point.

▯ **Information:** Am Markt 9, 74523 Schwäbisch Hall. ☎ (0791) 75 12 46. www.schwaebischhall.de.
▶ **Orient Yourself:** Schwäbisch Hall is tucked into the Kocher valley, south of the Hohenlohe plain, in north-eastern Baden-Württemberg.
👉 **Also See:** STUTTGART, ROMANTISCHE STRASSE.

Sights

Marktplatz★★ (Market Square)

This sloping central square is dominated by the monumental stone steps of the **Michaelskirche** (Church of St. Michael), which hosts a popular open-air theater festival in summer. It is flanked by houses in a variety of architectural styles from Gothic to Baroque.
Dating from 1509, the **Marktbrunnen** (fountain) stands against a decorative wall adorned with statues of Samson, St. Michael and St. George (copies, originals in the Hällisch-Fränkisches Museum). The rectangular design, unusual in a Gothic work, incorporates the old pillory post. The elegant 18C Late Baroque **Town Hall**★ and its beautiful clock tower stands opposite the church.
The two parallel streets of **Obere** and **Untere Herrengasse**, linked by stone stairways, are bordered by numerous 15C and 16C half-timbered houses.

Michaelskirche

Originally Romanesque, this church was transformed into a Gothic hall-church in the 15C and is reached via 53 steps. The Flamboyant chancel was added in the 16C.

Half-timbered houses on the banks of the Kocher

Hällisch-Fränkisches Museum (Regional Museum)

Keckenhof 6. ◐*Open year-round, Tue–Sun 10am–5pm.* ◐*Closed Good Fri, Dec 24, 25 & 31.* ◉*2.50€.* ☎*(0791) 75 12 89.*

This museum is housed in seven historical buildings, one of which is the 8-story **Keckenturm** (*tower*) from the 13C. Collections concentrate on the art, culture and everyday life of the townspeople, delving into the history of the Heller coins and the region's role in the salt trade. Highlights include the hand-painted wainscoting from a 18C synagogue and ivory carvings created during the Thirty Years' War.

Kunsthalle Würth (Fine Art Museum)

Lange Straße 35. ◐*Open year-round, daily 10am-6pm.* ◐*Closed Dec 24 & 31.* ☎*(0791) 946720. www.kunst.wuerth.com.*

Open since 2001, this ultramodern art temple created from a 19C brewery presents often exemplary changing exhibitions of art created after World War II.

Along the banks of the Kocher★

Attractive views of the half-timbered buildings across the river unfold from the **Henkersbrücke** (*Hangman's Bridge*). The view is perhaps even better from the junction of Am Spitalbach lane and the Salinenstraße quay, from where you can also spot the Church of St. John. **Views★** of the stepped silhouette of the old town lorded over by the Michaelskirche are especially appealing from Unterwöhrd island. Attractive roofed wooden bridges span the river.

Address Book

WHERE TO EAT

◒◒ **Sonne** – *Gelbinger Gasse 2.* ☎*(0791) 97 08 40. Closed Mon. Reservations recommended.* This pleasant restaurant in the center of Schwäbisch Hall serves regional specialties in two paneled dining rooms. In summer, you can relax in the Biergarten if the weather plays along.

WHERE TO STAY

◒◒ **Hotel Sölch** – *Hauffstraße 14.* ☎*(0791) 518 07. www.hotel-soelch.de. Closed Dec 24-Jan 6. 24 rooms.* This welcoming hotel is located 15min walk from the old town and has traditional rooms furnished in oak. The owners also operate the attached bakery, making breakfasts especially memorable.

The White Gold of Hall

The word Hala means "salt" in old German. The Celts found a salt water spring here and were using it as long ago as 500 BC. Rediscovered in AD 800, the saltworks quickly brought fame and fortune to the town of Hall. Green brine was pumped from a well that was dug where Haalplatz now stands, then processed by "distillers" who fed huge wood fires to evaporate the water. The resulting salt, said to be very white, very fine and of high quality, was used until 1924. The town was renamed Schwäbisch Hall in 1934.

Excursions

Benediktinerkloster Großcomburg★ (Benedictine Abbey of Grosscomburg)
3km/1.8mi south.

✎Church visit by guided tour (30min) only, Apr–Oct, Tue–Fri 10am, 11am, 2pm, 3pm, 4pm; Sat–Sun 2pm, 3pm and 4pm. ✆2.50€. ☎(0791) 93 81 85.

Dating from 1130, the crown-shaped **chandelier★★** in the church is made of copper-plated and gilded iron. In front of the high altar is an **antependium★** of the same period, showing Christ surrounded by the Apostles. The supporting framework is treated with *cloisonné* enamel and filigree work.

Hohenloher Freilandmuseum★ (Hohenlohe Open-Air Museum)

5km/3mi northwest. Herdgasse 2, in Schwäbisch Hall-Wackershofen.
◷Open mid-Mar–Apr & Oct, Tue–Sun 10am–5pm; May–Sept, daily 9am–5pm. ✆5.50€. ☎(0791) 97 10 10. www.wackershofen.de.

Over 50 buildings from the 16C to the 19C were moved here from throughout the region, faithfully recapturing rural life from the mid-16C to the 19C.

SCHWARZWALD★★★
BLACK FOREST

Although it gets its name from its thick pine forests, the Schwarzwald is actually a delightful pastiche of lakes, pastures, mountains and vineyards. Add to that picturesque villages, ubiquitous cuckoo clocks, excellent food and an abundance of year-round outdoor pursuits and it is easy to see why this mountainous region has long ranked at the top of Germany's most popular tourist destinations.

- **Information:** Ludwigstraße 23, 79104 Freiburg. ☎(0761) 296 22 71. www.blackforest-tourism.com.
- **Orient Yourself:** In the southwest corner of Germany, the Black Forest stretches for 170km/105.6mi from Karlsruhe to Basel. It is accessible from Stuttgart via the A81, and from Strasbourg or Freiburg via the A5.
- **Don't Miss:** A drive along the Crest Road, driving tour 1 below.
- **Organizing Your Time:** Allow four hours to travel the Crest Road, driving tour 1, one day each for driving tour 2 and 3.
- **Especially for Kids:** Outdoor pursuits throughout the Schwarzwald.
- **Also See:** RASTATT, ROTTWEIL, BAD SÄCKINGEN.

A Bit of History

Twin Sister of the Vosges – The Vosges and the Black Forest ranges both rise from a crystalline base to similar altitudes (the Feldberg at 1 493m/4 899ft and the Grand Ballon at 1 424m/4 672ft). Both drop steeply in the direction of the Rhine, and less abruptly to the Swabian plateaux and to Lorraine, respectively.

Varied resources – The region's economy has always been linked to the forest, wood being practically the only construction material in the Middle Ages and the base of all crafts.

Trees as long as 50m/164ft were floated along the Rhine all the way to the Netherlands for use by boat builders. Clock-making, including the famous cuckoo clock, remains a fruitful activity, although today much of the local economy is driven by tourism.

Driving Tours

1 Black Forest Crest Road★★★ (Schwarzwald-Hochstraße)

From Baden-Baden to Freudenstadt. 80km/49.7mi

Much of the Black Forest Crest Road runs at an elevation approaching 1 000m/3 280ft, skirting villages and ski slopes.

Baden-Baden★★ –
See BADEN-BADEN.

▸ *Follow signs 'Schwarzwald-Hochstraße/B500'.*

The road cuts through the Baden wine country and gradually climbs to quiet spa resorts such as Bühlerhöhe.

Mummelsee

This small, dark glacial lake at the foot of the **Hornisgrinde** (1 164m/3 819ft), the highest point of the northern Black Forest, is named after the "Mümmeln" (water sprites) that inhabit its icy depths, according to local legend. In former times, Black Forest breweries obtained blocks of ice chopped out of the frozen lake until well into spring.

▸ *At Ruhestein, leave the Hochstraße temporarily for a detour down to the* **Allerheiligen Valley**★*, then climb back from Oppenau to Zuflucht via an extremely steep mountain road.*

Allerheiligen★

The ruins of a 13C church still stand, along with a Gothic chapel. A 1.5km/1mi trail leads from the abbey ruins to the **Allerheiligen-Wasserfälle**★, a celebrated series of seven waterfalls with a total drop of 90m/295ft. Budget about 45min for the round-trip walk.

▸ *Continue along the Hochstraße towards Freudenstadt.*

Freudenstadt★

At the crossing of several tourist routes, this 17C town was destroyed by fire in 1945. It now follows a chessboard plan centered on the **Marktplatz**★, a huge square surrounded by Italianate arcaded buildings. The two naves of the 17C **Stadtkirche** *(parish church)*, built at right

Black Forest landscape

M. Hertlein/MICHELIN

Address Book

🪙 *For coin ranges, see the Legend on the cover flap.*

WHERE TO STAY

⊖**Berggasthaus Gisiboden** – *79674 Todtnau-Gschwend.* ☎*(07671) 99 98 21. 16 rooms. Restaurant*⊖. If you don't mind simple rooms and shared bathroom facilities, you will definitely enjoy the peace and quiet of this rustic mountain innat an altitude of 1 200m/3 937ft. It is an ideal base for hiking and mountain biking excursions. The pleasant restaurant serves rib-sticking regional fare.

⊖⊖**Hotel Belchen-Multen** – *79677 Schönau-Aitern-Multen.* ☎*(07673) 209.www.belchen-multen. de. Closed mid-Nov–mid-Dec. 39 rooms. Restaurant*⊖⊖. This well-kept hotel in the wilds of the Black Forest has simple rooms and an indoor swimming pool on those days when the sun is a no-show.

⊖⊖**Gasthof Gedächtnishaus** – *Fohrenbühl 12, 78730 Lauterbach.* ☎*(07422) 44 61. www.king-gastro.de. Closed 6 weeks from Jan 6. 7 rooms. Restaurant*⊖⊖. *Closed Wed dinner and Thu.* An ideal destination for tired hikers, this historic inn has newly renovated, modern rooms with a welcome degree of comfort. The rustic restaurant serves energy-restoring local fare.

⊖⊖**Hotel Sonne** – *Krumlinden 44, 79244 Münstertal-Obermünstertal.* ☎*(07636) 319. www.sonne-muenstertal. de. Closed mid -Nov- mid Dec. 13 rooms. Restaurant*⊖⊖, *closed Tue eve and Wed.* This pleasant little hotel snuggles into the romantic Münstertal valley and features that get a high charm quotient from blond wood furniture and good-sized balconies. Regional home cooking beckons in the traditional restaurant.

⊖⊖**Schwarzwaldhaus** – *Am Kurpark 26, 79872 Bernau-Innerlehen.* ☎*(07675) 365. www.sbo.de/schwarz waldhaus. Closed late Oct–late Nov. 14 rooms. Restaurant*⊖⊖, *closed Thu.* Sample classic Black Forest flair in this cozy farmhouse covered in wooden shingles typical of the region. After enjoying a delicious meal in the former stables, retire to handsome rooms decorated either farmhouse- or country-style.

⊖⊖⊖**Hotel Alemannenhof** – *Bruderhalde 21, 79822 Titisee.* ☎*(07652) 911 80. www.hotel-alemannenhof.de. 22 rooms. Restaurant*⊖⊖⊖. On the shores of the Titisee, this modern Black Forest hotel boasts a private beach and dock. In addition to the comfortable rooms, the establishment has a pleasant restaurant and a lakeside terrace.

⊖⊖⊖**Hotel Bären** – *Langestraße 33, 72250 Freudenstadt.* ☎*(07441) 27 29. www.hotel-baeren-freudenstadt.de. 25 rooms. Restaurant*⊖⊖, *closed Jan 7–23, Fri, lunch Mon–Sat.* Owned by the same family since 1878, this central inn has a homey feel and spacious rooms with rustic flair. The restaurant will tempt your tastebuds with creative Black Forest cuisine. Even vegetarians will not feel left out.

WHERE TO EAT

⊖⊖**Löffelschmiede** – *Löffelschmiede 1, 79853 Lenzkirch.* ☎*(07653) 279. www. sbo.de/loeffelschmiede. Closed Nov- mid Dec.* This little family-run restaurant is set in a small valley near Lenzkirch. Trout and simple regional dishes are served in the bright and welcoming restaurant with its earthenware stove.

⊖⊖⊖**Bareiss** – *Gärtenbühl-weg 14, 72270 Baiersbronn-Mitteltal.* ☎*(07442) 470. www.bareiss.com. 99 rooms. Restaurant*⊖-⊖⊖⊖. Charming décor and creaking wood make this upscale establishment a delightful refuge. Restore energies in the on-site pool and spa or choose from a menu of activities, including golfing, hunting and hiking. A farmhouse-style tavern serves Black Forest specialties, while the gourmet restaurant is among the region's best for upscale fare.

⊖⊖⊖**Jägerstüble** – *Marktplatz 12, 72250 Freudenstadt.* ☎*(07441) 23 87. www.jaegerstueble-fds.de.* The rustic setting and relaxed atmosphere make this central restaurant a popular choice with both locals and visitors.

angles, form one corner of Marktplatz. Inside, note the carved and painted 12C Romanesque **lectern**★★ supported by the Four Apostles. A further treasure is the 12C **baptismal font**★ with intricate animal decorations.

2 Central Black Forest★★

From Freudenstadt to Freiburg. 152km/94.4mi

The itinerary meanders through the Kinzig and Elz valleys, passing through bustling tourist villages before reaching the Upper Black Forest at Freiburg.

Alpirsbach★

About 18km/11mi south of Freudenstadt, Alpirsbach is worth a stop for its 11C red sandstone **Kloster Alpirsbach**★ (open mid-Mar–Oct, Mon–Sat 10am–5.30pm, Sun 11am–5.30pm, Nov–mid-Mar, Thu, Sat–Sun 1pm–3pm; 3€; (07444) 951 62 81; www.schloesser-und-gaerten.de), a former Benedictine abbey and the oldest Romanesque structure in the Black Forest. Inside the church, note especially the painted apse, the ornate pillars, the Romanesque choir and the late Gothic high altar. The attached museum showcases 16C objects from daily life at the monastery, unearthed during excavations in 1958.

Schwarzwälder Freilichtmuseum Vogtsbauernhof★★ (Black Forest Open-Air Museum)

In Gutach.
 Open Mar–Oct, daily 9am–6pm (Jul–Aug 7pm). 6€. (07831) 935 60. www.vogtsbauernhof.org.
Black Forest construction, craftwork, culture and agriculture are imaginatively presented in this open-air museum in the Gutach Valley. The 1612 Vogtsbauern farm, still in its original state, is set amid other farmhouses along with such outbuildings as a bakery, a smithy, a chapel and a granary.
All buildings were moved and reassembled here from throughout the region.

Traditional Black Forest house

R. Corbel/MICHELIN

▶ *Continue towards Triberg, enjoying fine* **views**★ *from the Landwassereck pass. Upstream from Oberprechtal, the beautiful cascades of the Elz parallel the route.*

Triberg★

The romantic (if busy) **Waterfall Walk**★ *(1hr round-trip; 2€)* follows the Gutach as it sprightly cascades over boulders and past tree-lined mossy banks. Back in town, **Maria der Tannen (Our Lady of the Firs)**★ is one of the most popular pilgrimage churches in the Black Forest. The **Schwarzwald Museum** *(Wallfahrtstraße 4; open May-Sept, daily 10am-6pm, Oct–Apr 10am-5pm; 4.50€; (07722) 44 34; www.schwarzwaldmuseum.com)* exhibits traditional costumes and local craftwork, including one of Europe's largest collections

A Bit of Advice

For a unique travel experience, travel the **German Clock Road** *(Deutsche Uhrenstraße)*, covering about 320km/198.8mi and taking in various cuckoo-clock sites: museums, factory tours, and remarkable clocks (details available from information offices in the region). For railway fans, the **Black Forest Train** *(Schwarzwaldbahn)* negotiates a 670m/2 198ft elevation change following the landscape on a route that avoids bridges. Despite the 39 tunnels required to manage the largest natural obstacles, the journey encompasses magnificent scenery, the most interesting section (27km/16.7mi) between Hornberg and St. Georgen.

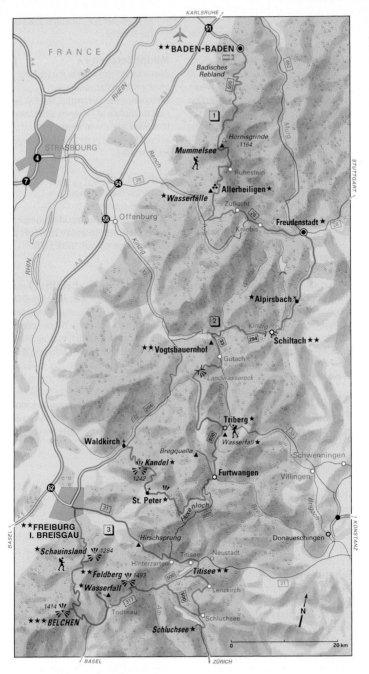

of barrel-organs. Another attraction is the **World's Biggest Cuckoo Clock** (*Schonachbach 27;* ⏰*open year-round, Mon–Sat 9am–6pm; Easter–Oct, Sun 10am–6pm;* 🎟*2€;* ☎ *(07722) 962 20; www.uhren-park.de*) which contains a clock shop and is even listed in the Guinness Book of Records. Its claim, however, is disputed by the world's 'other' biggest cuckoo clock about 1km/0.6mi further along in Schonach.

Furtwangen

The **Deutsches Uhrenmuseum** *(Robert-Gerwig-Platz 1;* ⏰ *open Apr–Oct, daily 9am–6pm; Nov–Mar, 10am–5pm;* ⏰ *closed Dec 24–26;* ⮕ *4€;* ♿ ☎ *(07723) 920 28 00; www.deutsches-uhrenmuseum. de)* displays the world's largest collection of Black Forest clocks and explains the ingenuity that artisans brought to the simple telling of time.

> ▸ *Soon after leaving Furtwangen, turn right for Hexenloch, a deep wooded gorge enlivened by waterfalls. Between St. Märgen and St. Peter, the twisting road treats you to plenty of fine* **views**★★.

St. Peter★

Two onion-domed towers top the splendid rococo **church**★ of this 18C former Benedictine abbey. Johann Anton Feuchtmayer carved the marvelous statues representing the Dukes of Zähringen who founded Freiburg. Several hiking trails leave from the parking lot.

Freiburg★★ – ⮕ See FREIBURG.

③ Upper Black Forest★★★ (Hochschwarzwald)

Round-trip leaving from Freiburg im Breisgau. 142km/88mi

This circuit skirts the three main peaks of the Black Forest (Schauinsland, Belchen and Feldberg) and also takes in its two best-known lakes (Schluchsee and Titisee).

Schauinsland★

An extremely twisty mountain road leads to the upper cable-car station. From the parking lot, follow the signs "Rundweg" and "Schauinsland Gipfel" to the viewing tower *(91 steps)*, which offers a **view**★ across upland meadows to the Feldberg *(30min round-trip walk)*.

> ▸ *Follow the road for 1km/0.6mi and take the right fork toward Stohren and the Münstertal. Meandering through meadows, the route finally plunges once more into the forest.*

> *At Wiedener Eck, turn right toward the Belchen.*

Mount Belchen★★

30min round-trip walk to the viewing platform from the parking lot.
Dominating the Wiesenthal, the Belchen rises to a height of 1 414m/4 637ft. When the skies are clear, views extend all across the Rhine plain, the High Vosges, and the Alps.

Todtnau Falls★

*1.5km/1mi from Todtnau,
1hr round-trip walk.*
Climbing through a wooded combe, a trail leads to an impressive series of cascades plunging down 97m/318ft.

Feldberg★★

The **Feldbergbahn chairlift** *(*⏰ *open Jul–Sept, daily 9am-5pm; May, Jun & Oct 9am-4.30pm;* ⮕ *7.20€ round-trip)* conveys sightseers up the Black Forest's tallest mountain, which is crowned by the Bismarck monument. Various **hiking trails** start near the top, taking in tremendous **views**★ as far as the Alps and down to the Feldsee, a small lake in the hollow of a glacial cirque. In winter, downhill and cross-country skiing are popular outdoor pursuits around the Feldberg.

Schluchsee★

This glacial lake became the largest body of water in the Black Forest when it was dammed in 1932.

> ▸ *The Titisee is reached via Lenzkirch. During the final part of the descent, the road overlooks the lake.*

Titisee★★

This clear glacial lake sits at the junction of several tourist routes and is popular for swimming, boating and windsurfing. In winter, cross-country skiing is the main outdoor activity. By the way, the name may sound funny to English-speakers but is actually said to have been derived from Roman emperor Titus.

> ▸ *Return to Freiburg via the romantic* **Höllental**★ *(Hell Valley).*

SCHWERIN★

POPULATION: 97 700

The state capital of Mecklenburg-Vorpommern, Schwerin is one of the most pleasant towns of northern Germany. Defined by numerous lakes surrounding it, the city is endowed with plenty of fine architecture, most famously the lordly castle on an island opposite the old town.

- **Information:** Am Markt 14, 19055 Schwerin. ☎(0385) 592 52 12. www.schwerin.de.
- ▶ **Orient Yourself:** Schwerin is situated in a landscape of lakes and forests. The A24 autobahn (Hamburg–Berlin) passes by about 20km/12.4mi to the south.
- **Parking:** Near the Old Town you'll find garages at Reiferbahn and Wittenburger Straße and on Geschwister-Scholl-Straße.
- **Don't Miss:** Schloßinsel and Ludwigslust (ⓒsee Excursion).
- **Organizing Your Time:** Allow two hours to visit the Schloßinsel.
- **Also See:** MECKLENBURGISCHE SEENPLATTE, WISMAR, LÜBECK.

A Bit of History

The oldest town in Mecklenburg

– The origins of Schwerin date to the 11C, when the Slavs built a fortress on what is now Schloßinsel. They were soon expelled by Henry the Lion, who colonized Schwerin in 1160 as the first German town east of the Elbe. In 1358 Schwerin was absorbed into the Duchy of Mecklenburg and became the seat of the local dukes from that time onward.

Schlossinsel★★

Schloss★ (Palace)

Lennéstraße 1. ◐Open mid-Apr–mid-Oct, daily 10am–6pm; mid-Oct–mid-Apr,

Tue–Sun, 10am–5pm. ⌨4€. ☎(0385) 525 29 20. www.schloss-schwerin.de.

Built as the residence of the Grand Dukes of Mecklenburg-Schwerin, the castle is today the home of the state parliament of Mecklenburg-Vorpommern and a harmonious hodgepodge of architectural styles ranging from Gothic to Neo-Renaissance. The oldest wing (15C–17C)

J. Bouraly/MICHELIN

Castle

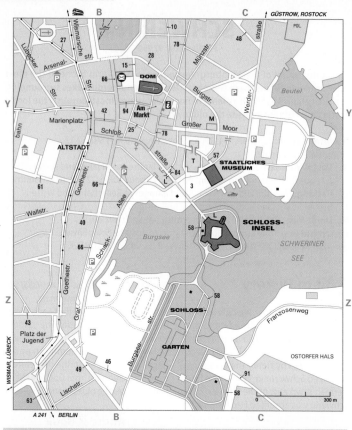

harbors the **Schlossmuseum**, which takes in a series of rooms richly decked out with 18C and 19C art, furniture and Meissen porcelain. The most impressive are the **Thronzimmer**★ (Throne Room) and the **Ahnengalerie** (Ancestors' Gallery), whose paintings are an uninterrupted roll call of all Mecklenburg dukes from the 14C to the 18C.

Schlosskirche★ (Palace Church)

This 16C Renaissance chapel was commissioned in 1560 by Duke Albrecht I as the first Protestant church in Mecklenburg as a simple, rectangular room with a gallery. In the 19C it was expanded by a Neo-Gothic choir with splendid stained-glass windows. A triumphal arch links the choir and the original chapel.

Schlossgarten★ (Palace Garden)

Created in the 19C, this formal Baroque garden is organized around canals, lime trees and ornamental flowerbeds. Lining the canals are statues by Balthazar Permoser.

Sights

Markt

Four 17C half-timbered houses are preserved beside the Town Hall. The 18C Neoclassical **Neues Gebäude** (new

Ludwigslust Cardboard Décor

Duke Friedrich's intensive building activity exhausted his funds but he was determined to decorate his palace in a manner befitting his social standing. Expensive material was replaced by Ludwigsluster Karton, a type of papier mâché that could be polished and painted and was even weather resistant. The Ludwigslust workshop achieved such mastery that its products were exported as far as Russia. Production ceased in 1835 due to lack of demand. The original formula was closely guarded and remains a secret to this day.

Building) is fronted by a monument of Henry the Lion.

Staatliches Museum Schwerin★ (State Museum)

Alter Garten 3.
Open year-round, Tue–Sun, 10am–6pm (5pm mid-Oct–mid-Apr). Closed Dec 24 & 31. 6€. (0385) 595 80. www.museum-schwerin.de.

This museum houses key 17C Flemish and Dutch paintings (Brueghel, Rembrandt, Rubens), European painting from the 16C to the 20C (Cranach, Gainsborough) and contemporary art (Cage, Polke).

Excursion

Schloss Ludwigslust★

40km/24.8mi south. Open mid-Apr–mid-Oct, daily 10am–6pm; mid-Oct–mid-Apr, Tue–Sun 10am–5pm. 5€. (03874) 571 90. www.schloss-ludwigslust.de.

This ducal palace has its origins in the early 18C as a hunting lodge but was significantly enlarged after Duke Friedrich made Ludwigslust the capital of his duchy in 1764.

The **Schloss**★ is an E-shaped, 18C Late Baroque building with some early Neclassical elements.

The 18 vases and 40 statues adorning the attic parapet represent the arts, sciences and virtues. The **Interior** is dominated by white and gold ornamentation, in German interpretations of Louis XVI style. Paintings, furniture, miniatures and gilded decorations made from papier mâché reflect the lifestyles of the ducal family. A particular highlight is the **Golden Room**.

The sprawling **Schloßpark**★ got its naturalistic English landscape design in the 19C under the supervision of star garden architect Peter Joseph Lenné Take a stroll to view streams, monuments, mausoleums and a grotto.

SPEYER★

POPULATION: 50 000

The old imperial city of Speyer lies in the Rhine plain and started out around 10 BC as a Roman camp, gaining in importance during the Middle Ages. Its main sight is the magnificent Romanesque cathedral, one of the largest in Europe and burial site of several Holy Roman Emperors.

- **Information:** Maximilianstraße 13, 67346 Speyer. (06232) 14 23 92. www.speyer.de.
- **Orient Yourself:** South of Heidelberg, Speyer is located between the wooded mountains of the Odenwald and those of the Pfalz.
- **Parking:** Garages are located throughout Speyer. The main train station has a garage convenient for travelers.
- **Don't Miss:** The Kaiserdom, Palatinate Museum.
- **Organizing Your Time:** Allow at least half a day to see the main sights.
- **Also See:** HEIDELBERG, KARLSRUHE, PFALZ.

A Bit of History

Imperial city – An episcopal seat since the 4C, Speyer gained in importance from the 11C onward under the Salian emperors. It was made an Imperial City in 1294 and hosted more than 50 Imperial Diets (parliament sessions) until 1570. The city was razed in 1689 by French troops. As a result, the only remaining evidence of Speyer's medieval splendor is the Kaiserdom, fragments of the town wall and the *Altpörtel*, a former city gate.

Kaiserdom★★

⊙*Open Apr–Oct, daily 9am–7pm; Nov–Mar, 9am–5pm.* ♿☎*(06232) 10 21 18. www.dom-speyer.de.*
Founded by Konrad II in 1030 and remodeled at the end of the 11C, Speyer's Kaiserdom is the largest Romanesque building in Europe and has been a UNESCO World Heritage Site since 1981.

The **interior**★★ is a masterpiece of unity and balance; the **Chapel of the Holy Sacrament** (*Afrakapelle, on the left, before the north transept*) houses two 15C low-relief sculptures: the *Bearing of the Cross* and the *Annunciation*. The two-tier central rotunda contains the

Speyer Cathedral

baptistry (Chapel of St. Emmeram) and, above, a chapel dedicated to St. Catherine.
The Kaiserdom's **crypt**★★ is the finest and largest Romanesque crypt in Germany. Groined vaulting features transverse arches of alternately pink and white sandstone. Four Holy Roman Emperors and four German kings, along with some of their wives, are buried in the **Royal Vault**.
In the gardens south of the cathedral is the 16C **Ölberg**, once the center of the cloister. A large stone trough, the **Domnapf**, stands in the forecourt. In former times, each time a bishop was installed, it was filled with wine and anyone who wished to do so could drink until he dropped.

Sights

Maximilianstraße
The main thoroughfare in Speyer's historic center runs west from the cathedral to the 12C–13C **Altpörtel**★, a gateway tower. It is a lively street lined by a number of ornate Baroque buildings, most notably the **Rathaus** (Town Hall) and the "Alte Münze" (Old Mint).

Judenhof (Jewish Courtyard)
South of the Town Hall, the Judenhof is at the center of the medievai Jewish quarter. Remains of the 12C synagogue

The *Protestants*

The Edict of Worms, in fact never enacted, was confirmed by the Diet of Speyer in 1529. The Lutheran states then made a solemn protest against the Diet's decisions, from which derives the label "Protestant" to identify partisans of the Reformation. The event is commemorated by the Neo-Gothic Gedächtniskirche, a church built early in the 20C on Bartholomä-us-Weltz-Platz.

and a ritual bath (*Mikwe*) are reminders of this once vibrant community.

Historisches Museum der Pfalz★ (Palatinate Museum)
Domplatz.
🕐*Open year-round, Tue–Sun 10am-6pm.* 🕐*Closed Dec 25 & 31.* ✎*4€, more for special exhibits.* ♿☎*(06232) 132 50. www. museum.speyer.de.*
This excellent museum is filled with treasures that illustrate the region's often tumultuous history. The rarest and most precious item on view is the solid gold, cone-shaped **Golden Hat of Schiffer-stadt**★★ from the 12C BC.

In the basement, the **Cathedral Treasury** (*Domschatzkammer*) houses tomb furnishings of the emperors, notably the funerary crown of Konrad II, the first Salian emperor. Also note the Imperial orb of Heinrich III and the crown worn by Heinrich IV during his penance walk to Canossa.

In the cellar is the **Wine Museum** (*Weinmuseum*), presenting 2 000 years of wine history, including a bottle of **Roman wine**★ from the 3C AD, the oldest wine in the world in a liquid state.

Technik Museum Speyer★ (Museum of Technology)
Am Technik Museum.
🕐*Open year-round, Mon–Fri 9am-6pm, 9am-7pm Sat–Sun.* ✎*12.50€.* ♿☎*(06232) 670 80. www.museumspeyer.de.*
Planes, trains and automobiles make up the bulk of the exhibit at this engaging museum. A highlight is a tour of a U 9 submarine from World War I, but the maritime displays and musical instruments also deserve attention.

SPREEWALD★★

A network of over 300 waterways crisscrosses this lush countryside, painstakingly drained to give it the appearance of a "Venice in the Woods." Another regional interest is its Sorbian minority, western Slavs who settled in Germany's Lausitz area in the 6C and who have managed to retain their language and culture to this day (👁*see BRANITZ*).

- 🛈 **Information:** Lindenstraße 1, 03226 Vetschau. ☎(035433) 722 99. www.spreewald.de.
- ▶ **Orient Yourself:** The Spreewald region is about 100km/62mi southeast of Berlin and covers about 260sq km/100sq mi.
- ☺ **Don't Miss:** A barge trip from Lübbenau.
- 🕐 **Organizing Your Time:** Allow at least half a day for a Spreewald barge trip.
- 🧒 **Especially for Kids:** A barge trip from Lübbenau.
- 👁 **Also See:** BRANITZ, FRANKFURT AN DER ODER.

Sights

Kahnfahrt (Barge Trips) 🧒
Boat trips are offered throughout the Spreewald, but **Lübbenau** *has established itself as the center for such trips.*

Boats leave from Grosser Hafen Lübbenau, Apr–Oct (weather permitting); 2–9hr, with stopovers. ✎*8.50–20€.* ☎*(03542) 22 25. www.spreewald express.de.*

Boating in the Spreewald

A favorite destination is **Lehde**★, a tiny lagoon village of 150 people with almost as many islands as houses. The **Freilandmuseum** (Open-Air Museum) consists of three 19C farms, complete with living quarters and outbuildings, furniture, folk art, costumes and agricultural tools. Alternatively, you could also walk from Lübbenau to Lehde in about 30min.

A longer trail goes to Leipe *(3hr round-trip)*.

Lübbenau

The 18C parish church of **St. Nikolai**★ (*open May–Oct, Tue–Sun 2pm–4pm; closed public holidays; donation requested;* (03542) 36 68) is an important example of the Dresden Baroque architectural style. Inside are impressive tombs and epitaphs, most notably the high **tomb** (c. 1765) of Prince Moritz Carl, count of Lynaer. To learn more about the region's cultural history, heritage and traditions, take a spin around the **Spreewald Museum** (*open Tue–Sun 10am–6pm (Oct–Mar 5pm;* 3€; (03542) 24 72).

ST. BLASIEN★

POPULATION: 4 000

The majestic domed church dedicated to St. Blaisen comes suddenly into view in the southern part of the Black Forest. It stands in the grounds of a medieval monastery founded in 835 by hermit monks.

Information: Am Kurgarten, 79837 St. Blasien. (07672) 414 30. www.stblasien.de.

Orient Yourself: St. Blasien is at the end of a wooded valley in the Hotzenwald.

Don't Miss: The Dom, the Hochkopf Massif (*see Excursion*).

Organizing Your Time: Allow half a day for the Hochkopf excursion.

Also See: SCHWARZWALD, BAD SÄCKINGEN.

Sights

Dom★★ (Cathedral)

Inspired by the Pantheon in Rome, French architect Pierre-Michel d'Ixnard pulled out all the stops in designing this early Neoclassical church. Completed in 1772, its central copper dome (33.5m/110ft in diameter) is the third largest in the world after those of St. Peter's in Rome and Les Invalides in Paris. Inside is a splendid Rococo high altar by Christian Wenzinger.

Excursions

The Hochkopf Massif
45km/28mi

▶ *Drive via Todtmoos to the Weißenbachsattel pass.*

Hochkopf
1hr round-trip walk.

From the parking lot, a trail leads to a look-out with **views**★★ of the barren peaks of the Belchen and the Feldberg and, on clear days, the Alps.

T. Krieger/MICHELIN

Cathedral with its impressive dome

Bernau★

At Bernau-Innerlehen, the **Town Hall** (*Rathaus*) houses the **Hans-Thoma-Museum** with an exhibition of paintings by this local artist.

The Alb Valley (Albtal)
30km/18.5mi south.
The road runs high above the Alb gorges, tunneling through the cliffs on its way to the Rhine at Albbruck.

STRALSUND★

POPULATION: 59 000

Stralsund, one of the most agreeable cities on the German Baltic, looks back on a long maritime tradition in fishing and ship building. Tourism is also a backbone of the local economy, thanks in large part to the beautifully restored and UNESCO-protected medieval city center.

- **Information:** Alter Markt 9, 18409 Stralsund. ☎(03831) 246 90. www.stralsundtourismus.de.
- ▶ **Orient Yourself:** Stralsund is on the Baltic at the far northeasterly point of mainland Germany. A causeway and a bridge link the town to the island of Rügen.
- **Don't Miss:** The Old Town or the Ozeaneum.
- ◷ **Organizing Your Time:** Allow two hours.
- **Especially for Kids:** The Oceanographic Museum and Ozeaneum.
- **Also See:** GREIFSWALD.

A Bit of History

A Coveted City – Stralsund was founded in the early 13C and quickly found itself in the crosshairs of the Free City of Lübeck, which felt its power threatened by the quickly growing settlement. After being razed by Lübeck in 1249, Stralsund was fortified with a sturdy city wall and rose in importance enough to become a member of the Hanseatic League in 1293. During the Thirty Years' War, the city was besieged by Wallenstein until Swedish and Danish troops arrived and forced the general to retreat. In 1815, it became part of Prussia.

Sights

Altstadt (Old Town)★

Stralsund's UNESCO-listed old town is anchored by the **Rathaus** (*Town Hall*), a splendid 13C and 14C edifice whose magnificent **north façade**★★ was added c. 1450. The ground floor arcades open onto a covered market hall leading to the west porch of the **Nikolaikirche** (*Church of St. Nicholas*).

A 13C hall church, it sports a magnificent altar with sculptures by Baroque artist Andreas Schlüter and Late Gothic frescoes.

STRALSUND

Deutsches Meeresmuseum★ (German Oceanographic Museum) Kids

Mönchstraße.

Open Jun–Sept, daily 10am–6pm; Oct–May, 10am–5pm. Closed Dec 24 & 31. 7.50€, 8.50€ with Nautineum (child 5.50€, 5€ with Nautineum). (03831) 265 02 10. www.meeresmuseum.de.

In a former abbey building, this beloved museum has displays on the flora and fauna of the Baltic Sea.

Among the aquariums the 50 000l/13 208gal shark tank and the 15m/49.2ft long fin-back whale skeleton are highlights.

The museum also operates the **Nautineum** (3€) on an islet off Stralsund, where you can learn about the fishing industry, ocean research and fishing boat construction in Stralsund.

Ozeaneum★★ Kids

Katharinenberg 14–20.

Open Jun–Sept, daily 9.30am–9pm; Oct–May, 9.30am–7pm; 14€, 18€ with Meeresmuseum. (03831) 265 06 01. www.ozeaneum.de.

Open since July 2007, this state-of-the-art aquarium takes visitors on an exciting underwater journey from Straulsund

Address Book

For coin ranges, see cover flap.

WHERE TO STAY

An den Bleichen – An den Bleichen 45. (03831) 39 06 75 Fax (03831) 392153 23 rooms In a residential area, this family-run place has pretty gardens. Close to the old town, port and beach.

Steigenberger Hotel Baltic – Frankendamm 22 (03831) 20 40 Fax (03831) 204999 www. stralsund.steigenberger.de. 134 rooms Restaurant . This hotel is located in a former barracks renovated in an elegantly modern style. Contemporary bistro-restaurant.

to the frigid Polar Sea. Along the way you pass 39 tanks introducing you to the flora and fauna of the Baltic Sea, the North Sea and the North Atlantic Ocean. Highlights include a giant tank where 2 500 herring swim their merry rounds and a 20m/65.6ft-high hall with life-size whale models, including a 28m/91.8ft long blue whale.

Marienkirche★
Neuer Markt.
Apart from the impressive 15C 104m/341ft west tower, the church's Gothic high altar with the Coronation of the Virgin Mary (15C) and an organ (c. 1659) by Lübeck organ builder Friedrich Stellwagen warrant attention.

STRAUBING
POPULATION: 44 500

Straubing evolved from a Roman military camp, but the present town center, the Neustadt, is a 13C Wittelsbach addition. Modern Straubing is still the regin's economic hub. In August, thousands of revelers descend for the Gäubodenfest.

- **Information:** Theresienplatz 20, 94315 Straubing. ☎ (09421) 94 43 07. www.straubing.de.
- ▶ **Orient Yourself:** Embraced by a loop of the Danube, Straubing's location in the fertile Gäuboden region, the granary of Bavaria, contributed in no small terms to its prosperity.
- **Parking:** There's a large, free garage on Am Hagen and another garage on Theresienplatz.
- **Organizing Your Time:** The sights of Straubing can be seen in half a day.
- **Also See:** REGENSBURG, LANDSHUT.

Sights

Stadtplatz★ (Town Square)
The elongated square is divided into the Theresienplatz *(west)*, with a wonderfully-adorned 17C Trinity column, and the Ludwigsplatz *(east)* with the 1644 Jakobsbrunnen fountain. The 14C tower in the center is the city emblem.

Jakobskirche
Just off Stadtplatz, the 15C Church of St. Jacob is the largest hall-church in Bavaria and best known for the impressive 'Moses Window' designed by Albrecht Dürer. The panels of the high altar **reredos**, bought in 1590 from a church in Nuremberg, frame 16C statuary.

Ursulinenkirche
This is the last joint project by the Asam brothers. It was built between 1736 and 1741 during the transition from Baroque to Rococo and features a rare blend of architecture and décor.

Basilika St. Peter
The 12C Romanesque church is surrounded by a walled cemetery with moss-covered graves from the 14C to the 19C. Note the Gothic Agnes-Bernauer-Chapel and the **Totenkapelle★** with a Dance of Death fresco by local painter Felix Hölzl (1763).

Agnes Bernauer

Agnes, a beautiful young barber's daughter from Augsburg, was married in secret to Albrecht III, son of Duke Ernst of Bavaria. The Duke took exception to the match and had Agnes condemned as a witch. In 1435 she was drowned in the Danube not far from Straubing. The tragic fate of this beautiful country girl captured many a heart, inspiring Friedrich Hebbel to write a political tragedy (1855) and Carl Orff to compose an opera (1947). Every four years there is a festival (Agnes-Bernauer-Festspiele) in her memory (next one in 2011).

STUTTGART★

POPULATION: 590 000

The capital of Baden-Württemberg is a commercial and industrial center whose name is often associated with automobiles. The name of the city, originally Stutengarten, derives from a seigniorial stud farm which flourished in the 10C. In the 14C the town became the home of the dukes and kings of Württemberg and centuries later prospered during the industrial revolution.

- **Information:** Königstraße 1a, 70173 Stuttgart. ☎(0711) 222 80. www.stuttgart.tourist.de.
- ▶ **Orient Yourself:** Stuttgart lies in a valley surrounded by vineyards and wooded hills opening onto the Neckar. The finest **view**★ of Stuttgart is from the upper platform of the 400m/1 312.3ft-high **Fernsehturm** (TV tower).
- 🅿 **Parking:** There is ample parking throughout Stuttgart. Visit http://wap.parkinfo.com for fees and locations.
- 🚫 **Don't Miss:** Car buffs should make time for the Mercedes-Benz and Porsche museums.
- **Especially for Kids:** Wilhelmina Park and Zoo.
- ⏱ **Also See:** TÜBINGEN, SCHWÄBISCH ALB, STIFT MAULBRONN.

A Bit of History

Two Auto Pioneers – An engineer born in Bad Cannstatt, **Gottfried Daimler** (1834–1900) pioneered the internal combustion engine needed to power vehicles. **Karl Benz** (1844–1929) envisaged an entire motor vehicle, which he elaborated in every detail at Mannheim. Soon he was able to start manufacturing autos in larger numbers; in 1899 he sold his 2 000th vehicle and thus became the world's leading automobile manufacturer. In 1901, Daimler's company marketed the **Mercedes**, a name that would make an automotive dynasty as well as no small fortune. Today, above the roofs of the city, the night sky over Stuttgart blazes with the illuminated three-point-star within a circle, the firm's world-famous trademark.

Urban Landscape – The only remnants of Stuttgart's medieval core are appar-

©Olaf Loose/istockphoto.com

Mercedes-Benz Museum

Address Book

&For coin ranges, see the Legend on the cover flap.

WHERE TO STAY

Hotel Geroksruhe – *Pischekstraße 70. ☎(0711) 23 86 90. 19 rooms.* Charming, functional rooms near the city center make this a convenient place to unpack your suitcase. The breakfast room with its terrace is pleasant. Apartments are available for longer stays.

Hotel Bergmeister – *Rotenbergstraße 16. ☎(0711) 268 48 50. www.hotel-bergmeister.de. Closed Dec 23–Jan 6. 46 rooms.* Bright rooms, many with balconies, welcome guests at this modern hotel that sports a good range of creature comforts.

Hotel Abalon – *Zimmermannstraße 7 (access via Olgasstraße 79). ☎(0711) 217 10. www.abalon. de. 42 rooms.* This modern building is in the city center but has comparatively quiet rooms that are spacious and functionally furnished. Views are great from the leafy rooftop terrace.

Wörtz zur Weinsteige – *Hohenheimer Straße 30. ☎(0711) 236 70 00. www.zur-weinsteige.de. 33 rooms. Restaurant.* The Scherle family takes exceptional care of its guests who reside in comfortable and elegant rooms in a miniature palace. For a special occasion book the Louis XVI junior suite. The restaurant is characterized by rustic décor.

WHERE TO EAT

Jägerhaus – *Obere Waiblinger Straße 110, 70374 Stuttgart-Bad Cannstatt. ☎(0711) 52 60 90. www.krehlgastronomie.de. Closed Tue.* You will receive a warm welcome in this rustic and pleasant restaurant with snug alcoves that are perfect for relaxing and sampling the tasty regional dishes.

Amici – *Lautenschlagerstraße 2. ☎(0711) 227 02 92. www.amici.de. Closed Sun.* Restaurant, café, bar or lounge— the choice is yours. Spectacular architecture, décor (including an original race car) and creative lighting set this site apart. Mediterranean dishes prepared in the glass-fronted kitchen and live music on weekends give it an edge with trendy types.

Délice – *Hauptstätter Straße 61. ☎(0711) 640 33 22. Closed Mar 15–24, Dec 23–Jan 6, Sat, Sun, holidays. Reservations required.* This upscale restaurant in ambience-laden vaulted cellars puts imaginative twists on classic cuisine, all prepared in an open kitchen. The wine selection includes some rare Rieslings.

Irma la Douce – *Katharinenstraße 21b. ☎(0711) 470 43 20. Closed Sun lunch.* An old propeller for a ventilator, a black baby grand and a 19C chandelier compete for attention with Matthias Hermann's inventive and often experimental cuisine at this trendy outpost in the old town.

TAKING A BREAK

Weinhaus Stetter – *Rosenstraße 32 (south of and parallel to Charlotten straße). ☎(0711) 24 01 63. www.weinhaus-stetter.de. Closed Sun, Dec 25–Jan 8, 2 weeks between late Aug and early Sept.* For over 100 years this rustic establishment has been offering an excellent choice of mainly regional wines to accompany its small selection of hearty local dishes. The attached wine shop has a huge selection of bottles to take home.

NIGHTLIFE

USEFUL TIPS

The **Bohnenviertel** between Charlotten- and Pfarrstraße brims with charming restaurants and bars. The mainly cobbled streets are pedestrian friendly.

Biergarten Karlshöhe – *Humboldtstraße 44 (no signposting; the path through vineyards leaves from the first bend in the street coming from Marienstraße and Mörikestraße; 10min walk). ☎(0711) 284 68 78. Closed Nov–Feb.* This idyllic self-service beer garden is a bit hidden but worth the effort for the fabulous city views, especially at sunset.

Brasserie Flo – *Marktstraße 1. ☎(0711) 211 16 61.* This modern bistro is in the Karlspassage arcades below the glass cupola of the Breuninger department store. Enjoy breakfast, lunch, cakes and light bistro fare.

Teehaus – Im Weißenburgpark (via Hohenheimer Straße and Bopserwaldstraße). ☎(0711) 236 73 60. www. teehaus-stuttgart.de. Closed Nov–Feb, weekdays Mar–Apr. Set in a public park, this Art Nouveau pavilion with its terrace is an idyllic place to enjoy a coffee, cake, ice cream or cold drink.

EVENTS

PUBLICATIONS

The annual *Highlights* brochure lists events taking place year-round. Pick it up at the tourist office or download it as a free PDF file from www.stuttgart-tourist.de. The monthly magazines *Lift Stuttgart* and *Prinz* highlight current happenings and are on sale in bookshops and newspaper kiosks.

SHOPPING

USEFUL TIPS

Stuttgart's main shopping district centers on Königstraße and its side streets. The main department store is *Breuninger* (on Marktplatz). South of the Altes Schloss, the *Markthalle* is an Art-Deco covered market. Craft shops and antique dealers are found in the *Bohnenviertel* (between Charlotten- and Pfarrstraße).

---

ent on **Schillerplatz**, flanked by the **Stiftskirche** (Collegiate Church) and the **Altes Schloss** (Old Castle). The statue of Schiller in the center of the square is the work of the Danish sculptor Thorwaldsen (1839). The Baroque **Neues Schloss** (New Palace) is now the home of regional ministerial departments.

Sights

Staatsgalerie★★ (Fine Arts Gallery)
Konrad-Adenauer-Straße 30–32. ◷Open year-round, Tue–Sun 10am–6pm; (Thu 9pm). ◷Closed Good Fri, Dec 24 & 25. ☞4.50€, Wed free. ♿☎(0711) 47 04 00. www.staatsgalerie.de.
The 19C building commissioned by King Wilhelm I of Württemberg houses a world-class collection of European painting from medieval times to Impressionism in the late 19C. Budget plenty of time for the 14C–16C **Old German Masters Section**★★ where the emphasis is on Swabian painting. Another jewel is the **Herrenberg Altar** by Jerg Ratgeb (1519), which portrays the Last Supper, the Crucifixion, and the Resurrection. Venetians and Florentines from the 14C dominate the Italian section.
Among the Dutch Old Masters are Hans Memling, Rembrandt, Jacob van Ruisdael and Rubens.

An annexe houses the department of 20C art. Among the modern classics on display are works by the Fauvists and French Cubists (Matisse, Braque, Juan Gris), Expressionists (Kokoschka), the artists of Neue Sachlichkeit (Dix, Grosz) and artists of the Bauhaus. The contemporary art section starts with Dubuffet and Giacometti and ends with works by Baselitz, Beuys and Kiefer as well as a representaive range of American Pop Art (Warhol, Segal).

Linden-Museum★★
Hegelplatz 1.
◷Open year-round, Tue–Sun 10am–5pm (Wed 8pm). ☞4€, Wed after 5pm free. ♿(0711) 202 23. www.lindenmuseum.de.
Take a journey back in time and around the world in a few hours at this ethnographic museum.
Exhibits are presented in six main departments. On the ground floor: America (Native Americans and Ancient Peruvian cultures) and the Pacific (Melanesia, Papua New Guinea and Australia). On the first floor: Africa and the Middle East; and on the second floor: the Far East and South Asia (Japan, China, India, Nepal and Tibet and Indonesia).

Altes Schloss (Old Palace)
Four wings flanked by round towers comprise this former ducal residence, most of which dates from the 16C. The

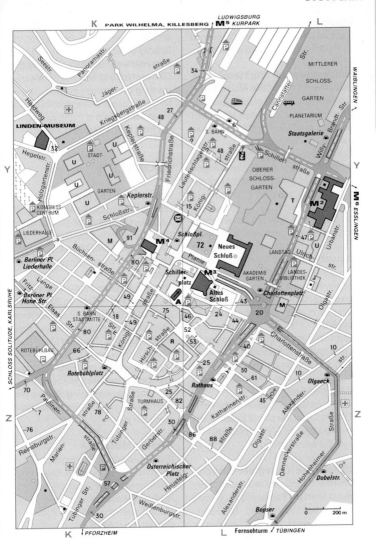

Renaissance Courtyard★ *(with access to the Schloßkirche, church)* is surrounded by three floors of arcaded galleries.

Landesmuseum Württemberg★ (Württemberg State Museum)

Schillerplatz 6, inside Altes Schloss.
Open year-round, Tue–Sun 10am–5pm.
4.50€. (0711) 27 94 98. www.landes museum-stuttgart.de.

The first floor displays collections from the Bronze and Iron Ages, with important finds from the excavation of the **royal tomb**★, a mid-6C BC Celtic burial site near Ludwigsburg.

On the second floor are collections of Ancient Roman artefacts, along with a section on South German **religious statuary**★★. Funerary objects (weapons, jewels and household items) are displayed in the **Franks and the Alemanni section**, tribes that dominated wide parts of Europe between the 3C and 8C.

Additional museum exhibits include a coin gallery, collections of furniture, clocks, scientific instruments, weapons, and the crown jewels of the kings of Württemberg.

A fine collection of musical instruments is on display in a separate building, the Fruchtkasten on Schillerplatz, not far from the Altes Schloss.

Stiftskirche (Collegiate Church)

This church combines architectural elements from the Romanesque (ground floor of the south tower, 12C), Early Gothic (chancel, 14C) and Late Gothic (the nave, 15C). A large **memorial**★ to the dukes of Württemberg stands in the chancel. Commissioned by Duke Ludwig III from Sem Schlör, it depicts 11 of the duke's ancestors dressed in armor and battle garb.

Kunstmuseum Stuttgart (Stuttgart Fine Arts Museum)

Kleiner Schlossplatz 1.
Open year-round, Tue, Thu–Sun 10am–6pm, Wed & Fri 10am–9pm. Closed Jan 1, Good Fri, Dec 24,25 & 31. 5€. (0711) 216 21 88. www.kunstmuseum-stuttgart.de.
The gallery owns some important works by famous artists from the Classical Modern and contemporary periods.

Neue Sachlichkeit artist **Otto Dix**★ is strongly represented. Famous for the ferocity of his social critique and anti-war sentiment, the artist's *Großstadt* (Big City) triptych and anti-war *Grabenkrieg* painting characterize his work. It is all housed in a impressive glass cube that glows from within at night. The mobile out front is by Alexander Calder.

Excursions

Mercedes-Benz Museum★★

Leave by Schillerstraße. Mercedesstraße 100, at factory in Stuttgart-Untertürkheim.
Open year-round, Tue–Sun 9am-5pm.
Closed Jan 1, Dec 24, 25 & 31. (07 11) 173 00 00. www.museum-mercedes-benz.com.

This new museum sits mere paces from the garage where Gottlieb Daimler first developed the gasoline engine some 120 years ago. Exhibits unfold in a spectacular building designed like a giant double helix wrapped around a towering, triangular atrium. Visitors descending from the top take a journey through time, encountering their gull-wing, prototype, racing and luxury car fantasies along the way.

Porsche Museum★

Porscheplatz 42, 70435 Stuttgart-Zuffenhausen. Leave via Heilbronner Straße, towards the autobahn. Before reaching the autobahn, take the exit 'Zuffenhausen-Industriegebiet', turn right on Porschestraße.
Open year-round, Mon–Fri 9am–4pm, Sat–Sun 9am–5pm. (0711) 911 256 85.
In 1934 Daimler-Benz engineer **Ferdinand Porsche** (1875–1951) successfully designed the famous "Beetle" for Volkswagen.

After 1948 he then devoted himself to creating a sports model bearing his own name, developed from the original VW chassis and engine and subsequently manufactured at Zuffenhausen. The museum displays several dozen different Porsches, along with high-performance engines. A much anticipated new, expanded museum is under construction nearby at Porscheplatz 1.

Wilhelma Park and Zoo★ Kids

4km/2.5mi northeast of the center. Neckartalstraße in Stuttgart-Bad Cannstatt. Leave via Heilbronner Straße.

🕐*Open daily 8.15am–dusk, 8pm latest.* 🎫*11.40€ (after 4pm, Nov–Feb daily 8€).* ♿☎*(0711) 540 20. www.wilhelma.de.*

Considered among Europe's finest botanical and zoological gardens, Wilhelma was laid out in the 19C. It features an amazing bonanza of plants, including rare orchids and cacti as well as more than 8 000 animals. Also worth seeing are the **aquarium**, **terrarium** and **Amazonian house**.

Höhenpark Killesberg

4km/2.5mi north via Heilbronner Straße.
West of the Rosenstein park, this park is a continuation of the green belt encircling the inner city. The Höhenpark integrates perfectly with the undulating terrain, including terraced cascades, fountains and brilliant flower beds, as well as a **miniature train** for touring the whole park. A look-out tower *(Aussichtsturm)* takes in sweeping views of the entire city.

Schloss Solitude★

9km/5.6mi southwest via Rotebühlstraße.
📷*Vist by guided tour only, Apr–Oct, Tue–Sat 9am–noon, 1.30pm–5pm, Sun 9am–5pm; Nov–Mar, Tue–Sat 1.30pm–4pm, Sun 10am–4pm.* 🎫*3.30€.* ☎*(0711) 69 66 99. www.schloss-solitude.de.*

The 18C former summer residence of the Württemberg court is built around a domed oval pavilion sitting majestically atop open arcades. Around this, the lower outbuildings spread out in a wide arc. The palace interior is decorated largely in the Neoclassical tradition; some apartments are French Rococo. The most opulent room is the White Hall (Weisser Saal) whose ceiling fresco celebrates Duke Carl Eugen as a wise, peace-loving ruler.

Esslingen am Neckar

13km/8mi southeast.
This Swabian town has been settled since the Bronze Age, was first mentioned in AD 777 and still possesses a largely intact historical town center. The finest building on the 19C **Mark-**

©Olaf Loose/istockphoto.com

Solitude Palace

tplatz★ is the Kielmeyer house. Marvelous **stained glass★** from the 13C and 14C is a key attraction of the Gothic **Stadtkirche St. Dionysius**, which has foundations dating back to the 8C city founding. The 15C and 16C **Altes Rathaus★** *(old Town Hall)* combines the charm of half-timbering with the gracefulness of Renaissance façades. And the Gothic **Frauenkirche**, which stands on a hillside *(reached from the Marktplatz via the Untere Beutau rise)*, has a beautiful ornate **church tower★**.

Schloss Ludwigsburg★

15km/9.6mi north.
Built by Duke Eberhard Ludwig von Württemberg, the 'Swabian Versailles' is a monumental four-winged 18C palace with 452 rooms, 75 of which are open to the public.

State Apartments★

📷*Visit by guided tour (90min) only, mid-Mar–Oct, daily half-hourly 10am–5pm; Nov–mid-Mar, Mon–Fri 10.30am, 11.45am, 1.30pm, 3pm and 4pm, Sat–Sun 10.30am, 11.45am, noon, half-hourly 1pm–4pm.* 🎫*6€.* ☎*(07141) 18 64 10. www.schloss-ludwigsburg.de.*

The most impressive rooms on a tour of the palace are the apartments of the first king of Württemberg, lavishly furnished in Empire style. Through the

Baroque Blooms

Schloss Ludwigsburg has not only richly furnished period rooms and museums, but from March to October, it also welcomes visitors to the Blooming Baroque (*Blühendes Barock*), a series of delightful and inspirational gardens. Unwind amid the Zen-like tranquility of the Japanese Garden, give your sweetie a kiss in the romantic Rose Garden, observe exotic birds fluttering around an aviary, trek up to a romantic medieval-style castle or catch a snooze by the lake. Kids are enchanted by the magical Märchengarten where they get to meet Hänsel and Gretel and other characters from classic fairytales, not to forget a paper-eating dragon. For more information, see www.blueba.de.

Green Baroque arbours and flowered terraces have been reconstituted in the southern part of the park, in front of the newest part of the palace. The terrain to the north and east has been landscaped in the English manner. In the **Märchengarten**★★ (Fairytale Garden), German fairytales and legends are illustrated.

Ahnengalerie (Ancestors' Gallery) and the Catholic church (*Schloßkirche*), decorated with lavish Italian stucco, visitors arrive at the Fürstenbau state apartments.

Museums

🕐*Open year-round, daily 10am–5pm.*
⊗*6€ for all museums.*
The vast Schloss is also home to half a dozen museums. The **Keramikmuseum** traces the evolution of porcelain, faïences and ceramics through five centuries. In the **Barockgalerie**, you are treated to a delightful survey of German and Italian paintings from the 17C and 18C. The **Modemuseum** exhibits fabulous fashions for men, women and children, including some fanciful frocks worn at court. There's also a small **Theatermuseum** as well as the interactive new **Kinderreich**, where kids get to dress up as princes or princesses and learn about life at court guided by Federico, the palace mascot.

Tiefenbronn★

38km/23.6mi west.
This village is home to the **Pfarrkirche St. Maria Magdalena**, which boasts an unusually rich interior. Besides 13C and 14C murals and stained glass and numerous tombs are some particularly fine Late Gothic altarpieces. The **high altar** by Ulm master Hans Schüchlin (1469) depicts scenes from the life of the Virgin Mary and the Passion of Christ. On the south aisle is a magnificent **altarpiece of St. Mary Magdalene**★★ (1432) by Lucas Moser.

Schwäbisch Gmünd

54km/33.5mi east.
Schwäbisch Gmünd has long been a center for the working of precious metals with dozens of companies still in operation today. The Baroque **Marktplatz** (*market square*) is framed by stately houses. The beautiful 14C **Heiligkreuzmünster**★ harbors chapels rich in statuary, including the Tree of Jesse (1520) in the Baptismal Chapel, adorned with 40 sculpted figurines.

Hohenstaufen★

14km/8.7mi southwest, plus 30min round-trip walk. 🅿*Park in the village square.*
From the two churches at the top of the town, a shady trail leads to the summit at 684m/2 244ft. Nothing remains of the Staufer castle, but the climb is worthwhile for the **panorama**★ of the Kaiserberge and, on the horizon, the Swabian Jura.

INSEL SYLT★★

Despite its modest area (100sq km/39sq mi), the landscape of this long, narrow island is quite varied: Sandy beaches and dunes, marshes and mudflats, fields and meadows, open heathland and primeval burial mounds. The island's spas, North Sea bathing and largely unspoiled nature make it popular with vacationers.

- **Information:** Stephanstraße 6, 25980 Westerland. ☎(04651) 820 20. www.sylt.de.
- ▸ **Orient Yourself:** Sylt extends north to for 40km/24.8mi; at its narrowest it is less than 457m/500yd across. The island is the largest of the Northern Frisian Islands and the most northerly part of Germany. Since 1927, it has been connected to the mainland via rail across the Hindenburgdamm causeway. You can reach Sylt via **train-car** ferry from Niebüll *(35min; car with passengers 86€ round-trip; ☎(04661) 93 45 67; www.syltshuttle.de)*. **Car ferries** leave from Havneby on the Danish island of Rømø—accessible by road *(5 to 7 ferries a day, up to 12 daily in Jul and Aug; 50min; 53€ round-trip per vehicle including passengers, 6.20€ round-trip for pedestrians; ☎(0180) 310 30 30; www.sylt-faehre.de)*.
- **Don't Miss:** The megalithic graves of Denghoog near Keitum.
- **Organizing Your Time:** Allow at least a full day to enjoy this island.
- **Especially for Kids:** Swimming and outdoor recreation on the North Sea.
- **Also See:** NORDFRIESISCHE INSELN, INSEL HELGOLAND.

Sights

Westerland★   Spa

This is the largest resort on Sylt and the most popular North Sea **spa** in Germany. Facilities include a boat-shaped water park and health spa, the **Sylter Welle** *(www.westerland.de/sport-freizeit/sylter-welle.html)*, and a 7km/4.3mi-long sandy beach.

The promenade is the place to see and be seen, as it is centered on a large music hall, and there is plenty of action in the bars, bistros and nightclubs. As the island's metropolis, Westerland has everything visitors desire, from window-shopping (Strandstraße and Friedrichstraße) and galleries to a casino (in the old *Jugendstil* spa). There are also various sports facilities and cultural events.

Keitum

This idyllic village and its craftshops presents a more relaxed, unpretentious face of the island. Keitum's traditional thatched Frisian houses hidden among trees and lilacs, the embankments of dog roses, and cliffs overlooking the sea and mudflats earn it the nickname "the green heart."

Kampen

This resort is popular with the German jet set (models, soccer players, aristocrats, etc.) and international VIPs. It brims with fancy international boutiques, while impeccably shiny BMWs and Mercedes patrol the streets.

The main "catwalk" is the Stroenwai, also known as Whiskey Alley. South of town, the **Rotes Kliff** towers above the sea. Embracing it is the **Uwe Dune**, at 52.5m/172ft the highest on Sylt. There are great **views★** over Sylt and neighboring islands from the top.

Wenningstedt

In Wenningstedt-Braderup, the **Denghoog★** is a 4 000-year-old megalithic grave open to the public. **Morsum-Kliff**, featuring ten million years of geological history, is an interesting geological feature.

List

Around the port of **List**, where ferries from Rømø drop off Danish day-trippers, the **Wanderdünen** are moving dunes extending 1 000m/3 280ft long and 30m/98.4ft-high.

Address Book

For coin ranges, see cover flap.

WHERE TO STAY

◎◎◎ **Parkhotel am Südwäldchen** – Fischerweg 45, 25980 Sylt-Westerland. ☎(04651) 83 63 00. www.parkhotel-sylt. de. 24 rooms. Set in a quiet residential area, this professionally kept hotel has an indoor pool and sauna.

◎◎◎**Seiler Hof** – Gurtstig 7, 25980 Sylt-Ost-Keitum. ☎(04651) 933 40. www. seilerhofsylt.de. 11 rooms. This former captain's house dates from 1761 and has a beautiful garden and time-lessly furnished rooms.

WHERE TO EAT

◎◎◎ **WebChristel** – Süderstraße 11, 25980 Sylt-Westerland. ☎(04651) 229 00. Closed Wed. Dinner only, reservations recommended. Cozy and rustic, in a reed-thatched Frisian house, this restaurant turns out refined regional dishes that sparkle with flavor.

◎◎◎ Morsum Kliff – Nösistig 13, 25980 Sylt-Ost-Morsum. ☎(04651) 83 63 20. www.hotel-morsum-kliff.de. Closed Jan 6–Feb 14. Reservations recommended. This reed-thatched upscale restaurant sits in a wonderfully isolated cliff-top location and generates a buzz with its tasty cakes, market-fresh regional cuisine and light lunches.

TAKING A BREAK

Kupferkanne – Stapelhooger Wai, 25999 Sylt-Kampen. ☎(04651) 410 10. www.kupferkanne-sylt.de. In a former bunker, this artsy café serves excellent coffee and cakes and has a large garden with views of the mudflats.

NIGHTLIFE

Salon 1900 – Süderstraße 40, 25980 Sylt-Ost-Keitum. ☎(04651) 93 60 00. www.salon1900.de. Closed mid-Jan–mid-Feb. A café, restaurant, bar and dance club are all under one thatched roof while the pleasant garden is perfect for lolling around in sunny weather.

THÜRINGER WALD★★
THURINGIAN FOREST

The Thuringian Forest is one of the most beautiful natural regions in Germany and hugely popular with hikers, cross-country skiers and outdoor types of all stripes. The massif is littered with charming villages where traditional skills and craftsmanship are kept alive.

- **Information:** Gräfenrodaer Straße 2, 98559 Oberhof. ☎(036842) 529 80. www.thueringer-wald.com.
- **Orient Yourself:** Around 100km/63mi in length, the Thuringian Forest separates the valleys of Swiss-Franconia from northern Thuringia.
- **Don't Miss:** Literature lovers should not miss Ilmenau, closely affiliated with Johann Wolfgang von Goethe.
- **Organizing Your Time:** Allow one day for the suggested driving tour.
- **Especially for Kids:** Marienglashöhle cavern.
- **Also See:** ERFURT, WEIMAR, OBERES SAALETAL, EISENACH.

Driving Tour

110km/68mi

Thüringer Hochstraße: Eisenach to Ilmenau

This delightful forest road mainly parallels the **Rennsteig**, a 168km/104mi-long hiking trail that keeps to the forest's

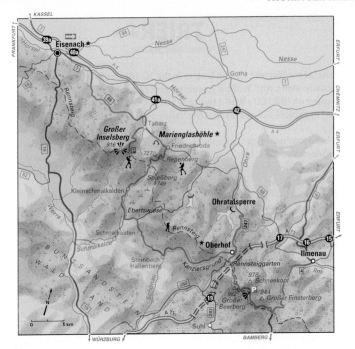

higher elevations, crossing the Großer Inselsberg (916m/3 005ft) and Großer Beerberg (983m/3 225ft) peaks.

Eisenach★ 👁 see EISENACH

▸ Go toward Gotha.

Großer Inselsberg

1hr round-trip walk.
The **views**★★ from the summit take in much of the forest.

Marienglashöhle★ 🄺🄸🄳🅂

👁*Visit by guided (45min) only, Apr–Oct, daily 9am–5pm; Nov–Mar, 9am–4pm. ⌾4€. ☎(03623) 30 49 53. www.schauhoehlen.de.*

This natural **mine** produces crystalline gypsum, a mineral used in the decoration of church altars and protection of pictures of the Virgin Mary. This watery gypsum was named *Marienglas* (Mary's glass) in the middle ages.

▸ *The road cuts across the Rennsteig and twists between the Regenberg and the Spießberg. Consider a hike through the Ebertswiese, a marsh- and meadowland.*

Steinbach is overlooked by the Hallenburg ruins. The road continues toward Oberhof via the grasslands of the Kanzlergrund.

Oberhof★

At 800m/2 625ft, Oberhof is the forest's most important winter sports center and the host of annual biathlon and nordic combined (cross-country skiing and ski-jumping) world cups. More than 4 000 plant species grow In the **Rennsteiggarten** botanical park. Follow the B247 to the parking lot of the **Ohratalsperre** reservoir which supplies water to Weimar, Jena, Gotha and Erfurt.

▸ *Leave Oberhof toward Schmücke.*

Ilmenau

On the forest's northern fringe, Ilmenau has always been associated with Goethe, said to have been particularly fond of its natural beauty. A plaque in his memory adorns the wall of the *Amtshaus* in Marktplatz, which now features a small Goethe museum. 🚶The **Goethewanderweg** (hiking trail) links sites associated with the great writer.

TRIER★★

POPULATION: 100 800

Capital of the Western Roman Empire in the 3C, Trier is one of the oldest cities in Germany, along with Worms. Its remarkable collection of Roman ruins earned it a place on UNESCO's World Heritage List in 1986. The city is an ideal starting point to explore the nearby Moselle Valley or Luxembourg.

- **Information:** An der Porta Nigra, 54290 Trier. ☎ (0651) 97 80 80. www.trier.de.
- ▶ **Orient Yourself:** Trier straddles the Moselle River, near the Luxembourg border. The Eifel mountains lie to the north and the Hunsrück massif to the southeast.
- **Parking:** Parking is found in garages throughout town. The Hauptmarkt has a lot convenient for visiting the Old City.
- **Don't Miss:** The Porta Nigra, the Cathedral, the Roman Baths and the Library Treasury.
- **Organizing Your Time:** Allow one day for a tour of the old town.
- **Also See:** MOSELTAL, UNTERES SAARTAL, IDAR-OBERSTEIN, EIFEL.

A Bit of History

The Oldest City in Germany – After the conquest of the Treveri, a Celtic tribe from eastern Gaul, the Roman Emperor Augustus founded on their territory the town of **Augusta Treverorum** (c. 16 BC). It evolved into a center of economic, cultural and intellectual activity until the invasion of Germanic tribes in AD 274. When Diocletian reorganized the Roman Empire, Trier was retaken and became capital of the western territories (Gaul, Spain, Germania and Britain). As the town regained its former eminence, the Emperor Constantine (306–37) sur-rounded it with a defensive wall within which magnificent buildings were erected.

In 313, the Edict of Milan ended the persecution of Christians, and a year later the See of Trier was created as the first on German soil.

Sights

Basilika St. Paulin★

Access via Thebäerstraße.
○*Open Mar–Sept, Mon, Wed-Sat 9am–6pm, Tue 11am–6pm, Sun 10am–6pm; Oct–Feb to 5pm.*

Porta Nigra

M. Hertlein/MICHELIN

Address Book

🪙 *For coin ranges, see the Legend on the cover flap.*

WHERE TO STAY

🛏️🛏️**Berghotel Kockelsberg** – *Kockelsberg 1, 54293 Trier-Kockelsberg.* ☎(0651) 824 80 00. www.kockelsberg. de. 32 rooms. Restaurant 🍽️🍽️m, closed Nov–Mar Sun dinner. Enjoy lovely views of Triers from this turn-of-the 20C hotel with its white façade and turrets. Rooms are charming and comfortable and the country-style restaurant has perfect pitch as well.

🛏️🛏️**Hotel Alte Villa** – *Saarstraße 133.* ☎(0651) 93 81 20. www.hotelaltevilla.de. 20 rooms. This hotel on the outskirts of the city occupies a charmingly restored Baroque villa from 1743. Rooms are well-proportioned and modern.

🛏️🛏️🛏️**Hotel Petrisberg** – *Sickingenstraße 11.* ☎(0651) 46 40. www. hotel-petrisberg.de. 35 rooms. Rooms are charming, balconied and well equipped, but its idyllic nature preserve location and magnificent views that set this property apart. Pleasant trails lead down to the city center.

WHERE TO EAT

🍽️🍽️**Pfeffermühle** – *Zurlaubener Ufer 76.* ☎(0651) 261 33. Closed Sun and Mon lunch. An aroma of the daily feast wasts from the kitchen of this riverside restaurant that welcome patrons with a traditional ambience, nicely set tables and classical cuisine.

TAKING A BREAK

Café Bley – *Simeonstraße 19.* ☎(0651) 736 80. This classic café in the 13C *Dreikönigenhaus* will spoil you for choice with its cake selection. The house specialty are the Riesling truffles, which makes great souvenirs for the folks back home.

NIGHTLIFE

Historischer Keller – *Simeonstraße 46.* ☎(0651) 46 94 96. www.historischer-keller.de. Closed Sun. The flair of the Middle Ages drips from this stone cellar built c. 1200. It is beneath the Karstadt department store and serves coffee, cakes and light meals.

Walderdorff's – *Domfreihof 1a.* ☎(0651) 994 44 12. www.walderdorffs. de. Thie place consists of a main café area, a wine cellar, and a jazz club. This café, club and wine bar is perfect for letting your hair down after a busy day on the tourist track.

Tall windows illuminate the single nave of this 18C church whose interior was designed by Balthasar Neumann. The martyrdom of St. Paul, citizens of Trier, and of the Theban Legion (AD 286) are illustrated in ceiling paintings by Christoph Thomas Scheffler of Augsburg. The high altar was based on Neumann's designs with woodcarving by Trier artist Ferdinand Tietz.

Amphitheater★ (Roman Amphitheater)

🕐*Open Apr–Sept, daily 9am–6pm, Oct–Mar to 5pm, Nov–Feb to 4pm.* 2.10€. ☎(0651) 730 10.

Once seating 20 000 spectators, this hillside arena was used as a quarry in the Middle Ages. The cellars housed theatrical equipment and machinery.

Every summer, the amphitheater hosts the **Antikenfestspiele** (Festival of Ancient Plays).

Barbarathermen

⚲*Closed for renovation.* ☎(0651) 442 62.

These Roman baths from the 2C are now in ruins and undergoing extensive restoration.

Thermen am Viehmarkt (Thermal Baths at Viehmarkt)

Viehmarktplatz. 🕐*Open year-round, Tue–Sun 9am–5pm.* 2.10€. ☎(0651) 994 1057.

These Roman baths were discovered by accident during excavations in the 1980s. They are protected by a glass shelter designed by OM Ungers.

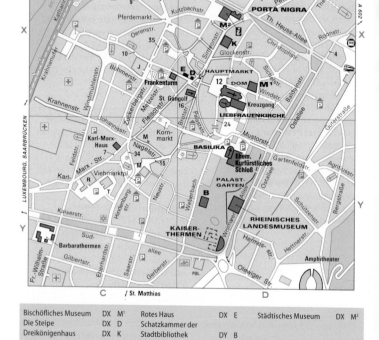

Old Town

Porta Nigra★★

🕒 *Open Apr–Sept, 9am–6pm; Oct and Mar, 9am–5pm; Nov–Feb, 9am–4pm.* 💶*2.10€.* ☎*(0651) 460 89 65.*

The **Porta Nigra** (Black Gate) is Trier's most famous landmark and the largest Roman edifice on German soil. This monumental gateway (2C), built to defend the northern town wall, is made of stones fitted together without mortar, held together only by iron crampons. The double arcade of the central block leads to an inner court with pierced upper arcades. Assailants that had broken through the outer gates would find themselves exposed to attack from all sides.

In the 11C, the fortified gateway was transformed into a church dedicated to St. Simeon. The Romanesque apse and Rococo decoration are still discernible. Napoleon ordered the monument restored to its original form in 1804.

Städtisches Museum Simeonstift

🕒*Open year-round, Tue–Sun 11am–6pm.* 🕒*Closed Jan 1, Dec 24, 25 & 31.* 💶*5€.* ♿ ☎*(0651) 718 14 59. www.museum-trier.de.*

This municipal museum occupies a Romanesque convent, the Simeonstift, built beside the Porta Nigra in the 11C.

Following a recent renovation, galleries again creatively illustrate the history of Trier with models, paintings, engravings, maps and sculptures.

The museum also encompasses a two-story Romanesque **cloister**.

Dreikönigenhaus★ (House of the Three Kings)

This Early Gothic town house (c. 1230), with arched windows, recalls the Italianate towers of the patricians of Regensburg.

Hauptmarkt★ (Main Square)

This is one of the finest old squares in Germany, anchored by a **Marktkreuz**★ (market cross) from 958 and a 16C **Brunnen** (fountain) surrounded by figures representing the cardinal virtues.

Standing next to the cross, you are surrounded by 15 centuries of architechtural history: To the north is the Porta Nigra; to the east the Romanesque cathedral; to the south the Gothic **Gangolfkirche**, its 16C tower once used as a look-out post; and half-timbered houses to the west. The **Steipe**, a 15C municipal building, is elegantly built over an open gallery. It now houses a toy museum. Beside it, the 17C **Rotes Haus** (Red House) bears the proud inscription: "There was life in Trier for 1 300 years before Rome even existed."

Frankenturm

This sturdy Romanesque tower (c. 1100) is named after one of its early owners, Franco of Senheim (14C).

Dom★ (Cathedral)

🕐Open Apr–Oct, daily 6.30am–6pm, Nov–Mar to 5.30pm.

With its six towers, Trier's cathedral looks more like a fortress than a church. A rounded apse projects from a massive, austere façade, which is a fine example of Early Romanesque architecture.

A flattened gable and rectangular plan, visible from the north side, point to the 4C Roman core of the building. West of this central block is the 11C Romanesque section; east of it the 12C polygonal chancel. A Baroque axial chapel crowned by a dome was added in the 18C.

The interior is primarily Baroque. Near the main door, note the fallen Roman **Domstein** (column) that supported part of the former church. A splendid **tympanum**★ in the south aisle depicts Christ flanked by the Virgin Mary and St. Peter.

Silver and gold plate, valuable ivories, and magnificently illuminated Gospels are on view in the **Domschatz**★ (Cathedral Treasury, 🕐open Apr–Oct, Mon–Sat 10am–5pm, Sun 12.30pm–5pm; Nov–Mar, Mon–Sat 11am–4pm, Sun 2pm–4pm; 🕐closed Jan 1, Easter Sun, Dec 25; 1.50€; (0651) 979 07 90; www.dominformation.de).

Liebfrauenkirche★ (Church of Our Lady)

⊶Closed until at least 2010.

One of the earliest Gothic sanctuaries in Germany (1235–60), this church was inspired by one in the French Champagne region and has a ground plan in the form of a Greek cross. Four apsidal chapels are flanked by two smaller, three-sided chapels, giving the entire church the layout of a rose with 12 petals. The church's interior has an incomparable elegance, enhanced by rings of foliage around each column and the lofty central vault.

Bischöfliches Dom - und Diözesanmuseum★ (Episcopal Museum)

🕐Open Apr–Oct, Mon–Sat 9am–5pm, Sun 1pm–5pm; Nov–Mar, Tue–Sat 9am–5pm, Sun 1pm–5pm. 🕐Closed Jan 1, Dec 24–26 & 31. 3.50€. (0651) 710 52 55. www.museum.bistum-trier.de.

The most interesting exhibits in this museum are the 4C ceiling frescoes that once decorated a residential palace which was demolished to make room for an early Christian church. The central picture is believed to represent Constantine's wife, Fausta. The rest of the museum is mainly devoted to sacred art.

Basilika★

This large rectangular building was once the **Aula Palatina** (main hall) of the Imperial palace, built by Constantine c. 310. Modified many times over the centuries, it was rebuilt in 1954 and is used today as a Protestant church.

Ehemaliges Kurfürstliches Schloss (Palace of the Electors)

Only the north and east wings remain of the Renaissance electoral castle, construction of which began in 1615. The 18C Rococo wings were designed by Johannes Seitz, student of Balthasar Neumann. His virtuosity is expressed in a magnificent staircase, one of the most beautiful creations of its kind in Germany.

Rheinisches Landesmuseum★★ (Rhineland Museum)

Weimarer Allee 1.

◷Open year-round, Tue–Sun 9.30am–5.30pm. ◷Closed Jan 1, Carnival, Dec 24–26. ⊚3€. ☎(0651) 977 40. www. landesmuseum-trier.de.

This museum of archeology has exceptional items from as far back as the **Paleolithic**, featuring Stone Age implements and ceramics; objects from the Bronze Age; and jewels set in gold from Iron Age sepulchres. A major highlight is the **Roman** section, featuring mar-

velous mosaics, bronzes and bas-reliefs as well as the famous Neumagen ship stone carving, a representation of a ship sailing down the Moselle loaded with wine. Note the figure of "the jolly sailor": A mariner with a broad grin who has passed into the folklore of the Moselle.

Kaiserthermen★★ (Imperial Roman Baths)

◷Open Apr–Sept, daily 9am–6pm, Oct–Mar to 5pm, Nov–Feb to 4pm. ⊚2.10€. ☎(0651) 460 89 65.

Among the largest in the Roman Empire, these baths date from the time of Constantine. The construction of the rounded walls is typically Roman.

Karl-Marx-Haus

Brückenstraße 10.

◷Open mid-Mar–Oct, daily 10am–6pm; Nov–mid-Mar, Mon 2pm–6pm, Tue–Sun 10am–1pm, 2pm–5pm. ◷Closed Jan 1, Dec 24–26 & 31. ⊚3€. ☎(0651) 97 06 80. www.museum-karl-marx-haus.de.

The birthplace of the socialist theoretician Karl Marx has been turned into a museum, displaying letters, manuscripts and a first edition of the *Communist Manifesto*.

TÜBINGEN★★

POPULATION: 83 000

Tübingen escaped World War II with nary a shrapnel wound and is therefore a virtual 3D textbook of its evolution from the Middle Ages to the 19C. The maze of narrow sloping lanes lined with ancient half-timbered houses and its animated student life create a delightful atmosphere.

- **Information:** An der Neckarbrücke, 72072 Tübingen. ☎(07071) 913 60. www.tuebingen-info.de.
- **Orient Yourself:** Tübingen is near Stuttgart, on the banks of the Neckar and Ammer, between the slopes of Schloßberg and Österberg.
- **Parking:** Garages are located throughout Tübingen. Visit http://wap.parkinfo.com for fees and locations.
- **Don't Miss:** A walking tour of the old town.
- **Organizing Your Time:** Allow a full day to absorb the history of Tübingen.
- **Also See:** STUTTGART, SCHWÄBISCHE ALB, SCHWARZWALD.

A Bit of History

The University – They say that rather than having a university, Tübingen *is* a university, so closely linked are the

town and its alma mater. It all began in 1477, when Count Eberhard founded the institution in a town of only 3 000. Tübingen University now has 16 faculties and 24 000 students registered in 74

Neckar riverfront, Tübingen

different fields of study. The university and the Protestant seminary of 1536 have educated such important figures as the poets Hölderlin, Mörike and Uhland, the philosophers Hegel and Schelling, the astronomer Kepler, the theologian Melanchthon, and Swiss biologist, Friedrich Miescher—discoverer of DNA. It has also produced nine Nobel Prize winners, most in the field of chemistry.

Sights

Old Town★★

Eberhardsbrücke (Bridge)

This bridge gives a scenic **view**★ over the Neckar with the Hölderlin Tower rising behind weeping willows. The **Platanenallee** is a beautiful walkway along the Neckar. Keep an eye out for the gondolas traveling from Hölderlin Tower past the riverfront.

Hölderlinturm (Tower)

Bursagasse 6. ◷*Open year-round, Tue–Fri 10am–noon, 3pm–5pm, Sat–Sun 2pm–5pm.* ✆*1.50€.* ☏*(07071) 220 40.*
Once part of the fortifications, this tower was the residence of Friedrich Hölderlin from 1807 until he died in 1843. Now a museum, it has displays on the life and work of the poet.

Schloss Hohentübingen (Palace)

The present Renaissance building was constructed on the foundations of an 11C fortress built by the archdukes of Tübingen. It as well as a **museum**★ (◷*open May–Sept, Wed–Sun 10am–6pm;*

Friedrich Hölderlin in Tübingen

Friedrich Hölderlin was born at Lauffen am Neckar in 1770. He studied theology at Tübingen's Protestant seminary, where he befriended philosophers Hegel and Schelling, in preparation for the ministry. Poetry continued to interest him in Tübingen, a craft he began while studying in Maulbronn. Finally rebelling against a career in the church, he worked as a tutor in Frankfurt, Switzerland and Bordeaux. The first sign of mental illness (thought to be schizophrenia) manifested itself in 1802. In 1806, he returned to Tübingen where he was promised recovery under the care of medical professor Autenrieth at a residential home. When treatment failed, Hölderlin resided in the tower room at the home of the Zimmers, a family of carpenters, at Bursagasse 6 for the remainder of his life.

TÜBINGEN

Am Markt	Y	Holzmarkt	Y 27	Pfleghofstr.	Y 48
Ammergasse	Y 5	Karlstr.	Z	Poststr.	Z 54
Derendinger Str.	Z 8	Kirchgasse	Y 30	Schmiedtorstr.	Y 60
Friedrichstr.	Z 12	Kronenstr.	Y 33	Wilhelmstr.	Y
Froschgasse	Y 15	Lange Gasse	Y		
Hirschgasse	Y 21	Mühlstr.	Y		
		Münzgasse	Y 39		
		Neckargasse	Y 42		

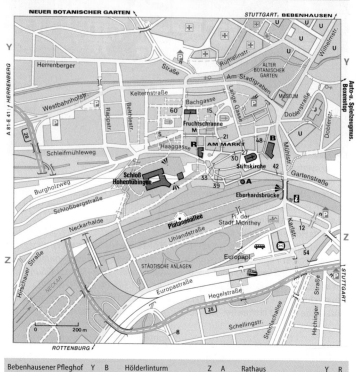

| Bebenhausener Pfleghof | Y | B | Hölderlinturm | Z | A | Rathaus | Y | R |

Oct–Apr to 5pm; ⏰closed Dec 24, 25 & 31; ☞4€; ☎ (07071) 297 73 84; www. uni-tuebingen.de/museum-schloss) on pre- and early history. A favorite exhibit is the tiny **"Vogelherdpferdchen"**★, an ivory horse figurine named for the cave near Ulm where it was discovered in 1931. It is one of the oldest works of art from the New Paleolithic Age.

There are also outstanding exhibits from Classical Antiquity, Ancient Egypt and the Ancient Orient.

Note in particular the **religious chamber**★ from an Old Kingdom tomb (third millennium BC), completely covered in bas-relief sculptures.

There is a good **view**★ of the Neckar and the roofs of the old town from the castle terrace.

Marktplatz★ (Market Square)

This charming historic square features a Renaissance fountain and a statue of Neptune and is surrounded by half-timbered houses.

It comes alive on market days (Mon, Wed and Fri). The 19C graffito decoration on the 15C **Rathaus** (Town Hall) depicts

Castle Residents

Schloss Hohentübingen houses the largest bat colony in southern Germany. Disturbed by roof renovations in 1995, the bats moved to the castle cellars, making it impossible for the public to view the giant 16C vat, with a capacity of 850hl/18 700gal.

Address Book

&For coin ranges, see the Legend on the cover flap.

WHERE TO STAY

⊖**Hotel Metropol** – *Reutlinger Straße 7.* ☎*(07071) 910 10. 12 rooms. Restaurant* ⊖⊖. This little hotel is on the edge of town within walking distance of the historic center. Rooms are rather basic but clean and modern.

⊖⊖**Hotel Am Bad** – *Am Freibad 2.* ☎*(07071) 797 40. www.hotel-am-bad. de. Closed Dec 18–Jan 6. 35 rooms.* This hotel is next to Tübingen's outdoor swimming pool. Some of the rooms have dark-wood furniture, others have a more natural look. Family rooms are available. Wi-Fi is free.

WHERE TO EAT

⊖⊖**Schwärzlocher Hof** – *Schwärzloch 1 (2.5km/1.5mi west of town, via Schwärzlocher Str. between Schleifmühleweg and Burgholzweg. ☎(07071) 433 62. www.hofgut-schwaerzloch.de. Closed Dec 25–mid-Feb.* The chancel of a 12C church has been incorporated into this farm inn. There is a beautiful view of the surrounding area from the terrace, shaded by lime trees. Sample the *Most* (dry cider) with traditional dishes.

⊖⊖**Weinstube Forelle** – *Kronenstraße 8. ☎(07071) 240 94. www. weinstube-forelle.de.* This restaurant is popular with students and tourists in the evenings for its friendly staff and creatively updated Swabian dishes.

TAKING A BREAK

Die Kelter – *Schmiedtorstraße 17.* ☎*(07071) 25 46 90. www.diekelter.de. Closed early Jan.* Follow the locals to this half-timbered building that combines a chic and charming café-restaurant, bar, delicatessen and wine shop (tastings available) under one roof.

NIGHTLIFE

Schöne Aussichten – *Wilhelmstraße 16.* ☎*(07071) 228 84. www.schoene-aussichten-tuebingen.de.* This relaxed café has a selection of sweet and savory nibbles, salads and light dishes. Breakfast is served until a hangover-friendly 6pm.

SPORT AND LEISURE

Boat Rentals H. Märkle – *Eberhardsbrücke (behind the tourist office)* ☎*(07071) 315 29. www.bootsvermietung-tuebingen.de. Closed in bad weather. Rowing boats from* ⊜*7.50€, pedaloes from 10€, Stocherkahn from 48€.* Row around Neckar island and enjoy beautiful views of the old town. Trips in a *Stocherkahn*—the Tübingen version of a Venetian gondola—are great fun, but must be booked four to five days in advance.

---

the allegories of Justice, Agriculture and Science. The astronomic clock dates from 1511.

Stiftskirche (Collegiate Church)

Am Holzmarkt.
🕐*Open from Easter to Harvest Festival (Erntedank) in early October; Fri and Sat, 11.30am–5pm, Sun, 1pm–5pm; during local school summer holidays, Tue–Sun, 11.30am–5pm.* ⊜*1€.*
This 15C Gothic hall-church was for centuries the burial place of the Württemberg princes. Note the funerary monument of Eberhard the Bearded, the original founder of the university, and the **Renaissance tombs**★★ of Duke Ludwig and his wife, which are adorned with fine alabaster relief work.

At the foot of the perron leading to the Stiftskirche stretches the *Holzmarkt* (woodwork market). The old Heckenhauer bookshop (now a travel agent) is where the writer and poet Hermann Hesse spent his apprenticeship from 1895 to 1899.

West of the church is the **Cottahaus**, the former home of Johann Friedrich Cotta (1764–1832), a leading publisher during the Enlightenment who was the first to print the works of Goethe and Schiller.

Excursion

Kloster Bebenhausen★

6km/3.7mi north via the Wilhelmstraße. ⟐*Open Apr–Oct, Mon 9am–noon, 1pm –6pm, Tue–Sun 9am–6pm; Nov–Mar, Tue–Sun 9am–noon, 1pm–5pm.* ⟐*Closed Jan 1, Dec 24, 25 & 31.* ⟐*3€.* ☎*(07071) 60 28 02. www.kloster-bebenhausen.de.*

Along with Maulbronn and Eberbach, this 12C abbey ranks among the best preserved Cistercian monastery in Germany. The landmark roof **turret**★ dates from the monastery's 15C heyday.

Schloss Bebenhausen

⟐*Visit by guided tour (45min) only, hourly, Apr–Oct, Tue–Fri 9am–5pm, Sat–Sun 10am–5pm; Nov–Mar to 4pm.* ⟐*Closed Jan 1, Dec 24, 25 & 31.* ⟐*3.50€.* ☎*(07071) 60 28 02.*

On the monastery grounds is **Schloss Bebenhausen,** the monastery house turned hunting lodge of King Karl of Württemberg.

This is where the last king of Württemberg, Wilhelm II, retired after his abdication. His widow, Charlotte, lived here until her death in 1946.

ÜBERLINGEN★

POPULATION: 21 300

This former Free Imperial City on Lake Constance was founded around 1180 by Frederick I Barbarossa and achieved great prosperity in the Middle Ages thanks to its vineyards and leading role in the salt and grain trade. Since the mid-19C, the tourist industry has become the local economic engine, especially after Überlingen became an official Kneipp spa resort in 1956.

- **Information:** Landungsplatz 14, 88662 Überlingen. ☎(07551) 99 11 22. www.ueberlingen.de.
- ▶ **Orient Yourself:** The town is on the northwest shore of Bodensee (Lake Constance) surrounded by orchards and a mild climate. West of the center, a pleasant **Stadtbefestigungsanlagen** (moat walk) leads to the **Seepromenade**.
- **Don't Miss:** The Münsterplatz and its Münster.
- **Organizing Your Time:** Allow three hours to see the sights of Überlingen.
- **Also See:** BODENSEE, KONSTANZ, SALEM.

Sights

Münsterplatz (Minster Square)

The square is bordered by the Gothic cathedral, the north façade of the Town Hall and the Renaissance **Alte Kanzlei** (municipal chancellery).

Münster (Minster)★

The Gothic cathedral proves its influence as a place of worship with its volume of donor altarpieces, including the High Altar by the Brothers Zürn in 1616.

A 16C Swabian work, the Virgin of the Crescent Moon, stands in St. Elizabeth Chapel.

Address Book

For coin ranges, see cover flap.

WHERE TO STAY

⟐⟐⟐**Hotel Seegarten** – *Seepromenade 7.* ☎*(07551) 91 88 90. www.seegarten-ueberlingen. com. Closed Dec to Feb. 21 rooms. Restaurant*⟐⟐. This hotel is beside the lake, with a terrace shaded by chestnut trees. Lovely terrace and comfortable guestrooms; ask for one with a view of the Überlinger See.

⟐⟐⟐**Hotel Rosengarten** – *Bahnhofstraße 12.* ☎*(07551) 928 20. www.haus-rosengarten.com. 15 rooms.* Modernized Jugendstil villa in the park (Stadtgarten) near the lake. Rooms fitted with every comfort.

ÜBERLINGEN

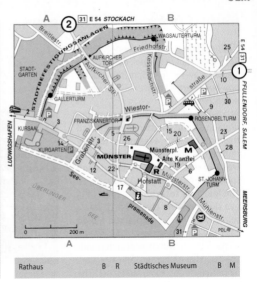

Bahnhofstr.	A	2
Christophstr.	A	3
Franziskanerstr.	B	5
Gradebergstr.	B	6
Hafenstr.	B	8
Hizlerstr.	B	9
Hochbildstr.	B	10
Hofstatt	B	
Jakob-Kessenring-Str.	A	12
Klosterstr.	A	14
Krummebergstr.	B	15
Landungspl.	B	17
Lindenstr.	B	19
Luziengasse	B	20
Marktstr.	AB	22
Münsterstr.	B	
Obertorstr.	B	23
Owinger Str.	B	25
Pfarrhofstr.	B	26
Schlachthausstr.	B	30
Seestr.	B	31
St. Ulrich-Str.	B	28

Rathaus	B	R	Städtisches Museum	B	M

Rathaus (Town Hall)

🕐 *Open May–Oct, Mon–Fri 9am–noon, 2pm–4.30pm, Sat 9am–noon.* ☎(07551) 99 10 11.

The first-floor **Ratssaal**★ (Council Chamber) is decorated with great finesse in the Gothic manner: paneled walls embellished with projecting arches; ribbed, slightly rounded wooden ceiling; and a series of 15C statuettes.

Städtisches Museum (Municipal Museum)

🕐 *Open year-round, Tue–Sun 9am–12.30pm, 2pm–5pm (Apr–Oct, also Sun 10am–3pm).* ◉3€. ☎(07551) 99 10 79. Exhibits in this late 15C mansion with Baroque touches include paintings and sculpture by local artists from the Gothic period to Classicism, a collection of 18C crèches (*Krippen*) and 50 dollhouses from the Renaissance to Jugendstil.

ULM★★

POPULATION: 121 000

The royal palace of "Hulma", recorded for the first time in 854, was one of Europe's most important medieval cities. Blessed with an exceptional cathedral, the Old City delights visitors and walks along the Danube. Ulm's most famous local figure is Albert Einstein, born here in 1879.

- ℹ **Information:** Münsterplatz 50, 89073 Ulm. ☎(0731) 161 28 30. www.tourismus.ulm.de.
- ▸ **Orient Yourself:** Ulm is separated from Neu-Ulm by the river Danube and is about midway between Munich and Stuttgart on the A8 autobahn.
- 🅿 **Parking:** Garages can be found near the main train station and the Town Hall.
- ⊚ **Don't Miss:** Ulm's Cathedral and the suggested walking tour.
- 🕐 **Organizing Your Time:** Allow at least an hour to tour Ulm's cathedral, including a climb up the world's tallest church spire.
- **Kids Especially for Kids:** Ascending Ulm Cathedral's spire (older children).
- 🖒 **Also See:** OBERSCHWÄBISCHE BAROCKSTRASSE, SCHWÄBISCHE ALB, ROMANTISCHE STRASSE, NÖRDLINGEN.

Münster★★★

🕐*Open Jul–Aug, daily 9am–7.45pm; Apr–Jun & Sept to 6.45pm; Mar & Oct to 5.45pm; Nov–Feb to 4.45pm (tower closes one hour earlier). Tower ⊛4€. www. muenster-ulm.de.*

At a height of 161m/528ft, Ulm's cathedral spire is the tallest in the world and the most distinctive feature of the city skyline Although the foundation stone was laid in 1377, the two towers and spire were only added in 1890.

The Minster's **interior** also draws the eye skyward. The chancel arch bears the largest fresco north of the Alps, a 1471 work depicting the Last Judgment. To the right on the chancel arch stands the 15C *Man of Sorrows*, an early work by native Ulmer, Hans Multscher. The pulpit is canopied by a splendid wooden sounding board from 1510, the work of Jörg Syrlin the Younger. There is a second pulpit in the Late Gothic style further up that is intended for the Holy Spirit, the invisible preacher. The four side aisles feature fine Late Gothic fan vaulting.

Left of the entrance to the chancel is the **tabernacle**★, at 26m/85ft the tallest in Germany. This masterpiece (c. 1460–70) was chiseled out of limestone and sandstone. Three rows of wooden figures depict the prophets and lawmakers. Note the small figures of people and animals carved into the handrail of the

M. Hertlein/MICHELIN

At 161m528ft, the spire of Ulm cathedral is the tallest in the world

banister on which the artist has allowed his imagination to run riot.

The **choir stalls**★★★ are a marvelous example of wood carving, executed by Jörg Syrlin the Elder between 1469 and 1474. Two series of characters, from the Bible and from pagan antiquity, face one another. Men are grouped on the left, women on the right, the upper gables being devoted to the Church's apostles and martyrs, and the high backs of the stalls to Old Testament figures.

For many cathedral visitors, the highlight is a 768-step **ascent of the spire**. The structure resembles stone lacework in its upper reaches, revealing a **panorama**★★ not only of the town and Danbue but as far as the plateaux of the Swabian Jura and the Alps.

Sights

Stadthaus (Town Hall)

Ulm's white and glass Town Hall is a daring design by avant-garde architect Richard Meier.

A modern counterpoint to the venerable cathedral, it generated a lot of controversy when first completed in 1993, but it actually lends a casual air to the Münsterplatz and has since been accepted as an attractive link between the past and the present.

The Iconoclasts

Konrad Sam, a virulent preacher, brought the Swiss Reformation to Ulm in 1530, advocating the destruction of religious imagery. Following a referendum approved by 87% of the population, he made the cathedral Protestant. Private donors removed their altars and sealed the cathedral's central door, the stalls and the tabernacle. Some altars were given to neighbouring villages, where they remain today. The rage of the iconoclasts was unleashed on June 21, 1531: The remaining cathedral icons (60 altars, numerous statues, altarpieces and hangings) were destroyed.

Ulmer Museum★

🕐*Open year-round, Tue–Sun 11am–5pm, Thu to 8pm (special exhibit only).* 🕐*Closed Dec 24, 25 & 31.* ⊛*3.50€, Fri free.* ☎*(0731) 161 43 12. www.museum.ulm.de.*

This rambling museum has some great works by local masters. Note especially the *Virgin Mary of Bihlafingen* by Hans Multscher and the charming 13C *Mary of Sorrows*, edged in blue and gold, by a master from the Lake Constance area. The archeological department boasts the 30 000-year-old Stone Age "Lion Man" statuette, masterfully carved from a mammoth tusk.

Also part of the museum is the Late Renaissance **Kiechelhaus**, which is the only suviving Patrician mansion from the 16C–17C and provides insight into the lifestyle of a wealthy merchant family. A new modern building makes a suitable setting for the **Kurt Fried Collection** of 20C art, including works by Klee, Kandinsky, Kirchner and Rothko.

Kunsthalle Weishaupt

Hans-und-Sophie-Scholl-Platz 1. 🕐*Open year-round, Tue–Sun 11am–5pm, Thu to 8pm.* ⊛*6€.* ☎*(0731) 161 43 60.www.kunsthalle-weishaupt.de.*

A spectacular, modern glass and steel building, designed by Richard Meier student Wolfram Wöhr, houses one of the Germany's most important private collections of 20C art. Feast your eyes on Concrete Art (Albers, Richard Paul Lohse), American colorfield paintings (Rothko, Kenneth Noland), Pop Art (Warhol, Rauschenberg) as well as sculptures and installations by such high-profile practitioners as Keith Haring and the late Nam June Paik.

Altes Rathaus (Old Town Hall)

This elegant Gothic and Renaissance building features painted façades and an astronomical clock on its west façade. It borders the market square with the *Fischerkasten* fountain, thus named

Address Book

WHERE TO STAY

Pension Rösch – *Schwörhausgasse 18.* ☎*(0731) 657 18. 16 rooms.* This simple little hotel provides good value and clean rooms at the entrance to the picturesque fishermen's district.

Schiefes Haus – *Schwörhausgasse 6.* ☎*(0731) 96 79 30. www.hotels chiefeshausulm.de. 11 rooms.* This restored medieval house harmoniously marries historic and modern touches.

WHERE TO EAT

Weinkrüger – *Weinhofberg 7.* ☎*(0731) 649 76.* Enjoy regional specialties in the comfortable ambience of this former tannery. Dark wood and whimsical, handpicked décor give the dining room a cozy country feel.

Zunfthaus – *Fischergasse 31.* ☎*(0731) 644 11. www.zunfthaus-ulm. de. Reservations recommended.* Set in the heart of the old town, this 600-year-old half-timbered building once served as the guild of the fishermen

and shipbuilders. Today its three floors house a country-style restaurant serving regional cuisine, including locally caught fish.

TAKING A BREAK

Café Ströbele – *Hirschstraße 4.* ☎*(0731) 637 79. Shop closed Sun.* This beloved café makes habit-forming cakes (try the Schwarzwald Torte—Black Forest gâteaux), deliciously roasted coffee, and 40 types of chocolate.

NIGHTLIFE

Alexandre – *Marktplatz 1.* ☎*(0731) 602 74 90. www.alexandre-welt.de/ulm.* This charming French bistro-lounge on the ground floor of the old Town Hall features 16C murals and *Jugendstil* interior. In good weather, camp out on the Marktplatz terrace.

Barfüßer – *Paulstraße 4, 89231 Neu-Ulm* ☎*(0731) 97 44 80. www.barfuesser-brauhaus.de.* On balmy summer days, there are few places more idyllic than this riverside beer garden. Sample the home-made suds along with tasty nibbles and traditional dishes.

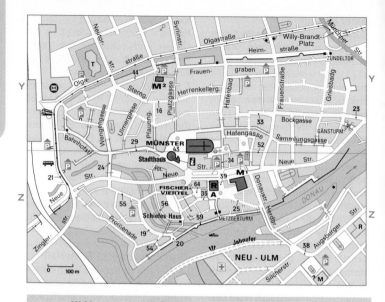

because fishermen would cool their wares in it. The spiral pedestal was fashioned by Jörg Syrlin the Elder in 1482.

Museum der Brotkultur★ (Museum of Bread Culture)

Salzstadelgasse 10.
⏱*Open year-round, daily 10am–5pm (Wed to 8.30pm).* ⏱*Closed Good Fri and Dec 24.* 🎫*3.50€.* ♿☎*(0731) 699 55. www. museum-brotkultur.de.*

8 000 years of the cultural and social history of bread is explored in this unique museum. Exhibits range from ovens, models, guilds, coins and stamps, to specially selected works of art (by Brueghel, Corinth, Kollwitz, Picasso), all related to grain or bread. The world's food supply is also critically examined.

Fischerviertel★ (Fishermen's Quarter)

The best place to begin an exploration of Ulm is in the narrow alleys emanating from the little Blau River in the quarter once inhabited by millers, fisherfolk and tanners. Begin in the Fischerplätzle, a small square shaded by a lime tree. Turn left into a narrow street and pass over

Baker's sign dating from 1820

Deutsches Brotmuseum, Ulm

Olympic Designs

Pictograms representing each of the Olympic disciplines were designed at the Ulm School of Design by German designer Otl Aicher for the Olympic Games in Munich in 1972. They have been used at each Games and are reproduced on the medals, to the great pride of the city.

the little bridge, which leads to the so-called mid-15C **Schiefes Haus** (crooked house) on the banks of the Balu. The tiny alley opposite is known as the **Kußgasse** (kissing alley) because the roofs of the houses touch one another. In the nearby 17C **Schwörhaus** (house of oaths) the town mayor swears allegiance to the 14C constitution and renews his oath of office on the first Monday of July.

The town **walls** afford a wonderful close-up of the gables of the old houses. The crooked **Metzgerturm** (butcher's tower), erected in 1349, stands out since it stands nearly 2.05m/6.7ft off center. Go through the rose garden to reach the **Adlerbastei** (eagle bastion), where the unfortunate "Tailor of Ulm" attempted to fly in 1811.

South bank of the Danube★

In fine weather, take a stroll along the pretty Jahnufer (the south bank of the Danube) to take in enchanting views of ornately gabled houses, the Metzgerturm and the cathedral.

Excursions

Kloster Wiblingen (Abbey)

5km/3mi south.
🕐*Open Apr–Oct, Tue–Fri 10am–1pm, 2pm–5pm, Sat–Sun, 10am–5pm; Nov–Mar, Sat–Sun 1pm–5pm.* 🕐*Closed Dec 24, 25 & 31.* 🎫*3.50€.* ☎*(0731) 502 89 75. www.kloster-wiblingen.de.*

Though founded in the 11C, final touches were not added to this abbey church until the 18C. As at Vierzehnheiligen (⬤*see WALLFAHRTSKIRCHE VIERZEHNHEILIGEN*), more than a third of the church's floor plan is occupied by the transept, where pilgrims worshipped

relics of the Holy Rood. Ceilings of the Baroque building are given the illusion of height with frescoes by painter Januarius Zick, who was also responsible for the high altar.

The **abbey library★**, completed in 1760, is one of the finest examples of the Rococo in Swabia; a column-supported gallery and false-relief ceiling fresco combine to create an ensemble rich in color and movement.

Blaubeuren★

18km/11mi west.

This village is renowned for its setting among the rocks and the **Blautopf** *(15min round-trip walk)*, a deep blue pool formed by a natural embankment of glacial origin. The shady approaches have been laid out as pleasant walks.

Nearby is the **Benedictine Abbey** *(allow 30min, follow the "Hochaltar" signs)*, which includes centuries-old half-timbered buildings. In the chancel of the **Klosterkirche** (abbey church) is a magnificent **Hochaltar★★** (altarpiece), a masterpiece of Gothic sculpture and a collective work created by the principal workshops operating in Ulm in the 15C. Themes treated are Christ's Birth and Passion, the life of St. John the Baptist, and the Virgin Mary surrounded by the saints. The beautiful choir **stalls★** of 1493 and the triple throne are the work of Ulm master Jörg Syrlin the Younger.

Old mill at the Blaubeuren village

INSEL USEDOM ★

Usedom's wonderfully unspoiled natural landscape is a pastiche of moors, estuaries, forests, dunes, sandy beaches and steep cliffs. The island is part of the Usedom-Oderhaff Nature Reserve and is dotted with elegant bathing resorts. For some time the island was known as "Berlin's bathtub" because of the large number of Berliners who came here to relax and recuperate.

- ⓘ **Information:** Waldstraße 1, 17429 Seebad Bansin. ☎(038372)-477 10. www.usedom.de.
- ▶ **Orient Yourself:** Usedom is Germany's easternmost island, although its far eastern portion, with the town of Swinoujscie, belongs to Poland. The flat northwest contrasts with the hilly south east, sometimes called Usedom's Switzerland.
- ☺ **Don't Miss:** The 19C beach resorts in the southeast.
- ⏱ **Organizing Your Time:** Allow one day to soak up the ambience of Usedom.
- **Kids Especially for Kids:** Outdoor recreation on sandy beaches and dunes.
- ⓖ **Also See:** GREIFSWALD, STRALSUND, INSEL RÜGEN.

Sights

Wolgast
On the mainland.
One point of access to Usedom is in the south at Zecherin; the other lies in the northwest, from Wolgast over the River Peene. The 14C **Pfarrkirche St. Petri** *(parish church;* ⏱*open May–Sept, Mon–Sat 10am–12.30pm, 1.30pm–5pm, Sun after the church service until noon;* ♿*☎(03836) 20 22 69)* is worth a visit. Its formidable octagonal tower and austere exterior contrast sharply with a sumptuous interior. Highlights include 15C–16C wall paintings and a 1700 *danse macabre* cycle painted by Caspar Sigmund Köppe based on a woodcut by Hans Holbein the Younger.

Krummin
East of Wolgast.
The most beautiful avenue of **lime trees**★ *(Lindenallee)* in Usedom leads to the right off B111 and extends to the little fishing village on the Krummin cove. The surfaced road is just 2km/1.2mi long but is marvelous; the arched canopy of leaves overhead gives the impression of being in a Gothic cathedral formed by Nature.

Peenemünde
In 1936, the German army located its V2 rocket-testing center to this spot on the northeastern tip of the island. A rocket museum, the **Historisch-Technisches Informationszentrum** *(*⏱ *open Apr–Sept, 10am–6pm; Oct–Mar to 4pm;*

Address Book

ⓖ *For coin ranges, see cover flap.*

WHERE TO STAY

⊜⊜⊜**Zur Post** – *Seestraße 5, 17429 Usedom-Bansin.* **Spa** ☎(038378) 560. *159 rooms. Restaurant* ⊜⊜⊜. A fine example of coastal architecture, this 1901 villa was enlarged with modern guesthouses and an elegant spa center. There are two restaurants, a casual one serving rib-sticking traditional cuisine, and an elegant dining room specialized in well-prepared international fare.

⊜⊜⊜⊜**Romantik Seehotel Ahlbecker Hof** – *Dünenstraße 47, 17419 Usedom-Ahlbeck.* **Spa** ☎(038378) 620. *70 rooms. Restaurant* ⊜⊜⊜. Set in a beautifully modernized Neoclassical mansion, this hotel satisfies even the most demanding patrons with its elegant and sumptuously outfitted rooms and spa complex. The crystal chandeliers and timeless ambience of the restaurant make this an unforgettable place to stay.

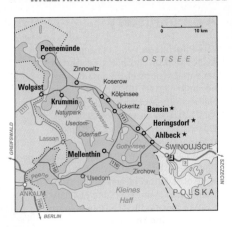

🕐*closed Dec 24–26, Nov–Mar, Mon;* ⬜6€; ♿☎*(038371) 50 50; www.peenemuende.de)* in the old power station, retraces the history of rocket development and its associated perils.

Usedoms "Taille" (Waist) [Kids]

At the island's narrowest point, the white sandy beaches of the resorts of **Zinnowitz**, **Kose-row**, **Kölpinsee** and **Ückeritz** lie side by side, protected by steep cliffs.

At Koserow, the island is barely 200m/220yd wide.

Bansin, Heringsdorf, Ahlbeck

These "three sisters" in the island's southeast are linked by a 10km/6.2mi-long beach promenade.

During the 19C, aristocrats and the merely moneyed convened in these fashionable resorts that were nicknamed "Kaiserbäder" (imperial spas). Numerous imposing and attractive late 19C beach villas and hotels with their typically frilly white wrought-iron decorations remain to this day.

Heringsdorf was an extraordinarily trendy resort and often visited Emperor Wilhelm II who resided in the still extant Villa Staudt *(Delbrückstraße 6)*. At 508m/1 666ft long, Heringsdorf's pier is the longest on mainland Europe.

Ahlbeck is also proud of its **historical pier**★, built in 1898. A restaurant was added in 1902. With its white walls, red roof and four green-roofed corner tow-ers, it is one of the most photographed subjects on the island.

Bansin is the westernmost of the resorts and maintains a more relaxed and fam-ily-friendly air.

Mellenthin

Northeast of the town of Usedom, 2km/1.2mi north of the B110.

This seldom-visited village and its Renaissance castle create a rural idyll. Although relatively plain, the three-winged castle surrounded by a moat boasts a colorfully mounted 17C Renais-sance fireplace in the entrance hall. The 14C village church in the town cemetery, though damaged, remains a little pearl with its 17C interior **decoration**★.

WALLFAHRTSKIRCHE VIERZEHNHEILIGEN★★

This pilgrimage church dedicated to the 14 Auxiliary Saints is a marvel of Baroque architecture created by the era's master builder Balthasar Neumann.

- **Information:** Vierzehnheiligen 2, 96231 Bad Staffelstein. ☎(09571)950 80. www.vierzehnheiligen.de.
- ▸ **Orient Yourself:** The church is 26km/16mi south east of Coburg, on an open hillside overlooking the Upper Main Valley.
- **Don't Miss:** The Rococo jewel, the Nothelfer Altar.
- **Organizing Your Time:** Allow one hour to see this pilgrimage church.
- **Also See:** BAMBERG, BAYREUTH, THÜRINGER WALD.

A Bit of History

The Pilgrimage – In 1445 and 1446, a shepherd on this hillside reported repeated visions of the Infant Jesus accompanied by the "Fourteen Holy Helpers". The worship of this group of saints, actively encouraged by German Dominicans and Cistercians, occurred in the early 15C, when Mysticism prevailed. Visions and voices were commonplace (those heard by Joan of Arc, born in 1412, were of St. Catherine and St. Margaret, themselves members of the Auxiliary Saints). Devotion to the Holy Helpers remained alive for many years, attracting crowds of pilgrims to a chapel which was superseded, in the 18C, by this sumptuous Rococo church.

Wallfahrtskirche

Visit

Exterior

The basilica is a handsome yellow ochre sandstone edifice built between 1743 and 1772 following designs by Balthasar Neumann. The west façade is framed by domed towers that are uncharacteristically tall for a Baroque building. The ornately decorated gables are adorned with a statue of Christ flanked by formerly gilded allegorical figures of Faith and Charity.

Interior

🕐*Open Mar–Oct, daily 6.30am–8.30pm; Nov–Feb, daily 7.30am–5.30pm.*

The interior layout is organized as a succession of three oval bays framed by colonnades and covered by low inner domes. The true center of the church is the bay containing the altar to the Auxiliary Saints. The church's Rococo decoration features outstanding color combinations inside the domes, delicate stuccowork, rich gold outlines defining the woodwork of the galleries, and graceful cherubs.

Nothelfer-Altar★★ (Altar to the Fourteen "Auxiliary Saints")

A Rococo pyramid with a pierced baldaquin, this remarkable work was designed by Johann Michel Küchel, a student of Balthasar Neumann, and executed by Johann Michael Feuchtmayr and his fellow stuccoworkers from the prestigious Wessobrunn School in 1764. It was placed in the physical center of the church, right where the shepherd's visions were believed to have occurred. Artistic representations include:

- **Balustrade**: 1) St. Denys 2) St. Blaise 3) St. Erasmus 4) St. Cyriacus (delivery from the Devil at the final hour).
- **Altar niches**: 5) St. Catherine, patron saint of the learned, of students and girls wishing to marry (signifying the model of Christian wisdom) 6) St. Barbara, patron saint of miners, artillerymen and prisoners (signifying the grace of a noble death).
- **Buttresses**: 7) St. Acacius (the agonies of death) 8) St. Giles, the only intercessor not to suffer martyrdom 9) St. Eustace (converted by the vision of a stag with a Cross between its antlers) 10) St. Christopher, patron saint of travelers.
- **Atop the baldaquin**: 11) St. Vitus 12) St. Margaret (intercession for the forgiveness of sins) 13) St. George, patron saint of peasants and their possessions 14) St. Pantaleon.

After exploring the abbey, trek up the slopes above the church for inspiring views of the edifice itself, the nearby fortress-like yellow sandstone abbey of Banz across the Main River, and the surrounding countryside.

WEIMAR★★

POPULATION: 64 400

To most non-Germans, Weimar recalls the ill-fated Republic which existed uneasily between World War I and the Hitler years. But the city's claim to a place in European history rests unerringly on the extraordinary flowering of intellectual and artistic talent over the centuries, attracting Luther, Cranach, Bach, Wieland, Schiller and Liszt. The one genius whose traces one cannot escape in Weimar is that greatest of all German classicists, Johann Wolfgang von Goethe.

- **Information:** Markt 10, 99423 Weimar. ☎(03643) 74 50. www.weimar.de.
- ▶ **Orient Yourself:** Set on the banks of the Ilm, Weimar is in the heart of Thuringia, around 20km/12.4mi from the state capital Erfurt. The A4 autobahn links the town with Dresden to the east and Frankfurt to the southwest (via the A5).
- **Parking:** Convenient central parking is in a garage near the Goethe House.
- **Don't Miss:** The suggested walking tour.
- **Organizing Your Time:** Allocate a full day to truly sample Weimar's legacy, especially if visiting Buchenwald.
- **Also See:** ERFURT, JENA, NAUMBURG.

A Bit of History

An Intellectual and Cultural Hotbed – Weimar's heyday coincided with the succession, in 1758, of Duchess Anna Amalia. It was during her reign that the town's intellectual reputation grew, largely because of **Goethe** (1749–1832). He was appointed minister of the small, provincial capital and produced here the majority of his life's work, including his dramatic masterpiece, *Faust*.

H. Champollion/MICHELIN

Goethe and Schiller, Weimar

Goethe's success went hand-in-hand with that of **Friedrich von Schiller**, who moved permanently to Weimar in 1799. The work produced by these two close friends, along with the writings of the theologian **Johann Gottfried Herder** (1744–1803), a disciple of Kant, raised Weimar's literary reputation to that of "home of German Classicism".

A couple of centuries earlier, from 1552 until his death a year later, **Lucas Cranach the Elder** had worked in Weimar on his final masterpiece: the altarpiece triptych for the parish church of St. Peter and St. Paul. **Johann Sebastian Bach** was organist and choirmaster here from 1708 to 1717. In 1848 **Franz Liszt** took the position, and became the driving force behind Weimar's School of Music, which still bears his name today.

In 1860, Grand Duke Alexander founded the **Weimarer Malerschule** (fine arts academy), where a veritable Who's Who of late 19C artists studied, including Hans Arp, Max Liebermann and Christian Rohlfs.

It was under the influence of such celebrated graduates as **Arnold Böcklin** (1827–1901) that painters spearheading the contemporary avant-garde movement developed "the Weimar School". Under Walter Gropius, the institution spawned the Bauhaus, a college of architecture and design.

The Weimar Republic (1919–33) – The constitution of the ill-fated Weimar Republic was drafted and adopted in 1919 by the German National Assembly, whose delegates convened at the Deutsches Nationaltheater (German National Theater).

The government itself, however, was never based in Weimar as members returned to Berlin just one week after adopting the text. The humanist tradition of Goethe's town had merely provided the budding democracy with a welcome counterpoint to the politically oppressive atmosphere of postwar Berlin.

Garden of Goethes Wohnhaus

Sights

Neues Museum
Weimarplatz 5.
🕐*Open Apr–Oct, Tue–Sun 11pm–6pm, Nov–Mar to 4pm.* *3.50€.* &♿*(03643) 54 59 63. www.klassik-stiftung.de.de.*
This 19C Neo-Renaissance building presents art by the international avant-garde since 1960, with emphasis on German art, Italian *Arte Povera*, and American Minimal and Conceptual Art. During the Third Reich it was the headquarters of Thuringia's Nazi administration.

Fürstengruft (Ducal Tomb)
Historischer Friedhof.
Johann Wolfgang von Goethe is buried alongside Grand Duke Carl August and other Weimar's ducal rulers in a **mausoleum** (🕐*open Apr–Oct, daily 10am–6pm, Nov–Mar to 4pm;* ⊜*2.50€)* on the 19C **Historischer Friedhof** (historical cemetery).
A 2006 investigation found that other remains believed to have been those of Schiller were in fact not.
The **Russian Orthodox Church** nearby was built in the 19C for Maria Pavlova, Grand Duchess and daughter-in-law of Carl August. Goethe's muse, Frau von Stein, is also buried in this cemetery.

Walking Tour

Historic Center★★

Weimar's chief highlights—mostly related to heroes of the German Renaissance or Enlightenment—cluster within a compact area in the lively pedestrian city center. The main squares are Theaterplatz, with the National Theater and Bauhaus Museum, and the neighboring Marktplatz.

Goethes Wohnhaus★★
(Goethe's Private Residene)
Frauenplan 1.
🕐*Open Apr–Sept, Tue–Sun 9am–6pm (Sat to 7pm); Oct to 6pm; Nov–Mar to 4pm.* ☛*Guided tours available.* 🕐*Closed Dec 24.* ⊜*6.50€.* ☎*(03643) 54 53 47. ww.klassik-stiftung.de.*
Germany's greatest man of letters lived in this 1709 Baroque mansion for 50 years, first as a tenant, then, after 1792, owner until his death in 1832. The interior is largely the way he left it. The living room, study, library and bedroom are all furnished with paintings and sculptures gathered by Goethe during his travels.

Goethe-Nationalmuseum
Frauenplan 1.
🕐*Same hours as Goethes Wohnhaus.* ⊜*3€. ww.klassik-stiftung.de.*
Next to Goethe's private home, the perment exhibit in this museum deals less with the man himself than the period of the Enlightenment and all the great minds that shaped it, including Wieland,

Herder, Schiller, Anna Amalia and her son, Duke Carl August.

▶ *Exit the museum and follow Ackerwand to to Haus der Frau von Stein.*

Haus der Frau von Stein
Ackerwand 25.
Goethe met Charlotte von Stein, lady-in-waiting to Anna Amalia, in November 1775. She was a young woman, then, who profoundly influenced him and his work. Today the building is home to the Goethe Institute language school and cultural center.

Platz der Demokratie
The equestrian statue of Grand Duke Carl August dominates this square. On the south side, the former palace (1757–74) is occupied by the **Franz Liszt Hochschule für Musik**. The 16C–18C **Grünes Schloss** (Green Palace) houses the **Duchess Anna Amalia Library** (🕐*open year-round, Tue–Sun 10am–3pm;* 🎫*6.50€;* ☎*(03643) 54 54 01*) with medieval manuscripts, early printed works, rare 16C–17C documents and 18C volumes. The library reopened in late 2007 after being partially destroyed in a devastating fire three years earlier

▶ *Leave Platz der Demokratie, head for the Markt and Cranach-Haus.*

Cranach-Haus
Markt 12.
The famous painter spent the last year of his life in this Renaissance house (1547–1549) adorned with scrolled gables. His studio was on the third floor.
The **Rathaus** (Town Hall), opposite, was built c. 1500 but was heavily remodeled in the mid-19C.

▶ *Take Schillerstraße toward Theaterplatz.*

Schillers Wohnhaus★ (Schiller's Private Residence)
Schillerstraße 12. 🕐*Open Apr–Sept, Wed–Mon 9am–6pm (Sat to 7pm); Oct, Wed–Mon 9am–6pm; Nov–Mar, Wed–Mon 9am–4pm.* 🕐*Closed Dec 24.* 🎫*4€.* ☎*(03643) 54 53 50. www.klassik-stiftung.de.*

Schiller moved here in 1802 to be near his great friend Goethe, and in this house wrote *William Tell* and *The Bride of Messina*. The museum examines his life and work.

▶ *Follow Schillerstraße until Theaterplatz.*

Deutsches Nationaltheater
Theaterplatz 2.
www.nationaltheater-weimar.de.
The present 1907 structure was built on the site of a 1779 Baroque building. It was in this previous theater that Schiller's great plays were staged and directed by Goethe, and it was here, in 1850, that Richard Wagner's *Lohengrin* was first performed. In 1919 the Weimar Republic constitution was adopted by the German National Assembly. In front of the present building stand the **statues★★** of Goethe and Schiller, sculpted in 1857 by Ernst Rietschel.

Bauhaus-Museum
Theaterplatz. 🕐*Open year-round, daily 10am–6pm.* 🎫*4.50€.* ☎*(03643) 54 59 61. www.klassik-stiftung.de.*
The Bauhaus School was founded in 1919 Weimar by Walter Gropius and cohorts and occupied this building until the group was forced to move to Dessau in 1925. The small permanent collection introduces the major players, their innovative approach to architecture and design and their impact on the modern aesthetic. Exhibits also pay homage to the School of Applied Arts founded in Weimar in 1908 by Henry Van de Velde.

Wittumspalais
Theaterplatz. 🕐*Open Apr–Oct, Tue–Sun 9am–6pm; Nov–Mar to 4pm.* 🕐*Closed Dec 24.* 🎫*4€.* ☎*(03643) 54 53 77. www.klassik-stiftung.de.*
After her husband's death, Anna Amalia moved to this Baroque palace where she held her illustrious salons with Goethe, Schiller, Herder and Wieland in attendance. Rooms are representative of the late 18C for a person of her standing. Note the Neoclassical ballroom and the late Baroque ceiling frescoes.

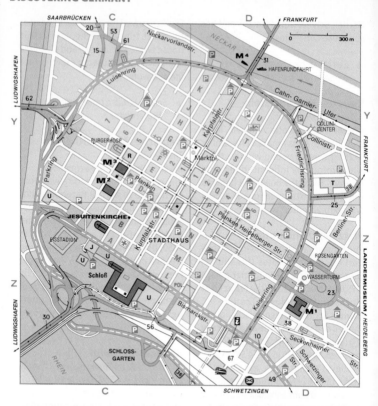

WEIMAR

		Frauenplan	BZ 18	Markt	BZ
		Frauentorstr.	BZ 19	Rittergasse	BZ 36
Am Poseckschen Garten	BZ 6	Heinrich-Haine-Str.	AZ 25	Schillerstr.	BZ 37
Amalienstr.	BZ 4	Jakobstr.	BYZ 27	Schloßgasse	BZ 39
Brennerstr.	BY 7	Karl-Liebknecht-Str.	BZ 30	Zeughof	BZ 42
Carl-August-Allee	BY 12	Kaufstr.	BZ 31		
Ernst-Kohl-Str.	AY 13	Marienstr.	BZ 34		

Bauhaus-Museum	BZ M¹	Herzogin Anna Amalia		Rathaus	BZ R
Deutsches National-		Bibliothek	BZB	Russich-orthodoxe	
Theater	ABZ T	Hochschule für Musik		Kapelle	BZ K
Haus der Frau von Stein	BZ A	Franz Liszt	BZ D	Wittumspalais	BZ M²

▶ *Go to Herderplatz via Zeughof, then Rittergasse.*

Stadtkirche St. Peter und Paul (or Herderkirche)

Am Herderplatz.

This triple-nave Gothic hall-church was built between 1498–1500 but thoroughly remodeled in the Baroque style in the 18C. It is also known as the Herderkirche, in memory of the sermons preached here between 1776 and 1803 by the philosopher, Johann Gottfried Herder, who is buried in the church.

The famous **Cranach Triptych**★★, begun by Lucas Cranach the Elder and finished by his son in 1555, represents the Crucifixion on its central panel and is surrounded by scenes from the Old and New Testaments. On the right are Luther and Cranach the Elder.

Schlossmuseum (Palace Museum)

🕐*Open Apr–Oct, Tue–Sun 10am–6pm, Nov–Mar to 4pm.* ⊕*5€.* ☎*(03643) 54 59 60. www.klassikstiftung.de.*

Address Book

For coin ranges, see cover flap.

WHERE TO STAY

Hotel Zur Sonne – *Rollplatz 2.* ☎*(03643) 862 90. www.thueringen. info/index.php?id=1229. 21 rooms. Restaurant.* This neat brick house is in the heart of the old town. Inside the style is modern, with attractively furnished rooms and no-nonsense tavern-style restaurant.

Romantik Hotel Dorotheen-hof – *Dorotheenhof 1, 99427 Wei-Mar–Schöndorf.* ☎*(03643) 45 90. www. dorotheenhof.com. 60 rooms. Restaurant*. This pretty hotel, in an idyllic park location abovethe town, used to belong to a 19C calvary captain and now delights guests with cozy country-style rooms. The elegant restaurant is cano-pied by a charming vaulted ceiling.

WHERE TO EAT

Sommer's Weinstube Restaurant – *Humboldtstraße 2.* ☎*(03643) 40 06 91. www.wein-sommer.com. Closed Sun.* This family-run restaurant has been popular for over 130 years and retains its old-fashioned charm. Thuringian specialties, often potato-based, go well with the regional and international wines.

Bratwurstglöck'l – *Carl-August-Allee 17a.* ☎*(03643) 20 28 75. Closed Mon.* Built in 1870, this traditional German sausage temple is close to the train station and has atmospheric wood-pan-elling and beautiful décor. Tasty links dominate the menu but other regional staples are served as well.

Gasthaus zum Weissen Schwan – *Frauentorstrase 23.* ☎*(03643) 90 87 51. www.weisserschwan.de. Closed Jan–Feb, Mon and Tue.* This historical inn was Goethe's favorite hang-out and still captures the rustic lyricism of his times.

NIGHTLIFE

Crêperie du Palais – *Am Palais 1 (east of Wittumspalais).* ☎*(03643) 40 15 81. www.creperie-weimar.de. Closed second week in Jan.* Run with charm and panache by a Franco-German couple, this delightful eatery has generated a buzz with its crêpes and galettes (buck-wheat-based pancakes) made with a great variety of delectable fillings.

Residenz-Café – *Grüner Markt 4 (near Stadtschloss).* ☎*(03643) 594 08. www. residenz-cafe.de.* This Weimar institution in an 1839 building caters to all tastes, budgets and times of days—breakfast to lunch, afternoon coffee to nightcap.

An early 19C palace built for Duke Carl August, the Stadtschloß features some of Germany's finest Neoclassicist apart-ments and important Weimar artworks. Highlights include an important **Cran-ach collection**★★; Flemish and Italian paintings; and work by Hans Baldung Grien, Albrecht Dürer and Bartholomäus Bruyn the Elder. The Weimar School and German Impressionists and Expression-ists (Max Beckmann, Max Liebermann) are also represented.

Ilm Park★★

"Weimar is in fact a park in which they happened to build a town," wrote Adolf Stahr in 1851. Expansive green spaces continue to shape modern Weimar. Its magnificent riverside park parallels both banks of the Ilm River from the palace of Tiefurt to the Belvedere and is only a few yards from the town center.

Goethes Gartenhaus★★

Open Apr–Oct, daily 10am–6pm, Nov–Mar to 4pm. 3.50€. ☎*(03643) 54 53 75. www.weimar–klassik.de.*
Duke Carl August gave this summer resi-dence as a gift to Goethe and the great man liked it so much that he frequently used it a retreat until the end of his life. *Wilhelm Meister's Theatrical Mission,* major parts of *Iphigenia,* and early drafts of *Egmont* and *Torquato Tasso* were written in this humble cottage.

▶ *Cross the park in the direction of the Belvederer Allee.*

Liszt-Haus

Open Apr–Oct, Wed–Mon 10am–6pm. Closed Nov–Mar. 4€. *(03643) 54 53 88. www.weimar–klassik.de.*

The great composer lived and taught in this converted garden house between 1869 and 1886. The period rooms are preserved so neatly, it feels as though Liszt could be returning any moment. His study, living-, dining- and bed rooms are filled with personal items; note the Bechstein grand piano.

Excursions

Schloss Tiefurt (Tiefurt Palace)

2km/1.2mi east, Hauptstraße 14. Open Apr–Oct, Wed–Sun 10am–6pm. Closed Nov–Mar. Park open year-round. 3.50€. *(03643) 85 06 66.*

Duchess Amalia's 18C summer residence sits amid English-style gardens. This is where she hosted many of her literary salons that often included Goethe and the Humboldt brothers. Furnishings provide a glimpse into the period.

Schloss Belvedere

4km/2.5mi southeast. Open Apr–Oct, Tue–Sun 10am–6pm. Closed Nov–Mar. Park open year-round. 4€. *(03643) 54 69 62.*

Delightful and artistically successful, this Baroque pleasure palace was built for Duke Ernst August in 1828 and served as Duchess Amalia's summer residence between 1756 and 1775. Rooms showcase 18C court life through a series of period rooms filled with fine furniture, porcelain, glass and weapons.

Buchenwald Museum & Memorial

8km/5mi northwest.

Open Apr–Oct, Tue–Sun 10am–6pm; Nov–Mar to 4pm. Grounds open until dusk. Closed Jan 1, Dec 24–26 & 31. *(03643) 43 02 00. www.buchenwald.de.*

Only a short distance from Weimar, in the Ettersberg beech forests, stood one of the largest Nazi concentration camps. Some 250 000 people were deported to Buchenwald; more than 50 000 died there. The camp was liberated by Americans troops on April 11, 1945.

The **Gedenkstätte Buchenwald** (Memorial Center) shows a film tracing the history of the camp. A tour of the camp starts at the gatehouse, still bearing the chilling slogan: "Jedem das Seine" ("You get what you deserve").

Each residential barrack is outlined on the ground; at the far end a building used for storing the inmates' possessions and effects is now a museum. Outside the camp, a road leads to the quarry where many prisoners were essentially worked to death.

From 1945 to 1950, the Soviet occupation force set up **Special Camp 2**, in which Nazi criminals, officials and political prisoners were interned. Over 7 000 are believed to have died here. From the entrance (*1km/0.6mi toward Weimar*) the Steles' Way leads to the **Avenue of Nations**, which links three mass graves. The last of these brings you to the **Mahnmal Buchenwald** (Buchenwald Memorial).

In August 1943, about 100km/62mi north of Weimar near Nordhausen, Nazis also set up an auxiliary camp called **Dora**. Prisoners were forced to convert underground shafts into a manufacturing plant for V-2 rockets. The factory's unsuitable location, appalling hygiene and inhumane working conditions resulted in the deaths of some 20 000 people in its 20 months of operation. Dora is also now a memorial and museum; some factory shafts are open to visitors as part of a guided tour.

WIESBADEN★

POPULATION: 272 000

Lying at the foot of the Taunus mountains and favored by the mild climate of the Rhine Valley, the capital city of Hessen has the refined atmosphere of a spa town and the flair of an elegant city.

- **Information:** Marktstraße 6, 65183 Wiesbaden. ☎(0611) 172 97 80. www. wiesbaden.de.
- ▶ **Orient Yourself:** Some 40km/24.8mi west of Frankfurt and across the Rhine from Mainz, Wiesbaden is reached via the A63 or the A67 autobahns from the south, and the A3 or the A5 from the north. Take the A66 if you are coming from Frankfurt.
- **Parking:** Old City parking garages can be found near the market on Bahnhofstraße and at Neugasse and Friedrichstraße.
- **Don't Miss:** A peak at the Kurhaus and its park and gardens.
- **Organizing Your Time:** Allow one hour each for the Old Town and the Spa Quarter.
- **Also See:** MAINZ, FRANKFURT AM MAIN, RHEINTAL.

A Bit of History

An International Spa Town – The ancient Romans were aware of the benefits of the 26 hot sodium chloride springs (46–66°C/115–150°F), and Pliny noted with surprise that the water from the springs stayed warm for three days. In the 9C, Wiesbaden was first called "Wisibada" (spa in the meadows).

The middle of the 19C saw the start of Wiesbaden's heyday as a spa town, when it became a gathering spot for the crowned heads and higher nobility of the world. Modern Wiesbaden enjoys an excellent reputation as a spa resort specializing in rheumatism and sports a state-of-the-art rehabilitation clinic.

Sights

Old Town

The largely pedestrianized town center wraps around the *Schlossplatz*. Shop-lined Landgasse and Neugasse are two particularly lively streets.

Schlossplatz (Palace Square)

This elegant and well-proportioned square is the heart of the town. It is lined with beautiful buildings and hosts a market twice weekly.

The former residence of the dukes of Nassau, the 19C **Schloss** was built in the unadorned Neoclassical style and today is the seat of the Hessen Parliament.

Altes Rathaus (Old Town Hall)

Built in 1609–10 and the city's oldest surviving building, the Old Town Hall retains its Late Renaissance style on the ground floor. The upper story dates

Address Book

For coin ranges, see cover flap.

WHERE TO STAY

Drei Lilien – *Spiegelgasse 3.* ☎*(0611) 99 17 80. www.dreililien.com. 15 rooms.* In a Jugendstil villa, this hotel offers individually furnished rooms mixed with historical details and a high degree of comfort. Days start with a lavish breakfast.

WHERE TO EAT

Käfer's Bistro – *Kurhausplatz 1 (inside the Kurhaus).* ☎*(0611) 53 62 00.* This restaurant is inside the lavish Kurhaus and Casino constructed in 1907 in Wilhelminian style. Paintings and wood dominate the décor of the beautiful dining room and there is a sunny terrace for those balmy summer days.

from 1828 and bears the Romantic Historicist style.

Neues Rathaus (New Town Hall)

Georg Hauberisser, architect of the Munich Town Hall, erected this building in the German Renaissance style in 1886–87. It was destroyed in World War II and has been rebuilt since.

Marktkirche (Market Church)

This first brick-built church in the Nassau region was erected in the mid-19C. Its architect, Carl Boos, copied the Schinkel-designed Friedrichwerder church in Berlin. A carillon chimes daily at 9am, noon and 5pm.

Spa Quarter Spa

The spa quarter has developed west of the old town.

Kaiser-Friedrich-Therme (Emperor Friedrich Baths)

Langgasse 38–42.
⊙*Open year-round, Sun–Thu 10am–10pm, Fri–Sat 10am–midnight.* ☞*3.50€ Apr–Sept, 5€ Oct–Mar.* ☎ *(0611) 172 96 60.*
This Jugendstil building boasts impressive frescoes in the entrance hall and a Roman-Irish steam bath festooned in glazed tiles. It is a fantastic place for visitors to enjoy Wiesbaden's famous thermal springs.

Kochbrunnen

This fountain is made up of 15 springs. Its hot salty water contains iron, evident from the reddish deposit on the granite basin. The octangular Kochbrunnen Temple dates from 1854.

Kurhaus★ (Casino & Conference Center)

A lawn as flat as a bowling green, flanked by colonnades and lofty plane trees, leads up to what Emperor Wilhelm II called "the most beautiful *Kurhaus* in the world." Built in 1907, the sumptuous interior has always been a social gathering spot for spa visitors. Today is it used as a conference center, but to enjoy its special ambience, you need to visit the Casino, where Dostoyevsky

Kurhaus, Wiesbaden

allegedly found inspiration for his novel *The Gambler.* ☞Men must wear a jacket and tie to get inside the Casino.

Staatstheater

The impressive 19C Renaissance-style building lies south of the theater colonnades. The taste for lavish decoration is evident in its Rococo foyer.

Kurpark★ (Spa Gardens)

A vast park, laid out in 1852, stretches east behind the Kurpark. Sonnenberger Straße *(to the north)* and Parkstraße *(to the south)* are flanked by magnificent villas from the Gründerzeit (late 19C).

Wilhelmstraße to Neroberg area

Museum Wiesbaden

⊙*Open year-round, Tue 10am–8pm, Wed–Sun 10am–5pm.* ⊙*Closed Jan 1, May 1, Dec 24, 25 & 31.* ☞*4€.* &☎*(0611) 335 22 50. www.museum-wiesbaden.de.*
This newly renovated museum comprises the **natural sciences collection**, the **collection of Nassau antiquities** and the **art collections**, including the world's largest **Jawlensky collection★**. (The artist lived in Wiesbaden from 1921 until his death in 1941.) Featured here are works from the 16C–17C, the Classical period and the present.

Wiesbaden's main street, **Wilhelm-straße**, is lined on one side by elegant shops and on the other by the "Warmer Damm" park, which leads to the Staatstheater. Antique dealers have set up along **Taunusstraße**, which leads to the **Nerotal** park.

Nerobergbahn★ `Kids`

🕐*Open Good Fri–Apr, Sept–Oct, Wed noon–7pm, Sat–Sun 10am–7pm; May–Aug, daily 9.30am–8pm.* 🎟*3€ round-trip (child 1.50€).* ☎ *(0611) 236 85 00. www. nerobergbahn.de.*

The water-powered funicular railway, which still runs as smoothly as when it was built in 1888, is a monument to technical achievement. It leads up the Neroberg, Wiesbaden's local mountain, 245m/804ft in height, from which you can enjoy panoramic **views**★.

Russisch-Orthodoxe Kirche (Russian Orthodox Church)

Christian-Spielmann-Weg 2.
🕐*Open May–Oct, Sat–Sun 10am–5pm; Nov–Apr, noon–4pm.* ☎ *(0611) 52 84 94.*

Atop the Neroberg, this church (which is also known as Greek Chapel) was built by Duke Adolf of Nassau in 1847–55 in memory of his wife Elisabeth, a Russian grand duchess who died at age 19. It includes a central building with five gilded cupolas, which overlook the whole city. The elegant marble tomb, a copy of Rauch's tomb for Queen Luise in Berlin-Charlottenburg, was created by Emil Alexander Hopfgarten.

WIESKIRCHE★★

CHURCH IN THE MEADOW

The Wieskirche, whose full name is Pilgrimage Church of the Scourged Savior, is a masterpiece of Bavarian Rococo masterminded by the architect Dominikus Zimmermann in the 18C. It has been on UNESCO's World Heritage List since 1983.

- **Information:** Wies 12, 86989 Steingaden. ☎ (08862) 93 29 30. www.wieskirche.de.
- **Orient Yourself:** The Wieskirche is in Steingaden, about 25km/15.5mi northeast of Füssen, at the foot of the Ammergau Alps.
- **Don't Miss:** The extraordinary Rococo detail of the cupola and upper walls.
- **Organizing Your Time:** Allow one hour to see the Wieskirche.
- **Also See:** DEUTSCHE ALPENSTRASSE, FÜSSEN, SCHLOSS NEUSCHWANSTEIN, SCHLOSS LINDERHOF, GARMISCH-PARTENKIRCHEN.

Visit

Exterior and Interior

🕐*Open May–Oct, daily 8am–7pm; Nov–Apr to 5pm.* 🎟*Donations appreciated.* ♿ ☎ *(08862) 93 29 30. www. wieskirche.de.*

The elegantly understated church exterior leaves visitors unprepared for the splendor of the interior. Gilded stucco, wood carvings and vivid frescoes stand out from the white walls, bathed in subtle light entering the windows.

The lower parts of the interior are sparsely decorated to symbolize the Earth. The upper reaches (the heavens) vibrate with a profusion of frescoes, stucco and gilded work. The immense **cupola fresco** represents the Second Coming, the Gates of Paradise (still closed) and the Last Judgment.

The decoration of the **choir** is unparalleled: columns, balustrades, statues, gilded stuccoes and frescoes form a glorious symphony of color.

In the center of the church is a figure of the flagellated Christ. In 1738, a local farmer noticed tears in the eyes of the statue.

This prompted such a pilgrimage rush that the local abbot commissioned this magnificent church to accommodate everyone. To this day, up to one million people visit every year.

BAD WIMPFEN★★

POPULATION 6 900

This small fortified town with its half-timbered houses along narrow streets is built overlooking the River Neckar. Along the foot of the hill are the Ludwigshalle salt works, the production of which once brought prosperity to the whole region.

- ▤ **Information:** Carl-Ulrich-Straße 1, 74206 Bad Wimpfen. ☎(07063) 972 00. www.badwimpfen.de.
- ▶ **Orient Yourself:** Bad Wimpfen is a short distance from the A6 (Mannheim–Nürnberg). From Heidelberg, travel along the Neckar via the stunning B37.
- 😋 **Don't Miss:** The suggested driving tour through the Neckar Valley.
- 🕐 **Organizing Your Time:** Allow one and a half hours for the suggested walking tour, four hours for the excursions.
- ⛄ **Also See:** KLOSTER MAULBRONN, HEIDELBERG, SCHWÄBISCH HALL.

Walking Tour

Wimpfen am Berg★★ (Upper Town)
Start from Marktplatz (see map).

Kaiserpfalz (Imperial Palace)
Behind the Rathaus (Town Hall) are remains of the Kaiserpfalz with the

Blauer Turm (Blue Tower) from which views extend over the town and the Neckar Valley. Farther on is the 16C Romanesque **Steinhaus** (Stone House), where a museum traces the history of Bad Wimpfen since Roman times.

▶ *Continue to follow the wall to the staircase on the right, which leads to*

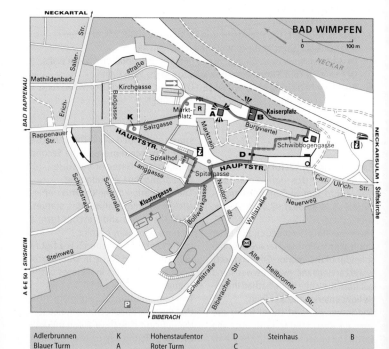

Adlerbrunnen	K	Hohenstaufentor	D	Steinhaus	B
Blauer Turm	A	Roter Turm	C		

View of Hirschhorn am Neckar

T. Krieger/MICHELIN

*the spur on which the town is
built, below the* **Roter Turm**
*(Red Tower)—the fortress' final
defensive point.*

Historic Streets
In **Klostergasse** are a number of half-
timbered houses. On the left are the
former bathhouses, recognizable by
their outside galleries. Explore more of
the town's streets via Langgasse, which
leads to **Hauptstraße**★ by way of a
narrow alley on the right. At no 45 is the
courtyard of a former hospital *(Spital-
hof)*, with half-timbered houses that are
among the oldest buildings in town.

▶ *Return along Hauptstraße, with its
picturesque, finely worked signs,
and pass the 1576* **Adlerbrunnen**
*(Eagle Fountain) before returning to
Marktplatz via Salzgasse.*

Wimpfen im Tal (Lower Town)
The Gothic Stiftskirche St. Peter und St.
Paul (parish church) has retained a strik-
ingly plain west façade from an earlier
Romanesque building. The **cloister**★★
shows the evolution of the Gothic style.
The north gallery (c. 1350), already more
angular in design, marks the transition
to the Renaissance. ☞ *Guided tour (1hr)
by prior appointment.* ☎(07063) 970 40.

Excursions

Neckartal★

Downstream from Bad Wimpfen, the
Neckar Valley cuts through the sandstone massif of the Odenwald, many of
its hills crowned by castles.

Neckarsulm
10km/6.2mi southeast.
The former Teutonic castle now houses
the bicycles and motorcycles of the
Deutsches Zweiradmuseum *(German Bi-ped Museum;* ◷*open year-round,
Tue–Sun 9am–5pm, Thu to 7pm;* ◷*closed
Dec 24 & 31.* ◠*4.50€.* &☎*(07132) 352
71).* Nearby is the Audi plant, originally
the NSU motor factory, which produced
Germany's first bicycles.

Sinsheim
25km/15.5mi west via Steinweg.
Mechanized vehicles of many types
comprise the 🅺🅸🅳🆂 **Auto- und Technik-
museum** *(Car & Technology Museum;*
◷ *open year-round, Mon–Fri 9am–
6pm, Sat–Sun to 7pm;* ◠*12.50€, 17€
with IMAX; up to 14yrs 10.50€, 13€ with
IMAX;* &☎*(07261) 929 90; www.technik-
museum.de).*
In the first building are early 20C trac-
tors, locomotives, luxury cars and a replica of a 19C hang-glider, the Lilienthal.
A second building exhibits military
vehicles.

An **IMAX cinema** shows 3D films such as *Abenteuer Grand Canyon* (The Grand Canyon Adventure), which will delight adults and children alike.

Burg Guttenberg

9km/5.6mi north of Bad Wimpfen. 🕐*Open Mar, Mon–Fri noon–6pm, Sat–Sun 10am–6pm; Apr–Oct, daily 10am–6pm; Mar & Nov on request.* 🎫4€. ☎(06266) 228. *www.burg-guttenberg.de.* A massive defensive wall protects this **castle**, which shelters rare collections of **objets d'art**★ and archives. Note the 18C "Library-Herbarium" in which plants are encased in 92 "wooden books".

Burg Hornberg

1.5km/1mi outside Neckarzimmern. 🕐*Open Thu-Fri from 6pm, Sat from 3pm, Sun from 11am.* 🎫3€. ☎(06261) 50 01. *www.burg-hornberg.de.*

Crowning a vine-covered hill, this **castle** is easily recognized from afar by its tall keep. A **museum** features the armor of Götz von Berlichingen, who died here in 1562. This knight, popularized in German folklore as a Robin Hood figure, was immortalized in a play by Goethe.

Hirschhorn am Neckar★

38km/23.6mi northwest of Burg Hornberg. The castle stands on a fortified spur. From the terrace and tower *(121 steps)* the **view**★ encompasses the wooded slopes of the Neckar Valley.

Neckarsteinach

Four castles stand on a narrow ridge overlooking the village: the Vorderburg and Mittelburg castles are privately owned. Hinterburg Castle (c. 1100) is the oldest and is now in ruins. Burg Schadeck, also in ruins, is a small 13C castle known as "swallow's nest".

WISMAR★

POPULATION 45 700

Midway between Rostock and Lübeck, Wismar is known for its fisheries and naval dockyards. Evidence of the Swedish reign in the 17C and 18C remains throughout town today. In 2002, the historic town center with its characteristic step-gabled red-brick houses was included on the UNESCO World Heritage List.

🛈 **Information:** Am Markt 11, 23966 Wismar. ☎(03841) 251 30 25. www.wismar.de.
▶ **Orient Yourself:** Wismar hugs a bay in the Baltic Sea opposite the island of Poel. The A20 links the town to Lübeck.
👁 **Don't Miss:** Meandering through the Old Town.
🕐 **Organizing Your Time:** Allow three hours to explore the Old Town.
👶 **Especially for Kids:** A visit to Poel Island.
🕯 **Also See:** BAD DOBERAN, ROSTOCK, LÜBECK, SCHWERIN.

D. Scherf/MICHELIN

Wismar harbour

A Bit of History

A trading town – Wismar dates back to 1229 and enjoyed a heyday as a member of the Hanseatic League. Breweries and wool-weaving were further sources of wealth. Wismar's downfall came at the end of the Thirty Years' War, when it fell under Swedish rule, staying until 1803.

Marktplatz★ (Market Square)

Situated in the old town, Wismar's Marktplatz—one of the largest town squares in Germany—is dominated by the white Neoclassical **Rathaus** (Town Hall), built between 1817–19. A permanent **exhibit** (🕐 *open year-round, daily 10am–6pm; ⊜1.50€) on* town history is to be found in the beautifully vaulted cellars.

Other gabled houses from various eras frame the rest of the square. The most eye-catching is the **Alter Schwede** (Old Swede) on the east side, which dates back to 1380. On the right is the **Reuterhaus**, a now-UNESCO building where the works of the Mecklenburg writer Fritz Reuter were published. Destroyed during the DDR, the building was fully reconstructed in the late 1980s, now housing a hotel/restaurant; the house on its left sports charming Jugendstil ornamentation. On the southeast side of the market stands an artistic pavilion, the **Wasserkunst★** (waterworks). It was built in 1580–1602 in the Dutch Renaissance style and supplied the town with water for centuries.

Marienkirchturm (Church of St. Mary's Tower)

🕐 *Open May–Sept, daily 8am–8pm, Apr & Oct, 10am–6pm, Nov–Mar 11am–4pm.* Only the 80m/262ft-high **tower** remains of the early 13C Marienkirche, which was destroyed during World War II. A carillon comes to life at noon, 3pm and 7pm.

Fürstenhof (Palace)

Originally the seat of the dukes of Mecklenburg, this large building was erected in two phases. The older, western, wing dates to 1512/13 and is Late Gothic in style, while the longer "New House" from 1553–55 shows off elements of the Italian Renaissance, including impressive pilasters and terracotta friezes. Those facing the road represent the Trojan Wars; those facing the courtyard, the parable of the Prodigal Son.

Grube ("Ditch")

The "Grube" is one of Germany's oldest artificial watercourses running through a town (1255). It served as a source of water for drinking and domestic use right up into the 20C.

Schabbellhaus★

Schweinsbrücke 8.
🕐 *Open May–Oct, Tue–Sun 10am–8pm, Nov–Apr to 5pm.* ⊜2€. ☎(03841) 28 23 50. www.schabbellhaus.de.
This sumptuously decorated red-brick building was built 1569–71 as the brewery and home of the later mayor, Hin-

Address Book

For coin ranges, see cover flap.

WHERE TO STAY

Willert – *Schweriner Straße 9. (03841) 261 20. www.hotel-willert. m-vp.de. 14 rooms.* This Jugendstil villa (1910) was meticulously restored in the 1990s. Rooms are modern and elegant; some stucco ceilings are original.

Reuterhaus – *Am Markt 19. (03841) 222 30. www.hotel-reuterhaus. de. 10 rooms. Restaurant .* This small hotel in a nicely renovated building on the market square has rather large, comfortable rooms tastefully outfitted with Italian furniture. The elaborately carved wainscoting lends traditional charm to the restaurant.

rich Schabbell, and is one of the oldest Renaissance buildings in the Baltic area. The house is now home to a local history museum with a special section on medical history.

St. Nikolaikirche★

Open Apr & Oct, daily 10am–6pm; May–Sept, 8am–8pm; Nov–Mar, 11am–4pm. 1€. (03841) 13 81 14 87.
Built between 1381 and 1487, this brick church's central nave soars skyward for 37m/121.4ft, making it the fourth highest in Germany. The **Altar der Krämergilde★** (Grocers' Guild Altarpiece), a 15C hinged, paneled altarpiece, is worth a closer look. The 1335 bronze font originally stood in the Marienkirche; it depicts the Life of Christ, the Last Judgment and the Wise and Foolish Virgins.

Alter Hafen (Old Harbor)

From the Grube and the idyllic street Am Lohberg, just a few steps lead to the harbor, at the end of which stands an unadorned Baroque building, the **Baumhaus** (tree house).

Excursion

Insel Poel   Kids

This little Baltic island north of Wismar makes a pleasant day trip. Poel's charming seaside villages and wild coastal stretches invite exploration.
The flat relief makes a perfect cycling destination; the local tourist office has bikes for hire.

LUTHERSTADT WITTENBERG

POPULATION: 46 770

Wittenberg was the center of Martin Luther's work and the place where, on October 31, 1517, he posted his famous "95 Theses" against Church corruption. This was a key step toward the Reformation and a new era in the religious and political history of the Western world. Sites related to Luther and his fellow reformer Philipp Melanchton were inscribed on UNESCO's list of World Heritage Sites in 1996. A renowned university town, Wittenberg also attracted many other talented people, including the master painter, Lucas Cranach the Elder.

- **Information:** Schloßplatz 2, 06886 Wittenberg. (03491) 49 86 10. www.wittenberg.de.
- **Orient Yourself:** Wittenberg enjoys a pleasant location between the wooded hills of Fläming and the Elbe. To reach the town from the A9, take exit 8 and follow the B187 toward Coswig, then Wittenberg.
- **Don't Miss:** The Castle Church and the Luther House.
- **Organizing Your Time:** Budget about one day for Wittenberg.
- **Also See:** WÖRLITZER PARK, DESSAU.

Philipp Melanchthon (1497–1560)

A gifted Humanist with a perfect command of Greek and Latin, Philipp Melanchthon entered Heidelberg University at age twelve and finished his studies at the Faculty of Philosophy in Tübingen. He became professor of Greek at Wittenberg in 1518 and made a strong impression on Martin Luther. The two men became close friends and Melanchthon became an ardent defender of the Reformation. The strength of his Loci communes of 1521 contributed greatly toward the spread of Protestantism. Melanchthon, who became head of the Lutheran church after Luther's death, was an open and tolerant man; driven by a desire to reconcile Protestant and Catholic dogmas, he was resented by the most orthodox Lutherans.

A Bit of History

A Key Town in the Reformation – Summoned by the Elector Friedrich the Wise (1502) to teach philosophy at his newly founded university, **Martin Luther** was at the same time appointed the town preacher. In 1547, a year after Luther's death, **Emperor Charles V** seized Wittenberg and reputedly meditated over the tomb of the great Reformer. The Lutherstadt prefix was added to Wittenberg in 1938.

Sights

Schloßkirche★ (Castle Church)
Am Schloßplatz.
⟳*Open Good Fri–Oct, Mon–Sat 10am–6pm, Sun 11.30am–6pm; Nov–Good Fri to 4pm; ⇆Contribution requested. Tower: Good Fri–Oct, Mon–Fri noon–4pm, Sat–Sun 10am–5pm; ⇆2€. ☎(03491) 40 25 85. www.schlosskirche-wittenberg.de.*
The original castle church burned down in 1760, destroying the original doors on which Luther pinned his famous 95 Theses condemning the abuses of the Church. The new door contains the text, which was cast in bronze in 1855. Luther's tomb is below the pulpit; next to his is that of his dear friend and supporter, Philipp Melanchthon. There is also a bronze epitaph to protector Friedrich the Wise.

Markt★ (Market Square)
Wittenberg's central square is bordered by gabled houses, including the birthplace of painter Lucas Cranach the Elder at no 4. The artist lived and worked nearby at Schloßstraße 1 from 1513–50. In front of the Late Gothic (1440) Town Hall stand 19C statues of Luther and Melanchthon.

Twin towers of Stadtkirche St. Marien over the houses of the market square

©Thomas Röske/Fotolia.com

Stadtkirche St. Marien
(Parish Church of St. Mary)

On Kirchplatz, east of the market square.
🕐*Open Easter–Oct, daily 10am–6pm;*
Nov–Easter to 4pm. ☎*(03491) 628 30. www.*
stadtkirchengemeinde-wittenberg.de.
Luther himself preached and was married to Katharina von Bora in this triple-aisle Gothic (14C–15C) church that got a Neo-Gothic makeover in the 18C. The key piece of artistry is Lucas Cranach's 1547 **Reformation Altar**★★. Cranach also crafted the elaborate epitaphs in the chancel. Older still is the **baptismal font**★ created by Hermann Vischer of Nürnberg in 1457.

Melanchthonhaus

Collegienstraße 60.
🕐*Open Apr–Oct, daily 10am–6pm;*
Nov–Apr, Tue–Sun 10am–6pm. ☞*2.50€.*
☎*(03491) 40 32 79. www.martinluther.de.*
The building in which Luther's companion lived and died is a Renaissance edifice topped by a gable of particularly

elegant form. Melanchton was a man of moderate temperament, more tolerant than Luther. The author of the Confession of Augsburg worked for most of his life trying to reconcile the different factions of the Reformation. His study and many documents relating to his work can be seen in this house.

Lutherhaus★

At the far end of Collegienstraße.
🕐*Open Apr–Oct, daily 9am–6pm;*
Nov–Mar, Tue–Sun, 10am–5pm. ☞*5€.*
☎*(03491) 420 30. www.martinluther.de.*
Luther fans and history buffs may spend a couple of hours in this excellent museum, dealing with all aspects of the Reformation through paneling, paintings (Cranach, Hans Baldung Grien), artifacts (Bibles, original editions of Luther's work, garments, coins) from Luther's time. There is also an exhibit on the role of mass printing (invented by Gutenberg in Mainz c. 1439) in spreading the Reformation throughout Europe.

WOLFENBÜTTEL★★

POPULATION: 54 700

For three centuries, until the court transferred to Brunswick in 1753, Wolfenbüttel was the seat of the dukes of Brunswick and Lüneburg. The precise, spacious plan, with perfectly straight streets linking large symmetrical squares, makes it one of the most successful examples of Renaissance town planning in Germany.

- 🅸 **Information:** Stadtmarkt 7, 38300 Wolfenbüttel. ☎(05331) 862 80. www.wolfenbuettel.com.
- ▸ **Orient Yourself:** Straddling the banks of the Oker, Wolfenbüttel is the ideal base for exploring the Harz massif.
- 🅰 **Don't Miss:** The city's half-timbered houses.
- 🕐 **Organizing Your Time:** Allow at least three hours to see everything,
- 🅲 **Also See:** BRAUNSCHWEIG, GOSLAR, HARZ, HILDESHEIM.

Sights

Fachwerkhäuser★★
(Half-timbered Houses)

The homes of High Court officials lining Kanzleistraße, Reichstraße and western Harzstraße, built c. 1600, are distinguished by majestic façades with overhangs flanking the main entrance. At Harzstraße 12 note the grimacing heads above cornices carved with

biblical inscriptions. The decoration of smaller houses owned by lesser dignitaries and merchants is, surprisingly, more elaborate. A single gable normally tops their wide, flat façades (Lange Herzogstraße, Brauergildenstraße, Holzmarkt, Krambuden). Even the simpler, two-story houses of the less well-to-do (Krumme Straße, Stobenstraße) are ornamented with colored fan designs. Corner houses with slightly projecting

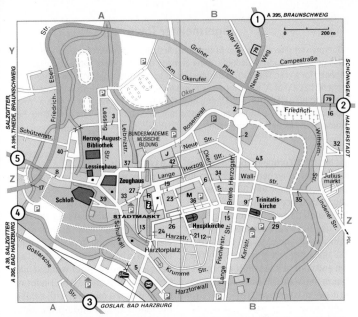

oriels are a particular characteristic of Wolfenbüttel and prevalent around the Stadtmarkt (main town square).

Stadtmarkt★
(Town Market Square)

The **Rathaus** (Town Hall) occupies a number of 16C and 17C buildings on the north and west of the square. The Weights and Measures Office has a distinctive arched doorway surmounted by King Solomon's Edict and the Wolfenbüttel coat of arms.

Schloss★ (Palace)

Open year-round, Tue–Sun, 10am–5pm. Closed Jan 1, Good Fri, May 1, Dec 24, 25 & 31. 3€. ☎(05331) 924 60. www.schloss-wf.de.

The palace is reached via an attractive narrow street bordered by arcades known as *Krambuden*. Originally a 12C stronghold conquered by Henry the Lion, the building experienced many transformations before it evolved into Lower Saxony's second largest palace (after the *Leineschloß* in Hanover).

The **Schlossmuseum** (palace museum) consists of the **Ducal Apartments** as they were 1690–1750. Rare furniture, tapestries, porcelain and paintings illustrate Baroque court life. Note the ivory scenes adorning the walls of the small study. *Access via the central courtyard and main stairway.*

Herzog August Bibliothek★
(Library)

Open year-round, Tue–Sun 10am–5pm. Closed Good Fri, Dec 24, 25 & 31. 3€, also good for Lessinghaus. ☎(05331) 80 80. www.hab.de.

Founded in 1572 by Augustus the Young, this was the largest, most impor-

Jägermeister Town

Jägermeister (literally, master of the hunt) first appeared in Wolfenbüttel in 1935. This uniquely-flavored alcoholic drink is made from 56 plants, roots and extracts ripened for a year. The stag on the label refers to St. Hubert, patron saint of hunters. Legend has it that 7C King Hubert rejected his wealth when his wife Floribana died, devoting himself to hunting. During one of his solitary outings a stag with a cross floating between its antlers appeared to him. The vision gave him his calling; he immediately forsook his wealth and title and founded several monasteries.

tant library in Europe in the 17C. Still a treasure for researchers and scholars, it houses today some 860 000 volumes. Among the priceless manuscripts and illuminated documents from the Middle Ages are a rare example of the 14C *Saxon Mirror*, and a gospel book from 1188 that once belonged to Henry the Lion and currently the most expensive book in the world *(shown periodically in the first floor vault room)*.

In the Globe Room are terrestrial and celestial globes from the 16C and 17C, as well as ancient maps. The Malerbuchkabinett hall contains books illustrated by great artists of the 20C.

Address Book

For coin ranges, see cover flap.

WHERE TO STAY

Parkhotel Altes Kaffeehaus – *Harztorwall 18.* (05331) 88 80. www.parkhotel-wolfenbuettel.de. *75 rooms. Restaurant*. Converted from a Turkish coffeehouse, this modern hotel has attractive, comfortable rooms Dine in the bright restaurant or in the vaulted wine cellar *(Weingrotte)*.

WHERE TO EAT

Ratskeller – *Stadtmarkt 2.* (05331) 98 47 11. *Closed Mon. Reservations recommended.* This pleasant restaurant occupies the basement of a 400-year-old house. Its brick façade has a grey-blue half-timbered frontage typical of the region. Also note the beautiful library.

Lessinghaus

Open year-round, Sat–Sun 10am–5pm. *3€, also good for Herzog August Library.* (05331) 80 82 14.

Gotthold Ephraim Lessing, the great innovator of German drama, spent eleven years working as official ducal librarian in Wolfenbüttel (1770–81) and penning, among other works, *Emilia Galotti* and *Nathan the Wise*. His former home is now a museum with exhibits providing insight into his life, times and work.

Beside the Lessing house is the **Zeughaus** (Arsenal, 1613), a distinctive Renaissance building with projecting gables, obelisks and scrolls.

Hauptkirche (Main Church)

Open year-round, Tue–Sun 10am–noon, 2pm–4pm. (05331) 311 72.

Built on Kornmarkt in 1608, this Protestant church was influenced by the Late Gothic hall-church tradition. The massive tower with its Baroque roof resembles the shape of the castle tower. The altar, pulpit and organ case date from the Late Renaissance.

Trinitatiskirche (Trinity Church)

Holzmarkt.

Open year-round, Tue, Wed 11am–1pm, Wed 2pm–4pm, Thu 3pm–5pm, Sat 11am–4pm. (05331) 311 72.

This Baroque church was built in 1719 on top of an existing, twin-towered structure, thus explaining its strangely flat silhouette. Near the church is a **park**, formed from the old city walls.

WÖRLITZER PARK★★

Wörlitz Park is the oldest landscaped park on the European mainland and part of the Garden Realm created by Prince Leopold III around Dessau between 1764 and 1800. Retaining all its original magic, the park has enchanting canalside trails, voluptuous hedges and lakes with small islands reached by ferry or gondola. In 2000, the gardens' special appeal was recognized by UNESCO, which placed Wörlitz on its list of World Heritage Sites.

🛈 **Information:** Förstergasse 26, 06786 Wörlitz. ☎ (034905) 202 16. www.wbticket.de.

▶ **Orient Yourself:** Wörlitz Park is 17km/10.5mi west of Dessau. From the A9 (Leipzig–Berlin), take exit 10 and follow the B185 to Orienbaum, then the B107 to Wörlitz.

☺ **Don't Miss:** A leisurely stroll through the gardens.

🕔 **Organizing Your Time:** Allow at least half a day to see the grounds and buildings.

Kids **Especially for Kids:** Exploring the lake and small islands by boat.

👣 **Also See:** DESSAU, WITTENBERG, LEIPZIG, MAGDEBURG.

A Bit of History

Prince Leopold III Friedrich Franz von Anhalt-Dessau (1740–1817), known as "Father Franz" to his subjects, was an enlightened ruler to whom the welfare of his small state was paramount (🕮 *see DESSAU).* His endeavors extended far beyond material matters; he sought to link the beautiful with the practical, promoting literature, music, architecture and garden design.

A number of trips to England provided him with food for progressive thought and paved the way for his planned reforms. It was also in England that he saw his first landscaped parks and was inspired to create such a park environment of his own. Master builder **Friedrich Wilhelm von Erdmannsdorff**, who had accompanied him on his trips, acted as his assistant and like-minded adviser. The gardens were completed around 1800.

©World Pictures/Photoshot

Admiring the scenery on board a gondola

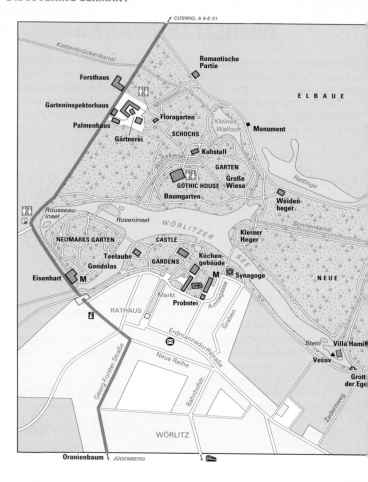

COSWIG, A 9-E 51

Kettenbrückenkanal

Forsthaus

Romantische Partie

Garteninspektorhaus

ELBAUE

Palmenhaus

Floragarten

Kleines Walloch

Monument

Gärtnerei

SCHOCHS

Kuhstall

Wolfskanal

GARTEN

Rettinge

GOTHIC HOUSE

Große Wiese

Baumgarten

Weidenheger

Rousseauinsel

Roseninsel

WÖRLITZER

Sonnenkanal

NEUMARKS GARTEN

CASTLE

Kleiner Heger

Teelaube

Gondolas

GARDENS

Küchengebäude

SEE

NEUE

Eisenhart

M

Markt

M

Synagoge

Amtsgasse

Probstei

Graben

RATHAUS

Erdmannsdorffstraße

Stein

Villa Hamil

Neue Reihe

Vesuv

Georg-Forster-Straße

Bahnhofstr.

Grott der Ege

Zedernweg

WÖRLITZ

Oranienbaum | JÜDENBERG

Visit

Schloss★ (Palace)

*Visit by guided tour (1hr) only; late Mar, Apr, Oct, Nov, Tue–Sun 10am–5pm; May–Sept to 6pm. 4.50€. (0340) 64 61 50. www.gartenreich.com.

Built by Erdmannsdorf between 1769 and 1773, this is the earliest Neoclassical palace outside of England; it replaced an earlier Baroque hunting lodge.

The two-story yellow and white building sits dignified against a backdrop of mature trees. Erdmannsdorff made ingenious use of the many technical innovations of the day, including water pipes, elevators, cast-iron stoves, folding beds and cupboards, all of which vastly improved the living standard of the ruling family.

The original interior has survived virtually intact and sports ceiling frescoes and murals inspired by antiquity. Most sculpture and carpentry work was undertaken by local people.

The elegant **Speisesaal** (dining room) with its elaborate stucco decoration and slim Corinthian pillars, and the great **Großer Festsaal** (banqueting hall) are striking. The **library** is richly hung with paintings (Snyders, Van Ruysdael, Antoine Pesne) and fitted with furniture, the highlight of which is the suite of Roentgen pieces.

Gotisches Haus★ (Gothic House)

*Visit by guided tour (1hr) only, late Mar, Apr, Oct & Nov, Sat–Sun, 10am–5pm; May–Sept, Tue–Sun, 10am–6pm. 4.50€. (0340) 64 61 50.

WÖRLITZER PARK

0   300 m

🅸   Information

🚻   Toilets

Pantheon

Großes
Walloch
Amalieninsel

Rotes
Wachhaus

ANLAGEN

Italienisches
Bauernhaus

Holzhof

One of the earliest Neo-Gothic buildings in Germany, the Gothic House was erected between 1773 and 1813. The canal-facing main façade was inspired by the church of Maria dell' Orto in Venice. While the palace served official purposes, this structure was the prince's private refuge. Through Swiss scholar Johann Caspar Lavater he acquired an outstanding **Swiss stained glass**★ collection from the 15C to the 17C. This has survived intact and adorns the windows of the Gothic house. All rooms house numerous 16C–18C paintings by Dutch, German and Italian masters, including Tintoretto and Lucas Cranach the Elder.

Wörlitz Park by Gondola★

Boats departs from the Pier (Gondolastation) Mar, Apr, Oct & Nov, daily 11am–4pm; May–Sept, daily 10am–6pm. 45min. ☜6€. www.woerlitz-information.de or www. gartenreich.com. Contact in advance to arrange group gondola tours.

An enchanting way to experience the charms of this extensive garden landscape is being poled around in a romantic gondola. Tours travel across Lake Wörlitz, glide through a canal and pass the Gothic House. Each boat seats up to 15 people comfortably.

WORMS★

POPULATION: 82 212

Worms is one of Germany's oldest cities and, along with Speyer and Mainz, was an Imperial residence on the banks of the Rhine. Its history is closely associated with the 5C kingdom of the Burgundians whose fate was immortalized in the 12C Nibelungenlied epic (☜see INTRODUCTION: Literature). Surrounded by vineyards, Worms makes a fantastic base for exploring the region.

🅸   **Information:** Neumarkt 14, 67547 Worms. ☏ (06241) 250 45. www.worms.de.
▶   **Orient Yourself:** Worms sits on the left bank of the Rhine, 20km/13mi north of Mannheim.
🅿   **Parking:** You'll find a parking garage at Römerstraße and Paulusstraße.
🅰   **Don't Miss:** St. Peter's Cathedral
🕐   **Organizing Your Time:** Allow half an hour for a tour of St. Peter's Cathedral.
🅲   **Also See:** PFALZ, MANNHEIM, MAINZ, HEIDELBERG.

Luther Before the Diet

Everyone knows the old story about Luther and the "diet of worms", bandied about in school history lessons. In fact this particular Diet had perhaps the most far-reaching consequences of any conference before the two world wars (*see INTRODUCTION: History – The Reformation and the Thirty Years' War*). Summoned before the Diet by Charles V in 1521 after a Papal Bull condemning everything he believed, Luther arrived in Worms "as though going to the torture chamber." He went nevertheless, troubled by the anxiety of his friends but acclaimed by enthusiastic crowds. Refusing to retract his beliefs, he was banned to the outer parts of the empire, but found protection in Wartburg castle in Eisenach (*see EISENACH*).

Sights

Dom St. Peter★★

Open May–Oct 9am–6pm; Nov–Apr 10am–5pm. www.wormser-dom.de.
Worms Cathedral, completed in 1181, is one of the finest Romanesque edifices in Germany. Entering through the south portal, you see a splendid Christ In Judgment statue from the 12C. In the older east chancel note the Baroque **high altar★** by Balthasar Neumann. The elegant west chancel sports rose windows, a chequered frieze and arched blind arcades. The five **Gothic relief sculptures★** in the north aisle represent the Annunciation, the Nativity, the Entombment, the Resurrection and the Tree of Jesse.

Lutherdenkmal (Luther Monument)

Unveiled in 1868, this monument shows Luther before the Diet of Worms surrounded by early Reformers, such John Wycliffe, Jan Hus and Savonarola, as well as Reformist theologians including Melanchthon and Reuchlin.

Museum Heylshof★

Stephansgasse 9. Open May–Sept, Tue–Sun 11am–5pm; Oct–Dec, mid-Feb–Apr, Tue–Sat 2pm–5pm, Sun 11am–5pm. 2.50€. (06241) 220 00. www.museum-heylshof.de.
This Gründerzeit mansion showcases an important collection of 15C–19C **paintings★**, including works by Rubens, Van Loo and Tintoretto, alongside precious ceramics, glassware and porcelain.

Jewish Sites

Worms was one of Germany's great centers of Jewish culture and is home to Europe's oldest Jewish **cemetery** (*open 9am–dusk, July–Aug to 8pm*), in use since the 11C. The old **synagogue** (*open Apr–Oct, 10am–12.30pm, 1.30pm–5pm; Nov–Mar to 4pm*) dates to the same period, but it had to be rebuilt in 1961 following its destruction in World War II. Steps lead down to the **Mikwe** (Bathhouse), while behind the

Address Book

For coin ranges, see cover flap.

WHERE TO STAY

Kriemhilde – Hofgasse 2. (06241) 911 50. www.hotel-kriemhilde.de. 19 rooms. Restaurant , closed Sat, Jan–Apr also Sun. This small hotel in the town center has friendly service and practical rooms furnished in pine or oak. The rustic, tastefully designed restaurant serves tummy-filling home-style meals.

WHERE TO EAT

Rôtisserie Dubs – Kirchstraße 6, 67550 Worms-Rheindürkheim (9km/6mi north, via the Nibelungenring). (06242) 20 23. www.dubs.de. Closed 2 weeks in Jan, Tue and Sat lunch. Owner-chef Wolfgang Dubs treats patrons to refined and varied German cooking in an intimate country inn. A separate restaurant is more rustic.

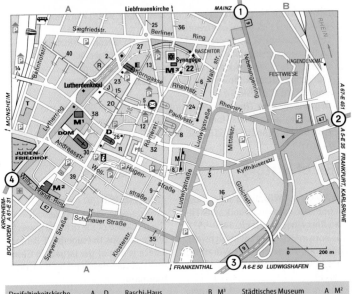

synagogue, the modern Raschi-Haus houses a **Jewish Museum** (☉*open Nov–Mar, Tue–Sun 10am–12.30am, 1.30pm–4.30pm; Apr–Oct to 5pm; ☞1.50€; ☎(06 241) 853 47 01*) that traces Jewish life in the Rhineland.

Museum der Stadt (City Museum)

☉*Open Tue–Sun, 10am–5pm.* ☉*Closed Jan 1, Good Fri, May 1, Dec 24–26 and 31 Dec.* ☞*2€.* ☎*(06241) 94 63 90.*
Five thousand years of artifacts are displayed in this former Romanesque monastery. The Ancient Roman section boasts one of Germany's largest collections of glassware from this period.

Nibelungen Museum★★

Fischerpförtchen 10.
☉*Open year-round, Tue–Fri 10am–5pm, Sat–Sun to 6pm.* ☞*5.50€.* ☎*(06241) 20 21 20.*

A wonderful addition to Worms' museum landscape, this modern multimedia exhibit brings to life the epic Nibelungen legend in two medieval towers and along a section of the old town wall. Budget about 90min.

Worms Cathedral

WÜRZBURG★★

POPULATION: 132 700

Würzburg lies at the starting point of the Romantic Road. Although much of the city center was destroyed by bombs in just 22 minutes on March 16, 1945, the main sights have been meticulously rebuilt. This includes the splendid prince-bishops residence, which has been a UNESCO World Heritage Site since 1981. It was in Würzburg that Wilhelm Conrad Röntgen discovered X-rays in 1895.

- **Information:** Am Congress Centrum & Marktplatz, 97070 Würzburg. ☎(0931) 37 23 35. www.wuerzburg.de.
- ▶ **Orient Yourself:** Former capital of the Duchy of Franconia, Würzburg lies on the banks of the Main, at the northwest border of Bavaria.
- P **Parking:** You'll find parking garages throughout Würzburg. Visit http://wap.parkinfo.com for fees and locations.
- ⊗ **Don't Miss:** The Residenz.
- ⊘ **Organizing Your Time:** Allow a couple of hours for the Residenz and its gardens and a full day for the suggested driving tour.
- ⊚ **Also See:** ROMANTISCHE STRASSE, BAMBERG, FRANKFURT-Am-MAIN.

A Bit of History

The Master of Würzburg – Flamboyant Gothic sculptor and woodcarver **Tilman Riemenschneider** (c. 1460–1531) was born in Heiligenstadt im Eichsfeld, Thüringia. He worked in Würzburg from 1483 and became town mayor in 1520–21.

His work was always more than purely decorative and largely centered on expressing human emotions.

Old bridge across the Main and Marienberg Fortress

M. Hertlein/MICHELIN

Residenz★★

♿☎(0931) 35 51 70.
www.residenz-wuerzburg.de.
The residence of the rich and powerful prince-bishops, this superb 18C Baroque palace is one of the largest in Germany and was designed by **Balthasar Neumann**.

Schloss★★ (Palace)

⊘Open Apr–Oct, daily 9am–6pm; Nov–Mar 10am–4.30pm; ticket office closes 1hr before closing. ⟿Some sections by guided tour only, offered throughout the day (11am and 3pm in English) ⊘Closed Jan 1, Shrove Tue, Dec 24,25 & 31. ⊜5€.
The monumental **Treppenhaus**★★ (Grand Staircase) occupies the whole northern part of the vestibule and is one of Neumann's masterpieces. The huge **fresco**★★ (600sq m/6 400sq ft) decorating the vaulted ceiling is by the Venetian, **Giovanni Tiepolo** (1753) and illustrates the four then-known continents. In the **Weißer Saal** (White Room), between the Grand Staircase and the Imperial Hall, the brilliant **stucco ornamentation** is the work of Italian artist Antonio Bossi.
The oval **Kaisersaal** ★★ (Imperial Hall) on the first floor is also splendidly-adorned with **frescoes by Tiepolo**.

WÜRZBURG

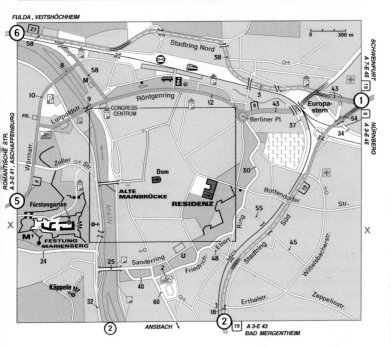

The **Paradezimmer** (Imperial Apartments) are a luxurious suite of restored rooms with Rococo stuccowork, tapestries and German furniture. The residence also houses a picture gallery with some fine **17C and 18C Italian paintings**, among them works by Bellucci, Canaletto and the Veronese school.

Hofkirche★ (Court Church)

The Residenz church is another work of Balthasar Neumann. Marble, gilding and warm ceiling frescoes by court painter Rudolf Byss all combine to form a colorful composition. Two more **Tiepolo** paintings hang above the side altars: *The Assumption* and *The Fall of the Angels.*

Hofgarten★ (Court Gardens)

Astute use of old, stepped bastions has produced a layout of terraced gardens. From the eastern side, the whole 167m/545ft of the palace façade, with its elegant central block, is visible.
The stucco is the work of Johann Peter Wagner.

Martin von Wagner Museum★
South wing.
Picture Gallery: *year-round, Tue–Sat 9.30am–12.30pm;* Collection of Antiquities: *Tue–Sat 1.30pm–5pm; Picture gallery and Collection of Antiquities open alternately on Sun, 10am–1.30pm.* Closed *Jan 1, Good Fri, May 1, Oct 3, 1 Nov, Dec*

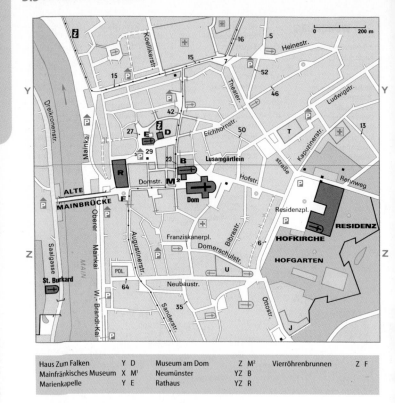

Haus Zum Falken	Y	D	Museum am Dom	Z	M²
Mainfränkisches Museum	X	M¹	Neumünster	YZ	B
Marienkapelle	Y	E	Rathaus	YZ	R
Vierröhrenbrunnen	Z	F			

24 & 31. ☎*(0931) 31 28 66. www.museum.
uni-wuerzburg.de.*

The university-affiliated museum houses
two grand collections. On the second
floor is the **Gemäldegalerie**★ (Picture
Gallery) with 14C–20C German and European works.

The most interesting exhibits include
altar paintings by the masters of Würzburg (14C–16C) and Franconian sculpture, especially that of Riemenschneider.
Dutch and Italian painters from the
16C to the 18C are well represented
(Tiepolo).

The **Antikensammlung**★ (Collection
of Antiquities) on the third floor specializes in works from the Mediterranean
countries dating as far back as the third
millennium BC. Pride of place goes to an
internationally renowned collection of
Greek vases★★ (6C–4C BC), but there
are also examples from Etruscan, Roman
and Egyptian civilizations.

Sights

Dom St. Kilian
(Cathedral of St. Kilian)

This basilica with columns and four towers, rebuilt after 1945, has retained its
original 11C–13C silhouette although
the interior was altered in subsequent
centuries. The modern **Altar of the
Apostles** holds three 16C **sculptures**★
by Riemenschneider. The 18C **Schönborn Chapel** by Balthasar Neumann off
the left transept contains the tombs of
the prince-bishops from that particular
family dynasty.

Neumünster (New Minster)

The imposing Baroque **west façade** of
this church (1710–16) is attributed to
Johann Dientzenhofer. In niches below
the cupola are a Riemenschneider *Virgin and Child* and a Christ figure in an
unusual pose with arms folded below
the chest (14C). In the west crypt is the
tomb of St. Kilian, the missionary who

A Masterpiece in 210 Days

Disappointment with other painters led Prince-Bishop Carl Philipp von Greiffenclau to commission the best fresco painter of the age, Giovanni Battista Tiepolo, to paint the palace. The painter arrived with his two sons on 12 December 1750. Tiepolo wanted for nothing; he was served eight courses at lunch and seven in the evening. In addition, he received three times the pay he earned in Venice. Tiepolo had a reputation for painting with great speed, but the artist surpassed all estimates during his short three years in Würzburg: He created frescoes in the Imperial Hall and staircase, two altars for the Würzburg court church, one for Schwarzach Abbey (now in Munich's Alte Pinakothek) and worked for other Würzburg families. Unable to paint during the winter, Tiepolo worked day and night for the rest of the year. It took him only 210 days to complete the staircase fresco, 32x19m/105x62ft in size with a wide range of people, allegories and details.

was martyred in Würzburg in 689 and has since become the patron of the Franconians. The exit to the left of the chancel leads to the idyllic **Lusamgärtlein**, a small garden where the 13C troubadour-poet Walther von der Vogelweide was buried.

Museum am Dom (Cathedral Museum)
Open Apr–Oct, Tue–Sun 10am–6pm; Nov–Mar to 5pm. 3.50€. www.museum-am-dom.de.
This museum presents religious art from the 11C to the 21C, including a fantastic crucifix by Riemenschneider. It follows a modern curatorial concept that organizes the exhibit into such themes as "Hoping", "Admonishing" and "Testifying" in order to encourage reflection and interaction on the visitors' part.

Marienkapelle (St. Mary's Chapel)
This fine Gothic chapel was built by the town burghers in the 14C and 15C and boasts an attractive *Annunciation* on the tympanum of the north doorway. Inside the western front is the 1502 tombstone of Konrad von Schaumberg, carved by Riemenschneider and, on the north side, a **silver Madonna** made by the Master of Augsburg, J Kilian, in 1680.

Rathaus (Town Hall)
The 13C Town Hall boasts a painted façade from the 16C and a charming interior courtyard. The western part, the **Roter Bau** (red building), is in Late Renaissance style, while the Baroque

Vierröhrenbrunnen (fountain) in front dates from 1765.

Festung Marienberg★ (Marienberg Fortress)
Open mid-Mar–Oct, Tue–Sun 9am–6pm. 4€. (0931) 35 51 70. www.schloesser.bayern.de
From 1253 to 1719, this stronghold was the home of the prince-bishops of Würzburg. Built above the west bank of the Main, the original 13C medieval castle was enlarged in the late Middle Ages and fortified after being stormed by Swedish troops in 1631 during the Thirty Years' War. The first-floor prince-bishops' apartments now house the **Fürstenbaumuseum** (Princes' Building Museum), richly furnished and hung with paintings and tapestries, including one from 1564 depicting the family of Prince-Bishop Julius Echter of Mespelbrunn. There is also a local history exhibit.

Mainfränkisches Museum★★ (Regional History Museum)
Second floor of Festung Marienberg, enter on the right in the first courtyard. Open Apr–Oct, Tue–Sun 10am–5pm, Nov–Mar to 4pm. Closed Shrove Tue, Dec 24, 25 & 31. 4€, combination ticket with Fürstenbaumuseum 5€. (0931) 20 59 40. www.mainfraenkisches-museum.de.
Housed in the former arsenal, the most important section of this collection of Franconian arts and crafts belong to 80 or so **sculptures by Tilmann Riemenschneider** *(first floor)*, including Adam and Eve, Virgin Mary and Child and The

Address Book

For coin ranges, see cover flap.

WHERE TO STAY

Hotel Alter Kranen – *Kärnergasse 11 (street parallel to Mainkai).* ☎ *(0931) 351 80. www.hotel-alter-kranen. de. 14 rooms.* This hotel sits on the banks of the Main, a mere stone's throw from the old town. The breakfast room offers fabulous views of the fortress.

Hotel Rebstock – *Neubaustraße 7.* ☎ *(0931) 309 30. www.rebstock. com. 70 rooms. Restaurant ⊜⊜⊜⊜, closed Aug and Sun.* Behind the Rococo façade of 1737, a range of rooms from elegant and modern to rustic and traditional awaits. The charming restaurant and bistro-style winter garden deliver continental cuisine.

WHERE TO EAT

Bürgerspital – *Theaterstraße 19.* ☎ *(0931) 35 28 80.* This mood-lit wine tavern with its cross-vaulted ceiling is operated by the Bürgerspital wine estate. Franconian specialties, including fish, accompany the excellent variety of local wines.

Weinhaus zum Stachel – *Gressengasse 1 (near Marktplatz).* ☎ *(0931) 527 70. www.weinhaus-stachel. de. Closed Sun. Reservations recommended.* This traditional Weinstube with an idyllic courtyard dates to the 15C. Excellent Franconian wines and regional cuisine. In the evening, a small menu of refined dishes is available.

NIGHTLIFE

USEFUL TIPS

Try the bars along Juliuspromenade north of the city center and Sanderstraße, south of the city center.

Gutsschenke Schützenhof – *Mainleitenweg 48.* ☎ *(0931) 724 22. Closed mid-Dec–early Mar.* A quiet and shady terrace graces this cafe slightly outside the city, which uses produce from its own garden in preparing the dishes.

Schönborn – *Marktplatz 30.* ☎ *(0931) 404 48 18.* Busy at all hours, this café has a large terrace. Choose from a wide variety of drinks from coffee to cocktails, and full meals.

Apostles. In the vaulted galleries of the **Echterbastei**, statues, gold and silver religious plate, Gothic easel paintings and

Käppele (Chapel)

A monumental Way of the Cross leads to this Baroque pilgrim chapel built by Balthasar Neumann in 1748. The adjoining chapel of mercy is connected via a "miracle passage".

The finest **view**★★ of Würzburg and the river is from the chapel terrace, with the fortress of Marienberg rising from the vineyards.

Driving Tour

Bocksbeutelstraße★ (Franconian Wine Route)

87km/55mi

▶ *Leave Würzburg via ③ on the town map.*

Medieval monks introduced viticulture to the Franconian region, which enjoys a mild climate and hot, dry summers. The region produces mainly dry white wines from the **Müller-Thurgau** and lightly more fruity more fruitier **Silvaner** grapes.

Ochsenfurt

Encircled by ancient **ramparts**★, Ochsenfurt's center is a hodgepodge of half-timbered houses and hotels adorned with wrought-iron statuettes or signs. A mechanical clock in the lantern turret strikes the hours at the 15C **Neues Rathaus**. The **Stadtpfarrkirche St. Andreas** built between the 13C and the 15C, has a fanciful interior.

▶ *Turn left off the B13 and drive alongside the Main.*

Sulzfeld

Sulzfeld's fortified town center features towers and gateways and half-timbered houses. A highlight of this pretty wine-growing village is the Renaissance **Town Hall** with its scrolled gables.

▶ *Pass through Kitzingen and Mainstockheim (on the east bank of the Main), and head for Dettelbach.*

Dettelbach★

Dettelbach clings to the northern slopes of the Main valley. Its charm lies in its Late Gothic (c. 1500) Town Hall and the 15C parish church, whose principal tower is linked by a wooden bridge to the smaller staircase tower. Northeast of the upper town is the **pilgrimage church "Maria im Sand"** (1608–13).

▶ *From Dettelbach to Neuses am Berg, the road crosses an open plateau of vineyards, with good views of the neighboring slopes. It then drops down again to the meandering Main valley before crossing to the other bank.*

Volkach★

This delightful wine-growing town lies on the eastern side of a wide oxbow in the Main. Of the original medieval enclave only two gates remain: the **Gaibacher Tor** and the **Sommeracher Tor**, one at each end of the main street. The 16C Renaissance **Town Hall** on the

Marktplatz contains the tourist office and is fronted by a 15C fountain bearing a statue of the Virgin Mary. Slightly farther south is the **Bartholomäuskirche** (Church of St. Bartholomew), a Late Gothic building with Baroque and Rococo flourishes.

At the northwestern edge of town (about 1km/0.6mi in the direction of Fahr) stands the 15C **pilgrimage church "Maria im Weingarten"** in an idyllic setting among vineyards covering the Kirchberg. Inside is the famous **Rosenkranzmadonna★** (Virgin with Rosary), a late work (1512–24) of Tilman Riemenschneider, in carved limewood.

▶ *Return to Würzburg via Schwarzach, turning right onto the B22.*

Excursion

Schloss Veitshöchheim★
7km/4.3mi northwest via ⑥ on the town map.
◷ Open Apr–Oct, daily 9am–6pm.
⊜3€. ☏ (0931) 35 51 70.
www.schloesser.bayern.de.
The 17C summer residence of the prince-bishops was enlarged in 1753 by Balthasar Neumann. Rooms brim with shiny Rococo and Empire furniture and are festooned with stucco ornamentation by Antonio Bossi. The lavish **park★** is a maze of shaded walks and arbors dotted with over 200 statues.

XANTEN ★

Xanten is one of the oldest towns in Germany, founded by the Romans around AD 100 as Colonia Ulpia Traiana. The Roman legacy is kept alive in an archeological park, while the town center itself still bears the stamp of the Middle Ages.

- **Information:** Kurfürstenstraße 9, 46509 Xanten. ☏ (02801) 715 70. www.xanten.de.
- **Orient Yourself:** Xanten is in the Lower Rhine region, about 69km/42.8mi northwest of Düsseldorf.
- **Don't Miss:** Archeological Park.
- **Organizing Your Time:** Budget at least half a day for Xanten.
- **Especially for Kids:** Playgrounds in the Archeological Park
- **Also See:** RUHRGEBIET, DÜSSELDORF.

Sights

Archäologischer Park★★
(Archeological Park) `Kids`
Warther Straße 2.
🕙*Open Mar–Oct, daily 9am–6pm, Nov to 5pm, Dec–Feb 10am–5pm.* 🕙*Closed Dec 24, 25 & 31.* ➽*6.50€; 9€ with museum and baths (child 2.50€, 4.50€ with museum and baths).* ☎ *(02801) 29 99. www.apx.de.*
Built on top of the ancient Roman settlement, this engaging park preserves the original foundations and ruins alongside replicas of actual buildings, including the amphitheater, the city wall, a temple and bathhouse, workshops and private residences.

Große Thermen
(Large Thermal Baths) `Kids`
➽*Combined museum and baths 5€ (child 2.50€).*
Take a peek at the **Grosse Thermen** west of the park (🕙*same hours as park*), which were built c. AD 125 during Emeror Hadrian's rule. The baths, which consisted of hot baths, warm baths, cold baths, saunas and a sports playing field, are protected by a large glass house. All parts have been carefully excavated.

RömerMuseum `Kids`
🕙*Same as park.*
➽*Museum alone, 5€ (child 2.50€).*
Treasures unearthed from the grounds are displayed in museum housed in a spectacularly modern building. The building is situated on an ancient Roman city called Colonia Ulpia Traiana. A staggering 2 500 objects are exhibited here, including the remains of a 12C Roman boat, which hangs from the ceiling.

Xanten Dom★
Propstei-Kapitel 8.
🕙*Open Mar–Oct, daily 10am–6pm; Nov–Mar to 5pm.* ☎*(02801) 713 10. www.st-viktor-xanten.de.*
The town's spiritual heart still beats in its cathedral, dedicated to its patron St. Viktor. Treasures inside the five-aisled Gothic basilica include the oldest choir stalls in the Rhineland (1250) and the **Marienaltar**★ carved by Heinrich Douvermann (1535)

ZUGSPITZE★★★

With a summit at 2 964m/9 724ft above sea level, the Zugspitze is the highest peak in Germany. Its matchless panorama and extensive ski slopes keep the mountain well-supplied with tourist facilities.

🛈 **Information:** ☎ (08821) 79 70. www.zugspitze.de.
▶ **Orient Yourself:** The Zugspitze is the northwest pillar of the Wetterstein limestone massif, a rocky barrier enclosing the valley of the Loisach and on the border with Austria. On clear days you have views extending to Germany, Italy, Switzerland and Austria.
🕙 **Organizing Your Time:** Plan at least half a day for the trip up the Zugspitze.
`Kids` **Especially for Kids:** The cable-car trip to the summit
👁 **Also See:** DEUTSCHE ALPENSTRASSE, SCHLOSS LINDERHOF, SCHLOSS NEUSCHWANSTEIN.

Visit

Summit Ascent `Kids`
➔*Wear warm clothing!*
➔*Only experienced hikers should attempt the ascent on foot.*
Getting to the Zugspitze summit involves riding either a cogwheel train, followed by a short cable-car ride, or a steep cable-car ride straight up from the Eibsee lake. Many people ascend the summit on the cogwheel train and return by cable-car, or vice versa.
Coming from from Ehrwald on the Austrian side, use the **Tyrolean Zugspitz Railway** (www.zugspitzbahn.at).

View of Zugspitze from Eibsee

From Garmisch-Partenkirchen

Duration 1hr 15min by cogwheel train and cable-car. Departs hourly from 8.15am to 2.15pm. ⌖45€ round-trip (34€ in winter). Last train to Garmisch 2.15pm, last train to Grainau 6.15pm. ☎(08821) 79 70.

The high-tech cogwheel trains depart from their own station behind the main train station in Garmisch and travel along the foot of the mountain past the Eibsee lake before starting their steep ascent through a 4.6km/2.8mi tunnel to the Zugspitzplatt station. From here, a cable-car *(Gletscherbahn)* ascends the last 350m/1 148ft to the summit.

From the Eibsee

Duration 10min by cable-car. Departs at least every 30min from 8am to 4.45pm (4.15pm in winter). ⌖45€ round-trip (34€ in winter). ☎(088 21) 79 70. www.zugspitze.de. Service reduced or suspended in bad weather.

This intensely steep cable-car makes the trip straight to the summit in a mere ten minutes and is not really suited for those suffering from fear of heights.

Zugspitzgipfel★★★ (Summit)

The upper terminals of the Gletscherbahn and the Eibsee cable-car are on the German side. The look-out terrace on the summit is 2 964m/9 724ft high. On the Austrian side is the upper station of the Tyrolean Zugspitzbahn.

The **panorama**★★★ to the east reveals the Kaisergebirge, the Dachstein and the Karwendel, the glacial peaks of the Hohe Tauern, the High Alps of the Tirol and the Ortler and the Bernina massifs. Nearer are the mountains of the Arlberg before the Säntis in the Appenzell Alps; farther away, to the west and northwest, are the Allgäu and Ammergau ranges. To the north, the Bavarian lowlands are visible, along with the Ammersee and Starnberger See lakes.

On good days, you can even spot Munich in the distance.

In fine snow conditions (usually from October to May), the lower Zugspitzplatt offers a **skiing** area of 7.5sq km/3sq mi, equipped with many rope tows. There is also a terrain park with half-pipes, kicker and rail areas.

Steep ride to Zugspitzgipfel

INDEX

INDEX

INDEX

WHERE TO STAY

WHERE TO EAT

MAPS AND PLANS

LIST OF MAPS

COMPANION PUBLICATIONS

MICHELIN MAP 718 GERMANY

- ◆ a practical map on a scale of 1:750 000 which shows the German road network and indicates isolated sites and monuments described in this guide;
- ◆ with index of place names.

MICHELIN TOURIST AND MOTORING ATLAS GERMANY/ AUSTRIA/BENELUX/SWITZERLAND/ CZECH REPUBLIC

- ◆ spiral-bound atlas on a scale of 1:300 000 for Germany;
- ◆ with index of place names and town maps.

MICHELIN REGIONAL MAPS (541-546)

- ◆ maps on a scale of 1:350 000 with detailed road mapping and maps of the main towns.

CITY PLANS:

- ◆ Berlin in map format (33)
- ◆ Berlin in spiral atlas format (2033)

TRAVELLING TO GERMANY

Michelin Tourist and Motoring Atlas Europe – A4 spiral (1136), A3 spiral (1129), A3 paperback (1135)

- ◆ the whole of Europe on a scale of 1:1 000 000 in one volume;
- ◆ major roads and 73 town plans and area maps;
- ◆ highway code of every country.

WWW.VIAMICHELIN.COM

Internet users can access personalised route plans, Michelin maps and town plans, and addresses of hotels and restaurants featured in The Michelin Guide Deutschland.

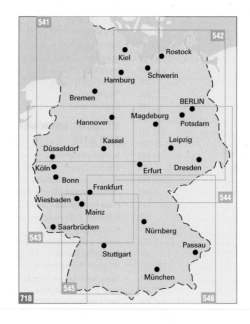

LEGEND

	Sight
Highly recommended	★★★
Recommended	★★
Interesting	★

Selected monuments and sights

●━━━ ➡	Tour - Departure point
🏛 ✝	Catholic church
🏛 ✝	Protestant church, other temple
✡ ☪	Synagogue - Mosque
🏛	Building
■	Statue, small building
✝	Calvary, wayside cross
◎	Fountain
━●━■▶	Rampart - Tower - Gate
✕	Château, castle, historic house
∴	Ruins
∪	Dam
✿	Factory, power plant
☆	Fort
∩	Cave
▢	Troglodyte dwelling
⊓	Prehistoric site
▼	Viewing table
Ⅶ	Viewpoint
▲	Other place of interest

Sports and recreation

🏇	Racecourse
⛸	Skating rink
≋ ≋	Outdoor, indoor swimming pool
🎥	Multiplex Cinema
⛵	Marina, sailing centre
⛺	Trail refuge hut
▫━■━■━▫	Cable cars, gondolas
▫++++++▫	Funicular, rack railway
🚂	Tourist train
◆	Recreation area, park
🎢	Theme, amusement park
🦌	Wildlife park, zoo
❀	Gardens, park, arboretum
◑	Bird sanctuary, aviary
🚶	Walking tour, footpath
☺	Of special interest to children

Special symbols

🅿	Park and Ride
🅿	Covered parking
19	Federal road (Bundesstraße).

Additional symbols

🛈		Tourist information
═══ ═══		Motorway or other primary route
❶ ❶		Junction: complete, limited
⊞══ ═══		Pedestrian street
ɪ═════ɪ		Unsuitable for traffic, street subject to restrictions
▥▥▥ ╌╌╌		Steps – Footpath
🚆	🚉 S.N.C.F.	Train station – Auto-train station
🚌	🚌 S.N.C.F.	Coach (bus) station
▬▬▬		Tram
◉		Metro, underground
Ⓟ Ⓡ		Park-and-Ride
♿		Access for the disabled
✉		Post office
☎		Telephone
▱		Covered market
⚔		Barracks
△		Drawbridge
∪		Quarry
✕		Mine
Ⓑ	Ⓕ	Car ferry (river or lake)
⛴		Ferry service: cars and passengers
⛵		Foot passengers only
③		Access route number common to Michelin maps and town plans
Bert (R.)...		Main shopping street
AZ B		Map co-ordinates

Abbreviations

J	Law courts (Justizgebäude)
L	Provincial government (Landesregierung)
M	Museum (Museum)
POL.	Police (Polizei)
R	Town hall (Rathaus)
T	Theatre (Theater)
U	University (Universität)

The German letter ß (eszett) has been used throughout this guide.

Michelin Apa Publications Ltd

A joint venture between Michelin and Langenscheidt

Suite 6, Tulip House, 70 Borough High Street, London SE1 1XF, United Kingdom

© 2009 Michelin Apa Publications Ltd
ISBN 978-1-906261-38-2
Printed: September 2008
Printed and bound: Himmer, Germany

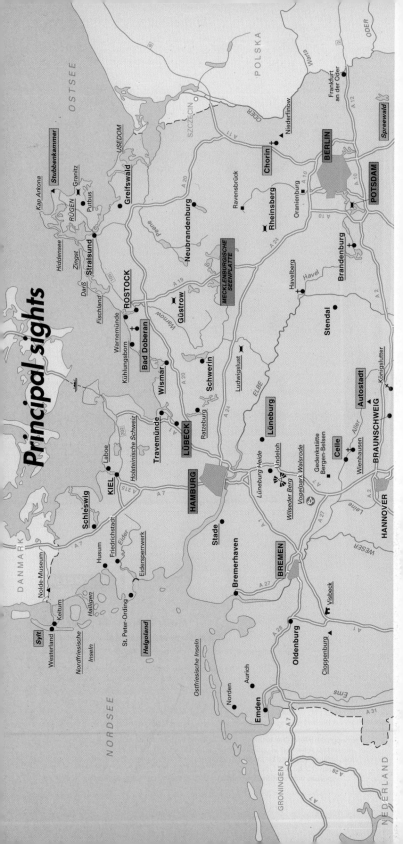

Principal sights

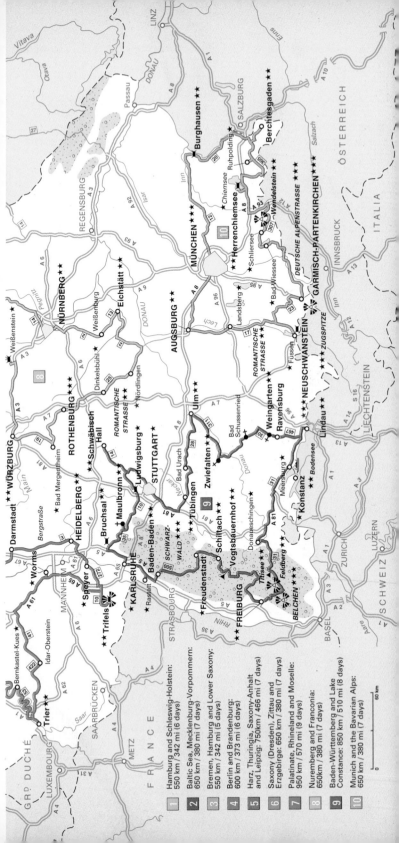

1 Hamburg and Schleswig-Holstein:
   550 km / 342 mi (6 days)

2 Baltic Sea, Mecklenburg-Vorpommern:
   650 km / 380 mi (7 days)

3 Bremen, Hamburg and Lower Saxony:
   550 km / 342 mi (5 days)

4 Berlin and Brandenburg:
   600 km / 373 mi (6 days)

5 Harz, Thuringia, Saxony-Anhalt
   and Leipzig: 750 km / 466 mi (7 days)

6 Saxony (Dresden), Zittau and
   Erzgebirge: 650 km / 380 mi (7 days)

7 Palatinate, Rhineland and Moselle:
   950 km / 570 mi (9 days)

8 Nuremberg and Franconia:
   650km / 380 mi (7 days)

9 Baden-Württemberg and Lake
   Constance: 850 km / 510 mi (8 days)

10 Munich and the Bavarian Alps:
   650 km / 380 mi (7 days)